CEREBRAL CONTROL OF SPEECH AND LIMB MOVEMENTS

ADVANCES IN PSYCHOLOGY

70

Editors:

G. E. STELMACH

P. A. VROON

NORTH-HOLLAND
AMSTERDAM • NEW YORK • OXFORD • TOKYO

CEREBRAL CONTROL OF SPEECH AND LIMB MOVEMENTS

Edited by

Geoffrey R. HAMMOND
Department of Psychology
The University of Western Australia
Nedlands, WA 6009, Australia

1990

NORTH-HOLLAND
AMSTERDAM • NEW YORK • OXFORD • TOKYO

NORTH-HOLLAND
ELSEVIER SCIENCE PUBLISHERS B.V.
Sara Burgerhartstraat 25
P.O. Box 211, 1000 AE Amsterdam, The Netherlands

Distributors for the United States and Canada:
ELSEVIER SCIENCE PUBLISHING COMPANY, INC.
655 Avenue of the Americas
New York, N.Y. 10010, U.S.A.

Library of Congress Cataloging-in-Publication Data

Cerebral control of speech and limb movements / edited by Geoffrey R. Hammond.
p. cm. -- (Advances in psychology ; 70)
Includes bibliographical references and indexes.
ISBN 0-444-88477-7
1. Aphasia. 2. Apraxia. 3. Extremities (Anatomy)--Movements. 4. Speech. 5. Cerebral cortex. I. Hammond, Geoffrey R., 1945- II. Series: Advances in psychology (Amsterdam, Netherlands) ; 70.
[DNLM: 1. Aphasia--physiopathology. 2. Apraxia--physiopathology. 3. Dominance, Cerebral--physiology. 4. Motor Acitivity--physiology. 5. Motor Skills--physiology. 6. Speech--physiology. W1 AD798L v. 70 / WL 335 C413]
RC425.C47 1990
612.8'25--dc20
DNLM/DLC
for Library of Congress 90-14304
CIP

ISBN: 0 444 88477 7

Preface

Michael Studdert-Kennedy wrote in 1981 that " ... the study of the connections between manual control and speech ... is a promising direction of research into the biology of language" (p77). This book reports a diversity of approaches along the path indicated by Studdert-Kennedy. The nature of the connections between the cerebral control of speech and skilled manual performance is examined in four sections.

The first section is concerned with the analysis of speech as motor activity, the features of movement that differentiate the motor abilities of the two hands, the emergence of articulatory skills and asymmetrical manual control during early development, and with the brain's control of movement.

The second section examines the associations between spoken language and manual gesture. The topics covered are the correspondence of speech and gesture in normal people; the changes in production and understanding of gesture that accompany aphasia; the structure of American Sign Language and its breakdown following brain damage in the deaf; and with the relationship of verbal and gestural explanations.

The third section examines the motor impairments associated with aphasias and the interpretations of the association of aphasia and apraxia: do speech and praxis suffer together because brain damage that is extensive enough to affect one also affects the other, or do they depend (at least to some degree) on common neural mechanisms?

The fourth section examines the interactions that are observed between speech and concurrent manual activity. The main questions of interest in this section are the nature of the interactions that are observed, and how these interactions can be understood both behaviorally and in terms of responsible neural mechanisms.

Some chapters review published literature, some report new findings. All present ideas that can be usefully applied to the common problem posed by the association of speech and language. A distinctive feature of the book is the inclusion of a diversity of approaches to this problem. Its worth comes from these individual contributions, and the credit is due to the contributing authors. A jockey remarked after winning a major Australian horse race that he couldn't have done it without the horse. I know what he meant.

Reference

Studdert-Kennedy, M. (1981). Cerebral hemispheres: specialized for what? *The Behavioral and Brain Sciences*, **4**, 76-77.

Table of Contents

Contributors

JOHN ANNETT
Department of Psychology
University of Warwick
Coventry, CV4 7AL
UNITED KINGDOM

MARIE-PAULE BOUCHAT
Unité de Neuropsychologie Cognitive
Voie du Roman Pays, 20
B-1348 Louvain-la-Neuve
BELGIUM

DOMINIQUE DÉRY
Unité de Neuropsychologie Cognitive
Voie du Roman Pays, 20
B-1348 Louvain-la-Neuve
BELGIUM

DARLYNNE A. DEVENNY
Department of Psychology
New York State Institute for
Basic Research in Developmental Disabilities
Staten Island, New York 10314
UNITED STATES OF AMERICA

JOSEPH R. DUFFY
Speech Pathology, Mayo Clinic
Rochester, Minnesota 55904
UNITED STATES OF AMERICA

ROBERT J. DUFFY
Department of Communication Sciences
University of Connecticut
Storrs, Connecticut 06269
UNITED STATES OF AMERICA

LISA ECKLUND-FLORES
Sub-program in Developmental Psychology
The City University of New York
New York, New York 10021
UNITED STATES OF AMERICA

ANATOL G. FELDMAN
Institute for Information Transmission Problems
Academy of Sciences
Moscow 101447
UNION OF SOVIET SOCIALIST REPUBLICS

PIERRE FEYEREISEN
Unité de Neuropsychologie Cognitive
Voie du Roman Pays, 20
B-1348 Louvain-la-Neuve
BELGIUM

J. RANDALL FLANAGAN
Department of Psychology
McGill University
Montreal, Quebec H3A 1B1
CANADA

GUILA GLOSSER
Department of Psychiatry
Medical College of Pennsylvania - Eastern Psychiatric Institute
Philadelphia, Pennsylvania 19129

VINCENT L. GRACCO
Haskins Laboratories
New Haven, Connecticut 06511-6695
UNITED STATES OF AMERICA

ADELE GREEN
Department of Psychology
Youngstown State University
Youngstown, Ohio
UNITED STATES OF AMERICA

KATHLEEN YORK HAALAND
Veterans Administration Medical Center
Albuquerque, New Mexico 87108
UNITED STATES OF AMERICA

GEOFFREY R. HAMMOND
Department of Psychology
The University of Western Australia
Nedlands, Western Australia 6009
AUSTRALIA

DEBORAH L. HARRINGTON
Veterans Administration Medical Center
Albuquerque, New Mexico 87108
UNITED STATES OF AMERICA

JOSEPH B. HELLIGE
Department of Psychology
University of Southern California
Los Angeles, California 90089
UNITED STATES OF AMERICA

MERRILL HISCOCK
Department of Psychology
University of Houston
Houston, Texas 77204-5341
UNITED STATES OF AMERICA

SHARON C. HOGG
Graduate Department of Speech Pathology
University of Toronto
Toronto, Ontario M5G 1L4
CANADA

GREGOR W. JASON
Division of Psychology
Foothills Hospital
Calgary, Alberta T2N 2T9
CANADA

DANIEL W. KEE
Department of Psychology
California State University
Fullerton, California
UNITED STATES OF AMERICA

RAY D. KENT
Department of Communicative Disorders
University of Wisconsin
Madison, Wisconsin 53706
UNITED STATES OF AMERICA

MARCEL KINSBOURNE
Department of Behavioral Neurology
The Shriver Center
Waltham, Massachsetts 02254
UNITED STATES OF AMERICA

ELENA T. LEVY
Department of Psychology
University of Connecticut
Storrs, Connecticut 06269
UNITED STATES OF AMERICA

MALCOLM R. MCNEIL
Department of Communicative Disorders
University of Wisconsin
Madison, Wisconsin 53706
UNITED STATES OF AMERICA

DAVID MCNEILL
Department of Psychology
The University of Chicago
Chicago, Illinois 60637
UNITED STATES OF AMERICA

DAVID J. OSTRY
Department of Psychology
McGill University
Montreal, Quebec H3A 1B1
CANADA

LAURA L. PEDELTY
Department of Psychology
The University of Chicago
Chicago, Illinois 60637
UNITED STATES OF AMERICA

MICHAEL PETERS
Department of Psychology
University of Guelph
Guelph, Ontario N1G 2W1
CANADA

HOWARD POIZNER
Center for Neuroscience
Rutgers University
Newark, New Jersey 07102
UNITED STATES OF AMERICA

ERIC A. ROY
Department of Kinesiology
University of Waterloo
Waterloo, Ontario N2L 3G1
CANADA

MONICA RUIZ
Unité de Neuropsychologie Cognitive
Voie du Roman Pays, 20
B-1348 Louvain-la-Neuve
BELGIUM

ANNE SMITH
Department of Audiology and Speech Sciences
Purdue University
West Lafayette, Indiana 47907
UNITED STATES OF AMERICA

PAULA A. SQUARE-STORER
Graduate Department of Speech Pathology
University of Toronto
Toronto, Ontario M5G 1L4
CANADA

JEFFERY J. SUMMERS
Department of Psychology
University of Melbourne
Parkville, Victoria 3042
AUSTRALIA

GERALD TURKEWITZ
Department of Psychology
Hunter College
The City University of New York
New York, New York 10021
UNITED STATES OF AMERICA

GIUSEPPE VALLAR
Istituto di Clinica Neurologica
Università di Milano
20122 Milano
ITALY

MORTON WIENER
Department of Psychology
Clark University
Worcester, Massuchusetts 01610
UNITED STATES OF AMERICA

GERALD YOUNG
Department of Psychology
Glendon College
York University
Toronto, Ontario M4N 3M6
CANADA

HOWARD ZELAZNIK
Department of Physical Education, Health, and Recreation Sciences
Purdue University
West Lafayette, Indiana 47907
UNITED STATES OF AMERICA

PART I

CONTROL OF LIMB AND SPEECH MOVEMENTS

Cerebral Control of Speech and Limb Movements
G.E. Hammond (editor)

Chapter 1

CHARACTERISTICS OF SPEECH AS A MOTOR CONTROL SYSTEM

Vincent L. Gracco
Haskins Laboratories

The structural and functional organization of any biophysical system provides potentially important information on the underlying control structure. For speech, the anatomical and physiological structure of the vocal tract and the apparent functional nature of speech motor actions suggest a characteristic control structure in which the entire vocal tract is the smallest functional unit. Sounds are coded as different relative vocal tract configurations generated from neuromuscular specifications of characteristic articulatory actions. Sensorimotor processes are applied to the entire vocal tract to scale and sequence changes in vocal tract states. Sensorimotor mechanisms are viewed as a means to adjust speech motor output predictively in the face of continuously changing peripheral conditions. An underlying oscillatory process is hypothesized as the basis for sequential speech adjustments in which a centrally-generated rhythm is modulated according to internal (task) requirements and the constantly changing configurational state of the vocal tract.

Speaking is a complex action involving a number of levels of organization and representative processes. At a cognitive level, speaking represents the manipulation of abstract symbols through a synthesis of associative processes expressed through a sophisticated linguistic structure. At a neuromotor level, at least seven articulatory subsystems can be identified (respiratory, laryngeal, pharyngeal, lingual, velar, mandibular, and labial) which interact to produce coordinated kinematic patterns within a complex and dynamic biomechanical environment. At an acoustic level, characteristic patterns result from complex aerodynamic manipulations of the vocal tract. The cognitive, sensorimotor, and acoustic processes of speech and their interaction are critical components in understanding this uniquely human behavior. As the interface between the nervous system and the acoustic medium for speech production/perception, speech motor processes constitute a direct link between higher level neurophysiological processes and the resulting aerodynamic/acoustic events.

In the following chapter, characteristics of the speech motor control process will be evaluated from a functional perspective emphasizing the structural and functional organization of the vocal tract and the timing characteristics associated with their continuous modulation. In contrast to perspectives which emphasize the large numbers of muscular/kinematic degrees of freedom, the current perspective is one that assumes that the overall vocal tract is the smallest unit of functional behavior. Sounds are encoded according to characteristic vocal tract shapes specified neuromuscularly and modulated through sensorimotor mechanisms to adapt to the constantly changing peripheral environment. Examination of the structural components and their interaction is consistent with this macroscopic organization as are a number of empirical observations. The functional organization is implemented by a limited number of sensorimotor control processes that scale overall vocal tract actions spatiotemporally within a frequency-modulated rhythmic organization characteristic of more automatic, innate motor behaviors.

Structural Properties

In order to describe speech from the perspective of a motor control system, a necessary step is to identify the components of the motor system to determine how their structural properties may reflect on the overall functional organization. The structures of the vocal tract include the lungs, larynx, pharynx, tongue, lips, jaw, and velum. Anatomically the vocal tract structures display unique muscular architecture, muscular connections, and muscular orientation that determine their potential contributions to the speech production process. For example, the orientation of the muscles of the pharynx, primarily the pharyngeal constrictors, is such that they generate a sphincteric action on the long axis of the vocal tract producing a change in the cross-sectional area and the tension or compliance of the pharyngeal tissues. The muscles of the velum are oriented primarily to raise and lower the soft palate separating the oral and nasal cavities. Perioral muscles are arranged such that various synergistic muscle actions result in a number of characteristic movements such as opening and closing of the oral cavity and protruding and retracting the lips. Some of the components, such as the tongue and larynx, can be subdivided into extrinsic and intrinsic portions each of which appear to be involved in different functional actions. Intrinsic tongue muscle fibers are oriented to allow fine grooving of the longitudinal axis of the tongue and tongue tip and lateral adjustments characteristic of liquid and continuant sounds. Extrinsic tongue muscles are arranged predominantly to allow shaping of the tongue mass as well as elevation, depression, and retraction of portions of the tongue. Intrinsic laryngeal muscles are arranged to open and close the glottis reciprocally and adjust the tension of the vibrating vocal folds, whereas extrinsic laryngeal muscles are oriented to displace the entire laryngeal complex (thyroid cartilage and associated intrinsic muscles and ligaments). Generally, movements of the vocal tract can be classified into two major categories; those that produce and release constrictions (valving) and those that modulate the shape or geometry of the vocal tract. The valving and shaping actions are generally associated with the production of consonant and vowels sounds, respectively (Öhman, 1966; Perkell, 1969).

In addition to the structural arrangement of the vocal tract muscles for valving and shaping actions, mechanical properties of individual vocal tract structures provide insight into the functional organization of the speech motor control system. The dynamic nature of the tissue load against which the different vocal tract muscles contract is extremely heterogeneous. For some structures such as the lips and vocal folds, inertial considerations are minimal, while for the jaw and respiratory structures inertia is a significant consideration. The tongue and lips are soft tissue structures that undergo substantial viscoelastic deformation during speech while the jaw and perhaps the lips display a degree of anisotropic tension (Lynn & Yemm, 1971). Even seemingly homogeneous structures, such as the upper and lower lips, display different stiffness properties (Ho, Azar, Weinstein, & Bowley, 1982), possibly contributing to their differential movement patterns (Kelso, Vatikiotis-Bateson, Saltzman, & Kay, 1985; Gracco & Abbs, 1986; Gracco, 1988). Considering the structural arrangement of the vocal tract, the different muscular orientations and the vast interconnection of muscles, cartilages, and ligaments, it is clear that complex biomechanical interactions among structures are the rule. Passive or reactive changes in the vocal tract due to inherent mechanical coupling is a consequence of almost any vocal tract action, with the relative significance varying according to the specific structural components and conformational change and the speed at which adjustments occur. As a result, a single articulatory action may generate primary as well as secondary effects throughout the vocal tract. Examination of individual articulatory actions is important to determine their contribution to the sound-producing process. However, individual articulatory actions never have isolated effects. The combination of the viscoelastic properties of the tissues, the different biomechanical properties of vocal tract structures, and the complex geometry of the vocal tract comprise a complex biomechanical environment. The kinematic and acoustic variability characteristic of speech production reflects in part the differential filtering of neural control signals by the peripheral biomechanics. Only through detailed biophysical models of the vocal tract and considerations of potential biomechanical interaction associated with various phonetic environments can the control principles of the speech motor control system be separated from structural or cognitive/linguistic influences.

Functional Organization

In order to characterize the speech motor control system accurately, and pose the motor control problem correctly, it is important to determine how the behavior is being regulated. That is, are the individual sound-influencing elements being independently controlled, or does the control structure involve larger units of behavior, and if so, what is the organizational structure? For speech, the simple observation that even an isolated vowel sound requires activity in respiratory muscles, tension and adduction of the vocal folds, adjustments in the compliance of the oropharyngeal walls, shaping of the tongue, positioning of the jaw, elevation of the velum, and some lip configuration is rather convincing evidence that speech is functionally organized at a level reflecting the overall state of the vocal tract. It is the interaction of all the neuromuscular components that provide each speech sound with its distinct character, not the action of any single component. The often-cited fact that speech production involves over 70 different muscular degrees of freedom, while perhaps anatomically factual, is a functional misrepresentation of the motor control system organization. As early as the birth cry and through the earliest stages of speech development, the infant's vocalizations involve the cooperative action of respiratory, laryngeal, and supralaryngeal muscles to produce sounds. A similar observation can be made for locomotion in that rhythmic stepping and other seemingly functional locomotion-like behaviors can be elicited well before the infant manifests upright walking (Thelen, 1985, 1986). It appears that functional characteristics of many human behaviors are present at birth or very early in the infant's development, suggesting that the "significant functional units of action" (Greene, 1972) may be innate properties of the nervous system. It is suggested that speech motor development reflects the ability to make finer and more varied adjustments of the vocal tract, not the mastering of the articulatory or muscular degrees of freedom.

As suggested above, the characteristics of speech as a motor control system include a control structure in which the smallest functional unit is the entire vocal tract. Recent studies have demonstrated examples of large scale manipulation of vocal tract actions rather than the modulation of separate articulatory actions. As shown in Figure 1, movements of individual articulators such as the upper lip, lower lip, and jaw demonstrate timing relations such that adjustments in one structure are accompanied by adjustments in all functionally-related structures. The coordinative process reflects a constraint on articulatory actions involved in the production of a specific sound. Similar results can be observed for other more spatially remote, but functionally related articulators.

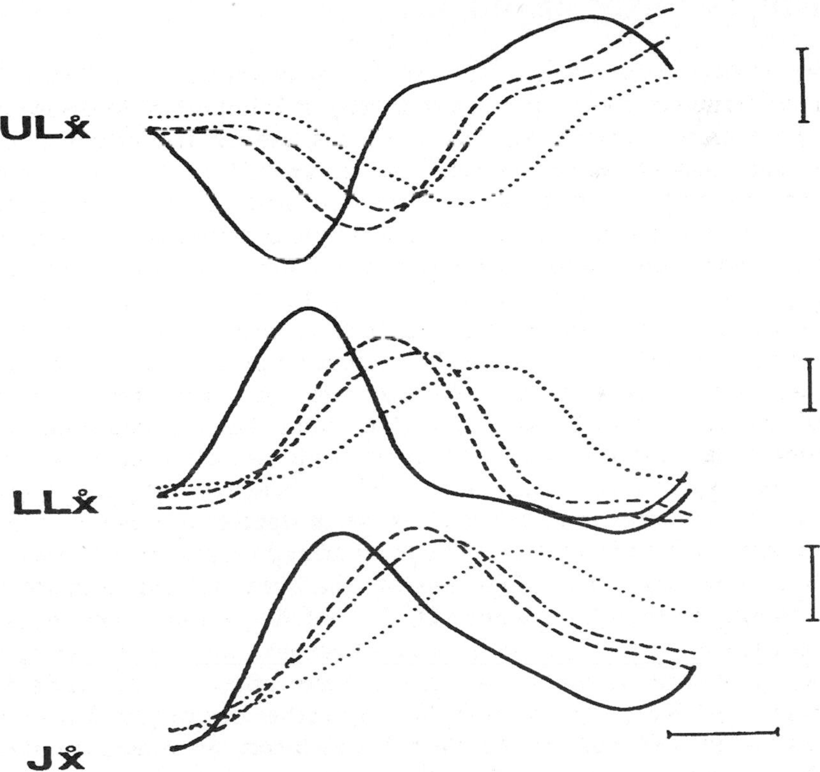

Figure 1. Upper Lip (UL), Lower Lip (LL), and Jaw (J) movement velocities associated with the first 'p' closing in 'sapapple'. Signals are aligned to the jaw opening peak velocity for the first 'a' in 'sapapple'. As the preceding vowel duration changes, the timing of the UL, LL, and J change in a consistent and unitary manner (from Gracco, 1988). Calibration bars are 50 mm/sec (vertical) and 100 ms (horizontal).

As shown in Figure 2, movements of the larynx and the lower lip demonstrate a similar timing dependency for the production of the 'f' in 'safety'. In order to generate the frication noise characteristic of the /f/, the glottal opening and labial constriction is appropriately timed. As the timing of one structure changes, the timing of the other functionally-related articulatory action also changes.

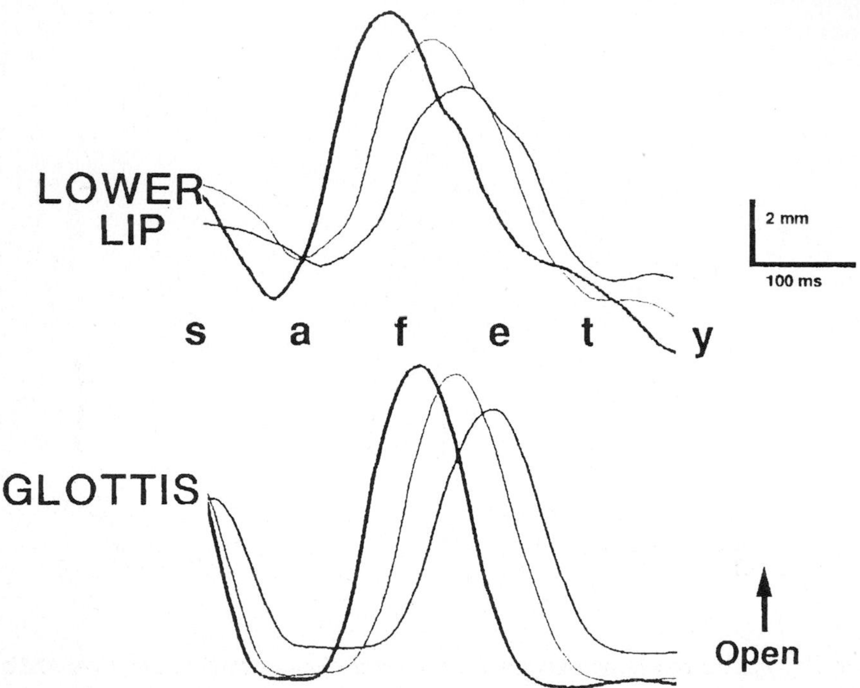

Figure 2. Lower lip closing and glottal opening for three repetitions of the word 'safety' produced in a carrier sentence "Its a _______ again"; signals were aligned to the peak glottal opening for the 'ts' in 'Its'. As the lower lip closing movement for 'f' varies, the timing of the glottal opening (devoicing) also varies (from Gracco & Löfqvist, 1989). Similar to Figure 1, the timing of the oral and laryngeal actions appears to be adjusted as a unit.

Similarly, for movements associated with resonance-producing vowel events, timing constraints can be observed between laryngeal voicing and jaw opening associated with tongue positioning for a vowel (Figure 3). Here, the laryngeal action associated with phonation and the change in jaw positioning to assist the tongue in vowel production demonstrate similar coordinative interdependency.

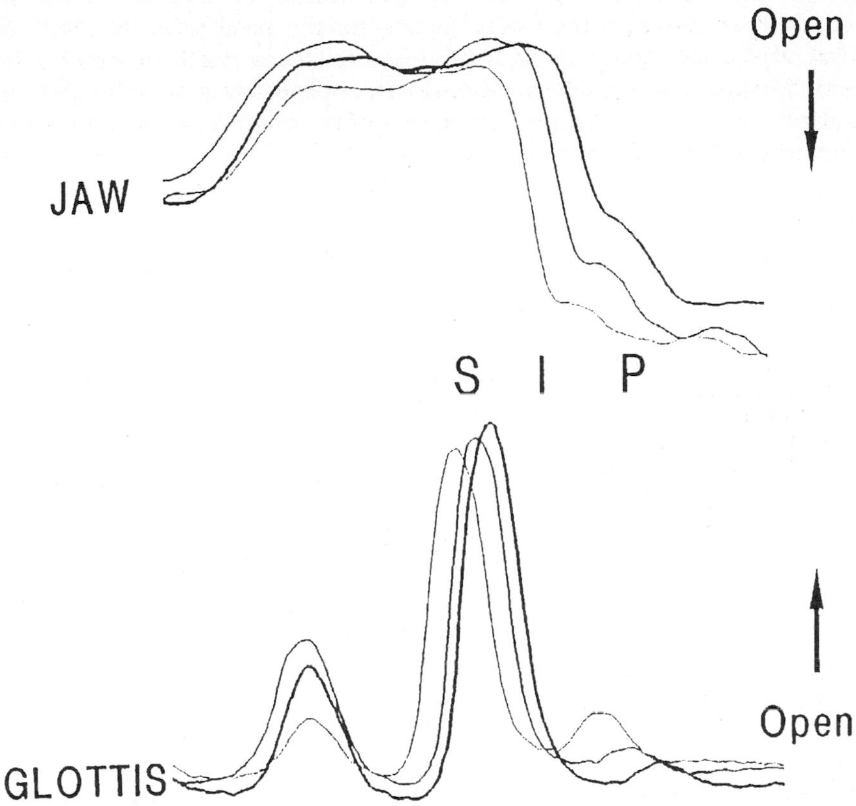

Figure 3. Timing relations between the glottal closing and the jaw opening associated with the vowel in 'sip'. As the glottal opening/closing associated with the 's' and subsequent vowel varies, the jaw opening (noted by the downward movement) also varies proportionally (from Gracco & Löfqvist, 1989). The signals are aligned as in the previous figure.

Some preliminary evidence further suggests that certain physiological changes associated with the production of emphatic stress result in an increase in the actions of all portions of the vocal tract rather than being focused on one specific articulator (Fowler, Gracco, & Vatikiotis-Bateson, 1989). In the presence of a potentially disruptive mechanical disturbance applied to one of the contributing articulators there is a tendency for the timing of all articulators to readjust (Gracco & Abbs, 1988). The timing of individual articulators is apparently not adjusted singularly but reflects a system level organization (see Löfqvist & Yoshioka, 1981, 1984; Tuller,

Kelso, & Harris, 1982, for other examples). It is not clear how general these observation are with regard to all speech sounds in all possible contexts. For example, the lip/jaw and laryngeal/supralaryngeal coordination observed in Figures 1 and 2 is modified when the sound is at the beginning of a word, apparently reflecting a change in the functional requirements of the task. The importance of these kinds of observations is not the specific observable pattern but the presence of characteristic patterns that are used for time-dependent articulatory adjustments.

Speech motor patterns reflect characteristic ways of manipulating the vocal tract, in the presence of a constant pressure source, to generate recognizable and language-specific acoustic signals (Ohala, 1983). The process through which such functional cooperation occurs has been described for many motor tasks in various contexts, with the assumption that the control actions involve the assembly of functional units of the system organized into a larger systems known as synergies or coordinative structures (Bernstein, 1967; Gelfand, Gurfinkel, Tsetlin, & Shik, 1971; Fowler, 1977; Fowler, Rubin, Remez, & Turvey, 1980; Turvey, 1977; Kugler, Kelso, & Turvey, 1980, 1982; Saltzman, 1979, 1986). In keeping with the interactive structural configuration outlined previously and the apparent functional nature of the task itself, a modification of this perspective is offered. Speaking appears to involve coordinative structures (or synonymously motor programs; see Abbs, Gracco, & Cole, 1984; Gracco, 1987) available for all characteristic vocal tract actions associated with the sound inventory of the language. It is not the case, however, that a coordinative structure or a motor program is a process but a set of sensorimotor specifications identifying the relative contribution of the vocal tract structures to the overall vocal tract configuration (see Abbs et al., 1984; Gracco, 1987). As such, coordinative structures may be more rigidly-specified than previously thought and the distinction between a flexible coordinative structure and a hard-wired motor program algorithm may be more rhetorical than real (cf. Kelso, 1986, for discussion of differences). In this regard, two observations are of note. When the contribution of jaw movement is eliminated, by placing a block between the teeth, jaw-closing muscle actions are still present (Folkins & Zimmermann, 1981). Further, in response to jaw perturbation, both functionally-specific responses and non-functional responses are observed, such as upper lip muscle increases when the subjects are not producing sounds requiring upper lip movement (Kelso, Tuller, Vatikiotis-Bateson, & Fowler, 1984; Shaiman, 1989). Together, these observations reflect on specific aspects of the speech motor control process and suggest that speech production may rely to some degree on fixed neuromuscular specifications. The presence of jaw muscle actions when jaw movement is eliminated is consistent with the previous suggestion that speech motor control is a holistic process involving the entire vocal tract. The presence of upper lip muscle increases (albeit small) when the sound being produced does not involve the upper lip, reflects on the underlying control process. The interaction of the phasic stimulus (from the perturbation) with activated motoneurons will produce the functionally-specific compensatory response. If the motoneurons are inactive, or slightly active, the phasic stimuli would result in small increases in muscle activation levels without any significant movement changes. This is a much simpler control scheme in that certain interactions and functionally-specific responses are a consequence of the activation of specific muscles and the actual synaptic interactions in the neural system controlling various vocal tract structures (Gracco, 1987). The advantage of this perspective is that certain properties of speech production result from the physiological organization and focus the functional organization of the speech motor control system on the neural coding of speech sounds and the characteristic sensorimotor processes that modulate and sequence vocal tract configurations.

Neural Coding of Speech Motor Actions

The coding of speech is viewed as the process by which overall vocal tract states are "represented and transformed by the nervous system" (see Perkel & Bullock, 1968). This coding is similar to what has previously been identified as the selection of muscular components associated with a specific motor act (cf. Evarts, Bizzi, Burke, DeLong, & Thach, 1972). In the following, the selection of characteristic vocal tract states will be evaluated with respect to two components of the hypothetical specification process, although the actual neural coding is viewed as a single process and is only presented separately for the purpose of clarity. As stated previously, the actions of the vocal tract are designed to either valve the air stream for different consonant sounds or to shape the geometry of the vocal tract for different vowel and vowel-like sounds. Considering the place of articulation for vowels and consonants naturally results in categorical distinctions which are apparent acoustically and aerodynamically (Stevens, 1972). However, rather than dichotomizing these apparently discrepant processes, it is suggested that valving and shaping can be conceptualized as a single physiological process. That is, speech sounds are coded according to overall vocal tract states which include primary articulatory synergies. When the appropriate muscles are activated, the resulting force vectors create characteristic actions resulting in vocal tract states which act to valve the pressure or change the geometry without creating turbulence producing constrictions. It is the orientation of the activated muscle fibers, the activation of synergistic and antagonistic muscles, and the fixed boundaries of the vocal tract (the immobile maxilla) that result in the achievement of characteristic shapes or constriction locations; certain muscular synergies can only result in certain vocal tract configurations. For example, selection of certain upper and lower lip muscles (orbicularis oris inferior and superior, depressor anguli oris, mentalis, depressor labii inferior) will always result in the approximation of the upper and lower lips for 'p', 'b', or 'm'. The magnitude or timing of the individual muscle actions may vary, but bilabial closure will always involve the activation of upper and lower lip muscles; otherwise bilabial closure could not be attained. Similarly, changing the focus of neural activation to regions representing lower lip muscles (orbicularis oris inferior and mentalis, with primary focus in mentalis) results in movements consistent with labiodental constriction for 'f' and 'v' achieved against the immobile maxillary incisors (Folkins, 1976). Different relative contributions of extrinsic and intrinsic tongue muscles result in various shapes and movements on the tongue tip, blade, and body, resulting in characteristic constrictions or shapes as a consequence. Constriction location and constriction degree are useful categories to describe different speech sounds because they specify what is distinctive to each phonetic segment. Control over the vocal tract configuration through the development of finer control over the neuromuscular organization provides a more reasonable description of the speech acquisition process because the entire vocal tract is manipulated, not just the distinctive attributes for each sound. The neuromotor differences in consonant and vowel sounds appear to be reflected in other characteristics of the control process.

One such characteristic involves the compliant states of the vocal tract consistent with the level of tension in the tissue walls. The importance of tissue compliance can be inferred from a number of observations. A major physical difference between voiced and voiceless consonants is in the level of air pressure associated with their production. Voiceless sounds are generally produced with higher vocal tract pressures than their voiced counterparts. The pressure difference, which has significant aerodynamic and acoustic consequences, results from changes in the tension in the pharyngeal and oral cavities as well as from pressure from the lungs (Müller & Brown, 1980). For example, subjects engaged in producing speech while simultaneously engaged in a valsalva maneuver (forceful closing of the glottis thereby eliminating the lung contribution) were able to maintain voiced/voiceless intraoral pressure differences apparently resulting from changes in the overall compliance of the vocal tract walls (Brown & McGlone, 1979). Together with experimental evidence that kinematic and electromyographic characteristics of lip and jaw movements are insufficient to differentiate voiced and voiceless sounds (Lubker & Parris, 1970; Harris, Lysaught, & Schvey, 1965; Fromkin, 1966), it appears that a major factor in generating voicing and voicelessness is the specification of overall vocal tract compliance. Two possible compliant states of the vocal tract are sufficient to categorize most speech sounds; low compliance associated with voiceless consonants and high compliance associated with voiced consonants and vowels. Compliant states of the vocal tract are associated with gross changes in the activity of at least the pharyngeal constrictors (Minifie, Abbs, Tarlow, & Kwaterski, 1974; Perlman, Luschei, & DuMond, 1989) and possibly other portions of the walls of the vocal tract (intraoral cavity). The specification of low compliance (resulting in high vocal tract pressures) would be associated with increased activity in larygneal muscles to assist in the devoicing gesture, and high compliance (resulting in low vocal tract pressures) would be associated with a relaxation of the muscle activity in the pharyngeal and oral cavities to allow cavity expansion for voiced stops and continuants (Bell-Berti & Hirose, 1973; Westbury, 1983; Perkell, 1969). Certain tense vowels may result from an intermediate level of compliance (between high and low) such that voicing is maintained but overall compliance is slightly higher than for lax vowels. It is important to note that modification in compliance is a process that produces a relatively slow change in the state of the vocal tract, with relaxation (high compliance) a slower process than constriction (low compliance). Together, specification of the compliant state of the vocal tract and selection of specific muscular actions is one means by which the vocal tract states may be specified neurally.

It should be noted, however, that the coding of speech motor actions is viewed primarily as a static process in which characteristic states of the vocal tract are identified prior to their actual implementation. Considering some dynamic properties of the speech motor control system provides some insight into the manner in which different sounds may acquire further acoustic and kinematic distinction. For example, lip closing movement associated with the voiceless bilabial stop 'p' is generally but not invariably associated with a higher velocity than the voiced bilabial 'b' or 'm' (Chen, 1970; Gracco, 1990; Summers, 1987; Sussman, MacNeilage, & Hanson, 1973). Lip and jaw closing movements are initiated earlier relative to vowel onset for voiceless 'p' than for voiced 'b' or 'm' (Gracco, 1990) resulting in shorter vowel durations. One possible explanation is that voiceless sounds are produced at a higher rate or frequency than their voiced counterparts, reflecting a different underlying frequency specification. Movement frequency is one dimension along which different speech sounds can be generally categorized. This hypothetical frequency modulation can be integrated with another dynamic property of the control system. Not only are closing movements generally faster for a voiceless than for a voiced consonant, but the preceding opening movement has also been observed to be faster (Gracco, 1990; Summers, 1987). It appears that not only may sounds be coded as a function of the frequency of individual vocal tract adjustments but that the functional requirements for specific sounds may be distributed across movement cycles rather than focused on a single movement phase. This observation suggests the operation of a look-ahead mechanism (Henke, 1966) similar to or identical with the mechanism underlying anticipatory coarticulation which predictively adjusts vocal tract actions. Speech motor control is a dynamic neuromotor process in which overall vocal tract compliance, the location of primary valving or shaping synergies, and frequency-modulated motor commands are specified by the immediate and future acoustic/aerodynamic requirements.

Invariance, Redundancy, and Precision

Before presenting some of the specific processes of the speech motor control system that are used to modulate overall vocal tract organization, two important and related issues should be addressed: invariance and precision. The search for invariance has a long and generally unsuccessful history in investigations of speech production with the obvious conclusion that invariance is not a directly observable event (alternatively, the appropriate metric has not been identified). From the perspective of speech as a motor control system, a more fundamental issue is the precision with which any quantity, variable, or vocal tract configuration is regulated. The presence of substantial acoustic, kinematic, electromyographic, and aerodynamic variability suggests that the speech motor control process operates at less than maximal precision (or within rather broad tolerance limits). The achievement of characteristic vocal tract configurations or individual articulatory actions is accomplished by a synthesis of general activation of most vocal tract structures (setting of overall vocal tract compliance) and focused activation of the relevant muscular synergies. This is consistent with neurophysiological evidence demonstrated in the studies of Kots (1975), in which voluntary movement is seen as a synthesis of diffuse excitation (pretuning), a more fixed and discrete increase in motoneuron excitability (tuning), and the final 'triggering' process. Similarly, brain potentials prior to the onset of muscle activity display rather diffuse activation over multiple cortical areas for discrete finger and toe movements (Boschert, Hink, & Deecke, 1983; Deecke, Scheid, & Kornhuber, 1969) and involve larger regions for production of speech (Larsen, Skinhøj, & Lassen, 1978; Curry, Peters, & Weinberg, 1978). One plausible perspective is that the nervous system modulates the focus of primary activation but that this process is not punctate. That is, activation and deactivation of cortical and perhaps subcortical cells involves diffuse and long term changes resulting in distributed tonic and phasic muscle activity. Specification of vocal tract configurations for specific sounds may involve characteristic patterns of activation and inhibition in all vocal tract muscles with only slightly greater focus on critical articulators involved in the more dominant or sound-critical movements. In some cases muscles may be partially activated just because of the proximity of their motoneurons to other activated motoneurones. One conclusion is that the neural processes underlying speech motor control are broadly specified and that the functional speech production goals (and the requisite perceptual properties) are only categorically invariant. As suggested by the apparent quantal nature of speech (Stevens, 1972), as long as the articulatory patterns are within a certain range (have not made a category change), the corresponding phonetic properties will be perceived, with kinematic variations producing very little perceptual effect. Perhaps speech perception and production should be appropriately represented as stochastic processes based on probability statements implemented through an adequate but imprecise control system. Strict determinism, invariance, and precision are most likely relegated to man-made machines working under rigid tolerance limits or simplified specifications, not to complex biological systems.

Sensorimotor Control Processes

Similar to the temporal organization for speech, spatial interactions are evident that reflect multiarticulate manipulations to achieve characteristic vocal tract states. The clearest examples of cooperative and functionally-relevant spatial interactions are observed when one articulator, such as the lip or jaw, is disturbed during speaking. Following the application of a dynamic perturbation impeding the articulatory movement, a compensatory adjustment is observed in the articulator being perturbed as well as other functionally-related, spatially-distant articulators (Abbs & Gracco, 1984; Folkins & Abbs, 1975; Gracco & Abbs, 1988; Kelso et al., 1984; Shaiman, 1989), reflecting the presence of afferent-dependent mechanisms in the control of speech movements. The distributed compensatory response to external perturbations is a direct reflection of the overall functional organization of the speech motor control process and is comparable to other sensorimotor actions observed for other motor behaviors such as postural adjustments (Marsden, Merton, & Morton, 1981; Nashner & Cordo, 1981; Nashner, Woollacott, & Tuma, 1979), eye-head interactions (Bizzi, Kalil, & Tagliasco, 1971; Morasso, Bizzi, & Dichgans, 1973), wrist-thumb actions (Traub, Rothwell, & Marsden, 1980), and thumb-finger coordination (Cole, Gracco, & Abbs, 1984). Changing the size of the oral cavity with the placement of a block between the teeth similarly results in compensatory changes in articulatory actions resulting in perceptually-acceptable vowel sounds (Lindblom, Lubker, & Gay, 1979;

Fowler & Turvey, 1980). It appears that the speech motor control system is designed to achieve functional behaviors through interaction of ascending sensory signals with descending motor commands.

Human and nonhuman studies have shown that sensory receptors located throughout the vocal tract are sufficient to provide a range of dynamic and static information which can be used to signal position and speed of physiological structures on a movement-to-movement basis (see Munger & Halata, 1983; Dubner, Sessle, & Storey, 1978; Kubota, Nakamura, & Schumacher, 1980; and Landgren & Olsson, 1982, for reviews). Studies utilizing perturbation of speech motor output indicate that the rich supply of orofacial somatic sensory afferents have the requisite properties to interact with central motor operations to yield the flexible speech motor patterns associated with oral communication (Abbs & Gracco, 1984; Gracco & Abbs, 1985; Gracco & Abbs, 1988; Kelso et al., 1984). Because of the constantly changing peripheral conditions during speaking, the absolute position of vocal tract structures can vary widely depending on the surrounding phonetic environment. The speech motor control system apparently adjusts for these movement-to-movement variations by incorporating somatic sensory information from the various muscle and mechanoreceptors located throughout the vocal tract. Considerations outlined elsewhere (Gracco & Abbs, 1987; Gracco, 1987) suggest that the speech motor control system appears to use somatic sensory information in two distinct ways; in a comparative manner to feed back information on the attainment of a speech goal and to predictively parameterize or adjust upcoming control actions. Structurally, there is strong evidence for the interaction of sensory information from receptors located within the vocal tract with speech motor output at many if not all levels of the neuraxis (see Gracco, 1987, and Gracco & Abbs, 1987, for a summary of the vocal tract representation in multiple cortical and subcortical sensory and motor regions). Furthermore, brain stem organization, evidenced by reflex studies, demonstrates a range of complex interactions in which sensory input from one structure such as the jaw or face is potentially able to modify motor output from lip and tongue as well as jaw muscles (Bratzlavsky, 1976; Dubner et al., 1978; Smith, Moore, Weber, McFarland, & Moon, 1985; Weber & Smith, 1987). It appears that there are multiple synaptic interactions possible throughout the neural system controlling the vocal tract, with the specific interaction dependent on how the system is actively configured.

Speech motor actions involve the activation or inactivation of various muscles of the vocal tract which are adjusted based on the peripheral conditions and the specific phonetic requirements. An important question related to the neural representation for speech is the character of the underlying activation process for different articulatory actions. A number of recent studies, evaluating the kinematic characteristics of different articulators, are consistent with a single sensorimotor process to generate a variety of articulatory actions. One method for evaluating the similarity in the underlying representation for multiple speech sounds and their associated movement dynamics is to compare the geometric (normalized) form of velocity profiles. A change in velocity profile shape accompanying experimental manipulation of phonetic context suggests a change in the movement dynamics, and by inference a change in the underlying neural representation. Conversely, a demonstration of trajectory invariance or scalar equivalence for a variety of movements suggests that different movements can be produced from the same underlying dynamics (Atkeson & Hollerbach, 1985; Hollerbach & Flash, 1982). That is, in order to produce movement variations appropriate to peripheral conditions and task requirements, it may be necessary only to scale the parameters of a single underlying dynamic relation; a much simpler task and, by inference, a simpler neural process. For movements of the vocal folds, tongue, lips, and jaw during speech it has been shown that changes in movement duration, and to a lesser extent movement amplitude, reflect a scaling of a base velocity profile (Gracco, 1990; Munhall, Ostry, & Parush, 1985; Ostry & Cooke, 1987; Ostry, Cooke, & Munhall, 1987; Ostry & Munhall, 1985). A scalar relation across a class of speech sounds involving the same articulators maintained for different initial conditions (different vowel contexts) suggests that the neural representation has been maximized and such a representation might reflect a basic component of speech production. That is, all speech movements may involve a simple scaling of a single characteristic dynamic (force-time) relationship (Kelso & Tuller, 1984) with the kinematic variations reflecting the influence of biomechanical and timing specifications. In addition, specification of control signals in terms of dynamics eliminates the need to specify individual movement trajectories since the path taken by any articulator is a consequence of the dynamics rather than being explicitly specified (see Kelso et al., 1985; Saltzman, 1986; Saltzman & Munhall, 1989). The scaling of individual actions appears to be another characteristic process that eliminates the need to store all possible phonetic variations explicitly. Rather, the control process is a scaling of characteristic motor patterns adjusted for endogenous conditions (speaking rate, emphasis, upcoming functional requirements) and the surrounding phonetic environment (sensorimotor adjustments). The classic central-peripheral, motor program-reflex perspectives have given way to more reasonable and realistic issues including when and how sensory information may be used and how the different representations are coded for the generation of all possible speech movements.

Movement Sequencing

A significant characteristic of many motor behaviors such as speech, locomotion, chewing, and typing is the production of sequential movements. Observations that interarticulator timing is not disrupted following perturbation (Gracco & Abbs, 1988), that speech rate can be modulated by changes in sensory input (Gracco & Abbs, 1989), and that perturbation induces minimal changes in speech movement duration (Gracco & Abbs, 1988; Lindblom, Lubker, Gay, Lyberg, Branderal, & Holgren, 1987) are consistent with an underlying oscillatory mechanism for speech. Further, somatic sensory-induced changes in the timing of oral closing action (due to lower lip perturbation) is consistent with an underlying oscillatory process (Gracco & Abbs, 1988; 1989). Qualitative observations of temporal consistency of sequential movements are also consistent with an underlying oscillatory or rhythm generating mechanism. Figure 4 shows 24 superimposed movements of the upper lip, lower lip, and jaw for the sentence "Buy Bobby a Poppy". These repetitions were produced as part of a larger study and were produced at different times during the experiment. The subject produced one repetition per breath and each repetition was produced at a comfortable subject-defined rate. As can be seen, there is a consistency to the repetitions that suggests an underlying periodicity indicative of a rhythmic process.

A few studies, attempting to address the periodicity and apparent rhythmicity of speech, have demonstrated the presence of some form of underlying frequency generating mechanism. Ohala (1975) recorded over 10,000 jaw movements within a 1.5 hour period of oral reading and was able to identify frequencies ranging from 2-6 Hz with significant durational variability. Kelso et al. (1985), using reiterant productions of the syllable 'ba' or 'ma', demonstrated a rather strong periodicity at approximately 5-6 Hz with minimal durational variability. The findings of Kelso et al. (1985) are consistent with an underlying oscillatory process. In contrast, the range of frequencies found by Ohala (1975) may reflect the frequency modulation associated with the sounds of the language, a factor minimized in the Kelso et al. (1985) study. The modulation of frequency, dependent on specific aerodynamic properties of the specific sounds and surrounding articulatory environment, may be a mechanism underlying speech movement sequencing (see also Saltzman & Munhall, 1989, for further discussion of serial dynamics). The fact that the frequency values reported by Kelso et al. (1985) were similar for 'ba' and 'ma' suggest that vowels may be a major factor in determining the local periodicity. However, it is the case that the individual movements or movement cycles are not the same; local frequencies are different depending on the phonetic context.

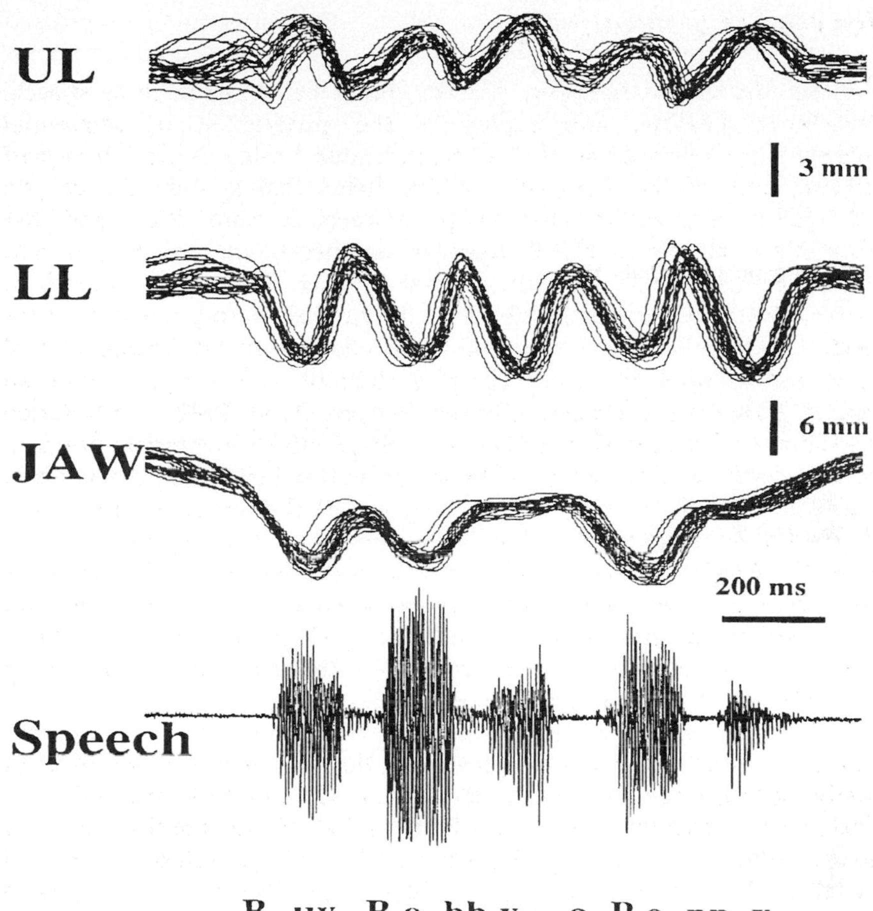

Figure 4. Superimposed Upper Lip (UL), Lower Lip (LL) and Jaw (J) movements associated with 24 repetitions of the sentence "Buy Bobby a Poppy"; the patterns are remarkably similar, displaying little spatiotemporal variation. Only the acoustic signal from a single repetition is shown. The signals are aligned to jaw opening peak velocity for the vowel in 'Buy'.

In addition, speech production involves many of the same muscles as such automatic behaviors as breathing, chewing, sucking, and swallowing. It has been suggested that the mechanisms underlying speech may incorporate, to some degree, the same mechanisms as more automatic motor behaviors but adapted for the specialized function of communication (Evarts, 1982; Gracco & Abbs, 1988; Grillner, 1982; Kelso, Tuller, & Harris,

1983; Lund, Appenteng, & Seguin 1982). Few studies have focused specifically on the similarity of speech with more innate, rhythmic motor behaviors (Ostry & Flanagan, 1989; Moore, Smith, & Ringel, 1988) with mixed interpretations. Recent experiments and theoretical perspectives on the organization of central pattern generators for rhythmic behaviors such as locomotion, respiration, and mastication suggest a more flexible conceptualization of the possible behavioral outputs than has previously been envisioned for the neural control of rhythmic behaviors (see Cohen, Rossignol, and Grillner, 1988, and Getting, 1989, for reviews). For example, *in vitro* results suggest that the central pattern generator for respiration may more appropriately be considered as two separate but interrelated functions; one generating the rhythm and one generating the motor pattern (Feldman, Smith, McCrimmon, Ellenberger, & Speck, 1988). The implication for other rhythmic and quasi-rhythmic behaviors such as speech is that each function can be modulated independently, thus generalizing the concept of a central pattern generator to a wider range of behaviors. Recently, Patla (1988) has suggested that nonlinear conservative oscillators are the most plausible class of biological oscillators to model central pattern generators in that they provide the necessary time-keeping function as well as independent shaping of the output (see also Kelso & Tuller, 1984). The recent demonstration by Moore, Smith, and Ringel (1988) that mandibular muscle actions for speech are fundamentally different than for chewing suggests that the patterning for each behavior is different. That is, speech and chewing may share the same generator but have different patterning or, conversely, rely on different generators and patterns. Conceptually and theoretically, a fundamental frequency oscillator and static nonlinear shaping function can generate a number of complex patterns. Although speculative, some current central pattern generator models have the necessary complexity to be tentatively applied and rigorously tested as to their appropriateness for speech motor control.

Summary

From the present perspective, the speech motor control system is viewed as a biophysical structure with unique configurational characteristics. The structure does not constrain the systems' operation but significantly affects the observable behavior and hence the resulting acoustic manifestations. Consideration of the structural organization and the potential contributions from biomechanical interactions are suggested as potential explanations for some speech motor variability. Sensorimotor mechanisms were implicated as the means by which adjustments in characteristic vocal tract shapes can be dynamically and predictively modified to accommodate the changing peripheral conditions. From the perspective of the vocal tract as the controlled system, the consistent coordinative timing relationships reflect the functional modification of all the control elements or articulatory structures. Rather than describing sound production as the modulation or assembly of discrete units of action, the current functional perspective suggests that entire vocal tract actions are modulated to regulate acoustic/aerodynamic output parameters. The different parameters are realized by manipulation of the frequency of the forcing function applied uniformly to the control elements of the system. Rather than a parametric forcing in which some parameter such as stiffness is viewed as a regulated variable, it is hypothesized that the system is extrinsically forced by manipulation of the frequency of neural output consistent with the spatial requirements (e.g. movement extent) of the task. The frequency-modulated neuromotor actions are then filtered by the biomechanical environment resulting in intricate kinematic patterns. Speech motor control is viewed as a hierarchically organized control structure in which peripheral somatic sensory information interacts with central motor representations. The control scheme is viewed as hierarchical from the standpoint that the motor adjustments are embedded within a number of levels of organization, reflecting the overall goal of the motor act, communication. Modifications in the control signals reflect the parallel processing of multiple brain regions to scale and sequence changes in overall vocal tract states (Gracco & Abbs, 1987). The organizational characteristics of speech as a motor control system are fundamentally similar to other sequential motor actions and are felt to involve a limited number of general sensorimotor control processes.

Acknowledgements

The author thanks E. Vatikiotis-Bateson and C. Fowler for editorial comments and Y. Manning for word processing. The writing of this paper was supported by NIH grants DC-00121 and DC-00594.

References

Abbs, J.H., & Gracco, V.L. (1984). Control of complex motor gestures: orofacial muscles responses to load perturbation of the lip during speech. *Journal of Neurophysiology*, **51**, 705-723.

Abbs, J.H., Gracco, V.L., & Cole, K.J. (1984). Control of multimovement coordination: sensorimotor mechanisms in speech motor programming. *Journal of Motor Behavior*, **16**, 195-232.

Atkeson, C.G., & Hollerbach, J.M. (1985). Kinematic features of unrestrained vertical arm movements. *Journal of Neuroscience* **5**, 2318-2330.

Bell-Berti, F., & Hirose, H. (1973). Stop consonant voicing and pharyngeal cavity size. *Journal of the Acoustical Society of America*, **53**, 295-315.

Bernstein, N. (1967). *The co-ordination and regulation of movements.* New York: Pergamon Press.

Bizzi, E., Kalil, R., & Tagliasco, V. (1971). Eye-head coordination in monkeys: evidence for centrally patterned organization. *Science*, **173**, 452-454.

Boschert, J., Hink, R.F., & Deecke, L. (1983). Finger versus toe movement-related potentials: further evidence for supplementary motor area (SMA) participation prior to voluntary action. *Experimental Brain Research*, **52**, 73-80.

Bratzlavsky, M. (1976). Human brainstem reflexes. In M. Shahani (Ed.), *The motor system: neurophysiology and muscle mechanisms* (pp. 133-154). New York: Elsevier.

Brown, W.S., & McGlone, R.E. (1979). Supraglottic air pressure during a valsalva maneuver. In J.J. Wolf & D.H. Klatt (Eds.), *Speech communication papers: proceedings of the 97th Meeting of the Acoustical Society of America* (pp. 157-160). New York: The Acoustical Society of America.

Chen, M. (1970). Vowel length variation as a function of the voicing of the consonant environment. *Phonetica*, **22**, 129-159.

Cohen, A.H., Rossignol, S., & Grillner, S. (1988). *Neural control of rhythmic movements in vertebrates.* New York: Wiley.

Cole, K.J., Gracco, V.L., & Abbs, J.H. (1984). Autogenic and nonautogenic sensorimotor actions in the control of multiarticulate hand movements. *Experimental Brain Research*, **56**, 582-585.

Curry, S.H., Peters, J.F., & Weinberg, H. (1978). Choice of active electrode site and recording montage as variables affecting CNV amplitude preceding speech. In D.A. Otto (Ed.), *Multidisciplinary perspectives in event-related brain potential research* (pp. 275-279). Washington, DC: US Environmental Protection Agency.

Deecke, L., Scheid, P., & Kornhuber, H.H. (1969). Distribution of readiness potential, pre-motion positivity, and motor potential of the human cerebral cortex preceding voluntary finger movements. *Experimental Brain Research*, **7**, 158-168.

Dubner, R., Sessle, B.J., & Storey, A.T. (1978). *The neural basis of oral and facial function.* New York: Plenum Press.

Evarts, E.V. (1982). Analogies between central motor programs for speech and for limb movements. In S. Grillner, B. Lindblom, J. Lubker, & A. Persson (Eds.), *Speech motor control* (pp. 19-41). Oxford: Pergamon Press.

Evarts, E.V., Bizzi, E., Burke, R.E., DeLong, M., & Thach, W.T. (Eds.). (1972). Central control of movement. *Neurosciences Research Symposium Summaries*, **6**.

Feldman, J.L., Smith, J.C., McCrimmon, D.R., Ellenberger, H.H., & Speck, D.F. (1988). Generation of respiratory patterns in mammals. In A.H. Cohen, S. Rossignol, & S. Grillner (Eds.), *Neural control of rhythmic movements in vertebrates* (pp. 73-100). New York: Wiley.

Folkins, J.W. (1976). *Multidimensional lower lip displacement resulting from activation of individual labial muscles: development of a static model.* Unpublished doctoral dissertation, University of Washington.

Folkins, J.W., & Abbs, J.H. (1975). Lip and jaw motor control during speech: responses to resistive loading of the jaw. *Journal of Speech and Hearing Research*, **18**, 207-220.

Folkins, J.W., & Zimmermann, G.N. (1981). Jaw-muscle activity during speech with the mandible fixed. *Journal of the Acoustical Society of America*, **69**, 1441-1445.

Fowler, C.A. (1977). *Timing control in speech production.* Bloomington, IN: Indiana University Linguistics Club.

Fowler, C.A., Gracco, V.L., & Vatikiotis-Bateson, E. (1989). Remote and local effects of stress within and among articulatory subsystems. *Journal of the Acoustical Society of America*, **86**, S115.

Fowler, C.A., Rubin, P., Remez, R.E., & Turvey, M.T. (1980). Implications for speech production of a general theory of action. In B. Butterworth (Ed.), *Language production* (pp. 373-420). New York: Academic Press.

Fromkin, V.A. (1966). Neuro-muscular specification of linguistic units. *Language and Speech*, **9**, 170-199.

Gelfand, I.M., Gurfinkel, V.S., Tsetlin, M.L., & Shik, M.L. (1971). Some problems in the analysis of movements. In I.M. Gelfand, V.S. Gurfinkel, S.V. Fomin, & M.L. Tsetlin (Eds.), *Models of the structural-functional organization of certain biological systems* (pp. 329-345). Cambridge, MA: MIT Press.

Getting, P.A. (1989). Emerging principles governing the operation of neural networks. *Annual Review of Neuroscience*, **12**, 185-204.

Gracco, V.L. (1987). A multilevel control model for speech motor activity. In H. Peters & W. Hulstij (Eds.), *Speech motor dynamics in stuttering* (pp. 57-76). Wien: Springer-Verlag.

Gracco, V.L. (1988). Timing factors in the coordination of speech movements. *Journal of Neuroscience*, **8**, 4628-4634.

Gracco, V.L. (1990). *Some organizational principles for speech movement control.* Manuscript submitted for publication.

Gracco, V.L., & Abbs, J.H. (1985). Dynamic control of the perioral system during speech: kinematic analyses of autogenic and nonautogenic sensorimotor processes. *Journal of Neurophysiology*, **54**, 418-432.

Gracco, V.L., & Abbs, J.H. (1986). Variant and invariant characteristics of speech movements. *Experimental Brain Research*, **65**, 156-166.

Gracco, V.L., & Abbs, J.H. (1988). Central patterning of speech movements. *Experimental Brain Research*, **71**, 515-526.

Gracco, V.L., & Abbs, J.H. (1989). Sensorimotor characteristics of speech motor sequences. *Experimental Brain Research*, **75**, 586-598.

Gracco, V.L., & Löfqvist, A. (1989). Speech movement coordination: oral-laryngeal interactions. *Journal of the Acoustical Society of America*, **86**, S114.

Greene, P.H. (1972). Problems of organization of motor systems. In R. Rosen & F. Snell (Eds.), *Progress in theoretical biology* (pp. 303-338). New York: Academic Press.

Grillner, S. (1982). Possible analogies in the control of innate motor acts and the production of sound in speech. In S. Grillner, B. Lindblom, J. Lubker, & A. Persson (Eds.), *Speech motor control* (pp. 217-230). Oxford: Pergamon Press.

Harris, K.S., Lysaught, G.F., & Schvey, M.M. (1965). Some aspects of the production of oral and nasal labial stops. *Language and Speech*, **8**, 135-147.

Henke, W.L. (1966). *Dynamic articulatory model of speech production using computer simulation.* Unpublished doctoral dissertation, Massachusetts Institute of Technology.

Ho, T.P., Azar, K., Weinstein, S. & Bowley, W.W. (1982). Physical properties of human lips: experimental and theoretical analysis. *Journal of Biomechanics*, **15**, 859-866.

Hollerbach, J.M., & Flash, T. (1982). Dynamic interactions between limb segments during planar arm movement. *Biological Cybernetics*, **44**, 67-77.

Kots, Ya.M. (1975). *The organization of voluntary movement.* New York: Plenum Press.

Kelso, J.A.S. (1986). Pattern formation in speech and limb movements involving many degrees of freedom. In H. Heuer & C. Fromm (Eds.), *Generation and modulation of action patterns* (pp. 105-128). Berlin: Springer-Verlag.

Kelso, J.A.S., & Tuller, B. (1984). Converging evidence in support of common dynamic principles for speech and movement coordination. *American Journal of Physiology*, **15**, R928-R935.

Kelso, J.A.S., Tuller, B., & Harris, K.S. (1983). A 'dynamic pattern' perspective on the control and coordination of movement. In P.F. MacNeilage (Ed.), *The production of speech* (pp. 137-173). New York: Springer-Verlag.

Kelso, J.A.S., Tuller, B., Vatikiotis-Bateson, E., & Fowler, C.A. (1984). Functionally specific articulatory cooperation following jaw perturbations during speech: evidence for coordinative structures. *Journal of Experimental Psychology: Human Perception and Performance*, **10**, 812-832.

Kelso, J.A.S., Vatikiotis-Bateson, E., Saltzman, E.L., & Kay, B. (1985). A qualitative dynamic analysis of reiterant speech production: phase portraits, kinematics, and dynamic modeling. *Journal of the Acoustical Society of America*, **77**, 266-280.

Kubota, K., Nakamura, Y., & Schumacher, G.H. (1980). *Jaw position and jaw movement*. Berlin: Verlag Volk und Gesundeit.

Kugler, P.N., Kelso, J.A.S., & Turvey, M.T. (1980). On the concept of coordinative structures as dissipative structures: I. Theoretical lines of convergence. In G.E. Stelmach (Ed.), *Tutorials in motor behavior* (pp. 1-47). Amsterdam: North Holland.

Kugler, P.N., Kelso, J.A.S., & Turvey, M.T. (1982). On the control and coordination of naturally developing systems. In J.A.S. Kelso & J.E. Clark (Eds.), *The development of movement control and coordination* (pp. 5-78). New York: Wiley.

Landgren, S., & Olsson, K.A. (1982). Oral mechanoreceptors. In S. Grillner, B. Lindblom, J.F. Lubker, & A. Persson (Eds.), *Speech motor control* (pp. 129-140). Oxford: Pergamon Press.

Larsen, B., Skinhøj, E., & Lassen, N.A. (1978). Variations in regional cortical blood flow in the right and left hemispheres during automatic speech. *Brain*, **101**, 193-209.

Lindblom, B., Lubker, J.F., & Gay, T. (1979). Formant frequencies of some fixed-mandible vowels and a model of speech motor programming by predictive simulation. *Journal of Phonetics*, **7**, 147-161.

Lindblom, B., Lubker, J.F., Gay, T., Lyberg, P., Branderal, P., & Holgren, K. (1987). The concept of target and speech timing. In R. Channon & L. Shockery (Eds.), *In honor of Ilse Lehiste* (pp. 161-181). Dordrecht, The Netherlands: Foris Publications.

Löfqvist, A., & Yoshioka, H. (1981). Interarticulator programming in obstruent production. *Phonetica*, **38**, 21-34.

Löfqvist, A., & Yoshioka, H. (1984). Intrasegmental timing: laryngeal-oral coordination in voiceless consonant production. *Speech Communication*, **3**, 279-289.

Lubker, J.F., & Parris, P.J. (1970). Simultaneous measurements of intraoral pressure, force of labial contact, and labial electromyographic activity during production of the stop consonant cognates /p/ and /b/. *Journal of the Acoustical Society of America*, **47**, 625-633.

Lund, J.P., Appenteng, K., & Seguin, J.J. (1982). Analogies and common features in the speech and masticating systems. In S. Grillner, B. Lindblom, J.F. Lubker, & A. Persson (Eds.), *Speech motor control* (pp. 231-245). Oxford: Pergamon Press.

Lynn, A.M.J., & Yemm, R. (1971). External forces required to move the mandible of relaxed human subjects. *Archives of Oral Biology*, **16**, 1443-1447.

Marsden, C., Merton, P., & Morton, H. (1981). Human postural responses. *Brain*, **104**, 513-534.

Minifie, F., Abbs, J.H., Tarlow, A., & Kwaterski, M. (1974). EMG activity within the pharynx during speech production. *Journal of Speech and Hearing Research*, **17**, 497-504.

Morasso, P., Bizzi, E., & Dichgans, J. (1973). Adjustments of saccade characteristics during head movements. *Experimental Brain Research*, **16**, 492-500.

Moore, C.A., Smith, A., & Ringel, R.L. (1988). Task-specific organization of activity in human jaw muscles. *Journal of Speech and Hearing Research*, **31**, 670-680.

Munger, B.L., & Halata, Z. (1983). The sensory innervation of primate facial skin. I. Hairy skin. *Brain Research Reviews*, **5**, 45-80.

Müller, E.M., & Brown, W.S. (1980). Variations in the supraglottal air pressure waveform and their articulatory interpretation. In N. Lass (Ed.), *Speech and language: advances in basic research and practice, Vol. 4* (pp 317-389). New York: Academic Press.

Munhall, K.G., Ostry, D.J., & Parush, A. (1985). Characteristics of velocity profiles of speech movements. *Journal of Experimental Psychology: Human Perception and Performance*, **11**, 457-474.

Nashner, L.M., & Cordo, P.J. (1981). Relation of automatic postural responses and reaction-time voluntary movements of human leg muscles. *Experimental Brain Research*, **43**, 395-405.

Nashner, L.M., Woollacott, M., & Tuma, G. (1979). Organization of rapid responses to postural and locomotor-like perturbation of standing man. *Experimental Brain Research*, **36**, 463-476.

Ohala, J.J. (1975). The temporal regulation of speech. In G. Fant & M.A.A. Tatham (Eds.), *Auditory analysis and perception of speech* (pp. 431-454). London: Academic Press.

Ohala, J.J. (1983). The origin of sound patterns in vocal tract constraints. In P.F. MacNeilage (Ed.), *The production of speech* (pp. 189-216). New York: Springer-Verlag.

Öhman, S.E.G. (1966). Coarticulation in VCV utterances: spectrographic measurements. *Journal of the Acoustical Society of America*, **39**, 151-168.

Ostry, D.J., & Cooke, J.D. (1987). Kinematic patterns in speech and limb movements. In E. Keller & M. Gopnik, (Eds.), *Motor and sensory processes of language* (pp. 223-235). Hillsdale, NJ: Lawrence Erlbaum Associates.

Ostry, D.J., Cooke, J.D., & Munhall, K.G. (1987). Velocity curves of human arm and speech movements. *Experimental Brain Research*, **74**, 1-10.

Ostry, D.J., & Flanagan, J.R. (1989). Human jaw movement in mastication and speech. *Archives of Oral Biology*, **34**, 685-693.

Ostry, D.J., & Munhall, K.G. (1985). Control of rate and duration of speech movements. *Journal of the Acoustical Society of America*, **77**, 640-648.

Patla, A.E. (1988). Analytic approaches to the study of outputs from central pattern generators. In A.H. Cohen, S. Rossignol, & S. Grillner (Eds.), *Neural control of rhythmic movements in vertebrates* (pp. 455-486). New York: Wiley.

Perkel, D.H., & Bullock, T.H. (1968). Neural coding. *Neurosciences Research Program Bulletin*, **6**, 223-344.

Perkell, J.S. (1969). *Physiology of speech production: results and implications of a quantitative cineradiographic study* (Research Monograph No. 53). Cambridge, Mass: MIT Press.

Perlman, A., Luschei, E., & DuMond, C.E. (1989). Electrical activity from the superior pharyngeal constrictor during reflexive and nonreflexive tasks. *Journal of Speech and Hearing Research*, **32**, 749-754.

Saltzman, E.L. (1979). Levels of sensorimotor representation. *Journal of Mathematical Psychology*, **20**, 91-163.

Saltzman, E.L. (1986). Task dynamic coordination of the speech articulators: a preliminary model. In H. Heuer & C. Fromm (Eds.), *Generation and modulation of action patterns* (pp. 129-144). Berlin: Springer-Verlag.

Saltzman, E.L., & Munhall, K.G. (1989). A dynamic approach to gestural patterning in speech production. *Ecological Psychology*, **1**, 333-382.

Shaiman, S. (1989). Kinematic and electromyographic responses to perturbation of the jaw. *Journal of the Acoustical Society of America*, **86**, 78-87.

Smith, A., Moore, C.A., Weber, C.M., McFarland, D.H., & Moon, J.B. (1985). Reflex responses of the human jaw-closing system depend on the locus of intraoral mechanical stimulation. *Experimental Neurology*, **90**, 489-509.

Stevens, K.N. (1972). The quantal nature of speech: evidence from articulatory-acoustic data. In E.E. David & P.B. Denes (Eds.), *Human communication: a unified view* (pp. 51-66). New York: McGraw-Hill.

Summers, W.V. (1987). Effects of stress and final-consonant voicing on vowel production: articulatory and acoustic analyses. *Journal of the Acoustical Society of America*, **82**, 847-863.

Sussman, H.M., MacNeilage, P.F., & Hanson, R.J. (1973). Labial and mandibular dynamics during the production of bilabial consonants: preliminary observations. *Journal of Speech and Hearing Research*, **16**, 397-420.

Thelen, E. (1985). Developmental origins of motor coordination: leg movement in human infants. *Developmental Psychology*, **18**, 1-22.

Thelen, E. (1986). Treadmill-elicited stepping in seven-month-old infants. *Child Development*, **57**, 1498-1506.

Traub, M.M., Rothwell, J.C., & Marsden, C.D. (1980). A grab reflex in the human hand. *Brain*, **103**, 869-884.

Tuller, B., & Kelso, J.A.S. (1984). The timing of articulatory gestures: evidence for relational invariants. *Journal of the Acoustical Society of America*, **76**, 1030-1036.

Tuller, B., Kelso, J.A.S., & Harris, K.S. (1982). Interarticulator phasing as an index of temporal regularity in speech. *Journal of Experimental Psychology*, **8**, 460-472.

Turvey, M.T. (1977). Preliminaries to a theory of action with reference to vision. In R. Shaw & J. Bransford (Eds.), *Perceiving, acting and knowing: toward an ecological psychology* (pp. 211-265). Hillsdale, NJ: Lawrence Erlbaum Associates.

Weber, C.M., & Smith, A. (1987). Reflex responses in human jaw, lip, and tongue muscles elicited by mechanical stimulation. *Journal of Speech and Hearing Research*, **30**, 70-79.

Westbury, J.R. (1983). Enlargement of the supraglottal cavity and its relation to stop consonant voicing. *Journal of the Acoustical Society of America*, **73**, 1322-1336.

Cerebral Control of Speech and Limb Movements
G.E. Hammond (editor)

Chapter 2

CONTROL OF HUMAN JAW AND MULTI-JOINT ARM MOVEMENTS

J. Randall Flanagan
McGill University

David J. Ostry
McGill University

and

Anatol G. Feldman
Academy of Sciences, Moscow

We present models based on the equilibrium point (EP) hypothesis for planar human jaw and arm movements. According to this hypothesis, central commands control the EP of the system by setting motoneuron recruitment thresholds (λs). In multiple muscle systems, these commands control the λs of many muscles in concert. We posit basic central commands which control specific motor functions via various combinations of λs. One command is associated with the level of co-activation of all muscles and other commands are associated with motions in specific degrees of freedom. Both models include two degrees of freedom either distributed across joints (arm) or located at a single joint (jaw). We suggest that arm motions are planned in equilibrium coordinates corresponding to the position of the hand in space whereas jaw motions are planned in equilibrium coordinates associated with rotation and translation of the jaw. In both cases, we argue that the nervous system need only specify the direction and rate of change of the EP (i.e., equilibrium velocity vector). In the absence of special constraints, we propose that the EP is simply shifted at a constant velocity. We show that the models can account for experimental kinematic and electromyographic records in speech, mastication, and reaching movements.

Introduction

In this chapter, we examine the organization of human multi-joint arm movements in reaching and motions of the mandible in speech and mastication. The control of these limb and orofacial behaviors is explored within the framework of the equilibrium point (EP) hypothesis (Feldman, 1986). This hypothesis suggests that voluntary movements arise as a consequence of shifts in the equilibrium state of the motor system. The equilibrium state is determined by the dynamic interaction of central control signals, spinal reflex mechanisms, muscle properties, and external loads. Central command signals control this process through the specification of motoneuron (MN) recruitment thresholds and thus are able to produce desired movements and postures. We present a vectorial representation of central commands (*command vectors*) which is especially convenient for modeling multi-muscle systems.

The EP hypothesis posits a common mechanism - the central parameterization of MN recruitment thresholds - underlying the control of unrestrained free motions (e.g., reaching) and compliant or restricted motions involving contact forces (e.g., mastication). The hypothesis can also be generalized to different articulatory systems including those involved in multi-joint arm movements, orofacial movements, and eye movements (Feldman, 1981). Thus, the EP hypothesis provides a vehicle through which the underlying control of these systems can be compared.

In this paper, mathematical models are used to examine and compare multi-joint human arm movements and jaw motions. The two models are applications of the EP hypothesis to motor systems with multiple degrees of freedom either distributed to different joints (the arm) or associated with one joint (the jaw). These models, which have been implemented in computer simulations, are used to explore the form of central control signals underlying the generation of trajectories (i.e., time sequences of positions and/or forces). Simulated trajectories, based on hypothetical central commands, are compared with experimental kinematic records. In addition, electromyographic (EMG) patterns predicted by the models are examined for different movements.

The EP hypothesis offers a fundamentally different view of motor control from what can be called the computational approach. According to the latter, motion trajectories are pre-planned by the nervous system which then *solves* the inverse-dynamics equations in order to determine the torques required to achieve the planned trajectory (see Hollerbach, 1985, for a discussion of this approach). In contrast, the EP hypothesis suggests that muscle activations and forces arise as a natural dynamic reaction to differences between the actual position of the system and its equilibrium position specified by central control signals.

The EP models described in this chapter are based on the λ model developed by Feldman and his colleagues (see Feldman, 1986, for a review) rather than the α model advocated by Bizzi and his co-workers (e.g., Bizzi, Accornero, Chapple, & Hogan, 1984). According to the α model, the central nervous system controls muscle activation, and consequently muscle stiffness, in order to shift equilibrium. Thus, the α model cannot explain how the motor system specifies the position of isoelectric loads which require a constant level of muscle activation regardless of position. Similarly, force control models cannot explain how the system specifies the position of isotonic loads which require a constant level of force regardless of position. The difficulty with the α model is that changes in muscle activation are considered as a cause of shifts in equilibrium. In the λ model, the causal sequence of events during movement production is quite different: another variable (recruitment threshold or λ) underlies shifts in the equilibrium whereas muscle activations are an effect of this process. Thus, the model offers an alternative to the traditional view that muscle activation is the prime reason underlying movement production.

Through their influence on the MN recruitment thresholds (λs) of muscles, central commands control specific motor functions. One command is associated with the level of muscle co-contraction and other commands correspond to motion associated with specific degrees of freedom. In the arm model, in addition to a co-contraction command, there are separate commands for motions about the shoulder and elbow. Likewise, in the jaw model there are commands for rotation and translation of the mandible as well as the command for co-contraction. In general, in multiple muscle systems, central commands act on the λs of several (or all) muscles. For example, in the jaw model, the λs of all three modeled muscles (closer, opener, and protruder) must be controlled in concert in order to rotate or translate the mandible or to produce co-activation without motion.

Physiologically, the parameter λ is associated with the threshold of MN recruitment. This corresponds, in biomechanical terms, to an invariant force-length (or torque-angle) characteristic (Feldman, 1966). Consequently, positional degrees of freedom associated with central commands are naturally transformed into force degrees of freedom. By specifying λs, the central nervous system can control both position as well as force involved in compliant or restricted motion including isometric conditions.

Recent studies of multi-joint arm pointing movements have focused on the issue of planning coordinates. On the basis of kinematic variables, researchers have debated whether these movements are planned in terms of hand coordinates or in terms of joint coordinates. Straight line hand paths and invariant bell-shaped hand speed profiles have been taken as evidence of hand planning (Abend, Bizzi, & Morasso, 1982; Flash & Hogan, 1985) whereas similarities in joint angular velocity profiles have been taken as evidence of joint planning (Hollerbach & Atkeson, 1988; Soechting & Lacquaniti, 1981). These studies assume that kinematics give a reliable measure of the central control signals underlying trajectory formation. However, the EP hypothesis views kinematics as a consequence of shifts in the equilibrium position of the system. Depending on movement dynamics, actual trajectories may deviate substantially from the underlying equilibrium trajectories (i.e., time sequences of equilibrium positions). Thus, according to the EP hypothesis, the issue of planning coordinates should focus on equilibrium trajectories rather than actual trajectories. Since the former cannot be directly measured, models are required so that simulated movements, based on hypothetical equilibrium trajectories, can be compared with empirical records.

We assume that trajectories are planned in neural control or equilibrium spaces which map onto external physical spaces. Specifically, it is suggested that multi-joint reaching movements are generally planned in terms of the equilibrium position of the arm endpoint (equilibrium hand coordinates). During movement execution, these coordinates are transformed into equilibrium joint coordinates. However, some movements may be planned directly in equilibrium *joint* coordinates thereby bypassing the equilibrium *hand* planning level. It is also suggested that jaw motions are planned in equilibrium spaces corresponding to rotation of the mandible about the temporo-mandibular joint (TMJ) and translation of the centre of rotation of the mandible (i.e., the mandibular condyle) along the articular eminence. Evidence from jaw movement in speech indicates the independence of rotation and translation (see below).

In this chapter, we argue that regardless of the particular equilibrium coordinates in which movements are planned, the nervous system need only plan the rate and the direction of the shift in the equilibrium position (i.e., the nervous system specifies an equilibrium velocity vector). However, information concerning movement amplitude is not required in order to plan or initiate a movement. Note that amplitude depends on both the speed and the duration of the shift. The latter may be planned prior to movement onset or determined during the movement. In contrast, Flash (1987) has suggested that human point-to-point arm movements are characterized by equilibrium velocity profiles which are bell-shaped and scale with both amplitude and duration. Consequently, amplitude must be specified during initial planning in order to scale the equilibrium trajectory appropriately.

In summary, the EP hypothesis provides a common departure point for the examination of the control of multi-joint reaching movements and jaw movements in speech and mastication. Computer simulations, based on the EP hypothesis, are used to explore the form of central control signals underlying the production of these behaviors. Although orofacial and multi-joint limb movements may be planned in different neural control spaces (or equilibrium coordinates), we suggest that essential features of the control signals are equivalent. Specifically, we argue that the central nervous system selects an equilibrium velocity vector which specifies the direction and rate of shift of the equilibrium state of the system.

The λ Model

In this section, we present a mathematical treatment of the λ model. Where relevant, differences between the multi-joint arm model and the jaw model will be emphasized. For further information concerning the mathematics of the λ model, see Feldman (1980), Feldman (1986), and Feldman, Adamovich, Ostry, and Flanagan (1990).

Figure 1 presents schematics of the two-joint planar arm model (1A) and the two degree of freedom planar jaw model (1B). The arm model has six muscles including single-joint antagonists at the shoulder and elbow and double-joint antagonists. Three muscles are represented in the jaw model: jaw closer, jaw opener, and jaw protruder. In the arm model, there is a single degree of freedom associated with each joint. In the jaw model, there are also two degrees of freedom which correspond to translation of the condyle along the articular eminence and rotation of the mandible about the condyle.

Muscle Activation

The λ model suggests that central commands are associated with changes in MN membrane potential. Specifically, central commands parameterize the threshold length (λ) of MN recruitment which may correspond to the threshold of the tonic stretch reflex. Under static conditions, when muscle length (x) exceeds λ, MNs are recruited and the muscle will be active. Consequently, the condition of muscle activation is $x > \lambda$. It follows that muscles can be activated either by stretching the muscle or by shifting λ via central commands.

MODEL BIOMECHANICS

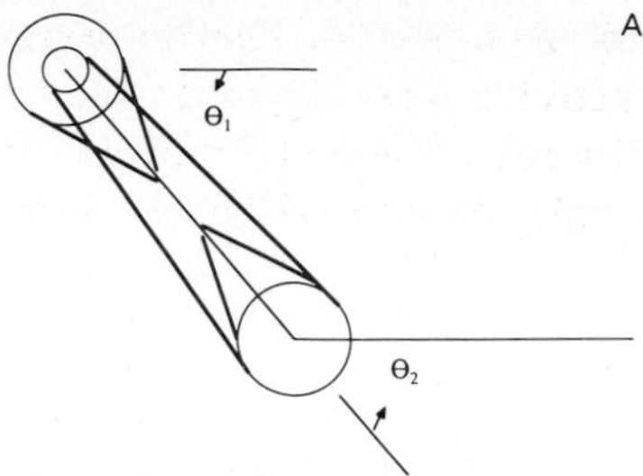

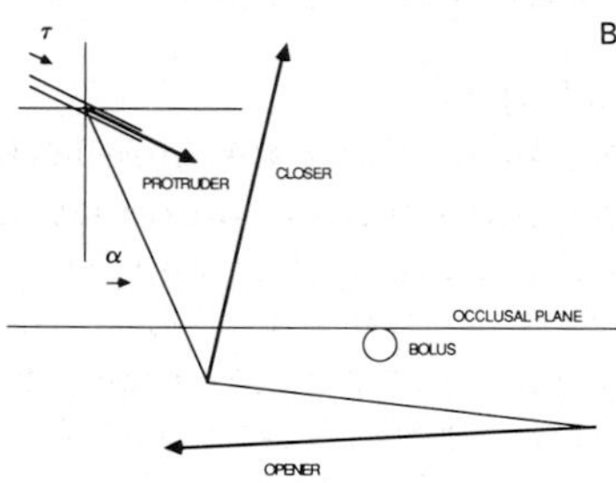

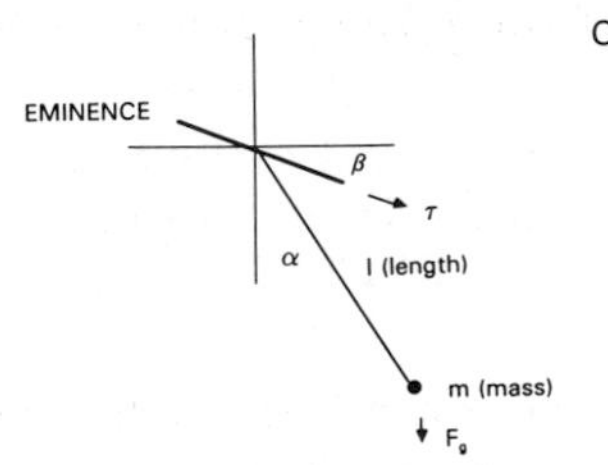

Figure 1. Schematics of the two-joint planar arm model (A) and two-degree of freedom planar jaw model (B). The arm model comprises three antagonistic muscle pairs including double-joint muscles. The jaw model includes a protruder muscle as well as closer and opener muscles which also act as retractors. Θ_1 and Θ_2 are the shoulder and elbow joint angles (A) and α and τ are jaw rotation and translation (B). To find the dynamics of jaw motion, the jaw was modeled as a pendulum with a point mass, m, located at length l. The pendulum is free to rotate, α, about a moving suspension point, τ, which is itself free to translate (C).

For simplicity, the level of MN recruitment (A) is assumed to increase linearly with the difference between the actual muscle length and the threshold length such that $A = x - \lambda$. Under dynamic conditions (i.e., during motion) muscle activity also depends on the rate of change of muscle length (x'). Activity increases with the rate of muscle lengthening and decreases with the rate of shortening. Thus, muscle activity in dynamics is:

$$A = x - \lambda^* \qquad (1)$$

where $\lambda^* = \lambda - \mu \cdot x'$ is the dynamic threshold length and μ is the coefficient of reflex damping due to homonymous muscle spindle afferents. In the present models, μ is assumed to be constant. However, this parameter may be under central control via gamma dynamic and beta MNs.

Muscle lengths and threshold lengths

In the arm model, we have made the simplifying assumptions that muscle moment arms (a_i) are constant and that muscle length varies linearly with joint angle(s). However, it should be noted that the moment arms of the elbow flexors (i.e., biceps brachii, brachialis and brachioradialis) vary by a factor of approximately two over the working range of the joint (An, Hui, Morrey, Linscheid, & Chao, 1982; van Zuylen, van Velzen, & Denier van der Gon, 1988). Although position-dependent moment arms will be included in future versions of the arm model, this will not alter its essential characteristics.

In general, the actual and threshold lengths of the muscle can be represented as angles:

$$\Theta_i = (x_i - b_i)/a_i \qquad (2)$$

$$\underline{\lambda}_i = (\lambda_i - b_i)/a_i$$

where b_i is a constant length which is independent of the actual joint angle (Θ_i) and $\underline{\lambda}_i$ is the threshold angle. In the special case of the double-joint arm muscles (e.g., biceps and triceps), muscle length (x_3) depends on both the shoulder angle (Θ_1) and the elbow angle (Θ_2). Therefore, we define a joint angle (Θ_3) and a threshold angle ($\underline{\lambda}_3$) as follows:

$$\Theta_3 = (x_3 - b_3)/(a_1 + a_2) \qquad (3)$$

$$\underline{\lambda}_3 = (\lambda_3 - b_3)/(a_1 + a_2)$$

where a_1 and a_2 are the moment arms at the elbow and shoulder respectively and $x_3 = a_1 \cdot \Theta_1 + a_2 \cdot \Theta_2 + b_3$. Note that Θ_3 defines a family of joint configurations (i.e., arm postures) subject to the kinematic constraint described in Equation 3. The transformation between linear and angular variables (Equations 2 & 3) has the same form for both muscle and threshold lengths.

In the jaw model, actual and threshold muscle lengths are based on an explicit representation of the geometry of the jaw system (see Figure 1B). Consequently, unlike the arm model, muscle length is a non-linear function of position (i.e., mandible rotation and translation).

Reciprocal Inhibition

Reciprocal inhibition of antagonist muscles mediated through Ia interneurons (INs) has been included in the multi-joint arm model. Ia INs receive effective inhibitory inputs from Renshaw cells (Hultborn, 1972). In addition, the Ia spindle afferents of agonists produce excitation of the Ia INs which inhibit the MNs of the antagonist muscles. Ia INs are also influenced by descending pathways (Grillner, 1981; Lundberg, 1975). Reciprocal inhibition (RI) has not been included in the mandibular model since Ia INs have not been found in the orofacial system (see Luschei & Goldberg, 1981).

Feldman & Orlovsky (1972) have shown that the threshold of the stretch reflex of the gastrocnemius muscle in the decerebrate cat increases when the antagonist is stretched. Thus, we suggest that the dynamic threshold length ($\lambda^{*\prime}$) modified by RI can be represented as the summation of the dynamic threshold length (λ^{*}) defined in Equation 1 and a value (λ^{*}_{S}) associated with antagonist spindle activity:

$$\lambda^{*\prime} = \lambda^{*} + \lambda^{*}_{S} \qquad (4)$$

When the muscle is stretched, the antagonist muscle is shortened and the magnitude of the inhibitory effect (λ^{*}_{S}) decreases. Thus, muscle activity, $A = (x - \lambda^{*\prime})$, increases more than it would in the absence of RI. Consequently, the effect of RI is to increase the magnitude of the muscle stiffness (in both agonists and antagonists) which also increases joint stiffness. RI also decreases the co-contraction area (in which both the agonist and antagonist are active) since both the threshold lengths of both the agonist and antagonist muscles are lengthened. The dependence of λ^{*}_{S} on antagonist muscle spindle activity can be controlled in different ways by central commands and has been described in detail (Feldman et al., 1990).

Muscle Forces and External Loads

An increase in muscle activation is associated with recruitment of MNs and an increase in their firing. As a result, both the muscle force and stiffness increase. To a first approximation, we assume that the stiffness increases linearly with A. Thus, muscle force (F) increases as a parabolic function of A:

$$F = (k_o + k' \cdot A) \cdot A \qquad (5)$$

where k_o is the initial muscle stiffness (when $x = \lambda^*$) and k' is the rate of change of stiffness with changes in A.

The form of Equation 5 defines an invariant characteristic (Feldman, 1966) which represents the force-length properties of the muscle together with afferent feedback. Both muscle activity (A) and muscle force (F) are velocity-dependent. Equation 5 must be considered as a simplification of the relationship between force and muscle activity which doesn't take into account either Hill's force-velocity relation or muscle fiber force decay properties.

In the two-joint arm model we have assumed that the moment arms and rates of change of stiffness (k') of antagonist pairs acting about a joint are equivalent. The moment arms of the single-joint muscles are assumed to be 3 cm and the moment arms of the double-joint muscles at the shoulder and elbow are assumed to be 1 cm and 3 cm respectively. The ratio of k' of the single-joint shoulder muscles to the single-joint elbow muscles is assumed to be 2:1 and the ratio of k' for the single-joint elbow muscles to the double-joint muscles is assumed to be 1:1.

In the jaw model, the ratio of k' of the jaw opener to the jaw closer is assumed to be 1:4 and the ratio of the jaw opener to the jaw protruder is assumed to be 1:2. The moment arms of the openers and closers are computed from a geometric model (see Figure 1B) and depend on the position of the mandible.

In the computer simulations, it is necessary to compute the kinematic consequences of the torques and forces acting on the limb or mandible. For the arm model, the Newton-Euler equations of motion are used (e.g., Hollerbach & Flash, 1982). To find the equations of motion for the jaw model, the mandible was represented as a moving pendulum with a point mass (m) located at length l (see Figure 1C). The pendulum is free to rotate (α) about a suspension point which is itself free to translate (τ) diagonally (at angle β). From the Lagrangian, a generalized torque (Q_α) and a generalized force (Q_τ) can be obtained:

$$Q_\alpha = m \cdot l \cdot \tau'' \cdot \cos(\alpha + \beta) + m \cdot l^2 \cdot \alpha'' + m \cdot g \cdot l \cdot \sin(\alpha) \qquad (6)$$

$$Q_\tau = m \cdot \tau'' + m \cdot l \cdot (\alpha \cdot \cos(\alpha + \beta) - \alpha'^2 \cdot \sin(\alpha + \beta)) - m \cdot g \cdot \sin(\beta)$$

It should be noted that rotation torque (Q_α) produces translation (τ) and that translation force (Q_τ) produces rotation (α). $Q\alpha$ is the sum of muscle, gravitational, and contact (e.g., bolus) torques about the condyle and Q_τ is the sum of the corresponding forces projected along the articular eminence.

To examine mastication movements with the jaw model, we included a simulated bolus and placed kinematic constraints on the motion of the mandible at occlusion. The width, compliance, and location of the bolus relative to the mandible can be specified (see Figure 1B). For simplicity, we assumed a bolus with linear stiffness such that force increased monotonically with compression. At occlusion (i.e., when any point on the mandible contacts the occlusal plane), neither rotation nor translation of the jaw is permitted. Once the jaw is in occlusion, it remains motionless until the force normal to the occlusal plane produces opening. In the model, the occlusal plane was assumed to be horizontal. Thus, the normal force at contact is equal to the sum of the vertical projections of muscle, gravitational, and bolus forces in addition to the vertical projection of the reaction force acting at the condyle perpendicular to the articular eminence. Although we have only examined restricted or compliant motion in the jaw model, the arm model can also be used to investigate motions such as grasping, drawing, and other behaviors involving external contact forces at the movement endpoint.

Central Commands: Vector Representation

In this section, we develop a vector representation of central commands which is especially convenient for modeling multi-muscle systems. The basic ideas are illustrated by considering a single-joint system and then extended to the modeling of mandibular and multi-joint arm motions.

Single degree of freedom

Consider a single joint with two antagonist muscles which can be controlled by two parameters, λ_1 and λ_2, which specify the MN recruitment thresholds (λs) of the flexor and extensor respectively. We define two functionally different commands which control the λs of antagonist muscle pairs as a single unit. The co-contraction command, Λ_c, gives rise to an increase in the activity of antagonist muscles (and therefore stiffness) while the joint remains motionless. The other command, Λ_Θ, shifts the equilibrium position of the joint and is associated with reciprocal changes in flexor and extensor activity. Both commands thus produce simultaneous changes in λs but they do so in different ways. Figure 2A shows these commands represented by vectors in the space of λ_1 versus λ_2. This space has orthogonal basis vectors $\mathbf{e_1}$ and $\mathbf{e_2}$ (vectors are bold-faced in this paper). The projections of vector $\mathbf{\Lambda_c}$ have the same sign and thus the Λ_c command produces changes of λs in the same direction. In contrast, the projections of vector Λ_Θ have opposite signs and consequently the Λ_Θ command produces changes of λs in different directions. The vector commands can be graded in magnitude to produce commands of varying strength. The vector commands are orthogonal and the corresponding functions can be controlled independently. Any voluntary movement control vector can be represented as a linear sum of these two basic command vectors (the principle of superposition). Unit activity recordings from motor cortex in monkeys support a distinction between central co-activation commands and movement related commands associated with reciprocal changes in muscle activity (Humphrey & Reed, 1983).

These basic command vectors can be expressed in terms of threshold angles ($\underline{\lambda}$s) as shown in Figure 2B. Figures 2C and 2D illustrate the effects of the command vectors in terms of shifts of invariant torque-angle characteristics (thick curves) of the flexors and extensors and changes in joint stiffness associated with the slope of the net torque-angle relationship of the joint (diagonal lines). The co-contraction command (Λ_c) shifts the two characteristics in opposite directions (2C). As a result, muscle torques and joint stiffness increase but the equilibrium position remains unchanged. (The equilibrium position under static conditions is the point at which the net joint torque is zero.) The reciprocal command (Λ_Θ) shifts the two characteristics in the same direction (2D). Consequently, the equilibrium position changes but the level of co-activation and joint stiffness in the new equilibrium position remains the same.

The two vector commands can be presented in the following general form:

$$\Lambda_c = c \cdot (p_1 \cdot \mathbf{e_1} + p_2 \cdot \mathbf{e_2}) \qquad (7)$$

$$\Lambda_\Theta = r \cdot (q_1 \cdot \mathbf{e_1} + q_2 \cdot \mathbf{e_2})$$

where c and r are the tunable strengths of the commands and p_i and q_i are the coordinates of the constant unit vectors which indicate the directions of the commands in the λ space. To determine the four coordinates of the unit vectors, we take into account that their lengths are equal to 1. In addition, the unit vectors are orthogonal so that their inner product is zero. This gives us three equations with four unknowns. The fact that the Λ_c command does not produce shifts in the equilibrium position of the joint gives the necessary fourth relation allowing us to find numerical values of the coordinates.

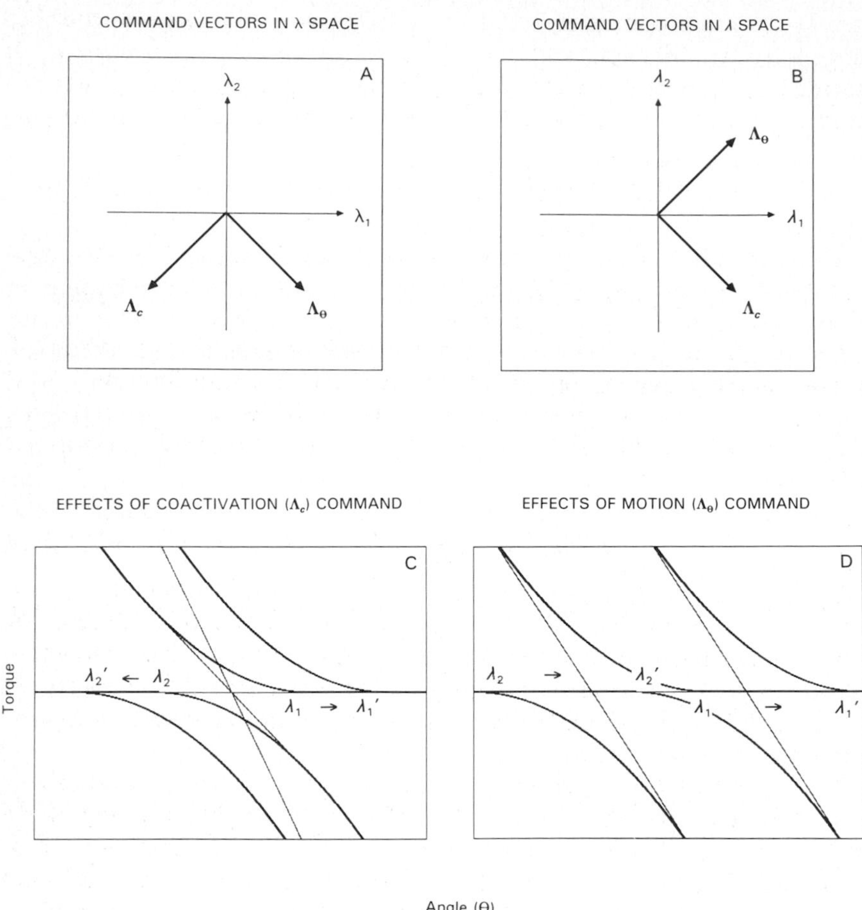

Figure 2. Co-activation (Λ_c) and movement (Λ_Θ) command vectors for single-joint motion shown in linear λ coordinates (A) and angular $\underline{\lambda}$ coordinates (B). The Λ_c command shifts the flexor ($\underline{\lambda}_1$) and extensor ($\underline{\lambda}_2$) threshold angles in opposite direction (C) whereas the Λ_Θ shifts them in the same direction (D). Each $\underline{\lambda}$ is associated with an invariant torque-angle relationship (thick curves) which summate to give the net stiffness (thin diagonal lines) about the joint equilibrium angle. Thus, the Λ_c command varies net stiffness without changing the equilibrium angle and the Λ_Θ command changes the equilibrium angle without altering stiffness.

Consider this last relation in more detail. When the joint is in equilibrium, the net joint torque (Q) is zero:

$$Q = T_1 + T_2 + L = 0 \tag{8}$$

where T_i are muscle torques and L is an external load. Assume that the system is in equilibrium and a small change in the Λ_c command is performed. To prevent a shift in the equilibrium position, the changes in individual muscle torques elicited by changes in the λs must be balanced:

$$\delta Q = \delta T_1 + \delta T_2 + \delta L = 0 \tag{9}$$

where:

$$\delta T_i = (\partial T_i / \partial \lambda_i) \cdot \delta \lambda_i = (\partial T_i / \partial \lambda_i) \cdot \delta c \cdot p_i \tag{10}$$

The partial derivatives are calculated for the equilibrium position. L does not explicitly depend on the control variables and therefore $\delta L = 0$. It can be shown that the following are the values of the vector coordinates: $p_1 = 1/\sqrt{(1+s^2)}$, $p_2 = s/\sqrt{(1+s^2)}$, $q_1 = p_2$, and $q_2 = -p_1$, where the parameter s is defined as:

$$s = -(\partial T_1/\partial \lambda_1)/(\partial T_2/\partial \lambda_2) = p_2/p_1 \tag{11}$$

The value $s = 1$ corresponds to the idealized case where the anatomical arrangement and the neural regulation of the antagonist muscles are identical as has been assumed in the two-joint arm model. The deflection of s from unity characterizes the degree of the asymmetry of the system. In the jaw model, the asymmetric muscle arrangement has been taken into account.

It is clear that the nervous system does not 'compute' the necessary vector commands (or the value of s). However, we suggest that these vectors are gradually approximated through evolutionary and developmental processes according to the basic constraint that one command produces co-activation without affecting the equilibrium position whereas the other changes the equilibrium position without affecting the level of co-activation.

In general, the basis command vectors will depend on the initial equilibrium position of the system. However, in the jaw model, simulations have shown that the command vectors change negligibly across equilibrium positions. For example, the same Λ_c command produces co-activation without jaw movement regardless of the equilibrium position of the mandible (and the load due to gravity). This is an important result since it indicates that the central nervous system can make use of an invariant set of basic functional control vectors independent of position and load.

A constant s parameter (Equation 11) characterizes the situation where the optimal central control vectors have been coordinated with the biomechanics of the system. We hypothesize that the neural regulation of muscle activity as well as muscle anatomy and mechanics are adjusted so that the s parameters (i.e., the basic command vectors) are invariant.

In a previous version of the λ model (Feldman, 1980), the co-contraction (C) command and the motion-related or reciprocal (R) command were defined in angular coordinates as:

$$C = (\underline{\lambda}_1 - \underline{\lambda}_2)/2 \qquad (12)$$

$$R = (\underline{\lambda}_1 + \underline{\lambda}_2)/2$$

These scalar commands are related to the magnitudes of the vector commands, c and r, in Equation 7 as follows: $R = r/\sqrt{2}$ and $C = c/\sqrt{2}$.

Two degrees of freedom: jaw motion

The vector representation of central commands can be generalized to multi-muscle systems with multiple degrees of freedom. In this section, we define the basis command vectors for the tri-muscle jaw model with two degrees of freedom. In principle, any three vectors can be combined or superimposed to generate all possible movements provided that they are not linearly dependent. However, we suggest that the three basis command vectors include a co-contraction vector (Λ_c) and two vectors associated with jaw rotation (Λ_α) and jaw translation (Λ_τ). These commands are represented in the space λ_1, λ_2, λ_3 (corresponding to the threshold lengths of the jaw closer, opener, and protruder). The Λ_c command affects the level of muscle co-activation without altering the equilibrium position whereas the Λ_α and Λ_τ commands produce pure rotation and translation respectively without changing the level of co-activation. The experimental records shown in Figure 4A demonstrate that the co-ordination between jaw rotation and translation can vary and that jaw rotation and translation can be produced independently. Consequently, the basic command vectors we have selected in the jaw model are consistent with experimental data.

To find the coordinates (p1, p2, p3) of the co-activation vector, we calculated two integral invariants of the system associated with the fact that the co-activation command gives neither rotation nor translation. Since, in our model, the protractor does not participate in rotation, the form of the invariant (s_α) associated with the rotational coordinate (α) corresponds to that defined before for single-joint movements (see Equation 11 for s):

$$s_\alpha = -(\partial T_1/\partial\lambda_1)/(\partial T_2/\partial\lambda_2) = p_2/p_1 \quad (13)$$

The second invariant (s_τ) is associated with the absence of translation during co-contraction. During equilibrium the translational components of the three muscle forces ($F_{\tau i}$) and the load acting along the translation surface sum to zero:

$$Q_\tau = F_{\tau 1} + F_{\tau 2} + F_{\tau 3} + L_\tau = 0 \quad (14)$$

and so do their changes during the translational command. The second integral invariant is:

$$s_\tau = -(\partial F_{\tau 1}/\partial\lambda_1 + s_\alpha \cdot \partial F_{\tau 2}/\partial\lambda_2)/s_\alpha \cdot (\partial F_{\tau 3}/\partial\lambda_3) = p_3/p_2 \quad (15)$$

In combination with the condition that p_1, p_2 and p_3 are components of a unit vector, these invariants allows us to calculate the components of the co-activation vector.

To find the components of the vector Λ_α, we used two constraints: the vector produces pure rotation and is orthogonal to Λ_c. The pure rotation constraint means that the variation of the net translation force (δQ_τ) elicited by central commands must be zero. From a theoretical point of view, the important point is that the unit vector associated with the command Λ_α is unique. To find the unit vector associated with Λ_α we selected, by trial and error, a voluntary vector command which produced rotation without translation. We then determined the component of this vector orthogonal to the co-activation vector (Λ_c) and normalized it. (In this way, lengthy calculations were avoided.) The same approach was used to find the unit vector associated with Λ_τ. According to the theorem formulated above, both of these vectors are unique.

The three basic control vectors in the space λ_{cl}, λ_{op}, λ_{pr} (corresponding to λ_1, λ_2, λ_3 above) are illustrated in Figure 3A. The two motion related vector commands, Λ_α and Λ_τ, are both orthogonal to Λ_c but are not themselves orthogonal. However, since Λ_α and Λ_τ are not linearly dependent, they can be combined with Λ_c to generate any voluntary movement command. Figure 3B-E shows simulated actions of the basic control vectors. Figure 3B demonstrates that the co-activation command (Λ_c) produces shifts in the three λs without motion in rotation (α) or translation (τ). (The extent of the changes in the λs is determined by the rate and duration of shifts in the magnitude of Λ_c.) The same Λ_c command is shown in 3C following a movement to another equilibrium position. This figure illustrates that regardless of the equilibrium position of the mandible, Λ_c produces co-activation without movement.

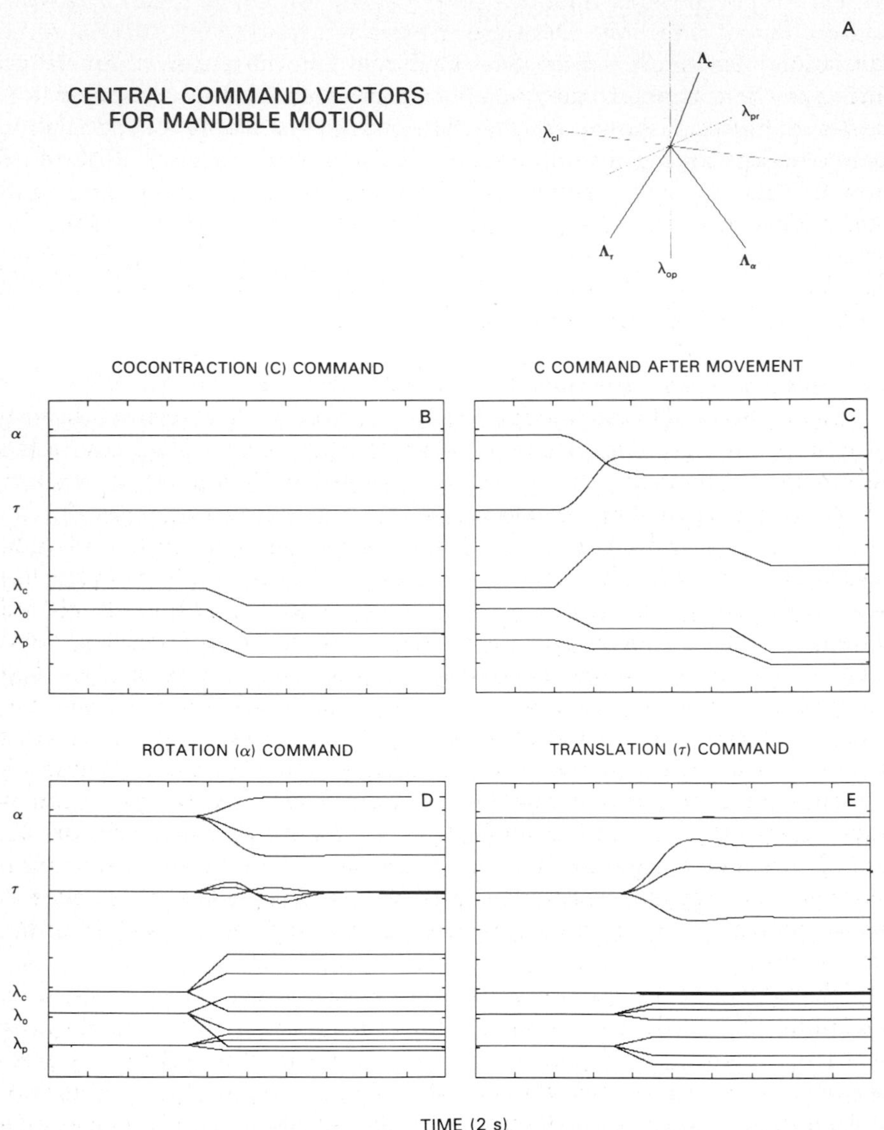

Figure 3. Three central command vectors for the jaw model shown in λ space (A). The co-activation command Λ_c produces shifts in the three λs without rotation α or translation τ (B). The same Λ_c command produces the same effect following a movement to another equilibrium position (C). The command produces rotation without translation (D) whereas the Λ_τ command produces translation without rotation (E).

Figure 3D presents rotations produced by Λ_α commands of varying magnitude and direction. During these rotation movements there is some translation due to dynamics (see Equation 6). However, there is no difference in τ between the initial and final equilibrium positions. A similar pattern is shown for translation movements produced by Λ_τ commands of varying magnitude and direction in 3E. Figures 3D and 3E show that the Λ_α and Λ_τ commands are able to produce pure rotation and translation (respectively) regardless of the extent to which they shift the system's equilibrium position in doing so. In summary, this figure shows that all three central control vectors function independently of the equilibrium state of the jaw system.

Two degrees of freedom: arm motion

In the two-joint arm model, we have selected three central control vectors: a co-contraction vector (Λ_c) and two other vectors ($\Lambda_{\Theta i}$) associated with motion at the two joints. We chose not to specify separate Λ_c vectors for each joint since there is some evidence that human subjects do not control shoulder and elbow joint stiffnesses independently (Mussa-Ivaldi, Hogan, & Bizzi, 1985). As in the case of single-joint motion (see Figure 2B), these command vectors may be represented in terms of joint threshold angles ($\underline{\lambda}$s). The Λ_c vector produces equal but opposite shifts in flexor and extensor $\underline{\lambda}$s for all three antagonist muscle pairs whereas the $\Lambda_{\Theta i}$ commands produce equal shifts in the flexor and extensor $\underline{\lambda}$s of the two (single- and double-joint) antagonist pairs acting at the ith joint in the same direction. The three command vectors produce shifts of equal magnitude in antagonist $\underline{\lambda}$s since the parameter s (Equation 11) of each muscle pair is unity. Unlike the jaw model, in which all three basic command vectors act on the threshold lengths (λs) of all muscles, only the co-activation commands has this property in the arm model. This reflects differences in muscle geometry and in the organization of the degrees of freedom in the two systems.

We assume that goal-directed arm movements are generally planned in equilibrium coordinates corresponding to the movement endpoint rather than joint angles. In particular, we suggest that the nervous system specifies the direction and the rate of change, u(t), of the equilibrium position of the endpoint (see Figure 6). In the absence of special constraints (e.g., obstacles to be avoided or precision targets), u(t) is assumed to be constant. Consequently, the equilibrium point shifts in a straight line and at a constant velocity towards the movement target. The equilibrium position of the endpoint is then transformed into equilibrium command vectors ($\Lambda_{\Theta i}$) associated with joint motion. Since the relationship between endpoint and joint coordinates is non-linear, the joint level command vectors will not, in general, be shifted at a constant rate.

Results

In this section, simulated trajectories based on assumed equilibrium trajectories are presented and compared with actual data from multi-joint reaching movements and motions of the mandible in speech and mastication (also see Ostry & Flanagan, 1989). We will demonstrate that simple constant velocity shifts in central command vectors can account for the movement kinematic patterns in each of these behaviors.

Speech Movements

The X-ray microbeam (University of Wisconsin, Madison) was used to record jaw kinematics in the mid-sagittal plane. X-ray tracking pellets were attached to the jaw (between the mandibular incisors and to both the left and right mandibular molars). Additional pellets were used to correct for planar head motion and to locate the occlusal plane. All pellet positions were projected onto the mid-sagittal plane. The jaw pellet motions were used to calculate the rotation of the condyle and the translation of its axis of rotation along the articular eminence.

Figure 4A shows a characteristic pattern of jaw rotation and translation in speech. In general, in both mastication and speech, jaw rotation (α) and jaw translation (τ) start and end simultaneously (see 4B) and their co-ordination is typically characterized by straight line paths. A number of manipulations involving both mastication and speech suggest that jaw rotation and jaw translation can be separately controlled. When jaw movements in speech were examined, the relationship between rotation and translation was not constant but varied in a systematic way with the composition of the utterance. Specifically, the slope of the relationship between translation and rotation appears to vary with the consonant (compare /sa/ with /ka/) but does not depend on the vowel or speech rate. In addition, when loud speech was compared to normal speech volumes, the jaw is translated forward but the slope of the relationship between rotation and translation is preserved (compare /sa/ loud versus fast). The co-ordination between jaw rotation and translation also varies under different mastication conditions. For example, at fast chewing rates, jaw rotation is observed without any accompanying translation whereas at slower rates, rotation and translation are coupled.

SIMULATED AND ACTUAL JAW
MOTION IN SPEECH

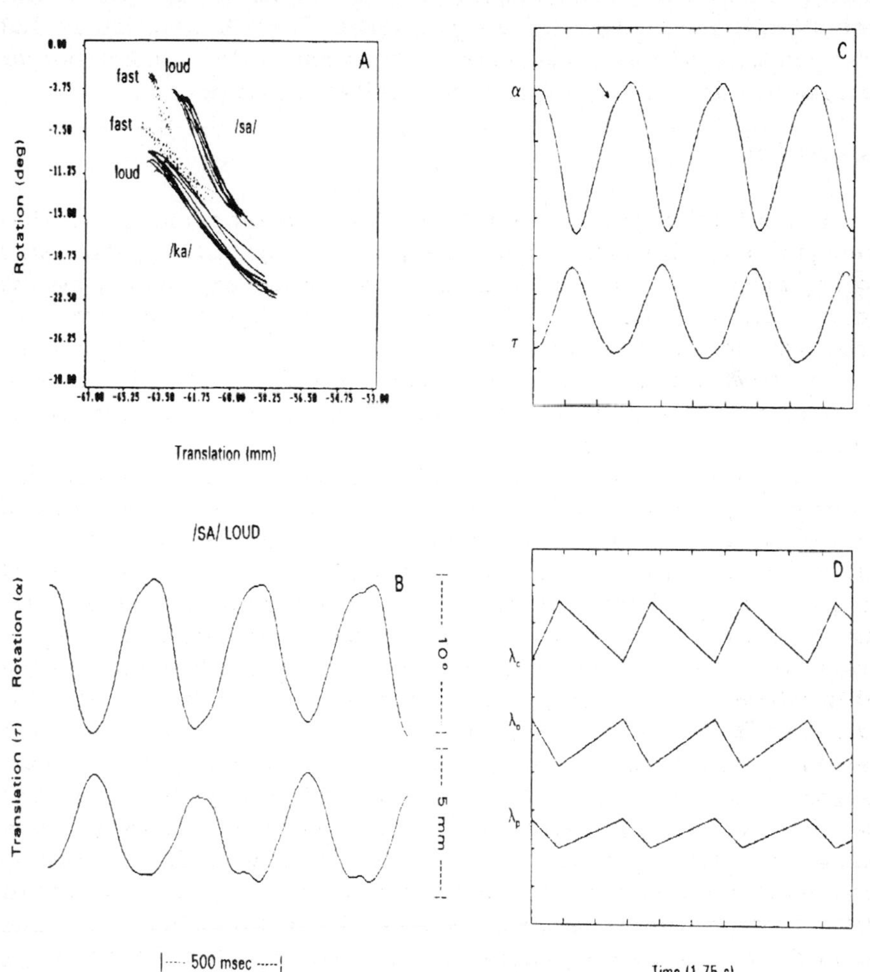

Figure 4. Speech movements recorded using the X-ray microbeam are shown in A and B. The slope of the relationship between jaw rotation and jaw translation depends on consonant (/sa/ versus /ka/). The condyle is translated forward in loud as opposed to fast speech (A). Empirical records of jaw rotation and translation during repetitions of /sa/ (B). These are well accounted for by simulated motions (C) based on simple constant velocity shift in central command vectors (D).

Figure 4B shows temporal patterns of jaw rotation and jaw translation recorded during a single trial in which the subject repeated /sa/ at a loud speech volume. (This record is one of those shown in 4A). Jaw opening (decreasing α) is associated with forward translation (increasing τ) of the centre of the condyle. This pattern of rotation and translation is simulated in 4C. The deceleration of jaw rotation towards the end of the closing phase of the movement (see ➘ in 4C) can be attributed, in the model, to decreases in the passive muscle force associated with shortening of the jaw closer. Figure 4D shows the changes in the muscle λs which produce this behavior. As shown in the figure, simple constant velocity shifts in the λs can generate the smooth patterns of rotation and translation observed experimentally. The changes in λs were produced by a combination of the basic command vectors Λ_α and Λ_τ with a constant level of co-activation (Λ_c). Notice that the rate and duration of the λ shifts differ for simulated opening and closing movements.

Mastication Movements

Simulated and empirical chewing movements are illustrated in Figure 5. Three chewing cycles are shown for both the simulated movements (5A-B) and the empirical movements (5C). Each cycle consists of an initial opening phase (in which α decreases and τ increases) followed by a closing phase. Figure 5A shows simulated patterns of jaw rotation (α) and translation (τ) as well as simulated bite forces. During the closing movement, when the bolus is contacted, an initial bite force is developed. At the same time, the velocity of jaw rotation (α) begins to decrease. This is consistent with the empirical pattern shown in 5C (as indicated by ➘). Empirically, bite force has only been measured under static conditions and consequently the simulated patterns observed with the model provide theoretical predictions to be tested experimentally.

Figure 5B shows the changes in the muscle λs corresponding to the simulated motions in 5A. These changes were produced with a combination of all three basis control vectors. The level of co-activation was increased during the closing phase of the movement. During occlusion, the positional degrees of freedom of the system are transformed into force degrees of freedom. At this point, the same central control vectors can be used to control and produce forces rather than motions. As in the case of speech movements, simple constant velocity shifts in muscle λs, determined by the rate and duration of shifts of the central commands vectors, can account well for the kinematic patterns observed in mastication. Note that subtle differences between cycles can be approximated by varying the delay between successive cyclical shifts in the λs and their magnitude (see Figure 5B).

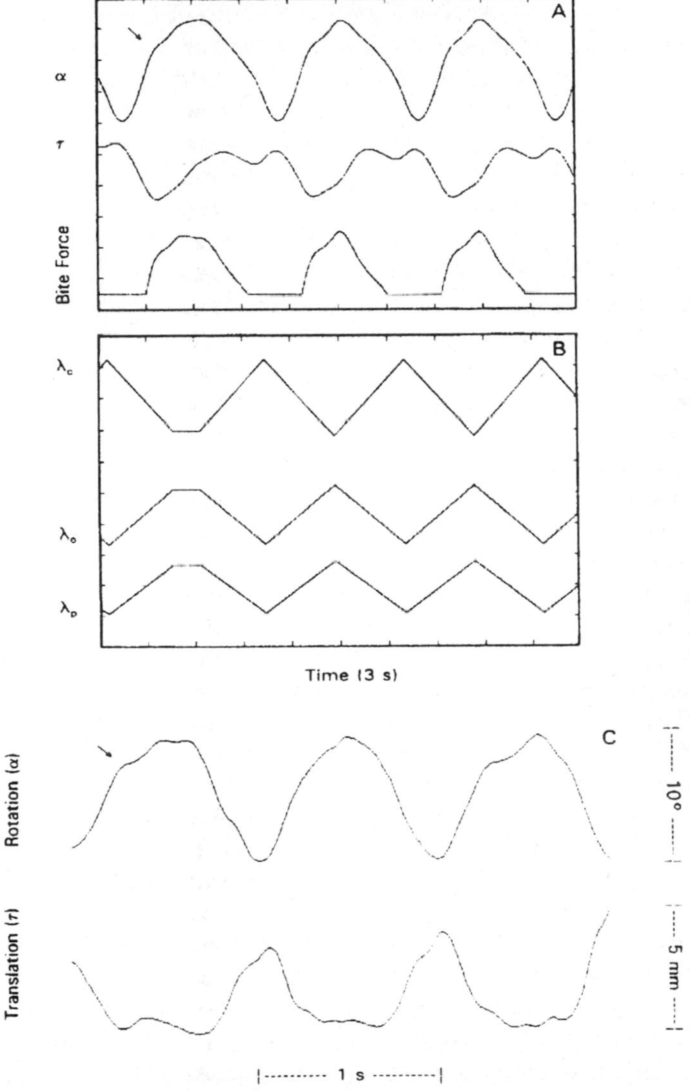

Figure 5. Simulated jaw rotation (α), translation (τ) and bite force (A) based on constant velocity shift in central control vectors (B). After contact with the bolus, the jaw rotation decelerates (↘). Empirical records of rotation and translation are shown in C.

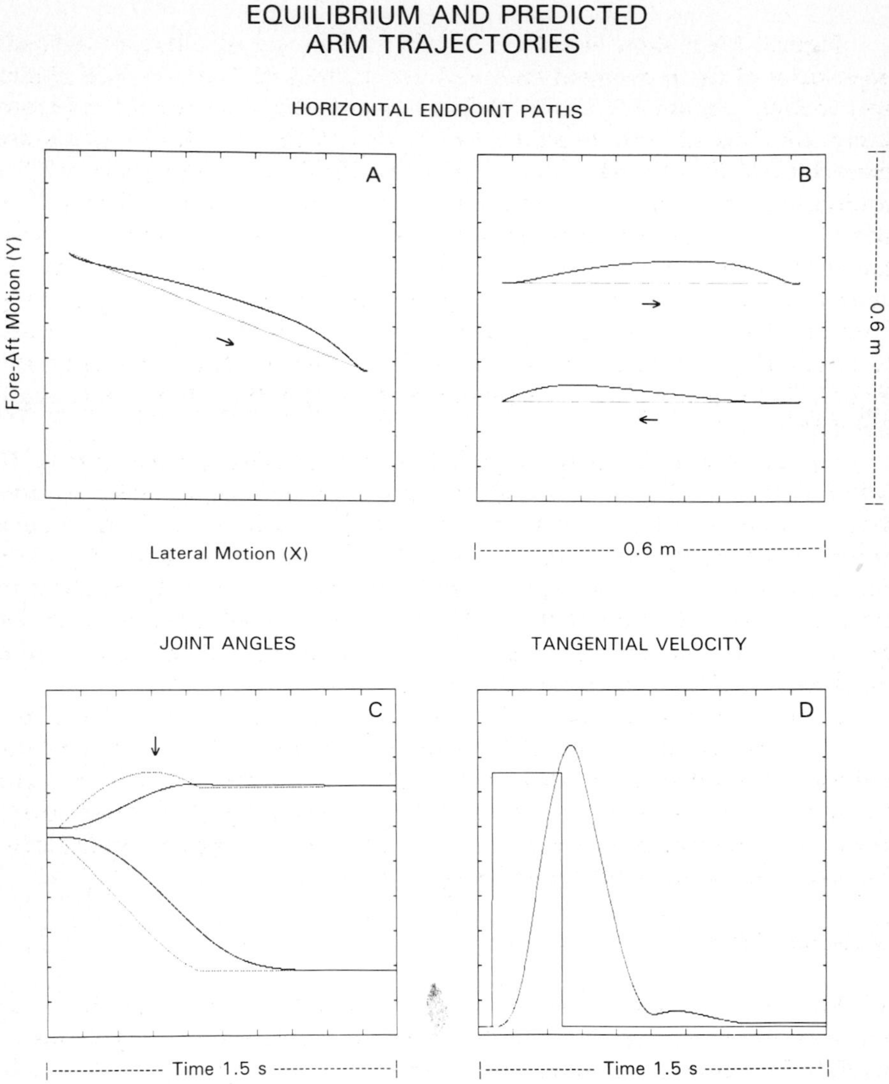

Figure 6. Equilibrium (dotted) and 'actual' (solid) endpoint paths generated by the two-joint planar arm model (A and B). Straight line constant velocity shifts (0.9 m/s) in the equilibrium position of the endpoint result in curved paths. Corresponding equilibrium joint angles (dotted) will not shift at a constant velocity and may result in joint reversals (C). Actual joint angles (solid) may nevertheless change monotonically. Constant velocity shift in the position of the movement endpoint (1.5 m/s) can produce smooth bell-shaped tangential velocity profiles (D).

Two-Joint Arm Movements

Figures 6A-B show simulated 'actual' (solid) and equilibrium (dotted) trajectories of the movement endpoint generated with the two-joint planar arm model. Figure 6A shows a (left to right) diagonal motion whereas lateral motions in both directions are shown in 6B. The actual paths are characteristically curved (Flash & Hogan, 1985) while the paths of the equilibrium position of the endpoint form straight lines. More subtle effects such as the dependence of curvature on movement direction are also consistent with experimental data (e.g., Flash & Hogan, 1985). Figure 6C illustrates the actual (solid) and equilibrium (dotted) joint angles as a function of time corresponding to the simulated movement shown in 6A. Although the equilibrium angle at the elbow reverses direction during the motion (indicated by ↓), a corresponding reversal in the actual elbow angle is not observed.

Equilibrium and actual tangential velocity profiles (corresponding to path 5 shown in 7C) are presented in Figure 6D. This figure demonstrates that the smooth bell-shaped tangential velocity profiles which have been reported for multi-joint arm movements (Atkeson & Hollerbach, 1985; Flash & Hogan, 1985) can be produced by simple constant velocity shifts in the equilibrium position of the endpoint. Thus, smoothness need not be specified at the motion planning level but may be considered as a natural consequence of the dynamics of the arm system.

Figure 7 shows shoulder EMG (7A) and kinematic patterns (7B) for the five movements shown in 7C in which the equilibrium position of the endpoint is shifted, at a constant velocity, in different directions. The magnitude and duration of the EMGs produced by the model are a function of movement direction. In the absence of joint motion reversals, the predicted agonist-antagonist EMG patterns are triphasic.

Discussion

We have illustrated three levels of threshold length (λ) regulation in our models: a *low* level associated with segmental reflex mechanisms mediated by muscle afferents, an *intermediate* level connected with basic command vectors, and a *high* level associated with the control of these basic command vectors.

The low level is associated with the tonic stretch reflex and intermuscular interactions including reciprocal inhibition (RI). The threshold of MN recruitment (λ) may correspond to the threshold of the tonic stretch reflex (Feldman & Orlovsky, 1972). RI, whereby spindle afferents of the agonist muscle give rise to an increase in the threshold length of the antagonist muscle and vice versa, is associated with an increase in total stiffness of the joint, a decrease in the level of co-activation area of the muscles, and a reduction in muscle activity in the equilibrium position without lose of stability. The tonic stretch reflex threshold and intermuscular interactions can be controlled by central commands of the intermediate level. These commands can affect the low level in different ways through their actions on α and γ MNs, Ia INs, and Renshaw cells.

The intermediate level consists of central commands which regulate threshold lengths independently of spindle afferents. We have hypothesized the existence of a set of basic commands classified according to the functional role they play in the control of equilibrium. Each command controls the λs of a set of muscles simultaneously and can be represented by a vector in λ space. These vectors have a constant part associated with their direction in λ space and a variable part representing their magnitude which is under high level control. Thus, the general form of a command vector Λ is as follows:

$$\Lambda = M \cdot \Sigma\, p_i \cdot \mathbf{e_i} \qquad (16)$$

where $\Sigma\, p_i \cdot \mathbf{e_i}$ is a unit vector indicating the direction of the vector Λ, p_i are its coordinates, $\mathbf{e_i}$ are basis vectors in λ space, and M is the magnitude of the command vector. The variable or controlled part of the vector can be represented as:

$$M = M_0 + u(t) \cdot (t - t_i) \qquad (17)$$

where M_0 is an initial magnitude of the command vector, u(t) is the rate of its change, t_i is the time of the onset of the command, and t is time.

There are several properties of command vectors which are worth emphasizing. The rate of change, u(t), of the magnitude of a command vector and the associated onset time (t_i) are under central control. In general, these parameters can differ for each command vector applied in a given movement. However, in the present chapter, we have only considered the simple case in which the onset of central commands is simultaneous. In movements without specific constraints, the rate u(t) is assumed to be constant. This assumption is supported by data on corrections in reaching and saccadic eye movements (Pélisson, Prablanc, Goodale, & Jeannerod, 1986). Pélisson et al. compared the trajectories of two movements, both directed to the same final target. In control trials only the final target was shown to the subject whereas, in 'correction' trials, the target was shifted to the final position from an intermediate position located along the path to the final target. The corrected movements coincided with non-corrected movements provided that the final target was exposed early in the movement towards the intermediate one. The same result was obtained for saccadic eye movements. This result is predicted by our model based on constant velocity control signals: to correct the movement, the control signal is simply continued (at constant velocity u) until the final equilibrium position is reached. Thus, the form of the control signal, and therefore the kinematics, will be the same for the corrected movements and the control movements.

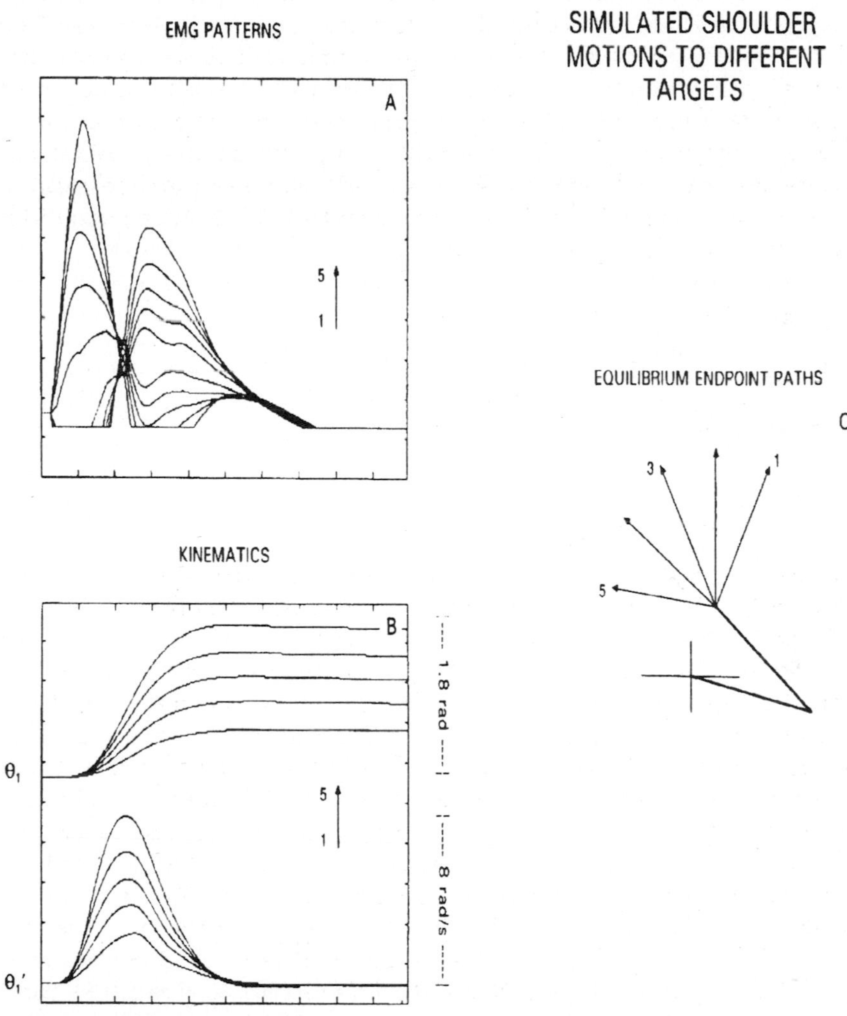

Figure 7. Shoulder EMG (7A) and kinematic patterns (7B) for five movements in which the equilibrium position of the endpoint is shifted, at a constant velocity, in different directions (7C).

Another important property of command vectors is that the coordinates (p_i) of a given vector are constant and can be considered as structural-functional invariants associated with a specific concordance among neuronal command structures, afferent systems, and biomechanics. For example, the invariance of the co-activation command (Λ_c) enables the system to produce co-activation of numerous, anatomically different muscles without motion in the joints regardless of position or external loads. In addition to a co-activation vector, we have suggested the existence of two other basic vectors associated with pure rotation and translation in jaw movements, and motion about the shoulder and elbow in the case of arm movements. Experimental records of jaw movements in speech (Figure 4A) are consistent with this suggestion but do not rule out an alternative basis vector set (e.g., associated with muscle co-activation, pure rotation, and another vector, orthogonal to the other two, associated with a combination of rotation and translation of the jaw). Vector commands can be applied in different combinations to produce different ratios of motion of each degree of freedom and co-activation.

Recent evidence on muscle synergies involved in the generation of isometric elbow torques in humans (Buchanan, Rovai, & Rymer, 1989; van Zuylen, Gielen, & Denier van der Gon, 1988) supports the notion that the activity of multiple muscles with different biomechanical functions can be controlled in concert in order to produce torques about specific degrees of freedom. Buchanan et al. (1989) have shown that when subjects produce a flexion torque at the elbow, pronator terres (a forearm pronator) activity compensates for the supination torque caused by the activation of the biceps. Thus, although the biceps both flexes and supinates the forearm, other muscles allow for the generate of pure flexion torques. (Likewise, when subjects were required to produce a forearm supination torque, triceps activity compensated for the flexion torque caused by biceps activity.)

The high level in the model of reaching movements is associated with a neuronal control or equilibrium space which maps onto the physical extrapersonal space in the sense that activation of a neuronal population localized about a point in the neuronal structure is associated with a point in the external space. In the case of multi-joint arm movements, this point coincides with the equilibrium position of the arm endpoint. It is also possible to present central commands generated at this level by goal-directed vectors which specify the rate and the direction of the shift in the equilibrium position of the endpoint to the target. This signal is then transformed into joint level commands according the scheme already described (Feldman et al., 1990). Analysis has shown that the commands which give rise to rotations of the joints are cosine functions of the angle between an optimal direction specific for each joint and the direction of the target vector. The corresponding dependence is characteristic of cortical neurons (Georgopoulos, 1988; Schwartz, Kettner, & Georgopoulos, 1988). This allows us to suggest that motor cortex neuronal activity not only reflects the direction and the magnitude of the target vector that produces shifts of the equilibrium position of the arm endpoint but also individual commands that produce shifts of the equilibrium angle for each joint.

Under certain conditions, both the rate of change, u(t), and the direction of the equilibrium vector can be modified in the course of movement. For example, u(t) may be reduced as the movement endpoint approaches the target zone in precision tasks and the direction of the vector may be altered to correct errors, react to sudden changes in the target position, or to avoid obstacles. Otherwise, if there are no specific constraints, the u(t) remains constant until the target is reached. This case has been realized in the two-joint model of reaching movements (Figures 6 and 7). Both kinematic and EMG patterns are consistent with experimental data (Flash & Hogan, 1985; Hasan & Karst, 1989).

In this chapter, we have argued that regardless of the particular equilibrium coordinates in which movements are planned, the nervous system needs only to plan the rate and the direction of the shift in the equilibrium point. Information concerning movement amplitude is not required in order to plan or initiate a movement. The amplitude of the shift in equilibrium depends on both the speed and the duration of the shift. The latter may be planned prior to movement onset or determined during the movement. In contrast, Flash (1987) has suggested that human point-to-point arm movements are characterized by equilibrium velocity profiles which are bell-shaped and scale with both amplitude and duration (i.e., u(t) is constantly varied during the movement). Consequently, amplitude must be specified during initial planning in order to appropriately scale the equilibrium trajectory.

An essential difference between Flash's (1987) model and our own concerns the role of smoothness in movement production. In the model by Flash, smoothness is considered to be a fundamental principle underlying the planning and production of movement by the nervous system (see also Hogan, 1984). In contrast, according to the λ model, movements are smooth because of the system's natural dynamics. In general, it is unnecessary to posit control signals which meet the maximal smoothness criterion. The λ model, with constant velocity shifts in the equilibrium position of the endpoint, is able to produce smooth bell-shaped tangential velocity profiles of the actual movement endpoint (see Figure 6).

References

An, K.N., Hui, F.C., Morrey, B.F., Linscheid, R.L., & Chao, E.Y. (1981). Muscles across the elbow joint: a biomechanical analysis. *Journal of Biomechanics*, **14**, 659-669.

Abend, W.E., Bizzi, E., & Morasso, P. (1982). Human arm trajectory formation. *Brain*, **105**, 331-348.

Atkeson, C.G., & Hollerbach, J.M. (1985). Kinematic features of unrestrained vertical arm movements. *Journal of Neuroscience*, **5**, 318-330.

Bizzi, E., Accornero, N., Chapple, W., & Hogan, N. (1984). Posture control and trajectory formation during arm movement. *Journal of Neuroscience*, **4**, 2738-2744.

Buchanan, T.S., Rovai, G.P., & Rymer, W.Z. (1990). Strategies of muscle activation during isometric torque generation at the human elbow. *Journal of Neurophysiology*, **62**, 1201-1212.

Feldman, A.G. (1966). Functional tuning of the nervous system with control of movement or maintenance of a steady posture. II. Controllable parameters of the muscles. *Biophysics*, **11**, 565-578.

Feldman, A.G. (1980). Superposition of motor programs. II. Rapid forearm flexion in man. *Neuroscience*, **5**, 91-95.

Feldman, A.G. (1981). Composition of central programs subserving horizontal eye movement in man. *Biological Cybernetics*, **42**, 107-116.

Feldman, A.G. (1986). Once more on the equilibrium-point hypothesis (λ model) for motor control. *Journal of Motor Behavior*, **18**, 17-54.

Feldman, A.G., & Orlovsky, G.N. (1972). The influence of different descending systems on the tonic stretch reflex in the cat. *Experimental Neurology*, **37**, 481-494.

Feldman, A.G., Adamovich, S.V., Ostry, D.J., & Flanagan, J.R. (1990). The origin of electromyograms - explanations based on the equilibrium point hypothesis. In J. Winters & S. Woo (Eds.), *Multiple muscle systems: biomechanics of movement organization*. Berlin: Springer-Verlag.

Flash, T., & Hogan, N. (1985). The coordination of arm movements: an experimentally confirmed mathematical model. *Journal of Neuroscience*, **5**, 1688-1703.

Flash, T. (1987). The control of hand equilibrium trajectories in multi-joint arm movements. *Biological Cybernetics*, **57**, 57-74.

Georgopoulos, A.P. (1988). Neural integration of movement: role of motor cortex in reaching. *Federation of American Societies for Experimental Biology*, **2**, 849-857.

Grillner, S. (1981). Control of locomotion in bipeds tetrapods and fish. In V.B. Brooks (Ed.), *Handbook of physiology: Sec. 1. The nervous system: Vol. II. Motor control* (pp. 1179-1236). Bethesda, MD: American Physiological Society.

Hasan, Z., & Karst, G.M. (1989). Muscle activity for initial of planar two-joint arm movements in different directions. *Experimental Brain Research*, **76**, 651-655.

Hogan, N. (1984). An organizing principle for a class of voluntary movements. *Journal of Neuroscience*, **4**, 2745-2754.

Hollerbach, J.M. (1985). Computers, brains and the control of movements. *Trends in Neuroscience*, **5**, 189-192.

Hollerbach, J.M., & Atkeson, C.G. (1987). Deducing planning variables from experimental arm trajectories: pitfalls and possibilities. *Biological Cybernetics*, **56**, 79-89.

Hollerbach, J.M., & Flash, T. (1982). Dynamic interactions between limb segments during planar arm movement. *Biological Cybernetics*, **44**, 67-77.

Hultborn, H. (1972). Convergence of interneurons in the reciprocal Ia inhibitory pathway of motoneurons. Acta Physiologica Scandinavica Suppl 375, 1-42.

Humphrey, D.R., & Reed, D.J. (1983). Separate cortical systems for control of joint movement and joint stiffness: reciprocal activation and coactivation of antagonist muscles. *Advances in Neurology*, **39**, 347-372.

Lundberg, A. (1975). Control of spinal mechanisms from the brain. In D.B. Tower (Ed.), *The nervous system, Vol. 2* (pp. 253-265). New York: Raven Press.

Luschei, E.S., & Goldberg, L.J. (1981). Neural mechanisms of mandibular control: mastication and voluntary biting. In V.B. Brooks (Ed.), *Handbook of physiology: Sec. 1. The nervous system: Vol. II. Motor control* (pp. 1237-1274). Bethesda, MD: American Physiological Society.

Mussa-Ivaldi, F.A., Hogan, N., & Bizzi, E. (1985). Neural, mechanical, and geometric factors subserving arm posture in humans. *Journal of Neuroscience*, **5**, 2732-2743.

Ostry, D.J., & Flanagan, J.R. (1989). Human jaw movement in mastication and speech. *Archives of Oral Biology*, **34**, 685-693.

Pélisson, D., Prablanc, C., Goodale, M.A., & Jeannerod, M. (1986). Visual control of reaching movements without vision of the limb. II. Evidence of fast unconscious processes correcting the trajectory of the hand to the final position of a double-step stimulus. *Experimental Brain Research*, **62**, 303-311.

Schwartz, A.B., Kettner, R.E., & Georgopoulos, A.P. (1988). Primate motor cortex and free arm movements to visual targets in three-dimensional space. I. Relations between single cell discharge and direction of movement. *Journal of Neuroscience*, **8**, 2913-2927.

Soechting, J.F., & Lacquaniti, F. (1981). Invariant characteristics of a pointing movement in man. *Journal of Neuroscience*, **1**, 710-720.

van Zuylen, E.J., van Velzen, A., & Denier van der Gon, J.J. (1988). A biomechanical model for flexion torques of human arm muscles as a function of elbow angle. *Journal of Biomechanics*, **21**, 183-190.

van Zuylen, E.J., Gielen, C.C.A.M., & Denier van der Gon, J.J. (1988). Coordination and homogeneous activation of human arm muscles during isometric torques. *Journal of Neurophysiology*, **60**, 1523-1548.

Cerebral Control of Speech and Limb Movements
G.E. Hammond (editor)

Chapter 3

MANUAL PERFORMANCE ASYMMETRIES

Geoffrey Hammond
The University of Western Australia

The performance characteristics of the hands will give clues to the cerebral mechanisms of handedness, which may in turn give clues to some of the cerebral mechanisms of language. One suggestion, that the hands differ in their precision of force control, with more precise control by the preferred hand, has little supporting evidence. Simple repetitive movements of the preferred hand (at least of right-handed males) are both faster and less temporally variable than those of the non-preferred hand. The greater temporal variability of response execution by the non-preferred hand persists when the speed differences between the hands are eliminated by providing external response-timing pulses, during slow performance, and by coupling the responses of the two hands in bimanual movements. More variable temporal control of the movements of the non-preferred hand may also account for the superior accuracy of the preferred hand in simple manual aiming tasks. Fast and precise processing may be one of the sensorimotor properties suitable for both fine motor control and perception and production of language. This may be characteristic of the neural organization of the left hemisphere in right handers.

Handedness has traditionally been thought of as the characteristic preference individuals show for one or the other hand for performing unimanual tasks. Commonly-used indicators of handedness (such as the Edinburgh Handedness Inventory, Oldfield, 1971) score an individual's hand preference on a range of tasks that are considered to require only one hand. A second conceptualization has been put forward recently: Guiard

(1987) has argued that the hands typically work together, even in tasks that have conventionally been thought of as unimanual, such as handwriting. Guiard argued that handedness is a matter of the performance of different movement patterns by each hand during bimanual cooperation. In either view, the behavioral phenomenon of handedness presumably results because the motor systems which control the two hands differ in some important ways. It is generally accepted that, at least for fine movements of the distal musculature (such as hand movements), the right hand is controlled by a left-hemispheric motor system and the left hand by a right-hemispheric motor system (see for example, Brooks, 1986; Goodwin & Darian-Smith, 1985; Phillips, 1986). There must be differences in neural organization that produce the obvious behavioral differences in manual performance. These differences in neural organization, whatever their nature, appear not to be specific to the motor-control systems but to be a more general feature of hemispheric organization. This is suggested by the remarkable association of handedness and the behavioral consequences of lateralized brain damage: disturbances of language (including signed language) follow appropriately-located left hemispheric damage but are seldom a consequence of right hemispheric damage in right-handers. This association is at first surprising -- why is an apparently low-level function of the nervous system (motor control of the preferred hand) associated with what is thought of as an exemplary high-level function, the use of language? Such surprise comes from a failure to keep different levels of function separate, leading to an inappropriate comparison of a complex psychological function (communication) with a more elementary function, motor control. The brain is a sensorimotor system and language, like manual control, is a sensorimotor function. This position is the one pioneered by Hughlings Jackson with his opinion that language is one of the highest sensorimotor developments of the brain (see, for example, the discussion by Marshall, 1980). The dependence of the effects of lateralized brain damage on handedness indicates that the neural organization which characterizes the left hemisphere of right handers that is suitable for fine manual control is also suitable for understanding and producing language.

Ojemann's cortical stimulation work has shown common or closely-related cortical zones for language functions (such as naming) and orofacial motor abilities (such as the ability to mimic orofacial movements; Ojemann, 1983; Ojemann & Creutzfeldt, 1987). This implies a common mechanism for the linguistic and motor functions. One suggestion is that fine motor control (as in mimicry of orofacial gestures) and language perception and production rely on neural systems that are capable of fast temporal control (e.g., Corballis, 1983; Hammond, 1982; Tallal, 1981).

Observations of manual performance may therefore offer insight into the nature of the neural organization that appears to be common to fine motor control and some of the basic processes that underlie language function. Performance differences between the left and right hands might suggest characteristics of the neural organization of the controlling motor systems that might be general to the left and right hemispheres.

Speculation about the significant differences in control of hand movements has followed two main lines (Carson, 1989). These are first, that the motor systems that control the two hands differ in the precision with which they are able to modulate force, and second, that the motor systems that control the hands differ in the variability of their output. Evidence relevant to these ideas (much of it from observations of repetitive finger tapping) will be discussed in turn.

Force Production

The idea that the preferred hand is capable of modulating force more precisely than the non-preferred hand is appealing. It appeals subjectively (we use the preferred hand for tasks that seem to require precise applications of force), and there is some neurophysiological evidence that force is a variable controlled by the nervous system when specifying movement (Stein, 1982). If the motor system that controlled the preferred hand were capable of finer force control, the phenomenon of handedness would be explicable.

Not much relevant evidence has been reported. Todor and Smiley-Oyen (1987) reported that the mean force level and the mean variability of the forces applied during repetitive finger tapping were greater for the non-preferred than the preferred hand. A second line of evidence is indirect: the faster and less temporally-variable finger tapping by the preferred hand have been reported to arise chiefly from briefer and less variable durations of the transition periods between flexion and extension (Peters, 1980; Todor & Kyprie, 1980). This finding has been taken to be consistent with the proposal that the non-preferred hand is less able to modulate force precisely, and therefore less efficient in making these movement transitions.

In three experiments (Hammond & Bolton, 1990) we set out to replicate the findings reported by Todor and Smiley-Oyen (1987) and to make some direct observations of the ability of right-handed subjects to control force with each hand. The first two experiments measured the peak impulsive force applied by each index finger during rapid unimanual finger tapping. Subjects tapped a circular disk (25 mm diameter) milled from an aluminum bar to which a strain gauge was attached. Two outputs were available from the strain gauge amplifier, a voltage that was proportional to the force applied by the tap and a one-shot signal synchronous with the onset of the tap.

In the first experiment, subjects (8 right-handed males) were given no instructions other than to tap as rapidly as possible. Each subject performed 10 trials with each hand, with a trial made up of 15 'warm-up' taps (which were not scored) followed by a 10-s period during which the interval between successive taps was scored to the nearest ms. Tapping force was measured as the peak force applied during the 20-ms period following the onset of a tap (pilot work showed that the peak force always occurred within this time window). The mean peak tapping force was calculated for each 10-s trial and the standard deviation of the peak forces produced in a trial was used as the measure of force variability. Tapping speed was measured as the mean inter-response interval (IRI, the interval between tap onsets) for each trial and the temporal variability of tapping was measured as the standard deviation of the IRIs produced in each trial.

Right-hand tapping was, as expected, faster and more temporally regular than left-hand tapping. Unlike the report of Todor and Smiley-Oyen (1987) however, there was no general asymmetry of either the mean force applied or of the mean within-subject variability of forces. An examination of individual performances gave no sign of any systematic asymmetry of either force score: two subjects produced reliably greater mean force with their right hand, and one with his left hand; two subjects showed reliably greater standard deviations of the forces applied by their right hand and one showed a reliably greater standard deviation of the forces applied by his left hand.

The second experiment repeated these observations in an independent sample of 10 right-handed males who were instructed to tap as rapidly as possible while restricting movement to the metacarpal-phalangeal joint. This was done to repeat the procedure of Todor and Smiley-Oyen (1987) more closely. Again, the expected hand asymmetries of speed and temporal regularity of tapping were obtained. And again, there was no general asymmetry of either force production measure. One subject tapped with reliably greater mean force with his right hand, and one with his left hand; one subject showed a reliably greater mean standard deviation of forces produced with his right hand, and one a reliably greater mean standard deviation of forces with his left hand. In both experiments, subjects who did not show statistically reliable asymmetries showed larger standard deviations as frequently with their right hand as with their left.

These two studies together give no support to the idea that force production is asymmetrical during rapid repetitive finger tapping. If it occurs, it is under specific circumstances that we have not been able to reproduce. There is no obvious reason that we were unable to replicate the results reported by Todor and Smiley-Oyen. Perhaps their apparatus (the subject's finger was strapped to the response key) or their procedure (the subjects performed three 8-s tapping trials successively with each hand, rather than alternating the hands) made tapping difficult or promoted the development of fatigue, which in turn caused a disproportionate increase in the forces and the variability of forces produced by the non-preferred hand.

In the third experiment we made direct observations of the ability of each hand to maintain a stable force level (with visual feedback) and to then make the smallest possible change, either an increase or a decrease, in the stable level (a 'just-producible difference', JPD). The JPD is a motor equivalent of the just-noticeable difference of sensory psychology, and was taken as the measure of the precision of force control. Eight right-handed males pressed the disk of the tapping apparatus used in the two previous experiments; the strain gauge output was sampled by a microcomputer every ms. In the first phase (which lasted 5 s) subjects produced a stable force that was either 20%, 40%, 60%, or 80% of a previously-determined maximum force that could be produced comfortably with that finger; a light-emitting diode (LED) in front of the subject was illuminated while the force was within a ±2% tolerance band around the target force for that trial. The end of the first phase was signaled by the illumination of a red or green LED that directed the subjects to increase or decrease the stable force by the smallest amount possible. Three trials were done in each of the eight conditions (four stable force levels maintained in the first phase and two directions of force change in the second phase). Figure 1 shows typical force records from one subject. Each tracing shows the forces produced by the subject in the different conditions on a single trial.

It can be seen that force levels were graded according to the experimental conditions and that the subject made the appropriate changes in force when instructed. This was characteristic of all subjects.

The JPDs increased as a linear function of the baseline force for both the force-increase and force-decrease conditions. There was no evidence that the JPDs were asymmetrical; neither hand showed a tendency to produce smaller JPDs which would have indicated more precise force control. Furthermore, there was no asymmetry of the variability of the sustained forces applied either during the first phase (during the period from the first force recorded in the target range to the end of the first phase) or during the second phase (during the last three s of the phase, following the prescribed change in force). These observations fail to reveal any difference between the hands in their control of force. Despite the appeal of the idea that handedness results from asymmetrical force control, there is at present insufficient evidence to support such a conclusion.

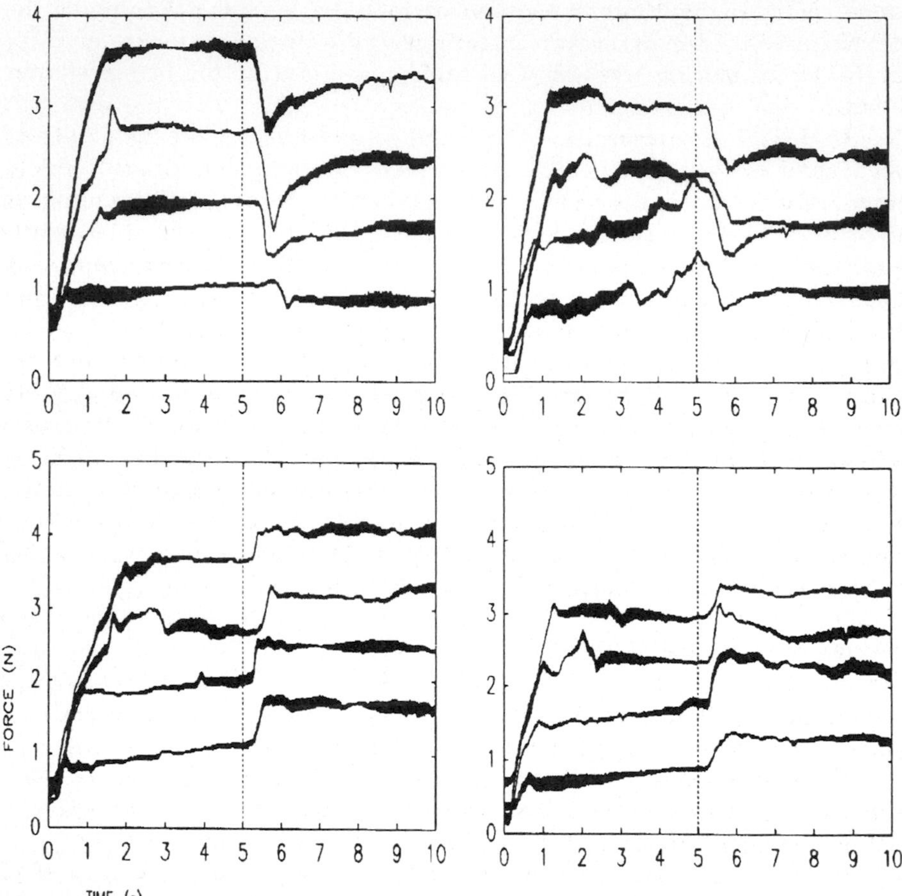

Figure 1. The four panels show the forces (in N) produced by one subject throughout both phases of the third trial for each condition. The top left panel shows the force decrement condition for the left hand, top right panel the force decrement condition for the right hand, the bottom left panel the force increment condition for the left hand, and the bottom right panel the force increment condition for the right hand. The four plots in each panel correspond to the four target force levels. The vertical line at 5 s shows the division of the two phases.

Output Variability

J. Annett, M. Annett, Hudson, and Turner (1979) observed that the non-preferred hand had to make more corrective movements during the final positioning phase of a task that required subjects to move pegs from holes in one row to those in an adjacent row. They argued that the output of the motor system of the non-preferred hand was 'noisier' than that of the preferred hand and the non-preferred hand was therefore less able to execute precise movements. Care needs to be taken with the idea that handedness is an expression of asymmetrical variability of motor control. As Peters (1989) pointed out in a response to Carson (1989), output variability is what is observed in performance, and therefore what is to be explained. To say that the non-preferred hand is more variable than the preferred hand does not explain its greater variability. The tautology can be avoided. More variable movement control by the nonpreferred hand may be an important determinant of hand preference; one hand may be preferred over the other because its performance is less variable. In turn, the greater observed performance variability of the non-preferred hand implies differences in the mode of control of the two hands. It is also necessary to specify which movement dimension is differently variable; to say only that the non-preferred hand is 'more variable' than the preferred hand is not a sufficient description. The next two sections present some observations of finger tapping and of more complex aimed movements that suggest there are differences between the hands in timing of movements.

Repetitive Finger Tapping

Keele (1986), in discussing the regularity of movement sequences, pointed out that precision of timing might be central to motor coordination. It may in turn be the case that an asymmetry of the precision with which movements are timed might be an important mechanism of handedness.

Fast repetitive finger tapping reveals asymmetries of both speed (the mean IRI from a series of taps by the preferred hand is usually shorter than that from the non-preferred hand) and temporal regularity (the standard deviation of the IRIs in a series of taps by the preferred hand is usually smaller than that of the non-preferred hand). The asymmetrical temporal variability evident in finger tapping may reflect a fundamental asymmetry of motor variability. An important question is whether the greater temporal variability of tapping by the non-preferred hand is a general characteristic of its performance or whether it occurs only in particular conditions (such as tapping as quickly as possible) that are at its performance limit. The following experiments were designed to answer this question; all observations were made on right-handed males.

We examined the performance of the left and right hands of eight subjects in Michon's (1967) continuation task (Truman & Hammond, 1990). In the synchronization phase of this task the subjects were required to tap in synchrony with a train of 30 regularly-spaced clicks delivered over headphones. This was followed by a continuation phase in which the subjects were required to produce another 30 taps at the rate established in the synchronization phase without the synchronizing clicks. Performance was tested over eight trials at each of four different rates, with inter-pulse intervals (IPIs) of 250, 500, 750, and 1500 ms. The temporal *accuracy* of performance in the synchronization phase was measured by the mean asynchrony of the timing clicks and their associated responses and in the continuation phase by the constant error of estimation of the responses (the mean difference between the produced IRIs and the target IRI, the IPI of the just-completed synchronization phase). The temporal *precision* of performance in both phases was measured as the standard deviation of the IRIs produced within each of the two phases.

There was no asymmetry of the synchronizing stimulus - response asynchronies in the synchronization phase or of the constant error of the intervals produced in the continuation phase: the left hand was no less accurate than the right in the temporal scheduling of responses. The standard deviations of the IRIs were, as expected from the work of Schmidt (1980), a linear increasing function of the base response rate. Furthermore, there was a small but statistically reliable asymmetry of the standard deviations of the IRIs in both the synchronization and the continuation phase: there was greater temporal dispersion of the responses produced by the non-preferred hand. The asymmetry was small in absolute terms (the standard deviations differed by several ms) but it may be behaviorally important. The task is simple, and as M. Annett (1985) pointed out, handedness may well be a consequence of apparently minor differences in sensorimotor capacity.

The greater variability of responding by the non-preferred hand was unexpected, especially as the hands were equally accurate and the tapping rates were well within the capability of the non-preferred hand to respond sequentially. In the next experiment we examined whether this greater variability of response timing by the non-preferred hand was more generally present. Right-handed male subjects tapped separately with their left and right index fingers in each of three rate conditions: as rapidly as possible, at a fast but steady rate, and at a 'natural comfortable rhythm'. The subjects had no difficulty adjusting their tapping according to these instructions: mean tapping rates were about 5/s in the fast rate, about 4/s in the fast steady rate, and about 3/s when tapping at a self-chosen comfortable rhythm. Different subjects adopted different rates in the latter condition, but they were themselves consistent, responding at a similar rate with each hand in the six trials. The speed asymmetry was graded in the three conditions: the mean IRI for the right hand was 27 ms shorter than that for the left hand in the fast condition, 13 ms shorter in the fast steady condition, and 3 ms shorter in the slow comfortable condition.

The mean standard deviations of the IRIs -- which indicate the temporal dispersion of responding -- were smallest in the fast steady condition and similar in the other two conditions. More importantly, the mean standard deviations were greater for the non-preferred hand by 3 ms in each of the three rate conditions. This asymmetrical dispersion of responding was present not only when the subjects were tapping as quickly as possible, but also when attempting to maintain a stable submaximal response rate and when responding at a subjectively comfortable rhythm that was the same for each hand.

The observations that the left hand showed greater temporal dispersion of responding when the hands were tapping at submaximal rates led us to look at the temporal dispersion of responding by each hand of right-handed males during fast bimanual tapping. Would the asymmetry be present when response output of the hands was coupled? In the first experiment subjects tapped in two conditions: unimanual tapping, and bimanual tapping with the responses of each hand synchronized (i.e., with the hands 0° out of phase). We were surprised that some subjects were unable to tap bimanually at a fast rate: their preferred hand responded more rapidly than their non-preferred hand despite their attempt to couple responding in the two hands. The results from five subjects who were able to tap synchronously at a fast rate are shown in Table 1.

Table 1. Means and standard deviations (in ms) of the IRIs for each hand during unimanual and synchronous bimanual tapping. The standard errors are in parentheses.

		Left Hand	Right Hand
Means	Unimanual	210 (7)	192 (6)
	Bimanual	223 (7)	223 (7)
Standard Deviations	Unimanual	14 (1)	11 (1)
	Bimanual	15 (1)	11 (1)

The subjects showed typical asymmetries of both speed and temporal variability in unimanual tapping. Response rate was slower with both hands during synchronous bimanual tapping, with the right hand showing a greater change from unimanual tapping than the left. Despite the temporal coupling of tapping by the hands, the left hand remained more variable; the asymmetry of variability of the IRIs was almost the same as that seen during unimanual tapping.

In a second experiment the bimanual task required alternate tapping (i.e., with the hands 180° out of phase). Again some subjects had difficulty with the task and could not maintain a 1:1 ratio of responses by the two hands. The results from four subjects who could do the task are shown in Table 2.

Table 2. Means and standard deviations (in ms) of the IRIs for each hand during unimanual and alternate bimanual tapping. The standard errors are in parentheses.

		Left Hand	Right Hand
Means	Unimanual	198 (3)	183 (3)
	Bimanual	247 (8)	247 (9)
Standard	Unimanual	20 (2)	16 (2)
Deviations	Bimanual	25 (3)	21 (3)

Again, the subjects showed speed and temporal variability differences between the hands in unimanual tapping that are typical of right-handers. The results from alternate bimanual tapping are similar to those seen with synchronous bimanual tapping. Tapping with each hand was slower during bimanual than unimanual tapping, and despite the coupling of response output, the difference between the hands in the variability of the IRIs persisted.

These findings with bimanual tapping show that the asymmetrical temporal dispersion of responding is present in simple bimanual tapping tasks where the nature of the motor task forces the same response rate for each hand. Results generally consistent with this finding have been reported for subjects engaged in more complex bimanual tapping tasks. The temporal dispersion of responses produced by the left hand of right-handers was greater for subjects performing a 2:1 tapping rhythm (with one hand executing two taps for each tap by the other) at either a self-chosen pace (Peters, 1985) or as rapidly as possible (Peters, 1987). The non-preferred left hand was also more temporally variable in subjects performing a more complex 2:3 rhythm with subjects instructed to count taps by the hand performing either the two-tap or the three-tap series. The IRIs produced by the left hand were more variable in each of the four conditions (2 or 3 taps produced, counted or not) although it is not clear whether the differences were statistically significant in each (Peters & Schwartz, 1989). An exception has been reported by Peters (1985) who required subjects to tap as quickly as possible with one hand while attempting to maintain a slow steady rhythm with the other. One hand began at either the slow or fast pace with the other hand joining in after the leading hand had completed a few taps. His results show greater temporal dispersion of left-hand responses at the fast rate, but a reversal with greater temporal dispersion of right-hand responses at the slow rate. This shows that there are some conditions in which the temporal variability of the preferred hand's output is greater than that of the non-preferred hand. Perhaps the preferred hand alters its temporal schedule of response to accommodate rapid tapping by the non-preferred hand, with a cost to the regularity of its own responding. A second possibility is that the requirement of tapping rapidly with the non-preferred hand and slowly with the preferred hand (which Peters has shown to be more difficult than the reverse pattern) draws attention to the rapidly-tapping left hand to the cost of the right-hand performance. When the right hand does the rapid tapping there may be no equivalent penalty for the left hand, which is maintaining the slower rhythm.

The presence of asymmetrical temporal variability with response rates of the two hands equated shows that it is not a simple statistical consequence of the association of larger standard deviations with larger means (McManus, Kemp, & Grant, 1986). Taken together, the behavioral observations show that the greater temporal variability of responding by the non-preferred hand is evident in conditions that are well within its performance capacities. Its greater temporal variability therefore does not result from an instability of control when it is operating near its performance limits. Instead, this greater variability appears to be a genuine -- and general -- feature of the scheduling of simple responses by the non-preferred hand. If so, it must be a consequence of an asymmetrical organization of the motor systems and may be an important determinant of hand preference.

The asymmetry of tapping speed (the faster response rate by the preferred hand) also seems to be genuine and does not appear to be secondary to some other factor. First, the speed asymmetry is not secondary to a more precise control of the spatial extent of the tapping movement in the preferred hand. We had thought that the longer IRIs produced by the non-preferred hand might result from less precise spatial control of movement, with a consequent greater distance traveled in the tapping movements; the preferred hand might in contrast show more restricted movement travel, allowing a greater number of responses to be completed within a specified time (and hence a shorter mean IRI). However, measurements of finger movement using reflection of infra-red light from the finger nail (Carey, 1985) showed that this was not the case. Between-hand differences in finger displacement during tapping were small, and the mean distance traveled by the preferred hand was (if anything) greater than that traveled by the non-preferred hand. (The usual speed asymmetry was found, with the preferred hand moving more rapidly.) Second, the greater mean IRI found for a sample of IRIs produced by the non-preferred hand is not an artifact of the greater temporal variability of tapping by that hand (the greater variability of IRIs from the preferred hand might be caused by a few very long IRIs which would inflate the mean). Hammond, Bolton, Plant, and Manning (1988) cumulated frequency distributions of the IRIs produced by each hand of each of eight right-handed male subjects over 20 10-s tapping periods. The distributions of IRIs from each hand were roughly normal. The IRIs produced by the non-preferred hand left hand were more dispersed than those produced by the preferred right hand, and they were shifted systematically to longer IRIs. The greater mean IRI of the non-preferred hand is not an artifactual inflation caused by a small number of large IRIs. Instead, there is a systematic production of longer IRIs by the non-preferred hand, and generally, the non-preferred hand cannot produce IRIs as short as the shortest IRIs produced by the preferred hand. The performance of the preferred hand in fast repetitive finger tapping is therefore both *faster* (it produces smaller IRIs) and *less variable* (it produces a more compact distribution of IRIs) than the non-preferred hand.

The asymmetry of temporal regularity implies an asymmetry of motor precision, with the preferred hand capable of more precise temporal scheduling of output. This view, that the non-preferred hand is an error-prone counterpart of the preferred hand, has been disputed recently (Guiard, 1987). Guiard has shown in a convincing series of demonstrations that the two hands perform different functions in normal bimanual movements. The non-preferred hand performs movements with low spatial and temporal frequencies while the preferred hand performs movements with high spatial and temporal frequencies. One illustration of this is handwriting, where the non-preferred hand makes infrequent, relatively large-amplitude movements of the paper while the preferred hand makes frequent low-amplitude movements of the writing instrument. Guiard interpreted this and other instances of bimanual cooperation as showing that the hands are not differently competent, but are specialized for complementary movement functions. Guiard's findings are important, but the fact that the hands adopt different functions during cooperative bimanual movements does not mean that they are specialized for those different functions. Different functions for the hands might be adopted because one hand is a more precise output timer than the other; the nervous system might make what appears to be a virtue out of a necessity. The finding that the non-preferred hand is usually more variable than the preferred hand at both fast and slow tapping rates questions Guiard's idea that the hands have complementary movement specializations with the non-preferred hand specialized for low frequency movements. Complementary movement specializations of the hands, with the preferred hand specialized for high frequency movements and the non-preferred hand for low frequency movements, should result in greater variability of the non-preferred than the preferred hand when tapping quickly and smaller variability of the non-preferred than the preferred hand when tapping slowly. The evidence is mixed, but on balance against this view. Most reports (discussed above) show greater temporal variability of tapping by the non-preferred hand for tapping at both fast and slow self-chosen rates for both unimanual and bimanual tapping. The single exception is Peters' (1985) fast/slow bimanual tapping task. Our results described above show also that the non-preferred left hand is more variable in a variety of conditions, including slow tapping. The findings together suggest that the hands do not have complementary 'roles', but rather do different things when working together because their different temporal precision makes them differently suited to different movement functions.

Furthermore, there are few examples in the literature of actions in which superior performance is shown by the non-preferred hand. There does not appear to be a specialized 'role' for the non-preferred hand. Kimura and Vanderwolf (1970) are frequently cited as showing a left-hand superiority for the ability to flex a single finger or a pair of fingers to about 90°, but the difference is neither large nor robust. A small but statistically significant left-hand superiority was found in their first experiment for the total mean accuracy score (apparently single and paired movements combined) but this was not replicated in their second experiment. Paired finger flexions were said to be more accurate by the left hand in both experiments but the standard errors of the means were not given and no inferential statistics were reported. Roy and MacKenzie (1978) found a clear superiority of the left hand on a task that required subjects to move both thumbs simultaneously to a mechanical stop, back to the start position, and to then return them to the stop position after the mechanical stop was removed. The superiority of the left hand was general across the subjects and was present in absolute error, constant error, and variable error. The task required kinesthetic perception of the initial stop position and recall of this information to reposition the thumb, and the performance asymmetry may reflect lateral differences in perceptual or recall processes (for which the right hemisphere may be superior) rather than revealing a specialized motor function for the left hand. Guiard, Diaz, and Beaubaton (1983) observed ballistic aiming movements to a visual target that could be presented to the left or right of a central fixation point. They found that the left hand had a significantly smaller constant error, which they took as a measure of the accuracy of programming the movement. The difference in variable error, which was taken as a measure of the accuracy of execution of the motor program, was greater for the left hand, but this difference was not statistically significant. Although there may be conditions in which the non-preferred hand outperforms the preferred hand, there is insufficient evidence at present to accept the view that the non-preferred hand has its own specialized function. Hand differences may instead emerge largely because the hands differ in the speed or temporal precision with which output is controlled.

Aiming Movements

The non-preferred hand has also been found to be less adept at performing precise aiming movements than the preferred hand. J. Annett et al.'s (1979) finding that hand differences in an aiming task were most pronounced in the final positioning phase of movement has been recently replicated by Todor and Cisneros (1985). They found that the preferred hand made fewer errors than the non-preferred hand in an aiming task that required the subjects to move a stylus from a position near the shoulder to a target in front of them. Their detailed behavioral analysis of the task showed two functional phases, an initial distance-covering phase and a succeeding target-homing phase in which error correction was assumed to occur. A hand asymmetry was evident only in this latter error-correction phase, where the non-preferred hand was slower than the preferred hand. The authors argued that the appearance of a hand asymmetry in this phase indicated an asymmetry in the efficiency of error correction, and that this differential efficiency might in turn be a major source of between-hand differences in variability of motor output. This position -- that the asymmetry in error correction is fundamental and the asymmetry in output variability secondary -- may be incorrect. It is clear that hand differences are present in movements (such as finger tapping) that do not require precise aiming and do not involve error correction. It is more parsimonious to account for the less efficient error correction by the non-preferred hand in terms of its more variable temporal control of movement rather than the reverse. Because the behavioral asymmetry emerges in the error-correction phase does not mean that its fundamental nature is one of 'error correction'. The differences in error correction might arise from differences in the variability of temporal control.

More variable temporal control of movement may also be responsible for asymmetries of spatial features of movement observed in aiming and pointing tasks. In two experiments, Roy and Elliott (1989) showed that the variable error (a measure of the spatial dispersion of the aiming movements) was greater for movements made by their subjects' non-preferred left hands. This asymmetry was present for aiming movements of different speeds to near and far targets, and when the movements were made with and without vision of the moving hand. Roy and Elliott used these results to dismiss the hypotheses that hand differences depend on an asymmetry in the capacity to utilize visual feedback (because the presence of visual feedback did not affect the size of the asymmetry) and that differences in force variability are important (because the asymmetry did not vary with movement force). They suggested that although variability of force production itself did not seem to be an important source of the asymmetry, the observed performance asymmetries might result from more consistent timing of force impulses to the preferred hand. More variable timing of response outflow by the non-preferred hand would increase the spatial dispersion of its movements because the end position of movement is determined by the timing of output forces as well as their magnitude. Roy and Elliott (1989), however, did not elaborate this idea, and they concluded that their performance asymmetries might have resulted from asymmetric noise in the motor control systems. Specifically, they argued that the neuromuscular system controlling the non-preferred hand might be less well 'damped' than that controlling the preferred hand, and therefore less capable of spatially precise movement.

Cortical Control of Hand and Finger Movements

The evidence described above shows that the non-preferred hand is slower and less temporally precise than the preferred hand in making simple repetitive movements in a variety of different conditions. The position taken here is that these behavioral differences result from differences in the operating characteristics of the responsible motor systems. A literal interpretation of the behavioral differences -- that the motor system controlling the non-preferred hand is slower and more temporally variable than that controlling the preferred hand -- is not helpful. All it does is transfer the observed characteristics to an unobserved level (the neurophysiological level). It is reasonable to argue, however, that the underlying mechanisms of hand control differ in such a way to cause the observed behavioral differences.

Recent developments in understanding the cortical control of hand movements put constraints on what the asymmetrical mechanisms might be, and may also give clues to the nature of the mechanisms. Reviews of these developments have been published by Humphrey (1986) and by Lemon (1988). Two principles of cortical control that might be relevant to the mechanisms of handedness have emerged. These are *divergence* (a single cortical locus can control more than one muscle) and *convergence* (a single muscle can be controlled from more than one cortical locus). These two organizational features result in motor structures called movement synergies (by Humphrey, 1986) and muscle fields (by Lemon, 1988). As an illustration of such a motor structure, a single corticomotoneuronal (CM) cell in precentral motor cortex might control several different (though related) muscles; another CM cell, distant from the first, might also control several different muscles, one or more of them common to those controlled by the first CM cell. These structures appear to be fundamental to the cerebral organization of movement, and so will be important to the lateral differentiation of motor control that is evident in handedness.

There are several lines of evidence for this organization. The spike-triggered averaging technique (in which the EMG activity from different muscles is averaged time-locked to impulses fired by a CM neuron) shows that single CM cells exert monosynaptic control over several different muscles. This diffusion apparently results from the intra-spinal branching of the axons of CM cells that has been shown by Shinoda, Zarzecki, and Asanuma (1979). Axonal branching would result in divergence (the CM cell would contact spinal motoneurons that control different muscles) and could also result in convergence (axonal branching would increase the likelihood that different CM neurons would synapse on the same spinal motoneuron). The intracortical microstimulation technique (Asanuma, 1981) shows that the same single motor unit can be excited by low-level electrical stimulation of separate cortical areas; there is an intermingling at the cortex of cells with different target spinal motoneurons.

The size of a muscle field (the number of muscles controlled by a CM cell) is associated with movement precision; larger muscle fields are found for proximal than distal muscles, and in particular, muscle fields of CM cells that control hand movements are restricted (Buys, Lemon, Mantel, & Muir, 1986; Cheney, Kasser, & Fetz, 1985; Muir, 1985). This relationship suggests a possible mechanism of handedness: the muscle fields or movement synergies of the preferred hand may be smaller than those of the non-preferred hand. The basic movement structures of the preferred hand may be simpler -- that is, include fewer muscles -- than the corresponding structures of the non-preferred hand. If this were the case, serial movement by the preferred hand would require switching between activation of motor structures that contained fewer component muscles than would serial movement by the non-preferred hand. Switching simpler motor synergies would, on average, be faster than switching more complex synergies. If the component muscles of a synergy were not activated synchronously from occasion-to-occasion, switching of simpler motor synergies would also be less temporally variable. This particular suggestion is not likely to be correct, but the search for mechanisms of handedness in what is known of the neurophysiology of motor control might prove fruitful. In any case, speculations about the mechanisms of handedness must comply with what is known about the cerebral control of movement generally.

Acknowledgements

I thank George Truman, Yvette Bolton, Clive Carey, and Sharyn Paul for their discussions and for working on the experiments described here.

References

Annett, J., Annett, M., Hudson, P.T.W., & Turner, A. (1979). The control of movement in the preferred and non-preferred hands. *Quarterly Journal of Experimental Psychology*, **31**, 641-652.

Annett, M. (1985). *Left, right, hand and brain: The right shift theory*. Hillsdale, NJ: Lawrence Erlbaum Associates.

Asanuma, H. (1981). The pyramidal tract. In V.B. Brooks (Ed.), *Handbook of physiology: Sec. I. The nervous system, Vol. II. Motor control, Part I* (pp. 703-733). Bethesda, MD: American Physiological Society.

Brooks, V.B. (1986). *The neural basis of motor control*. New York: Oxford University Press.

Buys, E.J., Lemon, R.N., Mantel, G.W.H., & Muir, R.B. (1986). Selective facilitation of different hand muscles by single corticospinal neurones in the conscious monkey. *Journal of Physiology*, **381**, 529-549.

Carey, C. (1985). *Asymmetry in free finger movement*. Unpublished honors thesis, The University of Western Australia.

Carson, R.G. (1989). Manual asymmetries: Feedback processing, output variability, and spatial complexity -- resolving some inconsistencies. *Journal of Motor Behavior*, **21**, 38-47.

Cheney, P.D., Kasser, R.J., & Fetz, E.E. (1985). Motor and sensory properties of primate corticomotoneuronal cells. In A.W. Goodwin & I. Darian-Smith (Eds.), *Hand function and the neocortex* (pp. 211-231). Berlin: Springer-Verlag.

Corballis, M.C. (1983). *Human laterality*. New York: Academic Press.

Goodwin, A.W., & Darian-Smith, I. (Eds.). (1985). *Hand function and the neocortex*. Berlin: Springer-Verlag.

Guiard, Y. (1987). Asymmetric division of labor in human skilled bimanual action: The kinematic chain as a model. *Journal of Motor Behavior*, **19**, 486-517.

Guiard, Y., Diaz, G., & Beaubaton, D. (1983). Left-hand advantage in right-handers for spatial constant error: Preliminary evidence in a unimanual ballistic aimed movement. *Neuropsychologia*, **21**, 111-115.

Hammond, G.R. (1982). Hemispheric differences in temporal resolution. *Brain and Cognition*, **1**, 95-118.

Hammond, G.R., & Bolton, Y.M. (1990). *Control of force production by the left and right hands*. Manuscript submitted for publication.

Hammond, G.R., Bolton, Y.M., Plant, M.Y., & Manning, J.J. (1988). Hand asymmetries in interresponse intervals during rapid repetitive finger tapping. *Journal of Motor Behavior*, **20**, 67-71.

Humphrey, D.R. (1986). Representation of movements and muscles within the primate precentral motor cortex: Historical and current perspectives. *Federation Proceedings*, **45**, 2687-2699.

Keele, S.W. (1986). Motor control. In K.R.Boff, L. Kaufman, & J.P. Thomas (Eds.), *Handbook of perception and human performance, Vol. II: Cognitive processes and peformance* (pp. 30.1-30.60). New York: Wiley.

Kimura, D., & Vanderwolf, C.H. (1970). The relation between hand preference and the performance of individual finger movements by left and right hands. *Brain*, **93**, 769-774.

Lemon, R.N. (1988). The output map of the primate motor cortex. *Trends in neuroscience*, **11**, 501-506.

Marshall, J.C. (1980). Clues from neurological deficits. In U. Bellugi & M. Studdert-Kennedy (Eds.), *Signed and spoken language: Biological constraints on linguistic form*. Weinheim: Verlag Chemie.

McManus, I.C., Kemp, R.I., & Grant, J. (1986). Differences between fingers and hands in tapping ability: Dissociation between speed and regularity. *Cortex*, **22**, 461-473.

Michon, J.A. (1967). *Timing in temporal tracking*. Soesterberg, The Netherlands: Institute for Perception, RVO-TNO.

Muir, R.B. (1985). Small hand muscles in precision grip: a corticospinal prerogative? In A.W. Goodwin & I. Darian-Smith (Eds.), *Hand function and the neocortex* (pp. 155-174). Berlin: Springer-Verlag.

Ojemann, G.A. (1983). Localization for common cortex for motor sequencing and phoneme identification. In M. Studdert-Kennedy (Ed.), *Psychobiology of language* (pp. 69-76). Cambridge, MA: MIT Press.

Ojemann, G.A., & Creutzfeldt, O.D. (1987). Language in humans and animals: contribution of brain stimulation and recording. In F. Plum (Ed.), *Handbook of physiology: Sec. 1. The nervous system: Vol. V. Higher functions of the brain, Part 2* (pp. 675-699). Bethesda, MD: American Physiological Society.

Oldfield, R.C. (1971). The assessment and analysis of handedness: The Edinburgh Inventory. *Neuropsychologia*, **9**, 97-114.

Peters, M. (1980). Why the preferred hand taps more quickly than the non-preferred hand: three experiments on handedness. *Canadian Journal of Psychology*, **34**, 62-71.

Peters, M. (1985). Constraints in the coordination of bimanual movements and their expression in skilled or unskilled subjects. *Quarterly Journal of Experimental Psychology*, **37A**, 171-196.

Peters, M. (1987). A nontrivial motor performance difference between right-handers and left-handers: Attention as an intervening variable in the expression of handedness. *Canadian Journal of Psychology*, **41**, 91-99.

Peters, M. (1989). Do feedback processing, output variability, and spatial complexity account for manual asymmetries? *Journal of Motor Behavior*, **21**, 151-155.

Peters, M., & Schwartz, S. (1989). Coordination of the two hands and effects of attentional manipulation in the production of a bimanual 2:3 polyrhythm. *Australian Journal of Psychology*, **41**, 215-224.

Phillips, C.G. (1986). *Movements of the hand.* Liverpool: Liverpool University Press.

Roy, E.A., & Elliott, D. (1989). Manual asymmetries in aimed movements. *The Quarterly Journal of Experimental Psychology*, **41A**, 501-516.

Roy, E.A., & MacKenzie, C. (1978). Handedness effects in kinesthetic spatial location judgements. *Cortex*, **14**, 250-258.

Schmidt, R.A. (1980). On the theoretical status of time in motor program representations. In G.E. Stelmach & J. Requin (Eds.), *Tutorials in motor behavior* (pp. 145-166). Amsterdam: North Holland.

Shinoda, Y., Zarzecki, P., & Asanuma, H. (1979). Spinal branching of pyramidal tract neurons in the monkey. *Experimental Brain Research*, **34**, 59-72.

Stein, R.B. (1982). What muscle variable(s) does the nervous system control in limb movements? *The Behavioral and Brain Sciences*, **5**, 535-577.

Tallal, P. (1981). Temporal processing as related to hemispheric specialization for speech perception in normal and language impaired populations. *The Behavioral and Brain Sciences*, **4**, 77-78.

Todor, J.I., & Cisneros, J. (1985). Accommodation to increased accuracy demands by the right and left hands. *Journal of Motor Behavior*, **17**, 355-372.

Todor, J.I., & Kyprie, P.M. (1980). Hand differences in the rate and variability of rapid tapping. *Journal of Motor Behavior*, 12, 57-60.

Todor, J.I., & Smiley-Oyen, A.L. (1987). Force modulation as a source of hand differences in rapid finger tapping. *Acta Psychologica*, **65**, 65-73.

Truman, G., & Hammond, G.R. (1990). Temporal regularity of tapping by the left and right hands in timed and untimed finger tapping. *Journal of Motor Behavior*.

Cerebral Control of Speech and Limb Movements
G.E. Hammond (editor)

Chapter 4

THE DEVELOPMENT OF HEMISPHERIC AND MANUAL SPECIALIZATION

Gerald Young
Glendon College, York University

An inhibition theory of complementary hemispheric specialization is considered from developmental and evolutionary perspectives. First, a review is undertaken of (a) prominent theories on the development and evolution of lateralization and of (b) recent research with adults and children on lateralization. For the former, the progressive view of lateralization development and the evolution of laterality in early nonhuman primates and hominids are described. For the latter, research on the effects of maturation, birth stress, and brain damage on fetal and neonatal lateralization is examined. Next, I describe a theory of complementary (related and not merely different) inhibition skills in the left and right hemispheres. Evidence in support of the theory is presented in terms of (a) perseverations in behavior after unilateral lesions, (b) irrelevant behavioral overflow on motor tasks, and (c) emotional expression. A 20-level model of lateralization development is introduced and is suggested as a possible model for understanding the evolution of lateralization. A concluding section focuses on the relationship of language development and lateralization, particularly as it pertains to the 20-level model. Neopiagetian models of development (e.g., Case, 1985) are critically compared to our own. It is shown that the current theory compared to the others can more precisely account for the steps in language development as described by Case.

1. Development, Lateralization, and Evolution

1.1. Lateralization in Development

"Laterality in human evolution". "Towards a central dogma for psychology". These are titles of recent articles (by Corballis, 1989, and N.D. Cook, 1989a, respectively) written on behavioral lateralization and hemispheric specialization in humans. The titles illustrate the increasing awareness that a core characteristic of our species centers on the asymmetric property of the brain and corresponding behavior. The present chapter is concerned with the development of human laterality in brain and behavior. Our major goals are, first, to describe a novel approach to understanding lateralization, and second, to present a novel theory of cognitive and related development. We also intend to show how these two areas interrelate and have implications for other aspects of behavior. The theory of complementary hemispheric specialization for inhibition described in a companion chapter by Young (1990) is underscored in the current chapter and is applied in new ways. [Key terms in the field are defined in the companion work.]

Although aspects of the development of lateralization seem constant from birth (Kinsbourne & Hiscock, 1987), there is progressive growth in lateralization both in isolated behavior (Molfese & Betz, 1987) and larger structures (Ramsay & Weber, 1986). Moreover, diverse organismic experiences can play a contributing role in this process (Michel, 1988). Thus, the various theories on the emergence of lateralization in humans seem complementary, although the specific ways all the relevant factors interrelate in lateralization development remain to be determined.

Another approach to the development of hemispheric specialization recently has been presented by de Schonen (de Schonen & Mativet, 1989; de Schonen, Mativet, & Deruelle, 1989). She proposed a complex scenario on the development of hemispheric specialization for the recognition of faces in infants. Factors hypothesized as important in this acquisition concern (a) experiential influences on neural interconnections, (b) the infant's limited sensitivity to the range of spatial frequencies inherent in encountered facial stimuli, (c) the more rapid maturation of the right hemisphere's temporo-occipital region early in life, etc. The question of maturation will be dealt with in section 2.1, but outside of this it is beyond the scope of the current work to present de Schonen's theory in detail. Suffice it to say that de Schonen deals mostly with a single lateralization in the developing person (face perception) and implicates experiential as well as endogenous determinants in its acquisition. Thus, it resembles Michel's progressive view of lateralization development. Previously, I have argued that my model of the development of lateralization (Young, 1990) resembles

Ramsay's work, in particular, since the model describes a series of parallel structures concerning asymmetries in the brain and behavior, neopiagetian cognition, and so on (as shall be shown in sections 5.2 and 5.3). However, I also showed how the model incorporates the perspectives of the other views on the development of lateralization. Nevertheless, the model is unique compared to the others in its emphasis on one organizing principle, that of inhibition.

1.2. Lateralization in Human Evolution

A major issue in the field of lateralization addresses the primary difference between the human's left and right cerebral hemispheres. The left hemisphere seems specialized for language and fine motor functions, in particular, while the right hemisphere appears to be especially primed for spatial and related functions. Consequently, traditional models of hemispheric specialization emphasize the left hemisphere's sequential, analytic skills and the right hemisphere's holistic, parallel ones (Springer & Deutsch, 1989). Variations of this approach have attempted to determine the specific types of sequences best amenable to left hemispheric control (e.g., Goodale, 1988), and the extent to which different arousal and affective components are intrinsic to the left and right hemispheres (e.g., Tucker & Williamson, 1984; Tucker & Frederick, 1989). However, there are recent, more far-ranging conceptualizations of cerebral hemisphere differences. For example, Corballis' (1989) generativity model of left hemispheric specialization is broad enough to allow implications about the evolution of laterality. My inhibition theory of hemispheric specialization permits the same (Young, 1990). Corballis' theory is presented at this juncture, whereas my model is presented especially in sections 3 and 5. The theories are compared at the end of section 5.

Corballis argues that the characteristic shared by the left hemisphere's superior language and fine motor (e.g., tool construction) skills is generativity. Humans excel in effortlessly assembling multiple components according to purposive rules in order to create novel combinations or assemblages. This may even apply to generating visual images by combining 'geons' or elements of visual perception (Biederman, 1987). That is, the left hemisphere's specialization for generativity enables us to produce novel amalgams of elemental units ranging from the visual/perceptual to sequential/motor to language domains. The same skill permits higher-order units to be integrated hierarchically (e.g., sounds into symbols, phonemes into morphemes, words into sentences, etc.). This process facilitates the formation of complex representations, even in the realm of music and art. Left hemisphere generativity may also involve decomposition or analysis through synthesis, as several rule-governed options can be invoked in such circumstances until matches are established. The right hemisphere is described in relatively traditional terms by Corballis. He attributes its spatial superiority (e.g., in spatial attention, mental rotation) to analog, holistic, appositional representation.

Corballis depicts a seven-step sequence in the evolution of human laterality, while admitting that such theorizing is speculative due to a paucity of data. The generative skills of the left hemisphere and the analog representation of the right hemisphere emerge in the fourth period of the evolutionary sequence according to Corballis. In the first step toward the evolution of human laterality beyond 5 million years ago, early ape ancestors did not evidence more than some asymmetries in behavior and brain organization. These were *weak* precursors at best of human laterality. For example, Corballis dismissed as "too weak" the evidence reviewed by MacNeilage, Studdert-Kennedy, and Lindblom (1987) on nonhuman primate left hand reaching and right hand manipulation (This issue will be re-examined in section 1.3). The first hominids, *Australopithecus afarensis*, emerged about 5 million years ago, and showed upright posture, bipedalism, and freeing of the hands. *Homo habilis* evolved a little over 2 million years ago, and was characterized by a tool culture with manufacture and design specification. Toth (1985) determined that the flakes formed in tool manufacture and sharpening dating from this period suggest that the majority of the individuals in the species were right-handers.

With the evolution of *Homo erectus* 1.5 million years ago, tool culture came to involve axes, and there are signs that left hemispheric anatomical adaptation for language emerged. Tobias (1987) observed imprints in fossil skulls which indicate that these hominids possessed a larger speech production (Broca's) area as well as a probably larger speech reception (Wernicke's) area in the left hemisphere. The next milestone saw the appearance of Neanderthal and other *Archaic homo sapiens* about 300,000 years ago. These relatively modern hominids were the first to possess a cranial size equivalent to contemporary humans. *Homo sapiens sapiens* evolved 200,000 years ago. They manifested (a) a vocal tract which permitted an extremely adaptive, rapid speech like our own (Lieberman, 1984) and also (b) a flexibility in tool blade manufacture and use. Finally, Cromagnon people appeared about 37,000 years ago, exhibiting an explosion in culture (see also Bradshaw, 1989).

Corballis has integrated several lines of research into a plausible account of both the nature of hemispheric specialization in humans and its evolution. However, (a) he may have prematurely excluded from consideration the nonhuman primate data; for example, there is growing evidence of a right hand preference for manipulation in nonhuman primates (MacNeilage, Studdert-Kennedy, & Lindblom, 1988; Vauclair &

Fagot, in press). (b) In his account, there are gaps at certain epochs in terms of advances in laterality, perhaps due to an absence of appropriate data; thus, a more coherent picture may emerge only by examining secondary sources, such as with children. By this, I am not suggesting that we accept the outmoded concept where ontogeny recapitulates phylogeny (Gould, 1977). Rather, it is being suggested that ontogenetic and phylogenetic sequences may manifest illuminating descriptive parallels. That is, a grade and not a clade view of evolution seems valid (Gould, 1976). (c) Young's (1990) inhibition theory of hemispheric specialization has led to a theory of lateralization development in humans consisting of 20 levels (see section 5.3). On the basis of this, I have extrapolated from ontogeny to phylogeny, and elaborated a theory of the evolution of laterality which consists of 20 steps (see section 5.4). Consequently, my theory can account for steps in evolution even prior to hominidization, unlike the case for Corballis. Moreover, the theory derives from one unifying principle, that of inhibition in lateralization, adding parsimony.

1.3. Lateralization in Primate Evolution

The evidence favoring asymmetries in nonhuman primates has been integrated into a schema for the evolution of laterality by MacNeilage et al. (1987, 1988). They hypothesized that early prosimians manifested a left hemisphere controlled whole-body postural organization (e.g., hold to balance with right hand while performing a task with the left arm). The complementary specialization of the right hemisphere in early prosimians concerned a control of predation through left hand visually-directed activities (e.g., reaching). Early higher primates evolved to locomote quadrupedally. Thus, the left hemisphere's penchant for whole-body postural control led it to become operative in bimanual, forceful foraging in the environment. This precipitated a role reversal in early higher primates relative to prosimian manual behavior, as the left hand now came to support right hand manipulation instead of dominating for visually-directed action. MacNeilage et al. (1988) admit to possible paleomammalian precursor steps in the evolution of laterality, and have also suggested possible intermediate nonhuman primate steps involving early monkeys versus apes, in particular (MacNeilage et al., 1987).

Despite emphasizing the nonhuman primates' *manual* laterality, MacNeilage et al. did not attribute a primacy to this source relative to brain asymmetry in the evolution of lateralization. Rather, they conceived a parallel evolution of manual and brain specialization in response to pressures for whole-body postural asymmetry in behavior. They also posited a possible similarity between left brain side specialization for vocal communication in monkeys and their other lateralizations. That is, monkey vocal output is dependent on much body musculature, usually takes place during arboreal activity involving continual postural adjustment, and typically involves associated whole-body postural coordinations. Thus, the left hemisphere's specialization for postural control of the whole body in early monkeys (inherited from early prosimians) may have served as a precursor onto which vocal communication was mapped. In summary, MacNeilage et al. (1987, 1988) propose a sequence of up to five steps in the evolution of manual laterality in nonhuman primates involving early mammals, prosimians, monkeys, apes, and hominids.

Although the evidence bearing on MacNeilage et al.'s (1987,1988) account is not always positive (Corballis, 1989; Vauclair & Fagot, in press), consistent patterns are emerging. For example, Kuhl (1988) found that all 30 macaque, rhesus, and pig-tailed monkeys that she tested over years used the right hand in manipulative keypress response during an auditory discrimination task. W.D. Hopkins, Washburn, and Rumbaugh (1989) had five rhesus monkeys and chimpanzees hit a moving target on a screen with a manually manipulated cursor, and the right hand emerged superior. (Fagot, in press) found that Guinea baboons preferred the right hand in object manipulation even in the neonatal period. Nevertheless, there are exceptions to the patterns in these data concerning nonhuman primate manual lateralization (e.g., left hand manipulation in monkeys, Hoerster & Ettlinger, 1985, but note that the task concerned haptic discrimination in the dark; right hand food reaching in monkeys, King & Landau, in preparation, cited in MacNeilage et al., 1988).

Moreover, research in this area has not been fully cognizant of the distinction between (a) handedness, or preference on common, practiced tasks, and (b) manual specialization, or asymmetry in skill or proficiency measures. Directional preferences for the latter compared to those for the former should be more revealing of underlying brain asymmetries (Vauclair & Fagot, in press; following Young, Corter, Segalowitz, & Trehub, 1983). For example, W.D. Hopkins et al. (1989) not only found right hand manipulation in rhesus monkeys and chimpanzees; they also found that these nonhuman primates showed no preference in reaching. Cunningham, Forsythe, and Ward (1989) found that an infant orang-utan observed longitudinally consistently preferred the right hand in nonfood reaching but not in food reaching or body touching. These latter behaviors were left hand activities (only as the infant got older for the first one). Thus, unilateral food reaching may not be an appropriate measure of nonhuman primate lateralization in the brain.

In conclusion, Corballis (1989) seems to have prematurely ascribed a weak precursor role to early nonhominid primates in the hominidization of laterality. Findings suggestive of right hand manipulation in the neonatal period in nonhuman primates (Fagot, in press) and in *all* 30 monkeys tested over years in a complex manipulation task (Kuhl, 1988) indicate that there may be a marked continuity across early nonhominid primates and hominids with respect to lateralization of manual behavior.

In this sense, Denenberg's (1988) contention that nonhuman primates have derived their laterality organization from early mammalian ancestors seems appropriate. Portions of the human subcortex demonstrate asymmetry in volume (Kooistra & Heilman, 1988; see section 2.1). A variety of mammals other than nonhuman primates evidence laterality in behavior comparable to trends in later evolving species (Denenberg, 1981). Denenberg's research with rats, in particular, is consistent with Young's (1990) inhibition theory of hemisphere specialization, for Denenberg underscores how diverse right hemisphere functions (e.g., emotional and spatial behavior) are under inhibitory control by the left hemisphere . Consequently, as suggested in section 1.2, it should be possible to create a theory of the evolution of laterality which encompasses all steps in the process under one unifying principle (i.e., inhibition). Ultimately this leads to a reinterpretation of MacNeilage et al.'s (1987, 1988) account of primate lateralization in terms of inhibition asymmetries in the brain and hand (see section 5.4).

1.4. Lateralization in Motor Behavior in Adults

Before the research on lateralization development is examined, recent investigations with adults are scrutinized. Haaland and Harrington (1989a,b) examined unilateral stroke patients and normals on various target tasks. Their data suggested that the left hemisphere excels in open loop (e.g., initial reaction in aiming) movements, whereas the right hemisphere seems specialized for certain closed loop (e.g., corrective) movements. This model needs to be integrated into a more general perspective, such as in the following. Sivak and MacKenzie (1989) and Goodale (1988) support the traditional notion that the left hemisphere is specialized for sequencing both sides of the body. Goodale, for example, begins by describing the work of Kimura (1982; Kimura & Archibald, 1974). Kimura argues that left hemisphere motor specialization is based in a selector mechanism which applies not only to sequential, verbal movements as in speech, but also to all types of movement (whether single or multiple, verbal or nonverbal, and symbolic or nonsymbolic). The mechanism especially selects movements and also facilitates their transition when multiple. Goodale maintains that this facilitation of movement transition in the left hemisphere essentially refers to the left hemisphere's capacity to orchestrate over time complex programs or patterns of integrated motor components, synchronizing parallel modalities (e.g., eye, limb) in the process.

In one type of research in support of his hypothesis, Goodale (Wolf & Goodale, 1987) observed right-handers' mouth movements during both verbal and nonverbal tasks (e.g., reproduce ma/bo/pi; open mouth, blow, retract lips, respectively). The right side of the mouth opened wider and faster, and this effect was more evident (a) in movements in series compared to in isolation, and (b) in serial movements after the initial movement compared to the initial movement, per se. In a second line of research, Fisk and Goodale (1985) recorded eye movements and pointing to small targets presented in different positions. Both the right hand and eye moved more quickly than their left counterparts, and this was found for eye movements even though they preceded pointing.

Kimura (Kimura & Watson, 1989) has differentiated her hypothesis of left hemispheric motor control by analyzing the lesion site for a large series of unilaterally brain-damaged adults. Damage to the left anterior region of the left hemisphere affected control of single motor elements, whether nonverbal oral or speech sounds, and whether the latter were isolated or part of rapid repeated syllable articulation. Posterior left hemispheric damage affected the production of multiple oral movements, whether verbal or nonverbal, implying a specialization for selection accuracy of movement. The posterior region seemed further differentiated into a parietal praxic or motor organizational system and a temporal auditory-verbal (word, vocalization, echolalic) component.

Thus, research supports the contention that the hands are not symmetric in behavior, but reflect the skills of the contralateral hemispheres that control them. If the left hemisphere is the supreme sequential organizer in this regard, then the right hemisphere better controls spatial activities of the hands. Right-handers have been shown to show left hand proficiencies in a variety of spatial tasks both in a children (Ingram, 1975; Walch & Blanc-Garin, 1989) and adults (e.g., Carson, 1989). This complementarity in manual asymmetries speaks to the issue raised in section 1.3 of how manual specialization reflects underlying hemispheric specialization.

Roy and Elliott (1989) investigated laterality differences in manual pointing to a target under several visual conditions. In both experiments, the left hand was more variable in aimed movements. The authors argued that this may take place because the right hand neuromuscular system is better damped than that of the left hand . This explanation speaks to our hypothesis of superior inhibition skills in the left hemisphere (Young, 1990; see section 3.1).

Handedness is no longer considered a unidimensional trait. Healey, Liederman, and Geschwind (1986) and Liederman and Healey (1987) factor-analyzed handedness questionnaires, showing that a possible distinction between items concerned to what extent they required distal (finger-wrist) vs. axial (arm-shoulder-whole body) musculature activity. However, the distinction did not apply to all items which loaded on the relevant factors and was not always replicated. Steenhuis and Bryden (1989) performed a similar study, and characterized the major factors in their data as skilled (e.g., manipulation) versus unskilled (e.g., pick up small object) rather than proximal versus distal musculature. Skilled behavior was more right lateralized than the unskilled. Other handedness factors concerned (a) strength and (b) bimanual activity as in batting, and again one factor (the former) seemed more right-lateralized than the other.

Factor analysis is notorious for reflecting the items chosen for analysis. Moreover, it does not permit what I would consider essential for a more complete understanding of handedness. That is, factor analysis cannot establish nested hierarchies in the behavior structure that it describes. Contrary to what factor analysis suggests, any one handedness item is not characterized just by one primary attribute; rather, it may vary along several dimensions simultaneously -- skilled vs. unskilled, distal vs. axial, unimanual vs. bimanual, and so on. Future research should consider choosing several items from each of the cells created by the intersection of the various relevant dimensions. Moreover, the statistical techniques used should permit hierarchical arrangements of the emergent groupings. Finally, cluster interpretation should be based on multiple characterization (e.g., dimension 1: unimanual, skilled, distal).

1.5. Lateralization in Language in Adults

When we turn to research with adults that is language- rather than motor-oriented, the recent research highlights the differentiation of the cerebral hemispheres. N.D. Cook (1989a,b) and Bryan (1988) both underscore the complementary relationship of the two hemispheres in language control. According to N.D. Cook, the left hemisphere is specialized for phonemic, syntactic, and lower-order, denotative semantic analysis. In contrast, the right hemisphere is considered better able to make judgments about and to utilize linguistic information in specific contexts. N.D. Cook based his dichotomy on a review of the literature which showed that right-hemisphere damaged patients had difficulty with semantically complex tasks such as understanding word connotations and proverbs. Moreover, their affective and confusional problems can be interpreted as deriving from their cognitive deficits with contextual processing in various language situations (e.g., conversation). Bryan's (1988) data support this view. He tested unilaterally damaged patients and controls (a) with a traditional aphasia or language battery, (b) with more subtle tasks involving the understanding of metaphorical comprehension, inferred meaning, and humor, and (c) during conversation using a discourse perspective. The right hemisphere patients were more impaired on the subtle language tasks and during functional conversation, in particular.

Prather, Gardner, and Brownell (1989) argued that the right hemisphere linguistic context hypothesis needs better operational precision. Moreover, there are intrahemispheric differences to consider. In this regard, the neurolinguistic approach of Goldberg (1989) is noteworthy for its qualification of how the different zones and axes of the left hemisphere are differently specialized for language-related activities. Prather et al. (1989) made a similar point about the right hemisphere. Nevertheless, what is important for our purposes is that the existence of language functions in the right hemisphere is no longer disputed, as the hemispheres are considered to possess complementary linguistic skills. Kosslyn (1988) and Corballis (1989) have adopted a parallel argument for mental image generation; traditionally, skills associated with this function were thought to be uniquely right hemisphere specializations, but now it is realized that some processes implicated in mental image activity are right-hemisphere lateralized while other complementary ones are left-hemisphere lateralized. This agrees with the view of manual specialization (see section 1.3) where each hemisphere seems to have its superiority. All this sets the stage for the complementary inhibition view of hemispheric specialization (Young, 1990), where each hemisphere is posited to specialize in different inhibitory skills (see section 3.1).

2. The Development of Lateralization

2.1. Differential Maturation of the Hemispheres

Whereas the common viewpoint a decade ago (e.g., Corballis & Morgan, 1978) was that the left hemisphere matures earlier than the right (exhibits a faster developmental rate or a left-right gradient), current opinion mostly subscribes to the opposite view (e.g., Best & Queen, 1989; Galaburda, Corsiglia, Rosen, & Sherman, 1987; Rothbart, S.B. Taylor, & Tucker, 1989; de Schonen & Mathivet, 1989). Moreover, the evidence in support of the latter view seems strong. De Schonen and Mathivet (1989) describe how portions of the right temporal lobe mature earlier than the left in the fetus (Chi, Dooling, & Gilles, 1977a,b). Also, compared to its homologous region in the left hemisphere, the fetal right temporal gyrus more quickly attains adult levels of choline acetyltransferase activity (Bracco, Tiezzi, Ginanneschi, Campanella, & Amaducci, 1984). To this list, we can add Simonds and Scheibel (1989) who studied basilar dendritic patterns in layer 5 cortical pyramids of human brains as young as 3 months. Measures of dendritic development revealed the right hemisphere to be more prominent than the left in the first year.

However, (a) the advantages in earlier right hemisphere maturation may not be long lasting (e.g., several weeks in Chi et al.), so their functional significance may be hard to determine and may be negligible; (b) Best (1988) described a three dimensional torque twisting in hemispheric maturation, which may complicate simplistic approaches to left-right hemisphere differences; (c) Work with normal children, using resting EEG coherence as an index of growth spurts, showed no hemispheric differences until the preschool period (Thatcher, Walker, & Giudice, 1987); (d) There may be multiple gradients of maturation, some favoring portions of the left hemisphere and others the right hemisphere (Greenough, 1988); (e) There may be several relevant levels of analysis of maturational left-right hemisphere differences. Simonds and Scheibel (1989) argue that at the cortical macrolevel or gross anatomical level the left compared to the right hemisphere language areas seem larger even in the fetal period. In contrast, at the cortical microenvironmental level, the dendritic data suggest a right hemisphere advantage, at least until the left hemisphere catches up after the first year, as we have seen.

The evidence favoring the view that fetally the left side of the brain is larger than the right now extends to subcortical motor areas. Witelson and Pallie (1973) and Wada, Clarke, and Hamm (1975) have established that language zones such as the planum temporale and Sylvian fissure are larger on the left side in neonates as early as 28 weeks of gestation. Recently, Kooistra and Heilman (1988) have expanded this perspective; they analyzed 18 normal brains as young as 28 weeks gestational age for asymmetry in volume of the subcortical globus pallidus, important in arm movement control. Most of the samples were larger on the left side, including all those below 4 years of age. In short, Simonds and Scheibel (1989) have put forward a useful model where different maturational gradients may coexist.

The behavioral data on neonatal target-directed activity indicates that there may be functional consequences of asymmetric globus pallidus volume already at birth. Ottaviano, Guidetti, Allemand, Spinetoli, and Seri (1989) observed 20 healthy, fullterm, first-born, 4-day-olds of both sexes for spontaneous movements and for reactions to a target. The neonates were placed supine at 30° on a mat having a hollow to minimize head rotation, and were videorecorded for 5 min for spontaneous movements. A grey board to which a red ball was attached was then placed above the subjects 20 cm away and in line with the starting direction of gaze. Five 1-min units were recorded, using the criterion that each had to commence with at least 6 s of gaze at the target. The tapes were decoded with high interobserver agreement for arm extensions, arm flexions, and semi-flexed arm movements to the midline with the hand at least half open. Separate analyses were applied to each behavior (the tests used did not account for the repeated nature of the two situations). The right hand manifested more movements in the target condition, suggesting a left hemisphere preference for target-directed activity.

As much as this conclusion seems reasonable and agrees with my predictions for neonates (e.g., Young, Segalowitz, Misek, Alp, & Boulet, 1983), future research should determine whether the neonate right hand manifests more midline movements to the target and not just to the body or space in front of the body. Moreover, it may be beneficial to try to disentangle target movements made while the head is turned and while it is centered. Nevertheless, this study by Ottaviano et al. (1989) extends von Hofsten's (1982) results on right hand reaching to targets in 3-week-olds by showing a possible precursor for this behavior in the neonatal period. Moreover, it agrees with B. Hopkins, Lems, Janssen, and Butterworth (1987) and Butterworth and B. Hopkins (1988) who found that neonatal hand-mouth coordination is more right-handed, especially when the head is turned right.

Greenough's (1988) and Simonds and Scheibel's (1989) comments underscore that the differential course of early maturation of the cerebral hemispheres is more complex than previously imagined. Corresponding to prior emphasis in this chapter on the complementary relationship between the hemispheres for any one domain, it seems that early in life each hemisphere will be shown to mature faster than the other in its own way and in a pattern where the gradients in the two hemispheres are interrelated.

2.2. Birth Stress, Familial Sinistrality, and Laterality

There are numerous theories on the origins of pathological and nonpathological left side preferences (e.g., Harris & Carlson, 1988). Beginning with birth, maturational and other factors seem to normally favor right hand preferences through contralateral left brain side control (as we have just seen in section 2.1). However, in the neonatal period this side of the brain is more vulnerable to unilateral focal lesions, intracranial hemorrhage, etc. (Schumacher, Barks, Johnston, Donn, Scher, Roloff, & Bartlett, 1988). Thus, birth stressors such as low birth weight and Caesarean delivery may also differentially affect the hemispheres, inducing left-to-right shifting in the hemispheres of neonatal motor control more than would be the opposite case. Specifically, Bakan (1977) suggested that compared to the right hemisphere, the left hemisphere needs more oxygen. A lack of oxygen in the neonate can affect Betz cells in the left pyramidal motor system, inducing a shift to right hemispheric control of motor behavior.

Searleman, Porac, and Coren (1989) reviewed the literature relating to this hypothesis. Nonright handedness (NRH) was related to birth stressors in three prospective studies, and in each a single predictive relationship was found. The newborn measures of (a) Caesarian delivery, (b) 2 min to establish normal breathing, and (c) very low birth weight in prematures (< 1,000 g) predicted later NRH in McManus (1981), Barnes (1975), and O'Callaghan, Tudehope, Dugdale, Mohay, Burns and F. Cook (1987), respectively. A retrospective study which used continuous measures of laterality (Coren, Searleman, & Porac, 1982) found reduced dextrality due to birth stress. When particular stressors are examined in retrospective research, Rh incompatibility, low birth weight, and Caesarian section all correlate with increased NRH when collapsed over boys and girls. However, the significant correlation values are small (about .03, significant because of the large N), and account for less than 1% of the variance in the data. When the sexes are examined separately, only boys exhibit significant relations between particular stressors and NRH (and this almost always with one- tailed tests). In terms of eyedness, multiple birth, low birth weight, and prematurity increased nonright values, but again at minimal levels of explained variance. Note that there were many measures without predictive power with respect to nonright side preference. This list included birth order, maternal age at birth, breech delivery, fast labor, and slow labor.

van Strien, Bouma, and Bakker (1987) found that left-handers compared to right-handers manifested more learning disorders and showed an increased incidence of birth stress. However, the list of specific birth stressors did not always show the same relationship in terms of significant prediction as compared to Searleman et al.'s review. M. Levander, Schalling, & S.E. Levander (1989) failed to replicate van Strein et al.'s (1987) findings using a more refined subject selection procedure. Only left eye dominance was associated with male left-handers who experienced birth stress. Segal (1989) found that left handedness in lower birth weight monozygotic co-twins seemed associated with prenatal insults. An interesting interaction effect was found as left handedness in higher birth weight twins seemed associated with delayed zygotic splitting and consequent disruption of the determination of asymmetry. This reminds us that handedness in general probably has several causal influences already at work in the fetal and neonatal periods.

There have been several studies which have examined birth stress in relation to neonatal and young infant laterality. Liederman and Coryell (1982) observed 4- to 10-week-olds on spontaneous head turning and situations involving the asymmetric tonic neck reflex (ATNR). The infants were categorized in terms of the presence or absence of perinatal complications and of right handedness in both parents. For the two general results derived from the infants (right head turning, more marked ATNR on the left side), an interaction of the presence of parental right handedness and perinatal complications negated the normal lateralization pattern. No clear relationship was found involving neonatal lateralization, parental non-righthandedness, and perinatal complications. Fox and Lewis (1982) studied how respiratory distress affected head turning in prematures born at 33 weeks (or less) gestational age and observed about 6 weeks later. The normal right side preference was absent in this group. J.F. Feldman (1983) found that 3-day-old head turning laterality varied with risk factors such as neurological test score, birth weight, gestational age, and perinatal complications. Saling (1982, 1983) supported Liederman and Coryell's conclusion that birth risk and familial sinistrality must be considered together in terms of influence on laterality. He studied 2-day-old spontaneous head turning, and found that birth stress and familial sinistrality interact in their effect on this behavior. However, the direction of the effect was opposite to the one found by Liederman and Coryell. That is, right side head turning was disrupted by conjoint birth stress and familial sinistrality, and not parental right handedness.

Young and Gagnon (1990) investigated the issue of how birth stress and familial sinistrality interact to affect neonatal laterality using several methodological refinements. These refinements included: (a) Familial sinistrality was measured using a continuous measure, or laterality coefficient, involving the ratio of right and nonright-handers in the families of the parents and the parents themselves. This variable was calculated separately for each parent, and it took into consideration the differential genetic weight of primary, secondary, and tertiary relatives. (b) Both spontaneous-related and directed or stimulus-responsive turning measures were employed. The latter measure may be less susceptible to disruption of normal lateral preferences due to birth stress and the like since it should better reflect underlying brain side specialization. The former measure should be more vulnerable to normal lateral preference disruption by birth stress and other factors, since it concerns a more limited motor skill. To elicit directed turning, low intensity speech and music stimuli 2 s in duration (and matched on several parameters) were presented from behind at the midline while the neonates were alert. (c) Manual as well as head turning behaviors were observed. This was facilitated by placing the neonates' hands on a bar as the stimuli were presented.

The results showed that the neonates turned more to the right to verbal compared to musical stimuli. For turning in the baseline or spontaneous condition, birth risk, familial sinistrality, and their interaction all predicted lateral preference. However, only the familial sinistrality measure predicted stimulus condition preferences, and the behaviors involved were manual, not head turning. These data confirm that (a) birth risk and similar factors can affect lateral preferences in the newborn, extending Searleman et al.'s (1989) conclusions on the topic to this young age period. However, only behavior in spontaneous conditions can have its laterality influenced by such stress. This obtains since stimulus-directed behavior reflects deep-seated brain functions which are not susceptible to short term negative conditions (e.g., anoxia) and other relatively minor negative conditions (e.g., low birth weight). (b) The data also speak to the issue raised by Liederman and Coryell (1982) and Saling (1982, 1983) that familial sinistrality and birth risk interact in their influence on early laterality. However, since the data did not specifically describe whether the familial sinistrality - birth risk interaction predicted left or right side preferences, we cannot help resolve the disagreement between Liederman and Coryell (1982) and Saling (1982, 1983) about how that interaction works to affect early laterality. More research is needed on this interesting question.

2.3. Other Research on Laterality Development

A study of more serious insult on the neonatal brain confirms the conclusion in a prior section (2.1) that already at birth the left side of the brain appears functional for some of its primary specializations. H. Feldman, Holland, and Keefe (1989) analyzed the language capacities of two dizygotic twin pairs in which one member of each pair was injured in the left hemisphere around the time of birth. Data were collected longitudinally during the preschool period. Standard testing revealed similar intelligence and receptive language scores in the twins. However, expressive naming and general expressive language skills were deficient in the injured member of each set of twins. Also, in one pair there were differences in vocabulary size and complexity of sentences. Thus, the left hemisphere may be programmed for certain of its language skills right from birth, and its impairment at this age will have subtle long term consequences for those behaviors. A similar conclusion can be drawn from the study of Bendersky and Lewis (1990) on preterm neonates who suffered ventricular dilatation due to intraventricular hemorrhage. They were tested at 16 months and only those with left dilatation were affected in their expressive language.

Bertoncini, Morais, Bijeljac-Babic, McAdams, Peretz, and Mehler (1989) used a dichotic discrimination procedure based on high-amplitude sucking to show the presence of laterality in four-day-olds. Syllabic changes in the right ear induced stronger reactions than in the left ear, unlike the case for music, matching the data on dichotic listening in children and adults.

Rochat (1989) placed objects in one hand of two- to five-month-olds and found more mouthing of a teether (especially at three to four months) when it was place in the left hand. This trend was found in one study but not in another. Fagard and Jacquet (1989) investigated bimanual coordination in 7- to 23-month-olds using both simpler and more complex tasks. The infants displayed an asymmetry in their manipulation as soon as it emerged at 10 months, as the right hand was more active and the left more supportive in function. When removing a lid in order to retrieve a cube, only the oldest subjects showed a right-left coordination. Connolly and Dalgleish (1989) studied the use of a spoon as an eating tool in two samples followed for six months beginning at 11 and 17 months respectively. The right hand was preferred 80% of the time in most subjects even in the younger infants, although this sample showed an increasing number of right-handers with age. Mount, Reznick, Kagan, Hiatt, and Szpak (1989) observed that eye movement orientation to the right member of a pair of moderately familiar pictures increased in the second year of life. Moreover, the correlation between degree of right preference in this behavior and mean utterance length (a measure of grammatical complexity) was highest at 20 months. Other cognitive measures such as symbolic play did not show the relationship. A spurt in central lateralization at about this age may be responsible. Together, these studies show various ways in which the standard right-side preference for key behaviors emerge and influence behavior in the first two years of life.

There are several models on the lateralization of gestural imitation. The traditional view (e.g., Kimura, 1982; Kimura & Watson, 1989), which is based on the study of unilateral brain damage in adults, is that the left hemisphere's fine motor skills permits it to control gestural imitation better than the right hemisphere. Dawson (1988) reported developmental research which supports this view, as children as young as 9 years manifested EEG patterns indicative of left hemispheric activation during attempted imitation, whether gestural or vocal, and whether single or sequential. However, Pizzamiglio, Caltagirone, Mammucari, Ekman, and Friesen (1987) found that facial expression imitation in brain- damaged patients reflected bilateral control, or even a right hemisphere control when the experimenters employed more lax scoring criteria of imitation accuracy. Similarly, Canavan, Passingham, Marsden, Quinn, Wyke, and Polkey (1989) suggested that the imitation of repetitive gestural sequences is a right hemispheric function, as determined in their research with brain-damaged adults. Finally, Ingram (1975) found that normal right-handed preschoolers imitated manual gestures and postures better with the left hand even though they performed other activities such as tapping better with the right hand. Again, right hemispheric specialization for gestural imitation is implied.

Young and Bowman (1989) performed a study similar to Ingram's using 18-month-olds. While these toddlers were right-handed in tapping and manipulating, in particular, they were not lateralized in their gestural imitation. The traditional point of view that the left hemisphere is specialized for gestural imitation may not apply to all ages and/or all tasks. Follow-up investigation seems required. It is hypothesized that each hemisphere will be found to manifest a specialization for imitation consonant with its underlying skills (e.g., appropriate manipulative versus certain spatial functions in the left and right hemispheres, respectively). This proposed complementarity in left- and right-hemisphere imitation skills may even fit with more basic functions, such as differential hemispheric inhibition skills (see section 3.1).

2.4. Laterality and Disturbances in Development

The possible role of abnormal hemispheric specialization in developmental psychopathology is now considered. Leboyer, Osherson, Nosten, and Roubertoux's (1988) literature review suggests an increased incidence of nonright handedness in infantile autism, with this asymmetry in behavior associated with lower performance on cognitive tasks. Dawson, Finley, Phillips, and Lewy (1989) found similar results with the EEG. Matched autistic, dysphasic, and normal children were tested for their AER to a simple speech sound (/da/) and a piano chord. A battery of standardized tests were used to assess language. Only the normals manifested the expected left hemisphere dominance for the speech stimulus. The more severe the autistics' language deficit, the more probable they exhibited reversed hemisphere asymmetry. Language skill was related to right hemisphere activity in the autistics and to left hemisphere activity in the dysphasics. Autistic children apparently suffer from an overactive right hemisphere, whereas the dysphasics' left hemisphere seems impaired. Elsewhere, Dawson (1988) has tentatively linked the apparent overactivation of the right hemisphere in autistics to problems in left hemispheric inhibition of the contralateral right hemisphere. This theme is evidently consistent with our own.

Gladstone, Best, and Davidson (1989) examined bimanual coordination in reading-disabled or dyslexic boys. On an Etch-a-Sketch type task, control subjects preferred bidirectional mirror movements compared to unidirectional parallel ones. In contrast, dyslexics were deficient in such mirror behavior, especially with their left hands, manifesting parallel clockwise rotation. Following Preilowski (1975), the normal subjects' behavior can be explained by (a) left hemispheric control of the right hemisphere in bimanual activity, and (b), within each hemisphere, a strong contralateral influence over manual control compared to the mirror-image ipsilateral one. However, traditional models of dyslexics' behavior cannot account for the specific nature of their bimanual deficits. For example, one can deduce from the interhemispheric coordination deficit view (e.g., Kershner, 1985) that dyslexics do not possess the standard left over right hemisphere influence and thus are deficient in inhibiting ipsilateral messages. But this hypothesis does not account for all of the dyslexics' performance in Gladstone et al.'s (1989) task. Thus, the authors offer the "quite speculative" suggestion that the ipsilateral pathways in dyslexics are also anomalous by their matching, not mirroring, of the direction of movement in the contralateral pathways. No justification was offered for this proposal, and possible mechanisms to explain it were not presented.

However, could it not be that a poorer inhibitory skill of the left hemisphere in dyslexics (coupled with their poorer interhemispheric communication) engenders an impairment in the suppression or inhibition of matched compared to mirror messages in the ipsilateral pathways? In this regard, Kinsbourne (1988) suggested that there may be left hemispheric inhibitory deficits in dyslexics. In a similar vein, Stout (1987) argued that left vs. right hemiplegia (i.e., right vs. left brain damage) in children lead to more severe motor and other consequences since there are inhibitory mechanisms in the left and not the right hemisphere, and these become damaged in such cases.

In this section, we have considered a possible causal role for left hemisphere inhibition problems in autistic, dyslexic, and hemiplegic children. It is even conceivable that a different inhibitory skill (or skill combination) in the left hemisphere is associated in a one-to-one relationship with various developmental abnormalities. Perhaps, different left (and right) hemisphere inhibition problems lead to different developmental disturbances.

3. The Inhibition Theory of Complementary Hemispheric Specialization

3.1. The Theory and Developmental Evidence

In this next section I examine more closely the model presented in Young (1990) that the cerebral hemispheres are differentially specialized for inhibition. The left hemisphere is considered the seat of inhibitory control, specializing in a sophisticated interweaving of activation and inhibitory skills. Activation/inhibition synchronization especially involves the suppression of interference due to inappropriate alternative behavior, both when selecting adaptive goal-directed activity and during its transitions. Through this skill, the left hemisphere can control the subtle, refined sequences in both language and fine motor activities, as successful unfolding of these functions demands activation/ inhibition intercoordination. The more focal somatosensory representation in the left hemisphere (Trotman & Hammond, 1989), along with its relative lack of transcortical connections and its greater regional variability (Gur, Packer, Hungerbuhler, Reivich, Obrist, Amarnek, & Sackeim, 1980), may contribute to the left hemisphere's superior inhibitory specialization. The right hemisphere may be specialized for less dynamic inhibition, as in general dampening of activity over time or activation/ inhibition synchrony instantaneously or for a short time period. The latter facility would be conducive to spatial processes, as a gestalt needs some information as figure to be highlighted and some as ground to be moderated.

Developmentally, the evidence is accumulating that the left side of the brain seems specialized for inhibition. Kooistra and Heilman (1988; see section 2.1) found greater left side volume of the globus pallidus both fetally and in the first years of life. This subcortical area is especially concerned with controlling the direction, amplitude, and velocity of arm movements. It is interesting to note for our purposes that with limb movement or turning, the globus pallidus has its tonic neuronal firing interrupted either by bursts of activity or pauses, apparently due to inhibitory striato-pallidal input. In short, neonatal and early directed arm movements seem partly governed by inhibition of one subcortical zone by another. This latter zone is larger on the left side of the brain even fetally, which may explain why neonatal target-directed arm movement seems right-sided (see section 2.1).

Young and Gagnon (1990) found that newborns turned their heads to the left more to musical compared to verbal stimuli (see section 2.2). While manifesting this turning pattern, the newborns moved away their right hand from a bar before them, and opened the hand. These data suggest that as the right side of the brain becomes more activated, secondary manual behaviors relative to bar contact increase in frequency on the right side. A parsimonious explanation of the results is that with less left hemisphere activation there is less inhibition of interfering manual activities, fitting Young's left-hemisphere inhibition hypothesis.

Liederman (1983) argued that left brain side inhibition either develops earlier or acts with greater strength. Thus, at about one month, left head turns better elicit the asymmetric tonic neck reflex because right-side reflex activity, in general, is more suppressed by the superior inhibitory skill of the left hemisphere. Kamptner, Cornwell, Fitzgerald, and Harris (1985) presented similar data on the stepping reflex. Young, Bowman, Methot, Finlayson, Quintal, and Boissonneault (1983) suggested that one-month-olds coordinate activation and inhibition better in the left than the right hemisphere, as they found that during right- compared to left-hand reaching there was more (a) hand opening/reaching synchrony and (b) unused hand inhibition.

McDonnell, Corkum, and Wilson (1989) investigated limb activity during stimulus present and absent periods in 10- to 18-week-olds. The infants were placed for 8 min supine in a featureless crib with an arched roof. Every second minute an interesting flashing rubber toy was presented. Movement sensors helped determine that there was less activity with the stimulus present, and that this occurred earlier in testing for the right hand than the left hand. The authors took this manual suppression to be indicative of an orienting reaction and thus cortical processing. One interpretation of these results is that beginning early in life the left hemisphere excels in inhibiting stimulus-irrelevant manual movements in order to direct activity to a newly presented target. This view is consistent with the left hemisphere inhibition model of hemispheric specialization, since a coordination of activation and inhibition seems necessary in the young infant's behavior in the described task.

One could add that the lateralization of a particular behavior may shift with age depending on whether it requires more or fewer subtle inhibitory mechanisms in its control at any one age, and depending to what degree it becomes automatized or simplified with respect to its inhibitory underpinnings. Thus, neonates may require complex left hemispheric inhibitory skills for apparently simple activities, whereas for similar movements adults may manifest an inverse pattern. Behaviors may shift in laterality consonant with inhibition requisites, although the underlying inhibition functions themselves should not exhibit such shifting.

3.2. Evidence from Perseverative Behavior

A critical type of evidence in support of the inhibition hypothesis of hemispheric specialization concerns perseverative behavior in brain-damaged adult patients. Instead of performing tasks smoothly, these patients show signs of a lack of appropriate behavioral inhibition or suppression, as they repeat behavior from previous tasks (recurrent perseveration), loop continuously, allow extraneous intrusions, etc. Some tasks do not manifest laterality effects in perseveration in brain-damaged adults. For example, perseveration in memory for drawings has been suggested to be a product of bilateral (Vilkki, 1989), right hemispheric (Jones-Gotman & Milner, 1977), and left hemispheric damage (Sandson & Albert 1984). The task where left hemisphere-damaged patients manifest perseverative behavior (especially of the recurrent variety) most clearly is picture naming (Albert & Sandson, 1986; Pietro & Rigrodsky, 1986), whereas the clearest task affected by right-hemispheric damage is card sorting (Heaton 1981; Hermann, Wyler, & Richey, 1988; A.L. Robinson,

Heaton, Lehman, & Stilson, 1980). [per contra, Milner (1963) found no laterality effect, although left-sided lesions were smaller, implying more left hemisphere perseverative behavior, and Drewe (1974) found left hemisphere perseverative behavior posteriorly, and a trend for right hemisphere perseverative behavior frontally.] Thus, the traditional verbal vs. spatial distinction between the left and right hemispheres seems to apply to the data on perseverative behavior. That is, once more it seems that inhibition-related measures can be affected by either left or right hemisphere damage, depending on the tasks involved. This speaks to the complementarity of the hemispheres for inhibition specialization.

There has also been a study where perseverative behavior has been examined in brain-damaged adults performing motor imitations. Mateer (1978) tested normal controls, right brain-damaged patients, and three types of left brain-damaged patients -- nonaphasics, fluent aphasics, who had some word usage, and nonfluent aphasics, who were more severely impaired. The subjects were administered a sequential oral imitation task (e.g., tongue to side, open mouth, protrude lip). Perseverative errors were defined as movements which had been correct movements either on previous trials or earlier in the same trial, but which were no longer appropriate. All left hemisphere-damaged groups imitated more poorly than the right hemisphere-damaged group. Moreover, both aphasic groups manifested more perseverative errors than the right hemisphere-damaged group, and no other error type (e.g., reversal) distinguished the groups. Thus, inhibition-related perseverative behavior as much as the quality of imitation data indicated a left hemispheric specialization for sequential oral imitation. Here we see the utility of examining inhibition-related behavior to understand better the nature of hemispheric specialization. Inhibition measures may supplement other ones on laterality tasks, providing a complementary view of lateralization of performance.

3.3. Evidence from Overflow Behavior

Another possible measure involving inhibition which may help in this regard is overflow or associated movement. For example, children performing a unimanual task, especially if it is repetitive, exhibit more involuntary movement of the unused hand when it is the preferred or right and not the nonpreferred or left one (e.g., Cohen, Taft, Mahadeviah, & Birch, 1967; Edwards & Elliott, 1987; D. Taylor, Powell, Cherland, & Vaughan, 1988, but only for left-handers; Todor & Lazarus, 1986). One explanation for this effect is that the left hemisphere alone possesses bilateral motor control (Geschwind, 1975), so that when it directs the right side of the body in a repetitive task it can suppress or inhibit unnecessary left side movements, either directly or indirectly. However, overflow movements are not unitary, as they can vary according to whether they are more overtly or covertly observed (Lazarus & Todor, 1987), and whether they are analyzed quantitatively or qualitatively (Noterdaeme, Amorosa, Ploog, & Scheimann, 1988).

A study by Chisolm and Karrer (1988) illustrates this principle and suggests that overflow movements may occur more in the left hand, unlike what prior research has found. They recorded movement-related readiness potentials while children and adults had to lift a finger to which an experimenter pointed. The subjects also had to fixate the target hand, react using their own timing, not blink or move the eyes, and not move the nontarget fingers. Thus, the task was not sequential in nature and explicitly required inhibition by suppression of movements over time. The results suggest that the left hand was less inhibited, as it manifested more overflow movements both when measuring the unused contralateral hand and when measuring the nontarget ipsilateral fingers.

The unused contralateral hand results are opposite to what is typically found, as we have seen. One suggestion is that these data were obtained due to the nature of the task employed. Typically, repetitive tasks are used, and so the left hemisphere's inhibition skills are favored. However, in the case of Chisolm and Karrer's study, the task was not repetitive and demanded activity dampening over time. As seen in section 3.1., I have postulated (Young, 1990) that the complementary right hemisphere inhibition skills are brought out by behavior exactly of this nature. Consequently, the direction of inhibition laterality for the unused contralateral hand in Chisolm and Karrer should not be considered surprising. This conclusion considers the following logic.

For contralateral hand inhibition during manual activity, which is almost always examined in this kind of research, there is uncertainty about how the left hemisphere is deployed in bimanual control. We have seen that Geschwind's (1975) standard model suggests that the left and not the right hemisphere possesses bilateral motor control. However, his conclusions were based on research with particular tasks (e.g., motor learning) and may not apply to others. Moreover, Gladstone at al. (1989) have argued that ipsilateral pathways participate in distal hand/finger control along with contralateral pathways (unlike what was traditionally thought). It is true that the former pathways are less important than the latter, but they can influence motor control. Thus, the specific nature of the left hemisphere's bimanual control has not been clearly delineated. The left hemisphere may possess better direct pathways to the ipsilateral upper limb including the hands and/or it may better access or somehow coordinate the contralateral (right) hemisphere to better control indirectly the ipsilateral upper limb.

The model supported here on bimanual control by the hemispheres argues that both hemispheres possess this capacity, but the left hemisphere is more efficient at it at least partly due to its superior ability to coordinate the contralateral hemisphere. This situation obtains probably because of the left hemisphere's more refined capacity compared to the right hemisphere to coordinate activation and inhibition not only intrahemispherically but also interhemispherically. Thus, given a task where one hand is active and the other is inactive or must be suppressed, the left hemisphere should be able to better deploy its activation/inhibition coordination resources than the right.

However, it is possible that task parameters may alter this dynamic and better elicit the right hemisphere's inhibition skills (e.g., the task does not require time constraint, allowing subjects to monitor carefully their behavior). That is, what I am arguing is that the standard model that the left hemisphere manifests efficient bimanual control compared to no or less bimanual control in the right hemisphere may have to be modified to allow better right hemisphere bimanual control in certain circumstances. For us, the latter relate to the particular inhibition skills of the right hemisphere which are complementary to those of the left. It should be noted that Chisolm and Karrer did not speculate on the nature of hemispheric differences in manual control based on their overflow results. Rather, the current theory on hemispheric inhibition specialization has provided the framework needed to ferret out the significance of the Chisolm-Karrer study for understanding hemispheric specialization.

The ipsilateral finger results in Chisolm and Karrer (1988) are also informative. Again, the left hand was less inhibited. Since these data refer to same-hand irrelevant finger movement suppression during finger lifting, they translate to mean that the hand that can better inhibit interfering movements deriving from itself while it is in action is the right and not the left hand. In the case of ipsilateral movements, then, a superior left hemisphere inhibition seems to have taken place in the task used by Chisolm and Karrer, which contrasts with the pattern obtained for the contralateral hand results. In inhibiting the unused fingers of a hand engaging in an active finger-lifting task, an activation/inhibition synchronization is obtained even if there is no time constraint on the task. It will be recalled that such coordination seems the prime characteristic of left hemisphere inhibition skill (see section 3.1). Thus, tasks which elicit this type of behavior seem the best ones to get at hemispheric superiority for complex inhibition since both the active and inactive fingers are under the same hemisphere control (i.e., the contralateral one), so that one hemisphere can be tested clearly against the other.

Parlow (1990) has recently performed a study which speaks to the issues raised in this section. Overflow activity was examined in children in grades 2 to 6. For right-handers, there was greater contralateral overflow in the unused hand during rapid, repetitive hand/forearm pronation/supination when the unused hand was the right one, not the left. The opposite pattern was obtained for contralateral overflow during careful, slow, isolated finger spreading, whereas no laterality effects were evident in ipsilateral unused fingers during any task. The contralateral results confirm those of Chisolm and Karrer (1988), and the opposition therein was attributed to the different specializations of the hemispheres "in an as yet unknown way". This argument resembles ours, except that we emphasize that the "way" relates to the hemispheres' complementary inhibition skills, as we have seen.

4. Hemispheric Specialization for Inhibition in Emotional Expression

4.1. Left Hemispheric Inhibition and Emotional Expression

There is a wide-ranging set of data on hemispheric inhibition of emotional expression, but interpretation is not always straightforward. Fisher (1966) found that awareness of the left side of the body in male college students is positively associated with heterosexuality measures. Thus, he argued that left side (right hemisphere) attention reflects greater spontaneity. That is, according to Fisher, the left hemisphere seems more controlling and inhibiting. Bakan (1969) examined lateral eye movements in response to questions and the relation of these movements to hypnotizability. Left eye movers (right hemisphere actives) were more susceptible to hypnosis. This result implies less spontaneity and more inhibition in the left hemisphere. Heilman, Schwartz, and Watson (1978) tested patients with unilateral lesions for galvanic skin response (GSR) to forearm stimulation ipsilateral to the lesion. Left hemisphere (aphasic) patients had higher GSRs than controls without brain damage. A disinhibition of sympathetic activity seems to have taken place in this patient group, suggesting a left hemispheric dominance for inhibition. Buck and Duffy (1980) observed that patients with left-sided brain damage were judged as more expressive emotionally, especially while viewing unpleasant slides. Thus, the left hemisphere seems to harbor the ability to inhibit voluntary responsiveness in emotivity.

Tucker has undertaken a series of studies which confirms the left hemisphere's inhibitory role in emotional expression. Tucker, Antes, Stenslie, and Barnhardt (1978) found that normal college students with high anxiety manifested a right ear (left hemisphere) attention bias and low levels of left eye movement. The results suggest that low anxiety may reflect right hemispheric activation and left hemisphere suppression. Shearer and Tucker (1981) asked college students to facilitate or inhibit their emotions when viewing sexual or aversive slides. A measure of auditory attention bias showed that right hemisphere activation is associated with greater success in facilitation and lesser success in inhibition of aversive affect. Tucker and Newman (1981) showed that left hemispheric cognitive strategies (e.g., verbal) in inhibiting emotions induced by sexual slides lead to reduced bilateral vasoconstriction or sympathetic arousal.

Swenson and Tucker (1983) found that a left hemispheric style of cognition is associated not only with high anxiety but also with greater introversion. (Levy, Heller, Banich, and Burton (1983) also found that left-hemisphere actives were more self-critical or less self-enhancing. Bear and Fedio (1977) found similar results with unilateral temporal lobe epileptics.) Dopson, Beckwith, Tucker, and Bullard-Bates (1984) observed that in adults the left side of the face is more intense for spontaneous expressions, in particular, and this was found whether the expressions were happy or sad. They postulated that left hemispheric inhibition may play a role in the data, as it could lead to suppression of emotional responsivity on the right side of the face.

Tucker (1987) interpreted data from diverse sources in terms of left hemispheric inhibition. For example, Kinsbourne (1974) trained the hemispheres of commissurotomy patients to perform in parallel some difficult tasks. However, the left hemisphere showed attentional priority, as the right one responded automatically, inappropriately, and without attentional competence. A left hemispheric inhibitory superiority is implied. Luria's (1973) research is also described at one point. He reported that *right* frontal lesions are associated with disinhibition of impulses. To me, this speaks to the complementary view of hemispheric specialization for inhibition (see section 3.1), since the inhibition of simpler activities seems specialized in the right hemisphere for emotional expression just as it is for motor behavior.

Then Tucker (1987) presented his diagonal localization model of emotional expression in the brain. It resembles my model of complementary inhibition specialization in the hemispheres, as it states that "the right anterior and left posterior regions appear to exert important inhibitory control on emotional functioning" (p. 282). In support of the model, Benson and Geschwind (1975/1982) found that posterior left lesions are associated with 'disinhibited' verbalizations. In contrast, R.G. Robinson, Kubos, Starr, Rao, and Price (1984) found that lesions nearer the frontal pole in the right hemisphere induced greater 'denial'. Both lesion sites produce inappropriate positive affective response. However, of the two sites, the right frontal one seems more important in interpersonal regulation according to Tucker (p. 284).

His model differs from ours in several primary ways with respect to the role of inhibition in emotion. First, our complementary view of hemispheric specialization for inhibition suggests qualitative differences between the hemispheres in inhibitory skill, whereas his localizes an equal skill in different parts of the left and right hemisphere. In this regard, we ascribe the more important role in inhibition control to the left hemisphere, since it performs the more qualitatively complex task of activation/inhibition coordination. Second, Tucker views the right hemisphere as more prominent in interpersonal exchange. However, Tucker's emphasis on right hemispheric social skill may have underestimated the role of the left hemisphere's inhibitory skills in the social realm. For example, activation/inhibition coordination must be important in social interchange. In this regard, Rinn (1984) contends that the left hemisphere, through regulation of behavior by language, is better at inhibiting or rationalizing away unwanted emotional episodes.

Three recent studies all underline the importance of left hemispheric inhibition of emotional expression. Lee, Loring, Meador, Flanigin, and Brooks (1988) found that extreme behavioral upset upon amobarbital injection in the right hemisphere took place in left compared to right frontal (structural) lesion patients. Thus, the left frontal region appears specialized for the inhibition of affective expression according to the authors. Vingiano (1989) found results similar to those Levy et al. (1983) and Swenson and Tucker (1983), reported above. He factor analyzed a personality questionnaire administered to a normal sample. Left compared to right hemisphericity was associated with the general trait of more control over impulses. Finally, Davidson and Fox (1989) found that 10-month-olds who cried versus those who did not cry due to maternal departure showed greater right frontal activation as measured by EEG during prior baseline activity. An inhibition interpretation of their data would argue that a relative lack of left hemispheric inhibitory activity when at rest predisposes to less inhibitory control in subsequent emotional expression. This study brings us back to lateralization in development, which continues in the next section.

The consensus seems to be that the left hemisphere is specialized for inhibition of emotion. However, the view of complementary hemispheric specialization for inhibition suggests parallel right hemispheric inhibitory skills in emotion (e.g., general dampening, simple impulse control). Moreover, a minority argue for the predominance of the right hemisphere in some general emotion-related activity (Levy et al., 1983; Tucker, 1987; also see Fridlund, 1988).

4.2. The Right Hemisphere View of Infant Emotional Expression

The issue of which hemisphere is specialized for inhibition of emotional behavior is an ongoing one as we have just seen. The same conclusion applies to the study of inhibitory specialization in the hemispheres in infant emotional expression. Some developmental researchers have proposed that the left hemisphere acquires inhibitory control over the right for emotional expression. Ramsay (1984) spoke to the age of about 8 months in this regard, and Fox and Davidson (1984) spoke of the period of about 18 months. However, these researchers did not directly use data concerning emotional expression when they made these suggestions. In contrast, Best and Queen (1989) have interpreted their findings on infant hemiface bias in emotional expression as supportive of the *right* hemisphere inhibition specialization view. They found that infants were judged to express emotions more intensely on the right side of the mouth region, in particular (see also Rothbart et al., 1989). Since the adult generally manifests more left than right hemiface emotional intensity (see section 4.1), this suggested a possible developmental shift or "developmental right-to-left gradient in maturation of cortical control" (Best & Queen, 1989; p. 273). Moreover, inhibition is part of this gradient. How?

First, the right hemisphere has been shown to mature earlier than the left one (e.g., Best, 1988). Second, as zones of the infant neocortex mature in development, the function of inhibiting subcortical reflexes precedes (often by several months) the function of activating voluntary control (e.g., Clifton, Morrongiello, Kulig, & Dowd, 1981). Together, these factors permit the inhibition of subcortical movement of the mouth more on the left side, and thus lead to a right side emotional expressiveness in infants. The second half of the first year is proposed as the age of onset for this phenomenon. This suggestion is consistent with the fact that the central zone responsible for the voluntary control of facial expression, the frontal cortex, begins to mature in this period (Rinn, 1984). Interhemispheric influences may also come into play through the maturing corpus callosum. In short, in contrast to what one finds with the adult, right hemispheric inhibition may predominate in the control of emotional expressivity of the face in the first year of life.

Best and Queen (1989) go on to hypothesize that the right hemisphere may manifest its specialization for inhibition even from birth for reflexive, involuntary movements. That is, the right hemisphere seems to inhibit newborn reflexes better than the left hemisphere, producing less left-sided reflex activity. Thus, one finds neonatal right-side biases in head turning (e.g., Michel & Goodwin, 1979). To Best and Queen, these right side biases indicate greater downward subcortical inhibition by earlier maturing right hemisphere (motor) areas of left body side activity. Moreover, to Best and Queen, the right hemisphere is not only specialized for inhibition early in life but may also be more *active* in organizing voluntary behavior in this period. For example, they cite McDonnell, Anderson, and Abraham (1983) who apparently found that 3- to 8-week-olds presented with visual targets moved the left hand more, while extending it farther and more appropriately. Carson (1989) defends a similar view in his literature review.

4.3. An Alternative View of Infant Emotional Expression

The first issue dealt with concerns Best and Queen's contention that early voluntary activity shows a left preference, while reflexive activity in this period takes place more clearly on the right side. Research generally shows that early reaching-related activity that is nonreflexive shows a *right-* and not left-sided preference (see section 2.1), in contrast to McDonnell et al.'s (1983) and Carson's (1989) conclusions. Moreover, in their study, McDonnell et al. (1983) did not measure forward movement, per se, as movements toward the midline were involved. Also, the early right-sided prevalence for reflexes and related behaviors may be based on their directed, active nature. Butterworth and B. Hopkins (1988) and B. Hopkins et al. (1987) have found that neonatal hand-mouth *coordination* is more right-sided, and that such activity usually takes place when the head is turned right. In short, from birth onward the right side of the body may be the more (and/or better) target-directed one, and only those reflexes which relate to this function will be right lateralized.

The apparent general neonatal right side advantage for directed activity is consistent with Fox and Davidson (1986) who found that newborns manifested left brain side EEG *activation* in the frontal and parietal regions in response to sucrose, whereas water and citric acid did not elicit this effect. Fox and Davidson's (1986) research, along with their similar investigation with older infants (1988), suggests (a) a left brain side specialization for certain positive expressions (see also Schiff & Lamon, 1989) that (b) does not apply to negative expressions, which are lateralized to the right brain side, (c) that begins at birth and persists throughout infancy in the same manner, (d) that is based on left brain side activation (as shown in the EEG), and (e) that does not change at seven months to involve right hemispheric inhibition.

According to Best and Queen (1989), the putative cortical zone responsible for voluntary facial expression control, the frontal cortex, begins to functionally mature at about the last quarter of the first year, which is *after* the 7 month age when their hemiface results were obtained. However, Chugani and Phelps (1987) have shown that the frontal region matures at 7 1/2 months, as determined by position emission tomography. Nevertheless, emotional expressivity in infancy may involve cerebral regions other than frontal ones, and these zones may mature earlier than 7 months. Recall that Fox and Davidson's (1986, 1988) results of left hemispheric activation for certain positive expressions in neonates concerned the parietal as well as the frontal region. Best and Queen's (1989) model also includes interhemispheric inhibition due to the maturation of the corpus callosum, which takes place after 7 months of age, according to them. However, this estimate may be conservative since corpus callosum growth begins fetally and is constant from birth to 2 years (Witelson & Kigar, 1988). Moreover, interhemispheric communication can also take place through subcortical channels (Liederman, 1983).

Best and Queen (1989) maintain that the right hemisphere matures earlier than the left, in keeping with a right to left developmental gradient. However, there may be multiple maturational gradients, e.g., several right-to-left and several left-to-right ones (see section 2.1). Moreover, perhaps this left vs. right opposition on which brain side is more involved in inhibition of emotional expression is a false dichotomy. That is, emotions are multi-layered constructions, and there may be several types of inhibition needed for their appropriate expressive manifestation, with both left and right hemisphere inhibition involved in complementary ways. Moreover, these multiple hemispheric inhibition specializations may not apply to emotions in the same way from one developmental epoch to the next.

5. The 20 Levels of Lateralization Development and Evolution

5.1. Complementary Hemispheric Inhibition

We can now examine Corballis's (1989) thesis that the left hemisphere is characterized by a rule-guided generativity in amalgamating components into higher-order complexes, while the right hemisphere is more holistic and analog (see section 1.2). The inhibition theory of complementary hemispheric specialization that I have emphasized throughout appears entirely compatible with Corballis's perspective. That is, rule-governed generativity can take place in the way Corballis describes because the left hemisphere can organize sophisticated sequences of behavior through its capacity to synchronize activation and inhibition.

Several facets of interference must be controlled in rule-governed serial organization, and the left hemisphere should be involved in many of them. (a) Alternative competing algorithms must be held in abeyance while appropriate evaluations take place. (b) Feedforward anticipation must occur through delayed response. (c) Memory of prior processes/behavior/components must be integrated into current planning, and this demands control of interference from inappropriate intrusions. (d) Ongoing unfolding of sequential processes must be protected from competition from grossly different processes. (e) Smooth transitions in components of the behavior stream must be facilitated by the ability to fend off subtly similar but highly ineffective substitute components. (f) The goal-appropriate components of an adaptive sequence must be ordered by coordinating (i) their selection and efficient activation one at a time with (ii) a simultaneous efficient inhibition of those not needed during each successive activation. (g) Effective discharge of the prior step must preclude maladaptive disorganization by repetitive cycling, perseverations, etc. (h) Formation of a hierarchy could take place as behavior becomes more automatic and task requirements more demanding. For example, (i) components could form higher-order units; (ii) the goal of rule application could come to include the notion that new, more complex and efficient rules should be formed in the generative process; (iii) parallel channels of behavioral processing or output could be integrated into a more coherent field of action (e.g., motor and language interdigitation).

In conclusion, the inhibition theory of hemispheric specialization can help explain how the left hemisphere may be generative in Corballis' sense of the word. We have already seen how the theory can help explain the right hemisphere's holistic spatial skills (see section 3.1). Thus, the current theory seems to have a broad- ranging generality. To what extent this conclusion applies to the evolution of lateralization is examined in the next sections.

5.2. A 20-Step Model of Cognitive Development

Corballis (1989) and MacNeilage et al. (1987, 1988) have investigated our phylogenetic heritage for steps in the evolution of behavior especially at the level of lateralization (as we have seen in sections 1.2 and 1.3). Corballis dealt with hominid precursors and suggested a seven-step sequence culminating in contemporary humans, and with no differentiation at the nonhominid level. In contrast, MacNeilage et al. dealt with nonhuman primate ancestors and posited up to five steps, with all hominids including contemporary humans sharing the last step. By combining the two phylogenetic progressions, one arrives at a sequence in primate and hominid evolution made up of up to 11 steps, after eliminating redundancies. The steps hypothesized to have taken place in evolution relate to the following levels: paleomammalian, early prosimian, early monkey, early ape, *Australopithecus afarensis, Homo habilis, Homo erectus, Archaic homo sapiens, Homo sapiens sapiens,* Cromagnon people, contemporary people. Corballis and McNeilage et al. may not agree with this suggested integration of their works. However, this marriage only reflects the evident validity of each of their endeavors.

In Young (1990) I presented a model of the ontogenetic development of lateralization in manual behavior which comprised 20 steps. I hypothesized that levels 9 to 12 of that sequence might correspond to the last four steps in MacNeilage et al.'s evolutionary sequence. At this juncture I expand my argument to include the work of Corballis (1989). But first, the theory that I elaborated is reviewed. The starting point of that theory centered on neopiagetian accounts of cognitive development. Case (1985; Case, Hayward, Lewis, & Hurst, 1988), Fischer (1980; Fischer & Lamborn, 1989), and Mounoud (1986) have all described cyclic recursions in cognitive growth. The individual passes through several major stages, and there are substages which recur from one stage to the next. [see Young (1990) for a review of the neopiagetian theories; note that some of Fischer's ages are slightly off.]

In my version of this approach, there are four stages with each going through five substages. In Tables 1 to 4, it can be seen that the stages concern (a) reflexive behaviors which begin to manifest fetally, (b) classic piagetian infant sensorimotor behavior, (c) a childhood stage combining preoperations and concrete operations, and (d) adolescent-adult formal, abstract thought. The substages begin with (a) a beginning coordination of relevant units, which (b) become fixed or hierarchized in terms of the direction of their relationship. Then, there is (c) a recruitment of what is needed to yield better systematic, on-target behavior. Following this, (d) systems multiply in chains, and then (e) further differentiate (integrate). Parallel socioemotional systems are also depicted; basic ones emerge in the odd-numbered substages, and they permit the first five Ericksonian stages to develop universally (in the starred periods). The extreme right hand column in each of Tables 1 to 4 indicates the evolutionary steps predicted to correspond to the developmental ones. The 11-step Corballis-MacNeilage et al. evolutionary sequence is embedded in this larger 20 step sequence, as will be shown in section 5.4.

The 20 hypothesized levels in development are presented in detail in sections 6.2 to 6.4. Examples of behavior are offered at the manual level to indicate that the theory has the potential to explain steps in areas other than cognitive development. There seems to be an increasing role of activation/inhibition coordination processes from level to level. (Bjorkland & Harnishfeger, 1990, and Pascuale-Leone & Johnson, in press, have also underscored the role of inhibitory processes in development.) That is, the 20-level progression in human development that has been postulated was formulated to reflect an increasing role for the left hemisphere's inhibitory skills from one level to the next. However, behavior is the product of the two cerebral hemispheres working in concert, and more thought is needed on the specific role of the right hemisphere at each of the 20 levels. (The notion that the right hemisphere is specialized for contextual placement of language (see section 1.5) and certain inhibition skills (see section 3.1) may help in this regard.)

5.3. 20 Steps in the Development of Left Brain Specialization

This section presents Tables 1 to 4, which concern the 20-step model of the development of lateralization described in Young (1990).

Table 1. The Reflex Stage of Cognitive Development

Control Unit in Substage	Age Range	Socio-emotional System	Evolutionary Origin
Reflex pair coordination	earlier fetal life	Distance acts	Reptilian I
Reflexive behavior hierarchization	quite premature		Reptilian II
Primitive schema (systematization)	somewhat premature	Outcome acts	Reptilian III
Patterned schema (multiplication)	fullterm newborn		Reptilian IV
Independent schema (integration)	0-1 mo	Emotional acts	Reptilian V

Table 2. The Sensorimotor Stage of Cognitive Development

Control Unit in Substage	Age Range	Socio-emotional System	Evolutionary Origin
Schema coordination	1-4 mo	Dyadic acts	Paleo-mammalian I
Schema coordinate hierarchization	4-8 mo	*	Paleo-mammalian II
Primitive representation (systematization)	8-12 mo	Sociabi-lity acts	Paleo-mammalian III
Linear plans (multiplication)	12-18 mo	*	Early prosimian
Symbolic plans (integration)	18-24 mo	Interact-ional acts	Early monkey

* Indicates levels when first Ericksonian stages emerge as important.

Table 3. The Perioperational Stage of Cognitive Development

Control Unit in Substage	Age Range	Socio-emotional System	Evolutionary Origin
Symbol plan coordination	2-3.5 yr	Superord-inate acts	Early ape
Symbol plan hierarchization	3.5-5 yr	*	*Australopith. afarensis*
Symbol plan systematization	5-7 yr	Gender acts	*Homo habilis*

Table 3 continued overleaf

Table 3 cont. The Perioperational Stage of Cognitive Development

Control Unit in Substage	Age Range	Socio-emotional System	Evolutionary Origin
Concrete operations (multiplication)	7-9 yr	*	*Homo erectus*
Logic in imagination (integration)	9-11 yr	Role acts	*Archaic homo sapiens*

Table 4. The Abstract Stage of Cognitive Development

Control Unit in Substage	Age Range	Socio-emotional System	Evolutionary Origin
Logic in imagination coordination	11-13 yr	Conscious acts	*Homo sapiens sapiens*
Abstract hierarchization	13-16 yr	*	Cromagnon people
Abstract systematization	16-19 yr	Nurturing acts	Contemporary people
Relativist abstraction (multiplication)	youth		Contemporary people
Abstract universality (integration)	adult	Universal acts	Contemporary people

5.4. Re-evaluating the Evolution of Laterality

The 20-step ontogenetic sequence presented in Tables 1 to 4 may be applicable to the phylogenetic emergence of our species. There may not be a one-to-one parallel in developmental stages and ancestral ones because of processes such as neoteny and acceleration (Gould, 1977), which function to alter or affect the former sequence in relation to the latter. (Neoteny concerns a retardation or delay in the appearance or full maturation of a developing behavior relative to the status predicted for it on the basis of prior evolution. Acceleration refers to the inverse of this process.) Nevertheless, the comparison of developmental and evolutionary trends can be instructive. In this regard, how would the 11-step MacNeilage et al.-Corballis sequence in evolution proposed in section 5.2 fit into the 20-step course in development in section 5.3? The most appropriate placement of the former in the latter still anchors around what I initially suggested for MacNeilage et al. by themselves in Young (1990). That is, the best fit of the MacNeilage et al. - Corballis 11-step evolutionary sequence and our 20-step developmental one would place the start of the former at the eighth level of the latter. This thesis is illustrated in the last column of Tables 1 to 4. It shows that the suggested four major stages in development (reflexive, sensorimotor, perioperational, formal operational) correspond to key reptilian, paleomammalian, nonhominid primate, and hominid ancestors. This tight correspondence in the current theory between major transition points in ontogenetic and phylogenetic advances seems noteworthy.

There are several major implications of the current theory for how we should conceptualize the steps in the evolution of lateralization. First, the tables predict quite precisely the nature of the various steps in the evolution of lateralization; they should concern cognitive underpinnings governed by left hemispheric activation/inhibition coordination as much as anything else. Thus, the skills ascribed to the diverse early hominids in this theory are more complex than current data collection methods have allowed us to intuit. For example, the early monkeys, the first hominids, *Homo erectus*, and the first *Homo sapiens sapiens* are hypothesized to have evolved lateralized behavior in terms of underlying symbolic plans, symbolic plan hierarchies, concrete operations, and a coordination of logic in imagination, respectively. Manual examples here would include a right hand preference in (i) resolving an embedded hiding task with a hand manipulated tool, (ii) symbolic gesturing to help communicate, (iii) manipulation necessary to solve a manual task requiring logical thought, and (iv) painting an abstract theme.

Second, the last several levels in the 20-step sequence characterize the unique attributes of contemporary humans. Corballis (1989) contemplated this issue, and considered his concept of left hemispheric generativity as crucial in this regard. However, the current perspective ascribes humanity's distinctiveness to the final five steps in our ontogenetic progression. That is, what makes us unique are the late-developing characteristics revolving around formal abstract thought which emerge in adolescents, youths, and adults (characteristics which unfortunately do not develop fully in all of us, which is perhaps why we have been confused in efforts to characterize ourselves).

Third, primate researchers should better consider developmental sequences in their studies on lateralization. The ontogenetic sequence hypothesized for contemporary humans may have applied in similar ways to nonhuman primate ancestors. For example, contemporary chimpanzees may develop their laterality in an 11-step sequence akin to the one presented for ancestral apes in Tables 2 to 4. Thus, according to the current theory Chevalier-Skolnikoff (1989a,b) is correct in arguing that chimpanzees can show preoperational thought, but is wrong in asserting that they will also be shown to possess concrete operations. Fourth, there should be more than one step in precursor laterality evident in species which evolved before the primates, as we predict eight steps which predate the one associated with early prosimians. Denenberg's (1981) description of bird and rodent laterality is a start in this direction, especially since he has implicated left hemisphere inhibition processes in this regard, like us, as we have seen in section 1.3. Fifth, other accounts of the evolution of cognitive and language behavior have been proposed recently (G. Richards, 1989; Wallace, 1989), and unlike the present account they are not based on lateralization of behavior and neopiagetian cognition. However, these views do not seem to be in conflict with the present one and complementary perspectives should not be excluded. Sixth, Gibson (1989) has suggested that Case's (1985) neopiagetian theory can provide a framework for understanding the phylogenesis of behavior in human and nonhuman primates. However, I feel that the following comparison of the present approach with Case's shows the present approach to be more useful.

6. The 20 Levels of Language Development

6.1. Hemispheric Specialization and Language

The exact relationship of language to hemispheric specialization for manual and other behavior remains an unresolved issue. There are divergent views on which evolved first (e.g., Corballis, 1989) and which is the engine of advance for the other in development (Young, 1990). The current emphasis on complementary hemispheric specialization would argue that each hemisphere possesses language skills, and that they are reciprocally related, fitting with the underlying inhibitory skills on which they are based (see section 3.1). By extension, it is predicted that there are 20 steps in the development of language lateralization in the left hemisphere, related to the 20 steps of general lateralization development described in section 5.3.

Thus, in the current perspective, advances in language are considered products of advances in hemispheric specialization (in terms of inhibition), and not vice versa. However, it is the inhibitory skill acquisition that is important at any one step, and not the fact that it is lateralized in the left hemisphere. In fact, developmental research needs to establish whether each complex inhibitory skill emerges bilaterally and then rapidly shifts to the left hemisphere or emerges immediately in the left hemisphere. Even if the latter perspective is correct, it may be easier to detect the signs of inhibition advance in general at any one step prior to their definitive lateralization. In short, developmental renewal depends on inhibition skill gains, in particular, and thus cognitive, language, lateralization, and other advances are dependent on this process. That is, the latter acquisitions can emerge simultaneously or after (but never before) in development compared to signs of corresponding inhibition skill acquisition. Moreover, they do not have to show a constant, universal relationship in the order of acquisition at anyone level. For example, early language and cognitive skills may be temporally associated with each other in development, but one need not develop first in all infants (the 'correlational' hypothesis; Kelly & Dale, 1989).

In the next section, the area of language is analyzed in relation to the 20 hypothesized levels in development. The work of Case (1985), in particular, is scrutinized. He has presented a theory of cognitive development involving four stages (sensorimotor, interrelational or preoperational, dimensional or concrete operational, abstract or formal) which go through three substages each (unifocal, bifocal, elaborated coordination). There is an initial precoordination phase, which gives a 13-level model of cognitive development (see Young, 1990, for a detailed description of this theory, as well as a critique). Case (1985) has performed an ambitious comparison between the cognitive levels that he describes in the first through sixth years and corresponding language- related behavior. For example, in the first year he shows how there are sensorimotor and vocal-verbal correspondences involving the use of vocalization for social purposes, the assignment of meaning to words, and the expression of recognizable words. The specific language-related behaviors that Case described at each cognitive substage are presented in Table 5. The 12-18 month period is listed in two ways (both as last sensorimotor substage and as first interrelational or preoperational one), fitting with the overlap found in the transition between cognitive stages in Case. The table gives all mentioned behavior for the sensorimotor period (condensed into one column), and considers spontaneous utterances for the interrelational period.

Table 5. Summary of Vocal-Verbal Development in Early Years in Case (1985)

Substage	Sensorimotor Period	Interrelational Period
Precoordination/ consolidation	Intentionally coo to elicit or sustain adult behavior. Coo when alone to produce interest. Use vowel or coo sequences (e.g., ah-ee-ya). [Up to 4 mo]	With adult, share/ relate to interesting event at distance (e.g., [see] Daddy). [12-18 mo]
Unifocal coordination	Babble consonant-vowel syllables loudly to call absent adult (also hand raising here). Coo when successful in making adult approach. Contribute to role exchange (e.g., make sound sequence then pause to listen). [4-8 mo]	Use two-word utterance with no referent present and with words relating to each other (e.g., daddy hit). [18-24 mo]
Bifocal coordination	Babble loudly to get adult to fetch object out of reach (also point, turn). Generate and imitate bisyllabic utterances (e.g., Mama) and use them to achieve goals. [8-12 mo]	Subject-verb-object sentences appear. Words qualified (e.g., Dad kicked the ball in garden). [2-3.5 yr]
Elaborated coordination	Add to above the use of object name (specific word or idio-syncratic attempt). Imitate novel adult utterances and use them to achieve goals. [12-18 mo]	Tell stories with episodes. Use sentences with embedded clauses. [3.5-5 yr]

Case has ingeniously woven these specific examples into the fabric of his theory. However, I will show that there is an alternative, better interpretation. In particular, it will be argued that the vocal/verbal examples provided by Case illustrate my own theory of neopiagetian cognitive development better than Case's own theory. Recall that I proposed a cyclic recursion of five substages (coordination, hierarchization, systematization, multiplication, integration) in each of four stages (see section 5.2). Case's precoordination and three coordinated sensorimotor substages correspond to the first four sensorimotor substages in Young (1990). His first interrelational substage, operational consolidation, is a transitional one and thus concerns our fourth sensorimotor substage along with Case's previous substage. His next interrelational substage corresponds to our fifth and last sensorimotor substage. The last two interrelational substages in Case's theory parallel the first two in what I termed the perioperational period.

Fischer (and colleagues; Fischer & Corrigan, 1981; Fischer & Hogan, 1989) has also presented a comparison of levels in neopiagetian cognitive development and parallel steps in language development, but only for three early cognitive levels. Instead of Case's (a) elaborated sensorimotor structures, (b) unifocal interrelations, and (c) bifocal interrelations beginning at 1, 1.5, and 2 years of life respectively, Fischer described (a) sensorimotor systems, (b) representational sets, and (c) representational mapping at about the same ages. Moreover, his examples of language acquisition which correspond to the cognitive levels resemble those of Case for the most part.

6.2. Sensorimotor Language Levels

In sensorimotor coordination from 1 to 4 months, I describe how schemas which have developed in the newborn during the reflexive period come to coordinate, but not in a fixed sequence. Thus, the very young infant shows primitive vision-movement coordination before an object target, but no successful visually-guided reaching. This behavior is similar to what Case describes for vocal behavior in sensorimotor precoordination, the substage equivalent to ours. That is, the infant at this age coos or performs other activity cycled with cooing in order to induce or maintain adult action. Also, separate vowel or sound units are serially sequenced. Clearly, these behaviors show that 1- to 4-month-olds already exhibit schema coordination in their vocal behavior. Thus, when Case labels them as "consolidating one operation" or "precoordinated", he does not do justice to the young infants' vocal skills.

With the next level of sensorimotor hierarchization, the current theory suggests that the schema coordinations of the prior substage become fixed in their temporal order in certain situations or exhibit a dominant-subordinate relationship. In the prior substage, the 3-month-old might exhibit hand watching while active before a target, but without movement to the target. He or she may also show ballistic reaching to a target, but without visual surveillance throughout to ensure target attainment. However, the 5-month-old in the sensorimotor hierarchization substage manifests refined visuomotor coordination in directed reaching, where reaching precedes hand opening and seizure and where vision is subordinated to manual aiming. This latter behavior of visually-directed reaching resembles the language-related examples in Case's equivalent stage of sensorimotor unifocal coordination. There, babbling loudly and hand-raising are both used to attain a specific goal, i.e., to call the absent adult. In social exchange, the active role and the passive role are appropriately alternated in time. In such behavior, we see more than just Case's unifocal sensorimotor coordination, for there is the added elements of appropriate order in behavior and of goal attainment. Moreover, related behaviors in the prior substage had already shown beginning coordination. Thus, once more Case's label does not adequately capture the essence of the examples he provides, a criticism which does not seem to apply to the current theory.

The next substage to develop according to the current theory, sensorimotor systematization, witnesses refinements of each component of schema hierarchies. Thus, visually-directed reaching can attain a new level of sophistication, as it can manifest intention at its outset and subtlety in its end search through primitive representation. Consequently, on object permanence tasks, the 10-month-old can seek a fully hidden object. Such behavior parallels the verbal ones found in Case's sensorimotor bifocal coordination. In babbling and pointing in order to induce an adult to get a hard-to- reach object and in using utterances to achieve goals, there is systematic organization from the outset towards a goal, which is reflective of a primitive image or representational guidance, even if coarse. Instead of visually-directed reaching without adjustment to unattainable objects, as would happen in the prior substage, personal reaching can be replaced by calling the other to reach. Visuomotor coordination is refined to the point that the other can perform part of the deed for the infant, as representation begins to function. Case's label of bifocal coordination for this substage is inappropriate, for behavior somewhat indicative of bifocal coordination seems to emerge in the prior substage. Moreover, in the current substage, the infant is systematically oriented to a goal from a behavior's onset, given his/her primitive representational capacity, and Case does not deal with this capacity.

The fourth sensorimotor substage of the current theory involves multiplication of sensorimotor systems through embedding or combination, so that chained plans can be formulated. Thus, the one-year-old comes to resolve embedded hidings or explore new ends for previously learned means, linearly organizing complex sequences of changing sensorimotor schemas. This cognitive skill fits the language behavior given in Case's sensorimotor elaborated coordination. He describes the repetition of novel adult utterances in this age period, as well as object naming in the context of efforts to enlist adults in object seeking. The former example illustrates well schema system multiplication by combination, whereas the latter one typifies such multiplication by embedding (or use of subprograms in plans). The interrelational operational consolidation example listed by Case also fits the current model, for language is used to share and link events. Again, Case's model needs reinterpretation, for there is more than a general sensorimotor elaboration in the year-old as specific multiplication, linkage, and chaining processes take place.

The last sensorimotor substage in the current theory, that of integration, refers to the embedding of branched plans (not just branched subprograms) in primary plans in order to allow for more flexible adaptation. In short, the toddler's plans are symbolically organized, permitting reversible secondary offshoots as in the resolution of a double embedded hiding. Case's substage of unifocal coordination in the interrelational period provides linguistic examples consistent with this model. That is, the young child at this age uses two-word utterances which relate to each other in a variety of ways and which can be uttered without any referent in the immediate context. In the prior substage, these utterances could be produced, but only through imitation. Now, the sensorimotor stage reaches its culmination point, as symbol-mediated words are used spontaneously with one related to another in order to communicate a larger whole appropriate to the child's world. Words combined one way in one circumstance can be used in other two-word utterances in different circumstances, as the child evidences "productive" syntax (Kelly & Dale, 1989). The child is exhibiting more than Case's unifocal interrelational coordination in his/her utterances, for they reflect our emphasis on reversible subprograms where embedding takes place in one circumstance only to be undone in order to prepare for a different circumstance.

6.3. Perioperational Language Levels

In the next stage of cognitive growth described in Young (1990), perioperational levels in thought emerge and they begin with the coordination of the symbol plans which had developed in the prior stage. The child can now balance these plans, permitting more appropriate dual channel symbol activity. Thus, a two- or three-year-old can simultaneously sort two subsets of a group of objects or translate the aural symbol into the written one (and vice versa) in learning to read and write letters. In terms of Case's examples in the bifocal coordination interrelational period, the child can structure two-word utterances into subject-verb-object sentences by coordinating different types of two-word utterances into large wholes (e.g., subject-verb with verb-object). (Sentence sequences or attempted stories, however, lack coordination and can be described as "heaps", Applebee, 1978.) Case's examples are concordant with my own theory, but in this view the child can perform more advanced linguistic-related functions than Case has described. That is, my model better captures the young child's nascent letter learning skills with its emphasis on a coordination of symbol plans.

Finally, the last substage that Case (1985) dealt with is considered. He stated that storytelling using sequential events (based on sentences with embedded clauses) marks the language skill of the five-year-old as he/she arrives at the elaborated coordination interrelational substage. This type of behavior is exactly the one that would best characterize Young's (1990) substage of perioperational symbol plan hierarchization in terms of language ability. This substage was described as one showing a dominant-subordinate relationship of symbol plans, so that, for example, symbolic gesturing could be used to supplement verbal utterances. Case's examples seem perfect here, as he shows that this age is marked by the subordination of clauses in sentences and events in stories.

Case has continued his analysis of story telling ability in the cognitive period following the interrelational one (Case, Marini, McKeough, Dennis, & Goldberg, 1986). His dimensional or concrete operational stage also manifests a "pre-", "uni-", "bi-", and "elaborated" substage sequence (3 1/2-5, 5-7, 7-9, 9-11, respectively). In Case et al. (1986) children had to tell a story about a "cute little lamb", and the stories were classified according to the four mentioned cognitive levels. The simplest story, corresponding to the first dimensional substage, consisted of one global episode of sequential events with no theme or plot. (Note that Case (1985) described story telling at this age as being comprised of "episodes", but I presume that the "episodes" in that context referred to the "events" in this one.) Next, the stories manifested clear plots with conventional themes, as two related episodes (problem, resolution) formed a coordinated higher-order unit. Older children embedded a minor plot (usually involving a secondary problem) in a major plot, and resolved both the major and minor plots (one after the other). In the most advanced level, resolutions of both the plot and subplot were usually more fully elaborated or unified, and took place in parallel, not sequentially.

Since the first level of story telling in Case et al. (1986) has already been reinterpreted in the prior paragraphs of this section, we will examine only the last three levels. They correspond to our own cognitive substages of perioperational systematization, multiplication, and integration, respectively. Thus, they afford us an opportunity to complete presentation of our perspective on the development of language to the end of the perioperational period. Perioperational systematization refers to the development of symbol plan systems through refinement of symbol plan hierarchies. This process takes place by adding to the latters' components so as to better produce target behavior. Ultimately, this systematization allows the child to better hold things in mind and use a precursor logic (e.g., in simpler concrete operational problems). In examining Case et al.'s description of story telling in this age period, we can see that a whole in the child's target story develops for the first time, as a major logical coordination of episodes over time emerges. Consequently, Case et al.'s description of story telling seems quite consistent with the current theory for this age period.

The next substage in the current model concerns perioperational multiplication. Here, the child tackles most of Piaget's concrete operations. Symbol plan systems can combine, chain, or sequence in intercoordinations, alternating patterns, etc., improving logic, rules, reversals in thought, etc. Again, Case et al.'s story telling data fit our model for they describe embedded minor plots in this age period. These embedded plots reflect the multiplicative nature of the symbol plans in the current theory. Moreover, the major and minor plots are resolved sequentially, fitting Piaget's description of thought reversals, where the child in this period returns to the starting on of his/her cognition before moving on.

The last substage dealt with in the current theory involves perioperational integration, where a limited logic in imagination comes to glimmer. The child differentiates optional branches or embeddings of logic in his/her thought and can deal with them simultaneously or in parallel to some extent since the ability to hold things in mind forms a larger integral whole. Once more, Case et al.'s data on story telling concords with the current view, as they describe in the age period of concern a parallel resolution of plot and subplot in a process of unity.

6.4. Comments

Case seems to have systematically underestimated the skills of the sensorimotor infant and early perioperational child. For each of the substages described, I pointed out how my theory depicted a more complex cognitive structure compared to Case's, and how it also better fit the data. This speaks to a point raised in Young (1990), who described how the current theory respected as much as possible Piaget's original account of the sequence of sensorimotor substages because of the apparent validity of that sequence, and built up from there. Case's model of cognitive development (as well as Fischer's) were not constructed in the same way, as data from the childhood period were especially emphasized to begin with.

Case has not analyzed language development in all possible stages. Thus, we now extend this analysis to other stages using our theory as a guide. Possible reflexive language levels are now suggested. Reflex coordination refers to fetal pairing of reflexes having no firing mechanisms. Moreover, temporal order is not specified. In terms of language precursors, such reflex pairs may control mouth movements associated with vegetative sounds in the womb. With reflexive behavior hierarchies of the quite premature newborn, a specific order for the behavior actions of coordinated reflexes develop and specific activating mechanisms for them emerge. Thus, cooing produced by appropriate organization of vocal chord and lip/mouth movement may manifest reflexively in certain relevant circumstances. In reflexive systematization, evident in the somewhat premature newborn, a more patterned behavior results from primitive schemas. Thus, nonreflexive components are added to the reflexive ones of the prior substage, refining their on-target orientation. In terms of vocalization, longer more varied coo units may be elicited in interest-provoking situations. This process accelerates in the next phase, as the fullterm newborn exhibits reflex multiplication, where combined series of sounds may be triggered in the optimal state. In reflex integration, the first month of life is devoted to exercising and differentiating reflexes and schema-guided behavior in order to render them more flexible. Vocalizations may come to differ in terms of intonation or sound variability for different circumstances, for example.

We end with possible formal, abstract language levels. Generally speaking, the stage begins with young adolescent coordination of logic in imagination, which allows classical piagetian formal operations to begin. In problem solving, one variable at a time is allowed to vary because the young teenager can orchestrate his/her logical thought pathways, even when no physical evidence is available to help in finding solutions. Thus, in story telling or writing the young teenager should be able to readily construct complex plots which subserve abstract themes being explored. The middle adolescent progresses to abstract hierarchization, where abstract approaches being explored are compared either among themselves or to a more general perspective. Story construction should reflect this by placing plots and/or themes being explored in various relations, juxtapositions, etc. The late adolescent develops abstract systematization where the approaches and their comparisons are qualified, leading to better understanding. Stories could reflect this logical advance by a refinement of the plots and themes therein, producing a more structured whole. The young person passes into dialectical, relativist abstraction, weighing larger systems organized into coherent multiple frameworks. Stories then should manifest creative, balanced combinations. Finally, in the adult's abstract integration, an empathic universality may emerge in stories, as differentiated branching in logic can come to include harmonization of self and others.

6.5. Conclusions

The '20-step' model of development proposed here may have practical applications. For example, it may be possible to qualify developmental differences in aphasia in terms of different language impairment predicted by the 20-step developmental theory. Also, different adult patients may manifest different language deficits depending on which of the 20 levels of language described in sections 6.3 and 6.4 are spared by their particular lesions.

The 20-step model of development may provide a basis for neuropsychological testing not only in language but also in cognitive, motor, and other areas (notwithstanding the model's lack of treatment of the right hemisphere, intrahemispheric differences, cortical vs. lower CNS differences, etc.). Young, Bowman, Methot, Finlayson, Quintal, and Boissonneault (1983) argued that the left hemisphere is an ideal hierarchical organizer because of its superior activation/inhibition coordination skills. A neuropsychological implication which stemmed from this position was that integration into the one stream that characterizes human action of the different modalities of behavior (motor, linguistic, socioemotional, etc.) would be more liable to disruption due to left compared to right hemisphere inhibition skill impairment.

> Does the motor, vocal, social, and/or processing activity in the patient suggest one inclusive model where there is an inability to select the appropriate hierarchy and/or to descend it (e.g., looping at a node or repeating it) and/or to exclude irrelevant parallel, lower, or higher nodes within a hierarchy, and/or to exclude nodes of unrelated hierarchies? Does the extent of recovery reflect reintegration in part along these lines? (p. 127)

Until now, 20 levels in development have been emphasized. In Young (1990), I raised the possibility of both sublevels within the levels and a twenty-first final level. The sublevels may consist of a sequence of initiation, application, maturation, and transition, or the like. Commons and F.A. Richards (1984) also see the repetition of four sublevels within each of the cognitive levels that they considered, but their conception borrows from signal detection theory. Fischer and colleagues (Fischer &

Corrigan, 1981; Fischer & Hogan, 1989) also described sublevels within cognitive levels, but these could vary from one task to another and are potentially limitless.

Karniol (1989) has described a 10-step sequence in the development of manual skill in the one month to nine month period. The first level of object rotation, which develops as early as 1 month and 7 days, would correspond to manual examples in the last reflexive level in our model of 20 steps in development. In Karniol, held objects are repeatedly twisted, for example, while in our model reflex-independent patterned behaviors manifest adjustment to objects. The next four steps in Karniol's manual sequence develop between 2 and 3.5 months and thus correspond to manual examples in the first sensorimotor level in our model. In this level, I describe a schema coordination (e.g., between vision and movement), but one that lacks a hierarchical fixity of two different schemas synchronized from the start in order to lead to successful outcomes (e.g., visually-directed reaching). Karniol gives four similar behaviors: (a) translation or changing object position (e.g., grasped object to mouth); (b) vibration or rapid periodic movement (e.g., with rattle); (c) bilateral hold or hold an object in one hand while actually exploring another in the other hand, and (d) two-handed hold in order to steady an object, hold a large one, or rotate one.

There are also four steps in Karniol's sequence of manual skill development in the 4.5 to 7 month period, which corresponds to our sensorimotor schema hierarchization level. She describes (a) hand to hand transfer of one object, (b) coordinated action on a single object (e.g., one hand holds while the other manipulates), (c) a similar coordination with two objects (e.g., an object in one hand is struck on another object in the other hand), and (d) object deformation by one or both hands (e.g., squeeze toy). In all cases two manual schemes are coordinated in a fixed way in order to actively produce a desired outcome, just what the current theory emphasizes for this age period. The last step in Karniol's sequence concerns instrumental sequential actions where the two hands are coordinated to attain a goal. Her example deals with complex bimanual coordination, where one hand lifts a lid of a container while the other grasps an object therein. This is also the example in our equivalent level of sensorimotor schema systematization. It seems clear that Karniol's (1989) developmental sequence of manual skills in infancy suggests that there may be four sublevels in the various levels that we have described. The exact nature of the sublevels, and to what extent they may be valid for all our levels and all the areas of development to which the model has been applied remains to be determined.

The proposed twenty-first supplementary level may be insufficient to capture the intent of the comment made in Young (1990). There it was suggested that the extra level concerned the relation of the individual to a communal intelligence or to human-machine interfacing. The intelligent individual can expand his/her intellectual limits by symbiotically sharing with the collective intelligence. In this regard, we can posit a fifth major stage of cognitive development reflective of this characteristic, and suggest that this stage can evolve through five substages like the others. The substages of coordination/hierarchization, systematization, and multiplication would then concern subdiscipline, discipline, and interdisciplinary levels of communal intelligence, respectively, while the integration substage would concern the larger collective level. This conception of humankind's ultimate cognitive advance borrows from F.A. Richards and Commons (1984) who suggested that some men can engage in cross-paradigmatic reasoning. The current approach emphasizes that in this stage (a) cognition needs to be conceived of beyond the individual; (b) paradigms or disciplines may concern complex practical, artistic, oral folk skills and the like as much as scientific endeavors; (c) at the individual level active mastery of the organization of the collective intelligence reflects this stage as much as creative acts in its reorganization. Together, these arguments suggest that this penultimate stage may be widespread in humans. In this regard precursors of this penultimate cognitive stage manifest in the prior one as the individual prepares the knowledge and experiential bases necessary for its realization.

Tables 1 to 4 indicate that socioemotional systems develop with each of the odd-numbered substages of the current theory and that the first five broad-ranging Ericksonian stages develop in conjunction with the even-numbered substages beginning in the infant sensorimotor period. Young (1990) described how the last three of the eight Ericksonian stages seem to develop in no set pattern with respect to the various substages of the current theory. With the present addition to the current theory of a fifth major stage in development concerning collective intelligence, an aesthetic closure can come to bear on the relationship of the current model of development and that of Erickson. That is, the last three Ericksonian stages (concerning intimacy, generativity, and integrity) would correspond with the three even-numbered substages in adult life that have yet to be assigned a specific Ericksonian stage (the last one in Table 4, plus the two new ones in the collective intelligence stage). The particular systems that are seen to develop with the odd-numbered substages of the latter stage are presented in Table 6. As with the other systems described in Young (1990), they vary along three dimensions, and only their positive portion is presented. The three dimensions relate to activity/reactivity, figure/ground or target vs. context, distance, etc., and positive/negative goal compatibility. The systems' passage through the substages of communal intelligence witnesses the transformation of metaphysical, penultimate mental states into more holistic, cathartic ones through catalytic cognitive conversion processes. See Young (in preparation) for a detailed description of all the systems, Ericksonian stages, and their relationship to the substages of the current theory.

Table 6. Positive Systems Corresponding to Odd-numbered Substages in Collective Intelligence

System Name	Dimension			
	Figure		Ground	
	Active	Reactive	Active	Reactive
Metaphysical Acts	Perspicacity	Awe (sense of)	Relativity (sense of)	Uncertainty (sense of)
Catalytic Acts	Emergent discovery	Chaotic attractors	Paradigmatic shift	Catastrophic inversion
Cathartic Acts	Wisdom	Reverence	Transcendence	Mystery

As a final conclusion, I offer the suggestion that whatever developmental domain is examined, the concepts of (a) left hemisphere inhibition superiority, (b) complementary inhibition specializations in the hemispheres, and (c) multiple (20 or more) progressive steps in their growth will prove to have some explanatory power and practical significance. The current theory strives to be both specific in the behavior it describes in areas such as motor, cognitive, and language development and general in its conceptualization. It seeks to establish how the brain and behavior relate especially using relatively novel models of lateralization in terms of inhibition and of cognitive and related development in terms of 20 neopiagetian levels. This union needs further exploration (see Hauert, 1990, for commentaries).[1]

1. Butterworth (1990) described my work as suggesting (a) a right hemispheric dominance from birth, (b) with especially interhemispheric inhibitory processes, (c) and not interhemispheric cooperation, as well as (d) with especially biological underpinnings even in cognitive development. It is evident from reading my work that he is incorrect or only partially correct on all these counts.

Acknowledgement

Many thanks to Laurie Miller for his helpful, challenging comments.

References

Albert, M.L., & Sandson, J. (1986). Perseveration in aphasia. *Cortex*, **22**, 103-115.

Applebee, A.N. (1978). *The child's concept of story. Ages two to seventeen.* Chicago: The University of Chicago Press.

Bakan, P. (1969). Hypnotizability, laterality of eye-movements and functional brain asymmetry. *Perceptual and Motor Skills*, **28**, 927-932.

Bakan, P. (1977). Left handedness and birth order revisited. *Neuropsychologia*, **15**, 837-839.

Barnes, F. (1975). Temperament, adaptability, and left-handers. *New Scientist*, **67**, 202-203.

Bear, D.M., & Fedio, P. (1977). Quantitative analysis of interictal behavior in temporal lobe epilepsy. *Archives of Neurology*, **34**, 454-467.

Bendersky, M., & Lewis, M. (1990). Early language ability as a function of ventricular dilatation associated with intraventricular hemorrhage. *Developmental and Behavioral Pediatrics*, **11**, 17-21.

Benson, D.F., & Geschwind, N. (1975/1982). The aphasias and related disturbances. In A.B. Baker & L.H. Baker (Eds.), *Clinical neurology, Vol. 1* (pp. 1-28). New York: Harper & Row.

Bertoncini, J., Morais, J., Bijeljac-Babic, R., McAdams, S., Peretz, I., & Mehler, J. (1989). Dichotic perception and laterality in neonates. *Brain and Language*, **37**, 591-605.

Best, C.T. (1988). The emergence of cerebral asymmetries for perceptual and cognitive functions in infancy. In D.L. Molfese & S.J. Segalowitz (Eds.), *Brain lateralization in children: Developmental implications* (pp. 5-34). New York: Guilford Press.

Best, C.T., & Queen, H.F. (1989). Baby, it's in your smile: right hemiface bias in infant emotional expressions. *Developmental Psychology*, **25**, 264-276.

Biederman, I. (1987). Recognition-by-components: a theory of human image understanding. *Psychological Review*, **94**, 115-147.

Bjorkland, D.F., & Harnishfeger, K.K. (1990). The resources construct in cognitive development: diverse sources of evidence and a theory of inefficient inhibition. *Developmental Review*, **10**, 48-71.

Bracco, L., Tiezzi, A., Ginanneschi, A., Campanella, C., & Amaducci, L. (1984). Lateralization of choline acetyltransferase (Ch.AT) activity in fetus and adult human brain. *Neurosciences Letters*, **50**, 301-305.

Bradshaw, J.L. (1989). *Hemispheric specialization and psychological function.* New York: Wiley.

Bryan, K.L. (1988). Assessment of language disorders after right hemisphere damage. *British Journal of Disorders of Communication*, **23**, 111-125.

Buck, R., & Duffy, R.J. (1980). Nonverbal communication of affect in brain-damaged patients. *Cortex*, **16**, 351-362.

Butterworth, G. (1990). Development in infancy: a quarter century of empirical and theoretical progress. In C.-A. Hauert (Ed.), *Developmental psychology: Cognitive, perceptuo-motor and neuropsychological perspectives* (pp. 183-190). Amsterdam: North Holland.

Butterworth, G., & Hopkins, B. (1988). Hand-mouth coordination in the newborn baby. *British Journal of Developmental Psychology*, **6**, 303-314.

Canavan, A.G.M., Passingham, R.E., Marsden, C.D., Quinn, N., Wyke, M., & Polkey, C.E.(1989). Sequencing ability in Parkinsonians, patients with frontal lobe lesions, and patients who have undergone unilateral temporal lobectomies. *Neuropsychologia*, **27**, 789-798.

Carson, R.G. (1989). Manual asymmetries: feedback processing, output variability, and spatial complexity -- resolving some inconsistencies. *Journal of Motor Behavior*, **21**, 38-47.

Case, R. (1985). *Intellectual development: Birth to adulthood.* Orlando, FL: Academic Press.

Case, R., Hayward, S., Lewis, M., & Hurst, P. (1988). Toward a neo-Piagetian theory of cognitive and emotional development. *Developmental Review*, **8**, 1-51.

Case, R., Marini, Z., McKeough, A., Dennis, S., & Goldberg, J. (1986). Horizontal structure in middle childhood: cross-domain parallels in the course of cognitive growth. In I. Levin (Ed.), *Stage and structure* (pp. 1-38). Norwood, NJ: Ablex.

Chevalier-Skolnikoff, S. (1989a). Spontaneous tool use and sensorimotor intelligence in *Cebus* compared with other monkeys and apes. *Behavioral and Brain Sciences*, **12**, 561-588.

Chevalier-Skolnikoff, S. (1989b). Tool use in *Cebus*: its relation to object manipulation, the brain, and ecological adaptations. *Behavioral and Brain Sciences*, **12**, 610-627.

Chi, J.G., Dooling, E.C., & Gilles, F.H. (1977a). Left-right asymmetries of the temporal speech areas of the human foetus. *Archives of Neurology*, **34**, 346-348.

Chi, J.G., Dooling, E.C., & Gilles, F.H. (1977b). Gyral development of the human brain. *Annals of Neurology*, **1**, 68-83.

Chisolm, R.C., & Karrer, R. (1988). Movement-related potentials and control of associated movements. *International Journal of Neuroscience*, **42**, 131-148.

Chugani, H.T., & Phelps, M.E. (1986). Maturational changes in cerebral function in infants determined by ^{18}FDG positron emission tomography. *Science*, **231**, 840-843.

Clifton, R.K., Morrongiello, B.A., Kulig, J.W., & Dowd, J.M. (1981). Developmental changes in auditory localization in infancy. In R. Aslin, J. Alberts, & M. Peterson (Eds.), *Development of perception, Vol. 1: Psychobiological perspectives* (pp. 141-160). New York: Academic Press.

Cohen, H.J., Taft, L.T., Mahadeviah, M., & Birch, H. (1967). Developmental changes in overflow in normal and aberrantly functioning children. *The Journal of Pediatrics*, **71**, 39-47.

Commons, M.L., & Richards, F.A. (1984). Applying the general stage model. In M.L. Commons, F.A. Richards, & C. Armon (Eds.), *Beyond formal operations: Late adolescent and adult cognitive development* (pp. 141-157). New York: Praeger.

Connolly, K., & Dalgleish, M. (1989). The emergence of tool using skill in infancy. *Developmental Psychology*, **25**, 894-912.

Cook, N.D. (1989a). Toward a central dogma for psychology. *New Ideas in Psychology*, **7**, 1-18.

Cook, N.D. (1989b). First things first: A reply to Prather, Gardner, and Brownell. *New Ideas in Psychology*, **7**, 27-32.

Corballis, M.C. (1989). Laterality and human evolution. *Psychological Review*, **96**, 492-505.

Corballis, M.C., & Morgan, M.J. (1978). On the biological basis of human laterality: I. Evidence for a maturational left-right gradient. *Behavioral and Brain Sciences*, **2**, 261-336.

Coren, S., Searleman, A., & Porac, C. (1982). The effects of specific birth stressors on four indices of lateral preference. *Canadian Journal of Psychology*, **36**, 478-487.

Cunningham, D., Forsythe, C., & Ward, J.P. (1989). A report of behavioral lateralization in an infant orang-utan (*Pongo pygmaeus*). *Primates*, **30**, 249-253.

Davidson, R.J., & Fox, N.A. (1989). Frontal brain asymmetry predicts infants' response to maternal separation. *Journal of Abnormal Psychology*, **98**, 127-131.

Dawson, G. (1988). Cerebral lateralization in autism: Clues to its role in language and affective development. In D.L. Molfese & S.J. Segalowitz (Eds.), *Brain lateralization in children: Developmental implications* (pp. 437-482). New York: Guilford Press.

Dawson, G., Finley, C., Phillips, S., & Lewy, A. (1989). A comparison of hemispheric asymmetries in speech-related brain potentials of autistic and dysphasic children. *Brain and Language*, **37**, 26-41.

Denenberg, V.H. (1981). Hemispheric laterality in animals and the effects of early experience. *Behavioral and Brain Sciences*, **4**, 1-21.

Denenberg, V.H. (1988). Handedness hangups and species snobbery. *Behavioral and Brain Sciences*, **11**, 721-722.

Dopson, W.G., Beckwith, B.E., Tucker, D.M., & Bullard-Bates, P.C. (1984). Asymmetry of facial expression in spontaneous emotion. *Cortex*, **20**, 243-251.

Drewe, E.A. (1974). The effect of type and area of brain lesion on Wisconsin Card Sorting Test performance. *Cortex*, **10**, 159-170.

Edwards, J.M., & Elliott, D. (1987). Effect of unimanual training on contralateral motor overflow in children and adults. *Developmental Neuropsychology*, **3**, 299-309.

Fagard, J., & Jacquet, A.-Y. (1989). Onset of bimanual coordination and symmetry versus asymmetry of movement. *Infant Behavior and Development*, **12**, 229-235.

Fagot, J. (in press). Early manual lateralization in baboons. In J. Ward (Ed.), *Current behavioral evidence of primate asymmetry*. New York: Springer Verlag.

Feldman, H., Holland, A., & Keefe, K. (1989). Language abilities after left hemisphere brain injury: A case study of twins. *Topics in Early Childhood Special Education*, **9**, 32-47.

Feldman, J.F. (1983, April). *Implications of the laterally asymmetric head position bias in newborns for behavioral development at 1 year*. Paper presented at 50th Biennial Meeting of the Society for Research in Child Development, Detroit, MI.

Fischer, K.W. (1980). A theory of cognitive development: The control and construction of hierarchies of skills. *Psychological Review*, **87**, 477-531.

Fischer, K.W., & Corrigan, R. (1981). A skill approach to language development. In R. Stark (Ed.), *Language behavior in infancy and early childhood* (pp. 245-289). New York: Elsevier.

Fischer, K.W., & Hogan, A.E. (1989). The big picture for infant development: Levels and variations. In J. Lockman & N. Hazen (Eds.), *Action in social context: Perspectives on early development* (pp. 275-305). New York: Plenum Press.

Fischer, K.W., & Lamborn, S.D. (1989). Mechanisms of variation in developmental levels: Cognitive and emotional transitions during adolescence. In A. de Ribaupierre (Ed.), *Transition mechanisms in cognitive-emotional child development: The longitudinal approach* (pp. 33-67). New York: Cambridge University Press.

Fisher, S. (1966). Body attention patterns and personality defenses. *Psychological Monographs*, **80**, 617.

Fisk, J.D., & Goodale, M.A. (1985). The organization of eye and limb movements during unrestricted reaching to targets in contralateral and ipsilateral visual space. *Experimental Brain Research*, 60, 159-178.

Fox, N.A., & Davidson, R.J. (1984). Hemispheric substrates of affect: A developmental model. In N.A. Fox & R.J. Davidson (Eds.), *The psychobiology of affective development* (pp. 353-381). Hillsdale, NJ: Lawrence Erlbaum Associates.

Fox, N.A., & Davidson, R.J. (1986). Taste-elicited changes in facial signs of emotion and the asymmetry of brain electrical activity in human newborns. *Neuropsychologia,* **24**, 417-422.

Fox, N.A., & Davidson, R.J. (1988). Patterns of brain electrical activity during facial signs of emotion in 10-month-old infants. *Developmental Psychology,* **24**, 230-236.

Fox, N.A., & Lewis, M. (1982). Motor asymmetries in preterm infants: Effects of prematurity and illness. *Developmental Psychology,* **15**, 19-23.

Fridlund, A.J. (1988). What can asymmetry and laterality in EMG tell us about the face and brain. *International Journal of Neuroscience,* **39**, 53-69.

Galaburda, A.M., Corsiglia, J., Rosen, G., & Sherman, G. (1987). Planum temporale asymmetry, reappraisal since Geschwind and Levitsky. *Neuropsychologia,* **25**, 853-868.

Geschwind, N. (1975). The apraxias: Neural mechanisms of disorders of learned movement. *American Scientist,* **63**, 188-195.

Gibson, K.R. (1989). Tool use in cebus monkeys: Moving from orthodox to neopiagetian analyses. *Behavioral and Brain Sciences,* **12**, 598-599.

Gladstone, M., Best, C.T., & Davidson, R.J. (1989). Anomalous bimanual coordination among dyslexic boys. *Developmental Psychology,* **25**, 236-246.

Goldberg, E. (1989). Gradiental approach to neocortical functional organization. *Journal of Clinical and Experimental Neuropsychology,* **11**, 489-517.

Goodale, M.A. (1988). Hemispheric differences in motor control. *Behavioral Brain Research,* **30**, 203-214.

Gould, S.J. (1976). Grades and clades revisited. In R. Masterson, W. Hodos, & H. Jerison (Eds.), *Evolution, brain and behavior: Persistent problems* (pp. 115-122). Hillsdale, NJ: Lawrence Erlbaum Associates.

Gould, S.J. (1977). *Ontogeny and phylogeny.* Cambridge, MA: Belknap.

Greenough, W.T. (1989). On detecting asynchronies in brain development: Interpretations of morphological data. *Cahiers de Psychologie Cognitive,* **9**, 77-79.

Gur, R., Packer, I., Hungerbuhler, J., Reivich, M., Obrist, W., Amarnek, W., & Sackeim, H. (1980). Differences in the distribution of gray and white matter in human cerebral hemispheres. *Science,* **207**, 1226-1228.

Haaland, K.Y., & Harrington, D.L. (1989a). Hemispheric control of the initial and corrective components of aiming movements. *Neuropsychologia,* **27**, 961-969.

Haaland, K.Y., & Harrington, D.L. (1989b). The role of the hemispheres in closed loop movements. *Brain and Cognition*, **9**, 158-180.

Harris, L.J., & Carlson, D.F. (1988). Pathological left-handedness: An analysis of theories and evidence. In D.L. Molfese & S.J. Segalowitz (Eds.), *Brain lateralization in children: Developmental implications* (pp. 289-372). New York: Guilford Press.

Hauert, C.-A. (1990). Developmental psychology: A brief inventory of fixtures. In C.-A. Hauert (Ed.), *Developmental psychology: Cognitive, perceptuo-motor and neuropsychological perspectives* (pp. 417-441). Amsterdam: North Holland.

Healey, J.M., Liederman, J., & Geschwind, N. (1986). Handedness is not a unidimensional trait. *Cortex*, **22**, 33-53.

Heaton, R.K. (1981). *Wisconsin Card Sorting Test Manual.* Odessa, FL: Psychological Assessment Resources.

Heilman, K.M., Schwartz, H.D., & Watson, R.T. (1978). Hypoarousal in patients with the neglect syndrome and emotional indifference. *Neurology*, **28**, 229-231.

Hermann, B.P., Wyler, A.R., & Richey, E.T. (1988). Wisconsin Card Sorting Test performance in patients with complex partial seizures of temporal-lobe origin. *Journal of Clinical and Experimental Neuropsychology*, **10**, 467-476.

Hoerster, W., & Ettlinger, G. (1985). An association between hand preference and tactile discrimination performance in the rhesus monkey. *Neuropsychologia*, **23**, 411-413.

von Hofsten, C. (1982). Eye-hand coordination in the newborn. *Developmental Psychology*, **18**, 450-461.

Hopkins, B., Lems, W., Janssen, B., & Butterworth, G. (1987). Postural and motor asymmetries in newlyborns. *Human Neurobiology*, **6**, 153-156.

Hopkins, W.D., Washburn, D.A., & Rumbaugh, D.M. (1989). Note on hand use in the manipulation of joysticks by rhesus monkeys (*Macaca mulatta*) and chimpanzees (*Pan troglodytes*). *Journal of Comparative Psychology*, **103**, 91-94.

Ingram, D. (1975). Motor asymmetries in young children. *Neuropsychologia*, **13**, 95-102.

Jones-Gotman, M., & Milner, B. (1977). Design fluency: The invention of nonsense drawings after focal cortical lesions. *Neuropsychologia*, **15**, 653-674.

Kamptner, N.L., Cornwell, K.S., Fitzgerald, H.E., & Harris, L.J. (1985). Motor asymmetries in the human infant: Stepping movements. *Infant Mental Health Journal*, **6**, 145-156.

Karniol, R. (1989). The role of manual manipulative stages in the infant's acquisition of perceived control over objects. *Developmental Review*, **9**, 205-233.

Kelly, C.A., & Dale, P.S. (1989). Cognitive skills associated with the onset of multiword utterances. *Journal of Speech and Hearing Research*, **32**, 645-656.

Kershner, J.R. (1985). Ontogeny of hemispheric specialization and relationship of developmental patterns to complex reasoning skills and academic achievement. In C.T. Best (Ed.), *Hemispheric function and collaboration in the child* (pp. 327-360). Orlando, FL: Academic Press.

Kimura, D. (1982). Left-hemisphere control of oral and brachial movements and their relation to communication. *Philosophical Transactions of the Royal Society*, **B298**, 135-149.

Kimura, D., & Archibald, Y. (1974). Motor functions of the left hemisphere. *Brain*, **97**, 337-350.

Kimura, D., & Watson, N. (1989). The relation between oral movement control and speech. *Brain and Language*, **37**, 565-590.

Kinsbourne, M. (1974). Mechanisms of hemispheric interaction in man. In M. Kinsbourne & W. Smith (Eds.), *Hemispheric disconnection and cerebral function* (pp. 260-285). Springfield, IL: Charles C Thomas.

Kinsbourne, M. (1988). Sinistrality, brain organization, and cognitive deficits. In D.L. Molfese & S.J. Segalowitz (Eds.), *Brain lateralization in children: Developmental implications* (pp. 259-280). New York: Guilford Press.

Kinsbourne, M., & Hiscock, M. (1987). Language lateralization and disordered language development. In S. Rosenberg (Ed.), *Advances in applied psycholinguistics, Vol. 1: Disorders of first language development* (pp. 220-263). New York: Cambridge University Press.

Kooistra, C.A., & Heilman, K.M. (1988). Motor dominance and lateral asymmetry of the globus pallidus. *Neurology*, **38**, 388-390.

Kosslyn, S.M. (1988). Aspects of a cognitive neuroscience of mental imagery. *Science*, **240**, 1621-1626.

Kuhl, P.K. (1988). On handedness in primates and human infants. *Behavioral and Brain Sciences*, **11**, 727-729.

Lazarus, J.C., & Todor, J.I. (1987). Age differences in the magnitude of associated movement. *Developmental Medicine and Child Neurology*, **29**, 726-733.

Leboyer, M., Osherson, D.N., Nosten, M., & Roubertoux, P. (1988). Is autism associated with anomalous dominance? *Journal of Autism and Developmental Disorders*, **18**, 539-548.

Lee, G.P., Loring, D.W., Meador, K.J., Flanigin, H.F., & Brooks, B.S. (1988). Severe behavioral complications following intracarotid sodium amobarbital injection: Implications for hemispheric asymmetry of emotion. *Neurology*, **38**, 1233-1236.

Levander, M., Schalling, D., & Levander, S.E. (1989). Birth stress, handedness and cognitive performance. *Cortex*, **25**, 673-681.

Levy, J. (1983). Commentary on Flor-Henry, 1983. *Integrative Psychiatry*, **4**, 52-53.

Levy, J., Heller, W., Banich, M.T., & Burton, L.A. (1983). Are variations among right-handed individuals in perceptual asymmetries caused by characteristic arousal differences between hemispheres? *Journal of Experimental Psychology: Human Perception and Performance*, **9**, 329-359.

Lieberman, P. (1984). *The biology and evolution of language*. Cambridge, MA: Harvard University Press.

Liederman, J. (1983). Mechanisms underlying instability in the development of hand preference. In G. Young, S.J. Segalowitz, C.M. Corter, & S.E. Trehub (Eds.), *Manual specialization and the developing brain* (pp. 71-92). New York: Academic Press.

Liederman, J., & Coryell, J. (1982). The origin of left hand preference: Pathological and non-pathological influences. *Neuropsychologia*, **20**, 721-725.

Liederman, J., & Healey, J.M. (1987). Independent dimensions of hand preference: Reliability of the factor structure and the handedness inventory. *Archives of Clinical Neuropsychology*, **1**, 371-386.

Luria, A.R. (1966). Higher cortical functions in man (B. Haigh, Trans.). New York: Basic Books. (Original work published 1962)

MacNeilage, P.F., Studdert-Kennedy, M.G., & Lindblom, B. (1987). Primate handedness reconsidered. *Behavioral and Brain Sciences*, **10**, 247-263.

MacNeilage, P.F., Studdert-Kennedy, M.G., & Lindblom, B. (1988). Primate handedness: A foot in the door. *Behavioral and Brain Sciences*, **11**, 737-746.

Mateer, C. (1978). Impairments of nonverbal oral movements after left hemisphere damage: A follow-up analysis of errors. *Brain and Language*, **6**, 334-341.

McDonnell, P.M., Anderson, V., & Abraham, W. (1983). Asymmetry and orientation of arm movements in three- to eight-week-old infants. *Infant Behavior and Development*, **6**, 287-298.

McDonnell, P.M., Corkum, V.L., & Wilson, D.L. (1989). Patterns of movement in the first 6 months of life: New directions. *Canadian Journal of Psychology*, **43**, 320-339.

McManus, I.C. (1981). Handedness and birth stress. *Psychological Medicine*, 11, 485-496.

Michel, G. (1988). A neuropsychological perspective on infant sensorimotor development. In C. Rovee-Collier & L. Lipsett (Eds.), *Advances in infancy research, Vol. 5* (pp. 1-37). Norwood, NJ: Ablex.

Michel, G., & Goodwin, R. (1979). Intrauterine birth position predicts newborn supine head position preferences. *Infant Behavior and Development*, **2**, 29-38.

Milner, B. (1963). Effects of different brain lesions on card sorting. The role of the frontal lobes. *Archives of Neurology*, **9**, 90-100.

Molfese, V., & Betz, J. (1987). Language and motor development in infancy: Three views with neuropsychological implications. *Developmental Neuropsychology*, **3**, 255-274.

Mounoud, P. (1986). Similarities between developmental sequences at different age periods. In I. Levin (Ed.), *Stage and structure* (pp. 40-58). Norwood, NJ: Ablex.

Mount, R., Reznick, J.S., Kagan, J., Hiatt, S., & Szpak, M. (1989). Direction of gaze and emergence of speech in the second year. *Brain and Language*, **36**, 406-410.

Noterdaeme, M., Amorosa, H., Ploog, M., & Scheimann, G. (1988). Quantitative and qualitative aspects of associated movements in children with specific developmental speech and language disorders and in normal pre-school children. *Journal of Human Movement Studies*, **15**, 151-169.

O'Callaghan, M.J., Tudehope, D.I., Dugdale, A.E., Mohay, H., Burns, Y., & Cook, F. (1987). Handedness in children with birthweights below 1000 g. *Lancet*, **1**, 1155.

Ottaviano, S., Guidetti, V., Allemand, F., Spinetoli, B., & Seri, S. (1989). Laterality of arm movement in full-term newborn. *Early Human Development*, **19**, 3-7.

Parlow, S.E. (1990). Asymmetrical movement overflow in children depends on handedness and task characteristics. *Journal of Clinical and Experimental Neuropsychology*, **12**, 270-280.

Pascuale-Leone, J., & Johnson, J. (in press). Psychological unit and its role in task analysis: reinterpretation of object permanence. In M. Chandler & M. Chapman (Eds.), *Criteria for competence: Controversies in the assessment of children's abilities*. Hillsdale, NJ: Lawrence Erlbaum Associates.

Pietro, M.J.S., & Rigrodsky, S. (1986). Patterns of oral-verbal perseveration in adult aphasics. *Brain and Language*, **29**, 1-17.

Pizzamiglio, L., Caltagirone, C., Mammucari, A., Ekman, P., & Friesen, W. (1987). Imitation of facial movements in brain damaged patients. *Cortex*, **23**, 207-221.

Prather, P., Gardner, H., & Brownell, H.H. (1989). Providing an anchor for neurolinguistic processing: Should the right hemisphere step forward? A response to Cook. *New Ideas in Psychology*, **7**, 19-25.

Preilowski, B. (1975). Bilateral motor interaction: Perceptual motor performance of partial and complete 'split brain' patients. In K. Zulch, O. Creutzfeldt, & G. Galbraith (Eds.), *Cerebral localization* (pp. 115-132). Berlin: Springer.

Ramsay, D.S. (1984). Onset of duplicated syllable babbling and unimanual handedness in infancy: Evidence for developmental change in hemispheric specialization? *Developmental Psychology*, **20**, 64-71.

Ramsay, D.S., & Weber, S.L. (1986). Infants' hand preferences in a task involving complementary roles for the two hands. *Child Development*, **57**, 300-307.

Richards, F.A., & Commons, M.L. (1984). Systematic, metasystematic, and cross-paradigmatic reasoning: A case for stages of reasoning beyond formal operations. In M.L. Commons, F.A. Richards, & C. Armon (Eds.), *Beyond formal operations: Late adolescent and adult cognitive development* (pp. 92-119). New York: Praeger.

Richards, G. (1989). Human behavioral evolution: A physiomorphic model. *Current Anthropology*, **30**, 244-255.

Rinn, W.E. (1984). The neuropsychology of facial expression: A review of the neurological and psychological mechanisms for producing facial expressions. *Psychological Bulletin*, **95**, 52-77.

Robinson, A.L., Heaton, R.K., Lehman, R.A.W., & Stilson, D.W. (1980). The utility of the Wisconsin Card Sorting Test in detecting and localizing frontal lobe lesions. *Journal of Consulting and Clinical Psychology*, **48**, 605-614.

Robinson, R.G., Kubos, K.L., Starr, L., Rao, K., & Price, T.R. (1984). Mood disorders in stroke patients: Importance of location of lesion. *Brain*, **107**, 81-93.

Rochat, P. (1989). Object manipulation and exploration in 2- to 5-month-old infants. *Developmental Psychology*, **25**, 871-884.

Rothbart, M.K., Taylor, S.B., & Tucker, D.M. (1989). Right-sided facial asymmetry in infant emotional expression. *Neuropsychologia*, **27**, 675-687.

Roy, E.A., & Elliott, D. (1989). Manual asymmetries in aimed movements. *Quarterly Journal of Experimental Psychology*, **41A**, 501-516.

Saling, M. (1982). *Determinants of lateral organization in neonates*. Unpublished doctoral dissertation, University of Witwatersrand, Johannesburg, South Africa.

Saling, M. (1983). Familial handedness, prenatal environmental adversity, and neonatal lateral organization. In G. Young, S.J. Segalowitz, C.M. Corter, & S.E. Trehub (Eds.), *Manual specialization and the developing brain* (pp. 275-284). New York: Academic Press.

Sandson, J., & Albert, M.L. (1984). Varieties of perseveration. *Neuropsychologia*, **22**, 715-732.

Schiff, B.B., & Lamon, M. (1989). Inducing emotion by unilateral contraction of facial muscles: A new look at hemispheric specialization and the experience of emotion. *Neuropsychologia*, **27**, 923-935.

de Schonen, S., & Mathivet, E. (1989). First come, first served: A scenario about the development of hemispheric specialization in face recognition during infancy. *Cahiers de Psychologie Cognitive*, **9**, 3-44.

de Schonen, S., Mathivet, E., & Deruelle, C. (1989). A timing puzzle. *Cahiers de Psychologie Cognitive*, **9**, 147-161.

Schumacher, R.E., Barks, J.D.E. Johnston, M.V., Donn, S.M., Scher, M.S., Roloff, D.W., & Bartlett, R.H. (1988). Right-sided brain lesions in infants following extracorporeal membrane oxygenation. *Pediatrics*, **82**, 155-160.

Searleman, A., Coren, S., & Porac, C. (1989). Relationship between birth order, birth stress, and lateral preferences: A critical review. *Psychological Bulletin*, **105**, 397-408.

Segal, N.L. (1989). Origins and implications of handedness and relative birth weight for IQ in monozygotic twin pairs. *Neuropsychologia*, **27**, 549-561.

Shearer, S.L., & Tucker, D.M. (1981). Differential cognitive contributions of the cerebral hemispheres in the modulation of emotional arousal. *Cognitive Therapy and Research*, **5**, 85-93.

Simonds, R.J., & Scheibel, A.B. (1989). The postnatal development of the motor speech area: A preliminary study. *Brain and Language*, **37**, 42-58.

Sivak, B., & MacKenzie, C.L. (1989). Evidence for cerebral asymmetries in a finger sequencing task. *Brain and Cognition*, **9**, 109-122.

Springer, S.P., & Deutsch, G. (1989). *Left brain, right brain.* New York: Freeman.

Steenhuis, R.E., & Bryden, M.P. (1989). Different dimensions of hand preference that relate to skilled and unskilled activities. *Cortex*, **25**, 289-304.

Stout, J.L. (1987). Hemispheric specialization for motor function and hemiplegic cerebral palsy: Is there a difference in function between children with right and left hemiplegia? *Physical & Occupational Therapy in Pediatrics*, **7**, 53-65.

van Strien, J.W., Bouma, A., & Bakker, D.J. (1987). Birth stress, autoimmune diseases, and handedness. *Journal of Clinical and Experimental Neuropsychology*, **9**, 775-780.

Swenson, R.A., & Tucker, D.M. (1983). Lateralized cognitive style and self description. *International Journal of Neuroscience*, **21**, 91-100.

Taylor, D., Powell, R., Cherland, E., & Vaughan, C. (1988). Overflow movements and cognitive, motor and behavioral disturbance: A normative study of girls. *Developmental Medicine and Child Neurology*, **30**, 759-768.

Thatcher, R.W., Walker, R.A., & Giudice, S. (1987). Human cerebral hemispheres develop at different rates and ages. *Science*, **236**, 1110-1113.

Tobias, P.V. (1987). The brain of *Homo habilis*: A new level of organization in cerebral evolution. *Journal of Human Evolution*, **16**, 741-761.

Todor, J.I., & Lazarus, J.C. (1986). Exertion level and the intensity of associated movements. *Developmental Medicine and Child Neurology*, **28**, 205-212.

Toth, N. (1985). Archeological evidence for preferential right-handedness in the Lower and Middle Pleistocene, and its possible implications. *Journal of Human Evolution*, **14**, 607-614.

Trotman, S.C.A., & Hammond, G.R. (1989). Lateral asymmetry of the scalp distribution of somatosensory evoked potential amplitude. *Brain and Cognition*, **10**, 132-147.

Tucker, D.M. (1987). Neural control of emotional communication. In D. Blanck, R. Buck, & R. Rosenthal (Eds.), *Nonverbal communication in the clinical context* (pp. 258-301). New York: Pennsylvania State University Press.

Tucker, D.M., Antes, J.R., Stenslie, C.E., & Barnhardt, T.M. (1978). Anxiety and lateral cerebral function. *Journal of Abnormal Psychology*, **87**, 380-383.

Tucker, D.M., & Frederick, S.L. (1989). Emotion and brain lateralization. In H. Wagner & A. Manstead (Eds.), *Handbook of social psychophysiology* (pp. 27-70). New York: John Wiley & Sons.

Tucker, D.M., & Newman, J.P. (1981). Verbal versus imaginal cognitive strategies in the inhibition of emotional arousal. *Cognitive Therapy and Research*, **5**, 197-202.

Tucker, D.M., & Williamson, P.A. (1984). Asymmetric neural control systems in human self-regulation. *Psychological Review*, **91**, 185-215.

Vauclair, J., & Fagot, J. (in press). Manual specialization in gorillas and baboons. In J. Ward (Ed.), *Current behavioral evidence of primate asymmetries*. New York: Springer Verlag.

Vilkki, J. (1989). Perseveration of memory for figures after frontal lobe lesion. *Neuropsychologia*, **8**, 1101-1104.

Vingiano, W. (1989). Hemisphericity and personality. *International Journal of Neuroscience*, **44**, 263-274.

Wada, J., Clarke, R., & Hamm, A. (1975). Cerebral hemispheric asymmetry in humans. *Archives of Neurology*, **32**, 239-246.

Wallace, R. (1989). Cognitive mapping and the origin of language and mind. *Current Anthropology*, **30**, 518-526.

Walch, J.-P., & Blanc-Garin, J. (1989). Spatial performance and perceptual asymmetries in beginning readers: Shift of hand advantage in dichhaptic tasks. *Brain and Cognition*, **10**, 1-17.

Witelson, S.F., & Kigar, D.L., (1988). Anatomical development of the corpus callosum in humans: A review with reference to sex and cognition. In D.L. Molfese & S.J. Segalowitz (Eds.), *Brain lateralization in children: Developmental implications* (pp. 35-58). New York: Guilford Press.

Witelson, S.F., & Pallie, W. (1973). Left hemisphere specialization for language in the newborn: Neuroanatomical evidence of asymmetry. *Brain*, **96**, 641-646.

Wolf, M.E., & Goodale, M.A. (1987). Oral asymmetries during verbal and non-verbal movements of the mouth. *Neuropsychologia*, **25**, 375-396.

Young, G. (1990). Early neuropsychological development: Lateralization of functions - hemispheric specialization. In C.-A. Hauert (Ed.), *Developmental psychology: Cognitive, perceptuo-motor and neuropsychological perspectives* (pp. 113-181). Amsterdam: North Holland.

Young, G., & Bowman, J.G. (1989, July). *Laterality of gestural imitation in toddlers.* Paper presented at the First International Conference on Action Memory, Toronto, Ontario.

Young, G., Bowman, J.G., Methot, C., Finlayson, M., Quintal J., & Boissonneault, P. (1983). Hemispheric specialization development: What (inhibition) and how (parents). In G. Young, S.J. Segalowitz, C.M. Corter, & S.E. Trehub (Eds.), *Manual specialization and the developing brain* (pp. 119-140). New York: Academic Press.

Young, G., Corter, C.M., Segalowitz, S.J., & Trehub, S.E. (1983). Manual specialization development and the developing brain: An overview. In G. Young, S.J. Segalowitz, C.M. Corter, & S.E. Trehub (Eds.), *Manual specialization and the developing brain* (pp. 3-12). New York: Academic Press.

Young, G., & Gagnon, M. (1990). Neonatal laterality, birth stress, familial sinistrality, and left brain inhibition. *Developmental Neuropsychology*, **6**, 127-150.

Young, G., Segalowitz, S.J., Misek, P., Alp, I.E., & Boulet, R. (1983). Is early reaching left-handed? Review of manual specialization research. In G. Young, S.J. Segalowitz, C.M. Corter, & S.E. Trehub (Eds.), *Manual specialization and the developing brain* (pp. 13-32). New York: Academic Press.

Cerebral Control of Speech and Limb Movements
G.E. Hammond (editor)

Chapter 5

DISORDERS OF MOTOR FUNCTION FOLLOWING CORTICAL LESIONS: REVIEW AND THEORETICAL CONSIDERATIONS

Gregor W. Jason
Foothills Hospital and University of Calgary

Cerebral cortical mechanisms for limb praxis are reviewed, with an emphasis on lesion studies of humans and monkeys. There are multiple components in the cortical control of motor behavior. Prefrontal cortex is important for the direction of behavior when environmental demands are somewhat ambiguous. There are bifrontal and contralateral frontal and parietal mechanisms for the execution and exact control of movements. Premotor cortex and the supplementary motor area each appear to be involved in movement coordination as well as in the selection of movements. There is also a system for the bihemispheric integration of behavior, which involves at least the supplementary motor area and corpus callosum. In humans, there are left-hemispheric processes for the generation of specific movements from memory. Evidence supports the view that the human and monkey brain are organized very similarly, although published research has not addressed the issue of hemispheric specialization for motor tasks in the monkey.

In this chapter I shall provide an overview of cerebral cortical mechanisms for limb praxis. The emphasis will be almost entirely on cortical areas other than primary motor cortex. I shall attempt to integrate findings from research with both humans and monkeys, and in doing so will first consider anatomical divisions of the cortex, focusing largely on the effects of focal cortical lesions. This is primarily because focal cortical lesions provide a common ground for comparison of work on humans and monkeys, but also because of limitations in the amount of material which can be reviewed in the chapter.

Figure 1 illustrates areas of monkey and human cortex which will be discussed in the text.

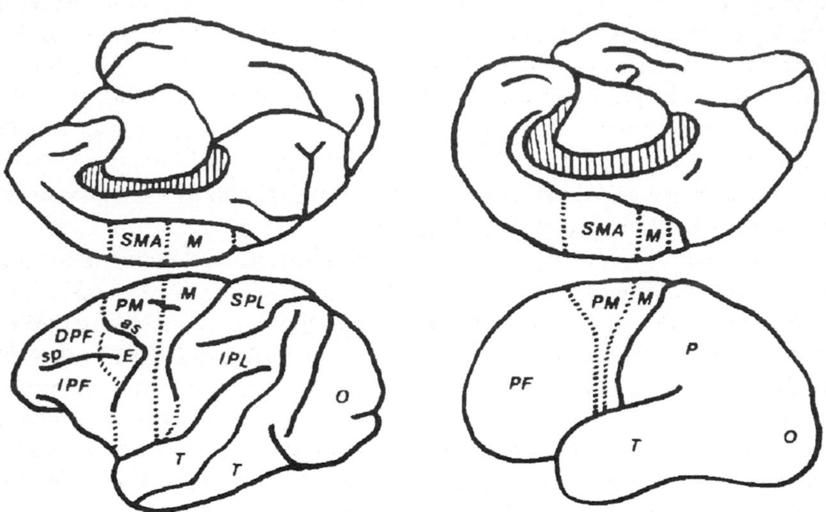

Figure 1. Lateral and medial views of the cerebral cortex of monkey (*Macaca mulatta*) and human. Exact boundaries of premotor cortex and the supplementary motor area vary from source to source (cf. Fuster, 1981; Wiesendanger, 1986). There is also functional and neuroanatomic evidence that monkey premotor cortex dorsal to the bow of the arcuate sulcus is different from that ventral to the bow (Pandya & Barbas, 1985; Rizzolatti, 1987).

PF - Prefrontal; DPF - Dorsal Prefrontal; IPF - Inferior Prefrontal; E - Frontal Eye Fields; PM - Premotor Cortex; SMA - Supplementary Motor Area; M - Primary Motor Cortex; P - Parietal Lobe; SPL - Superior Parietal Lobule; IPL - Inferior Parietal Lobule; T - Temporal Lobe; O - Occipital Lobe; sp - sulcus principalis; as - arcuate sulcus

Parietal Lobes

One source of evidence for a role of the parietal lobes in praxis is the clinical literature on ideomotor apraxia. Ideomotor apraxia has usually been assessed by asking patients to demonstrate meaningful movements such as waving goodbye or brushing their teeth, either in response to verbal command or by imitation. Geschwind (1965, 1975) elaborated a model in which the left parietal lobe (including Wernicke's area) played an important role in the genesis of movements in response to verbal commands and by imitation. Heilman (1979) proposed that the left parietal lobe is the site of visuokinetic motor engrams, which are involved in programming motor association cortex as to what movements are necessary, and reported that apraxic patients with left-parietal lesions had difficulty learning lists of gestures because of an inability to consolidate the information in memory (Gonzalez-Rothi & Heilman, 1984). Kertesz and Ferro (1984) reviewed the CT scans of 177 patients with left-hemispheric stroke who had been examined on a test of ideomotor apraxia. Their findings provided only partial support for a role of parietal cortex itself, in that lesions of deep parietofrontal and occipitofrontal fibers seemed to be more important than parietal cortex *per se*.

Ideational apraxia is assessed by presenting patients with actual objects and asking them to demonstrate their correct use. Some investigators have argued that the critical deficit in ideational apraxia is a problem with ordering actions (Hécaen, 1978; Lehmkuhl & Poeck, 1981), but detailed analysis of the errors made has not borne out this interpretation (Jason, 1983a; De Renzi & Lucchelli, 1988). Jason (1983a) and De Renzi and Lucchelli (1988) argued instead that the deficit was one involving defective memory for the actions. De Renzi and Lucchelli found that ideational apraxia was frequently associated with damage to the left posterior temporoparietal junction.

Some investigators have taken the approach of demonstrating complex non-meaningful limb movements to patients, and asking them to reproduce the movements. Kimura (1982) and De Renzi, Faglioni, Lodesani, and Vecchi (1983) both found deficits after left-parietal lesions, primarily of vascular origin. Kolb and Milner (1981) examined patients with surgical excisions for the control of epilepsy, and also found deficits after left-parietal lesions.

One role of the parietal lobes in motor function is the visuospatial guidance of movements. Thus, misreaching is found after bilateral parietal lesions in humans (Holmes, 1918; Ratcliff & Davies-Jones, 1972; Rondot, De Recondo, & Ribadeau Dumas, 1977; Damasio & Benton, 1979; Hausser, Robert, & Giard, 1980) and monkeys (Ettlinger & Kalsbeck, 1962; Deuel, 1977; Faugier-Grimaud, Frenois, & Stein, 1978). After unilateral lesions in monkeys, most investigators have found that only the contralateral limb misreaches (Ettlinger & Kalsbeck, 1962; Hartje & Ettlinger, 1973; Faugier-Grimaud, Frenois, & Stein, 1978; Lamotte & Acuna, 1978; Deuel & Regan, 1985), although Stein (1976) found that cooling parietal area 7 unilaterally did affect reaching of the ipsilateral arm in the contralateral visual field. Other effects include abnormal shaping of the hand while approaching the target (Faugier-Grimaud, Frenois & Stein, 1978; Deuel & Regan, 1985). Results from human work have been more complex, with effects of visual field as well as hand (Cole, Schutta, & Warrington, 1962; Ratcliff & Davies-Jones, 1972; Boller, Cole, Kim, Mack, & Patawaran, 1975; Rondot et al., 1977; Levine, Kaufman, & Mohr, 1978; Perenin & Vighetto, 1983). Unilateral disconnection of parietal cortex from geniculostriate visual input causes monkeys to misreach with the contralateral hand (Jason, 1983b). The evidence thus supports the importance of intrahemispheric parietofrontal pathways in accurate reaching of the contralateral hand.

There is another way in which the parietal lobe is involved in the visual direction of movement. Halsband and Passingham (1982) found that monkeys with bilateral lesions of the superior parietal lobule were very impaired on a task in which a visual instruction (color of a panel) told the animal which of two movements to make (pull or rotate a handle). Here the problem was not with the coordination of the movement, but rather with the choice of which movement to make.

Somesthetic information from a limb has long been considered very important in the control of movements of that limb. With respect to the role of the parietal lobes in this, Freund (1987a) discussed the issue of whether deficits observed are solely due to the primary sensory deficits, or whether there is additional impairment of motor mechanisms. He commented that the degree of impairment of tactile exploration and prehension is often disproportionate in comparison to impairment in cutaneous sensibility, thus supporting the view that the motor deficits are not simply due to primary sensory impairment. Peripheral deafferentation of monkeys initially is very disruptive to limb movement, but there can be remarkable (albeit incomplete) recovery given time (Bossom, 1974; E. Taub, Goldberg, & P. Taub, 1975; Gilman, Carr, & Hollenberg, 1976). A peripherally deafferented man had a number of problems of motor control, including absence of automatic reflex correction, inability to sustain muscle contraction without visual feedback, and inability to maintain long sequences of simple acts without visual feedback; this disabled him for many uses of his hands in daily life (Rothwell, Traub, Day, Obeso, Thomas, & Marsden, 1982). Nevertheless, the patient could perform a number of other tasks even with his eyes closed, including touching his thumb to each of his fingers in turn, tapping, and outlining shapes in the air. Remarkably, he was even able to drive his old car at night (although he was unable to learn to drive his new car). Jeannerod, Michel, and Prablanc (1984) reported on a woman who suffered hemianesthesia following a unilateral parietal lesion not affecting primary motor cortex. Deficits in the contralateral hand were similar to the case of Rothwell et al. but she also was unable to touch her thumb to her other fingers without watching and could not draw figures in the air without watching. These additional problems of hers cannot be attributed simply to a more severe sensory deficit, since with visual control she was able to use her hand for tasks such as manipulating objects, eating, and writing, whereas the peripherally deafferented man could not. The sum of human and monkey evidence, therefore, indicates a role of parietal cortex in somatosensory guidance of movements which is not entirely attributable to primary sensory loss.

Temporal Lobes

Jason (1985b) demonstrated that left-temporal excisions for the control of epilepsy in human subjects impaired the ability to learn series of hand positions. First-trial performance was not affected, nor was delayed recall of positions which had already been learned: this suggests that the deficit was one of initial acquisition rather than perceptual encoding or retrieval from memory. The deficit was the same whether or not the positions had to be ordered.

Memory for motor acts in this sense may be considered an example of declarative memory (Cohen & Squire, 1980), in that subjects declare their knowledge by showing hand positions upon demand. A clear distinction should be made between this and procedural learning of motor skills, which is intact following medial temporal-lobe excisions (Corkin, 1968; Milner, 1972). Jason (1986) reinforced this distinction by demonstrating that the same patients who were impaired on the learning task described above were unimpaired in acquiring a motor skill involving rapidly copying the same types of hand positions. Similarly, monkeys with medial temporal-lobe excisions are not impaired on acquisition of motor skills (Zola-Morgan & Squire, 1984).

Petrides (1985) tested patients on a visuomotor conditional learning task in which the color of a stimulus informed the patients which of six hand postures to perform. Impairment was seen in patients with left-temporal surgical excisions including extensive resection of the hippocampus and parahippocampal gyrus. Hemispheric lateralization depended on the motor nature of the task (or verbal recoding) because the same patients were unimpaired when the response was spatial; in this case impairment was seen after right-temporal lesions with extensive hippocampal and parahippocampal gyrus removal.

Gaffan and Harrison (1988) tested monkeys on a similar visuomotor conditional task. They found that learning rate was impaired by unilateral inferotemporal ablation contralateral to the hand used, combined with transection of the anterior corpus callosum. They concluded that learning of this task required cortico-cortical interaction between the inferotemporal areas and the frontal lobe contralateral to the hand in use. The impairment was not a general impairment of visual learning, because the same animals learned a visual discrimination task normally.

Frontal Lobes

This section will initially review evidence from work with human subjects in which the nature of the lesions does not allow a clear distinction among the different areas comprising the frontal lobes, followed by discussions of prefrontal cortex, premotor cortex, and the supplementary motor area.

Kertesz and Ferro (1984), in their review of CT scans of people with left-hemispheric stroke who were studied for ideomotor apraxia, found that small lesions producing moderate or severe apraxia were mostly frontal and close to the body of the lateral ventricle. These lesions would have the effect of disconnecting the left-parietal and left-frontal lobes, thus supporting models of ideomotor apraxia stressing connections between these two areas (Geschwind, 1965, 1975; Heilman, 1979). Although the most common site of damage in De Renzi and Lucchelli's (1988) patients with ideational apraxia was the left temporoparietal junction, a number of their patients had lesions localized by CT scan to the left-frontal lobe.

People's ability to copy complex non-meaningful movements is also impaired after left-frontal lesions (Kolb & Milner, 1981; Kimura, 1982; De Renzi et al., 1983). With respect to the effects of right-frontal lesions, Kolb and Milner (1981) found that epileptic patients with right-frontal excisions were also impaired, whereas Kimura (1982) found that patients with right-frontal lesions of varied etiology were not.

The tasks just cited require the subject to perform the movements from memory, because the experimenter's model is no longer present when it is time for the subject to perform the movement. The movements are also complex enough to tax performance skills in addition to memory. Jason (1985b, 1986) dissected these components by devising two tasks. His Manual Sequence Learning task maximized memory demands (by requiring memory of a series of hand positions), but minimized performance demands (by using discrete hand positions and imposing no time limit). His Metronome-Paced Performance task maximized performance demands (by requiring the subjects to demonstrate hand positions one after another at an increasing rate), but minimized memory demands (by providing a constant model for the subjects to copy). Left- but not right-frontal surgical excisions (sparing primary motor cortex) resulted in impairment on the Manual Sequence Learning task. In contrast, excisions from either frontal lobe resulted in impairment on the Metronome-Paced Performance task. Interestingly, the latter impairment was present in both hands, suggesting ipsilateral as well as contralateral frontal-lobe involvement in manual performance. For both tasks, ordering demands were shown not to be important, because the same deficits were present whether the positions were ordered or not.

Canavan, Passingham, Marsden, Quinn, Wyke, and Polkey (1989) provided additional evidence for a role of the frontal lobes in memory for hand positions. Their patients with frontal-lobe lesions (of varying etiology and including some bilateral lesions) were impaired in reproducing sequences of three gestures from memory. They thought the 'sequencing' aspect of this test was critical because only a few errors were seen in control conditions involving only one gesture. Nevertheless, their data show the rate of errors in frontal-lobe patients on single gestures to be more than three times as high as any of the comparison groups (controls and patients with left- or right-temporal lesions). Additionally, seven of ten patients with frontal-lobe lesions made at least one error on a very simple test requiring reproduction of one familiar hand position after a delay of 10 sec in which the subject sat quietly. Only one of ten controls and one of ten patients with right-temporal lesions made such an error. Four of nine patients with left-temporal lesions made an error; as discussed above patients with left-temporal excisions are impaired at a manual learning task.

Leonard, Milner, and Jones (1988) demonstrated that patients with unilateral surgical excisions from either frontal lobe (sparing primary motor cortex) were impaired on a bimanual tapping task requiring coordination of different simultaneous movements of the two hands. They were also impaired with both hands on a unimanual sequential tapping task, but the authors could not demonstrate a differential impairment in the frontal-lobe groups compared to groups with unilateral temporal-lobe excisions.

Frontal-lobe lesions in humans may result in a decrease in spontaneous general activity (Hécaen, 1964; Hécaen & Albert, 1975; Luria, 1980), and patients with surgical excisions from the frontal lobes are impaired on a formal test of gesture fluency (Jason, 1985a). Left-frontal lesions produced impairment in the ability to generate novel finger positions, and left- or right-frontal lesions produced impairment in the ability to produce meaningful gestures.

Prefrontal Cortex

Some patients with inferior prefrontal lesions of either side have a compulsion to use objects which are presented to them without instructions (Lhermitte, 1983), or to imitate the examiner without instructions to do so (Lhermitte, Pillon, & Serdaru, 1986). These phenomena, termed 'utilization behavior' and 'imitation behavior', may have a parallel in the increased reactivity seen in monkeys with prefrontal lesions (Gross & Weiskrantz, 1964; Jacobsen, 1931).

It has been known for some time that prefrontal lesions in monkeys produce a marked deficit in delayed-response tasks (Jacobsen, 1936; see Fuster, 1981, for review). In one version, the animal is first shown a piece of food being placed under one of two objects. After a delay of some seconds in which the objects are out of reach, the animal is allowed to choose one object and retrieve the food if it is there. An important factor in demonstrating impairment after prefrontal lesions is that the choice must be made on the basis of memory of a recent event; there is no sensory information available at the time of response which can help in making the choice (Fuster, 1981; Goldman-Rakic, 1987).

The deficit also extends to conditions in which the animal must remember its own responses in order to avoid repeating them. Thus, Pinto-Hamuy and Linck (1965) and Passingham (1985a) found that prefrontal lesions in monkeys produced impairment on tasks in which the animal had to perform series of responses without repetition. Petrides and Milner (1982) found similar results in people with unilateral surgical excisions from the frontal lobes. Patients with left-frontal lesions were impaired regardless of the verbal or nonverbal nature of the stimuli; patients with right-frontal lesions were impaired only when the stimuli were nonverbal.

Passingham (1985a) showed that the deficit after prefrontal lesions in the tasks just described depended on memory, because if there was no delay the same animals were able to indicate which of two locations they had touched. This deficit was attributable to lesions in the sulcus principalis within prefrontal cortex. Passingham (1978) has also shown a role of a different area of prefrontal cortex (dorsal prefrontal convexity) in a different aspect of memory for movements. In this task, the animals had to tap a key until a light went out, and then repeat the same number of taps in order to receive a food reward. Combined lesions of the dorsal prefrontal convexity and sulcus principalis produced impairment on this task, whereas lesions of the sulcus principalis alone did not. The deficit was the same whether or not the monkeys were required to wait between the first and second sets of taps, but it should be noted that while the second set of taps was being made, the only information which the monkey had to help determine the number of taps was in memory.

The frontal eye field (corresponding largely to area 8) has been shown to be important in conditions where the animal must respond in different places at different times. Thus, Halsband (1987) found that lesions in this area produced impairment on a task in which monkeys had to respond to three different manipulanda in order. The deficit was not present on a very similar task requiring a sequence of three responses to one manipulandum, emphasizing the spatial rather than the sequential motor aspects of the task

(Halsband & Passingham, 1982). Deuel (1977) had earlier reported a similar deficit in animals in which the lesions encompassed both the frontal eye field and part of premotor cortex. Frontal eye field lesions also impair performance on a task in which a color cue tells an animal to which of two objects it should respond (Passingham, 1985b). Finally, Collin, Cowey, Latto, and Marzi (1982) reported that monkeys with frontal eye field lesions were deficient on a task requiring them to make a series of responses in different locations without repeating themselves. As already described, more anterior prefrontal lesions in the sulcus principalis also produce impairment on this task (Passingham, 1985b).

Goldman-Rakic (1987) has commented upon other aspects of the behavior of prefrontally lesioned people and monkeys: they are distractible (responding inappropriately to extraneous stimuli) and perseverative (inappropriately repeating previous responses). She theorized that the essence of prefrontal function was the regulation of behavior by internal models of reality. In the absence of such a regulatory function, delayed-response tasks are failed, people and animals respond to external stimuli rather than internal models (distractibility), and therefore they repeat the same responses when external stimuli stay the same but task requirements change (perseveration). These internal models of reality were thought to rely strongly on working memory (Goldman-Rakic, 1987).

Fuster (1981) proposed that the prefrontal lobes were important in the temporal organization of complex structures of behavior. This temporal organization involved anticipatory preparation for coming events, memory of recent events, and suppression of interference. His proposal and that of Goldman-Rakic are similar in that both emphasize memory and behavior which is responsive to internal processes rather than the sensory input of the moment.

Premotor Cortex

Deficits after premotor lesions appear to fall into two broad categories. One type of deficit has to do with the selection of movements under certain conditions; the other to do with movement coordination and with strength.

Passingham and Halsband, in a series of experiments, have demonstrated that premotor lesions in monkeys cause impairments in visuomotor conditional tasks in which 'contextual' cues tell the monkey which of two movements to make (Halsband & Passingham, 1982, 1985; Passingham 1985b, 1986, 1988). In the most recent paper, for example, monkeys with premotor lesions were unable to choose whether to pull or turn a handle according to the color of a panel immediately behind the handle (Passingham, 1988). Animals with similar lesions are able to decide which of two objects to choose in accordance with a color cue (Halsband &

Passingham, 1985; Passingham, 1985b). They are also able to perform the task if the manipulandum itself provides the cue as to which movement to make. This is true if the color of the handle provides the cue (Passingham, 1985b). It is also true if the cue is kinesthetic, and the type of movement possible with a manipulandum in one part of a trial tells the monkey which movement to perform in the next part of the trial (Passingham, 1986). Petrides (1982) also found that monkeys were impaired on a visuomotor conditional learning task after a lesion combining premotor cortex with the frontal eye field. It is interesting that the deficit is present even when the cue is still present at the time of response (Passingham, 1988), unlike the situation with prefrontal lesions which impaired delayed response tasks only when the cue was absent at the time of response.

Patients with unilateral surgical excisions of the frontal lobes are also impaired on a visuomotor conditional learning task (Petrides, 1985), although it was not possible to identify the critical area within the frontal lobes in this study. Perhaps because of the variability of lesion site, these findings did not depend upon the specific motor nature of the task: the same patients with frontal lesions were also impaired when the response was spatial rather than motor. A similar study of patients with more focal lesions, restricted to or sparing premotor cortex, will be necessary to provide results strictly comparable to the studies with monkeys.

An interesting deficit has been reported in animals with large unilateral lesions of the premotor cortex, supplementary motor area, and part of caudal prefrontal cortex (Moll & Kuypers, 1977). The monkeys were impaired when required to use their contralateral hand to reach around a transparent barrier for food; instead they tended to reach straight toward the food. More precise localization of the lesion responsible for the deficit was not accomplished but a large removal seemed necessary: the deficit was not there when arcuate cortex was spared, nor when it alone was lesioned.

Passingham (1987) argued that the premotor area directed actions on the basis of visual rather than proprioceptive cues. He pointed out that animals with lesions in this area could not learn visuomotor conditional tasks in which the cue is separate from the manipulandum, but performed normally on a proprioceptive-motor conditional task. Unfortunately, the type of cue (visual or proprioceptive) is confounded with the location of the cue (separate from the manipulandum or part of the manipulandum). The latter consideration may be crucial; monkeys with premotor lesions are not impaired if even a visual cue is part of the manipulandum (Passingham, 1985b). There is also indirect evidence against this proposal, in that a considerable proportion of single neurons within premotor cortex respond to proprioceptive input (cf. Wiesendanger, Hummelsheim, & Bianchetti,

1985), although Passingham (1987) has argued that this does not mean that proprioceptive information is used in selecting actions.

If Passingham is right, then perhaps proprioceptive input to the premotor area is used in actual coordination of the movement, rather than in selection of actions. Consistent with this notion is the finding that shortly after monkeys were given premotor lesions they were clumsy and showed less spontaneous movement (Deuel 1977; Passingham, 1985b). Although the monkeys improved considerably within two weeks postoperatively, a deficit remained on a demanding visually guided reaching task (Passingham, 1985b).

Poorly coordinated movements of the contralateral limb have also been reported in people with unilateral lesions of premotor cortex (Freund & Hummelsheim, 1985; Freund, 1987b). The deficit was greatest when the patients were required to coordinate movements of the two sides, and there was some evidence of a topographic organization in which high premotor lesions affected mainly proximal movements and low premotor lesions affected more distal movements (Freund, 1987b).

Freund and Hummelsheim (1985) reported that unilateral premotor lesions produced contralateral weakness of proximal muscles. Leonard, Jones, and Milner (1988) found that some people with unilateral surgical excisions from the frontal lobe, sparing primary motor cortex, had residual loss of grip strength. Although the lesions were rather variable in location, the authors hypothesized that premotor involvement was responsible for the deficits observed.

It is interesting to note that in the study by Leonard et al. (1988), women with left-frontal excisions were weak with both hands. This pattern was not present in all patient groups (the men with left-frontal excisions were normal with both hands, and men and women with right-frontal excisions were weak with the contralateral hand), but it is reminiscent of Jason's (1986) finding that unilateral frontal-lobe excisions produced impairment in either hand on a speeded manual performance task.

There is additional evidence for premotor involvement in ipsilateral as well as contralateral movements. Roland, Skinhøj, Lassen, and Larsen (1980; Roland 1984) recorded regional cerebral blood flow in people performing a variety of unimanual tasks. They found that there was bilateral increase in blood flow to the premotor cortex under conditions when a new motor program was being established, or when a previously learned motor program was being modulated. An example of such a task was when the subjects moved their index finger around a maze in accordance to verbal commands given for each move. In monkeys, bilateral cooling of premotor cortex interrupted reaction-time movements more than unilateral cooling contralateral to the hand being used (Sasaki &

Gemba, 1986). In addition, neurons in premotor cortex in monkeys may fire selectively before ipsilateral, contralateral, or bilateral movements (Rizzolatti, Gentilucci, Fogassi, Luppino, Matelli, & Ponzoni-Maggi, 1987; Tanji 1987; Tanji, Okano, & Sato, 1987). Rizzolatti (1987; Rizzolatti et al., 1987) has shown that some neurons in inferior premotor cortex discharge only in relation with certain motor acts, and described 'grasping-with-the-hand' neurons, 'grasping-with-the-hand-and-mouth' neurons, 'holding' neurons, and 'tearing' neurons. He suggested that this area contains a 'vocabulary' of motor acts related to hand-mouth movements.

Supplementary Motor Area

The structure and function of the supplementary motor area (SMA) have been the focus of a considerable number of research papers, and two thorough reviews have appeared in recent years (Goldberg, 1985; Wiesendanger, 1986). These reviews cover a wider range of topics in more detail than is possible here. As with premotor cortex, the effects of SMA lesions can be divided broadly into impairment of movement selection and impairment of movement coordination.

Brinkman (1984a) reported that after unilateral SMA lesions in monkeys, a deficit appeared in a task requiring one hand to do one thing (push on a currant with the index finger) while the other hand did another thing (catch or retrieve the currant). She found that the hand contralateral to the lesion tended to behave similarly to the other hand, thus interfering with efficient task performance. Remarkably, subsequent transection of the corpus callosum immediately abolished the deficit. Furthermore, bilateral SMA lesions did not produce this deficit (Brinkman, 1984b). She interpreted her results as implying that the SMA normally gives rise to discharges informing the contralateral hemisphere of intended and/or ongoing movements. Goldberg (1985) suggested instead that after unilateral SMA lesion the remaining SMA dominated control of both limbs through projections to primary motor cortex of both hemispheres, thus increasing the tendency for mirror movements. Cutting the corpus callosum released motor cortex in the lesioned hemisphere from control of the contralateral SMA, with the result that mirror movements no longer were evident.

Chan and Ross (1988) reported similar findings in a patient with lesion of the right SMA but without a lesion of the corpus callosum. This Chinese patient made mirror image characters when writing with the left hand, and also made mirror movements during certain other movements such as demonstrating how to drive a car, or eating with both hands.

Other investigators have reported instances of intermanual conflict after unilateral SMA lesions (Goldberg, Mayer, & Toglia, 1981; Goldenberg,

Wimmer, Holzner & Wessely, 1981; McNabb, Carroll, & Mastaglia, 1988). The deficit in these patients was different from Chan and Ross's patient, or Brinkman's monkeys, in that the conflicting acts were not mirror movements, but instead could be well-coordinated acts with conflicting purposes. This is illustrated well by one of the patients studied by Goldberg et al., whose right hand came up to keep her glasses on after the left hand started to remove them: here, mirror movements would have helped rather than hindered. Part of the explanation may lie in the possibility that these patients had corpus callosal damage in addition to their SMA lesions. Intermanual conflict has also been reported after callosal lesions (see below). Callosal damage cannot entirely account for the findings, however, since in right-handed patients with SMA damage the conflicting acts were seen in the contralateral hand regardless of side whereas in right-handed patients with callosal damage the conflicting acts were always seen in the left hand.

Ideomotor apraxia was reported after left-SMA lesions in two patients (Watson, Fleet, Gonzalez-Rothi, & Heilman, 1986). The apraxia affected both limbs, and was restricted to transitive movements with sparing of intransitive movements.

Monkeys with bilateral SMA lesions were impaired on the ability to learn a series of three movements (Halsband, 1987). This same task was performed normally by animals with bilateral premotor lesions (Halsband & Passingham, 1982).

SMA lesions may result in a lack of spontaneous movements (Meador, Watson, Bowers, & Heilman, 1986). A contralateral 'grasp reflex' has been reported (Penfield & Welch, 1951; Gelmers, 1983), but the 'reflex' nature of this behavior is unclear since patients may actually reach out to grasp something rather than just grasp it when it is placed in their palm (Goldberg et al., 1981; Gelmers, 1983). Motor perseveration has also been reported (Goldberg et al., 1981; Gelmers, 1983).

The deficits described above may all be characterized as a failure to select the appropriate movement in certain circumstances. Other deficits after SMA lesions seem more to involve coordination or accurate execution of movements which otherwise are appropriate. Thus, an immediate effect of SMA ablation in monkeys is transient clumsiness of the contralateral hand (Brinkman, 1984a). Additionally, there is a lasting deficit in the ability to reach to a target zone in the dark after bilateral SMA lesions; the monkeys initiated reaching properly but were inaccurate (Passingham, 1987). Movements of the left limb in a man with a right-SMA lesion were slow and of inadequate extent (Meador et al., 1986). Dick, Benecke, Rothwell, Day, and Marsden (1986) reported that a right-SMA lesion disrupted coordination when more than one movement was performed, either simultaneously or sequentially. Both arms were affected, although the contralateral one was affected the most.

A study of regional cerebral blood flow in humans by Roland, Larsen, Lassen, and Skinhøj (1980) was very influential in establishing the idea that the SMA played an important role in programming movements. They found that blood flow was increased bilaterally to the SMA during a complex task performed with one hand (sequential finger tapping), but not simpler tasks (repetitive flexion or isometric contraction of finger and thumb). Actual execution of the complex task was not required: an increase in blood flow to the SMA was seen even when the subjects imagined doing the task. Further work, reviewed by Roland (1984), showed that a number of other voluntary movements similarly activated the SMA, and that activation was always bilateral. Consistent with this is the finding that SMA neurons in the monkey may fire before ipsilateral, contralateral, or bilateral movements (Tanji, 1987; Tanji et al., 1987).

Goldberg (1985) has proposed that the SMA is part of a medial system which is crucial in the programming and fluent execution of movements on the basis of internal models of reality. He hypothesized that there are two stages in the microgenesis of movement, each stage being a loop consisting of a number of cortical and subcortical structures. The first stage involves the selection of a context-appropriate behavioral strategy, and the second involves the specification of the details required to execute the action. In his model, the SMA plays a critical role in the transition from the first to the second stage, in that it is the final step in processing in the first stage and the origin of activity in the second. His proposal fits well with the observations that SMA lesions can impair both the selection and coordination of movements. These observations are also consistent with the suggestion of Wiesendanger (1986) that the SMA exerts a double control. The 'low-level' control, in his formulation, depends on direct projections of the SMA to the spinal cord and acts to set appropriate excitability levels of spinal circuits in preparation for voluntary movements. The 'high-level' control was deliberately not precisely defined, but referred to processes involved in the initiation of voluntary movements.

Corpus Callosum

A commonly recognized consequence of callosal transection is an inability of the left hand to demonstrate some act in response to verbal command (Bogen, 1985); this is usually interpreted as being a result of disconnecting the right hemisphere from the language areas of the left hemisphere. In a similar fashion, if the examiner places one hand of the patient in a particular position (screened from sight), the patient cannot demonstrate that position with the other hand (Bogen, 1985). The failure is observed regardless of which hand is performing, and the patient can copy the single positions with either hand if allowed to see them, and therefore the deficit is interpreted as being due to failure of interhemispheric transfer of proprioceptive information.

Lesions of the corpus callosum may disrupt the ability to execute bimanual coordination tasks smoothly in both humans (Preilowski, 1972; Zaidel & Sperry, 1977) and monkeys (Trevarthen, 1978). A need for callosally mediated interhemispheric integration may not be surprising for bimanual tasks, but it also is necessary for complex unimanual tasks. Thus, Milner and Kolb (1985) found that patients with surgical transection of the corpus callosum were impaired in the ability to copy complex unimanual movements with either hand. They also noted that patients with anterior callosal transection were as impaired as those with complete transection, suggesting that the disconnection between the frontal lobes was responsible for the deficit.

Akelaitis (1945) reported two cases of what he termed 'diagonistic dyspraxia' after section of the corpus callosum for the control of epilepsy. He said it consisted of an apparent conflict between the desired act and the actually performed act, and manifested itself as conflict between the two hands or between stated intentions and actual behavior. Since then, a number of reports of intermanual conflict have appeared (Gazzaniga, Bogen, & Sperry, 1962, 1965; Sperry, 1966; Trevarthen & Sperry, 1973; Wilson, Reeves, Gazzaniga, & Culver, 1977; Bogen, 1985; Graff-Radford, Welsh, & Godersky, 1986; Jason & Pajurkova, 1987), although Sperry (1964, 1966) has stressed that in general the hands cooperate well. Conflict is most commonly seen immediately after the surgery (Wilson et al., 1977), and Bogen (1985) has stated that almost all of their patients demonstrated some degree of intermanual conflict in the early postoperative period.

Another way in which conflict may be evident is when two disconnected hemispheres appear to compete for control over the same musculature (Levy, Nebes, & Sperry, 1971; Blanc-Garin, 1983; Jason & Pajurkova, 1987). In these cases only one hand is involved, and the conflict is between the two hemispheres for control of that hand. The deficit, therefore, is not one of bimanual control but rather one of interhemispheric cooperation.

Hemispheric Asymmetries

The evidence reviewed above on human patients with lateralized lesions supports a distinction between two broad classes of manual tasks. One type of task requires patients to reproduce a manual act which, at the time of performance, is based on an internal representation. Because of this, they may be thought of as including a memory component. The other type of task emphasizes performance demands rather than memory, because at the time of performance there is a model available on which to base the performance. There is evidence for left-hemisphere predominance in the tasks emphasizing memory, and bilateral involvement in tasks emphasizing performance.

The clearest evidence for this comes from work with manual sequences. When the task is to learn a series of manual movements, patients with left-temporal or left-frontal excisions are worse than those with comparable right-hemisphere excisions (Jason, 1985b). When the task is to copy a rapidly changing series of manual movements, with the experimenter providing a continually available visible model, there is no difference between left- and right-sided lesions; instead impairment is seen after frontal-lobe excisions from either side (Jason, 1986).

Other evidence supports this distinction. Ideomotor and ideational apraxia, for example, are considerably more common after left- than right-sided lesions (De Renzi, Pieczuro, & Vignolo, 1968; Hécaen & Albert, 1978). In both of these tasks, the patient must perform the acts when no model is present (even if a demonstration is given, the model is not available to the patient at the time of performance).

In other tasks a complex movement is demonstrated for the patient, who then must repeat the movement from an internal representation. These tasks are difficult to interpret, because there is both a memory component (the model has disappeared by the time the patient must make the movement) and a performance component (the movements are difficult by virtue of their complexity and demands for correct spatiotemporal integration). Most investigators using these types of tasks have noted left-hemispheric predominance (Kolb & Milner, 1981; Kimura 1982; De Renzi et al., 1983), but it is notable that right-frontal involvement has also been demonstrated (Kolb & Milner, 1981).

The regional cerebral blood flow studies of Roland and his collaborators (Roland et al, 1980a; 1980b) found bilateral increases in premotor cortex and the SMA, even for unilateral tasks. This is consistent with the idea that performance aspects of the tasks are represented bilaterally. But the SMA was activated bilaterally even when the subjects only thought about the movements without actually executing them. Primary motor cortex was not activated in this situation. This suggests that some aspect of the internal representation of movements is bilaterally represented in a way that can operate independently of the actual descending commands from primary motor cortex to spinal cord.

Evidence with respect to hemispheric involvement in monkeys is incomplete. There is indirect evidence for bilateral involvement in unilateral performance, in that single neurons in premotor cortex and the

SMA may be related to movements of either or both hands (Tanji 1987; Tanji et al., 1987), and bilateral cooling of premotor cortex affects unimanual performance more than just contralateral cooling (Sasaki & Gemba, 1986). To my knowledge, however, hemispheric asymmetries for manual memory tasks have not been looked for. This would be an interesting question to examine, because of evidence that hemispheric asymmetries in monkeys do exist for some tasks which also reflect asymmetries in the human brain (cf. Jason, Cowey, & Weiskrantz, 1984; Hamilton & Vermeire, 1988). Investigators have often looked, without success, for handedness in monkeys which might be comparable to human handedness (Warren, 1980). Although individual monkeys do show hand preferences for individual tasks, this seems different from human handedness in that for any given task there are equal numbers of left-handed and right-handed monkeys. Furthermore, if the tasks are sufficiently different in the movements required, then individual monkeys may not have the same hand preference for the different tasks. These negative results should not be discouraging, however, since even in humans the preferred hand is not always the one contralateral to the hemisphere specialized for motor functions. Milner (1976), for example, demonstrated that interference with a manual memory task was observed after injection of sodium Amytal to the hemisphere in which speech was represented (but rarely after injection to the other side), regardless of which was the preferred hand.

Discussion

Table 1 presents a summary of the results of studies of human patients with focal cortical lesions. Studies with monkeys are not included in this summary because of a lack of studies looking for hemispheric asymmetries, although as noted throughout this review there is considerable evidence that in other respects the human and monkey brain are organized very similarly. The basis for the organization of Table 1 is that different types of tasks may be grouped together on the basis of apparent similarity of functions assessed, as well as similar patterns of interhemispheric and intrahemispheric involvement.

The first group of tasks are those in which the environmental demands are somewhat ambiguous, and normal or correct behavior is loosely defined. In the studies of utilization behavior or imitation behavior, for example, the examiner deliberately withholds specific instructions. The result is that some people with prefrontal lesions misinterpret the situation and incorrectly infer that an implicit command is present.

Table 1. Results of Studies of Human Patients with Focal Cortical Lesions

DEFICIT	SITE OF DAMAGE*			
	L	B	C	CC
Utilization Behavior		PF		
Imitation Behavior		PF		
Self-Ordering	F	F		
Gesture Fluency	F	F		
Manual Sequence Learning	F,T			
Ideomotor & Ideational Apraxia	F,P,SMA			
Copy Complex Movements	F,P	F		CC
Visuomotor Conditional Learning	TH	(F)		
Metronome-Paced Performance		F		
Coordination / Smoothness		SMA	PM,SMA,P	
Misreaching			P	
Strength		F	F,PM	
Mirror Movements			SMA	
Reaching Out to Grasp			SMA	
Intermanual Conflict			SMA	CC
Internal Conflict over One Limb				CC

* L - Left; B - Both Left and Right; C - Contralateral to Limb; CC - Corpus Callosum; F - Frontal; PF - Prefrontal; P - Parietal; T - Temporal; TH - Temporal with extensive Hippocampal removal; PM - Premotor Cortex; SMA - Supplementary Motor Area. See text for details of tasks and references. Entries are made in two columns when different investigators have found different results, or when an experimenter has found different results depending on specific task conditions. For example, frontal lesions on either side impaired self-ordering when stimuli were visuospatial but only left-frontal lesions produced impairment when stimuli were verbal. The frontal-lobe impairment for visuomotor conditional learning was not specific to the motor nature of the task, and therefore is entered in brackets.

The test of gesture fluency provides guidelines as to which types of actions are correct, but no guidance as to exactly which actions should be performed. The self-ordering test allows the subject to order responses in any way, with only the requirement that responses not be repeated. Depending on the exact nature of the stimulus or task requirements, it may be seen that either the left-frontal lobe or both frontal lobes are implicated in tasks where the response is ambiguously determined. Within the frontal lobe, the most important area is probably prefrontal cortex. In a general sense, these tasks all place high demands on the guidance of behavior on the basis of internal models of reality, which according to Goldman-Rakic (1987) is the essence of prefrontal function.

The second group of tasks has in common the requirement that specific movements be produced, and that these movements be based on an internal representation of the correct act. The subject must either remember hand positions, demonstrate acts on verbal command or when given real objects, or perform movements after a demonstration but when the model is no longer present. The left-frontal lobe (including, in one study, the SMA) is implicated in all of these tasks, and also the left-temporal or -parietal lobe depending on the specific task. One study also demonstrated a role of the right-frontal lobe in copying complex non-meaningful movements; as argued above this may be attributable to that task's performance demands rather than its memory demands. The deficit seen in patients with callosal lesions may be interpreted in a similar way. Visuomotor conditional learning is also included with this group of tasks. Although the left-temporal involvement depended upon the motor nature of the tasks, the bilateral frontal involvement was not dependent upon the motor response but instead was also seen when the response was spatial.

The tasks in the third group have in common an emphasis on the execution of the movement, including speed, strength, timing, and coordination of movements involving multiple joints. The frontal lobes, especially the premotor cortex and SMA, as well as the parietal lobes appear necessary for these types of tasks. Although deficits in the contralateral hand are most consistently reported, a number of studies have emphasized bilateral involvement of the frontal lobes or, more specifically, the SMA.

The final group consists of inappropriate positive actions which are in some way not in accordance with the apparent wishes of the patient. They include mirror movements even when these are recognized as errors, automatically reaching out to grasp objects, intermanual conflict or other acts which are at cross purposes to those desired by the patient, and internal struggle over the control of a limb. These behaviors are all associated with either unilateral SMA lesions, or complete or anterior corpus callosal lesions. This suggests that the SMA and corpus callosum are important not just in controlling the fine aspects of bimanual coordination, but that they also participate in higher-level integration of bihemispheric control of behavior.

In conclusion, the evidence suggests that there are multiple components in the cortical control of motor function: bilateral prefrontal processes for the direction of behavior in conditions of ambiguity, left-hemispheric processes for the generation of specific movements from memory, bifrontal and contralateral frontal and parietal mechanisms for execution and exact control of movements, and a system for maintaining bihemispheric integration of behavior in which at least the SMA and corpus callosum play a role. Although subcortical structures have not been discussed, this omission should not be interpreted as meaning that they are of little importance. Indeed, there is now a large and growing body of data clarifying the roles of the basal ganglia, cerebellum, and thalamus in movement control (cf. Paillard, 1982; Goldberg, 1985), and it is clear that these subcortical structures interact with cortical structures at a number of different levels of control. An understanding of the contributions of cortical and subcortical regions and the spinal cord will be essential for a complete model of the neural control of motor behavior.

Acknowledgments

I wish to thank Dr. Eva Pajurkova and Dr. Stuart Coupland for their help in the preparation of the figure.

References

Akelaitis, A.J. (1945). Studies on the corpus callosum. IV. Diagonistic dyspraxia in epileptics following partial and complete section of the corpus callosum. *American Journal of Psychiatry*, **101**, 594-599.

Blanc-Garin, J. (1983). Elaboration of representations in a left-handed subject with callosal damage. *Cortex*, **19**, 493-508.

Bogen, J.E. (1985). The callosal syndromes. In K.M. Heilman & E. Valenstein (Eds.), *Clinical neuropsychology* (2nd Ed.) (pp. 295-338). New York: Oxford University Press.

Boller, R., Cole, M., Kim, Y., Mack, J.L., & Patawaran, C. (1975). Optic ataxia: clinical-radiological correlations with the EMI scan. *Journal of Neurology, Neurosurgery and Psychiatry*, **38**, 954-958.

Bossom, J. (1974). Movement without proprioception. *Brain Research*, **71**, 285-296.

Brinkman, C. (1984a). Supplementary motor area of the monkey's cerebral cortex: short- and long-term deficits after unilateral ablation and the effects of subsequent callosal section. *Journal of Neuroscience*, **4**, 918-929.

Brinkman, C. (1984b). Effects of bilateral supplementary motor area lesions in the monkey. *Neuroscience Letters*, **Suppl 15**, S23.

Canavan, A.G.M., Passingham, R.E., Marsden, C.D., Quinn, N., Wyke, M., & Polkey, C.E. (1989). Sequencing ability in Parkinsonians, patients with frontal lobe lesions and patients who have undergone unilateral temporal lobectomies. *Neuropsychologia*, **27**, 787-798.

Chan, J.-L., & Ross, E.D. (1988). Left-handed mirror writing following right anterior cerebral artery infarction: evidence for nonmirror transformation of motor programs by right supplementary motor area. *Neurology*, **38**, 59-63.

Cohen, N.J., & Squire, L.R. (1980). Preserved learning and retention of pattern-analyzing skill in amnesia: dissociation of knowing how and knowing that. *Science*, **210**, 207-210.

Cole, M., Schutta, H.S., & Warrington, E.K. (1962). Visual disorientation in homonymous half-fields. *Neurology*, **12**, 257-263.

Collin, N.G., Cowey, A., Latto, R., & Marzi, C. (1982). The role of frontal-eye fields and superior colliculi in visual search and non-visual search in rhesus monkeys. *Behavioral Brain Research*, **4**, 177-193.

Corkin, S. (1968). Acquisition of motor skill after bilateral medial temporal-lobe excision. *Neuropsychologia*, **6**, 255-265.

Damasio, A.R., & Benton, A.L. (1979). Impairment of hand movements under visual guidance. *Neurology*, **29**, 170-178.

De Renzi, E., Pieczuro, A., & Vignolo, L.A. (1968). Ideational apraxia: a quantitative study. *Neuropsychologia*, **6**, 41-52.

De Renzi, E., Faglioni, P., Lodesani, M., & Vecchi, A. (1983). Performance of left brain-damaged patients on imitation of single movements and motor sequences. Frontal and parietal-injured patients compared. *Cortex*, **19**, 333-343.

De Renzi, E., & Lucchelli, F. (1988). Ideational apraxia. *Brain*, **111**, 1173-1185.

Deuel, R.K. (1977). Loss of motor habits after cortical lesions. *Neuropsychologia*, **15**, 205-215.

Deuel, R.K., & Regan, D.J. (1985). Parietal hemineglect and motor deficits in the monkey. *Neuropsychologia*, **23**, 305-314.

Dick, J.P.R., Benecke, R., Rothwell, J.C., Day, B.L., & Marsden, C.D. (1986). Simple and complex movements in a patient with infarction of the right supplementary motor area. *Movement Disorders*, **1**, 255-266.

Ettlinger, G., & Kalsbeck, J.E. (1962). Changes in tactile discrimination and in visual reaching after successive and simultaneous bilateral posterior parietal ablations in the monkey. *Journal of Neurology, Neurosurgery and Psychiatry*, **25**, 256-268.

Faugier-Grimaud, S., Frenois, C., & Stein, D.G. (1978). Effects of posterior parietal lesions on visually guided behavior in monkeys *Neuropsychologia*, **16**, 151-168.

Freund, H.-J. (1987a). Abnormalities of motor behavior after cortical lesions in humans. In F. Plum (Ed.), *Handbook of physiology: Sec. 1. The nervous system: Vol. V. Motor control, Part* 2 (pp. 763-810). Bethesda, MD: American Physiological Society.

Freund, H.-J. (1987b). Differential effects of cortical lesions in humans. In G. Bock, M. O'Connor, & J. Marsh (Eds.), *Motor areas of the cerebral cortex* (CIBA Foundation Symposium 132, pp. 269-281). Chichester: Wiley.

Freund, H.-J., & Hummelsheim, H. (1985). Lesions of premotor cortex in man. *Brain,* **108**, 697-733.

Fuster, J.M. (1981). Prefrontal cortex in motor control. In V.B. Brooks (Ed.), *Handbook of physiology, Sec. 1. The nervous system: Vol. II. Motor control, Part 2* (pp. 1149-1178). Bethesda, MD: American Physiological Society.

Gaffan, D., & Harrison, S. (1988). Inferotemporal-frontal disconnection and fornix transection in visuomotor conditional learning by monkeys. *Behavioral Brain Research,* **31**, 149-163.

Gazzaniga, M.S., Bogen, J.E., & Sperry, R.W. (1962). Some functional effects of sectioning the cerebral commissures in man. *Proceedings of the National Academy of Sciences of the United States of America,* **48**, 1765-1769.

Gazzaniga, M.S., Bogen, J.E., & Sperry, R.W. (1965). Observations on visual perception after disconnexion of the cerebral hemispheres in man. *Brain,* **88**, 221-236.

Gelmers, H.J. (1983). Non-paralytic motor disturbances and speech disorders: the role of the supplementary motor area. *Journal of Neurology, Neurosurgery and Psychiatry,* **46**, 1052-1054.

Geschwind, N. (1965). Disconnexion syndromes in animals and man. *Brain,* **88**, 237-294, 585-644.

Geschwind, N. (1975). The apraxias: neural mechanisms of disorders of learned movement. *American Scientist,* **63**, 188-195.

Gilman, S., Carr, D., & Hollenberg, J. (1976). Kinematic effects of deafferentation and cerebellar ablation. *Brain,* **99**, 311-330.

Goldberg, G., Mayer, N.H., & Toglia, J.U. (1981). Medial frontal cortex infarction and the alien hand sign. *Archives of Neurology,* **38**, 683-686.

Goldberg, G. (1985). Supplementary motor area structure and function: review and hypotheses. *Behavioral and Brain Sciences,* **8**, 567-616.

Goldberg, G., Wimmer, A., Holzner, F., & Wessely, P. (1985). Apraxia of the left limbs in a case of callosal disconnection: the contribution of medial frontal lobe damage. *Cortex,* **21**, 135-148.

Goldman-Rakic, P.S. (1987). Circuitry of primate prefrontal cortex and regulation of behavior by representational memory. In F. Plum (Ed.), *Handbook of physiology, Sec. 1. The nervous system: Vol. V. Motor control, Part 1.* (pp. 373-417). Bethesda, MD: American Physiological Society.

Gonzalez-Rothi, L.J., & Heilman, K.M. (1984). Acquisition and retention of gestures by apraxic patients. *Brain and Cognition*, **3**, 426-437.

Graff-Radford, N.R., Welsh, K., & Godersky, J. (1986). Callosal apraxia and the supplementary motor area. *Neurology*, **36** (Suppl 1), 343.

Gross, C.G., & Weiskrantz, L. (1964). Some changes in behavior produced by lateral frontal lesions in the macaque. In J.M. Warren & K. Akert (Eds.), *The frontal granular cortex and behavior* (pp. 74-101). New York: McGraw-Hill.

Halsband, U. (1987). Higher disturbances of movement in monkeys (*Macaca fascicularis*). In G.N. Gantchev, B. Dimitrov & P. Gatev (Eds.), *Motor control* (pp. 79-85). New York: Plenum Press.

Halsband, U., & Passingham, R.E. (1962). The role of premotor and parietal cortex in the direction of action. *Brain Research*, **240**, 368-372.

Halsband, U., & Passingham, R.E. (1985). Premotor cortex and the conditions for movement in monkeys (*Macaca fascicularis*). *Behavioral Brain Research*, **18**, 269-277.

Hamilton, C.R., & Vermeire, B.A. (1988). Complementary hemispheric specialization in monkeys. *Science*, **242**, 1691-1693.

Hartje, W., & Ettlinger, G. (1973). Reaching in light and dark after unilateral posterior parietal ablations in the monkey. *Cortex*, **9**, 346-354.

Hausser, C.O., Robert, F., & Giard, N. (1980). Balint's syndrome. *Canadian Journal of Neurological Sciences*, **7**, 157-161.

Hécaen, H. (1978). Les apraxies idéomotrices. Essai de dissociation. In H. Hécaen & M. Jeannerod (Eds.), *Du contrôle moteur à l'organisation du geste* (pp. 343-358). Paris: Masson.

Hécaen, H., & Albert, M.L. (1978). *Human neuropsychology*. New York: Wiley.

Heilman, K.M. (1979). The neuropsychological basis of skilled movement in man. In M.S. Gazzaniga (Ed.), *Handbook of behavioral neurobiology, Vol. 2: Neuropsychology* (pp. 447-461). New York: Plenum Press.

Holmes, G. (1918). Disturbances of visual orientation. *British Journal of Ophthalmology*, **2**, 449-468, 506-516.

Jacobsen, C.F. (1931). A study of cerebral function in learning. The frontal lobes. *Journal of Comparative Neurology*, **52**, 271-340.

Jacobsen, C.F. (1936). Studies of cerebral function in primates. *Comparative Psychology Monographs*, **13**, 1-68.

Jason, G.W. (1983a). Hemispheric asymmetries in motor function: II. Ordering does not contribute to left-hemisphere specialization. *Neuropsychologia*, **21**, 47-58.

Jason, G.W. (1983b). Misreaching in monkeys after combined unilateral occipital lobectomy and splenial transection. *Experimental Neurology*, **81**, 114-125.

Jason, G.W. (1983b). Misreaching in monkeys after combined unilateral occipital lobectomy and splenial transection. *Experimental Neurology*, **81**, 114-125.

Jason, G.W., Cowey, A., & Weiskrantz, L. (1984). Hemispheric asymmetry for a visuo-spatial task in monkeys. *Neuropsychologia*, **22**, 777-784.

Jason, G.W. (1985a). Gesture fluency after focal cortical lesions. *Neuropsychologia*, **23**, 463-481.

Jason, G.W. (1985b). Manual sequence learning after focal cortical lesions. *Neuropsychologia*, **23**, 483-496.

Jason, G.W. (1986). Performance of manual copying tasks after focal cortical lesions. *Neuropsychologia*, **24**, 181-191.

Jason, G.W & Pajurkova, E.M. (1987). Conflict in motor control after lesion of the corpus callosum. *Journal of Clinical and Experimental Neuropsychology*, **9**, 73.

Jeannerod, M., Michel, F., & Prablanc, C. (1984). The control of hand movements in a case of hemianaesthesia following a parietal lesion. *Brain*, **107**, 899-920.

Kertesz, A., & Ferro, J.M. (1984). Lesion size and location in ideomotor apraxia. *Brain*, **107**, 921-933.

Kimura, D. (1982). Left-hemisphere control of oral and brachial movements and their relation to communication. *Philosophical Transactions of the Royal Society of London*, **B298**, 135-149.

Kolb, B., & Milner, B. (1981). Performance of complex arm and facial movements after focal brain lesions. *Neuropsychologia*, **19**, 491-503.

Lamotte, R.H., & Acuna, C. (1978). Defects in accuracy of reaching after removal of posterior parietal cortex in monkeys. *Brain Research*, **139**, 309-326.

Lehmkuhl, G., & Poeck, K. (1981). A disturbance in the conceptual organization of actions in patients with ideational apraxia. *Cortex*, **17**, 153-158.

Leonard, G., Jones, L., & Milner, B. (1988). Residual impairment in handgrip strength after unilateral frontal-lobe lesions. *Neuropsychologia*, **26**, 555-564.

Leonard, G., Milner, B., & Jones, L. (1988). Performance on unimanual and bimanual tapping tasks by patients with lesions of the frontal or temporal lobe. *Neuropsychologia*, **26**, 79-91.

Levine, D.N., Kaufman, K.I., & Mohr, J.P. (1978). Inaccurate reaching associated with a superior parietal lobe tumor. *Neurology*, **28**, 556-561.

Levy, J., Nebes, R.D., & Sperry, R.W. (1971). Expressive language in the surgically separated minor hemisphere. *Cortex*, **7**, 49-58.

Lhermitte, F. (1983). 'Utilization behavior' and its relation to lesions of the frontal lobes. *Brain*, **106**, 237-255.

Lhermitte, F., Pillon, B., & Serdaru, M. (1986). Human autonomy and the frontal lobes. Part I: Imitation and utilization behavior: a neuropsychological study of 75 patients. *Annals of Neurology*, **19**, 326-334.

McNabb, A.W., Carroll, W.M., & Mastaglia, F.L. (1988). 'Alien hand' and loss of bimanual coordination after anterior cerebral artery territory infarction. *Journal of Neurology, Neurosurgery and Psychiatry*, **51**, 218-222.

Meador, K.J., Watson, R.T., Bowers, D., & Heilman, K.M. (1986). Hypometria with hemispatial and limb motor neglect. *Brain*, **109**, 293-305.

Milner, B. (1972). Disorders of learning and memory after temporal lobe lesions in man. *Clinical Neurosurgery*, **19**, 421-446.

Milner, B. (1976). Hemispheric asymmetry in the control of gesture sequences. *Proceedings of the XXI International Congress of Psychology*, 149.

Milner, B., & Kolb, B. (1985). Performance of complex arm movements and facial-movement sequences after cerebral commissurotomy. *Neuropsychologia*, **23**, 791-799.

Moll, L., & Kuypers, H.G.J.M. (1977). Premotor cortical ablations in monkeys: contralateral changes in visually guided reaching behavior. *Science*, **198**, 317-319.

Paillard, J. (1982). Apraxia and the neurophysiology of motor control. *Philosophical Transactions of the Royal Society of London*, **B298**, 111-134.

Pandya, D.N., & Barbas, H. (1985). Architecture and connections of the premotor areas in the rhesus monkey. *Behavioral and Brain Sciences*, **8**, 595-596.

Passingham, R.E. (1978). Information about movements in monkeys (*Macaca mulatta*) with lesions of dorsal prefrontal cortex. *Brain Research*, **152**, 313-328.

Passingham, R.E. (1985). Prefrontal cortex and the sequencing of movement in monkeys (*Macaca mulatta*). *Neuropsychologia*, **23**, 453-462.

Passingham, R.E. (1985a). Memory of monkeys (*Macaca mulatta*) with lesions in prefrontal cortex. *Behavioral Neuroscience*, **99**, 3-21.

Passingham, R.E. (1985b). Premotor cortex: sensory cues and movement. *Behavioral Brain Research*, **18**, 175-185.

Passingham, R.E. (1986). Cues for movement in monkeys (*Macaca mulatta*) with lesions in premotor cortex. *Behavioral Neuroscience*, **100**, 695-703.

Passingham, R.E. (1987). Two cortical systems for directing movement. In G. Bock, M. O'Connor, & J. Marsh (Eds.), *Motor areas of the cerebral cortex* (CIBA Foundation Symposium 132, pp. 151-165). Chichester: Wiley .

Passingham, R.E. (1988). Premotor cortex and preparation for movement. *Experimental Brain Research*, **70**, 590-596.

Penfield, W., & Welch, K. (1951). The supplementary motor area of the cerebral cortex. A clinical and experimental study. *Archives of Neurology and Psychiatry*, **66**, 289-317.

Perenin, M.T., & Vighetto, A. (1983). Optic ataxia: a specific disorder in visuomotor coordination. In A. Hein & M. Jeannerod (Eds.), *Spatially oriented behavior* (pp. 305-326). New York: Springer-Verlag.

Petrides, M. (1982). Motor conditional associative-learning after selective prefrontal lesions in the monkey. *Behavioral Brain Research*, **5**, 407-413.

Petrides, M. (1985). Deficits on conditional associative-learning tasks after frontal- and temporal-lobe lesions in man. *Neuropsychologia*, **23**, 601-614.

Petrides, M., & Milner, B. (1982). Deficits on subject-ordered tasks after frontal- and temporal-lobe lesions in man. *Neuropsychologia*, **20**, 249-262.

Pinto-Hamuy, T., & Linck, P. (1965). Effect of frontal lesions on performance of sequential tasks by monkeys. *Experimental Neurology*, **12**, 96-107.

Preilowski, B.F.B. (1972). Possible contribution of the anterior forebrain commissures to bilateral motor coordination. *Neuropsychologia*, **10**, 167-177.

Ratcliff, G., & Davies-Jones, G.A.B. (1972). Defective visual localization in focal brain wounds. *Brain*, **95**, 49-60.

Rizzolatti, G. (1987). Functional organization of inferior area 6. In G. Bock, M. O'Connor, & J. Marsh (Eds.), *Motor areas of the cerebral cortex* (CIBA Foundation Symposium 132, pp. 171-186). Chichester: Wiley.

Rizzolatti, G., Gentilucci, M., Fogassi, L., Luppino, G., Matelli, M., & Ponzoni-Maggi, S. (1987). Neurons related to goal-directed motor acts in inferior area 6 of the macaque monkey. *Experimental Brain Research*, **67**, 220-224.

Roland, P.E. (1984). Organization of motor control by the normal human brain. *Human Neurobiology*, **2**, 205-216.

Roland, P.E., Larsen, B., Lassen, N.A., & Skinhøj, E. (1980a). Supplementary motor area and other cortical areas in organization of voluntary movements in man. *Journal of Neurophysiology*, **43**, 118-136.

Roland, P.E., Skinhøj, E., Lassen, N.A., & Larsen, B. (1980b). Different cortical areas in man in organization of voluntary movements in extrapersonal space. *Journal of Neurophysiology*, **43**, 137-150.

Rondot, P., De Recondo, J., & Ribadeau Dumas, J.L. (1977). Visuomotor ataxia. *Brain*, **100**, 355-376.

Rothwell, J.C., Traub, M.M., Day, B.L., Obeso, J.A., Thomas, P.K., & Marsden, C.D. (1982). Manual motor performance in a deafferented man. *Brain*, **105**, 515-542.

Sasaki, K., & Gemba, H. (1986). Effects of premotor cortex cooling upon visually initiated hand movements in the monkey. *Brain Research*, **374**, 278-286.

Sperry, R.W. (1964). The great cerebral commissure. *Scientific American*, **210**, 42-52.

Sperry, R.W. (1966). Brain bisection and mechanisms of consciousness. In J.C. Eccles (Ed.), *Brain and conscious experience* (pp. 298-313). New York: Springer-Verlag.

Stein, J.F. (1976). The effect of cooling parietal lobe areas 5 and 7 upon voluntary movement in awake rhesus monkeys. *Journal of Physiology (London)*, **258**, 62P-63P.

Tanji, J. (1987). Neuronal activity in the primate non-primary cortex is different from that in the primary motor cortex. In G. Bock, M. O'Connor, & J. Marsh (Eds.), *Motor areas of the cerebral cortex* (CIBA Foundation Symposium 132, pp. 142-150). Chichester: Wiley.

Tanji, J., Okano, K., & Sato, K.C. (1987). Relation of neurons in the nonprimary motor cortex to bilateral hand movement. *Nature*, **327**, 618-620.

Taub, E., Goldberg, I.A., & Taub, P. (1975). Deafferentation in monkeys: pointing at a target without visual feedback. *Experimental Neurology*, **46**, 178-186.

Trevarthen, C., & Sperry, R.W. (1973). Perceptual unity of the ambient visual field in human commissurotomy patients. *Brain*, **96**, 547-570.

Trevarthen, C. (1978). Manipulative strategies of baboons and origins of cerebral asymmetry. In M. Kinsbourne (Ed.), *Asymmetrical function of the brain* (pp. 329-391). Cambridge: Cambridge University Press.

Warren, J.M. (1980). Handedness and laterality in humans and other animals. *Physiological Psychology*, **8**, 351-359.

Watson, R.T., Fleet, W.S., Gonzalez-Rothi, L., & Heilman, K. (1986). Apraxia and the supplementary motor area. *Archives of Neurology*, **43**, 787-792.

Wiesendanger, M. (1986). Recent developments in studies of the supplementary motor area of primates. *Reviews of Physiology, Biochemistry and Pharmacology*, **103**, 1-59.

Wiesendanger, M., Hummelsheim, H., & Bianchetti, M. (1985). Sensory input to the motor fields of the agranular frontal cortex: a comparison of the precentral, supplementary motor and premotor cortex. *Behavioral Brain Research*, **18**, 89-94.

Wilson, D.H., Reeves, A., Gazzaniga, M., & Culver, C. (1977). Cerebral commissurotomy for control of intractable seizures. *Neurology*, **27**, 708-715.

Zaidel, D., & Sperry, R.W. (1977). Some long-term motor effects of cerebral commissurotomy in man. *Neuropsychologia*, **15**, 193-204.

Zola-Morgan, S., & Squire, L.R. (1984). Preserved learning in monkeys with medial temporal lesions: sparing of motor and cognitive skills. *Journal of Neuroscience*, **4**, 1072-1085.

Cerebral Control of Speech and Limb Movements
G.E. Hammond (editor)
Elsevier Science Publishers B.V. (North-Holland), 1990

Chapter 6

COMPLEX MOVEMENT BEHAVIOR: TOWARD UNDERSTANDING CORTICAL AND SUBCORTICAL INTERACTIONS IN REGULATING CONTROL PROCESSES

Kathleen York Haaland and Deborah L. Harrington
Veterans Administration Medical Center and University of New Mexico

Deficits in the cognitive aspects of complex motor skills have been shown after basal ganglia damage secondary to Parkinson's disease and after damage to the cerebral cortex. Despite the existence of several neuroanatomical circuits interconnecting areas in the cerebral cortex and basal ganglia, studies of complex motor function in these two areas have proceeded independent of one another. This chapter assesses the literature relevant to complex motor function in these areas, emphasizing the importance of isolating deficits in specific cognitive aspects of movement. Research methods and findings from cortical and subcortical studies are contrasted and, whenever possible, integrated as a preliminary step toward gaining insight into the importance of these areas for regulating specific components of complex motor skills. The combined study of motor control and motor learning, which have traditionally been treated as separate research domains, is proposed as a method to further our understanding of motor programming processes and their neuroanatomical basis.

1. Introduction

The development of a comprehensive model describing the neural control of complex motor skills will come about only through an understanding of the shared roles of cortical and subcortical areas. In this chapter the cognitive aspects of complex movements are compared between patients with cortical or subcortical damage to determine the similarities and differences in their deficits. Dysfunction of the basal ganglia, as evidenced by Parkinson's disease (PD), is used as a model of subcortical damage as complex movements have been most extensively studied in this patient group. PD is a good clinical model of basal ganglia dysfunction, and the relationship of the basal ganglia to cerebral cortex, in part because it is possible to differentiate putamen and caudate nucleus damage (Nahmias, Garnett, Firnau, & Lang, 1985). Although concomitant metabolic changes in the frontal cerebral cortex of PD patients have been reported (Perlmutter & Raichle, 1985), there is controversy regarding structural abnormalities in the cerebral cortex. Some (Boller, Mizutani, Roessman, & Gambetti, 1980) have emphasized the presence of general pathological changes while others (Chui, Mortimer, Slager, Zarow, Bondareff, & Webster, 1986) have reported minimal changes even in the face of cognitive deficits. The neuropathological basis of cognitive deficits is still controversial (Pirozzolo, Swihart, Rey, Jankovic, & Mortimer, 1988) but the problem of cortical involvement is decreased by examining patients with few or no cognitive deficits.

This does not imply that the basal ganglia are the only important subcortical structures for controlling complex movements (Brooks, 1986). For example, deficits in programming sequences with cerebellar damage (Inhoff, Diener, Rafal, & Ivry, 1989) demonstrate the importance of studying complex movements in these patients. Further, we are not suggesting that PD is the only human model of basal ganglia dysfunction. Huntington's disease (HD) and basal ganglia infarcts also are useful models, but the neurotransmitter abnormalities are not as specific, and in HD concomitant cortical damage is more common. Unfortunately, central programming deficits involved in complex motor skills have received little attention in studies of HD or basal ganglia infarcts.

This chapter begins with an overview of the neuroanatomical and behavioral basis for cortical-subcortical interactions followed by a discussion of some of the methodological problems in studying patients with cortical or subcortical damage. Cortical and subcortical studies of complex movements are then discussed in some detail with an emphasis on identifying deficits in specific aspects of motor control processes. Finally, the convergence of research findings from cortical and subcortical studies is examined to suggest future directions.

2. Overview of Cortical-Subcortical Interactions

2.1. Rationale for Studying Cortical-Subcortical Interactions

As the complexity of the behavior increases there is a greater likelihood that a larger number of areas at cortical and subcortical locations will interact to influence the behavior. The emphasis upon the interaction of structures or the importance of neuroanatomical *systems* in regulating complex behaviors has been useful in better understanding a wide variety of deficits including aphasia, apraxia, agnosia, and memory (Geschwind, 1965; Heilman, Rothi, & Valenstein, 1982; Luria, 1966; Mishkin, 1982; Nauta, 1971). Although the focus of early studies was upon the interaction of cortical areas, the more recent work has expanded to include cortical-subcortical interactions (Goldman-Rakic, 1988; Mishkin, 1982; Nauta, 1971).

The subcortical sites which most directly influence movement are the basal ganglia, their thalamic relays and the cerebellum (Brooks, 1986). In the cerebral cortex, the parietal and frontal cortex and their interconnections have been most frequently studied with particular emphasis on the left hemisphere because a variety of complex motor skills are more impaired after left hemispheric lesions (see Haaland & Yeo, 1989). Over the years several models of neuroanatomical control of movement have been suggested (Allen & Tsukahara, 1974; Brooks, 1986; Paillard, 1982), but with one exception (Paillard, 1982) these models have generally not considered the cognitive aspects of movement in any detail and have frequently omitted any but a passing reference to the cerebral cortex. In contrast, the neuroanatomical models of limb apraxia have focussed upon the role of the cerebral cortex with little or no reference to subcortical structures (Geschwind, 1965; Heilman, et al., 1982). Work in patients with PD is beginning to acknowledge the importance of relationships between basal ganglia and cerebral cortex (especially frontal cortex).

2.2. Neuroanatomy and Function of Cortical-Subcortical Connections

Parallel neuroanatomical circuits (the motor circuit and the 'complex' loops; Alexander, DeLong, & Strick, 1986) linking the basal ganglia and cerebral cortex have been described, but their function in programming and executing movements is not well understood. The motor circuit, which originates in supplementary motor area (SMA) and motor and somatosensory cortex, projects to the putamen and returns to the SMA via the globus pallidus and thalamus. The presence of input from the parietal lobe to the putamen has not been thoroughly evaluated, but if it does exist it could serve as an additional link to cortical areas which affect praxis

(Basso, Faglioni, & Luzzatti, 1985; Haaland, Rubens, & Harrington, 1989). The motor circuit is topographically organized throughout and has been related to movement preparation (Alexander, 1984) and movement direction and velocity in animals (Crutcher & DeLong, 1984). The possible functions of the SMA and its interconnection with the basal ganglia should also not be overlooked. SMA lesions in humans have been associated with response initiation deficits (Damasio & Van Hoesen, 1980) and a decreased ability to inhibit the grasp reflex (Erickson & Woolsey, 1951). The activity of SMA has also been shown to be influenced by preparation to respond (Tanji, Taniguchi, & Saga, 1980), especially for sequential movements (Roland, Larsen, Lassen, & Skinhøj, 1980). In addition, one case report has demonstrated limb apraxia after left SMA infarct (Watson, Shepherd, Gonzalez-Rothi, & Heilman, 1986).

The complex loop is composed of two circuits, both of which project through the caudate nucleus and back to their respective cortical sites in the dorsolateral prefrontal area and lateral orbitofrontal area. Both of these loops have input from the posterior parietal cortex, but parietal and frontal inputs do not overlap precisely within the basal ganglia (Selemon & Goldman-Rakic, 1985). The functions of these circuits are poorly understood, but they may be the anatomical basis for some of the cognitive deficits seen in PD (Cools, Van Den Bercken, Horstink, Van Spaendonck, & Berger, 1984; Taylor, Saint-Cyr, & Lang, 1986) which could also influence complex motor skills.

3. General Methodological Problems

3.1. Comparing Cortical-Subcortical Deficits Across Tasks

Studies of cortical and subcortical patients have been concerned with identifying central programming deficits in movement but there has been little overlap in the specific aspects of programming investigated or the experimental tasks used. Experiments with cortically damaged patients have focused upon whether deficits are due to the performance of isolated versus sequences of movements. The paradigms have emphasized errors in performance whereas programming processes prior to and during the performance of correct movements have been largely ignored. By comparison, studies of basal ganglia abnormalities have been primarily concerned with PD patients' ability to utilize advance or predictable information to facilitate response initiation and execution. The conditions under which PD patients seemingly can and cannot employ predictive strategies have served as a basis for speculating about the nature of programming deficits. Few studies, however, have systematically examined deficits in specific levels of programming, particularly during movement. In both cortical and subcortical research, long-term acquisition of complex skills has received little or no attention and, as a consequence, studies have focused more on processes associated with performance than learning and memory for skills. We will argue that research into these two latter domains will offer more promise of understanding motor skills and their neuroanatomical underpinnings.

Despite the use of different tasks, some general comparisons in motor deficits can be made between patients with cortical or subcortical damage. Limb apraxia and hand posture sequencing deficits are more common after left hemispheric damage, particularly of the parietal lobe (Basso, et al., 1985; Haaland, et al., 1989). Sequencing deficits or limb apraxia can also occur after frontal or basal ganglia damage (Agostini, Coletti, Orlando, & Tredici, 1983; Kolb & Milner, 1981; Sharpe, Cermak, & Sax, 1983), but the deficits with basal ganglia damage are not as severe or as frequent as those reported for cortical patients. Patients with prefrontal damage and basal ganglia damage due to PD show analogous cognitive deficits which could influence complex motor performance. These deficits include set switching (Cools, et al., 1984; Luria, 1966; Taylor, et al., 1986); initiating a series of different responses (Jones-Gotman & Milner, 1977; Taylor, et al., 1986); planning (Morris, Downes, Sahakian, Evenden, Heald, & Robbins, 1988); maintaining set (Flowers & Robertson, 1985); and temporal ordering (Sagar, Sullivan, Gabrieli, Corkin, & Growdon, 1988). Despite similarity of deficits in frontal and subcortical groups, it is unclear whether the same mechanisms underlie the deficits in these groups. Therefore, from a neuroanatomical and behavioral standpoint it is important to explore how cortical and subcortical structures interact to control specific aspects of movement using similar tasks.

3.2. Definition and Description of Patient Groups

Discrepancies in the definition and description of subject populations have also introduced problems interpreting data both within and across patient groups. In cortical studies, the major problems are in the description of lesion size, location, and etiology (Haaland & Yeo, 1989). Although lesion size and location can now be measured directly by radiological methods, recent studies have usually not considered lesion size even though it has been related to apraxia (Kertesz & Ferro, 1984). An additional problem with anatomical correlations is the validity of lesion size and location measures derived from CT scans obtained soon after an acute infarct. We are aware of only one study in this area which has adequately controlled this variable (Haaland, et. al., 1989). In this study, lesion size was related to apraxia severity, which points to the possibility that variation in lesion size especially as a function of lesion location could confound conclusions pertaining to the behavioral functions of neuroanatomical systems.

Lesion location is usually defined by an experienced rater who designates whether a particular lobe or structure is damaged. Typically the damage is not restricted to that lobe, and it is rare for interrater reliabilities to be included. The studies using lobectomy patients are better controlled in terms of additional cortical involvement but are problematic because the patients frequently had injuries in childhood which could affect neural development. In addition, only one of these studies (Kolb & Milner, 1981) included a parietal group, the lobectomies frequently involved structures other than neocortex (e.g. amygdala, hippocampus, cingulate gyrus), and lesion size varied.

The etiology of damage is also a potential confounding variable especially since more rapid onset problems, such as strokes, are likely to cause greater disruptions in behavior and to be more reflective of the role of the damaged structure (Finger & Stein, 1982) in comparison to problems with more gradual onset (e.g., tumor). In one study (De Renzi, Motti, & Nichelli, 1980), trauma cases were included along with those with vascular disease. However, trauma patients also frequently show generalized neuropathological abnormalities making it difficult to interpret focal lesion effects.

One factor which influences the interpretation of findings from PD studies is the severity of Parkinsonian symptoms (e.g. bradykinesia and akinesia, tremor, rigidity). Rating scales of Parkinsonian symptoms are quite gross psychometrically, but at least provide a rough index allowing other investigators to gauge disease severity (Lieberman, 1974). This is important as when primary motor deficits were controlled, one study found that only PD patients with more advanced symptoms showed motor learning deficits (Harrington, Haaland, Yeo, & Marder, 1990).

3.3. Specifying Cognitive Deficits

Most studies of cortical and subcortical groups do not provide information regarding general cognitive functioning. This is a problem in studies of cortical patients where deficits on motor tasks may simply reflect a variety of broader deficits such as generalized memory problems or an inability to use verbal encoding strategies due to language deficits. This is also a problem in PD studies where cognitive deficits may be a sign of dysfunction of the basal ganglia and their cortical (especially prefrontal) projections (Chui, et al., 1986), and/or generalized degenerative changes as a higher than normal percentage of PD patients have neuropathological evidence of Alzheimer's disease (Boller, et al., 1980).

Information regarding a variety of cognitive skills also affords an opportunity to relate these measures to cognitive aspects of motor performance. This has been done in one PD study where some aspects of programming hand posture sequences were associated with visuospatial deficits but not other cognitive deficits (Harrington & Haaland, 1990). This finding demonstrates that the deficit is specific rather than indicative of generalized impairment. However, correlational data of this type should also be cautiously interpreted as whether there are significant correlations with motor skills clearly depends on the specific cognitive deficit being assessed.

4. Cortical Control of Complex Movements

4.1. Sequencing Finger and Hand Movements

The left hemisphere is widely viewed as more important than the right hemisphere in controlling many movements in *both* arms (see Haaland & Yeo, 1989). However, findings are contradictory concerning the left hemisphere's role in the sequencing of actions. The predominant task used for studying sequencing has been copying of multiple finger/hand movements in the limb ipsilateral to lesion (De Renzi, et al., 1980; Kimura, 1982; Kimura & Archibald, 1974; Kolb & Milner, 1981). Typically the experimenter demonstrates a single finger or hand position whereupon the subject imitates the position. This method presumably ensures that subjects can accurately perceive and execute the individual positions although few studies have rigorously tested this assumption. Subsequently, subjects imitate a sequence of the previously performed hand positions as demonstrated by the experimenter. The accuracy of performance is usually measured.

4.2. Single Versus Sequences of Movements

A number of cognitive processes underlie performance in this paradigm. Deficits in sequencing must be separated from deficits in the execution of the *same* individual movements comprising the sequences. Several studies have found deficits following left hemispheric damage in copying both individual movements and sequences of movements (De Renzi, et al., 1980; De Renzi, Faglioni, Lodesani, & Vecchi, 1983; Kimura, 1982) concluding that it is not the sequencing requirements of complex actions that produces deficits. However, different movements were used for copying isolated and multiple positions, and some isolated movements contained several movement components rendering them more similar to sequences. The high correlations reported between performance of single and multiple movements is consistent with this observation (Kimura, 1982). Although deficits in copying isolated movements have not been consistently reported (Kimura & Archibald, 1974), in order to examine processes underlying sequencing patient groups should be equated on the performance of individual movements through practice and tests of recall. With this procedure, processes specific to the sequencing of actions can be studied independently from those associated with the perception, memory, programming, and/or execution of individual movement components.

4.3. Memory for Sequences

Typically, subjects must remember the sequence of actions after they are demonstrated which introduces the possibility that a simple deficit in immediate memory could account for the findings. When memory was a component of movement copying, left hemisphere lesioned patients, especially those with frontal or parietal damage, were consistently impaired in sequencing multiple hand movements (De Renzi, et al., 1980; Kimura, 1982; Kolb & Milner, 1981) although patients with right frontal damage also were impaired to a lesser extent in one study (Kolb & Milner, 1981). However, memory demands were not manipulated and performance on independent tests of memory span were not reported.

One study varied memory demands in a unique task in which subjects copied one sequence of four movements (Roy, 1981). In the perceptual phase, which did not include a memory component, a single sequence was performed in the presence of an action-picture card depicting a movement, each associated with one of four knobs (pull, point, turn, slide) on an apparatus. When subjects reached criterion performance, the action-picture card was removed and the sequence was performed from memory (the memory phase). The results showed that, relative to the right-hemisphere group, the left-hemisphere group had a higher proportion of perseverative errors in the perceptual and memory phase which was interpreted as a deficit controlling postural transitions. When there was a memory component to sequencing, the left-hemisphere group also had more difficulty than the right-hemisphere group in ordering responses as reflected by more complex sequencing errors (i.e., more than one position and order error per trial) but not simple sequencing errors (i.e., one position and order error per trial), which was interpreted as an ordering deficit. These findings contrast with Kimura (1977) who found more perseverative but not ordering errors in left-hemisphere patients when they were learning to execute from memory a sequence of three hand positions on an apparatus. This discrepancy most likely reflects the difference between studies in the sequential ordering demands of the tasks. Roy's sequences contained more responses and the manipulanda for different responses did not cue the response as does Kimura's manual sequence box task.

One concern, however, pertains to the use of error types to infer specific cognitive processes. Perseverative and sequencing errors may reflect processing deficits other than those involved in postural transitions and ordering actions, such as generating or retrieving an internal motor program, forgetting, failure to monitor movement, or inattention. Measures that allow for an examination of performance on correct trials (e.g., reaction time) *together* with experimental manipulations designed to affect specific processes (i.e., sequential ordering versus position transitions) need to accompany an analysis of error types in order to verify that the proposed underlying cognitive processes are indeed different.

Memory factors have been controlled in other studies by examining movement copying when photographs of sequences were available during performance (De Renzi, et al., 1983). Left parietal but not left frontal patients were impaired on this task relative to controls (no right hemisphere group was studied), but the left parietal group also showed deficits in the copying of single movements. This latter finding suggested to the authors that the left parietal area was critical for selecting actions and that this process was the basis for impaired copying of multiple movements as well. This interpretation, however, was clouded by the operational definition of single movements which included both repetitions of the same movement and those with more than one movement component. Thus, deficits reported for single movements could also reflect sequencing problems.

Jason (1983a, 1983b, 1985, 1986) has conducted the most thorough investigations of memory demands in movement copying concluding that the left hemisphere is specialized only for memory of movements. Left-hemisphere patients were consistently impaired relative to right-hemisphere patients (Jason, 1983a, 1983b, 1985) and normal controls (Jason, 1985) in reproducing hand positions from memory. This finding was consistent with the left-hemisphere group's relatively worse memory for a sequence of two hand positions in a Brown-Peterson memory task (Jason, 1983a). To eliminate memory factors from the task, sequences of movements were performed to a criterion and then executed as rapidly as possible with pictures of the action sequences available during performance (Jason, 1983a). No difference was found between the left- and right-hemisphere groups in movement time (MT) but the left-hemisphere group made more errors. To control for immediate memory factors better (Jason, 1986), patients performed a metronome-paced task in which they imitated three hand positions immediately after each was demonstrated at a speed ranging from .3 to 2.0 s per position. When a patient failed at one rate, the previous rate, which was .1 s slower, was used as the measure of performance. All patient groups (left and right frontal and temporal) were impaired on this task relative to controls. While this task eliminated memory for a sequence as each movement was performed immediately after presentation, it also emphasized speed. The speed factor is important as all patient groups made more errors (but were not slower) than controls in copying single finger positions when task instructions emphasized speed and accuracy. Similarly, left and right frontal and temporal patients (Leonard, Milner, & Jones, 1988) showed slower sequential tapping rates and a trend for slower repetitive tapping rates ($p < .07$) which suggests deficits in speeded performance. While it appears that speeded tasks are more sensitive in identifying deficits in all patients with cortical damage, these tasks involve several different cognitive abilities, such that deficits could be due to one or more of these processes. Thus, patients with damage to different areas of the cortex may all show motor sequencing problems, but perhaps for different reasons.

To summarize, the outcomes from investigations of memory factors in sequencing are not conclusive. No studies have provided data showing patient groups and controls are equivalent on tests of immediate or short-term memory for sequences of movements so as to eliminate memory factors as an explanation for findings. When appropriate methods have been utilized for controlling memory factors (i.e., pictures of the sequence remain available during performance) conclusions have been marred by the absence of normal controls or the use of only error data to infer sequencing deficits. Other methods for controlling memory factors (Jason, 1986) also emphasized speed of copying movements such that the role of memory in nonspeeded tasks with left or right hemispheric damage is not clear. Most studies also have not controlled for memory and performance of isolated postures by training subjects on the individual hand positions that are used in the sequencing tasks and then testing for recall of these positions. In fact, Jason (1985) has shown that left- and right-hemisphere patients show no sequential ordering deficits relative to normal controls when they have had more extensive practice on the same hand positions used in earlier experiments. Finally, the distinct possibility that deficits in memory for movements following left hemispheric damage may be due, in part, to poor verbal mediation strategies has received practically no attention. This is critical since aphasic patients are particularly prone to limb apraxia.

4.4. Sequential Ordering

An important question that emerged from the study of memory was whether movement copying performance reflected deficits in the ordering of actions irrespective of memory requirements. Movement copying studies typically use sequences containing no more than four responses which may not be sensitive to sequential ordering deficits especially when examining performance on repeated trials of the same sequence (Kimura, 1977; Roy, 1981). Further, the rationale that sequential ordering deficits can be inferred through an examination of error types (Kimura, 1977, 1982; Roy, 1981) is clearly problematic because the mechanisms for the errors are not explicitly assessed.

A more promising method for uncovering ordering deficits is to experimentally manipulate variables that should influence sequencing difficulty (Jason, 1985, 1986). In one study (Jason, 1985), subjects copied sequences containing five hand positions under three different conditions. In one condition (restricted) the five hand positions were always demonstrated and reproduced in the same order whereas in another condition (unrestricted) the sequence could be reproduced in any order. Only left frontal and left temporal groups (no parietal groups were examined) were impaired relative to controls, but the amount of impairment when reproduction order was not constrained (unrestricted) was similar to when positions were reproduced in the same order as demonstrated (restricted), indicating that deficits were not due to sequential ordering. However, there also was no difference in absolute performance levels between the restricted and unrestricted conditions suggesting that the ordering manipulation was not robust.

Jason (1983a, 1986) has also reported that when memory factors are minimized, sequential ordering does not explain impaired movement copying performance in left- and right-hemisphere-damaged patients. In these studies, three hand positions were copied either in a repeated or varied order from trial to trial in a metronome-paced task. Left and right frontal groups were slower than left and right temporal groups in the speed with which movements were accurately imitated for either condition, but all patient groups were impaired relative to controls (Jason, 1986). All patient groups were equally impaired on the copying of single movements, but the frontal groups were more impaired on sequencing. However, as ordering demands increased, performance of the frontal groups did not deteriorate more than the temporal groups which indicates ordering deficits cannot account for these findings.

It has been suggested that sequential ordering may not generally explain movement copying deficits (with or without a memory component) because subjects do not have to generate a program for a sequence as the order is externally defined by the experimenter (Jason, 1986). An alternative interpretation is that failures to produce undisputed evidence for ordering deficits may be due to the small number of items used in motor sequencing tasks rather than the self-ordered nature of the tasks. While no experiment has directly manipulated internal and external ordering demands, two studies have separately examined internal ordering (Petrides & Milner, 1982) and external ordering (Shimamura, Janowsky, & Squire, 1989) using non-motor tasks, and both reported deficits in patients with frontal damage. In both of these studies, however, subjects ordered a large number of items which may account for the ordering deficits. Whether these findings generalize to the motor modality awaits future investigation.

4.5. Posture Transitions

Reported movement copying deficits may also be due, at least in part, to problems making position or posture transitions. This explanation has not been directly examined as studies have not been designed to separate this factor from sequential ordering or other processes. Studies comparing the execution of a single position with sequences of positions have not always used the same positions in both tasks or the positions frequently are complex to achieve, rendering them similar to sequences. Another method for examining this issue is to compare the execution of sequences containing repetitions of the same posture with those containing changes in postures. The rationale is that if posture transitions are a source of difficulty, performance should be relatively more impaired when changing postures than when repeating postures (Harrington & Haaland, 1987; 1990).

4.6. Movement Recognition

The ability to recognize movements has been largely ignored with one notable exception. Heilman and colleagues (1982) investigated whether apraxia in patients with anterior or posterior left hemispheric damage (as inferred from type of aphasia) could be explained by deficits in different processes. In a recognition task, patients were asked to identify a target act, which was verbally specified, from three pantomimed acts (e.g., using a saw, hammering). The two distractor acts were either poor performance of the target act or different acts. Posterior apraxics made more errors relative to anterior apraxics and anterior and posterior non-apraxics. These findings point to a disturbance in posterior apraxics possibly related to a disruption in the storage and/or retrieval of visuokinesthetic motor engrams (Heilman, et al., 1982) or perhaps deficits integrating information from visuoperceptual and motor modalities. Because anterior apraxics showed deficits in performing gestures to command or imitation but could discriminate between actions on the recognition test, their apraxia was attributed to a processing disorder related to the programming of movements, as others have suggested (Geschwind, 1965). However, no direct test of this hypothesis was provided. Although intriguing, a replication of these findings is necessary using radiological specification of lesion location and a control group along with data describing immediate memory capacities and visuoperceptual skills of patient groups as these factors may also interact with recognition performance in this task. Further, the existence and nature of programming deficits in all groups need to be directly assessed, perhaps using some of the paradigms that will be discussed in the section on subcortical motor deficits.

4.7. Concluding Remarks

It should be apparent from this review that much is still unknown about the role of the cerebral cortex in the cognitive control of complex movements. In addition to using better methods to isolate specific processes, our knowledge of central programming deficits with cortical damage may be enhanced by investigations into perceptual processes involved in the programming of complex movements. Although some studies have examined short-term learning of sequential movements, the study of motor performance and related processes has largely excluded serious investigations into the long-term learning and retention of complex motor skills. The importance of examining the role of learning is illustrated, in part, by a study showing that left- but not right-hemisphere patients were impaired initially on a manual sequence learning task, but subsequently showed no such deficits when transferring to a similar task which used the same hand positions but a different order (Jason, 1985). While it is not clear from this experiment whether the equivalent transfer of training effects among groups was due to savings from learning individual positions, position transitions, and/or procedures for sequential ordering, it points to the importance of examining motor learning.

5. Subcortical Control of Complex Movements

A theory of motor control and learning and the neuroanatomical underpinnings cannot be complete without knowledge of the role(s) of subcortical areas/pathways in the regulation of complex movements. PD has served as one human model for studying basal ganglia dysfunction. It is widely believed that part of the motor problem observed in PD is due to central programming deficits although explanations for these deficits are disputed.

Studies of central programming deficits in PD have adopted an information processing approach in which components of programming have been inferred by manipulating factors that presumably affect the duration of these stages. Investigators have typically manipulated advance information (e.g., precue versus no cue) and target predictability to study general programming deficits in response initiation and execution. Some studies also have focused on identifying specific aspects of programming prior to and during the execution of action sequences that may be dysfunctional in PD. As will become evident, few of these paradigms overlap with those employed in studies of cortical damage, rendering immediate integration of these areas premature.

5.1. Response Predictability During Movement

Research examining electromyographic (EMG) activity showed that PD patients could not produce a large enough EMG in the agonist muscle when initiating a movement although the duration of the first burst was normal as was the pattern of subsequent agonist and antagonist activity (Hallett, Shahani, & Young, 1977). PD patients produced a repetitive series of small agonist bursts which seemed to explain why they could not make preprogrammed, rapid movements, but rather appeared to rely on external cues and visual feedback (Flowers, 1976). Early studies attempted to specify the nature of this programming deficit better by determining whether PD patients could utilize predictable information to guide movements. The rationale was that if PD patients can utilize predictable information as controls do, this would indicate they are capable of formulating motor programs. Flowers (1978) reported that PD patients were impaired in predicting the movement of a target they were tracking. PD patients made consistently more errors in anticipating the direction of a predictable target when the target path briefly disappeared from view or when the target jumped to a different spatial location. More recently these findings were reaffirmed in a task where the accuracy and speed of movement were measured as subjects traced predictable patterns containing varying numbers of deleted segments (Stern, Mayeux, & Rosen, 1984). Prior to each trial, subjects compared the patterns with and without deleted segments. On each trial they were asked to trace the partially deleted pattern. Despite an absence of group differences in movement velocity, the PD group was less accurate than controls especially as the patterns contained more deleted segments. This suggested PD patients showed deficits primarily when the task emphasized performance based on an internal motor representation, perhaps reflecting problems planning movements in advance without external guidance, generation of inaccurate motor programs, retrieval problems, and/or a failure to monitor the accuracy of their movements. For the PD group but not controls, poorer performance on drawing tasks was related to greater error and reduced speed on patterns containing the most missing segments. This finding suggests that poor visuospatial skills may also partially explain the programming deficits on this task.

To explore whether the previous deficits were due to the discrete nature of the movement rather than problems generating an internal motor program, performance was examined on continuous tracking tasks in which movements were always externally guided (Bloxham, Mindel, & Frith, 1984; Day, Dick, & Marsden, 1984). Subjects tracked a slow-moving target that moved in a predictable or an unpredictable pattern. Data from the first 30 to 60 s of each trial were discarded to minimize the influence of bradykinesia. The results from both studies showed no differences between PD patients and control groups in mean tracking lag for predictable patterns suggesting PD patients could employ predictive strategies. However, in one study (Bloxham, et al., 1984) differences between PD and control groups in primary motor function were 'controlled' by matching groups on initial tracking performance to unpredictable targets such that PD patients who had difficulty in this condition were excluded. The rationale of the matching procedure, that unpredictable targets require little or no programming relative to predictable targets, is controversial. Less predictable targets also require programming operations in which case the matching procedure very likely equated groups not just in initial motor speed but also on cognitive processes that are involved in programming more demanding movements. Second, in both studies, tracking movements were very slow such that PD patients could still be less effective than controls at employing a predictive strategy, but the task may have been too easy to be sensitive to these possible deficits.

Apart from these concerns, both of these studies show that PD patients are able to track predictable targets, but whether this is due to the slowness of targets and/or the fact that movements were externally guided is unclear as neither factor was experimentally manipulated. A recent study of sequencing in a button-pressing task (Robertson & Flowers, 1990) has shown PD patients were less accurate than controls when sequences were generated by the subject than when they were guided by stimulus cues. This points to the importance of distinguishing between the types of processes involved in programming movements that are visually guided and those that are not. Similarly, in most tasks where external guidance has been provided continuous movements were required (Bloxham, et al., 1984; Day, et al., 1984), whereas when external guidance was not available the movements were discrete or segmented (Flowers, 1978; Stern, et al., 1984). The cognitive requirements for these two types of movements may also be different irrespective of whether external guidance is provided. For example, performance of discrete or segmented movements emphasizes response initiation and shifting processes whereas performance of continuous movements is more reflective of on-line processing perhaps involving monitoring of the movement. Further, both studies of continuous movements (Bloxham, et al., 1984; Day, et al., 1984) discarded the first 30 to 60 s of data on each trial, which precluded an examination of the initial programming of the movement.

5.2. Using Advance Information: Choice versus Simple RT

This latter limitation prompted the investigations concerning PD patients' ability to effectively use advance information. In some studies, this question was approached methodologically by comparing simple and choice RTs where the response was very simple (e.g., key press or release). In simple RT tasks subjects receive cues about the impending movement before the imperative stimulus whereas in choice RT tasks no such prior information is provided before the imperative stimulus. In one study (Bloxham, et al., 1984), subjects responded to a visual imperative stimulus, 'GO LEFT' or 'GO RIGHT', by lifting their left or right index finger. Either 250 or 2000 ms prior to the imperative stimulus, one of three possible warning cues were presented: READY (unpredictable condition, choice RT) or READY LEFT or READY RIGHT (predictable conditions, simple RT). In the unpredictable condition there was no difference in RT between PD patients and controls regardless of delay interval but in the predictable condition RTs of PD patients showed little improvement with a longer delay in contrast to controls who showed a large benefit. Simple but not choice RT deficits are paradoxical as they seem to imply programming deficits when responding to anticipated but not unanticipated events. However, additional work suggests that these findings are controversial.

Another study (Sheridan, Flowers, & Hurrell, 1987) investigated this paradox by examining whether utilization of advance information was dependent on the complexity of simple aiming movements. Response complexity was manipulated by varying the index of difficulty (ID; where ID level = $\log_2$ ((2 X Amplitude)/Target Width)). The finding of simple but not choice RT deficits in PD was replicated. However, PD patients made more errors than controls in choice RT indicating they had problems programming unanticipated events. Thus, the paradoxical RT findings could be due to a speed-accuracy trade off, such that if error rates were equated between groups, choice RTs of PD patients should be longer than those of the control group. As for response complexity, a significant interaction of group by RT condition by ID level was not reported, indicating response complexity affected simple and choice RTs of both groups similarly. Furthermore, RTs did not always systematically vary with ID level. Other manipulations of response difficulty, which will be described soon, may better test for programming deficits related to response complexity.

Stelmach and colleagues (1986) further pursued the reasons for deficits in simple but not choice RT in PD by examining whether this was due to problems in using advance information to select movements. Subjects received extensive training on a task in which they learned to press one of six keys in response to a light cue. The lights precued subjects as to hand (left or right), direction (forward or backward), and extent (near or far), and precues were always valid. There were four different precue conditions which were randomly presented: No precue (choice RT condition) and one, two, or all three movement dimensions precued (simple RT conditions). The results showed that RTs were longer for the PD group, regardless of precue condition, indicating that PD patients had difficulty with both predictable and unpredictable events. However, both groups showed the same amount of benefit from a precue (i.e., direction, extent, and/or arm) about the forthcoming movement, demonstrating that PD patients' longer simple and choice RTs were not due to response selection processes. Moreover, as subjects had to hold the precue in working memory for 1 s prior to response initiation, these findings dispel the notion that simple RT deficits are due to problems in maintaining information in short-term memory. The longer RTs shown by the PD group may be due to impaired stimulus detection and classification, response programming, initiation, or production. Alternatively, PD patients may have difficulty translating precues and target stimuli into overt responses especially as other studies which required less stimulus translation have not found choice RT deficits in PD (Bloxham, et al., 1984; Sheridan, et al. 1987).

The simple and choice RT paradox has not been resolved, but an important outcome from the above investigations is that discrepant findings regarding PD deficits are due in part to the level of analysis. Abnormalities in some aspects of programming are not always observed, especially when the amount of subject-initiated processing is minimized as in precuing studies where subjects are highly practiced (Stelmach, et al., 1986), in simple RT paradigms where the same response is repeated on successive trials (Rafal, Posner, Walker, & Friedrich, 1984), or when movements are externally guided (Bloxham, et al., 1984; Day, et al., 1984). When subjects must construct an internal motor representation to guide movement, cognitive deficits seem to be more evident (Flowers, 1978; Robertson & Flowers, 1990; Stern, et al., 1984). The issue of practice is particularly relevant here as organizational processing should be more important during the initial stages of learning even a relatively easy task, such as those used in some simple RT precuing studies (Bloxham, et al., 1984; Sheridan, et al., 1987). The organizational processing demands of a task should also be greater as the complexity of movements increases.

5.3. Programming Sequences of Movements

Motor planning in PD has been less well studied using tasks that require more organizational processing such as the sequencing of movements. A few studies have examined programming in PD using gesture or multiple-movement copying tasks similar to those described in cortical studies. In one study (Sharpe, et al., 1983), performance of PD patients and controls was examined on representational (e.g., 'Show me how you would eat with a spoon') and non-representational gestures (e.g., dorsal side of hand under chin, fingers extended and abducted) to imitation. PD patients made more spatial errors than controls but only on non-representational gestures. These findings were suggestive of deficits in PD related to the generation and/or execution of movements, but impairments were relatively mild. In a recent study (Canavan, Passingham, Marsden, Quinn, Wyke, & Polkey, 1989), PD patients were as accurate as controls in copying sequences of three hand positions whereas those with frontal lesions and right but not left temporal lobectomies were impaired on this task. As noted previously, these types of studies have not identified the mechanism(s) for observed deficits.

In an effort to describe programming deficits in PD better, Benecke and colleagues (1986,1987) examined sequencing and simultaneous bilateral performance of two types of movements performed in isolation, simultaneously with both hands, or sequentially: (1) squeeze with the thumb and fingers (or isotonic opposition of thumb and finger) and (2) elbow flexion. Subjects were precued verbally as to which movement(s) to perform, and after five practice trials performed 10 consecutive RT trials without cues. MTs were measured from records of force and velocity, and inter-onset latency (IOL) was the interval between the onset of both movements. For the PD group but not controls, MTs were longer for individual movements when performed sequentially or simultaneously than when executed in isolation. IOLs were also slowed in PD relative to controls. While these findings were suggestive of deficits in programming sequential and simultaneous actions, it is unclear as to whether this is due to a difficulty switching between different motor programs, problems programming a series of force requirements, difficulty retrieving or activating motor programs, or inefficient programming prior to movement initiation.

Some studies of programming deficits in PD have manipulated variables which presumably affect the duration of certain aspects of programming sequential movements but not others. Deficits in the utilization of advance information were examined in a simple RT paradigm in which subjects performed sequences containing one, two, or three finger-press responses (Rafal, Inhoff, Friedman, & Bernstein, 1987). Because performance was examined on consecutive trials of the same sequence, it was assumed that a motor program was already constructed prior to RT and, therefore, RT reflected the retrieval of subprograms from a motor buffer. Despite longer overall RTs and IRTs (but not higher error rates) for the PD group, RT increased with sequence length similarly for both groups suggesting PD patients were not impaired in retrieval processes.

Impaired motor programming of sequences has been reported in PD when the order of trials was randomized such that on each trial a motor program must be assembled for a sequence. In one study (Stelmach, Worringham, & Strand, 1987), subjects executed sequences of repetitive finger taps that required one to five key presses. On each trial a precue (e.g., R, RR, RRR, RRRR, or RRRRR) was presented for 2 s followed by a rehearsal delay of 2.5 s, two warning beeps, and then the imperative stimulus. The results showed that despite no group differences in overall RT, RTs increased linearly with sequence length for normal controls, but there was no sequence length effect on RT for the PD group suggesting that they did not program the sequence prior to movement initiation. This is not to say that they cannot construct a motor program, but rather they do not appear to do so for all movements contained within the sequence.

A recent study in our laboratory (Harrington & Haaland, 1990) examined programming processes prior to and during movement as a function of the complexity of the sequences. We were interested in whether programming deficits in PD were due to problems generating motor programs only for more complex sequences, and if deficits in the utilization of motor programs for the individual movements depended upon the composition of others within the sequence. Processing deficits were inferred based on the manipulation of variables that should affect the duration of certain processes. To test for deficits utilizing advance information, the delay interval was varied between the onset of the stimulus and the signal to begin movement. Deficits in planning a series of movements prior to movement initiation were examined by varying the number of responses contained within a sequence. Deficits in changing between different responses were examined by comparing the execution of repetitive and nonrepetitive movements.

In this study, sequences of hand postures were executed across the face of an apparatus (see Figure 1) containing a row of vertical plates (P) which required contact with the side of the hand, a row of recessed buttons (B) which required contact with the index finger, and row of handlebars (H) which required the four fingers to wrap around the bar from underneath. A start plate was located to the left of the manipulanda and subjects always moved from the left to the right using their right hand. A monitor presented pictorial displays of the sequences (see Figure 1).

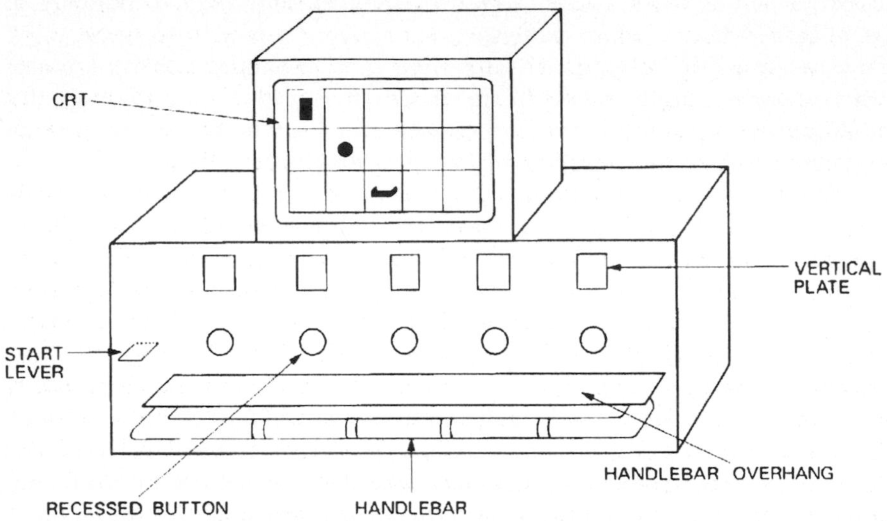

Figure 1. The hand posture sequencing apparatus

Subjects started each trial by resting their index finger on the start plate which caused the sequence to appear on the monitor. After a random delay of 250 ms or 2000 ms, a tone signaled subjects to begin the sequence. To control for memory factors, the visual display remained available until completion of the last response in the sequence. Subjects performed sequences of repetitive hand postures that varied in length from one to five responses (e.g., P, PP, PPP, PPPP, PPPPP) and heterogeneous hand postures that varied in length from two to five responses (e.g., PB, PBP, PBPP, PBPPP).

The results showed that prior to movement PD patients programmed sequences of repetitive hand postures similarly to controls. There was no difference between groups in overall RT, and for both groups sequence length had only a small effect on RTs with isolated hand postures having faster RTs than repetitions of the same hand postures (regardless of length). This finding suggests repetitive sequences were programmed as a single unit (Harrington & Haaland, 1987), and contrasts with those of others (Stelmach, et al., 1987) perhaps because in our study subjects could more easily group repetitive movements due to the spatial location cues provided by the apparatus.

For heterogeneous sequences, RTs increased linearly with sequence length for both groups because they had to assemble a motor plan consisting of motor programs, one for each response in the sequence. However, RTs of the PD group were less affected by sequence length, indicating that in PD a motor program is constructed that is dissimilar to that of controls even when more time is available to do so. Interestingly, RTs in a group of PD patients with normal visuospatial skills increased with sequence length similarly to those of controls, introducing the possibility that assembling a motor program for nonrepetitive movements may rely in part on the integration of visuospatial information.

PD patients showed as much improvement as controls with a longer delay prior to the imperative stimulus, and this was true for both types of sequences. However, unlike controls, their performance continued to benefit with a longer delay during the first inter-response time (IRT). These findings contrast with those of others (Bloxham, et al., 1984; Sheridan, et al., 1987) and demonstrate that PD patients can benefit from advance information despite their apparent deficits in planning more complex movements. The delay interval effects for the first IRT were not related to the complexity of sequences suggesting that longer delays facilitated the initiation or programming of the first response. PD patients may take longer to activate the motor program (which specifies the movement parameters) for the first hand posture which is consistent with EMG studies (Hallett, et al., 1977), or they may have difficulty programming force-time parameters of the first hand posture (Stelmach & Worringham, 1988).

However, regardless of delay, the PD group's IRTs were *faster* with *longer* sequences of repetitive hand postures whereas for controls sequence length had no effect on IRTs. These findings suggest a deficit in utilizing motor programs to control execution, even of repetitive movements. One proposal is that the PD group had difficulty resolving where a sequence would terminate such that hand postures contained in longer sequences were more quickly executed because they had more time to identify the end of the sequence. Execution of shorter sequences had to be delayed in order to coordinate identification of the terminal response with scheduling the execution of individual movements. Deficits of this nature may be similar to those where PD patients made more errors than controls concerning the number of repetitive finger taps in a sequence (Stelmach, et al., 1987).

For heterogeneous sequences, PD patients had difficulty switching from one motor program to another (i.e., longer IRTs and more errors, but only when changing to a different hand posture), as others have suggested (Benecke, et al., 1987). The mechanisms underlying this deficit were not clear from our studies as we do not know whether deficits were due to, for example, problems switching between different motor programs or selecting force parameters of a new movement.

The above findings suggest that deficits in PD are specific to different levels of motor programming. PD patients did not evidence problems utilizing advance information, initiating movements (i.e., no group differences in overall RT), or assembling motor programs for particular hand postures (i.e., no group differences in RTs for different hand postures). They did demonstrate deficits in assembling a motor plan for heterogeneous sequences only (i.e., PD patients' RTs less effected by sequence length), planning the termination of a sequence (i.e., IRTs of patients became faster as sequences increased in length), switching between different responses (i.e., patients had longer IRTs and greater errors when changing hand postures), and activating a motor program or programming force parameters of movements (i.e., the first IRT of patients continued to improve with a longer delay).

5.4. Concluding Remarks

Investigations of complex motor function in PD patients is in its early stages, but studies are gaining insight into possible central processing deficits. Findings suggesting that PD patients cannot use advance information in simple RT paradigms to facilitate response initiation are clouded by possible speed-accuracy tradeoffs and response complexity issues, and have not been consistently replicated. Recent work suggests that PD patients can use advance information to formulate a motor program but that the motor program may be different from that of controls (Harrington & Haaland, 1990). Organizational processes should be studied as programming deficits in PD are especially evident when an internal motor representation must be constructed (Flowers, 1978; Robertson & Flowers, 1990; Stern, et al., 1984). Such processes are multifaceted, but there are some clues as to aspects that may be relevant in the study of complex movements such as sequencing. Findings that RTs are less affected or not affected by sequence length (Harrington & Haaland, 1990; Stelmach, et al., 1987) may suggest that PD patients have difficulty constructing a motor program for all responses within a sequence when movements are sufficiently complex. Sequential ordering is another component of response organization that has received practically no attention in studies of PD despite such deficits in patients with frontal lobe damage (Petrides & Milner, 1982; Shimamura, et al., 1989) and related deficits (i.e., temporal ordering of words) in patients with PD (Sagar, et al., 1988).

Some research has suggested that the ability to integrate visuospatial information may also affect organizational processing or other aspects of motor programming (Harrington & Haaland, 1990; Stern, et al., 1984) especially as PD patients appear to rely on the use of visual information for performing movements (Flowers, 1976, 1978). Many (Boller, Passafiume, Keefe, Rogers, Morrow, & Kim, 1984; Pirozzolo, Hansch, Mortimer,

Webster, & Kuskowski, 1982) but not all studies (Brown & Marsden, 1986) assessing cognitive deficits in PD have demonstrated visuospatial deficits but these studies have not examined motor programming processes.

Frequently it has been observed that PD patients exhibit difficulty learning tasks during practice trials and some studies have confirmed that they indeed show deficits in motor learning (Frith, Bloxham, & Carpenter, 1986; Harrington, et al., 1990; Saint-Cyr, Taylor, & Lang, 1988). Although impaired motor learning may be explained by deficits in some of the previously described cognitive processes, the basal ganglia may regulate other processes that are more specifically important in motor learning. Reasons for impaired learning in PD have not been defined as studies have not examined the cognitive processes underlying motor learning or how motor representations change with learning.

6. Implications for Future Directions

One of the difficulties in studying neuroanatomical correlates of complex motor skills is the absence of a theoretical account of complex motor function that provides enough specificity to guide research. Open and closed loop control theories (Adams, 1971; Keele, 1968) and schema theories (Schmidt, 1975) have dominated cognitive views of motor skills, but they have not supplied the necessary specificity to guide systematic investigations into the processes that frequently seem relevant to understanding abnormalities in motor systems. In contrast, research concerned with the neuroanatomical basis of motor control processes has typically ignored long-term learning and retention which has largely been the emphasis of motor theories. We believe that integration of these two separate lines of research holds promise for furthering our knowledge of motor programming processes and their neuroanatomical basis.

6.1. Cortical and Subcortical Roles

Both cortical and subcortical studies of motor sequencing have been primarily concerned with examining deficits in the cognitive control of movements, but the studies differ in terms of which aspects of motor control have been examined. Studies of inter- and intra-hemispheric roles in performing sequences of movements lack specificity for identifying deficits in levels of motor programming. Thus, studies are not able to address the reasons underlying motor deficits reported in patients with left- or right-hemispheric damage or in patients with amage to the frontal, temporal, or parietal cortex. By comparison, studies of movement regulation with basal ganglia dysfunction have made more progress in isolating deficits in specific aspects of motor control but more work is needed to identify the mechanisms that explain these deficits.

The effects of internal and external contextual states (e.g., goals, motivation, arousal, familiarity, strategies, instructions, stimulus cues) on motor control processes have received little or no attention in either area. Internal and external contextual states have been shown to influence performance in normal controls but how these factors directly relate to deficits in specific aspects of motor programming is unknown. Although there is some evidence that PD patients (Flowers, 1978; Stern, et al., 1984; Robertson & Flowers, 1990) may rely on the presence of external stimulus cues to facilitAte motor programming, no study has directly compared how internally versus externally generated cues affect different motor programming levels. The importance of such cues is perhaps also reflected by studies of memory factors in motor performance showing deficits in left- but not right-hemisphere damaged patients in the acquisition of hand position sequences with but not without a memory component (Jason, 1985, 1986). When subjects reproduce an action sequence from memory this may require more self-generated motor programming such that the demands on certain levels of programming are greater. Similarly, the development of goals and strategies and the importance of state dependent factors such as depression and arousal are typically not considered in regards to their potential influence on cognitive aspects of performance.

This leads us to the topic of learning. Motor representations are established and continually modified by the motor programming or control processes that operate upon actions thereby allowing for learning. Yet studies of motor control and motor learning have traditionally proceeded independently of one another which may, in part, explain why our knowledge of motor representations and the processes that presumably formulate these representations (Kolers & Roediger, 1984) is extremely limited. Processes involved in motor programming likely vary with learning (Marteniuk & Romanow, 1983). Still, few studies of neurologically intact individuals and none of patients with motor abnormalities have interrelated these components of the motor system. How is this relevant to studies of cortical and subcortical motor deficits? Studies of short-term learning are suggestive of impaired motor learning in left-hemisphere-damaged patients (Jason, 1983a, 1983b, 1985; Kimura, 1977; Wyke, 1971), and motor learning deficits have also been found in PD (Frith, et al., 1986; Harrington et al., 1990; Saint-Cyr, et al., 1988). However, because the relative importance of specific motor programming processes early versus late in practice have not been studied, we do not know if the reasons for learning impairments are different in patients with cortical or subcortical damage. Similarly, if skill learning is a process of developing increasingly more accurate and coordinated motor programs or, in other terms, moving from a closed-loop (i.e., feedback based) to an open-loop (i.e., preprogrammed) mode of control, recent findings showing left hemisphere damage produces deficits in performing simple aiming movements that are largely open-loop (Haaland & Harrington, 1989) may account for apparent motor learning impairments in these patients. These findings must be extended in experiments designed to examine how the contribution of specific cognitive processes changes with learning in patients with and without motor abnormalities.

As a final comment, recent proposals suggestive of functionally and neuroanatomically separate systems for acquiring certain types of knowledge (Cohen & Squire, 1980; Squire, 1987) also point to the importance of studying motor control processes across the course of learning. Briefly, some of these studies suggest that the diencephalic-medial temporal lobe system may be important for learning declarative information such as required in tests of recall and recognition (Graf, Squire, & Mandler, 1984; Moscovitch, 1984; Squire & Cohen, 1984;) whereas the basal ganglia may regulate some procedural functions such as rotary pursuit learning (Harrington, et al., 1990; Heindel, Butters, & Salmon, 1988; Mishkin & Petri, 1984). However, the mechanisms behind slower learning for certain skills are not known. This is an important point as it is unlikely that neuroanatomical systems are specialized for certain tasks but rather for certain processes that regulate learning, some of which may be common to both procedural and declarative tasks. This may explain why some patients with damage to the medial temporal lobe system can learn some declarative tasks (Glisky, Schacter, & Tulving, 1986; Hirst, Johnson, Phelps, & Volpe, 1988; Schacter, Harbluk, & McLachlan, 1984) but not some procedural tasks (Butters, Wolfe, Martone, Granholm, & Cermak, 1985), and why PD patients can learn a visuoperceptual but not a motor procedural task (Harrington, et al., 1990). Future studies examining similar levels of programming on motor and non-motor based procedural and declarative tasks may provide some insight into the neuroanatomical basis for specific processing deficits and whether they generalize across sensory modalities.

Acknowledgements

This research was supported by the Research Services of the Veterans Administration. The authors would like to thank Kenneth A. Flowers and Gregor W. Jason for their helpful suggestions on the manuscript.

References

Adams, J.A. (1971). A closed-loop theory of motor learning. *Journal of Motor Behavior*, **3**, 111-149.

Agostini, E., Coletti, A., Orlando, G., & Tredici, G. (1983). Apraxia in deep cerebral lesions. *Journal of Neurology, Neurosurgery, and Psychiatry*, **46**, 804-808.

Alexander, G.E. (1984). Instruction-dependent neuronal activity in primate putamen. *Society of Neurosciences Abstract*, **10**, 515.

Alexander, G.E., DeLong, M.R., & Strick, P.L. (1986). Parallel organization of functionally segregated circuits linking basal ganglia and cortex. *Annual Review of Neurosciences*, **9**, 357-381.

Allen, G.I., & Tsukahara, N. (1974). Cerebrocerebellar communication systems. *Physiological Reviews*, **54**, 957-1006.

Basso, A., Faglioni, P., & Luzzatti, C. (1985). Methods in neuroanatomical research and an experimental study of limb apraxia. In E.A. Roy (Ed.), *Neuropsychological studies of apraxia and related disorders* (pp. 179-202). Amsterdam: North-Holland.

Benecke, R., Rothwell, J.C., Dick, J.P.R., Day, B.L., & Marsden, C.D. (1986). Performance of simultaneous movements in patients with Parkinson's disease. *Brain*, **109**, 739-757.

Benecke, R., Rothwell, J.C., Dick, J.P.R., Day, B.L., & Marsden, C.D. (1987). Disturbance of sequential movements in patients with Parkinson's disease. *Brain*, **110**, 361-379.

Bloxham, C.A., Mindel, T.A., & Frith, C.D. (1984). Initiation and execution of predictable and unpredictable movements in Parkinson's disease. *Brain*, **107**, 371-384.

Boller, F., Mizutani, T., Roessman, U, & Gambetti, P. (1980). Parkinson's disease, dementia, and Alzheimer's disease: clinicopathological correlations. *Annals of Neurology*, **7**, 329-335.

Boller, F., Passafiume, D., Keefe, N.C., Rogers, K., Morrow, L., & Kim, Y. (1984). Visuospatial impairment in Parkinson's disease. *Archives of Neurology*, **41**, 485-490.

Brooks, V. B. (1986). *The neural basis of motor control.* New York: Oxford University Press.

Brown, R.G., & Marsden, C.D. (1986). Visuospatial function in Parkinson's disease. *Brain*, **109**, 987-1002.

Butters, N., Wolfe, J., Martone, M., Granholm, E., & Cermak, L.S. (1985). Memory disorders associated with Huntington's disease: verbal recall, verbal recognition and procedural memory. *Neuropsychologia*, **23**, 729-743.

Canavan, A.G.M., Passingham, R.E., Marsden, C.D., Quinn, N., Wyke, M., & Polkey, C.E. (1989). Sequencing ability in Parkinsonians, patients with frontal lobe lesions and patients who have undergone unilateral temporal lobectomies. *Neuropsychologia*, **27**, 787-798.

Chui, H.C., Mortimer, J.A., Slager, U., Zarow, C., Bondareff, W., & Webster, D.D. (1986). Pathologic correlates of dementia in Parkinson's disease. *Archives of Neurology*, **43**, 991-995.

Cohen, N.J., & Squire, L.R. (1980). Preserved learning and retention of pattern-analyzing skill in amnesia: dissociation of knowing how and knowing that. *Science*, **210**, 207-210.

Cools, A.R., Van Den Bercken, J.H.L., Horstink, M.W.I., Van Spaendonck, K.P.M., & Berger, H.J.C. (1984). Cognitive and motor shifting aptitude disorder in Parkinson's disease. *Journal of Neurology, Neurosurgery, and Psychiatry*, **47**, 443-453.

Crutcher, M.D., & DeLong, M.R. (1984). Single cell studies of the primate putamen. II. Relations to direction of movement and pattern of muscular activity. *Experimental Brain Research*, **53**, 244-258.

Day, B.L., Dick, J.P.R., & Marsden, C.D. (1984). Patients with Parkinson's disease can employ a predictive motor strategy. *Journal of Neurology, Neurosurgery, and Psychiatry*, **47**, 1299-1306.

Damasio, A.R., & Van Hoesen, G.W. (1980). Structure and function of the supplementary motor area. *Neurology*, **30**, 359.

De Renzi, E., Motti, F., & Nichelli, P. (1980). Imitating gestures: a quantitative approach to ideomotor apraxia. *Archives of Neurology*, **37**, 6-10.

De Renzi, E., Faglioni, P., Lodesani, M., & Vecchi, A. (1983). Performance of left brain-damaged patients on imitation of single movements and motor sequences. Frontal and parietal-injured patients compared. *Cortex*, **19**, 333-343.

Erickson, T.C., & Woolsey, C.N. (1951). Observations of the supplementary motor area in man. *Transactions of the American Neurology Association*, **76**, 50-52.

Finger, S., & Stein, D.G. (1982). *Brain damage and recovery: Research and clinical perspectives*. Orlando, FL: Academic Press.

Flowers, K.A. (1976). Visual 'closed-loop' and 'open-loop' characteristics of voluntary movement in patients with Parkinsonism and intention tremor. *Brain*, **99**, 269-310.

Flowers, K.A. (1978). Lack of prediction in the motor behaviour of parkinsonism. *Brain*, **101**, 35-52.

Flowers, K.A., & Robertson, C. (1985). The effect of Parkinson's disease on the ability to maintain a mental set. *Journal of Neurology, Neurosurgery and Psychiatry*, **48**, 517-529.

Frith, C.D., Bloxham, C.A., & Carpenter, K.N. (1986). Impairments in the learning and performance of a new manual skill in patients with Parkinson's disease. *Journal of Neurology, Neurosurgery, and Psychiatry*, **49**, 661-668.

Geschwind, N. (1965). Disconnexion syndromes in animals and man. *Brain*, **88**, 237-294, 585-644.

Glisky, E.L., Schacter, D.L., & Tulving, E. (1986). Computer learning by memory-impaired patients: acquisition and retention of complex knowledge. *Neuropsychologia*, **24**, 313-328.

Goldman-Rakic, P. (1988). Topography of cognition: parallel distributed networks in primate association cortex. *Annual Review of Neuroscience*, **11**, 137-156.

Graf, P., Squire, L.R., & Mandler, G. (1984). The information that amnesic patients do not forget. *Journal of Experimental Psychology: Learning, Memory, and Cognition*, **10**, 164-178.

Haaland, K.Y., & Harrington, D.L. (1989). Hemispheric control of the initial and corrective components of aiming movements. *Neuropsychologia*, **27**, 961-969.

Haaland, K.Y., Rubens, A.B., & Harrington, D. L. (1989). Anatomical correlates of recovery from apraxia. *Journal of Clinical and Experimental Neuropsychology*, **11**, 42.

Haaland, K.Y., & Yeo, R.A. (1989). Neuropsychological and neuroanatomic aspects of complex motor control. In E.D. Bigler, R.A. Yeo, & E. Turkheimer (Eds.), *Neuropsychological function and brain imaging* (pp. 219-244). New York: Plenum Publishing.

Hallett, M., Shahani, B.T., & Young, R.R. (1977). Analysis of stereotyped voluntary movements at the elbow in patients with Parkinson's disease. *Journal of Neurology, Neurosurgery, and Psychiatry*, **40**, 1129-1135.

Harrington, D.L., & Haaland, K.Y. (1987). Programming sequences of hand postures. *Journal of Motor Behavior*, **19**, 77-95.

Harrington, D.L., & Haaland, K.Y. (1990). Sequencing in Parkinson's disease: abnormalities in programming and controlling movement. *Brain*.

Harrington, D.L., Haaland, K.Y., Yeo, R.A., & Marder, E. (1990). Procedural memory in Parkinson's disease: impaired motor but not visuoperceptual learning. *Journal of Clinical and Experimental Neuropsychology*, **12**, 323-339.

Heilman, K.M., Rothi, L.J., & Valenstein, E. (1982). Two forms of ideomotor apraxia. *Neurology*, **32**, 342-346.

Heindel, W.C., Butters, N., & Salmon, D.P. (1988). Impaired learning of a motor skill in patients with Huntington's disease. *Behavioral Neuroscience*, **102**, 141-147.

Hirst, W., Johnson, M.K., Phelps, E.A., & Volpe, B.T. (1988). More on recognition and recall in amnesics. *Journal of Experimental Psychology: Learning, Memory, and Cognition,* **14**, 758-762.

Inhoff, A.W., Diener, H.C., Rafal, R.D., & Ivry, R. (1989). The role of cerebellar structures in the execution of serial movements. *Brain,* **112**, 565-581.

Jason, G.W. (1983a). Hemispheric asymmetries in motor function. I. Left hemisphere specialization for memory but not performance. *Neuropsychologia,* **21**, 35-45.

Jason, G.W. (1983b). Hemispheric asymmetries in motor function. II. Ordering does not contribute to left hemisphere specialization. *Neuropsychologia,* **21**, 47-58.

Jason, G.W. (1985). Manual sequence learning after focal cortical lesions. *Neuropsychologia,* **23**, 483-496.

Jason, G.W. (1986). Performance of manual copying tasks after focal cortical lesions. *Neuropsychologia,* **24**, 181-191.

Jones-Gotman M., & Milner, B. (1977). Design fluency: the invention of nonsense drawings after focal cortical lesions. *Neuropsychologia,* **15**, 653-674.

Keele, S.W. (1968). Movement control in skilled performance. *Psychological Bulletin,* **70**, 387-403.

Kertesz, A., & Ferro, J.M. (1984). Lesion size and location in ideomotor apraxia. *Brain,* **107**, 921-933.

Kimura, D. (1977). Acquisition of a motor skill after left- hemisphere brain damage. *Brain,* **100**, 527-542.

Kimura, D. (1982). Left-hemisphere control of oral and brachial movements and their relation to communication. *Philosophical Transactions of the Royal Society of London,* **B298**, 135-149.

Kimura, D., & Archibald, Y. (1974). Motor functions of the left hemisphere. *Brain,* **97**, 337-350.

Kolb, B., & Milner, B. (1981). Performance of complex arm and facial movements after focal brain lesions. *Neuropsychologia,* **19**, 491-503.

Kolers, P.A., & Roediger H.L. (1984). Procedures of mind. *Journal of Verbal Learning and Verbal Behavior,* **23**, 425-449.

Leonard, G., Milner, B., & Jones, L. (1988). Performance on unimanual and bimanual tapping tasks by patients with lesions of the frontal or temporal lobe. *Neuropsychologia,* **26**, 79-91.

Lieberman, A. (1974). Parkinson's disease. A clinical review. *American Journal of Medical Sciences,* **267**, 66-80.

Luria, A.R. (1966). *Higher cortical functions in man.* New York: Basic Books.

Marteniuk, R.G., & Romanow, S.K.E. (1983). Human movement organization and learning as revealed by variability of movement, use of kinematic information, and fourier analysis. In R.A. Magill (Ed.), *Memory and control of action* (pp. 167-196). Amsterdam: North-Holland.

Mishkin, M. (1982). A memory system in the monkey. In D.E. Broadbent & L. Weiskrantz (Eds.), *Neuropsychology of cognitive function* (pp. 85-95). London: The Royal Society.

Mishkin, M., & Petri, H.L. (1984). Memories and habits: some implications for the analysis of learning and retention. In L.R. Squire & N. Butters (Eds.), *Neuropsychology of memory* (pp. 287-296). New York: Guilford Press.

Morris, R.G., Downes, J.J., Sahakian, B.J., Evenden, J.L., Heald, A., & Robbins, T.W. (1988). Planning and spatial working memory in Parkinson's disease. *Journal of Neurology, Neurosurgery, and Psychiatry*, **51**, 757-766.

Moscovitch, M. (1984). The sufficient conditions for demonstrating preserved memory in amnesia: a task analysis. In L.R. Squire & N Butters (Eds.), *Neuropsychology of memory* (pp. 104-114). New York: Guilford Press.

Nahmias, C., Garnett, E.S., Firnau, G., & Lang, A. (1985). Striatal dopamine distribution in Parkinsonian patients during life. *Journal of the Neurological Sciences*, **69**, 223-230.

Nauta, W.J.H. (1971). The problem of the frontal lobe: a reinterpretation. *Journal of Psychiatric Research*, **8**, 167-187.

Paillard, J. (1982). Apraxia and the neurophysiology of motor control. *Philosophical Transactions of the Royal Society of London*, **B298**, 111-134.

Perlmutter, J.S., & Raichle, M.E. (1985). Regional blood flow in hemiparkinsonism. *Neurology*, **35**, 1127-1134.

Petrides, M., & Milner, B. (1982). Deficits on subject-ordered tasks after frontal- and temporal-lobe lesions in man. *Neuropsychologia*, **20**, 249-262.

Pirozzolo, F.J., Hansch, E.C., Mortimer, J.A., Webster, D.D., & Kuskowski, M.A. (1982). Dementia in Parkinson's disease: a neuropsychological analysis. *Brain and Cognition*, **1**, 71-83.

Pirozzolo, F.J., Swihart, A.A., Rey, G., Jankovic, J., & Mortimer, J.A. (1988). Cognitive impairments associated with Parkinson's disease and other movement disorders. In J. Jankovic & E. Tolosa (Eds.), *Parkinson's disease and movement disorders* (pp. 425-439). Baltimore: Urban & Schwartzenberg.

Rafal, R.D., Inhoff, A.W., Friedman, J.H., & Bernstein, E. (1987). Programming and execution of sequential movements in Parkinson's disease. *Journal of Neurology, Neurosurgery, and Psychiatry*, **50**, 1267-1273.

Rafal, R.D., Posner, M., Walker, J.A., & Friedrich, F.J. (1984). Cognition and the basal ganglia. *Brain*, **107**, 1083-1094.

Robertson, C., & Flowers, K.A. (1990). Motor set in Parkinson's disease. *Journal of Neurology, Neurosurgery, and Psychiatry*.

Roland, P.E., Larsen, B., Lassen, N.A., & Skinhøj, E. (1980). Supplementary motor area and other cortical areas in organization of voluntary movements in man. *Journal of Neurophysiology*, **43**, 118-136.

Roy, E.A. (1981). Action sequencing and lateralized cerebral damage: evidence for asymmetries in control. In J. Long & A. Baddeley (Eds.), *Attention and performance IX* (pp. 487-500). Hillsdale, NJ: Lawrence Erlbaum Associates.

Sagar, H.J., Sullivan, E.V., Gabrieli, J.D.E., Corkin, S. & Growdon, J.H. (1988). Temporal ordering and short-term memory deficits in Parkinson's disease. *Brain*, **111**, 525-539.

Saint-Cyr, J.A., Taylor, A.E., & Lang, A.E. (1988). Procedural learning and neostriatal dysfunction in man. *Brain*, **111**, 941-959.

Schacter, D.L., Harbluk, J.L., & McLachlan, D.R. (1984). Retrieval without recollection: an experimental analysis of source amnesia. *Journal of Verbal Learning and Verbal Behavior*, **23**, 593-611.

Schmidt, R.A. (1975). A schema theory of discrete motor skill learning. *Psychological Review*, **82**, 225-260.

Selemon, L.D., & Goldman-Rakic, P.S. (1985). Common cortical and subcortical target areas of the dorsolateral prefrontal and posterior parietal cortices in the rhesus monkey. *Society of Neurosciences Abstract*, **11**, 323.

Sharpe, M.H., Cermak, S.A., & Sax, D.S. (1983). Motor planning in Parkinson's patients. *Neuropsychologia*, **21**, 455-462.

Sheridan, M.R., Flowers, K.A., & Hurrell, J. (1987). Programming and execution of movement in Parkinson's disease. *Brain*, **110**, 1247-1271.

Shimamura, A.P., Janowsky, J.S., & Squire, L.R. (1990). *Memory for the temporal order of events in patients with frontal lobe lesions and amnesic patients.* Manuscript submitted for publication.

Squire, L.R. (1987). *Memory and brain.* New York: Oxford University Press.

Squire, L.R., & Cohen, N.J. (1984). Human memory and amnesia. In J. McGaugh, G. Lynch, & N. Weinberger (Eds.), *Neurobiology of learning and memory* (pp. 3-64). New York: Guilford Press.

Stelmach, G.E., & Worringham, C.J. (1988). The preparation and production of isometric force in Parkinson's disease. *Neuropsychologia*, **26**, 93-103.

Stelmach, G.E., Worringham, C.J., & Strand, E.A. (1986). Movement preparation in Parkinson's disease. *Brain*, **109**, 1179-1194.

Stelmach, G.E., Worringham, C.J., & Strand, E.A. (1987). The programming and execution of movement sequences in Parkinson's disease. *International Journal of Neuroscience*, **36**, 55-65.

Stern, Y., Mayeux, R., & Rosen, J. (1984). Contribution of perceptual motor dysfunction to construction and tracing disturbances in Parkinson's disease. *Journal of Neurology, Neurosurgery, and Psychiatry*, **47**, 983-989.

Tanji, J., Taniguchi, K. & Saga, T. (1980). SMA: neuronal response to motor instructions. *Journal of Neurophysiology*, **43**, 60-68.

Taylor, A.E., Saint-Cyr, J.A., & Lang, A.E. (1986). Frontal lobe dysfunction in Parkinson's disease. *Brain*, **109**, 845-883.

Watson, R.T., Shepherd, F., Gonzalez-Rothi, L., & Heilman, K.M. (1986). Apraxia and the supplementary motor area. *Archives of Neurology*, **43**, 787-792.

Wyke, M. (1971). The effects of brain lesions on the learning performance of a bimanual co-ordination task. *Cortex*, **7**, 59-72.

PART II

LANGUAGE AND GESTURE

Cerebral Control of Speech and Limb Movements
G.E. Hammond (editor)

Chapter 7

SPEECH AND GESTURE

David McNeill
University of Chicago

Elena T. Levy
University of Connecticut

and

Laura L. Pedelty
University of Chicago

When people talk they can be seen making spontaneous movements called 'gestures'. These are usually movements of the arms and hands and they are closely synchronized with the flow of speech. Gestures and speech occur in very close temporal alignment and often have identical meanings, or 'idea units' (Kendon, 1980). Yet they express these idea units in fundamentally different ways. While speech is segmented (into phonemes, words, phrases, etc.), gestures are global and synthetic. There is no gesture 'language'. Comparing speech to gesture thus enables us to observe the same idea unit expressed in two different ways at the same time. A comparison of this kind produces an effect on our understanding of the linguistic system and gesture something like the effect of triangulation in vision. Many new details, previously hidden, spring out in the new dimension of seeing. Rather than analytically slicing the person into modules, taking into account gesture encourages seeing something like the entire personality as a single theoretical entity -- thinking, speaking, acting as a unit.

Our goal in this chapter is to describe the variety of relationships that hold between speech and gesture -- temporal, semantic, and functional. We also discuss the gestures of aphasic patients and what they suggest about the cerebral control of this type of meaning-bearing movements. The types of gesture we consider are the unwitting gestural accompaniments of spoken discourse, and among these gestures we identify several types: *iconic gestures* (in which form, space and movement depict a concrete action or object), *metaphoric gestures* (in which form, space, and movement depict an abstract idea), *beats* (small rapid movements synchronized with speech rhythms), and *deictic gestures* (pointing, especially 'abstract' pointing in which an overt target is lacking).

We present our topic in seven sections. The first describes in general the types of gesture that appear during speech. To distinguish gesture types presupposes a classificatory system for movements, and we describe the classificatory system that we have used. The next section describes the experimental paradigm we have followed for collecting and coding gestures. The third section analyzes the kinesic structure of gesture forms. Our fourth section presents detailed examples of the varieties of gesture that occur during narrative discourse -- iconic, metaphoric, beat, and deictic -- that appear in the experimental setting (most of our examples are drawn from narratives, as we will explain). In this section, also, we present the basic statistics on gesture occurrence in relation to speech. The fifth section analyzes the various relationships of gestures to speech. In the sixth section we explore issues of the cerebral control by discussing investigations of handedness of gesture movements and the gestures of brain-damaged patients. Finally, we propose some unifying themes that tie together our observations of gestures and speech.

Types of Gesture

Kendon's Continuum

In a paper first circulated in 1983, Kendon (1988) distinguished among gestures on what we shall call 'Kendon's continuum':

Gesticulation → 'Language-like' gestures → Pantomime → Emblems → Sign Languages

As we move from left to right on the continuum several changes take place: (1) the obligatory presence of speech declines, (2) the presence of language properties in the gesture increases, and (3) the gestures themselves change from idiosyncratic to socially regulated.

Kendon's continuum is important for sorting out gestures of fundamentally different kinds. Many authors refer to all forms of nonverbal behavior as 'gesture', failing to distinguish among different categories, with the result that behaviors that differ fundamentally are confused or conflated. (Hécaen, 1967, 1978, proposed a scheme that recognized many of the distinctions above, but did not perceive them as falling on a continuum.) We use the term 'gesture' in this chapter specifically to refer to the leftmost, 'gesticulation' end of the spectrum.

Gestures in this sense are idiosyncratic spontaneous movements of the hands and arms accompanying speech. An example is the hand rising upward while the speaker says 'and he climbs up the pipe'. Gestures ('gesticulation') almost never occur in the absence of speech. 'Language-like gestures' are similar in form and appearance to gesticulation but differ in that they are grammatically integrated into the utterance; an example is 'the parents were all right, but the kids were [gesture]', where the gesture fills the grammatical slot of an adjective. In pantomime the hands depict objects or actions, but speech is not obligatory. This weakened speech presence locates pantomime in the middle of Kendon's continuum. There may be either silence or just inarticulate onomatopoeic sound effects ('whoops!' 'click!' etc.). Moreover, successive pantomimes can create sentence-like demonstrations, and this is different from gesticulation where successive gestures do not combine. Emblems also occupy the middle area of Kendon's continuum. Which one -- emblem or pantomime -- belongs more to the right is arbitrary. These are the familiar 'Italianate' gestures, mostly insults but some of them praise, and all attempts to control other people's behavior (Kendon, 1981). Emblems have standards of well-formedness, a crucial language-like property that gesticulation and pantomime lack. For example, the 'OK' sign must be made by contacting the thumb and index finger; contacting the thumb and second finger is not the 'OK' sign. Emblems have as their characteristic use production in the absence of speech (indeed, this is probably their raison d'etre: they offer a way of getting around speech taboos). Emblems have been described by Efron (1941), Ekman and Friesen (1969), Morris, Collett, Marsh and O'Shaughnessy (1979), and Kendon (1981). Sign languages, finally, such as ASL, are full-fledged linguistic systems with segmentation, compositionality, a lexicon, a syntax, distinctiveness, arbitrariness, standards of well-formedness and a community of users (see Klima & Bellugi, 1979).

These distinctions between the different types of communicative manual actions are crucial. Not only do the different types of movements bear different logical and behavioral relations to speech, they also are affected differently following cerebral lesions. Thus highly codified sign languages such as ASL may be disrupted in ways that result in 'sign aphasias' much like the aphasias observed in speaking patients (Poizner, Klima & Bellugi 1987). Emblems and pantomimes might be expected to replace or supplement language to the extent that linguistic capacities remain to be exploited via another channel. Production of emblems and pantomimes, which are often tested in an attempt to 'quantify' gestural skills (see Peterson & Kirshner, 1981, for a review) do not vary systematically with the type of aphasia, but seem to be related to overall severity of the communicative deficit. Gesticulation, as we will see, bears a more complex relationship to speech, and varies in subtle and intricate ways in relation to the speech it accompanies.

Classification Schemes

A number of classification schemes for gestures have been proposed over the years. For example, Ekman & Friesen (1969) distinguished between kinetographs, pictographs, spatials, batons, ideographs, underliners, rhythmics and deictics. Freedman (1972) recognized representational gestures, concretization gestures, pointing, and gestures with speech failures. All gesture classification schemes refer to the same movements and seem to recognize a distinction between content-carrying gestures and other forms, but categorize them in somewhat different ways depending on the purpose of the investigation.

Table 1. Three Gesture Classification Schemes

Freedman et al.	Ekman & Friesen	Present Categories
representational	kinetographs	iconix
	pictographs	
concretization	ideographs	metaphorix
	underliners	
	spatials	
pointing	deictics	deictix
	batons	beats
	rhythmics	
speech failures		Butterworths

Our scheme is close to that of Freedman, and is different from Ekman & Friesen's only in that it combines several of their categories into a smaller number of more macro-categories. Our purpose in classifying gestures is to bring out semiotic values, and this entails finding fundamentally different types of signs. To do this we build semiotic distinctions directly into the gesture classification; that is, to classify the gesture means asking (1) is the movement a symbol? and (2) what type of symbol is it? The categories we have used are iconic, metaphoric, beat or deictic -- fundamental signs of semiology (Peirce, 1931-58). To make clear the differences and similarities among the three schemes mentioned, we offer the accompanying chart (Table 1).

Experimental Paradigm

Basic Situation

Most of our gesture examples have been recorded during narrative discourse. The situation is quasi-experimental in that a speaker is shown a narrative 'stimulus' -- a film, animated cartoon or comic book -- and then immediately tells the story of the stimulus from memory to a listener, and we videotape the performance. The listener is a genuine listener who does not have prior knowledge of the stimulus and does not see it. The speaker is told to present the story in as clear and complete a fashion as possible, for the listener will have to retell it later to a third person. Neither the speaker nor the listener knows that gestures are of the slightest interest and the instructions take care not even to mention the word. The speakers have been adults or children, and some have been speakers of non-English languages (German, French, Italian, Georgian, Swahili, Chinese and Japanese -- the last four non-Indo-European). In addition, we have tested both Broca type and Wernicke type aphasics and one commissurectomized patient (a 'split brain'). A major methodological advantage of our procedure is that since we know the source of the narration independently of the narration itself, comparisons among speakers narrating the same episodes are possible. A detailed description of this research project will be presented in McNeill (forthcoming).

Coding

The following is a sketch of the method that we have followed in coding iconic, beat, metaphoric and deictic gestures.

All visible movements by the speaker are first differentiated into gestures and non-gestures; the latter are self-touching (e.g., stroking the hair) or object-manipulations. The rest are 'gestures' and are classified as to type.

A gesture is *iconic* if it bears a close formal relationship to the semantic content of speech. The definition is that an iconic gesture displays, in its form and manner of execution, aspects of the same scene that speech also is presenting (McNeill & Levy, 1982). A gesture is *metaphoric* if it depicts the vehicle of a metaphor, an image of an abstract concept (Richards, 1936). A gesture is a *beat* if it does not depict any recognizable image but is timed to occur with the rhythmical pulses of speech. A gesture, finally, is *deictic* if it points to a locus in the gesture space.

The coding scheme is hierarchical in that some coding categories are introduced only for gestures of the imagistic type (iconix, metaphorix). Coding proceeds by answering a series of questions. For those gestures considered to be iconic or metaphoric gestures, each gesture is coded in terms of: (1) Hands (handedness, shape of hand, palm and finger orientation, and gesture space); (2) Motion (shape of trajectory, space where motion is articulated, and direction), and (3) Meaning (for the hand, what does it represent, and what viewpoint does it entail; for motion, what does it represent and what viewpoint does it entail; in addition, what marked features, if any, does it have, such as manner, direction, kind of path, or locus). For the body, is it representing a different entity from the hand or motion? For metaphoric gestures, we specify both the vehicle of the metaphor (the image that the gesture is depicting) and the tenor (what the abstract meaning is that is being presented in the metaphoric image). If the gesture is a beat, we code timing with respect to speech but not the form of the gesture, unless this varies from the typical (i.e., if the shape is other than an open palm and the movement other than short and up-and-down or side-to-side strokes. If the gesture is deictic, we code only the handedness, shape and the locus where the hand (finger) is directed.

To time gestures in relation to speech a movement is located in slow motion, the tape stopped, and then the tape released and the speech recorded: this provides an alignment within a syllable (it is crucial to have a VCR modified so that it reproduces sound in slow motion). To aid the temporal alignment, we add to each video field a sequential number and oscilloscope trace of the speech wave form. With such data, based entirely on visual information, speech and gesture can be lined up to an accuracy of ±1/60th sec. The auditory and visual methods can be used jointly.

Beat filter

This is an example of a completely formal method of differentiating imagistic (iconic and metaphoric) from non-imagistic (beat) gestures. It is called a 'beat filter' because it filters out imagistic gestures: what passes through are the beats. The filter is a series of questions, and a score of 1 is added for each 'yes' answer: (1) Does the gesture have other than two movement phases (i.e., either 1 phase or 3 phases, or more)? (2) How many times does wrist or finger movement or tensed stasis appear in any movement phase not ending in a rest position? (add this number to the score). (3) If the first movement is in a non-center part of space, is any other movement performed in center space? (4) If there are exactly two movement phases, is the space of the first phase different from the space of the second?

A score of 0 means no imagery on formal grounds, and the gesture probably is a beat. A score of 5 or 6 means high imagery on formal grounds, and the gesture is probably iconic or metaphoric (which it is depends on the relationship to meaning).

The beat filter is useful as an aid to classification. In addition, meaning judgments can be rated on a confidence scale with 1 = marginally convinced and 5 = totally certain.

Kinesic Structure of Gestures

Gesture Form

Kendon (1972, 1980) analyzed gesture movements into several levels. He wrote of this hierarchy that it "may be seen to provide at least a partial diagram of the relations between the units of the speaker's discourse" (Kendon, 1972, p. 207); we have found ample reason to agree with this statement. The following diagram summarizes the gesture levels.

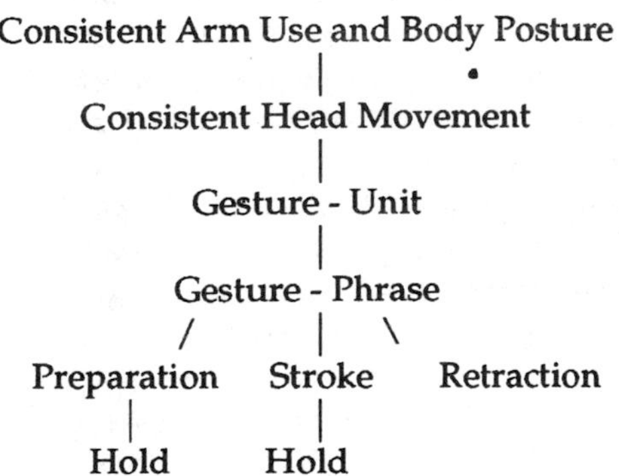

Arm use and body posture

Within units on this level, the speaker adopts different body postures and arm usage patterns. Kendon observed stretches in which all gestures were made with the right arm or left arm, or both. Shifting between arm options and body postures defines a kinesic unit on this level. The discourse stretches marked by consistent arm usage and body postures correspond roughly to a 'paragraph' (Kendon, 1972).

Head movements

Within stretches of a consistent arm and body use shorter stretches occur in which the same head movements take place; for example, first the head moves from the center of the gesture space to the right, and this occurs several times.

Gesture-unit

Gesture-unit is defined as the period of time between successive rests of the limbs; a G-unit begins the moment the limb begins to move and ends when it has reached a rest position again.

Gesture-phrase

Gesture-phrase occurs within a G-unit (several G-phrases may cluster together within one G-unit).

A G-phrase in turn consists of one or more movement phases (preparation, various holds, stroke, retraction):

1. *Preparation* (optional), in which the limb moves away from its rest position to a position in the central gesture space where the stroke begins. The preparation phase typically anticipates the linguistic segments that are co-expressive with the gesture's meaning.

1h. *Preparation-hold* (optional) is the position and hand posture reached at the end of the preparation itself; this may be held more or less briefly until the stroke begins.

A *hold* is a temporary cessation of movement without leaving the gesture hierarchy (in contrast to a rest, which means canceling the existing hierarchy).

2. *Stroke* (obligatory) is the peak of effort in the gesture. It is in this phase that the meaning of the gesture is expressed. The stroke is synchronized with the linguistic segments that are co-expressive with it. It typically is performed in the central gesture space bounded roughly by the waist, shoulders and arms; the head also becomes involved occasionally.

2h. *Stroke-hold* (optional) is the final position and posture of the hand reached at the end of the stroke; this may be held more or less briefly until the retraction begins.

3. *Retraction* (optional) is the return of the hand to a rest position (not necessarily the one occupied before the G-phrase).

While a G-phrase cannot exist without a stroke, by definition, the other phases are optional. However, the option to omit the preparation phase is rarely taken in our narratives. Virtually all gestures contain a preparation component, and one may be added, apparently superfluously. Retraction phases are often omitted when one gesture passes directly into a succeeding gesture. The preparation- and stroke-hold phases can compensate for mismatches of speech-gesture synchrony (see the section on temporal relationships). To illustrate these phases we will use the following examples from Kendon (1980):

1. The hand rises up and takes an 'umbrella' form, and then moves down sharply:
- Preparation: hand rising up and taking 'umbrella' form;
- Stroke: hand moving down sharply;
- Stroke-hold: hand held in position reached at end of stroke;
- Retraction: fingers relax into loose bunch.

2. The arm rises up and sweeps side-to-side two times:
- Preparation: arm rises upward;
- Stroke: arm swings in and out twice; note that this is considered to be one stroke, even though the arm moves in and out two times;
- Retraction: arm returns to the rest position it was in before the gesture.

In this chapter most of our observations refer to the lowest level of the kinesic hierarchy, and within this level, just to the stroke phase (the brackets in examples show stroke phases). The preparation phase will become crucial for the question of gesture timing, which we consider separately below.

Length of G-units

Given that G-units can encompass more than one G-phrase, or gesture, how long in fact do G-units tend to be? Table 2 answers this question for the six cartoon narratives, and shows the percentage of G-units that contain 1, 2, 3, etc., G-phrases. About half of all G-units consist of a single gesture, a few of 2 successive gestures, and the rest of a range of longer sequences.

Table 3 gives the converse distribution, the empty spans between G-units. These are stretches of speech where there were no gestures; the length of a span is indexed in terms of clauses. Most G-units had no clauses between them. This means that 70% of the time the hands returned to rest between successive clauses. Of the remaining spans, two-thirds contained just one clause. Thus, while gesture activity is fairly continuous, there are almost as many rests as there are gestures.

From Tables 2 and 3 we learn that most gestures occur one gesture at a time. Gestures tend to occur as singletons and between gestures the hands return to a rest position. (Along with the obligatory presence of speech, this fact also differentiates gestures from pantomime.)

Table 2. Percent of G-Units of Different Lengths

	Number of G-Phrases in G-Unit							
	1	2	3	4	5	6	>6	Number G-Units
Percent G-Units	56	14	8	8	4	2	8	254

Table 3. Percent of Non-Gesture Intervals of Different Lengths

	Number of Clauses Between G-Units								
	0	1	2	3	4	5	6	>6	Number Intervals
Percent Intervals	70	19	5	3	1	2	-	1	275

Gesture Space

This can be visualized as a flattened disk in front of the speaker. Adults usually gesture within a limited space (with children the gesture space is more like a sphere with the child at the center; see McNeill, 1986, for a description of children's gestures). The fore-aft dimension is shortened and almost never extends behind the body; gestures behind the frontal plane of the body are rare and have marked status.

For transcription purposes, the gesture space can be divided into sectors using a system of concentric squares; the sector directly in front of the chest is Center-Center; surrounding this is the Center, then the Periphery (divided into upper, lower, right, left), and finally, at the outer limit, the Extreme Periphery (also divided).

Iconix, Metaphorix, Beats and Deictix

Statistics on Gesture Occurrence

These statistics are based on the descriptions of 6 cartoon narratives mentioned earlier by young adult English language speakers (university students). The statistics provide a general orientation to the incidence of gestures and their distribution in relation to speech during narrative discourse.

Frequency of Gesture Types

Table 4 is an expanded version of a table in McNeill and Levy (1982).

Table 4. Frequency of Gesture types in Different Contexts

	Type of Gesture					
Type of Clause	Iconic	Beat	Meta-phoric	Deic-tic	None	Total
Narrative	226	134	12	25	146	543
Extranarrative	35	134	31	3	44	247
Total	261	268	43	28	190	790

It shows the relative frequency of iconix, metaphorix, beats, and deictix, as well as the frequency of clauses with no gestures accompanying them at all.

The clause type variable will be explained briefly; for more details, see McNeill and Levy (1982). A narrative clause presents a step in the plot-line development of the story; it is therefore subject to sequential constraints (Labov & Waletzky, 1967; Hopper, 1979; Hopper & Thompson, 1980). An extranarrative clause is any other clause in the storytelling act that is not on the plot-line (e.g., describing the setting, summing up the action, introducing characters, forecasting what is to come, mentioning the video, etc.) and is not subject to sequential constraints. Extra-narrative clauses can be differentiated into subvarieties ('metanarrative' and 'paranarrative'), but the distinction is not crucial for present purposes and can be overlooked (see McNeill, forthcoming, for discussion).

More than half of the clauses in narratives were accompanied by gestures and narrative and extranarrative clauses did not differ in their gesture density.

One generalization that fits Table 4 is this: although there are similar numbers of iconix and beats, iconix occur overwhelmingly in narrative clauses, while beats can occur in both narrative and extranarrative clauses. Thus, iconic gestures are limited by the sequentiality constraint, but beats can appear anywhere. The difference in distribution reflects the different functions of the two kinds of gesture. The events that iconix exhibit inherently progress in temporal and causal sequences in the real or fictive world, while beats occur at points of significant discontinuity in discourse and function to highlight atemporal relationships (Silverstein, 1984).

Another generalization is the following: abstract pointing occurs chiefly with narrative clauses, whereas metaphorix appear chiefly with extranarrative clauses.

Thus, while each type of gesture has its own way of correlating with narrative and extranarrative contexts, the gestures fall into two larger groups:

(1) *Sequence-related* iconix and deictix appear in narrative contexts;

(2) *Structure-related* beats and metaphorix appear in extranarrative contexts. Of these 'structure related' gestures, beats appear in all contexts, while metaphorix appear only in extranarrative contexts.

Gesture : clause correspondence

As a general rule there is one gesture to one clause. Gestures begin, run their course, and end within the span of a single linguistic clause. Narrators, however, can depart from this rule and depart in both directions. Some clauses have more than one gesture and some gestures cover more than one clause. Table 5 tallies the correspondence of gestures and clauses in the 6 cartoon narrations.

Table 5. Proportions of Gesture: Clause Ratios

	Gesture : Clause Ratio						
	1gst: 4cls	1gst: 3cls	1gst: 2cls	1gst: 1cls	2gst: 1cls	3gst: 1cls	N of gsts
Normal Speakers	.005	.01	.04	.67	.19	.08	433

As can be seen, most departures are in the multiple gesture : one clause direction. If we equate gestures with 'idea units' (Kendon, 1980), we can say that the speaker is attempting to unpack more than one idea unit with a single clause. Not surprisingly, given the overloading of the linguistic program this implies, multiple gesture: single clause utterances are often accompanied by dysfluencies. For example, one speaker performed two distinct gestures during the following: '[and she ...][grabbed a knife].' A lengthy pause interrupted the speech flow at the gesture boundary. In the section on cerebral control we will present parallel data for aphasics.

Iconic Gestures

Basic iconix

As mentioned earlier, gestures are 'iconic' if they bear a close formal relationship to the semantic content of speech. An example is a speaker recounting a comic book story and describing a scene in which one of the characters grasped a tree and bent it to the ground. As the speaker described this scene ('and he bends it way back') he appeared to grip something in his own hand and pull it back toward his shoulder. The grip shape of the hand and the backwards trajectory display aspects of the scene that speech also was presenting. Thus the gesture is classified as iconic (in citing gesture examples, square brackets [ ] indicate the temporal extent of the stroke phase of the gesture; italics mark the description of the gesture itself; and the utterance is underlined):

and he [bends it way back]
(1)

(1) Right hand in a grip posture moves backwards and down from the front, ending up near the shoulder.

Note that to judge this or any other gesture iconic, we compare it to our knowledge of the scene, not to the speech. Speech is necessary inasmuch as we rely on the spoken text to know which scene the speaker is describing; but the iconicity of the gesture is determined by whether it exhibits aspects of the same scene described in speech, not the speech itself. It is our independent knowledge that a character seized hold of and bent back a tree that enables us to recognize iconicity in the gesture above. This may seem like an overly precious distinction, but it is logically important. It underlies the concept of gestures and speech complementing each other -- presenting overlapping but different aspects of the same scene. This is a frequent occurrence, but if all we had to go on was the information in the speech, we could not say that a gesture is iconic when it adds to the information conveyed in the speech. Since we refer the gesture to the independently known scene, we can logically define cases of complementarity involving iconic gestures.

The gesture above in fact complemented speech, in that it presented a somewhat different aspect of the scene from the utterance. We note that the gesture was performed with a single hand; from this we can infer that the object being bent back was fastened down at one end (in fact, it was a tree). A two-handed gesture would have been used to depict an object like a stick or ruler that had to be held in place to be bent back. Speech doesn't convey this detail, but we see that it was part of the speaker's active representation of the scene from his gesture.

Examples such as this imply that gesture and speech jointly comprise a single integrated expression of meaning (see McNeill, 1985 for arguments in support of this view). Gesture and speech convey information about the same scenes, but each can include something that the other leaves out. The bending way back example is in no way unique. Many other iconic gestures display this relationship to speech, co-expression combined with complementation.

While the basic definition of iconic gestures refers to the content of the gesture, it is theoretically and practically possible to pick out iconic gestures without any reference to the accompanying speech. Gestures have been coded as beat or iconic based solely on the formal characteristics of movements; this method has been crucial for coding the gestures of non-normal speakers, such as aphasics (Pedelty, 1987). The method requires having a known source of narrations and a corpus of gestures produced by normal speakers in narrations of this source. Because we have repeatedly used the same narrative stimuli we have been able to examine the gestures of many speakers narrating these stories, and to derive 'canonical' gesture forms used to depict certain scenes. Gestures of special populations of subjects (such as aphasics) can then be classified and even interpreted with high reliability by comparing their movement features with the movement features of the 'canonical' gestures.

McNeill and Levy (1982) found a strong association between the meaning features of verbs in speech and movement features of the co-occurring iconic gestures. Thus a gesture accompanying 'climbs up' might have an upward trajectory and clambering manner of execution, and show kinesic end-marking for the destination; it would never display a downward or circular trajectory or a hopping manner of execution. In general, iconix change their form and motion when there is a change in the concurrent meaning.

Iconix in Georgian, Swahili and English

The following demonstration takes advantage of the fact that we have shown the same stimulus to speakers of different languages. At one point in the cartoon story a character is shown climbing up the inside of a drainpipe to reach another character; but the second character somehow fetches a bowling ball and drops it into the pipe and onto the first character. Most narrators remember this scene and describe it with one or more accompanying gestures. The gesture that depicts the second character's putting the bowling ball into the pipe is synchronized with the particular expression in each language that describes this act. First, the Georgian speaker's version (transcription and translation by Kevin Tuite; the first line is the Georgian text, the second a morpheme-by-morpheme transcription, and the third line an idiomatic English translation):

GEORGIAN:
da uzarmazar rk'inis burts ... cha[agdebs]
(1)
and enormous iron ball.....[throw-down]
'and throws down this enormous iron ball'

(1) Both hands at head level push down on what appears to be a large round object.

The speaker appears to grasp a large round object and push it down into the space before her.

An essentially identical gesture appears in the Swahili narration (even though the narrator took the bowling ball to be a tire):

SWAHILI:
i-ka-chuku-a li-mpira [fulani i-ki-]
(1)
take tire [certain]
'and found a certain tire'

(1) Hands join and rise up as if squeezing something together.

[...tum]buk- iz-a
(2)
[...push down]
'and pushed it'

(2) Hands, still joined, push this thing down

(Recorded in Tanzania by Karen Peterson, who also provided the transcription and translation.)

Here also the speaker takes the part of the character dropping the bowling ball. The shape depicted in the gesture is pressed together, and this seems to reflect the speaker's belief that the object was a rubber tire (the speaker was the only one not living in the United States).

Finally, here is an English language speaker's rendition of the same scene:

ENGLISH:

and Tweetie Bird runs and gets a bowling ball
and drops it [down] the drainpipe
(1)
(1) Both hands push down a large round object.

This narrator also seizes a large round object and appears to shove it into the space in front of her.

Thus, three languages: one gesture. A character is depicted as pushing a large round object into a space in front the speaker. Looking at the video tapes, it is quite easy to follow this part of the story with no other information than the gestures. The Swahili speaker added the unique feature of compressing the round object as it went into the pipe, presumably because of her belief that it was made of a pliable substance, but otherwise the gesture depictions are very similar.

The gestures are similar despite the radically different linguistic systems within which each speaker couched her verbal descriptions. In English the sentence structure was the standard SVO transitive verb sentence pattern; in Georgian it was an OV pattern with an elided subject; in Swahili there was a single polymorphic verb into which was built a subject marker, a conditional marker, a verb root (with which the gesture stroke coincided), a causative suffix and a final vowel that signaled the indicative mood. Thus, even though each language forced its speakers to construct what on the surface are highly unalike sentences, the combination of gesture and speech in each case was essentially the same. In each version the gesture coincided exactly with the segment of speech that conveyed the idea of downward motion; this was true even in Swahili, where this idea of downward motion was embedded in the middle of a long polymorphic word and had to be, as it were, sought out by the gesture.

Although the surface locus and context of this downward motion segment varies greatly between languages, the gestures teach us to look at the underlying development of sentences. The gestures imply that in each language the image exhibited in the gesture comes into contact with the equivalent linguistic segments. In each language the gesture lined up with the word that encodes downward motion. The growth point for the utterance would be this word with which the gesture coincided, 'down' in English (the particle of the verb giving the direction of motion), throw-down in Georgian ('chaagdebs'), push-down in Swahili ('tumbuk'). It is this growth point that the gesture synchronizes with, and from this common seed the rest of the sentence grows. An essential similarity of thought is what we unearth via iconic gestures.

Metaphoric Gestures

'Metaphoric' gestures are like iconix in that they present a picture of something but the picture they present is not of a concrete object, but an abstract idea. The gesture depicts the vehicle of a metaphor (Richards, 1936). The vehicle is felt to be similar to the abstract idea, and thus the gesture seems similar as well. Metaphoric gestures presuppose a capacity for abstract thought, and an ability to think in terms of spatial images. They imply that abstract thinking is based on concrete images of objects and space.

Mathematician's gestures

Based on a worldwide survey of mathematicians, Hadamard (1945) concluded that mathematicians primarily think in terms of images, both visual and kinesthetic. One of Hadamard's informants was no less than Einstein, who wrote that

> The psychical entities which seem to serve as elements in thought are certain signs and more or less clear images which can be 'voluntarily' reproduced and combined. ... The above mentioned elements are, in my case, of visual and some of muscular type. Conventional words or other signs have to be sought for laboriously only in a secondary stage... (Hadamard, 1945, pp. 142 - 143).

It is not surprising that there should be gestural manifestations of these kinds of images. Mathematicians indeed perform gestures in which mathematical concepts are realized as visual-kinesic forms; e.g., the concept of a mathematical dual accompanied by gestures in which the hand rotates between two positions (in a dual, a relation is replaced by its converse). The following is an illustration (from McNeill, 1987):

<u>[the duals] will be the inverse limit of finite</u>
(1)
(1) Right hand loops upward.

Conduit metaphors

Lakoff and Johnson (1980) described a family of linguistic metaphors that they termed 'conduit metaphors', following Reddy (1979). For example, someone saying 'I got a lot out of that lecture' is implicitly presenting the lecture as a bounded object (a container) and the contents of the lecture as a substance inside the container. This substance the lecturer brought out, and the amount of this stuff was a lot, the speaker is saying. An example of a non-mathematical conduit gesture for an abstract concept is the following, where the speaker is announcing the genre of his upcoming narrative:

<u>it [was a Sylves][ter and] [Tweet]ie cartoon</u>
(1) (2) (3)
(1) Both hands rise up as if holding up an object.
(2) Hands support object motionlessly.
(3) Hands appear to pull object open.

The speaker created an object and presented it to the listener. The 'object' was the idea of a cartoon and/or of the upcoming narration; either way, an abstract concept. In conduit gestures, abstract concepts like language, knowledge, a work of art, etc., are presented as bounded manipulable containers; 'substance' goes inside the container; and to communicate one conveys a container filled with substance over a conduit -- the space between the speaker and the listener. To conceive of 'a Sylvester and Tweetie cartoon' as an object and hold it up to the listener is thinking in terms of the conduit metaphor. Indeed, after creating the object and holding it up, the speaker proceeded, in true conduit fashion, to pry it open at (3), revealing the contents (viz., the cartoon genre). In contrast to iconix which appear to follow the same rules in different languages, conduit metaphoric gestures are not universal. We have found excellent conduit examples in the Georgian language narrative (a non-Indo-European language but western culture), but no convincing examples of conduits in the Chinese or Swahili narratives. These narratives contain abundant metaphoric gestures of other kinds, but do not depict abstract ideas as bounded supported containers. In a context where an English narrator could have used a conduit, for example, the Chinese speaker created a bound*less* substance that she patted on (this is a metaphoric gesture also used by English narrators, but it is not a conduit).

Spatial metaphors

Space also can be used metaphorically. The speaker can conceive of the plot-line as an object with extent in space. Thus one part of the story can be set aside as space A and a contrasting part as space B; the relationship in space can then diagram the story. Here is an example where space is dichotomized to represent the distinction between true morality and apparent morality, a difference that the narrator took to be the crux of the story (from a narration of a full-length film in which the central figures are a murderer, her boyfriend, who helps her cover up, and a would-be blackmailer):

everyone's morals are very ambiguous
cause [they're sup]posed to be the good guys
(1)
(1) Both hands move to front.

[but she] really did kill him
(2)
(2) Both hands move to left.

and [he's a] bad guy
(3)
(3) Both hands move to front again.

[but he really] didn't kill him
(4)
(4) Both hands move to left again.

The left side of the space stands for the true guilt or innocence of the characters, while the front stands for their surface respectability. The moral dilemma or ambiguity the speaker found in the film story was unfolded, then, and laid out in space like map (presumably the left vs front locations had no significance in themselves; it was the fact of their opposition that mattered).

The metaphoric use of space appears in all narratives regardless of the language being spoken. It is too early for us to say if spatial metaphors are the same in every language.

An implication of the phenomenon of metaphoric gestures (of every kind) is that the abstractness of an idea is no barrier to its receiving a concrete reality in gesture form. Movements of the hands are perfectly capable of expressing abstractions. Conduit and spatial metaphors are instantly available. Metaphoric gestures are outnumbered by iconix in narratives, but this is because of the content of the narrative, not the gesture itself, and they are among the most frequent of all gestures in conversations (in particular among academics).

Beats

The beat is the simplest of gesture movements. Unlike iconic gestures, beats tend to have the same form regardless of the content of what the person is saying. The gesture is a short rapid flick of the hand or fingers, up and down or back and forth; the movements occur at the rhythmical pulses of speech. Beats don't have a special space where they are localized, but are performed wherever the hands happen to find themselves, including the periphery of the gesture space. Given such unprepossessing qualities, it is all the more surprising that beats perform a vital role in the narrative structure.

The beat signals that a significant discontinuity of some kind has occurred. It implies that the word it accompanies is important, not for its own content, but for its relationships to something else in the verbal or nonverbal context. Beats thus appear when the narrator momentarily withdraws from the main plot-line of the story to, e.g., introduce a new character, introduce a new development in the plot, summarize the story, make a metalinguistic remark, make a repair, etc. -- the occasions are multiple and various. The beat gesture can be thought of as a temporal index of the moment of a discontinuity when a linguistic segment steps out of its normal referential role. Here is an English language example in which, first, there is a nonnarrative clause with a metaphoric gesture; then a narrative clause with no gesture; and finally another nonnarrative clause, and this one with beats (from a narration of the full length film):

Nonnarrative:

and the way the story takes place is [as the film]
(1)
opens we see
(1) Right hand conduit metaphor presents the film as an object.

Narrative:
Frank going about his detective duties.

Nonnarrative:

as would [be expected]
(2)
(2) Left hand beats (2X).

The metaphoric gesture at (1) presented the idea of the film as an object. The narrator next resumed the story line itself, but immediately switched back to make a nonnarrative comment. This discontinuity of levels at (2) was signaled by beats that accompanied the phrase 'be expected.' A normal referential use of 'expected,' however, would have called for a second conduit gesture, rather than the beats that took place. The beats emphasize that the words are significant for their relationships to the story structure, not for their inherent content (referring to expectations).

Deictic Gestures

Pointing gestures in narratives can have a referential function. The speaker describes a location or the motion of something into a location, and sets up a spot in the gesture space to represent this locus. For example,

and [throws him off] the window sill
(1)
(1) Right hand points to lower right space.

The gesture depicts the trajectory and final destination of the character.

Pointing also has a discourse function in narratives, and it is this kind of pointing -- abstract pointing -- that we will focus on. Pointing has an obvious denotative function when someone points at a concrete object or event, but the kind of pointing that we will emphasize is abstract, aimed at abstract targets. This is a gesture where the speaker appears to be pointing at empty space, but in fact the space is full. A metaphoric use of space implies an object or array of objects for potential referents and this space can be indexed by pointing. The objects aren't actually present, but the compulsion to point at their space remains. In the following example, the speaker is at a point of transition and is introducing a new character and new development in the plot:

and in fact a few minutes later we see [the artist]
(1)
(1) Points to left side of space.

The gesture was synchronous with mentioning the artist. A key point is that there were no gestures that synchronized with succeeding mentions of the artist; the next reference to this character ('him') was in a clause that happened to co-occur with an identical pointing gesture, but the gesture now was timed with the action (of looking at the artist) and not with the artist:

and uh she [looks over] Frank's shoulder at him
(1)
(1) Points to left side of space again.

Thus the spatial assignment of the artist to the left was retained but now was used to provide the locus for an action directed to the artist. The gesture depicted the action, but was no longer used to establish the reference itself, and this shift of function reveals itself in the timing of the gestures.

Note that the same discourse functions can be performed by more than one kind of gesture. The discourse function of initiating new episode sequences of narrative text is particularly well suited to the deictic gesture. As we will show later, deictic gestures are overrepresented at the beginnings of new episode units in narratives. Beats also can initiate new episodes since such a juncture in a narrative involves a discontinuity -- the special emphasis of the beat -- and indeed we also find that this function is marked by beats as well as deictix.

Relationships

Gestures interrelate on many levels in their co-occurrences with speech. In this section we consider the multiplicity of these relationships -- phonological, syntactic, semantic, viewpoint, pragmatic function, and temporal.

Gestures and Phonology

In an analysis of the tone units composing a natural conversation, Kendon (1972) found that the kinesic hierarchy mentioned earlier was accompanied by a parallel phonological hierarchy (Kingdon, 1958). On the lowest phonological level is the *most prominent syllable*, the phonological peak within a single clause. Just above this is the *tone unit*, a grouping of syllables over which there is a complete intonation tune (e.g., rise-fall, etc.). Tone units in turn form *locutions*, mapping typically onto complete sentences. A locution is separated from its neighbors by distinct pauses and begins with increased loudness. A series of locutions forms a *locution group*. At this level there may be phonological variation but some common phonological feature will be preserved throughout, such as the same, e.g., low-rise tune. The highest level is the *locution cluster*, which is marked by pauses, repeated or repaired phrases, altered pitch and/or voice quality, and a thematic shift of content. The phonological and kinesic hierarchies line up such that boundaries between the highest, middle and lowest levels of each modality co-occur in time (Table 6, based on Kendon, 1972, 1980). It appears from Table 6 that each speech unit has its equivalent unit of body motion, and the larger the speech unit, the greater the change in the kinesic sphere, perhaps as a form of working memory control (Kendon, 1972).

Table 6. Kinesic and Phonological Hierarchies Combined

Kinesic Hierarchy	Phonological Hierarchy
Consistent Arm Use and Body Posture	Locution Cluster
Consistent Head Movement	Locution Group
One G-Unit	Locution
One G-Phrase	Tone Group
One Stroke	Most Prominent Syllable

Gestures and Syntax

The syntactic structures of utterances are less fundamental for explaining gestures than one might suppose. In our earlier table we demonstrated that most gestures are one to a clause. However, this is best explained by saying that both the gesture and the clause are dependent variables, each trying to cover the same idea unit (Kendon, 1980). Some purely syntactic effects on gesture however are suggested in the cross-linguistic comparisons.

Georgian uses an object-verb sequence in verb phrases as an unmarked order (as in the earlier example, where the speaker said 'burts [ball] chaagdebs' [throw-down]). The gesture with this phrase was carried out in two steps: first the hands statically held the ball, then the hands showed the ball plunging downward. Perhaps this use of two phases, first static then dynamic, corresponds to the OV grammatical pattern. In contrast, English language narrators, following a VO pattern, start the gesture with a dynamic phase and have never been observed to perform gestures for this event in two phases. So the temporal subdivision or unity of the gesture may have its origin in the syntax of the verb phrase.

The Chinese narrative also includes a potential example of a syntactic influence on gesture. The continuative aspect (which in English is conveyed with a progressive verb, as in 'he keeps on climbing') is conveyed in Chinese with a verbal particle 'zai', which grammatically is a separate word from the verb. At one point the Chinese narrator said the equivalent of 'he keeps on looking' and performed two gestures simultaneously. One was a head movement that seemed to convey looking, and the other a lateral back and forth movement of the hand, which seemed to depict the aspect in a 'continuous' manner. Thus the grammatical separation of aspect and verb was paralleled in a gestural separation. We don't have an English language example to compare to this Chinese one, but it seems to us likely that English speakers would convey continuative aspect by sustaining or repeating a single gesture rather than by separating the action and the aspect into two gestures.

Examples of syntactic relationships in gesture are scattered and hard to find. The situation contrasts with the ubiquity of the semantic and pragmatic relationships of gesture and speech.

Gestures and Semantics

In an earlier paper (McNeill & Levy, 1982) we analyzed how the form of the gesture corresponds to meaning by comparing each gesture's movement features to the meaning features of the verbs in the accompanying speech. We defined altogether 44 movement features; a few examples are: fingers curled or extended; index finger extended; palm down, up, right, left, toward self; motion up, down, sideways (left or right), and so forth. The meaning features were inspired by Miller & Johnson-Laird's (1976) analysis of English verbs and included such semantic dimensions as Entrance/Exit (as in 'he swallows the bowling ball'); Downward ('he comes down the pipe'); Horizontal ('he runs ahead of it'); and End-State ('it catches up to him' and again 'he swallows the bowling ball'). We intended the meaning features to capture the meanings of the verbs in the specific not always canonical senses with which the narrators used them in the narratives.

Given the two kinds of features, we could compare the featural composition of gestures to their co-occurring meaning features. For example, we found that 54% of verbs with the Downward meaning feature co-occurred with gestures in which there was downward movement; 0% co-occurred with gestures in which there was upward movement. Seventy-three percent of verbs with the Horizontal meaning feature occurred with gestures that included a left-right movement feature, compared to only 8% of gestures that moved downward and 17% that went upward.

The Downward meaning feature not only went with downward movements, but also with curled fingers more than 60% of the time. Curled fingers seem to depict passive movement, such as falling under the influence of gravity. The Downward meaning feature did not appear with the contrary feature of extended fingers, nor with both hands moving in the same direction, nor with reduplicated arm movements suggesting running. This total pattern of positive and negative associations with Downward suggests a coherent picture in which there is falling, falling under the influence of gravity, only one object moving, and motion other than locomotion. Such a gesture occurred repeatedly in the cartoon narrations. It exhibits a prototypical situation. The character was constantly falling from great heights, falling alone and involuntarily, definitely not moving in a way he would have been had he been locomoting on his own. The aggregate gesture profile that emerges from the correlations with Downward thus presents a picture that is typical of the cartoon narrative.

Two-handed gestures are a specially interesting case. These are gestures in which the two hands perform different movements but the movements are coordinated; for example, one hand depicts a character's open mouth while the other hand becomes a bowling ball going inside. The gestures that appeared with End-State verbs tended to be made with two coordinated hands (68%) and those with Entrance/Exit verbs very strongly so (90%). End-State and Entrance/Exit imply actions that reach a goal; such actions have been termed accomplishments by Vendler (1967). For example, 'to swallow' means that something has not merely moved toward the appropriate orifice but that it enters it, passes inside; otherwise one has not swallowed but perhaps bitten. 'To catch up to' similarly requires not only movement but that a certain end state be reached; otherwise one has not caught up to but chased. Thus the kinesic form of the gestures co-occurring with these kinds of verbs was shaped to reflect the logical element of accomplishment. Verbs lacking the End-State or Entrance/Exit features went with two-handed gestures only 40% of the time.

Viewpoint

We come now to an aspect of iconic gestures that has a radical effect on gesture form. The question is how does the narrator 'see' the event as he recounts it. Viewpoint is directly part of the form of the gesture. The gesture that accompanied 'and he bends it way back' revealed not only the speaker's memory of the scene, but also his point of view towards the event. The speaker was 'seeing' the event as if he were the person performing the act, rather than taking the viewpoint of an onlooker, or observer of the event. There are two major options: character viewpoint and observer viewpoint (C-VPT and O-VPT). The example of bending back the tree was C-VPT. C-VPT simulates the performance of the character; the speaker's hands play the part of the character's hands, his body becomes the character's, and his space is the space in which the character performs the act. In the bending back example, the speaker's hand rose up in front of his own chest and appeared to grasp something round; then he pulled this round thing backwards towards his own shoulder, i.e., pulled it not directly onto his body, but off to the side, as one would with a tree. The speaker clearly was, at that moment, the character.

An O-VPT can be inferred from the following:

and you see him swinging [across a rope]
(1)
(1) Right hand forms a bloblike figure moving from rear to front.

In contrast to a C-VPT gesture, the speaker's hands here play, not hands, but the character as a whole; his body is that of an observer of the event, and the gesture space represents a field of view in which the event takes place. Each perspective thus has is own distinctive gesture appearance. This makes viewpoint into one of the most readily coded aspects of gesture.

The viewpoints also have different linguistic contexts. Viewpoint is directly displayed in the gesture channel, but once we see gestural viewpoints we find linguistic manifestations of viewpoint as well. The C-VPT tends to appear with simple sentences and where possible with transitive verbs. The 'and he bends it way back' example is an illustration: it has one clause and a transitive verb. The O-VPT tends to appear with complex sentences (multiple clauses) and where possible with intransitive or stative verbs. In the O-VPT example above the speaker said 'and you see him swinging across a rope,' in which the higher clause ('you see S') implies an observer, and the lower clause ('[he] swings across a rope') describes the action this observer is witnessing (with an intransitive verb). This is typical of O-VPT sentences: the very sentence structure embodies distance from the narrative event. Thus, in an unexpected way, two kinds of sentence structure (simple and complex) are co-expressive with gestural viewpoints.

The speaker's choice of viewpoint is neither random nor arbitrary. C-VPT appears when the speaker recounts a central story event and O-VPT when the event is peripheral. The table below is based on an analysis of 3 cartoon narratives by Church, Baker, Bunnag and Whitmore (1989). Based on story grammar categories (Stein & Glenn, 1979), she classified story events as Central or Peripheral: Central events were (1) initiation of goal actions, (2) main goal actions, and (3) outcomes of goal actions; Peripheral events were (4) setting statements, (5) subordinate actions, and (6) responses to actions and outcomes (one further category -- describing a goal -- was never depicted in gestures and was rarely described in speech). Using these definitions, the two view-points can be shown to appear in quite different contexts, as displayed in Table 7.

Table 7. Percent of Events with Each Viewpoint

Event Type	Viewpoint C-VPT	O-VPT	Uncod-able	Number Events
Central	71	24	5	66
Peripheral	6	93	1	72

Thus there was a sharp separation of viewpoints in terms of the contexts in which they appear: C-VPT with Central events, O-VPT even more strongly with Peripheral events. This functional separation suggests that the C-VPT is taken when events are salient. At important moments in the narrative the narrator begins to play the part of characters directly, and this shifts the gesture mode to the C-VPT, and in the process totally altering the meaning of the hands, limbs, movement and space.

Gestures and Pragmatic Function

Each of the different types of gesture can carry out pragmatic operations, including cohesively linking together temporally separated but thematically connected parts of the discourse, dividing the discourse into episodic units, tracing out different hierarchical levels of discourse structure, and highlighting what is relevant to the speaker at the moment of speaking. We discuss here an important pragmatic function performed by beats and pointing gestures, to introduce new information as potential discourse topics. We focus on this in the following section as a case study of gesture function.

New themes

An accumulation of beats and pointing gestures at transitional points in narratives and other forms of discourse (cf. the tables and examples below) suggests a more general phenomenon: that gestures are used to introduce new information as potential discourse topics. We explain this pragmatic function, focusing on the role of beats and abstract pointing.

A number of lines of evidence converge on this hypothesis. First, within a clause, information that cannot be presupposed on the basis of earlier linguistic or gesture context is accompanied by gestures more often than highly presupposed information. Kendon (1972) found that G-phrases tended to accompany only those tone units that conveyed new information. Tone units that linked new information to a previous or succeeding argument of the discourse were not accompanied by gestures. Consistent with this observation are various of our examples cited earlier; e.g., the stroke in 'he bends it way back' began only after the highly presupposing pronoun 'he' was uttered, even though the preparation for the stroke started during the preceding sentence. The stroke phase thus synchronized with the speaker's current focus of attention.

Analysis of units of text larger than the clause shows that changes in body motion accompany transitions to new informational units. Kendon (1980) suggested that: "... gesticulation may, in various ways, make visible the organization of the discourse ... at times one may observe gesticulatory patterns that appear to have this function particularly." (p. 22).

Within the broad hierarchical structure created by changes in body motion, changes in gestural form reflect distinctions between different levels of discourse. McNeill and Levy's (1982) study, cited earlier, showed that different types of gesture accompany different narrative functions: iconic gestures co-occurred with narrative statements that reproduced the chronology of the events in the original story, while beats accompanied extranarrative statements that lacked this sequentiality constraint (Table 4). Many extranarrative clauses were scene-introducers and summaries of events. These findings suggest that beats often accompany transitions to new narrative episodes.

Similarly, abstract pointing also reveals changes in discourse structure. In a highly unstructured situation of a conversation between two strangers whose task was to become acquainted in front of a video camera, the participants began by trying to establish a shared topic.[1] Abstract pointing gestures accompanied these initial efforts during which new information was the dominant discourse relationship. Subsequent coreferences (i.e., old information) were not accompanied by gestures of any kind. Table 8 summarizes the first two co-referring chains of the conversation (the contributions of the two participants have been combined).

---

1. We are grateful to Starkey Duncan of the University of Chicago for letting us examine the videotape of this conversation.

The occurrence of pointing was used, then, as an accompaniment to the introduction of *potential conversational topics.* The rest of the conversation confirmed this pattern. Following these initial coreferential chains pointing gestures continued to accumulate until a conversational topic was firmly established. Once this topic was successfully negotiated (and this took many clauses), the amount and density of pointing subsided, to be supplanted by mostly metaphoric gestures. This conversation points toward the role of deictic gestures in fulfilling a particular discourse function: that of introducing new material as potential discourse topics. Similarly, beats signal transitions to other levels of structure, some of which also are introducing new material.

Table 8. First Co-Referring Chains in a Conversation

Coref Chain	Position in Coref Chain	Referent	Referring Expression	Pointing Gesture	Other Gesture
1	1	`Mary'	Mary	yes	--
	2	"	we	yes	--
	3	"	she	--	--
	4	"	she	--	--
	5	"	Mary	--	--
2	1	`Cindy'	Cindy	yes	--
	2	"	she	ys	--
	3	"	zero	yes	--
	4	"	we've	--	--
	5	"	Cindy	--	--
	6	"	her	--	--
	7	"	we've	--	--

In narratives as well as non-narrative conversations, deictix and beats participate in introducing new discourse themes. In Marslen-Wilson, Levy and Tyler (1982), a narrator recounted a comic book story, and as he spoke held a copy of the comic book on his lap. This arrangement generated a large number of pointing gestures, since the speaker used the picture that appeared on the comic book cover to point to figures of the two central characters in the story. Although the picture was constantly available, pointing was not uniformly spread out through the narrative. 100% of the episode-initial references to the characters were accompanied by pointing, but only about 40% of the within-episode references were. This distribution, like that in the conversation above, suggests that pointing was used to establish the referents that would be thematic in the subsequent discourse. The following extract from the narrative occurred when the speaker was reintroducing the two main characters for a new episode of the story, and shows that the first mention of the characters was accompanied by a point at the comic book cover (the preparation phase coinciding with 'the Hulk' and the stroke with 'the Thing'); in contrast, the immediately following references to the same characters were gestureless ('the Hulk is getting stronger'; 'the Thing keeps catching him off guard'):

so then it cuts back to [the Hulk] [and the Thing]
(Prep) (1)
(Prep) Raises right hand to prepare for pointing.
(1) Points at comic book cover.
and they're still battling and knocking
down chimneys and nobody's really getting
any temporary advantage and the Hulk is
getting stronger but the Thing keeps
catching him off guard and tripping him up

In Levy (1984), beats appeared in a narrative with the function of introducing new information as potential discourse topics. The subjects were shown a full length film 'stimulus' and retold the story to a listener. Levy divided the resulting half-hour-long narratives into episode units using such formal criteria as explicit references to scene changes, e.g., 'they show one scene,' and so forth. Of 37 episode-initial references to characters made with full noun phrases (e.g., 'the central character figure'), 22 were accompanied by gestures; most of these were beats. Of 64 references to characters with full noun phrases that appeared later in episodes, only 17 had co-occurring gestures of any kind. Thus, again, gestures -- in this case, beats -- accompanied the introduction of discourse themes (as in the beat example cited earlier, the gestures that appeared within-episode units occurred with other than references to the character, e.g., with verbs, verb particles, clauses, etc.). Another way to show the use of beats with this function is to look at the first time a character is mentioned in the narrative. How is this done? Table 9 lists the eight most frequent gestural and linguistic devices employed by one speaker to introduce each of eight characters into her narrative. The characters are ranked according to their overall frequency of mention in the narration, where the frequency of mention is an operational definition of how central a character is (Levy, 1984). As can be seen, gestures accompany the first mentions of the more central characters but not the first mentions of the more peripheral characters (since these are *first* mentions, this accumulation of gestures with the main characters reflects the perceived centrality of a character, not the past history of mentioning it -- a history that doesn't yet exist).

Table 9. Formal Means Used to Introduce Characters into Narration

Character Ranked by Overall Frequency of Mention in Narration	Linguistic Form	Gesture
1	Def. article + NP: 'the central character figure'	yes
2	Def. article + NP: 'the second character in the film'	yes
3	Possessive + noun: 'his father'	--
4	Indef. article + NP: 'one of the enlisted men'	yes
5	Demonstrative + NP: 'this pompous officer'	--
6	Indef. article + NP: 'one of the members'	--
7	Indef. article + NP: 'a friend'	--
8	Indef. article + NP: 'a cousin'	--

Finally, the use of gestures to introduce themes also appears in non-English narratives. The Georgian-speaking narrator whom we described earlier used many explicit verbal devices for scene-changing. At such points the first speech references to the characters were synchronized with gestures, whereas later mentions of the same characters were not accompanied by gestures (gestures might occur in the same clause, but not synchronously with the character). Table 10 is parallel to the earlier table for the two conversation participants (Table 8), and shows for the Georgian narrative the first two coreferential chains in a new scene, their subject-slot referring expressions, and the occurrence or non-occurrence of synchronous gestures (translation by Kevin Tuite). It is striking that gestures synchronize with the introductory references to the 'young woman' and 'this man,' and then shift to elsewhere in the clause or disappear altogether with the immediately succeeding references to the same characters; this is exactly equivalent to the phenomenon with Marslen-Wilson et al.'s (1982) English-speaking narrator. As in that narration, the Georgian speaker produced gestures timed to co-occur with episode-initial references to characters, suggesting that in her narrative system she too used gestures for creating and introducing thematic referents.

Table 10. Co-Referring Chains in a Georgian Language Narration

Coref Chain	Position in Coref Chain	Referent	Referring Expression	Pointing Gesture
1	1	'young woman'	es axalgazrda kali (= this young woman)	yes
	2	"	es kali (= the woman)	
	3	"	es kali (= the woman)	
	4	"	es kali (= this woman)	
2	1	'man'	es k'aci (= this man)	yes
	2	"	es ka- k'aci (= this m- man)	yes
	3	"	es k'aci (= this man)	

The text represented in Table 10 is from a passage that begins and ends with explicit scene-changing devices (start: 'the next scene is ...'; and end: 'and the whole scene gives us the impression that this woman is doing something wrong'). In between are the two animate coreferential chains, one for the 'young woman' and the other the 'man,' with gestures as shown. The chains intertwine, yet each has its own identity and controls precisely where referring forms are accompanied by gestures. To demonstrate this interweaving of the two chains we quote the portion of the Georgian text that underlies Table 10 (only those gestures accompanying full NP referring forms are included; gestures elsewhere are irrelevant to the point and are omitted, to avoid clutter; numbers refer to the co-referring chains, as in Table 10: thus '1.1' is Chain 1-Position 1; '2.2' is Chain 2-Position 2, etc.; also to avoid clutter, we omit a literal morpheme-by-morpheme transcription):

shemdeg uh scena aris imisa
'the next scene is'

1.1 rom ai [es axalgazrda kali]
(1)
'here's this young woman'
(1) Both hands present object to right side.

2.1 romelsac [es k'a]ci mos c'ons
(2)
'who likes this man'
(2) Both hands present object to left side.

da ep'ranch'eba da un inazeba
'and is flirting with him and playing cute'

2.2 da [es ka k'aci ro]melic aghelvabulia imit
(3)
'and this man who is all excited because'
(3) Both hands present object to center.

rom mis otaxshi gvian ghame axalgazrda kalia
'there's a young woman in his room late at night'

1.2 da es kali dainaxavs balerinas pachk'as
'and the woman notices a ballerina's tutu'

ici ai balerinas k'abas
'you know, it's a ballerina's dress'

da miizomebs da eubneba
'and holds it up to herself and says'

o uh gindata me viknebi me viq'o tkveni modelio
'oh do you want me to be your model?'

2.3 es k'aci eubneba o es saint'ereso azriao
'the man says: oh that's an interesting idea'

rat'om ar chaicmevto
'why don't you put it on?

cot'a un ise gapranchebis da uaris shemdeg
'after a bit more of this flirtation and refusal'

1.3 es kali isev chaicmevs uhh am uh chaicmevs am
'this woman again puts on this puts on this dress'

amasobashi es k'aci uk 'ravs p'ianinoze
'meanwhile the man is playing the piano'

uh da mteli scena gadmovcems im grdznobas
'and the whole scene gives us the impression'

1.4 rom es kali schadis raghaca cuds
'that this woman is doing something wrong'

Cohesion

Gestures are cohesive in the same sense that linguistic devices are cohesive, but achieve cohesion by a different mechanism. Cohesive devices, gestural or linguistic, link together thematically connected but temporally separated parts of the discourse. Linguistic devices do this by presupposing parts of the discourse (examples of such linguistic devices are third person pronouns, demonstrative pronouns, ellipsis, and others; cf. Halliday & Hasan (1976; a third person pronoun, for instance, presupposes a coreferring explicit noun phrase elsewhere in the text). Gestures, in contrast, produce cohesion by recreating parts of earlier gestures. Any gesture type can do this, so long as its form or space allows a recognizable repetition. In the following example, an iconic gesture provided the cohesive linkage. A speaker was recounting the cartoon story but interrupted herself to explain how a streetcar works. Her explanation done, she returned to the plot-line and repeated her last iconic gesture; this repeated gesture was the cohesive linkage back to the interrupted plot-line:

[the network of wires that hooks up the cable car]
(1)

(1) Both hands contact at the tips and hold a criss- cross for the network of wires.

[um you know the trolley] (Listener: oh a c-)
(2)

(2) Right hand shifts next to head and moves forward and backward for pantograph.

right and there's [a whole] network of these wires
(3)

(3) Both hands contact at tips for second crisscross.

The repeated gesture at (3) showed the point in the narration to which the listener should return, after the side comment (and the listener's own question). Note that the cohesive gesture anticipated the cohesive linguistic device (the pronoun 'these,' which also links back to the earlier reference to wires). It should also be noted that the explanation of how a streetcar hooks up to the wires at (2) was carried exclusively in the gesture channel.

Salience

The following two examples appeared successively in one person's description of a character climbing up a pipe. The character's first attempt was on the outside of the pipe, and the gesture was undifferentiated as to path; the second attempt was inside the pipe and the gesture highlighted this contrasting feature. The two hand shapes contrast in that the second adds a hollow region that conveys the new information, that the path was inside the pipe. The movement features of the second gesture thus incorporate what was relevant at the moment of speaking and made this salient.

The first attempt:

he crawls [up a pipe]
(1)

(1) Right hand rises up in blob shape.

and when he gets up to the bird the grandma hits him over the head with the umbrella ... and he goes back

The second attempt:
and [he goes up THROUGH the pipe] this time
(2)
(2) Right hand rises in hollow basket shape.

Thus, we can infer that, at the moment of speaking, the narrator saw the interiority of the path as particularly relevant. This same highlighting of interiority was marked concurrently in speech with contrastive stress on 'through.' It appears that concurrent gesture performance offers an avenue for the empirical investigation of 'relevance,' a topic that has attracted theoretical interest in linguistics (Sperber & Wilson, 1986) but little in the form of concrete empirical investigation.

Gestures and Time

We give here three rules governing how speech and gesture combine in time; then we point out the phenomenon of gesture anticipation, and discuss the implications of this anticipation for the mental operations underlying speech production.

Phonological synchrony

The rule at the phonological level is that the stroke phase of the gesture precedes or ends at, but does not follow, the phonologically most prominent syllable of the co-expressive speech segment (Kendon, 1980). For example, the stroke phase of the gesture that accompanied 'he bends it way back' ended at the word 'back,' which was the stress peak of the utterance. Hold phases appear when this phonological synchrony threatens to break down. In the 'umbrella' hand example cited earlier from Kendon (1980; Bull, 1987), there was a downward stroke followed by a static hold. The effect of the hold was to maintain the 'umbrella' hand shape until the phonologically most prominent part of the utterance could be completed (from Kendon, 1980, Fig. 1):

this patient has been a problem so far as a history is
concerned uh y'know [a] [very formal one] uh or any
(1) (2)
(1) *Stroke*: 'umbrella' hand moves sharply down.
(2) *Hold*: 'umbrella' hand posture held statically.

According to the transcription that accompanied this example, the intonation contour was flat and low during 'uh y'know a', ascended through 'very formal one', and then abruptly fell after the word 'one'. Thus the stroke phase of the 'umbrella' gesture took place during the low intensity part of the utterance but then the speaker held onto the form of the gesture while the phonological peak was being reached.

Semantic synchrony

The rule at this level says that if gestures and speech co-occur they must cover the same idea unit, or meaning. In the 'and he bends it way back' example, the idea unit was a character seizing a tree and bending it back toward the ground. The gesture depicted this act, plus the unique information that the object was fastened at one end, and co-occurred with the utterance segment that described the same act. We have seen no counterexamples to semantic synchrony. Some gestures and/or utterances are so vague that it is hard to say if they really present the same idea unit, but there are no examples of speech presenting one idea unit and gesture another. For instance, we do not find such pairs as 'he bends it way back' with a gesture that depicts a running person. Thus, speakers do not present separate units of meaning in the two channels.

Pauses

When there are pauses within a tone unit (the lowest level phonological unit) a semantically co-expressive gesture stroke will continue through the pause, thus showing that the semantic structure of the interrupted tone unit remains intact (Kendon, 1980). Despite the interruption of the flow of speech, semantic synchrony holds in that the semantic structure of the sentence is preserved. Kendon gives this example:

they wheel a big table in
[with a with a ... (1 sec.) ...] cake on it
(1)

(1) Series of circular motions with hand pointing down and index finger extended -- outlining the cake.

Multiple gestures

Multiple gestures. As we saw from the statistics given earlier on gesture : clause correspondences, a small but not insignificant proportion of clauses have two or more distinct gestures accompanying them. How do these cases of multiple gestures preserve semantic synchrony? Basically, they work in the same way as single gestures that complement speech. When more than one gesture occurs during a clause, the gestures are not related like the constituents of a sentence. Gestures do not combine into more complex hierarchically organized gestures. Rather, successive gestures are like snapshots of a single event from different angles, bringing out different aspects or temporal phases, but each is a complete gesture symbol in itself. For example (cited earlier),

[... and she ...] [grabs] the knife
(1) (2)

(1) Right hand gropes in circling movements with palm facing down and fingers spread out.

(2) Right hand grasps by turning up, closing to a fist, and rigidly holding this pose in front of the chest.

The scene was one in which a character flails about and encounters a knife by accident. The successive gestures depict the temporal phases of this event. The gestures however do not combine into a single complex gesture that maps onto the clause. In fact, there was maximization of kinesic contrast between the two gestures: horizontal movement to vertical, open hand to closed, circling motion to tensed cessation of motion, etc. Semantic synchrony is preserved since the two gestures depict the same event in the story but provide a more complete record of what occurred in the event than the clause does alone.

Pragmatic synchrony

The rule here says that if gestures and speech co-occur they must perform the same pragmatic functions. In the example of a conduit metaphoric gesture, 'it was a Sylvester and Tweetie cartoon', the utterance was identifying the genre of the upcoming narrative, and the gesture was presenting this same genre as a bounded object. The utterance and gesture thus came together on the pragmatic level of presenting the narration. The illustrations of beats and pointing that introduced new themes co-occurred with utterances carrying out the same discourse function. Pragmatic synchrony has no exceptions, so far as we are aware.

Pragmatic synchrony implies that speakers are limited to one function at a time. This does not exclude (and in fact helps to explain) a hierarchical ordering of functions. The only way in which a speaker can carry out more than one function at a time without violating pragmatic synchrony is to embed one function inside another. Thus, a narrative comment (with an iconic gesture that conveys this) can be inserted inside a nonnarrative comment (with a gesture that conveys this) without interrupting the nonnarrative comment. One illustration of this kind of embedding is making a series of iconix (for narrative content) in the extreme upper left corner of the gesture space, rather than in the central gesture space as usual; the speech with these iconix being carried out up next to the ear is perceived as literally a nonnarrative 'side comment' that incorporates descriptive content (see McNeill, forthcoming, for this particular example).

Gesture Anticipation and its Meaning

The synchrony rules apply specifically to the gesture stroke phase. It is now appropriate to consider the implications of the preparation phase (which is almost invariably present, as observed earlier). This phase regularly anticipates by a slight interval not only the stroke but also the co-expressive linguistic segments (Kendon, 1972, 1980). The following is the familiar 'he bends it way back' example, now with the preparation phase shown along with the stroke:

he grabs a big [oak tree and he] [bends it way back]
(Prep) (1)

(Prep) Hand rises from armrest of chair and moves into the gesture space at eye level; also takes on grip shape.

(1) (Stroke) Hand moves backwards and down, ending up near the shoulder.

The gesture both anticipated and synchronized with the sentence; anticipated it in its preparation phase and synchronized with it in its stroke. The implication of the preparation phase is that it, and not the stroke, marks the moment at which the representation of the event that the stroke exhibits takes form in the speaker's mind. There is no other reason why the speaker's hand would suddenly shoot forward and take the shape of a grip than that he had formulated the idea of the character grasping and pulling back on the tree. Thus, we see the mental development underlying the utterance most clearly in the timing of the gesture preparation phase. As many psycholinguists have assumed, the speaker formulates the next utterance in running discourse while still producing the previous one. However, it has not been possible to actually observe this anticipatory formulation and gesture provides a window onto it.

Cerebral Control of Gestures

Gesture Handedness

Although gestures may be performed with either the right hand or left hand, or both together, most speakers tend to prefer one hand over the other for performing gestures during an extended stretch of discourse. We know that the dominant hand for most complex motor tasks is preferentially controlled by the language-dominant (left) hemisphere in most right-handers; left-handers exhibit more complex relationships (Rasmussen & Milner, 1975; Milner, Branch & Rasmussen, 1974). Thus, observing patterns of gesture hand preference can potentially yield interesting insights into the cerebral laterality of gesticulation, and the neurological underpinnings of gesture in relation to speech.

Sousa-Poza, Rohrberb, and Mercure (1979) reported a right hand preference among normal speakers for the performance of meaningful gestures but not for meaningless movements or self-touching movements. Similarly, Kimura (1973 a,b) found that right-handers in a conversational setting preferred their right hand for 'free movements' (presumably gesticulation in Kendon's sense) but not for self-touching. Moreover, the right-hand preference seems to be associated with left-hemisphere dominance as assessed by dichotic listening; the few speakers who preferred the left hand for gesture performance were more likely to have a left-ear advantage (implying a right-hemisphere involvement in language). Left handers with an inferred right-hemisphere superiority for language tended to make gestures preferentially with their left hands, while left handers with inferred left-hemisphere language showed no strong manual preferences in gesture.

Thus, the cerebral hemisphere that is dominant for language appears also to be a significant locus for the production of the gestures that accompany speech. Kimura (1976) and Kimura and Archibald (1974) proposed that the specific quality of the language dominant hemisphere responsible for lateralization is the programming of complex movement sequences. This hypothesis economically accounts for both gesture and speech lateralization, since complex movements, both oral and manual, would engage the left hemisphere. Other interpretations exist, however. Stephens (1983) was able to tease apart some of the issues by observing the spontaneous gestures during narrations by left- and right-handed speakers. Kimura did not classify movements into types of gesture, but Stephens did this by utilizing the standard roster of types that we have followed in our work (beats, iconix, metaphorix). This classification allowed Stephens to evaluate the influence of motoric complexity and imagistic content of gestures on hand preference. She found that right handers preferentially performed iconic gestures with their right hands; left handers, with their left hands. Moreover, with the left handers, the degree of left-hand preference for iconic gesture performance varied directly with the strength of left-hand preference in various one-handed tasks (right handers did not vary in their right-hand preference on any task).

Thus, Stephens replicated Kimura's result that right-handers prefer to use their right hands for gesture performance while left-handers favor their left hands, and added to this observation the identity of the type of gesture for which the result obtains (iconix). There was no such clear-cut hand preference for beats. Beats, being motorically simple, could be simple enough for the non-language hemisphere to program.

Stephens, however, also observed that metaphorix are preferentially performed with the dominant hand. These gestures combine the motoric simplicity of beats with the imagistic content of iconix (the metaphorix in

Stephens' study were generally conduits and spatial metaphors, and such gestures tend to be executed with simple movements; e.g., a simple rotation of the hand for a conduit, or the hand flicking out in an arc and returning for a spatialized metaphor of a time-line). If complexity of movement alone were responsible for lateralization, the lateralization pattern with such metaphorix should have been like beats; but in fact the pattern was like iconix. Metaphorix went to the dominant hand. It thus appears that more than motoric complexity underlies the role of the language-dominant hemisphere in the production of gestures, and that the movement's symbolic character also must be taken into account.

Gestures in Aphasia

This conclusion is borne out by studies with brain-damaged patients. Goldblum (1978) noted that even patients with ideomotor and ideational apraxia continue to gesture. Similarly, Pedelty (1987), studying a group of 9 aphasic patients, found that while the motoric complexity of gestures correlated significantly with practic skills, as assessed by standard tests, the propensity to produce iconix, i.e., the proportion of iconic gestures produced by the patient, did not correlate with indexed practic skill. Thus, while motoric skill is an important component of gesticulation, it is neither necessary nor sufficient to explain the role of the language-dominant hemisphere in the production of gestures.

What do we expect to see when language is disrupted -- when words are not available, or when a speaker is unable to generate full syntactic sentences? Damage to the anterior portions of the language dominant hemisphere tends to result in a language pattern first described by Paul Broca (1861). Broca's, or anterior, aphasics have relatively spared comprehension and 'drive to communicate', but are able to speak only haltingly, dysfluently, and with great difficulty. The resulting 'telegraphic' speech is largely lacking in grammatical functors (articles, prepositions and other structure words) and relies heavily on content-bearing, open-class words. Somewhat the converse pattern is seen in patients with more posterior damage, a syndrome first described by Karl Wernicke (1874). Wernicke's, or posterior, aphasics have fluent, even hyperfluent speech that makes use of a rich variety of syntactic patterns, but the speech is notoriously devoid of meaningful content.

Nonetheless, both types of patients produce gestures, but their gesture systems do not survive intact. Gestures, too, are impaired and, described globally, the deficits are parallel to those in their linguistic systems. Several investigators (Cicone Wapner, Foldi, Zurif and Gardner, 1979; Goldblum, 1978; Feyereisen, 1983) have said that anterior aphasics tend to produce meaningful interpretable gestures, while posterior aphasics produce vague, meaningless, uninterpretable gestures. Cicone et al. (1979) described gestures from anterior aphasics that, like their speech, are brief and isolated, while the gestures from posterior aphasics occur in fluent streams. They also found that anterior aphasics are more likely to gesture in silence.

Pedelty (1987) studied 9 aphasic patients, 4 of whom were nonfluent Broca-like patients with anterior damage, and 5 were fluent Wernicke-like patents with damage to the posterior regions of the left hemisphere. The patients recounted the standard cartoon 'stimulus' to a listener (Pedelty). The coding of their gestures was independent of the spoken narration, as described earlier; thus linguistic content had no influence on judgments of iconicity. The gestures also were coded in terms of movement complexity (taking into account the number of movement phases, and the shape and trajectory of the stroke phase). The patients in this study, unlike those in previously reported studies, did not differ substantially in most physical characteristics of their gestures. There was no special tendency for either group to gesture more than the other. While there was some individually specific variation in the average number of G-phrases included in G-units, these differences were uncorrelated with the type of aphasia.

The one physical characteristic of gesture that did distinguish the two kinds of aphasics was the type of gesture space. The posterior patients used a space similar to that of normal adults: a flat plane parallel to the torso. The nonfluent patients, in contrast, had extremely large gesture spaces of a type also seen in young children (McNeill, 1986), with gestures taking place high above their heads and often reaching far out into the periphery. The reason for this expanded gesture space is unclear, but it may be related to the phenomenon described next, the range of gesture activity in the two groups.

Posterior aphasics resembled normals in another way: their gestures arose almost exclusively from the 'gesticulation' end of Kendon's continuum: beats, occasional deictix, iconix and metaphorix, but little from the more language-like regions of the continuum. The nonfluent aphasics, in contrast, produced communicative movements from all points along Kendon's continuum. They performed unique, usually clearly interpretable iconix, much like those described for normals; but they also ranged into more codified movements. In addition to iconix, they produced emblems (e.g., a wave hello, yes, no, the 'ok' sign, etc.), spelled out words with their fingers in the air, and performed whole-body pantomimes of the kind also found in children (McNeill, 1986), often replete with vocal sound effects. Thus anterior, nonfluent aphasics seem to exploit more fully the entire range of nonverbal communication and produce a wider range of physical movements in the process.

Iconic : beat ratios

When only gesticulation is considered, nonfluent anterior patients have a more heavily iconic, imagistic gesture system. Table 11 compares anterior and posterior aphasics in terms of their production of iconic and beat gestures. The comparison is expressed as the ratio of the frequency of iconix to the frequency of beats for each of Pedelty's 9 subjects. This ratio is much higher in the anterior aphasics than in the posterior. The posteriors, in two cases, had more beats than iconix, whereas every anterior had more iconix than beats (and two had no beats at all, but did have iconix). No posterior aphasic had as many iconix relative to beats as any anterior aphasic.

Table 11. Production of Iconix and Beats by Non-Fluent and Fluent Aphasics

Type of Patient		Frequency Ratios Iconic : Beat
Anterior (Nonfluent)	1	2.63
	2	no beats
	3	3.84
	4	no beats
Posterior (Fluent)	1	1.54
	2	0.22
	3	0.45
	4	1.67
	5	1.00

The ratios show that the anterior patients have a strong preference for representational iconix. The posterior patients are also capable of producing iconix, but their gestures are weighted to varying extents toward motorically simple gestures that are more strongly related to language form than to content. Thus, the agrammatic anterior aphasics tended to avoid the specific gesture type (beats) that emphasize relationships, while the 'semantically empty' posterior aphasics tended to avoid the specific gesture type (iconix) that present semantic content. In this global sense, gesture and speech dissolve in parallel in the two aphasias. It is important to emphasize, however, that patients of each type produced both kinds of gesture, and that the gestures were patterned in their narratives much as did those of normals. Specifically, the iconix of both the anterior and the posterior aphasics appeared in narrative contexts, while their beats accompanied extranarrative clauses conveying background information, locating events in time and otherwise overtly structuring the narration. The gestures of these patients, despite their gross linguistic abnormalities, are clearly tied to their linguistic systems in ongoing narrative performance. Their gestures seem to play a role vis-a-vis language that is similar to the role of the gestures with normals.

Compensation with gestures

Observations such as these suggest that gestures in aphasic speakers are closely linked to their speech. This is certainly true globally, but it does not mean that gestures and speech of aphasic speakers are necessarily tightly yoked in every utterance. Gestures can compensate for speech, replace speech, or repair it when language fails. Both the anterior and posterior patients had lapses of language, but of different kinds. The nonfluent anterior patients often were unable to produce a word or sentence to describe a particular entity or event from the cartoon. In such cases, iconic gestures could take over. The following illustrates one such case:

(Experimenter: What was the cat doing?)
ah ah [ ]
(1)

(1) Left hand with index finger pointing up, rises up over head and then straight down to lap: the cat plunging to earth.

Although the speaker could not say anything at all, he could perform a clear iconic gesture that was appropriate to the scene in which a character was rolling out of a drainpipe with a bowling ball inside him.

More surprising are the gestural repairs that we find with fluent posterior patients. Their semantically empty, neologism-ridden speech seems to reflect an equally unorganized and empty conceptual store. Indeed, most neologistic and paraphasic utterances with these patients were accompanied by simple nonimagistic beats or by no gestures at all; thus compensation was not attempted in such cases. There were a few rare but striking cases, however, where paraphasias were accompanied by iconix, and in these cases the gesture was always appropriate to the target word, never to the erroneous word (as discerned from the context, since all speakers were narrating the same cartoon story).

For example, a posterior patient substituted the word 'person' for 'umbrella', but performed a grasping gesture appropriate for the standard movement of the umbrella in the cartoon (the umbrella used as a weapon):

and she had to use a [person] for a ... a stick and a
(1)
(1) Curled hand grasps 'umbrella' and moves outward and to the right.

Another posterior patient described a cartoon scene in which a character had a bowling ball dropped on him while inside a drainpipe, and produced the word 'pillow' followed by a nonfluent neologism 'tscher'. All of this was accompanied by very clear iconic gestures depicting the locus and shape of the pipe, and the character's dramatic descent through it:

see he went through the [pillow] and [all around]
(1) (2)
(1) Index finger rises and moves down, indicating locus of drainspout.
(2) Hand curls to grasp the 'bowling ball.'

through [that tscher] ...
(3)
(3) Hand swoops down, depicting descent of ball and character.

Such uses of gesture to replace or compensate for speech suggest that with aphasics, as with normals, speech and gesture are the parallel but potentially nonredundant unfolding into communicative behavior of idea units. When the spoken output is flawed, gesture may, in some cases, proceed fluently, and an idea unit may be conveyed in an appropriate iconic gesture.

Gesture : clause correspondence

Table 5 presented earlier showed that for normal speakers most gestures are one to a clause, and that where there are departures from this rule, the speaker most often produced multiple gestures with a single clause, implying an attempt to unpack more than one idea unit with one linguistic program. The output of speech in such cases is usually dysfluent, suggesting that the speaker experienced difficulty in mapping the idea units onto the single clause. The gesture : clause ratios for anterior and posterior patients differ from each other in interesting ways that may provide some insight into the nature of the aphasic deficits in speech. Table 12 shows gesture : clause ratios for anterior and posterior aphasics with the normals repeated for comparison. As the table reveals, with aphasics as well as for normals, most gestures are one to a clause. However, when the two kinds of aphasic speakers stray from this pattern they move off in different directions. The fluent posterior patients are more likely to span several clauses with a single gesture, while the nonfluent anterior patients are more likely to perform several gestures during a single clause. The relative fluency and ease of production of speech by the posterior patients may thus be related to an unfolding of a single idea unit into several grammatical clauses.

Table 12. Proportion of Gesture: Clause Ratios

	Gesture : Clause Ratio						
	1gst: 4cls	1gst: 3cls	1gst: 2cls	1gst: 1cls	2gst: 1cls	3gst: 1cls	N of gsts
Nonfluent	.00	.01	.04	.77	.15	.02	92
Fluent	.03	.06	.14	.74	.03	.00	117
Normal	.005	.01	.04	.67	.19	.08	433

This interpretation is supported by the grammatical structure of these utterances, which tend to be simple declarative clauses either multiply embedded into other clauses or clauses concatenated in stereotyped frames. In contrast, the nonfluent anterior patients seem to suffer from a mismatch of too many idea units in relation to their linguistic resources, with several idea units (as revealed by the individual iconic gestures) being squeezed into a single, dysfluent clause. This interpretation is consistent with Friederici's (1988) proposal that agrammatism is due to an inability to quickly retrieve closed class items (grammatical function words).

Comparison to deaf aphasics

Poizner et al. (1987) describe in detail the linguistic performance of several deaf aphasics, both nonfluent and fluent types. Fundamentally, the same pattern of symptoms appears in the ASL aphasias as in hearing/speaking aphasias. While this appears superficially similar to our observations of the spontaneous gestures of hearing aphasics, it is crucial to consider that ASL is a complete structured language and thus not comparable to spontaneous gestures (they are on opposite poles of Kendon's continuum). In ASL many of the same formal characteristics of kinesic form and space are used as in spontaneous gesture, but they are organized into a system of contrasts and standards of well-formedness that have no counterpart with gestures. In particular, ASL syntax is conveyed spatially, and this spatial syntax is differentially impaired by left hemispheric damage, while nonlinguistic uses of space by ASL users are differentially impaired by damage to the right hemisphere. With right-lesioned deaf ASL users, an interesting finding emerged from comparing their performance on purely spatial tasks to their use of space for linguistic purposes. Such patients employ the full sign-production space, including the area left of the midline. However, non-linguistic uses of space for representational purposes were grossly distorted, with a total avoidance of the left side -- the very space that linguistic signs were placed in. Thus, the left hemisphere seems to be involved in the organization of manual activity insofar as it is linguistic, but the right hemisphere plays a crucial role in spatial aspects of non-ASL gestures.

The gestures of deaf signers have not been described, although informal observation of several ASL cartoon narrations suggests that true gesticulation does accompany sign language use. If signers have spontaneous gestures along with their sign production, we would expect, in the case of sign aphasia, that the gestures would behave like the gestures of hearing aphasics.

Gestures of a Commissurectomized Speaker

We have been able to obtain one narration by a commissurectomized patient (a 'split-brain'), a 35 year-old man (right hander) whose corpus callosum had been completely severed surgically for treatment of intractable epilepsy (the corpus callosum, the anterior commissure, and the hippocampal commissure were all disconnected, confirmed by a MRI scan).[2] The subject was shown the cartoon 'stimulus' (in three segments, to improve chances for recall), and attempted to retell the story after each segment. Vision was free, so visual input was available to each cerebral hemisphere. The subject's memory is impaired, but there was some recall of 8 of 12 episodes. His narration included some 55 clauses and there were 47 gestures. Both the narration and the gestures, however, were different from those of normal speakers.

The difference in his narration is difficult to quantify, but obvious on inspection. The narration was conducted at a level of abstractness that, in the speech of a normal person, we would regard as nonnarrative. That is, rather than recount the events of the cartoon, which requires thinking of the sequence of cartoon events as primary, the speaker appears to remain in the real world and tell a story about looking at the cartoon. For example,

---

2. We are grateful to Dalia Zaidel of UCLA who kindly collected this narration for us, and to Kaaren Bekken who transcribed the narration and analyzed the gestures.

here are two contrasting versions of the scene from the cartoon where a character swallows a bowling ball:

A normal speaker (the most laconic available):

Tweetie drops a bowling ball. The bowling ball falls into Sylvester's mouth. Sylvester falls back down the drainpipe.

The commissurectomized speaker:

He had a bowling ball dropped on him among other things, while he was coming up.

The normal speaker's description is more detailed and, crucially, was in the same order as the order of events in the cartoon. The commissurectomized narrator's version reversed this order, and this can occur only in nonnarrative texts.

Thus rather than describe the cartoon events directly, the patient's style was to distance himself from these events. The narrative was thus primarily a description of looking at a visual text and it thereby slighted the story text. While a normal speaker's narrative also will make extensive use of nonnarrative perspectives, they are always for the purpose of organizing and presenting the narrative content of the story. It is conceivable that a nonnarrative perspective without strong narrative content is the form in which the left hemisphere apprehends, stores and reproduces visually presented narrations, such as a cartoon.

In keeping with the universal observation of speech-gesture co-expression, the subject's gestures were parallel to his spoken narration. There was not any use of the gesture channel to compensate for the lack of visual content in the speech channel. Whereas a normal speaker's gestures are highly iconic during the narration of a cartoon story, this speaker's gestures were highly noniconic, small in size, and often of such generic form as to be impossible to relate to any of the narrative content. In general, the subject's gestures are what one would expect from an image-poor left cerebral hemisphere. If this is the correct interpretation, it implies that the gestures of the subject were organized in his left hemisphere, along with his speech, and did not draw on the (presumed) greater resources of visual memory and organization in the right hemisphere.

The subject performed gestures with either the right or the left hand, and several times performed gestures bimanually. All but one of the bimanual gestures were symmetrical -- the hands simultaneously performing the same movements in mirror images. It would seem likely that such symmetrical bimanual gestures could arise from a single hemisphere.

Although one might have supposed that each hemisphere would control its own process, this study suggests that the left hemisphere was controlling both speech and gesture, to the detriment of each channel of expression. Both speech and gesture were in a strangely depleted condition in this subject, apparently cut off from a possibly richer store of visual information in the right hemisphere.

Summary of Cerebral Control and a Hypothesis

We can sum up our observations in 4 points that we consider to be of importance for understanding the cerebral control of speech and gesture:

1. Fluent aphasics appear to unpack single idea units into several clauses; this shows that semi-autonomous speech is possible with scant imagistic content.

2. Nonfluent aphasics try to squeeze several idea units into single clauses; this shows that imagery is not sufficient for fluent speech production.

3. The peculiar speech and gesture patterns of the commissurectomized patient suggest that the 'nonlinguistic' hemisphere normally supplies imagery to the speech production process.

4. The handedness results suggest that it is precisely the imagistic content of gestures that requires the linguistic hemisphere's action. Beats, since they do not incorporate images, are less tied to the specific processes of integration in the speech hemisphere.

All of these observations point to the conclusion that, in addition to controlling specific linguistic operations and skilled movement, the linguistic hemisphere integrates imagistic and verbal processes.

Thus we make the following proposal, which we put forth very tentatively. Normal speech production involves the cooperative interaction of both hemispheres, each making its own specific contribution. The close temporal, semantic and functional relationships of speech to gesture arise because the language-dominant hemisphere is the locus of a convergence and interaction of imagistic and linguistic operations. This interaction is an essential part of what makes it the 'linguistic' hemisphere. The imagistic aspects of speech are contributed by the 'non-linguistic' hemisphere and converge on the linear-segmented aspects of speech in the 'language-dominant' hemisphere. The result is an integral whole that contains both imagistic and linear-segmented aspects. Although the aphasic patients had intact right hemispheres, imagistic data could not interact normally with verbal processes in their left hemispheres. Damage in the linguistic part of the brain disturbs the convergence but leaves open the gesture channel itself; hence the globally parallel speech and gesture disruptions that we observed but also the rare instances of gestural compensations.

Unifying Themes

We will describe ideas in this section that pull together some of the observations laid out in this chapter.

A major unifying idea is that speech and gesture reflect different parts of a single system of mental operations. That gesture and speech are manifestations of a single computational process appears in the timing of gestures and speech, in the mutual complementation of gesture and speech, in the breakdown of gestures along with speech in aphasia, and in the differentiation among gesture types to perform different linguistic and discourse functions. If we assume that the surface linguistic structure of speech is but the final stage of an evolutionary process that begins as a primitive stage of global imagery (McNeill, 1985, 1987), we can say that speech and gesture necessarily have a constant relationship in time. The preparation phase of the gesture arises directly out of the primitive stage of the utterance, while the stroke is delivered together with its co-expressive linguistic segments. We in fact find that the preparation phases of iconix anticipate their co-expressive speech, and a preparation phase may even be added to a gesture, seemingly superfluously, to maintain this constant temporal relationship. In other utterances, a stroke may be held statically, in order not to get ahead of the co-expressive speech. The stroke itself is always synchronous with the co-expressive part of the utterance. In this hypothesis, speech and gesture are manifestations of different evolutionary stages of one continuous mental process. What ties them together is the presentation of meanings at rhythmical pulses. Tuite (1989) has presented an argument that conceptualizes gesture and speech production in terms of presenting symbols in synchrony with rhythmical pulses. In his proposal, speaking:

> consists in the presentation of signs -- linguistic and gestural -- accompanied by a more or less regular rhythmic pulse which is, like the semiotic content, expressed through both verbal and kinesic channels. (Tuite, 1989, p. 7).

The synchrony of the gesture stroke with the phonological apex is taken to manifest this rhythmical pulse: both the utterance peak and the gesture stroke occur at the same pulse. If we also assume that each sign is integrated into its full semantic and pragmatic context at the moment that it is generated, the other two levels of synchrony would follow. What the speaker is doing at the rhythmic pulse is presenting a sign realized as part of a definite context of meaning and pragmatic function; thus, the stroke and the linguistic segment coincide in time and are in agreement on the idea unit that they cover and the functions that they carry out. This synchrony is possible, we propose, precisely because the utterance is an evolutionary outcome of process in which imagery plays an integral role;

thus gesture and speech are linked organically, and can be timed to coincide with the same rhythmical pulsations.

At the level of cerebral control, we have proposed that in normal speech production both cerebral hemispheres must cooperate and provide specific elements of the linguistic performance. For effective speech production, there must be a balance and meshing of two forms of representation -- linear-segmented with global-synthetic; this balance we can see in the statistical predominance of one gesture (idea unit) : one clause co-occurrences. The non-dominant hemisphere may thus be the origin of the primitive global form of the utterance in normally functioning brains, passing imagery to the language-dominant hemisphere to attain a final communicative form of the utterance. The commissurectomized patient's results suggest that the opposite hemisphere is needed to supply imagery to the speech production process, while the handedness results suggest that imagery is integrated with speech in the language-dominant hemisphere. The gestures of Wernicke's aphasics demonstrate the possibility of semi-autonomous speaking capacity with minimal imagery input; those of Broca's aphasics demonstrate that imagery input is not sufficient. Insofar as speech is the outcome of an internal temporal evolution that begins in an imagistic and turns into a linear-segmented state, speaking, understanding and communication necessarily involve both hemispheres cooperatively interacting.

Acknowledgments

Preparation of this chapter was supported by grants BNS 8211440 and BNS 8518324 from the National Science Foundation, by a Biomedical Research Support Grant PHS 2S07 RR-07029-23, and by grants in 1981 and 1989 from the Spencer Foundation. We wish to thank Justine Cassell for commenting on the manuscript.

References

Broca, P. (1861). Remarques sur le siege de la faculte du langage articule, suivies d'une obsevation d'aphemie. *Bulletin de la Société Anatomique*, **36**, 330-357.

Bull, P.E. (1987). *Posture and gesture.* (International Series in Experimental Social Psychology, Vol 16). Oxford: Pergamon Press.

Church, R.B., Baker, D., Bunnag, D., & Whitmore, C. (1989, April). *The development of the role of speech in and gesture in story narration.* Paper presented at the Biennial Meeting of the Society for Research in Child Development, Kansas City, MO.

Cicone, N., Wapner, W., Foldi, N.S., Zurif, E., & Gardner, H. (1979). The relation between gesture and language in aphasic communication. *Brain and Language*, **8**, 324-349.

Efron, D. (1941). *Gesture and environment*. Morningside Heights, New York: King's Crown Press.

Ekman, P., & Friesen, W.V. (1969). The repertoire of nonverbal behavioral categories -- origins, usage, and coding. *Semiotica*, **1**, 49-98.

Feyereisen, P. (1983). Manual activity during speaking in aphasic subjects. *International Journal of Psychology*, **18**, 545-556.

Freedman, N. (1972). The analysis of movement behavior during the clinical interview. In A. Siegman & B. Pope (Eds.), *Studies in dyadic communication* (pp. 153-175). New York: Pergamon Press.

Friederici, A.D. (1988). Agrammatic comprehension: Picture of a computational failure. *Aphasiology*, **2**, 279-284.

Goldblum, M.C. (1978). Les troubles des gestes d'accompagnement du langage au cours des lésions corticales unilatérales. In H. Hécaen & M. Jeannerod (Eds.), *Du contrôle moteur à l'organisation du geste*. (pp. 383-395). Paris: Masson.

Hadamard, J. (1945). *The psychology of invention in the mathematical field*. Princeton: Princeton University Press.

Halliday, M.A.K., & Hasan, R. (1976). *Cohesion in English*. London: Longman.

Hécaen, H. (1967). Approche semiotique des troubles du geste. *Langages*, **5**, 67-83.

Hécaen, H. (1978). Les apraxies ideomotrices. Essai de dissociation. In H. Hécaen & M. Jeannerod (Eds.), *Du contrôle moteur à l'organisation du geste* (pp. 333- 358). Paris: Masson.

Hopper, P. (1979). Aspect and foregrounding in discourse. In T. Givon (Ed.), *Syntax and semantics* (pp. 213-241). New York: Academic Press.

Hopper, P., & Thompson, S. (1980). Transitivity in grammar and discourse. *Language*, **56**, 251-299.

Kendon, A. (1972). Some relationships between body motion and speech. In A. Siegman & B. Pope (Eds.), *Studies in dyadic communication* (pp. 177-210). New York: Pergamon Press.

Kendon, A. (1980). Gesticulation and speech: Two aspects of the process of utterance. In M.R. Key (Ed.), *The relationship of verbal and nonverbal communication* (pp. 207-227). The Hague: Mouton.

Kendon, A. (1981). Geography of gesture. *Semiotica*, **37**, 129-163.

Kendon, A. (1988). How gestures can become like words. In F. Poyatos (Ed.), Cross-cultural perspectives in nonverbal communication (pp. 131-141). Toronto: Hogrefe Publishers.

Kimura, D. (1973a). Manual activity during speaking -- I. Right-handers. *Neuropsychologia*, **11**, 34-50.

Kimura, D. (1973b). Manual activity during speaking -- II. Left-handers. *Neuropsychologia*, **11**, 51-55.

Kimura, D., & Archibald, Y. (1974). Motor functions of the left hemisphere. *Brain*, **97**, 337-350.

Kingdon, R. (1958). *The groundwork of English intonation.* London: Longmans Green.

Klima, E.S., & Bellugi, U. (1979). *The signs of language.* Cambridge, MA: Harvard University Press.

Labov, W., & Waletzky, J. (1967). Narrative analysis: oral versions of personal experience. In J. Helm (Ed.), *Proceedings of the 1966 Annual Spring Meeting of the American Ethnological Society* (pp. 12-44). Seattle, WA: University of Washington Press.

Lakoff, G., & Johnson, M. (1980). *Metaphors we live by.* Chicago: University of Chicago Press.

Levy, E.T. (1984). *Communicating thematic structure in discourse. The use of referring terms and gestures.* Unpublished doctoral dissertation, University of Chicago, Chicago.

Marslen-Wilson, W., Levy, E.T., & Tyler, L.K. (1982). Producing interpretable discourse: The establishment and maintenance of reference. In R. Jarvella & W. Klein (Eds.), *Speech, place, and action* (pp. 339-378). Chichester, England: Wiley.

McNeill, D. (1985). So you think gestures are nonverbal? *Psychological Review*, **92**, 350-371.

McNeill, D. (1986). Iconic gestures of children and adults. *Semiotica*, **62**, 107-128.

McNeill, D. (1987). *Psycholinguistics: A new approach.* New York: Harper & Row.

McNeill, D. (forthcoming). *Mirrors of gesture.* Chicago: University of Chicago Press.

McNeill, D., & Levy, E.T. (1982). Conceptual representations in language activity and gesture. In R. Jarvella & W. Klein (Eds.), *Speech, place, and action* (pp. 271-295). Chichester, England: Wiley.

Miller, G.A., & Johnson-Laird, P.N. (1976). *Language and perception.* Cambridge, MA: Harvard University Press.

Milner, B., Branch, C., & Rasmussen, T. (1964). Observations on cerebral dominance. In A.V.S. de Reuck & M. O'Connor (Eds.). *Disorders of language* (pp. 200-214). London: Churchill.

Morris, D., Collett, P., Marsh, P., & O'Shaughnessy, M. (1979). *Gestures, their origins and distribution.* New York: Stein & Day.

Peirce, C.S. (1931-1958). *The collected works of Charles Sanders Peirce.* (C. Hartshorn & P. Weiss, Eds.). Cambridge, MA: Harvard University Press.

Pedelty, L.L. (1987). *Gesture in aphasia.* Unpublished doctoral dissertation, University of Chicago, Chicago.

Peterson, L.N., & Kirshner, H. (1981). Gestural impairment and gestural ability in aphasia: A review. *Brain and Language,* **14**, 333-348.

Poizner, H., Klima, E.S., & Bellugi, U. (1987). *What the hands reveal about the brain.* Cambridge, MA: MIT Press.

Rasmussen, T., & Milner, B. (1975). Clinical and surgical studies of the speech area in man. In K.J. Zulch, O. Creutzfeldt, & G.C. Galbraith (Eds.), *Cerebral localization.* Heidelberg: Springer-Verlag.

Reddy, M. (1979). The conduit metaphor -- a case of frame conflict in our language about language. In A. Ortony (Ed.), *Metaphor and thought* (pp. 284-324). Cambridge, England: Cambridge University Press.

Richards, I.A. (1936). *The philosophy of rhetoric.* New York: Oxford University Press.

Silverstein, M. (1984). On the pragmatic 'poetry' of prose: Parallelism, repetition, and cohesive structure in the time course of dyadic conversation. In D. Schiffrin (Ed.), *Meaning, form and use in context* (pp. 181-199). Washington, DC: Georgetown University Press.

Sousa-Poza, J.F., Rohrberb, R., & Mercure, A. (1979). Effect of type of information (abstract-concrete) and field dependence on asymmetry of hand movements during speech. *Perceptual and Motor Skills,* **48**, 1323-1330.

Sperber, D., & Wilson, D. (1987). *Relevance.* Cambridge, MA: Harvard University Press.

Stein, N.L., & Glenn, C.G. (1979). An analysis of story comprehension in elementary school children. In R. O. Freedle (Ed.), *New directions in discourse processing: Vol. 2* (pp. 53-120). Hillsdale, NJ: Lawrence Erlbaum Associates.

Stephens, D. (1983). *Hemispheric language dominance and gesture hand preference.* Unpublished doctoral dissertation, University of Chicago, Chicago.

Tuite, K. (1989). *Towards a production-based model of gesture.* Unpublished manuscript, University of Chicago, Department of Psychology.

Vendler, Z. (1967). *Linguistics in philosophy.* Ithaca, NY: Cornell University Press.

Wernicke, K. (1874). *Der aphasische Symptomenkomplex.* Breslau: Cohn & Weigert.

Cerebral Control of Speech and Limb Movements
G.E. Hammond (editor)

Chapter 8

GESTURES AND SPEECH: EVIDENCE FROM APHASIA

Guila Glosser
Medical College of Pennsylvania - Eastern Pennsylvania Psychiatric Institute

and

Morton Wiener
Clark University

Four proposed explanations of the relationship between verbal and gestural communication are reviewed: 1) Gestures and speech are separate and unrelated communication channels for representing different types of information and serving different communication functions; 2) Gestures and speech are parts of the same psychological structure. They arise from common semantic-conceptual representations and share a computational stage in symbolic formation; 3) Gestures and speech are related by virtue of the fact that they rely on common motor systems for production; 4) Gestures are primarily manifestations of effortful or disrupted speech encoding; gestures and speech arise independently, and gestures occur specifically when speech is disrupted. Each of the proposed explanations includes predictions about the behavior of aphasic speakers. Data from studies of aphasic speakers pertaining to these predictions are described and critically assessed.

The relationship of gestural and verbal communication was an issue raised in some of the earliest writings on aphasia (Duffy & Liles, 1979;

Taylor, 1932). Initially, the apparent association of verbal and gestural disorders was explored in studies of apractic disorders, specifically ideomotor apraxia, which co-occur with aphasic disorders following damage to the left cerebral hemisphere. In many of the earliest formulations both the verbal and the gestural impairments were interpreted as manifestations of a single generalized disorder of "symbolic formulation and expression" (Head, 1926). Later investigators, however, showed that aphasic and apraxic disorders do occur independently. Thus, one could not claim that apraxia is the basis for an association between impairments in verbal and gestural communication in aphasia. The notion of a generalized disorder of symbolic representation has also been abandoned, with evidence that aphasics do demonstrate intact performance on some kinds of tasks which require manipulation of nonverbal symbolic materials.

The relationship between impairments in gestural and verbal communication for aphasics remains a reasonable concern despite refutations of the early 'apraxic' and 'symbolic' explanations. Co-occurrence of verbal and gestural communication impairments among aphasic patients has been consistently demonstrated (e.g., Cicone, Wapner, Foldi, Zurif, & Gardner, 1979; Glosser, Wiener & Kaplan, 1986; Pedelty, 1987). New explanations have been put forth to account for the apparent association. These current explanations derive from models which specify particular types of relationships of verbal and gestural communication for normal speakers. Recent studies on gestural communication in aphasia have addressed issues which are relevant not only to the neuropsychological characterization of aphasic disorders, but are also important for understanding the apparently ubiquitous relationships between gestural and verbal communication.

Before considering the newer explanations and the evidence from aphasia pertaining to these explanations, it is necessary to define the events which are the object of study. It is generally agreed that there is a subset of spontaneous movements which are considered communicative. Kendon (1983) terms these movements 'gesticulations', while Ekman and Friesen (1969) and Wiener, Devoe, Rubinow and Geller (1972) use the term 'communicative gestures'. These movements, which we will refer to as 'gestures', are distinguished from other behaviors by the following criteria: 1) gestures occur almost exclusively during speech production (McNeill, 1985; Wiener et al., 1972); 2) observers reliably distinguish gestures as intentionally expressive movements (Kendon 1978, Wiener et al., 1972). Gestures function as 'signals' in the same sense that words are signals, while most other movements may be taken as 'signs' which only incidentally accompany verbal communications; 3) gestures have traditionally been identified as a subset of movements of the upper limbs that are distinctive in their spatio-temporal-kinetic characteristics (Kendon, 1986); and 4) gestures are reliably categorized by members of a social-cultural-ethnic group in terms of a set of shared meanings in the same way as words and utterances are (Wiener et al., 1972).

There has been remarkable unanimity in classifying different types of gestures. Most formulations identify a class of gestures which appear to represent aspects of the content in the accompanying verbalization concretely. These gestures are termed 'iconic' by McNeill (1985), 'physiographic' by Efron (1941) and 'improvisational pantomimics' by Wiener et al. (1972). An example of such a gesture to indicate the act of opening a door is a single clockwise rotation of the hand which is configured as if it is grasping a small object. A second class is comprised of gestures that represent abstract aspects of the content in the accompanying verbalization metaphorically. For example, back and forth rotation of the open hand where the palm and back of the hand are alternately facing up, is a gesture which is taken to metaphorically indicate the concept of alternatives (either-or) or a relationship of similarity, but nonidentity, between concepts ('sort of'). These gestures have been termed 'metaphorix' by McNeill (1985) and 'semantic modifying and relational' by Wiener et al. (1972). A third class includes nonrepresentational gestures that denote *relationships* among propositions. They are typically small, simple, rapid movements that are not related to the verbal content iconically. Short, rhythmic, vertical chopping movements of the hand and arm, for example, denote separations between ideas or segments of an utterance. Such gestures have been termed 'beats' by McNeill (1985), 'batons' by Ekman and Friesen (1969), and are identified as a subgroup of 'semantic modifying and relational gestures' by Wiener et al. (1972).

Three other categories of movements have been identified by numerous investigators. These movements are typically dealt with separately, however, as they do not fulfill all of the criteria for gestures specified above. 'Regulators' (Wiener et al., 1972) or 'coverbal' behaviors (Markel, 1975) include movements and orientation usually of the head and eyes (as well as variations in pitch and in timing of speech onset and offset) while the person is speaking. Unlike the other categories of gestures, regulators or coverbal behaviors occur not only during speech production but also sometimes when listening to a speaker (e.g., head nods, focusing gaze, frowning). These movements appear to manage the communication exchange (e.g., turn-taking), rather than communicating content. Another subset of communication gestures has been called 'emblems' (Ekman & Friesen, 1969; Efron, 1941). These are movements with highly conventional, stylized culture-specific forms (e.g., the 'OK' sign). Emblems do not necessarily accompany speech and often occur in the absence of speech (Kendon, 1981). Finally, 'self adaptors' (Ekman & Friesen, 1969) or 'self-touching' movements (Kimura, 1973) are body movements usually produced for a practical purpose (e.g., grooming). These are not considered to be signals or deliberately communicative behaviors, although they may be interpreted as signs from which one may infer something about the person, content, or other aspect of the communication exchange matrix. These behaviors seem to be only incidentally related to speaking, in that they are not specific to communication or speech situations.

Proposed Explanations

Four types of explanations or hypotheses can be identified, each of which attempts to specify a basic relationship between verbal and gestural communication. From the behavior of normal speakers a considerable data base has been constructed for each of the proposed views. Each of these hypotheses also includes predictions about the behaviors of aphasic speakers. We will review each of the explanations and describe evidence found in studies of aphasic speakers pertaining to the proposals.

1. Gestures and Speech are Separate and Unrelated Communication Channels

This view is most apparent in the psychoanalytic literature (e.g., Mahl, 1968) where a theoretical distinction is made between 'primary and secondary processes'. Within the psychoanalytic tradition, verbal communication is thought to be driven principally by secondary processes; speech expresses consciously intended meanings. Gestures, on the other hand, are thought to be driven by primary processes and convey unintended, connotative, emotional information. The two channels of communication are conceived as systems which represent different types of information, serve distinctly different functions in communication, and are not necessarily coordinated or related at conceptual or production stages. The primary evidence for this view is that the communicator is most often not 'aware' of the symbolic information inferable from his or her nonverbal productions.

Although it is generally acknowledged that there are instances where the information in verbal and gestural communications may be unrelated in terms of meanings, all of the other current conceptions appear to regard these cases as exceptional rather than normative. In both normal and pathological groups, parallels in the semantic content and the pragmatic functions of gesture and speech are clearly demonstrable (McNeill, 1985). Verbal and gestural productions are highly synchronized both temporally and pragmatically. Not only are there predictable temporal relationships between the production of speech and gesture (e.g., Butterworth & Beattie,

1978), but information in these channels is also interchangeable (McNeill, 1987). Moreover, manipulation of informational content or form in one channel has predictable effects on the complexity and form of communication in the other channel (Glosser, Wiener & Kaplan, 1988; McNeill, 1987). That representation of information is interchangeable and complementary for the gestural and speech channels seems to argue for the notion that these are interdependent rather than separate communication channels.

Perhaps the most persuasive counter-evidence for the posited independence of gestural and verbal communication comes from studies of patients with linguistic disorders associated with left hemisphere dysfunction. A claim of no relationship between gestures and speech would predict that gestural communication is not altered with disturbance in verbal communication. Despite disagreements about the nature and/or locus of the conjoint disturbance, there appears to be unanimous agreement that gestural communication is never completely normal in aphasic individuals. This first of the proffered explanations, therefore, does not seem to warrant further consideration.

2. Gestures and Speech are Intrinsically Related and are Parts of the Same Psychological Structure

This explanation has been most fully articulated by Kendon (1983) and McNeill (1985) who state that gestures and speech arise from common semantic-conceptual representations and share a computational stage in symbolic formulation. Gesture and speech are viewed as separate vehicles or channels for representing meanings, but they are employed in the service of the same communicative-pragmatic functions and they represent common underlying semantic-conceptual content. The prediction derived from this claim is that to the extent that linguistic impairments arise from a central disruption of the organization, activation, or access to semantic-conceptual representations in aphasia, there will be parallel disruption in the types of meanings and forms of expression in the gestural communication channel.

Results of several investigations are consistent with this view. Studies of communicative gestures have generally not found significant differences in the total quantity of hand and arm gestures (measured as a function of speaking time) produced by different aphasic subgroups nor differences between aphasics and normal speakers, when the degree of primary motor impairment (i.e., hemiplegia) is taken into account (Cicone et al., 1979; Feyereisen, 1983; Glosser, Wiener, & Kaplan, 1986; Pedelty, 1987). However, consistent and significant *qualitative* differences have been documented among aphasic and nonaphasic groups in the types of gestures produced and in the representational adequacy of communicative gestures. These results come from studies that have specifically focused on the *semantic* properties of gestural communication in natural communication exchanges (e.g., conversation, narration and description).

The first such exploratory study by Cicone et al. (1979) reported simultaneous 'propositional' analyses of the gesture and speech of two anterior (Broca) and two posterior (Wernicke) aphasics. It was found that these patients' gesture and speech exhibited the same configurational properties. The authors concluded that disruption in a 'central organizer' most parsimoniously accounted for the observed parallels between gestural and verbal impairments in aphasia. This postulation of a central organizer is compatible with McNeill and Kendon's notion of shared semantic-conceptual representation and computations. Cicone et al. reported that anterior aphasics produced a higher proportion of referential (iconic) gestures than did posterior aphasics. The latter patients produced more 'nonreferential' gestures, that is, gestures which are noniconic, emphatic or rhythmic, and which are nonspecific for meaning. Anterior aphasics' gestures were simple, unelaborated and generally clear; posterior aphasics' gestures were more elaborate and complex, but often unclear. This pattern, of course, parallels anterior aphasics' sparse speech which is composed primarily of high information bearing substantive words, and posterior aphasics' fluent, grammatically complex speech that is noninformative and unclear in meaning.

Pedelty (1987) replicated Cicone et al.'s major findings with a slightly larger sample of patients, and she extended the analogies between aphasics' speech and gestural patterns through additional qualitative analyses. She, too, observed a high proportion of iconic gestures in the productions of nonfluent aphasics. She further noted that although these iconic gestures were generally recognizable, they tended to be 'schematic', unelaborated and produced with frequent hesitations and 'repair'. Nonfluent aphasics also produced a greater number of discrete, unrelated, gestures per verbal clause or per idea than did fluent aphasics. This gestural segmentation of clausal units appears to parallel the manner in which these patients segment clauses telegraphically in their spontaneous speech and writing. Fluent aphasics were found to produce fewer (but often more elaborate) iconic gestures than nonfluent patients. The ostensible iconic gestures of fluent patients were stereotypic and perseverative, or more often idiosyncratic in form, and they were not predictably related to the content of the spontaneous speech. Throughout discourse fluent aphasics produced a disproportionate number of 'beats' as compared to iconic gestures. Among normals, beats typically occur in conjunction with extra-narrative reference in speech (McNeill & Levy, 1982; Stephens, 1983). These gestures appear to serve structural functions in discourse, but, by definition, they are 'empty' of propositional content. Pedelty's detailed observations show a remarkable parallel between fluent aphasics' elaborate but noninformative gestures and these patients' fluent but nonsubstantive language productions.

The results of these descriptive studies are consistent with the view that gestures and speech are functionally related in communication. The findings reviewed thus far, however, do not contribute to identifying the locus of interaction of verbal and gestural communication. These findings would be predicted not only by positing a shared semantic-conceptual representation source for gesture and speech, but they may also be compatible with alternative claims that the gestural impairment in aphasia is secondary to the speech disorder. For example, if speech is viewed as the dominant channel of communication that directs gesturing at the level of motor planning or execution of output, it is possible that modifications in the rate and quality of speech output would result in changes in the accompanying gestures.

Other investigations provide data which begin to focus more directly on the locus of the interaction between speech and gesture in aphasic communication. Glosser et al. (1986) examined mild and moderate aphasics' use of 'semantic modifying and relational' gestures. Evidence from developmental studies indicates that these gestures are conceptually more complex than, for example, iconic and deictic gestures (Jancovic, Devoe & Wiener, 1975). As expected, semantic modifying and relational gestures were found to be most vulnerable to disruption within the aphasic groups. Furthermore, a significant positive correlation was found between the proportions of these gestures (but not of representationally simpler gestures) produced by aphasics and scores on formal tests of auditory comprehension and naming. A significant negative correlation was also found between auditory comprehension scores and the production of referentially unclear, ambiguous gestures. Thus, independent of characteristics of the actual speech production during a particular communication exchange, relationships were found between the severity of semantic-linguistic impairments and the representational adequacy and complexity of gestural communications. It seems reasonable to interpret these findings as being consistent with the view that the interaction of speech and gesture takes place at some early phase in symbolic representation.

Glosser et al. (1986, 1988) also found that manipulating visual access between the speaker and listener (i.e., conversing through an opaque barrier versus face-to-face conversation) resulted in *complementary* changes in verbal and gestural communication, which would suggest a shared source in earlier phases of message formulation rather than in motor output. As might be expected, aphasics' gestural production *declined* when visual access between the speaker and listener was restricted. This was taken as evidence that the observed gestures (deictic and semantic modifying and relational gestures) serve a communicative function for the listener, rather than merely accompanying speech encoding and production. Furthermore, it was found that when gestural production decreased with restricted visual access, aphasics produced linguistically *more complex* speech (e.g., greater syntactic complexity and lower frequency words). This result would be predicted if gesture and speech encode common underlying information. With restricted visual access, gestures can no longer carry information for the listener. For the communication to be successful, the equivalent message or information must be encoded with a more restricted set of behaviors, in this case the verbal channel. The outcome is a 'transfer' of message information from the gestural to the verbal channel. Such transfer of complexity between gestures and speech, according to McNeill (1987), provides strong evidence for the claim that "speech and gestures arise as interacting elements of a single system".

Butterworth, Swallow and Grimston (1981) approached the question of the relationship of speech and gesture from a very different perspective. They analyzed the verbal and gestural productions of a patient with jargonaphasia, focusing on possible speech planning impairments. Their results are surprisingly consonant with the claim that gestures and speech share common representations of meaning. Butterworth et al. found that incomplete, unidentifiable movements accompanied neologistic paraphasias. Complete and identifiable 'speech-focused movements', on the other hand, occurred in conjunction with (actually slightly before) literal paraphasias in spontaneous speech. In the latter case it was argued that lexical search had failed at the point at which phonological representations are accessed for speech production. The conceptual information appeared to have been accessed and was represented both linguistically and gesturally. The meaning was recognizable but failed to be completely realized in the verbal channel because of distortion in surface level phonological features. If gesture and speech share a common conceptual-semantic basis, this failure in phonological access/activation would not be expected to show parallel disruption of gestures. Neologistic paraphasias, by contrast, were taken to reflect failure to access semantic-lexical information. The aborted gestures accompanying neologistic paraphasias, it was argued, resulted from failure at an earlier stage in conceptual formulation, one that is shared by speech and gesture. McNeill (1985) predicted such findings on the assumption that gestures undergo less complex transformations from their conceptual-semantic representation to their motoric expression. Gestures, for example, appear to be immune to the transpositional errors that characterize speech production. For normals, gestures also often show anticipatory references, ones that are expressed linguistically only later because of grammatical constraints. For aphasic speakers, the anticipatory gesturally conveyed information may not be followed by linguistic reference because of impairments in syntactic production, lexical retrieval failure, or disrupted phonological access/activation.

Before proceeding with our review of the other proffered explanations it is important to reiterate that the arguments in support of an intrinsic shared conceptual base for verbal and gestural communication are concerned with a limited class of movements which accompany speech, those we termed 'gestures'. This explanation does not address the issue of whether or not other types of movements which accompany speech may be intact in aphasics' communication. For example, Katz (1977) found no group differences in the occurrence of coverbal behaviors (e.g., eye contact, smiles, eyebrow raises and head tilts) for mildly and moderately impaired aphasics. These behaviors, of course, regulate social aspects of the communication exchange but do not convey propositional content. The documented preservation of coverbal behaviors (also found by Labourel, 1986) is consistent with aphasics' well recognized competence in other pragmatic communicative functions (Foldi, Cicone & Gardner, 1983). The hypothesized concurrent dissolution of semantic aspects of speech and gesture in aphasia also does not preclude the possibility that speech-related movements which specifically index linguistic encoding failures may be increased for aphasic patients as the individual struggles to express him/herself verbally. This class of movements, termed 'search and correction' by Wiener et al. (1972), has not been directly studied in aphasia. It seems reasonable, however, that with the negative symptoms in aphasia (i.e., decreases in the complexity of verbal and gestural communications) there may also be positive symptoms (i.e., increased 'search and correction') that serve an adaptive function.

There is considerable evidence from studies of aphasic patients which is consistent with the hypothesis that speech and gesture are indeed related and may interact computationally in their conceptual-semantic representation. Data which are unequivocally consistent only with this view do not exist, either in studies of aphasics or normal speakers. One of the prerequisites for further testing of this hypothesis, and contrasting this hypothesis with other proposed explanations, is a further articulation of the posited representations/processing shared by speech and gesture.

3. Gestures and speech arise from separate structures and interact incidentally

Several models postulate that speech and gesture in principle are independent systems, but they interact peripherally in motor representation, planning and execution. Common to these models is the assumption that the relationship between gesture and speech is incidental rather than intrinsic. These models, by and large, do not differentiate between communicative gestures and other speech-related movements, and thus, are not in opposition to the preceding explanation which deals specifically with communicative gestures. The issue that gestures and speech may interact at loci other than the semantic-conceptual representation is part of the following explanations:

a) In one formulation it has been proposed that all communicative behaviors are related by virtue of the fact that they rely on common motor systems. Kimura (1976) postulated that

> ... brain regions considered to be important for symbolic-language processes might better be conceived as important for the production of motor sequences which happen to lend themselves readily to communication.

The brain regions referred to are posterior, specifically parietal, left hemispheric structures (Kimura, 1982). Taken in its broadest extent, this proposal suggests that verbal and gestural communication depend on common motor control programs and are related at the level of motor planning, organization and programming. The prediction, then, is that when there is left hemispheric damage, there will be disruption of all communicative behaviors (speech, gesture, manual sign language), and what is common to all of the disorders is an impairment in motor programming. If this claim is taken as an alternative to the previous one (which it need not be), it would predict that the amount of impairment in motor control will account for more of the shared variance between verbal and gestural communication disorders in aphasia, than will the degree of conceptual-semantic impairment.

Unfortunately, this prediction has not been tested directly. The indirect evidence for this view comes from studies of apraxia. For example, Kimura and Archibald (1974) observed that patients with left hemispheric lesions were impaired in their performance of meaningless manual sequences, as well as in the traditional tests of apraxia which assess performance of familiar meaningful movements. There was a high positive correlation between these two abilities among patients with left hemispheric damage. However, *no* relationship was found between linguistic abilities (auditory comprehension and naming) and performance on the motor tests. The underlying relationship between language, praxis and skilled motor productions, therefore, was attributed to a facility in motor control rather than in verbal symbolic processing. It should be noted that these data and the conclusions drawn from these empirical findings have not gone unchallenged (e.g., Duffy, 1987). The continuing debate regarding the symbolic/motoric basis for apraxia will not be detailed here as we will argue that apraxia, at least in the way it is conventionally defined, does not seem to be relevant to understanding gestural communication.

There are several reasons to believe that apraxia is not relevant to understanding gestural *communication.* Clinically, an apraxic disorder is determined to be present when a patient fails to correctly perform familiar movements to verbal command or fails to imitate these movements when demonstrated by the examiner. Speech is explicitly suppressed in this assessment. The individual is required to produce an emblem or conventionalized pantomimic movement in a decontextualized manner, independent of a communication exchange. The movement serves no communicative function within this context. As was noted above, emblems are not necessarily used in conjunction with verbal communication even in natural settings. Pantomimic movements, of the types sampled in the assessment of apraxia, are exceedingly rare in natural communication exchanges (Glosser et al., 1986; Hermann, Reichle & Lucius-Hoene, 1988). It is not clear, therefore, that studies of these kinds of apraxic difficulties are relevant in exploring the relationships between speech and gestural communication (McNeill, 1987). In fact, several investigators of gestural communication in aphasic patients have reported no relationships between the presence and severity of apractic disorders and impairments in gestural communication (Cicone et al., 1979; Goldblum, 1978).

To our knowledge only two studies address directly the possible associations between gestural communication and the production of complex nonrepresentational movements. Such data would be relevant to a motor control explanation. Stephens (1983) examined the manual preferences of normal speakers when producing communicative gestures which differed on orthogonal dimensions of motor complexity (e.g., number of component motor sequences comprising the gesture) and symbolic complexity (e.g., 'distance' between the referent and symbol). Relative right or left hand utilization was taken as the measure of lateral cerebral control. The question posed was whether motor complexity or symbolic complexity best accounted for the neural relationships (i.e., lateral manual preference) among different classes of communicative gestures. The results are generally consistent with the claim that communicative gestures are neurally (laterally) related on the basis of their semantic-functional communicative characteristics, rather than by their motoric characteristics. The strongest right hand - left hemisphere preference, for example, was evident for motorically simple, but representationally complex, metaphoric gestures ('conduit metaphors').

In the context of her study of communicative gestures in fluent and nonfluent aphasics, Pedelty (1987) also assessed performances on traditional tests of ideomotor apraxia and on Kimura's task which requires copying nonrepresentational movement sequences. Pedelty reported several pertinent relationships: 1) performances on the tests of praxis and motor sequencing - but not the type and severity of aphasia - correlated moderately with overall gestural rate as a function of time; 2) performances on tests of apraxia and motor sequences, however, did not correlate with the relative distribution of gestures which varied in terms of their semantic symbolic characteristics (e.g., the ratio of beats/iconic gestures); 3) the degree of elaboration of iconic gestures was computed as a sum of the number of changes in the physical parameters of the gesture with respect to the preceding state of the hand. A significant positive correlation was found between degree of motoric elaboration of iconic gestures and scores on the motor sequences task. Pedelty concluded from all of these results that the types of communicative gestures produced by aphasics depend on the nature of the underlying language disorder, but the *form* of the representational gesture relies on degree of motor skill which is indeed independent of language ability.

Returning to the issue of the posited relationship between verbal and gestural communication, it would appear that the data from aphasia are not consistent with a claim that shared motor control systems form the *sole* basis for the relationship between gesture and speech. The empirical results, however, do raise the possibility that gestures and speech may interact at multiple loci, conceptual-semantic and motoric, for example. As Kinsbourne (1986) emphasized, gestures do not comprise a neuropsychologically distinct category. By virtue of their motoric, symbolic and pragmatic characteristics they may involve multiple neural/psychological systems in their expression. Just as a distinction is made between dysarthria and aphasia, there may be a distinction to be made between impairments in the motoric and symbolic aspects of gestural communication. The semantic and pragmatic aspects of gestures are related to speech (or manual signing for that matter) in conceptual formulation, whereas the practic-motoric aspects of gesture may be related to systems specialized for motor organization and control of speech production (or manual signing).

The motor programming deficit explanation, we believe, is partially complementary to the conceptual deficit hypothesis in explaining some of the correlated speech and gestural disorders among aphasics. The two hypotheses make predictions about different aspects of behavior. As was noted above, the conceptual explanation deals specifically with semantic features of a subclass of speech-related movements, communicative gestures. The motor programming explanation appears to deal with a broader range of movements, both those related and unrelated to speech, and focuses on the physical, rather than semantic representational characteristics of the behaviors.

b) In several other formulations of the relationship between speech and gesture the claim is made that movements accompanying speech are a byproduct of the cerebral activation which occurs with effortful encoding in certain instances of speech production (Dittman, 1972; Feyereisen, 1986; Marcos, 1979). Within this view speech and gestures are assumed to arise independently, but they interact coincidentally during speech production. The speech channel has primacy in communication and gestures occur when speech is disrupted. This view derives from a more general notion that because of the multitude of interconnections in the brain, focal patterned neural activation (especially that associated with more complex effort-demanding processing) overflows to contiguous brain regions. The overflow is manifest in resonant activity in effector organs that are represented in the proximal neural regions.

In contrast to the preceding kinds of explanations, the speech encoding/activation hypothesis predicts that gesturing will *increase* with greater disruption (i.e., effort) in speech encoding or production. Evidence from the behavior of aphasics is quite pertinent to this hypothesis. The argument is that to the extent that aphasics are impaired in lexical search, syntactic encoding and articulation they should demonstrate increased gestural production (Marcos, 1979).

Feyereisen (1983) found *increased* total duration of speech-related movements for both fluent and nonfluent aphasics, compared to normals, during informal narration. Total movement duration was computed as a function of total conversation time. Since movement durations were increased in both aphasic groups, it was concluded that neither fluency nor verbal symbolic facility determined the motoric production. Rather, the amount of movement was related to more effortful linguistic-verbal encoding which presumably characterizes all forms of aphasia. Other results which have been replicated by several investigators (Feyereisen, 1983; Glosser et al., 1986; Goldblum, 1978) have also been cited as supportive of the notion that as speech production becomes more effortful in nonfluent, anterior aphasics, gestural production increases proportionately. These studies have all shown higher gesture/spoken word ratios among nonfluent aphasics.

There are several problems with the interpretation of these limited data. First, the central finding of an overall increase in the *duration* of speech-related movements (and the trend for longer durations of individual movements) in aphasic speakers could well reflect severity of the motor impairments of these hemiparetic/hemiplegic patients. Longer durations of individual movements and longer overall movement times might be expected with primary motor disturbance. Recall that the actual numbers of movements and gestures recorded per unit time do not appear to differ among groups. The trend is typically for increased frequency of hand-arm movements in the fluent aphasia patients and decreased frequency in nonfluent patients who overtly appear to struggle more to speak.

Second is the more important fact that qualitative analyses of the movements or kinds of gestures which may be associated with speech encoding failures are lacking. Research on normal speakers indicates that *nonrepresentational* speech-related movements (noniconic, short, rhythmic movements that tend to occur in bursts) are those specifically associated with hesitations and speech encoding failures (Marcos, 1979). The results of Glosser et al. (1986) also suggest that the gestures associated with verbal dysfluencies are those which are also less clear and nonspecific in terms of representational form. As Butterworth et al. (1981) observed, different gestural types may correspond to different kinds of speech encoding difficulties (i.e., paraphasias). An adequate test of the speech encoding claim, therefore, entails a more detailed qualitative assessment of the movements which may be associated with effortful speech production.

A third problem, which is related to the previous one, is that the noted increases in certain types of movements among aphasic speakers are not always associated with speech hesitation, dysfluency, or effortful speech encoding. Although movements may increase for aphasic speakers, one can not assume that they are due to speech encoding failures. For example, we along with other investigators (Hermann et al., 1988; Katz, 1977) have noted increased head movements indicating assent and denial especially among nonfluent aphasic patients. The amount of these head movements, unlike representationally complex hand and arm movements, correlates positively with reduced verbal fluency (phrase length), but not with the degree of naming or auditory comprehension impairments. These head nods, however, frequently appear to be produced by aphasic speakers in response to the behaviors of the nonaphasic participants in the communication exchange (Hermann et al., 1988). When communicating with aphasics, particularly with nonfluent patients, normal speakers often assume a greater burden in the communication exchange and structure it with more questions to which the patient can respond simply with verbal or gestural assent or denial. As illustrated in this example, it is important to distinguish between instances where increased production of a particular movement is the result of a deficit or disruption for the aphasic speaker and cases where increased production is in response to a change in the behavior of another participant in the communication exchange. Such distinctions rest on qualitative differences among the types of movements, as well as on analyses of co-occurring variables in the communication exchange matrix (e.g., properties of the listener, physical aspects of the setting, social aspects of the communication exchange, etc.).

The fourth problem with the evidence presented in support of the speech encoding hypothesis concerns the presumed causal relationship between disrupted speech encoding and gestural production. Even if increased gesturing may be shown to co-occur with aphasics' effortful speech encoding or production, one may conceive of at least two ways in which the gestures are related to effortful speech encoding that do not rely on the notion of undifferentiated overflow of cerebral activation: one possibility which has been raised is that certain nonreferential movements (Helm, 1979), or, in some cases, referential movements (Pedelty, 1987) are associated with effortful speech encoding in a manner which might suggest that the gesture activates speech rather than vice versa. This self-cuing function of limb movements has been reported anecdotally but has not been explored empirically. Another alternative is that movements (primarily head movements) associated with hesitations, pauses and dysfluencies in aphasics' verbal communications serve a 'place holding' function. They are social behaviors which are produced deliberately as compensations for, rather than expressions of, the verbal encoding difficulties (Hermann et al., 1988; Katz, 1977). Both of these alternatives posit that increased gestures in aphasic patients are pragmatically determined, compensatory, positive symptoms, rather than signs of failure in speech encoding.

The hypothesis that speech-related movements are primarily a function of effortful, disrupted speech encoding is not supported by the available, but limited data, from aphasia. Based on the preceding review of other studies of gesturing among aphasics, it seems that the evidence from aphasia will not support the claim that communicative gestures are formulated independently of speech and are only incidentally related to the effort associated with speech production. It still remains possible that further examinations of aphasics' gestural expressions will reveal a subset of behaviors (most likely nonreferential head movements) which co-occur specifically with hesitations in speaking. Hesitations are commonly accepted as external indicators of speech encoding/planning difficulties (Butterworth & Beattie, 1978; Goldman-Eisler, 1968). As noted above, caution must be taken in interpreting movements which occur in conjunction with hesitations as signs only of speech encoding difficulties. These movements also may be pragmatically determined and served a communication exchange function. Most investigators have analyzed aphasics' verbal as well as gestural communication abilities independent of social variables in the communication matrix. In fact, we have shown that the complexity of aphasics' verbal communications varies significantly with changes in the nonlinguistic social context of communication (Glosser et al., 1988). It seems quite reasonable to suppose that speech encoding deficits might interact with social pragmatic factors in determining the verbal and gestural communication behaviors of aphasics.

Conclusions

Four kinds of explanations to account for the observed relationships between verbal and gestural communication have been reviewed here. Each approach makes predictions with respect to the ways in which aphasics' gestural communication is altered. Relevant data from research with aphasics were presented as evidence for each of the proposals. As noted, not all of the explanations are mutually exclusive, and the presented evidence from studies of aphasic patients are consistent with at least two of the proposed models of the interaction between speech and gesture. Clearly further research is required to refine each of the models and then to test predictions derived from these models in normal speakers as well as aphasics.

Evidence from aphasia is likely to continue to be important in assessing the relative merits of the different explanations offered to account for the noted relationships of gesture and speech. The evidence from aphasia is certainly not conclusive, but may be combined with other sources of data. Three issues must be considered in evaluating the evidence from aphasia: First, the interpretation of observed disrupted gesturing and its relation to speech in aphasia depends critically on how one characterizes the linguistic disorder of aphasics. If, for example, one believes that a semantic-linguistic impairment underlies impaired comprehension and speech production in certain aphasic syndromes (e.g., Berndt, Caramazza & Zurif, 1983), then it is reasonable to test for the hypothesized concurrent conceptual-semantic dissolution of gestures. If, on the other hand, aphasia is viewed only as a disorder in lexical access, then one would not use this population to test predictions about semantic-conceptual disruption in speech and gestures. There is not yet general agreement with respect to the nature of the underlying conceptual/linguistic impairment in different aphasic groups. Thus, inferences about any relationships found for gestural and speech impairments in these groups must be tentative.

A second, and obviously related, issue is that aphasic patients can not be dealt with as a homogeneous group. The surface symptoms as well as the presumed underlying cognitive impairments differ among traditionally defined aphasic subtypes. Subgroups of aphasics may be expected to evidence different patterns of gestural impairment, and the data from each subgroup might be pertinent to different hypotheses about the interaction of speech and gesture. For example, many investigators believe that in anomic aphasia there is a selective disruption in lexical access, with relatively intact activation and organization of semantic-conceptual representations (Blumstein, 1981; Butterworth, Howard & McLoughlin, 1984). Patients with pure anomia would not be expected to show changes in the semantic representational characteristics of their communicative gestures. These patients are expected to evidence preserved gesturing, and even possibly increased use of gestures to compensate for failures in lexical retrieval. This group of patients may be ideal for testing the speech encoding explanation of gestural production.

Third, it must be recognized that aphasics are impaired in numerous nonlinguistic domains (e.g., motoric, visuo-perceptual, etc.), and that these impairments may also contribute significantly to alterations in their gestural communications. Irrespective of whether the nonlinguistic impairments are viewed as intrinsic or coincidental to the language disorder, these concurrent deficits constrain the kinds of inferences which can be made about relationships of language and gesture in aphasic patients.

It is clear that the study of aphasia can inform about the ways in which gesture and speech interact psychologically and neurologically. Conversely data from normal speakers which leads to further articulation and empirical validation of each of the models presented above can be informative with respect to the underlying neuropsychological systems which are impaired and spared in aphasia. Whether one believes that gestural disorders arise from a conceptual-semantic impairment, a motor-practic impairment, or disturbance in speech planning, gestures provide alternate means for exploring basic neuropsychological functions in aphasia.

There are two final concerns about the exploration of the relationship between gesture and speech which pertain not only to investigations of aphasic speakers, but also to normal speakers. Much has been made about the commonalities between gesture and speech in terms of their shared symbolic and motoric basis. It is obvious, however, that gestures and speech differ in their structural properties: in speech, information is represented in discrete, temporally-ordered units, while in gesture information is more often represented in large, simultaneous spatially-organized configurations. The view that equivalent information can be represented in verbal and gestural channels is not incompatible with the idea that it is 'easier' or more 'efficient' for a communicator to represent different or specialized types of meanings in the two channels. Some kinds of gestures, for example, appear particularly suited for representing spatially organized scenes. Speech, on the other hand, appears to be better specialized for analytic, explanatory, conceptual content. This formulation suggests that the content, as well as the setting, of the communication exchange in which gestures and speech are assessed may well contribute to the forms of observed gestural and verbal communications. The specialization of gestural and speech channels for particular contents for one or another cultural group is not necessarily a hindrance to exploring the conceptual bases and relationships of speech and gesture. It may also provide an opportunity for assessing conceptual representation of different contents or types of information in normal and aphasic speakers.

More broadly, a concern may be raised that the whole endeavor of looking for an explanation of a relationship between speech and gesture is so narrowly drawn that we fail to explore other components that co-occur in a communication matrix (Hymes, 1974) and which may bear on the apparent relationships of speech and gesture. We know of no communication exchange, oral or graphic, that does not also include many facets other than the two components in this review. There are 'channels' other than hand-arm gestures and semantic content of speech (e.g., eye movements and tonal variations) each of which may contribute to the totality of the communication exchange or may modify information in the other channels. No speech or gesture is completely understandable independent of the physical context of the communication exchange, the content, and the participants, to name just a few facets. In our review of the data we have indicated some instances where these variables obviously bear on the interpretation of the relationship between speech and gesture. From our perspective, it is important to view each instance of communication as a social act (Austin, 1962). Just as an account of the social and pragmatic aspects of oral and written language entails consideration of multiple facets of the communication exchange matrix, so too, the relationships of speech and gesture must be evaluated within a broader perspective of communication as social action.

References

Austin, J.L. (1962). *How to do things with words.* Oxford: Claredon Press.

Berndt, R.S., Caramazza, A., & Zurif, E. (1983). Language functions: syntax and semantics. In S.J. Segalowitz (Ed.), *Language functions and brain organization* (pp. 5-28). New York: Academic Press.

Blumstein, S.E. (1981). Neurolinguistic disorders: language - brain relationships. In S.B. Filskov & T.J. Boll (Eds.), *Handbook of clinical neuropsychology* (pp. 227-256). New York: John Wiley and Sons.

Butterworth, B., & Beattie, G. (1978). Gesture and silence as indicators of planning in speech. In R.N. Campbell & P.T. Smith (Eds.), *Recent advances in the psychology of language: Formal and experimental approaches, Vol 4* (pp. 247-360). New York: Plenum Press.

Butterworth, B., Howard, D., & McLoughlin, P. (1984). The semantic deficit in aphasia: the relationship between semantic errors in auditory comprehension and picture naming. *Neuropsychologia*, **22**, 409-426.

Butterworth, B., Swallow, J., & Grimston, M. (1981). Gestures and lexical processes in jargon aphasia. In J.W. Brown (Ed.), *Jargon aphasia* (pp. 113-124). New York: Academic Press.

Cicone, M., Wapner, W., Foldi, N., Zurif, E., & Gardner, H. (1979). The relation between gesture and language in aphasic communication. *Brain and Language*, **8**, 324-349.

Dittman, A.T. (1972). The body movement-speech rhythm relationship as a cue to speech encoding. In A.W. Siegman & B. Pope (Eds.), *Studies in dyadic communication* (pp. 135-151). New York: Pergamon Press

Duffy, J.R. (1987, February). *The asymbolia explanation for impairment of propositional nonverbal communication in aphasia*. Paper presented at the meeting of the International Neuropsychological Society, Washington, D.C.

Duffy, R.J., & Liles, B.Z. (1979). A translation of Finkelburg's (1870) lecture on aphasia as 'asymbolia' with commentary. *Journal of Speech and Hearing Disorders*, **44** 156-168.

Efron, D. (1941). *Gesture and environment*. New York: King's Crown Press.

Ekman, P., & Friesen, W.V. (1969). The repertoire of nonverbal behavior: origins, usage and coding. *Semiotica*, **1**, 49-98.

Feyereisen, P. (1983). Manual activity during speaking in aphasic subjects. *International Journal of Psychology*, **18**, 545-556.

Feyereisen, P. (1986). Lateral differences in gesture production. In J.L. Nespoulous, P. Perron & A.R. Lecours (Eds.), *The biological foundations of gestures: Motor and semiotic aspects* (pp. 77-94). Hillsdale, NJ: Lawrence Erlbaum Associates.

Foldi, N., Cicone, M., & Gardner, H. (1983). Pragmatic aspects of communication in brain damaged patients. In S.J. Segalowitz (Ed.), *Language functions and brain organization* (pp. 51-86). New York: Academic Press.

Glosser, G., Wiener, M., & Kaplan, E. (1986). Communicative gestures in aphasia. *Brain and Language*, **27**, 345-359.

Glosser, G., Wiener, M., & Kaplan, E. (1988). Variations in aphasic language behavior. *Journal of Speech and Hearing Disorders*, **53**, 115-124.

Goldblum, M.C. (1978). Les troubles des gestes d'accompagnement du langage au cours des lésion corticales unilatérales. In H. Hécaen & M. Jeannerod (Eds.), *Du contrôle moteur à l'organisation du geste* (pp. 383-395). Paris: Masson.

Goldman-Eisler, F. (1968). *Psycholinguistics*. London: Academic Press.

Head, H. (1926). *Aphasia and kindred disorders of speech*. Cambridge: Cambridge University Press.

Helm, N.A. (1979). *The gestural behavior of aphasic patients during confrontation naming.* Unpublished doctoral dissertation, Boston University.

Hermann, M., Reichle, T., & Lucius-Hoene, G. (1988). Nonverbal communication as a compensative strategy for severely nonfluent aphasics? - A quantitative approach. *Brain and Language*, **33**, 41-54.

Hymes, D.H. (1974). *Foundations in sociolinguistics: An ethnographic approach.* Philadelphia: University of Pennsylvania Press.

Jancovic, M., Devoe, S., & Wiener, M. (1975). Age-related changes in hand and arm movements as nonverbal communication: some conceptualizations and an empirical exploration. *Child Development*, **46**, 922-928.

Katz, R.C. (1977). *Coverbal behavior elicited by aphasic subjects during conversational turns.* Unpublished doctoral dissertation, University of Florida.

Kendon, A. (1978). Differential perception and attentional frame: two problems for investigation. *Semiotica*, **24**, 305-315.

Kendon, A. (1981). Geography of gesture. *Semiotica*, **37**, 129-163.

Kendon, A. (1983). Gesture and speech: how they interact. In J.M. Wiemann & R.P. Harrison (Eds.), *Nonverbal interaction* (pp. 13-45). Beverly Hills, CA: Sage Publications.

Kendon, A. (1986). Current issues in the study of gesture. In J.L. Nespoulous, P. Perron & A.R. Lecours (Eds.), *The biological foundations of gestures: Motor and semiotic aspects* (pp. 23-48). Hillsdale, NJ: Lawrence Erlbaum Associates.

Kimura, D. (1973). Manual activity during speaking - I. Right handers. *Neuropsychologia*, **11**, 45-50

Kimura, D. (1976). The neural basis of language qua gesture. In H. Whitaker & H.A. Whitaker (Eds.), *Studies in Neurolinguistics, Vol 2* (pp. 145-156). New York: Academic Press.

Kimura, D. (1982). Left-hemisphere control of oral and brachial movements and their relation to communication. *Philosophical Transactions of the Royal Society London*, **B298**, 135-149.

Kimura, D., & Archibald, Y. (1974). Motor functions of the left hemisphere. *Brain*, **97**, 337-350.

Kinsbourne, M. (1986). Brain organization underlying orientation and gestures. Normal and pathological cases. In J.L. Nespoulous, P. Perron & A.R. Lecours (Eds.), *The biological foundations of gestures: Motor and semiotic aspects* (pp. 65-76). Hillsdale, NJ: Lawrence Erlbaum Associates.

Labourel, D. (1986). Shrugging shoulders, frowning eyebrows, smiling agreement: mimic and gesture communication in the aphasic experience. In J.L. Nespoulous, P. Perron & A.R. Lecours (Eds.), *The biological foundations of gestures: Motor and semiotic aspects* (pp. 295-308). Hillsdale, NJ: Lawrence Erlbaum Associates.

Mahl, G.F. (1968). Gestures and body movements in interviews. In J. Schlein (Ed.), *Research in psychotherapy, Vol 3* (pp. 295-346). Washington, D.C.: American Psychological Association.

Marcos, L.R. (1979). Non verbal behavior and thought processing. *Archives of General Psychiatry*, **36**, 940-943.

Markel, N.N. (1975). Coverbal behavior associated with conversational turns. In A. Kendon, R. Harris & M.R. Key (Eds.), *Theory of behavior in face-to-face interaction* (pp. 189-197). The Hague: Mouton.

McNeill, D. (1985). So you think gestures are nonverbal? *Psychological Review*, **92**, 350-371.

McNeill, D. (1987). So you do think gestures are nonverbal! A reply to Feyereisen (1987). *Psychological Review*, **94**, 499-504.

McNeill, D., & Levy, E.T. (1982). Conceptual representations in language activity and gesture. In R. Jarvella & W. Klein (Eds.), *Speech, place and action: Studies in deixis and related topics* (pp. 271-295). Chichester, England: Wiley.

Pedelty, L.L. (1987). *Gestures in aphasia*. Unpublished doctoral dissertation, University of Chicago.

Stephens, D. (1983). *Hemispheric language dominance and gesture hand preference*. Unpublished doctoral dissertation, University of Chicago.

Taylor, J. (1932). *Selected writings of Hughlings Jackson*. London: Hodder & Stoughton.

Wiener, M., Devoe, S., Rubinow, S., & Geller, J. (1972). Nonverbal behavior and nonverbal communication. *Psychological Review*, **79**, 185-214.

Cerebral Control of Speech and Limb Movements
G.E. Hammond (editor)
Elsevier Science Publishers B.V. (North-Holland), 1990

Chapter 9

THE CONCOMITANCE OF SPEECH AND MANUAL GESTURE IN APHASIC SUBJECTS

Pierre Feyereisen, Marie-Paule Bouchat, Dominique Déry, and Monica Ruiz
University of Louvain

Contradictory findings about the gestural behavior of aphasic subjects during speaking have been reported. In the present paper, a first study of 12 aphasic and 6 normal control subjects was aimed at demonstrating that different patterns of association between gestures and speech may be found, and that this variability does not relate to aphasia type defined by fluency or use of content words. In a second part, a single case study was used to analyze the relationships between gestures and speech in a subject who suffered from semantic impairments without deficits in the output phonological processing (transcortical sensory aphasia). Four tasks were designed from a single set of items: picture naming, elicitation of communicative gestures from pictures and names, and word-to-picture matching. In the visual input conditions, verbal and gestural performance were significantly associated, but in the auditory input conditions, the number of correct gestures was not related to correct word-to-picture matching. Furthermore, gestures were more often judged correct in the auditory than in the visual condition, and the two performances were not related to each other. These results partially support the hypothesis of association between verbal and gestural behavior in a patient suffering from defective semantic processing, and they do not support the hypothesis of a direct link between visual object recognition and motor programming.

1. Introduction

1.1. Working hypotheses

The neuropsychological study of manual activity while speaking has mainly been devoted to the analysis of two rival hypotheses. The first is the assumption of shared mechanisms controlling both manual and oral performances. According to the authors, emphasis was put on different aspects of these performances, either their communicative value (e.g., R.J. Duffy, J.R. Duffy, & Mercaitis, 1984; Kendon, 1983) or their motor realization (e.g., Kimura, 1976). From such a perspective, the left hemisphere's contribution is thought to extend beyond language processing and left-brain damage may result in concomitant verbal and gestural impairments. The alternative hypothesis is to conceive the possibility of gestural compensation for momentary or permanent word-finding difficulties (see e.g., Butterworth, Swallow, & Grimston, 1981). Several explanations may account for the ability to perform gestures in relation to concepts which cannot be expressed by verbal means. First, a modality-specific impairment may disturb access to word forms in the lexical store but visual or semantic information is still available to program a gesture. Second, the component which is shared by the gestural and the verbal systems may be more efficient in one modality and thus, performances may dissociate though they depend on a single process (Dunn & Kirsner, 1988; Shallice, 1988). More specifically, a gestural response may be less difficult to select, for instance, because there are more words than plans for action, and motor programs for gestures may be less demanding than those used in speaking, for instance, because the sequence of movements which constitutes gestures like pointing or nodding may be shorter than the sequence of oral movements in uttering correspondent words (for reviews, see Feyereisen, 1988, in press).

1.2. Supporting Evidence

Arguments for the first hypothesis of a common mechanism underlying speech and gestures were found in systematic observations of spontaneous manual activity of aphasic subjects. In a pilot study, Cicone, Wapner, Foldi, Zurif, and Gardner (1979) analyzed small portions of conversations of four subjects, two being described as 'anterior' or Broca's aphasics, the two other as 'posterior' or Wernicke's aphasics. The posterior aphasics performed more movements per time unit than the anterior aphasics and their gestural units showed greater complexity, i.e., longer chains of components. Similarly, referential value of manual movements was found to correlate with the informative content of speech production.

A higher proportion of gestures carrying information was found in anterior than in posterior aphasics. From a similar perspective, Pedelty (1987) carefully compared the performance of five fluent and four nonfluent aphasics in a story-telling task and she demonstrated several differences between these two groups. Narrations of fluent aphasics were longer and syntactically more complex but their noun to pronoun ratios were lower than in the nonfluent group. Neither the rate of gesturing nor the complexity of gestures related to verbal fluency, but nonfluent subjects used a larger portion of space which corresponds to a higher proportion of representational gestures. McNeill (1985, 1989) argued from these results that linguistic and gestural abilities dissolve simultaneously in aphasia. Converging evidence was gathered in another study, in which the percentage of interpretable gestures during an interview did correlate positively with auditory comprehension and naming scores, and the percentage of uninterpretable gestures negatively; the most severely impaired aphasics performed communicative gestures in a lower proportion than the less severely impaired aphasics and the normal control subjects (Glosser, Wiener, & Kaplan, 1986). From these observations, the conclusion was drawn that left-hemisphere lesions disrupt communication both in the verbal and the gestural modality.

However, other studies contradicted these observations. Feyereisen (1983) found no significant differences in hand movement duration and frequency between four nonfluent and eight fluent aphasics. These measures did not correlate with speech rate or noun to pronoun ratio. Both aphasic groups displayed higher manual activity than normal control subjects. Similarly, Smith (1987a,b) observed more hand and arm movements in aphasic than in nonaphasic subjects, and in nonfluent than in fluent aphasic subjects. With a different technique of automatic recording of arm movements, Hadar (1989) found increased level of coverbal activity in aphasic subjects as compared to control subjects. In other studies, special attention was devoted to the communicative value of gestures. When the frequency of batonic, deictic, and illustrative gestures was compared in four Broca's and three Wernicke's aphasics, the Broca's aphasics were found to display an increased manual activity for the three categories of gestures, as compared to Wernicke's aphasics and to control subjects (LeMay, David, & Thomas, 1988). In a heterogeneous group of 11 aphasics, appropriate usage of gestures did not relate to measures of verbal skills but fluent aphasics tended to perform gestures which supported oral expression whereas nonfluent aphasics more often substituted gestures for verbal communication (Behrmann & Penn, 1984). Finally, higher reliance on gestural mode of communication was observed in severe nonfluent aphasics (Broca's and global aphasics) as compared to their normal partners and in a referential communication task, more gestures were performed by the more severely impaired aphasics whose residual language was less efficient (Feyereisen, Barter, Goossens, & Clerebaut, 1988; Hermann, Reichle, Lucius-Hoene, Wallesch, & Johannsen-Horbach, 1988).

In summary, only one study has shown reduced gestural activity in aphasics as compared to control (Glosser et al., 1986) whereas several others have shown increased gestural activity in cases of language impairment. Highest gesture rates have been observed either in nonfluent aphasics (Smith, 1987b) or in fluent aphasics (Feyereisen, 1983). The proportion of representational gestures is usually higher in nonfluent aphasics (e.g. Pedelty, 1987) but these subjects sometimes performed more batonic (i.e., nonrepresentational) gestures than fluent aphasics (LeMay et al., 1988). How can these discrepancies be explained? To begin with, the possible influence of several methodological decisions on experimental results must be examined.

Subject characteristics

A small sample size and the well-known heterogeneity of aphasic population may yield discrepant results. As shown by a Monte Carlo simulation, chance alone can account for a small number of 'significant' differences in favor of one or another group when actually no difference exists between them. Furthermore, the group composition may affect the outcome of statistical comparison. In some studies, 'prototypical' subjects were selected whereas in others, diagnostic criteria were not used for inclusion in the sample. The distinction between fluent and nonfluent aphasics does not identify with the presence or the absence of conceptual impairments which would affect gesture production. In both groups, subjects may suffer from semantic impairments and spoken word comprehension disorders (non-fluent global aphasics and fluent Wernicke's aphasics) or not (some nonfluent Broca's aphasics and, by definition, the fluent conduction aphasics and the anomics). Finally, if the use of gestures results from strategic adaptations to language impairments, educational or cultural background, time since onset, and training communication effectiveness during speech therapy may influence the behavior of the subjects. There are little indications, however, that studies may be distinguished in function of these variables.

Situation

In most studies, gestures were observed in conversation-like situations, with the exception of Pedelty (1987), who devised a narrative task. Gestural behavior may vary with communication condition. For instance, aphasic subjects were more influenced than normal subjects by visual access to the partner, in interviews by telephone, through an opaque barrier, face-to-face, or through a closed-circuit television system (Glosser,

Wiener, & Kaplan, 1988). A more critical variable could be the behavior of the partner who may be a relative discussing spontaneously with the subject (e.g. Hermann et al., 1988) or an interviewer attempting to limit his or her participation (e.g. Glosser et al., 1986). However, these variables cannot account for differences between experimental results obtained in apparently similar conditions.

Gesture coding

Some observations bear on 'manual activity' irrespective of its functional value, whereas others are concerned with 'communicative hand gestures'. Thus, an increased rate of speech-related movements is compatible with a reduction of communicative gestures if fewer movements may be interpreted by the observer in the aphasic than in the normal population. This was the case in the study of Glosser et al. (1986) who noted a lower proportion of 'semantic modifying and relational gestures' and a higher proportion of 'other', i.e. unclassifiable, gestures in moderate aphasics than in controls. However, this result was not confirmed by the functional analyses of LeMay et al. (1988) or of Smith (1987a) who reported that only 4% of aphasic gestures were 'ineffective'.

Interim conclusions

In summary, no isolated variable can be identified to account for the discrepancies in the literature on gestural behavior of aphasic subjects. Thus, the two working hypotheses presented in Section 1.1. can both be supported in some cases or be questioned on the basis of contradictory findings. No general conclusion which would be true for the whole aphasic population can be drawn, but the individual characteristics of performances have to be considered. The present study will illustrate such a position.

2. The Production of Gestures in Story-Telling by Aphasic Subjects: The Case for Dissociations

2.1. Overview

The procedure of Feyereisen, Verbeke-Dewitte, and Seron (1986) was modified for the purpose of the present study. Twelve aphasic and six normal control subjects were individually videotaped in two conditions: conversation and story description. In a preliminary stage, an instantaneous time sampling procedure was used to code the verbal and the manual behavior every 5 s: silence or vocalization and hand immobility or gesturing were recorded. Groups and situations were compared in nonparametric analyses. During conversations, aphasics were found to speak in a lower proportion of the observation time than control subjects but to gesture at the same extent. Consequently, the proportion of vocalizations accompanied by gestures was higher in aphasics. In both groups, the majority of gestures were considered nonreferential. During narratives, only one normal subject was observed to perform gestures while all aphasics gestured to some extent. A majority of these gestures were considered to refer to some aspects of the picture stories. In the following section, special attention will be paid to the gestures performed by the aphasic subjects during this second condition in relation to the lexicon used in the narratives.

2.2. The Relationship of Lexical and Gestural Representations in Aphasic Subjects

2.2.1. Methods

Subjects. Twelve aphasic subjects were referred to by the members of the neuropsychological rehabilitation unit of the Saint-Luc clinics in Brussels and of the Centre William Lennox in Ottignies. The main demographic and neurologic characteristics of the sample are given in Table 1. Aphasia type was assessed by means of standard evaluations of performance in spontaneous speech, repetition, naming, and auditory comprehension. Apraxia was examined by a test in which subjects were verbally requested to show the use of 32 objects (Ska & Nespoulous, 1987; Feyereisen et al., 1988). Six non-brain-damaged subjects, in the same range of age and educational level, acted as control subjects. All subjects were native French speakers and right-handers.

Procedure. The subjects were invited to sit or led in their wheelchair in front of a table, facing the experimenter. The camera was located at an angle of 45° to the frontal plane and focused on the subject. No attempt was made to hide the recording apparatus or the fact that a recording was being made. A timer was included in the frame. At the end of an interview of about ten min, the subjects were given the narrative task. The pictures used in a previous study (see Feyereisen, 1984) had been redrawn to avoid some ambiguities. Five pictures describing one story were presented together. After a first narrative, the pictures were removed and the subject was asked an immediate recall. Five narratives were elicited in this way. The same order was followed by each subject: (1) the shaving story, (2) the chicken and the fox, (3) the tree cut down, (4) the jumping, and (5) the fishing.

Table 1. Demographic and clinical data concerning the aphasic subjects. Education refers to the duration of schooling: superior is more than 12 years and medium between 6 and 12 years. The CT-scan localization of lesions refers to the Frontal (F), temporal (T), or parietal (P) lobes.

Subject	Age (years)	Sex	Educ.	Etiology	CT scan	Time since onset (mo)	Associated motor deficits	Type of aphasia
Des	67	M	S	CVA	FTP	58	R hemiplegia (& apraxia)	Global
Gr	48	M	S	CVA	TP	48	R hemiplegia	Broca
Ro	55	F	S	CVA	TP	68	R hemiplegia (& apraxia)	Broca
Vd	28	M	S	Trauma	P	43	R hemiplegia	Broca
Sta	42	M	M	CVA	TP	28	Articulatory disorders	Mixed
Cor	64	M	M	Tumor	FP	2*	R hemiplegia	Anomia
Str	56	M	S	CVA	T	29	None	Wernicke
Ma	56	M	M	CVA	T	20	R hemiplegia	Wernicke
Mo	64	M	M	Tumor	T	2*	None	Wernicke
La	25	M	S	Encephalitis	T	13	None	Sens. transcort.
Coo	30	F	M	CVA	TP	2	R hemiplegia	Sens. transcort.
Del	58	M	M	CVA	T	1	Articulatory disorders	Mixed

* Post-operative

Scoring. The video recordings of the narratives were coded in three steps. First, the vocal signal was automatically analyzed into a sequence of pauses and vocalizations at a sampling rate of 250 ms by a program written for an Apple II+ computer (see Feyereisen et al., 1986). The experimenter's interventions were then identified and removed. Two variables per story were computed from these data. The narrative time is the interval between the beginning of the first utterance of the subject and the end of the last, pauses included. The speaking time was the sum of the durations of the different utterances, pauses excluded. Second, the verbal content of the narrative was transcribed and the number of words counted. Interjections, onomatopoeia, fragments of words, neologisms and phonemic paraphasias were not considered in this computation. Semantic paraphasias and extranarrative comments were not excluded. The proportion of different categories of content words (nouns, verbs, and qualifying adjectives) was then calculated. Noun proportion was highly correlated with the proportion of content words. Third, manual movements, i.e. visible departures from rest positions by one or both hands during the whole narrative time were identified and classified in several categories: deictic gestures were pointing movements towards the pictures or towards some parts of them, iconic gestures described some aspects of a referent, batonic gestures were small movements like thumb raising which usually related to peaks of loudness or larger extra-narrative gestures which were associated with word finding difficulties and expressions like "this is not the right term". The self-touching movements that did not belong to these categories were not considered.

The reliability of gesture identification and classification was assessed from time sampling data. Indeed, instantaneous time sampling is the easiest way to estimate the probability of immobility and gestures. The nonverbal behavior of four aphasic subjects was coded by two observers at a sampling rate of one observation every 5 s (N = 311). The observed probability of agreement was 0.785 and the kappa statistic 0.67 ($p < .001$). Disagreements occurred most often for batonic gestures, partially because of their short duration (a batonic gesture may have been identified by the two observers but seen terminated or not yet begun by one of them; however, some gestures were also coded batonic by one observer and iconic by the other). A relatively low reliability was also achieved for deictic gestures because touching the picture with the extended index finger may be considered a gesture or a rest position. Obviously, these deictic gestures were only elicited in the picture description condition (only one subject was observed to point to the location of the removed pictures in the recall condition). These gestures will not be considered in the computations presented in the following section.

2.2.2. Results

Pathology can be identified in verbal behavior from several criteria. A first quantitative dimension is the reduction of speech tempo which may relate to qualitatively distinct impairments (Tables 2 and 3). Eight subjects of the aphasic sample uttered fewer than 1.2 words per s (normal range in the six control subjects: 1.6 - 2.9). The production of Mr Des, a global aphasic, was limited to the adverbs 'oui' (yes) and 'non', the conjunction 'mais' (but) and the stereotyped utterance 'c'est' (it's). Mr Gr typically used an agrammatic, telegraphic speech. The proportion of content words, specially nouns, was above normal (the proportion of nouns in the normal sample was between 16% and 22%). The indefinite article 'un' (a) and the conjunction 'et' (and) were almost the only available function words. Verbs were sometimes used in the infinitive form. The cases Vd and Roc displayed a similar but less characteristic behavior. Noun proportion was lowered by the frequent use of the form 'c'est' (it's). The four other subjects were nonfluent for probably different reasons: long silent pauses when word finding difficulties were met (cases Str, Sta, and Cor), or utterances of unrecognizable word forms (case Ma). The noun proportion was below normal in the narratives of Cor and Ma while it was normal in Str and Sta who were only mildly impaired and usually found the words after a time of search.

Table 2. Individual performance in the story description task

Subj	Time (s)	Silent pauses (%)	Words (total)	Words per s	Nouns (%)	Sum of gestures (icon & bat)	Gestures per s	Iconic gestures (%)
Des	78	59	14	0.18	0	17	0.22	53
Gr	328	41	111	0.34	27	56	0.17	77
Ro	703	52	551	0.78	11	14	0.02	64
Vd	315	79	141	0.45	18	20	0.06	50
Sta	522	68	315	0.60	21	11	0.02	36
Cor	150	71	144	0.96	14	14	0.09	43
Str	457	71	287	0.63	18	24	0.05	46
Ma	145	30	92	0.63	5	33	0.23	76
Mo	321	61	414	1.29	9	19	0.06	21
La	312	40	388	1.24	17	24	0.08	42
Coo	290	32	575	1.98	13	32	0.11	56
Del	101	25	jargon	--	0	0	0.00	--

Similar patterns were observed among fluent aphasics. Noun proportion was reduced in the narratives of Coo and Mo and normal in that of La. No word was identifiable in the speech of Mr Del. Fluency and use of content words were consistent across the two situations. Speech rate was higher and narratives were usually shorter in the recall than in the description task, but one subject (Coo) tended to embellish the stories in the second trial.

Table 3. Individual performance in the free recall task

Subj	Time (s)	Silent pauses (%)	Words (total)	Words per s	Nouns (%)	Sum of gestures	Gesture per s	Iconic gestures (%)
Des	50	70	0	0.00	--	20	0.40	85
Gr	265	46	82	0.31	28	51	0.19	80
Ro	437	65	384	0.88	11	23	0.05	22
Vd	174	72	103	0.59	19	21	0.12	52
Sta	310	58	272	0.88	22	5	0.02	40
Cor	108	62	134	1.24	16	281	0.26	68
Str	372	62	295	0.79	17	16	0.04	56
Ma	79	24	60	0.83	15	32	0.40	81
Mo	200	47	284	1.42	7	21	0.10	48
La	210	34	305	1.45	19	31	0.15	58
Coo	376	34	771	2.05	12	65	0.17	55
Del	154	17	jargon	--	--	3	0.02	00

Gestural behavior was not found to relate systematically to this verbal performance. Let us first consider the relative frequency of gestures (sum of iconic and batonic gestures divided by the narrative duration). This measure did not correlate with speech fluency in the description and the recall conditions (Spearman's rho = 0.10 and 0.03 respectively). Numerous gestures were observed in severely impaired aphasics (cases Des and Ma) whereas subjects Sta and La who spoke almost normally performed many fewer gestures. This is not a general rule, however. Mr Del, a severe jargonaphasic, uttered unintelligible speech without hand movements whereas the richer narratives of Coo were illustrated by numerous gestures. Several factors influenced the rate of gesturing. In Mr Str, word search was often accompanied by face touching and thus the production of illustrative gestures was inhibited. The frequency of iconic and batonic gestures was also higher in the recall task than in picture description which elicited deictic movements.

Likewise, the proportion of gestures scored iconic or batonic did not relate to the proportion of nouns in the narratives (Spearman's rho = 0.01 and 0.29 in the two conditions respectively). Any kind of association which was theoretically possible was observed in at least one case. The patterns that were expected from the literature were found, for instance, in Gr (high proportion of nouns, high proportion of iconic gestures), and in Mo (low proportion of nouns, high proportion of batonic gestures). The reverse was noted in Sta (high proportion of nouns, high proportion of batonic gestures) and in Ma (low proportion of nouns, high proportion of iconic gestures). In this context, it is also worth describing the occurrence of batonic gestures in the most agrammatic subject, Gr:

Time:	14 min 31 s		34 s	38 s	47 s
Speech:	"C'est...	euh oui...	une poule...	et...	poussin"
	(It's	uh yes	a hen	and	chicken)
Gestures:			batonic	iconic	batonic
			(rotation	(describing	(palm
			of the wrist)	a fence)	raising)

Time:	18 min 30 s		35 s	40 s	45 s
Speech:	"Euh...	euh...	*un route...	euh...	un arbre"
	(Uh	uh	a road	uh	a tree)
Gestures:		iconic		iconic	batonic
		(drawing		(describing	(hand
		on the table)		a tree)	opening)

* ungrammatical article

In these contexts, batonic gestures might relate to the propositional attitude of the speaker toward the utterance (having found the right term or an approximate form), or to the effort in articulation, but not to the syntactic complexity of the sentence.

2.2.3. Discussion

Different patterns of association between gestures and speech were found in the observation of an unselected sample of aphasic subjects. In spite of the attempt to devise a standardized situation, high variability was observed in the response length, the speech rate, its informativeness, and in the use of gesture. A special problem is raised by the fact that most of the normal subjects did not perform any gesture during their narratives. Thus, it appears that people who would be able to use gestures in other circumstances did not actually rely on these means in some experimental conditions. The strategic choice of the communication channel constitutes a source of variance which is difficult to isolate from the true cognitive impairments of subjects suffering from brain lesions.

Furthermore, in the present observation as in previously published studies, analyses were conducted at a general level with indices computed across the whole speech sample: total number of words and gestures, noun proportion, proportion of iconic gestures, etc. These measures enable comparisons between subjects globally characterized by variables like severity of aphasia, communicative skills, or fluency. A typical feature of the pathology that is neglected is that aphasic subjects usually perform below normal but above floor level. Moreover, naming errors may consist of responses like circumlocutions, semantic or phonemic paraphasias, and, in spoken word-to-picture matching tasks, selection of a distractor which relates to the target is the most frequent error. Thus, a partial processing of the verbal information is demonstrated. Accordingly, one may wonder whether referential gestures correspond to these residual verbal abilities or to compensations for verbal impairments. The hypothesis of a central communication deficit predicts that when an idea cannot be expressed by means of language, gestures will also fail. Nevertheless, gestures may accompany or even anticipate spoken utterances. The alternative hypothesis is that at least some aphasic subjects remain able to substitute gestures for unavailable word forms. However, as these gestures stem from semantic processes which may also be impaired by brain lesions, compensation cannot be expected in all cases of aphasia, and characterization of the performances remains an empirical matter. In the following section, we will sketch a model that can predict several patterns of association or dissociation between gestures and speech and we will present a single case study to illustrate it.

3. Gestural and Verbal Performances: a Single-Case Study

3.1. Theoretical Framework

Oral and manual responses may be elicited by auditory and visual information. Within an information-processing approach, this behavior has to be analyzed into more elementary components. For instance, naming and object-related gesture are assumed to result from several, partially parallel, operations: stimulus identification from perceptual analysis, response selection, and response programming (e.g., Feyereisen & de Lannoy, in press; Humphreys, Riddoch, & Quinlan, 1988; Riddoch, Humphreys, & Price, 1989). Modality specificity is hypothesized for input processing: object recognition, for instance, may be impaired in the visual but not in the tactile and auditory modalities. Likewise, modality effects may be observed in output processing, for example, in cases of aphasia without apraxia. Two conceptions are opposed about the more central operations which are involved between input and output or when a transfer between modalities is required, as in a word-to-picture matching task (see for example Shallice, 1988). First, one may assume an 'abstract', propositional coding of the information under the format of conceptual nodes or semantic features. This semantic system would be unitary and modality-independent. Alternatively, the cognitive system may be shaped by modality-specific properties. A 'visual-semantic system' may be more particularly involved in action planning or in semantic decision about functional features of objects whereas a 'verbal-semantic system' would control responses such as defining the meaning of an abstract term. Intermodal transfer would be achieved by the application of correspondence rules between the different semantic systems.

Some independent variables may selectively affect one of these operations and a brain lesion may impair one process while it spares the others. Thus, from such an information-processing model, different patterns of association or dissociation between gestural and verbal performances may be predicted. Impairments of the central semantic processes result in associated deficits in the two domains, whereas in a case of specific inability to access the word form from conceptual or semantic information, gestural processing or spoken word comprehension are spared. Furthermore, if several semantic systems (or regions within the semantic system) are to be distinguished, performances may dissociate in relation to the input modality. For instance, the case CD described by Riddoch et al. (1989) was able to gesture in responses to auditory commands but not in front of actual objects, visually and kinesthetically presented, and correctly recognized in a word-to-picture matching task. The authors assumed a direct route between the visual system and the action system (the unilateral character of the deficit which was restricted to the right hand, and the conception of Riddoch et al. who distinguished structural-visual knowledge and conceptual-abstract knowledge instead of visual and verbal semantic systems will not be discussed here).

To test the different predictions of the model, several single-case studies should be made to compare the behavior of aphasic patients suffering from language impairments of various kinds. On this preliminary stage, only one of these studies has been completed. An aphasic subject suffering from comprehension disorders was presented several tasks: picture naming, word-to-picture matching, and performing gestures referring to pictures and to spoken names. As the words and pictures presented in the different modalities corresponded to the same referents, three questions might be answered: (1) Is the subject more impaired in naming than in gesturing? (2) Are gestural performances better when pictures than when spoken words are presented? (3) Are the responses consistent across modalities (for instance, does the subject perform better gestures for the objects which were correctly named)?

The Case

At the beginning of the study, J.N. was a retired 69-year-old woman. Educational level was low; she was previously occupied as hairdresser assistant, after six years of schooling. She was not exempt from psychiatric problems and had three times attempted to commit suicide. Eleven months ago, J.N. suffered a stroke and was hospitalized in the Saint-Luc clinics at Brussels. A CT-scan examination showed a lesion of the anterior part of the left temporal lobe. Disorders of naming and auditory comprehension were demonstrated but repetition of single words and of short sentences was spared and thus, the diagnosis of sensory transcortical aphasia was proposed. Six months later, J.N. remained aphasic but had recovered from depression, perhaps because of anosognosia. Naming score was 40/72 with special difficulties with infrequent or long words. The most frequent errors were circumlocutions and verbal and semantic paraphasias. Semantic impairments were also shown in word-to-picture and picture categorization tasks. In the test for ideomotor apraxia (pantomime of object use on verbal request), J.N. scored 15/16 for unimanual movements and 11/16 for bimanual movements.

Material and Procedures

One hundred pictures were chosen in the series of Snodgrass and Vanderwart (1980) or among similar pictures used in previous studies on confrontation naming. To elicit naming errors, selection was biased toward low-frequency names (for 77 words, relative frequency was below 1400 per 100 million occurrences in the second part of the 20th-century in the CNRS dictionary). Furthermore, the objects had to give the possibility to be evoked gesturally in relation to some of their visual (e.g., mushroom) or functional features (e.g., needle). The material was presented to three normal subjects with the instruction to "perform a gesture in such a way as to get another person who does not see the picture to guess what it means". Some items of a preliminary list of pictures were disregarded because one normal subject was unable to represent them by gestures (e.g. 'sea' to which another subject referred by an horizontal, palm down movement of the hand). Nonetheless, pictures that elicited a gesture in relation to some visual features of the stimulus (for instance, the sharp tip of the 'mountain') were retained. Thus, the task differed from the elicitation of action in the classical examination of apraxia.

Two tasks were devised from this material: a naming task and a gesture production task with the same instruction as for the normal subjects. The material was presented twice to assess the test-retest reliability and the stability of the performances. The two tasks and their replications were distributed over six sessions in which 20 to 45 pictures were used.

In a second step, 40 words corresponding to pictures used in these tasks were selected in order to test the processing of auditory information. A majority of these items corresponded to errors in the preceding naming tasks (31 were not named at the first presentation, 33 in the replication). One may assume, indeed, that words correctly produced in naming would also be understood. Two tasks were proposed: a gesture production task (with the same instructions as previously in the visual conditions) and a semantic decision task in which the 40 stimuli were presented twice with the question "is it an X?". In half of the cases, X was the name of the item and the correct answer was 'yes'. In the other half, a distractor name was used and the correct answer was 'no'. The names either corresponded to an item which was visually similar to the target item (e.g. "Is it a glass?" -- thimble picture), semantically related (e.g. "Is it a loud speaker?" -- microphone picture), visually similar and semantically related (e.g. "Is it a shoe?" -- roller skate picture), or unrelated (e.g. "Is it a lance?" -- sled picture). There was 10 items in each condition. The two tasks were completed in one session.

Responses in the naming tasks were classified as correct (target noun or other plausible name) or incorrect (semantico-visual error, circumlocutions, no response). The subject did not produce errors of other types. The gestures were videotaped and two judges scored the response as correct (the gesture enables somebody to guess which item the subject refers to) or incorrect. Cases of disagreement were disregarded and thus, the total number of items was inferior to 100 (or to 40).

3.4. Results and Discussion

3.4.1. *Visual input*

3.4.1.1. *Response homogeneity and consistency.* As the aim of the study was to examine the relationship between verbal and gestural responses which were observed at different times, it was necessary in a preliminary analysis to assess the homogeneity of the error probability and the consistency of responses within each modality. Homogeneity was tested by means of the Haber's unconditional Z test (formula 6 in Overall,

Rhoades, & Starbuck, 1987) and consistency by means of the Goodman and Kruskal's *Gamma* (Marascuilo & McSweeney, 1977).

The results are given in Table 4 (Haber's Z was computed from row and column totals, *Gamma* from cells of the matrices). A nonsignificant Haber's Z means that the probabilities of correct responses did not change from the first trial to the replication. High values of *Gamma* demonstrate consistency of responses in each modality. Thus, one may presume that in the further analyses comparing verbal and gestural responses the intraindividual variability will not be too great.

Table 4. Homogeneity and consistency of responses to pictures in the naming and the gesture production tasks (N = 100).

(a) Naming

		Replication		
		Correct	Incorrect	Total
First trial	Correct	51	8	59
	Incorrect	10	31	41
	Total	61	39	100

Haber's $Z = 0.29$, NS; *Gamma* $= 0.90$; $Z = 8.60$, $p < .001$

(b) Gesture

		Replication		
		Correct	Incorrect	Total
First trial	Correct	38	8	46
	Incorrect	11	38	49
	Total	49	46	95

Haber's $Z = 0.43$, NS; *Gamma* $= 0.88$; $Z = 7.64$, $p < .001$

3.4.1.2. Comparison of the verbal and gestural responses. The Haber's Z showed a trend toward a higher probability of correct response in the verbal than in the gestural modality but the statistics did not reach the 0.05 significance level (see Table 5).

Table 5. Relations between responses to pictures in the naming and the gesture production tasks: (a) first trial, (b) replication (N= 100).

(a) First trial

		Gesture		
		Correct	Incorrect	Total
Naming	Correct	32	25	57
	Incorrect	15	26	41
	Total	47	51	98

Haber's Z = 1.43, $p < .076$; *Gamma* = 0.38; Z = 1.44, $p < .075$

(b) Replication

		Gesture		
		Correct	Incorrect	Total
Naming	Correct	38	20	58
	Incorrect	11	27	38
	Total	49	47	96

Haber's Z = 1.31, $p < .095$; *Gamma* = 0.65; Z = 3.06, $p < .001$

The meaning of such a comparison deserves discussion, however, and the respective demands of the two experimental tasks have to be examined. Picture naming requires activation of a stored verbal form and the response is judged from its similarity to expected word. A circumlocution is considered incorrect. On the contrary, gesture improvisation requires the selection of a characteristic visual or functional feature to feed a motor program. A larger degree of freedom is allowed, but correlatively, the number of alternative responses is higher. However, a more liberal criterion for response acceptance was used and any gesture found related to the target was considered correct.

3.4.1.3. Relationships between the verbal and the gestural performances. During the first trials, the capacity to refer to the pictured items was only moderately associated with the naming performance (see Table 5). However, in the replication, a slight diminution of the number of responses which were discrepant across modalities had dramatic effect on the *Gamma* statistics, and thus, gestural and verbal performances were found highly associated.

3.4.2. Visual and auditory input

3.4.2.1. Responses in the gesture production and semantic decision tasks. In the semantic decision task, Mrs J.N. made only 5 errors when the correct answer was positive, but 23 errors when she had to reject a proposed word as the name of the visually presented item (3 errors when the name was unrelated to the picture). Making the two kinds of error occurred three times out of 40. The errors most often concerned items which had not been correctly named in previous sessions with three exceptions: the words 'micro' (microphone) and 'traineau' (sled) were given twice correctly in the naming task and the word 'poupée' (doll) once, but the subject also accepted wrong names in the semantic decision task (respectively loud speaker, lance, and girl).

Strangely enough, the spoken words correctly understood in the semantic decision task did not elicit a higher proportion of correct gestures than the words giving rise to errors (Table 6).

Table 6. Relations between performances in the gesture production task (auditory input) and the semantic decision task (visual and auditory input: n = 40).

		Responses to the yes-no questions		
		Both Correct	1 or 2 Errors	Total
Gesture	Correct	6	15	21
	Incorrect	9	9	18
	Total	15	24	39

Gamma = - 0.43; Z = - 1.04, $p < .149$

The *Gamma* statistics even showed a nonsignificant inverse relationship between the two performance measures. One can understand that a correct comprehension of spoken word does not imply the ability to represent it by a gesture. The inverse dissociation may be explained in different ways. First, the subject may suffer from defective access to the semantic system from visual information, and the semantic decision task will be impaired because it requires interpretation of a picture. Second, a response bias toward the answer 'yes' might have influenced the decisions in the semantic decision task, or imprecise notions about the borders of a concept may have led the subjects to accept, for instance, the word 'violin' for a guitar; the typical gesture of guitar playing was nevertheless performed when the word was auditorily presented. Third, some gestures were judged correct but they might refer to both the target word and the semantic distractor. For instance, a screwing gesture was performed when the word 'boulon' (bolt) was given and the subject also accepted the word 'vis' (screw) when the question about the picture of a bolt was asked.

3.4.2.2. Gestures in responses to visual and auditory input. In the last analyses, gestural performances in responses to pictures and to spoken words were compared (Table 7).

Gestures of Mrs J.N. were significantly more often judged correct in the auditory condition (Haber's Z) and the results of the two conditions were not associated (see *Gamma* statistics). Again, a deficit in access to semantic system from vision may be assumed, but there was little support for such an explanation in the neuropsychological examination of the subject.

4. Conclusions

The case J.N. was selected because she suffered from naming disorders which were assumed to depend on defective semantic processing. Thus, impairments in the gestural modality were also expected with two reservations: (1) J.N., like the global aphasic subjects who still remain able to perform some communicative gestures, might be more impaired in naming than in gesturing: (2) If there are privileged connections between visual processing and the action system, better gestural performances might be elicited by pictures than by spoken words.

In the first experiment in which input was visually presented, consistent responses were found across modalities and, as expected, the subject performed better gestures for the objects which were correctly named. Thus, support was provided for the conception of a shared component underlying oral and manual responses. The proportion of errors was similar in the two tasks. Hence, one cannot conclude from the behavior of this subject that gestural responses are easier to produce than verbal ones.

Table 7. Relations between gestural responses to pictures and to spoken words (N = 40)

(a) First trial

		Gesture to visual input		
		Correct	Incorrect	Total
Gesture to auditory input	Correct	5	15	20
	Incorrect	3	15	18
	Total	8	30	38

Haber's $Z = 2.85$, $p < .002$; *Gamma* = 0.25; $Z = 0.46$, NS

(b) Replication

		Gesture to visual input		
		Correct	Incorrect	Total
Gesture to auditory input	Correct	5	15	20
	Incorrect	3	14	17
	Total	8	29	37

Haber's $Z = 2.87$, $p < .002$; *Gamma* = 0.22; $Z = 0.39$, NS

Contrary to the expectations, the frequency incorrect gestural responses did not increase when input was presented in the auditory modality, and performance in the two modalities was not positively associated. Notwithstanding the difficulties in interpreting these results (we have no evidence of J.N.'s impairments in object recognition from vision), the observed modality effect considerably weakens the conclusion of a common semantic process underlying speech and gesture. Control experiments should be conducted in order to test gesture production under other modalities of presentation and in patients suffering from other pathologies. Different patterns of result might be obtained and thus, several cases studies have to be conducted to provide a more complete picture of the relationships of speech and gestures in aphasia.

Acknowledgements

This work was done while the first author was Research Associate of the National Fund for Scientific Research (Belgium). Video recording equipment was funded by a research grant to Xavier Seron and Pierre Feyereisen (National Fund for Scientific Research: 1.5.121.87F). Gratitude is expressed to the members of the clinical teams who referred the patients and conducted the language examinations, and particularly to Marie-Pierre de Partz, Michel Frederix, and Dominique Rectem.

References

Behrmann, M. & Penn, C. (1984). Non-verbal communication of aphasic patients. *British Journal of Disorders of Communication*, **19**, 155-168.

Butterworth, B., Swallow, J., & Grimston, M. (1981). Gestures and lexical processes in jargonaphasia. In J. Brown (Ed.), *Jargonaphasia* (pp. 113-124). New York: Academic Press.

Cicone, M., Wapner, W., Foldi, N., Zurif, E., & Gardner, H. (1979). The relation between gesture and language in aphasic communication. *Brain and Language*, **8**, 324-349.

C.N.R.S. (1971). *Etudes statistiques sur le vocabulaire français. Dictionnaire des fréquences. Vocabulaire littéraire des XIX et XX siècles* (sous la direction de P. Imbs). Paris: Didier.

Duffy, R.J., Duffy, J.R. & Mercaitis, P.A. (1984). Comparison of the performances of a fluent and a nonfluent aphasic on a pantomimic referential task. *Brain and Language*, **21**, 260-273.

Dunn, J.C. & Kirsner, K. (1988). Discovering functionally independent mental processes: the principle of reversed association. *Psychological Review*, **95**, 91-101.

Feyereisen, P. (1983). Manual activity during speaking in aphasic subjects. *International Journal of Psychology*, **18**, 545-556.

Feyereisen, P. (1984). How do aphasic patients differ in sentence production? *Linguistics*, **22**, 687-710.

Feyereisen, P. (1988). Nonverbal communication. In F.C. Rose, R. Whurr, & M.A. Wyke (Eds.), *Aphasia* (pp. 46-81). London: Whurr.

Feyereisen, P. (in press). Brain pathology, lateralization, and nonverbal behavior. In R.S. Feldman & B. Rimé (Eds.), *Fundamentals of nonverbal behavior*. Cambridge: Cambridge University Press.

Feyereisen, P., Barter, D., Goossens, M., & Clerebaut, N. (1988). Gestures and speech in referential communication by aphasic subjects: channel use and efficiency. *Aphasiology*, **2**, 21-32.

Feyereisen, P., & de Lannoy, J.-D. (in press). *Gestures and speech*. Cambridge: Cambridge University Press.

Feyereisen, P., Verbeke-Dewitte, C., & Seron, X. (1986). On fluency measures in aphasic speech. *Journal of Clinical and Experimental Neuropsychology*, **8**, 393-404.

Glosser, G., Wiener, M., & Kaplan, E. (1986). Communicative gestures in aphasia. *Brain and Language*, **27**, 345-359.

Glosser, G., Wiener, M., & Kaplan, E. (1988). Variations in aphasic language behaviors. *Journal of Speech and Hearing Disorders*, **53**, 115-124.

Hadar, U. (1989). *Speech-related body movement in aphasia: period analysis of upper arms and head movements*. Unpublished manuscript.

Hermann, M., Reichle, T., Lucius-Hoene, G., Wallesch, C.W., & Johannsen-Horbach, H. (1988). Nonverbal communication as a compensative strategy for severely nonfluent aphasics? A quantitative approach. *Brain and Language*, **33**, 41-54.

Humphreys, G.W., Riddoch, M.J., & Quinlan, P.T. (1988) Cascade processes in picture identification. *Cognitive Neuropsychology*, **5**, 67-103.

Kendon, A. (1983). Gesture and speech: how they interact. In J.M. Wiemann & R.P. Harrison (Eds.), *Nonverbal interaction* (pp. 13-45). *Sage Annual Reviews of Communication Research, Vol. 11*. London: Sage.

Kimura, D. (1976). The neural basis of language qua gesture. In H. Whitaker & H.A. Whitaker (Eds.), *Studies in neurolinguistics, Vol. 2* (pp. 145-156). New York: Academic Press.

LeMay, A., David, R., & Thomas, A.P. (1988). The use of spontaneous gesture by aphasic patients. *Aphasiology*, **2**, 137-145.

Marascuilo, L.A., & McSweeney, M. (1977). *Nonparametric and distribution-free methods for the social sciences*. Monterey, CA: Brooks Cole.

McNeill, D. (1985). So you think gestures are nonverbal? *Psychological Review*, **92**, 350-371.

McNeill, D. (1989). A straight path -- to where? Reply to Butterworth and Hadar. *Psychological Review*, **96**, 175-179.

Overall, J.E., Rhoades, H.M., & Starbuck, R.R. (1987). Small-sample tests for homogeneity of response probabilities in 2 x 2 contingency tables. *Psychological Bulletin*, **102**, 307-314.

Pedelty, L.L. (1987). *Gesture in aphasia*. Unpublished doctoral thesis. University of Chicago.

Riddoch, M.J., Humphreys, G.W., & Price, C.J. (1989). Routes to action: evidence from apraxia. *Cognitive Neuropsychology*, **6**, 437-454.

Shallice, T. (1988). *From neuropsychology to mental structure*. Cambridge: Cambridge University Press.

Ska, B., & Nespoulous, J.L. (1987). Pantomimes and aging. *Journal of Clinical and Experimental Neuropsychology*, **9**, 754-766.

Smith, L. (1987a). Nonverbal competency in aphasic stroke patients' conversation. *Aphasiology*, **1**, 127-139.

Smith, L. (1987b). Fluency and severity of aphasia and non-verbal competency. *Aphasiology*, **1**, 291-295.

Snodgrass, J.G., & Vanderwart, M. (1980). A standardized set of 260 pictures: norms for name agreement, image agreement, familiarity, and visual complexity. *Journal of Experimental Psychology: Human Learning and Memory*, **6**, 174-215.

Cerebral Control of Speech and Limb Movements
G.E. Hammond (editor)

Chapter 10

LANGUAGE AND MOTOR DISORDERS IN DEAF SIGNERS

Howard Poizner
Rutgers University

The study of sign language probes the intersection of the brain's control of language and of movement. We combine new techniques of three-dimensional computergraphic movement analyses with linguistic analyses to illuminate neural mechanisms controlling language and movement from a striking new perspective: Investigation of processing deficits of signers with distinct language and movement disorders. Lesions in the left but not in the right hemisphere in deaf signers are seen to produce sign language aphasias. These aphasias differentially affect phonological, morphological, and syntactic organization within a visual-gestural language. Thus it would appear that the left cerebral hemisphere in man has an innate predisposition for language, independent of language modality. Our ability to create digital records of the spatiotemporal patterns of signing allows us to investigate signing not only as linguistic behavior, but also as motor behavior. In contrast to the representational-linguistic deficits of signers with aphasia, a signer with Parkinson's disease is shown to have motor implementation deficits that markedly alter his signing. These alterations parallel the effects of Parkinson's disease on speech, and are likely due to common motor requirements for language in the two modalities. Analysis of patterns of breakdown of linguistic structure and motor control for sign language following brain damage in deaf signers is providing new input into models of brain function for language.

The study of language and motor disorders in deaf signers provides a special window into the nature of brain function for language and for limb movement, since sign language utilizes a transmission modality different from that of spoken language On the one hand, language in the visual-gestural modality allows us to begin to solve the problem of how the brain is organized for language in general. Sign language can serve as such a vehicle, since it allows us to sort neural organization central to language from that determined by particular modalities of language transmission and reception. On the other hand, the study of sign language allows us to address the interplay between the neural control of language and of movement. Sign language stands at the intersection of the study of how the brain controls arm movement and how it controls language expression. Sign language shares with spoken language the conveyance of linguistic messages through complex gestures that occur in a very well controlled fashion. It differs from spoken language, however, in that the movements of the articulators are not hidden from view, but are available for direct measurement. Movement of the hands and arms can thus serve as a universal element for the study of disorders of language and disorders of motor control.

The selective breakdown of language and movement in deaf signers under conditions of brain damage is turning out to provide intriguing new clues to the neural basis of language and motor behavior. This chapter first reviews aspects of the breakdown of sign language following localized lesions in the brains of deaf signers. The objective of these studies is to gain insight into the basis of cerebral specialization for language. We then turn to the study of a deaf signer, not with a linguistic disorder, but with a motor disorder, that of Parkinson's disease. By contrasting linguistic and motor disorders of signing, the underlying nature of each of these disturbances of signing can be better revealed. In order to bring these issues into focus, and to highlight the ramifications of how the linguistic system of hand signs is represented in the brain, a brief description of American Sign Language is first presented.

Language in the Visual-Gestural Modality

American Sign Language (ASL) is the visual-gestural language that has arisen in deaf communities in the United States. ASL is a completely autonomous language not derived from spoken language, passed from deaf parents to their deaf children as a native language. It is a full-fledged language, serving everyday conversation, philosophical discussion, humor and poetry. As with spoken languages, signed languages differ from one country to the next. The independence of sign languages used in different areas of the world is clearly demonstrated by the fact that the signed language used in England is mutually incomprehensible with that developed in the U.S., despite the fact that the spoken language is essentially the same. In the absence of hearing and speech, these communication systems of deaf people have developed as separate and complete languages (Klima & Bellugi, 1979; Lane & Grosjean, 1980; Poizner, Klima, & Bellugi, 1987; Wilbur, 1987).

Levels of Structure and Layers of Form

Like spoken languages, ASL exhibits formal structuring at two distinct levels, one involving internal structure to the lexical units and a second involving rules governing the relations between signs in sentences. ASL displays the complex organizational properties found in all natural languages of the world, but does so in ways that are highly conditioned by the visual-gestural modality.

Gestural 'phonology'

Signs themselves are fractionated into sublexical elements, being composed of three major parameters: configuration of the hands, location of the hands relative to the body, and movement of the hands and arms (Stokoe, Casterline, & Croneberg, 1965; Klima & Bellugi, 1979). Each of these parameters comprises a limited inventory of discrete components which combine concurrently rather than linearly. They function separately, however, to contrast minimally different signs, much as phonemic segments of spoken languages minimally differentiate words. Thus, for example, the sign HOME,[1] with a change in hand configuration, is YESTERDAY; with a change in location, is FLOWER; and with a change in movement, is PEACH (Klima & Bellugi, 1979). Although the representatives of the different parameters are combined concurrently, there is sequentiality in the sublexical structure when more than one representative of a parameter occurs in a single sign: two Hand Configurations, for example, or two Movements (Liddell 1984; Liddell & Johnson 1986; Wilbur 1987; Padden, 1988; Supalla, 1985).

Three-dimensional morphology

The form that grammatical structuring assumes in a visual-gestural language is deeply rooted in the modality in which the language develops.

---

1. Words in capital letters represent English glosses for ASL signs. The gloss represents the meaning of the uninflected, basic form of a sign. Morphological processes are indicated by the specification of grammatical category of change, as in LOOK [Exhaustive].

ASL differs from English in the mechanisms by which its lexical units are modified. Like spoken languages, ASL has developed grammatical markers that serve as inflectional and derivational morphemes; these are regular changes in form across syntactic classes of lexical items associated with systematic changes in meaning (Klima & Bellugi, 1979). Strikingly, these grammatical processes are conveyed by particular patterns of movement and spatial contouring. That movement information alone is sufficient to convey these processes has been demonstrated by presenting sign forms as patterns of moving points of light, following Johansson's (1973) classic procedures for isolating biological motion (Poizner, Bellugi, & Lutes-Driscoll, 1981). Small incandescent lights were placed on the major joints of the arms, and signs were videotaped in the dark yielding patterns of moving light. Signs presented as these dynamic point-light displays have a strong perceptual coherence. Deaf signers are able to identify accurately grammatical processes so presented, often from only three moving points of light. These studies demonstrate the isolability of grammatical layers of structure in ASL, pointing to the fact that separate layers of grammatical function in ASL are mirrored by separate layers of form (Poizner, 1981; 1983; Poizner et al., 1986).

Spatially organized syntax

The requirements of a spatially organized syntax may be especially revealing for the neurological substrate of language, since in this domain, the nature of the apparatus used in ASL may have its most striking effect. The most distinctive use of space in ASL is in its role in syntax and discourse, especially in pronominal reference, verb agreement, anaphoric reference, and the referential spatial framework for discourse (Padden 1988; Lillo-Martin 1986; Klima & Bellugi, 1979; Poizner, Klima, & Bellugi, 1987). ASL specifies syntactic relations among signs in large part through the manipulation of sign forms in space. A horizontal plane in front of the signer's torso plays an important role in the structure of the language. For example, noun signs introduced into ASL discourse may be assigned to arbitrary loci in a plane of signing space. Pronoun signs directed to a specific locus clearly 'refers back' to the previously mentioned noun, even with many other signs intervening. The ASL system of verb agreement is also essentially spatialized. Verb signs move among the abstract loci in signing space in order to specify grammatical subject and object (Lillo-Martin & Klima, in press). ASL is thus markedly different in surface form from English, and from spoken languages in general. Many syntactic functions fulfilled in spoken languages by word order or case marking are expressed in ASL by essentially spatial mechanisms. In sign, language space itself carries linguistic meaning.

Three-Dimensional Computergraphic Analysis

To investigate the nature of grammatical processes in ASL, we have developed new systems which allow the real-time, three-dimensional tracking and computergraphic analysis of hand and arm movements (Poizner, Wooten, & Salot, 1986; Poizner, Mack, Verfaillie, Rothi, & Heilman, 1990; Jennings & Poizner, 1988). Two optoelectronic cameras directly sense the positions of infra-red emitting diodes that are attached to the hands and arms (see Figure 1). A microcomputer synchronizes the sequential flashing of the diodes with the digitizing of the camera signals. The three-dimensional coordinates are then computed from the two sets of camera data. The positions of each of the diodes are sampled at 100 Hz. Finally, the movement is reconstructed on a computergraphic system allowing the interactive manipulation and dynamic display of the reconstructed movement in three-dimensions.

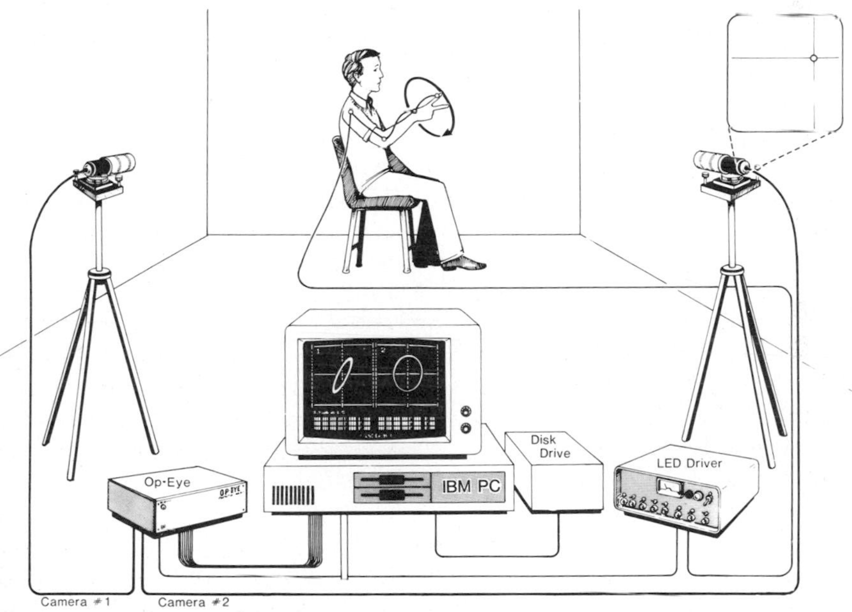

Figure 1. Three-dimensional movement monitoring system. The main hardware components and the positioning of LEDs on a subject are shown. Three-dimensional coordinates are calculated by triangulation, with knowledge of relative camera position and orientation.

Figure 2 presents three-dimensional reconstructions of the sequence of hand and arm positions for three grammatically inflected ASL signs.

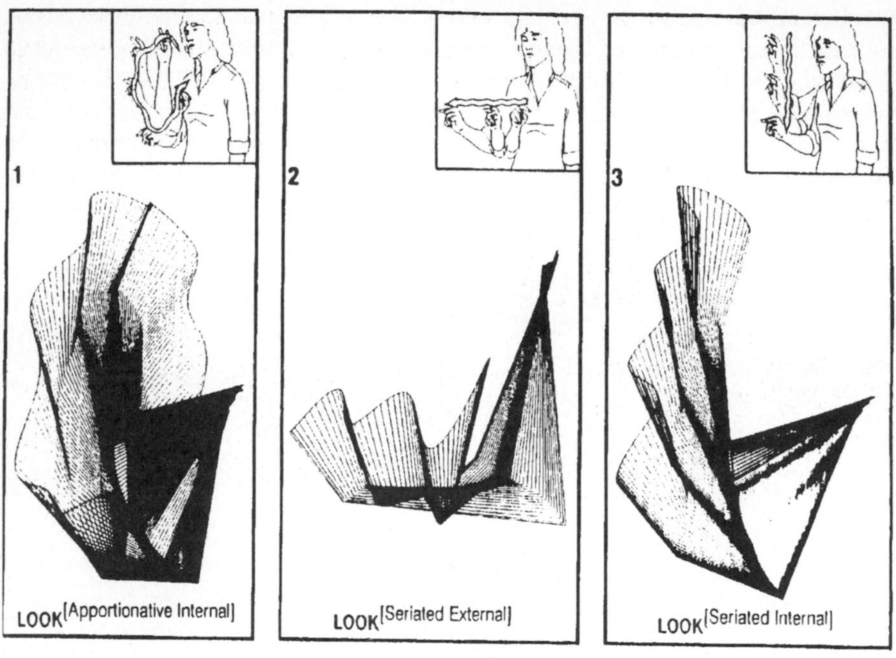

Figure 2. Three-dimensional computergraphic reconstructions of three grammatically inflected ASL signs. The images show all the sequential positions of the hand and arm during the course of the movements.

Figure 2 illustrates the structured use of spatial contrasts within ASL's rich morphological system. The Apportionative Internal inflection contrasts minimally with the Seriated Internal inflection in trajectory shape: the former inflection is made with a circular path shape in the vertical plane of signing space, whereas the latter inflection is made with a linear path shape (these inflections and the Seriated External inflection convey different class membership distinctions, as described in Klima & Bellugi, 1979). The Seriated Internal inflection, however, contrasts minimally with the Seriated External inflection, not in trajectory shape, but in planar locus. Variation in planar locus for a variety of ASL inflections for temporal aspect, number, and distributional aspect are presented in Figure 3. These movements were digitized and the best fitting plane of the hand motion computed. Figure 3 shows several groupings of movements. Movements conveying temporal aspect distinctions, which specify recurrence and duration of events over time, (points H, J, and K) are grouped together in a sagittal plane, whereas those for number and distributional aspect, which specify such distinctions as plurality and specific distributional relations between actions and recipients, (points A, B, C, D, E, and L) cluster in either the horizontal or vertical plane relative to the body. These clusterings based on the spatial properties of the movements markedly correspond to the independent linguistic classifications of these forms.

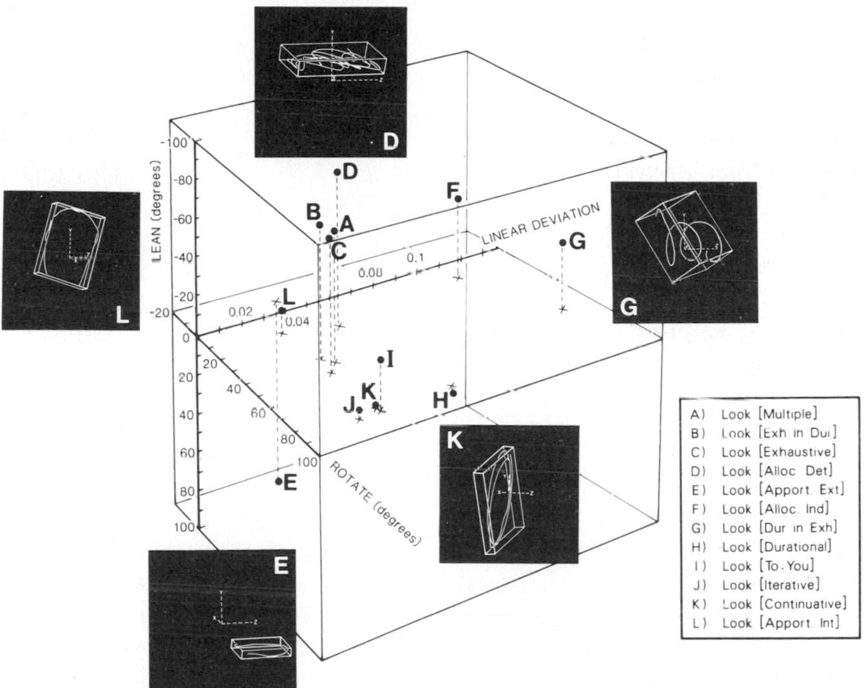

Figure 3. Three-dimensional visual-phonetic analysis of the linguistic dimension Planar Locus. The two axes Lean and Rotate provide two angles (elevation and azimuth) that specify the particular plane of motion of the hand. The third axis, Linear Deviation, specifies how planar a motion was. Spatial clusterings of movements correspond to independent linguistic classifications of these forms.

Thus, spatial contrasts such as trajectory shape and planar locus are key formational building blocks of ASL's morphology. Furthermore, spatial loci in a horizontal plane of signing space are actively manipulated in ASL's syntax and discourse. Thus, sign language displays complex linguistic structures in large part by manipulating spatial relations.

Because the left cerebral hemisphere in man has been considered specialized for linguistic functions, and the right for visuospatial functions, ASL exhibits properties for which each of the hemispheres of hearing people shows an opposing specialization. What then is the effect on the organization of the brain for language when spatial relations have grammatical function?

Brain Function for Sign Language

A series of recent studies has examined the effects of unilateral brain damage on language and nonlanguage performance in deaf signers (Poizner, Klima, & Bellugi, 1987; Bellugi, Klima, & Poizner, 1988; Klima, Bellugi, & Poizner, 1988; Poizner, Bellugi, & Iragui, 1984; Bellugi, Poizner, & Klima, 1989; Poizner, Bellugi, & Klima, 1990). The general program included an array of probes involving an adaptation, for ASL, of the Boston Diagnostic Aphasia Examination (BDAE; Goodglass & Kaplan, 1983), linguistic tests for processing the structural levels of ASL, an analysis of ASL production, and tests of nonlanguage spatial processing and motor control. The battery of language and nonlanguage tasks was administered to deaf brain-lesioned subjects and to matched deaf control subjects.

Studies of six brain-lesioned signers will be discussed here, three with left-hemisphere damage (Paul D., Gail D., and Karen L.) and three with right-hemisphere damage (Brenda I., Sarah M., and Gilbert G.). All subjects were members of deaf communities, had been educated in residential schools for deaf children, and had deaf or hard-of-hearing spouses. All were right handed before their strokes. For each subject, the primary form of communication with family and friends was ASL.

Figure 4 presents lateral reconstructions of brain lesions and summary characteristics of the six deaf, brain-lesioned subjects. Of the left-lesioned signers, Paul D. has a subcortical lesion in his left hemisphere, with an anterior focus deep to Broca's area, and including major portions of the basal ganglia. The lesion extends posteriorly into the white matter underlying the left supramarginal and, to a lesser extent, angular gyri. Gail D. has a large left-hemisphere lesion that involved most of the convexity of the frontal lobe, including Broca's area and the anterior portions of the superior and middle temporal gyri. This lesion is typical of those that produce agrammatic aphasia in hearing-speaking individuals. Finally, Karen L. has a circumscribed cortical lesion in the region of the left inferior parietal lobule, that extended subcortically into the postcentral and precentral gyri, as well as into the posterior portion of the middle frontal gyrus. Both the traditional Broca's area and Wernicke's area were spared.

LEFT HEMISPHERE DAMAGED SIGNERS

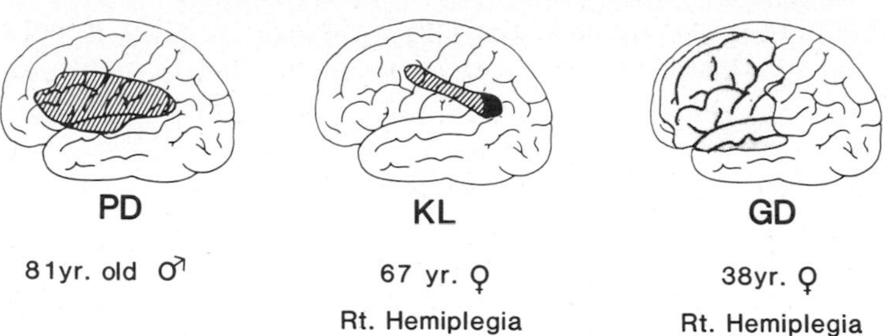

RIGHT HEMISPHERE DAMAGED SIGNERS

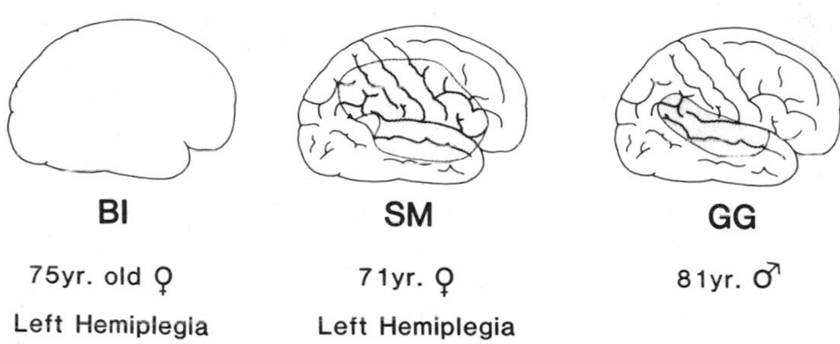

Figure 4. Lateral reconstructions of brain lesions of the brain-damaged signers.

Of the right-lesioned signers, Sarah M. has a massive lesion involving most of the territory of the right middle cerebral artery. The lesion extends from the frontal operculum (the homologous area of the right hemisphere to Broca's area), involves premotor, motor, and somatosensory areas, and includes the inferior parietal lobule, superior parietal lobule, and the middle and superior temporal gyri. Large critical areas of the right hemisphere were thus damaged. Gilbert G.'s lesion involves the cortex and underlying white matter in the superior temporal gyrus, extending inferiorly to involve in part the middle temporal gyrus. Posteriorly, the lesion extends into the lower portion of the inferior parietal lobule. Unfortunately, no CT scan was available for Brenda I., but like Sarah M., she showed a dense paralysis of her left arm and hand (see Poizner, Klima, & Bellugi, 1987 for more detailed neurological information on the six signers).

Preserved Language in Right-Lesioned Signers

Quite remarkably, the signers with right-hemisphere damage were not aphasic for sign language. They exhibited fluent, grammatical, virtually error-free signing. Figure 5 (top) shows the rating scale profiles from the ASL adaptation of the BDAE for the three left-lesioned signers. The middle part of the figure presents the rating scale profiles of three matched deaf control subjects, showing normal performance. Performance of the right-lesioned signers is shown in the bottom panel of the figure. The rating scale profiles of their sign characteristics, shown in the lower portion of the figure, reflect their grammatical (nonaphasic) signing; in fact, their profiles are much like those of the control subjects. Furthermore, the right-lesioned signers, but not those with left-hemisphere damage, were unimpaired on tests for processing the various levels of structure of ASL.

Importantly, this preserved signing was in the face of marked deficits the right-hemisphere damaged signers showed in processing nonlanguage spatial relations. Across a range of tests, including drawing, block design, attention to visual space, perception of line orientation, facial recognition, and visual closure, right-lesioned signers showed many of the classic visuospatial impairments seen in hearing patients with right-hemisphere damage. In contrast, left-lesioned signers showed relatively preserved nonlanguage spatial functioning. These nonlanguage data indicate that the right hemisphere in deaf signers can develop cerebral specialization for nonlanguage visuospatial functions (Poizner, Kaplan, Bellugi, & Padden, 1984). However, despite their nonlanguage spatial deficits, the signing (including spatially expressed syntax) of the right-lesioned signers was virtually unimpaired. The correct use of the spatial mechanisms for syntax in the production of right-lesioned signers points to the abstract nature of these mechanisms in ASL.

Sign Language Aphasias in Left-Lesioned Signers

The three signers with left-hemisphere damage, however, show clear sign language impairments, as indicated by their results on the sign language adaptation of the BDAE, on tests for processing the structural levels of ASL, and on a linguistic analysis of their signing. Figure 5 shows the marked contrasts in the rating scale profiles from the sign adaptation of the BDAE for the three left-lesioned signers, with those of the right-lesioned signers and control subjects. On each scale the scores of the left-lesioned signers are scattered, spanning virtually the entire range of values. These profiles reflect frank sign language aphasias. Moreover, the sign language impairments are not uniform, but rather diverge along lines of linguistically-relevant components.

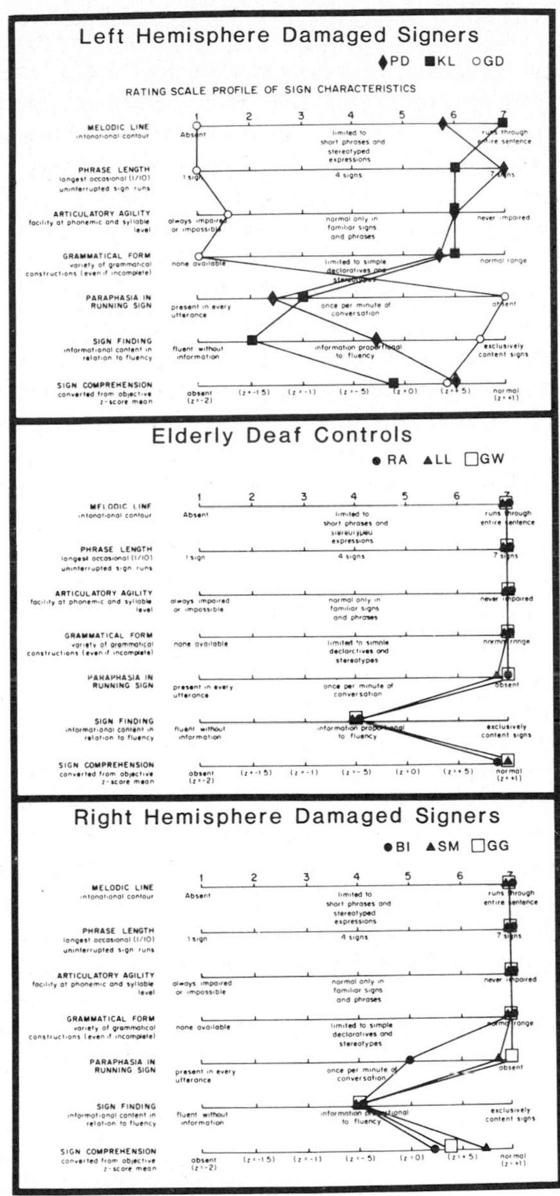

Figure 5. Rating scale profiles from the ASL adaptation of the Boston Diagnostic Aphasia Examination for left-lesioned signers, right-lesioned signers, and control signers. Note that performance of the right- lesioned signers is similar to that of the controls.

Agrammatic sign aphasia

Of the three deaf signers with left hemisphere damage, one (Gail D.) was grossly impaired in her sign output after her stroke. Her signing was dysfluent, reduced to single sign utterances of largely referential signs, shorn of syntactic and morphological markings. These omissions of grammatical markers occurred even though American Sign Language is a heavily inflected language, in which signs frequently involve many grammatical morphemes concurrently expressed with the sign stem. Her language profile was, in fact, classically like that of hearing patients classified as Broca's aphasic; her signing was agrammatic. Gail D.'s limited output was generated through continuous prompting by the examiner. Her signs were produced in an extremely effortful manner much of the time, and she was clearly frustrated in her attempts to communicate further information. She tended to have great difficulty in expression. Her narratives were severely limited, effortfully produced, and, significantly, without any of the grammatical apparatus of ASL. Gail D. omitted all grammatical formatives, including most pronouns, inflectional and derivational processes, as well as all aspects of spatially organized syntax. Her case shows the devastating effect that left hemisphere damage can have on a visual-gestural language (Bellugi et al., 1988; Poizner et al.,1987).

Impaired phonological representation

Unlike Gail D., Karen L. produced long strings of signs effortlessly which showed a wide range of correct morphological and syntactic forms. However, this left-lesioned signer showed primary impairment at the phonological (sublexical) level, making frequent errors in the selection of the correct hand configurations, movements, and places of articulation from which signs are formed. These were not articulatory problems, but rather were substitutions within the sublexical parameters of signs. These errors of the selection of the correct formational components of signs, in the context of motorically facile output, are the equivalent of phonemic paraphasias in a spoken language, and reflect a disruption in the representation or processing of phonological information within sign language.

In addition, Karen L.'s signing appeared vague. Linguistic analysis revealed that she exhibited a specific problem with specifying who or what she was referring to with her use of pronouns. She tended to use pronominal indices in ASL very freely and also indexed verbs to spatial loci frequently. In ASL, both pronouns and indexed verbs involve association with spatial loci. Karen L.'s deficit arose in failing to specify the nouns associated with the indices. Her frequent use of pronouns and spatially indexed verbs without specifying associated nouns gave rise to the impression that her signing was 'vague' and somewhat empty of content.

In summary, her signing errors were in two domains -- in selection of incorrect handshapes, movements, and locations within signs, and in failure to specify nominal referents for pronouns. These errors were in contrast to her well preserved lexical semantics and her inclusion of derivational and inflectional morphology. Finally, Karen L. had a marked and lasting sign comprehension loss (Bellugi et al., 1988; Poizner et al., 1987).

Impaired morphological representation

Paul D., like Karen L., had a fluent sign aphasia, producing long strings of motorically facile signs. However, the nature of his sign language breakdown was in many respects opposite to that of Karen L.'s. Whereas Karen L. showed preserved morphology and syntax, and impaired phonology, Paul D. exhibited impaired morphology and syntax, but relatively preserved sign phonology. What was remarkable about Paul D.'s signing was the occurrence of selection errors within ASL morphology. These errors involved substitutions of one inflectional form for another, or the addition an inappropriate inflection or derivation to a root form. On occasion, Paul D. even produced nonsense inflections and sign neologisms, created by illegally combining root forms and morphological processes. In general, he had a tendency to select morphologically complex forms where simple ones would be linguistically appropriate. Paul D.'s grammatical impairment was evident not only in his frequent paragrammatisms, but also in his use of the spatially organized syntax and discourse. He tended to overuse nouns and appeared to avoid spatial indexing (the equivalent of pronouns in ASL). Furthermore, he often failed to use verb indexing, even where it is required. When he used it, the verb agreement, as conveyed through spatial indexing, was often incorrect (Bellugi et al., 1988; Poizner et al., 1987).

Paul D.'s specific problems at the inflectional and derivational level indicate that lexical and grammatical structure can break down independently in a sign language. The structure of Paul D.'s lexical signs was relatively preserved in the face of marked grammatical deficits. This is particularly interesting, given that ASL conveys the two levels of structure concurrently, rather than sequentially.

Summary: Brain Organization for Language

Patterns of language breakdown in left- as opposed to right-lesioned signers help illuminate the nature of neural organization for language. Because the left-lesioned signers showed frank sign language aphasias and the right-lesioned signers showed preserved language function, it appears that it is, indeed, the left cerebral hemisphere that is specialized for sign language. Moreover, components of sign language (lexicon and grammar) were found to be selectively impaired following lesions in the left hemisphere, reflecting differential breakdown of sign language along linguistically relevant lines. Thus, there appear to be neural circuits within the left hemisphere that emerge specialized for linguistic processing in persons who have profound and lifelong auditory deprivation and who communicate with a linguistic system that uses radically different channels of reception and transmission from that of speech. In this crucial respect, brain organization for language in deaf signers parallels that in hearing, speaking individuals. Thus, the specialization of the left hemisphere for language appears independent of language modality.

The study of visual-gestural languages can not only inform us about brain function for language, but can also serve as a new vehicle for probing the intersection of the brain's control of language and of movement. Sign language differs from spoken language in an important regard. In sign language, unlike in spoken language, movements of the articulators are directly observable, rather than hidden from view, and are thus available for non-invasive measurement. Our ability to create digital records of the spatiotemporal patterns of signing allows us to investigate signing not only as linguistic behavior, but also as motor behavior. The study of signers with distinct motor disorders can provide clues to the neural substrate underlying language as motor behavior, and, in turn, can illuminate the functional properties of the motor systems of the brain. We turn next to the analysis of a deaf signer, not with a linguistic disorder, but with a motor disorder, that of Parkinson's disease.

Motor Disorders in Deaf Signers

Movement of the hands and arms serves both as linguistic articulation in sign language, and as complex upper limb motion. Thus, the study of deaf signers with motor disorders can illuminate the interplay between the neural control of language and of movement. Moreover, such studies in deaf signers can provide insight into otherwise obscure functional properties of certain motor systems of the brain. The basal ganglia are one such system. The basal ganglia are large, complex subcortical brain structures whose output signals are closely coded to movement. They receive motor instructions from the cerebral cortex and issue instructions to initiate and drive movement. A human model of basal ganglia dysfunction is provided by Parkinson's disease (Marsden, 1982). Studies of subjects with Parkinson's disease indicate that the basal ganglia seem to be responsible for the automatic execution of sequences of motor programs (Marsden, 1982), delivering instructions to higher motor areas in such a way as to set up the correct motor programs required for the next motor actions (Marsden, 1987). Interestingly, patients with Parkinson's disease seem to have lost the ability to predict the end position of their hand following a rapid movement (Flowers, 1975; 1976), and they have prosodic disturbances of speech (Netsell, 1983).

The speech of hearing patients with Parkinson's disease is characterized by imprecise articulation, loss of variation in pitch and loudness, reduced stress, variable rates and short rushes of speech, inappropriate silences, and other prosodic abnormalities (Darley, Aronson, & Brown, 1969). These impairments are assumed to be a manifestation of rigidity, slowed movements, or reduced movements of the speech production system, although motor impairments in these patients are generally characterized for movements of the limbs rather than of the vocal tract (Abbs, Hunker, & Barlow, 1983). In contrast, the analysis of sign language impairments due to Parkinson's disease can be made directly.

A Signer With Parkinson's Disease

We have had the opportunity to investigate the signing of a 64 year-old congenitally deaf signer with Parkinson's disease (Poizner, Kritchevsky, O'Grady, & Bellugi, 1988). The subject had attended residential schools for deaf children, had married a deaf spouse, had deaf children, was an integral member of the deaf community, and was fluent in American Sign Language. Neurological examination revealed typical findings of Parkinson's disease, including micrographia, expressionless face, mild rigidity of the arms, resting tremor, and stooped, shuffling gait. We conducted a linguistic analysis of his spontaneous and elicited signing and a three dimensional computergraphic analysis of both his signing and nonlanguage motor behavior. In the latter, movements of the hands and arms were tracked in three-dimensional space, reconstructed computergraphically, and analyzed numerically and graphically.

Errors of joint use

The signing of the subject was markedly abnormal, although the abnormalities were of a different sort than those seen in the signers with aphasia. The most striking alteration was a great reduction in the amplitude of all sign movements. Few arm movements through space were produced. Most of the signing was made in a single, small location in front of the signer's torso, without the normal variation in the location of the hand in space. Rather than generating movements proximally, the signer with Parkinson's disease used distal movements of the fingers and wrist almost exclusively, reducing the extent of the movement and stripping off required movement repetitions. Thus, the Parkinsonian signer omitted the appropriate path movement of the arm through space, substituting instead hand internal movement. Moreover, many of his signs were indistinctly articulated. His signing appeared 'slurred', although it could be understood. Importantly, the subject did not appear to be aphasic. For example, he did not make selection errors (paraphasias), either within ASL phonology, as did left-lesioned Karen L., or within ASL morphology, as did Paul D. He did, however, show disturbances of ASL prosody.

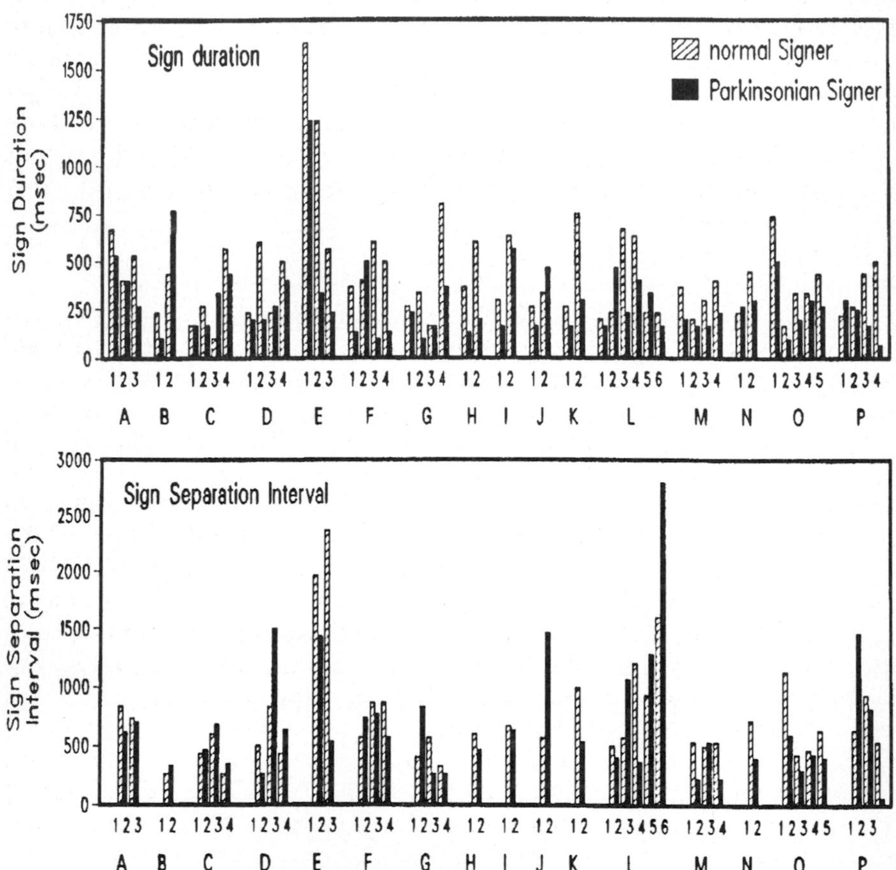

Figure 6. Impaired rhythm and timing in the flow of signs in a Parkinsonian signer. Sign durations and intervals separating signs are presented for 16 consecutive signed sentences produced by a Parkinsonian signer (solid bars), and the same sentences produced by a control signer (dashed bars). Capital letters refer to different sentences, and Arabic numerals, individual signs in those sentences.

Disruption of rhythm and timing

Rhythmic and timing processes both within ASL signs and within sign sentences were disrupted. Figure 6 presents durations of signs and intervals separating signs for a passage of spontaneous conversation consisting of 16 signed sentences. The capital letters in the figure refer to the different sentences, and the Arabic numerals to the individual signs in those sentences. The solid bars represent the data from the Parkinsonian signer, and the dashed bars the data from a normal control signer, who signed the same 16 sentences produced by the Parkinsonian signer. Figure 6 shows that the signer with Parkinson's disease produced signs of short duration, a finding consistent with the reduced amplitudes of his sign movements. However, the intervals separating his signs were quite variable. There were inappropriate pauses between signs, with occasional very short, and occasional extremely long pauses separating the signs within his sentences.

Sequential blends of signs

The disruption in the flow of the signs of the Parkinsonian signer was reflected also by the fact that signs at times ran into each other and were incorrectly merged. There were many occurrences of interesting blends of signs. These blends appeared to be compressions of two signs in a sequence into a single rhythmic unit. This was often accompanied by a restructuring of handshapes, usually a merging of the two individual handshapes into a composite. For example, the Parkinsonian signer in trying to sign WHERE FROM merged the two distinct handshapes of the two signs into one, and the two movements into one. The sign WHERE is normally made with the index finger extended from a fist, palm facing outward, with repeated lateral movement of the hand in the frontal plane. The sign FROM is made with the index finger bent in a hook from the fist, moving inward towards the body from a base hand contact. The Parkinsonian signer merged the two signs into one. He used the bent index finger hand configuration of FROM, and combined the lateral movement from WHERE, with repetition omitted, with the inward movement of FROM. Such blends show marked rhythmic-temporal abnormalities, and are quite distinct from the representational/selection errors of the signers with aphasia. Moreover, the Parkinsonian signer's substitution of distal movement of the fingers for proximal path movement of the arm, and his omission of movement repetition of signs reflect additional reductions and compressions in sign production that appear to reduce motor demands. Single rather than repeated movement is used, and articulators of small mass are substituted for articulators of much larger mass. These compressions result in sign forms having improper prosodic contours.

Deficits occur for signs in sentences

Quite remarkably, isolated signs or gestures could often be made quite well, but the disorder became particularly prominent when sequences of signs were required. Figure 7 presents production data of the Parkinsonian signer for a single gesture, 'erase a blackboard,' and of an inflected sign, LOOK [Exhaustive], meaning, 'look at each of them.' The sign was not produced in isolation, as was the gesture, but was graphically edited from a digitized signed sentence. Figure 7 presents computergraphic reconstructions of the motions together with the tangential velocities of the hand, and the cumulative distances the hand moved during the course of the two movements. The movement trajectory of the isolated gesture, or of isolated signs, could be quite normal. The movement was fully and precisely articulated, of proper trajectory shape, velocity, and amplitude. Figure 7 shows that the velocity and amplitude profiles of the Parkinsonian signer for production of the single gesture was virtually indistinguishable from that of a control subject. However, the movement of the sign taken from sentential context showed the marked alterations found in his conversational signing. The spatial trajectory was reduced and indistinct, and the movement was of lower velocity, smaller amplitude and smaller duration than that of a control signer. Thus, we are finding that this signer with Parkinson's disease could often make isolated gestures or signs normally, but showed marked alterations and distortions for signs in sentential context.

Parallel Disturbances of Sign and Speech as Motor Systems

There is every reason to expect different effects of Parkinson's disease on sign and speech due to differences in the articulators that must be moved. Abbs et al. (1983) have even shown that Parkinson's disease has differential effects on different articulators within the vocal tract. However, a number of features of this subject's signing are strikingly parallel to abnormalities of sentence-level prosody seen in Parkinsonian speech. The lack of variation in the height of the hand relative to the body and the lack of facial expressions of the signer give rise to the impression that the signing of the subject is 'monotone'. The disruption of rhythmic and timing processes within sign sentences reflect additional prosodic impairments in the flow of signs. Furthermore, there was a lack of emotional content and emphasis in his signing, as well as the 'monotone' delivery. The greatly reduced amplitudes of the signs is in many ways similar to the reduced speech volume and micrographia of hearing subjects with Parkinson's disease. This impaired signing should not be misconstrued as whispering in sign, even though both show reduced movement amplitude and reduced variation in sign location. The Parkinsonian signing is more extreme in the reductions made, does not use compensatory head and body shifts to help make clear intended movement targets, has impaired rhythm and timing, and shows improper sign mergings and other alterations.

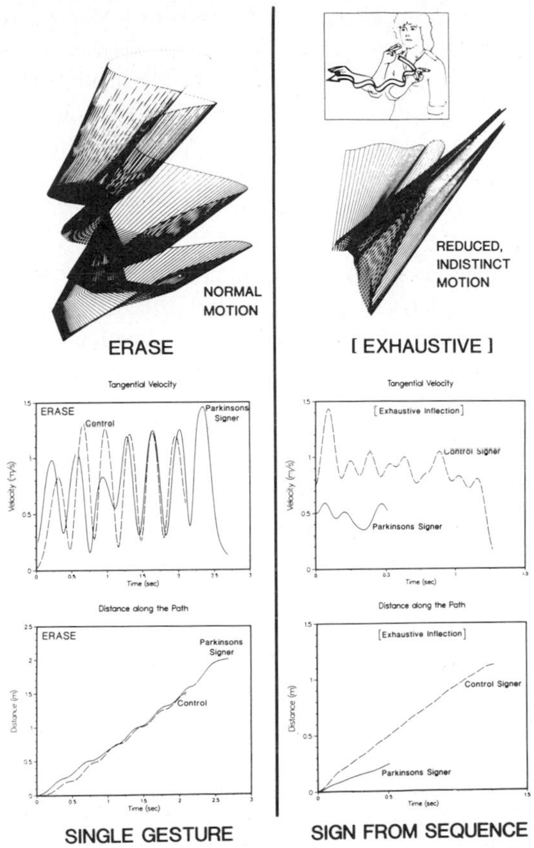

Figure 7. Preserved single gestures but impaired production of signs in sentences by a Parkinsonian signer. The upper panels present three-dimensional reconstructions of a single gesture, 'erase a blackboard,' and an inflected sign, LOOK [Exhaustive], graphically edited from a digitized signed sentence. The lower panels present tangential velocities of the hand and the cumulative distances the hand travelled over the course of the two movements.

The parallel linguistic breakdown between signed and spoken language that occurs in deaf and hearing individuals following lesions to anatomic structures of the left hemisphere reflects the specifically linguistic functions and processing operations required of language in either modality. Unlike cases of sign language aphasia, however, this case of a Parkinsonian signer reflects a motor rather than a language disorder. This is apparent in part from the fact that the surface forms of the Parkinsonian signer often reflected preserved underlying form. The correct production of these forms in isolation shows that the signer had knowledge of the phonological constraints, but suggests that he relaxed them under motor demands inherent in sentential signing. The motoric rather than the linguistic nature of his signing breakdown is also apparent from the nature of his errors. His use of the distal rather than the proximal musculature, his sequential blending of signs, his compression of prosodic structures and his other reductions all differ markedly from the kinds of representational/selection errors found in the signers with aphasia. Thus, the disorder of signing in Parkinson's disease does not appear to be at the representational level, but, rather, at a motor implementation level.

Parkinson's disease itself appears to produce certain parallel disturbances on signing and speaking as evidenced by the disruption of prosodic processes in languages in the two modalities. The parallel disturbances that occur at this level are likely due to disruption of common motor requirements. Both sign and speech require a rapid series of ballistic movements that are executed in large part in 'open loop' mode, that is, are preprogrammed and do not rely heavily on sensory feedback. It has been proposed that patients with Parkinson's disease cannot make large amplitude ballistic movements because they cannot initiate sufficient force of muscle contraction to move the arm rapidly to a required point of aim (Hallett & Khoshbin, 1980). The present case of a signer with Parkinson's disease is consistent with this position, since large-amplitude ballistic movements were lost. In addition, the data suggest that the signer was attempting to minimize the energy expended, and thus may point to the role of the basal ganglia in maintaining or programming computed forces over time. The basal ganglia provide an important motor substrate for sign and speech, particularly with respect to prosodic patterning.

Conclusions

Analysis of the breakdown of language and motor control in deaf signers is providing new perspectives on the nature of the neural substrate underlying the human capacity for language and movement. Since congenitally, profoundly deaf signers exhibit hemispheric specialization, even though sign language is conveyed in large part via spatial manipulation, hearing and speech cannot be necessary prerequisites for the development of such specialization. Furthermore, since lesions in the left hemisphere of deaf signers, but not in the right, produce sign language aphasias, it would appear that the left cerebral hemisphere in man has an innate predisposition for language, independent of language modality. The very distinctive patterns of spoken language breakdown that occur after damage to certain anatomical structures of the left hemisphere point to the importance of particular neural structures and their interconnecting pathways for spoken language. Alternate views of speech centers are beginning to emerge, however, couched not in terms of hard-wired connectivity patterns, but rather in terms of coalitions of brain structures that are called into play. Processing becomes an emergent property of the interaction of a variety of brain centers, both cortical and subcortical (Petersen, Fox, Posner, Mintun, & Raichle, 1988; Posner, Petersen, Fox, & Raichle, 1988). Studies of the neurological control of sign language and limb movement allow factors relevant to language modality to now be considered. Differential disturbances of signing at various levels of representation and motor execution, in signers with aphasias and Parkinson's disease, are providing fresh insights into neural processes underlying language and movement, and into the interplay between these processes. Clearly, many more cases are needed before one can attempt to map the neural substrate underlying the linguistic use of limb movement. But, if one can uncover the neural circuitry essential for sign language, one will illuminate the ways in which the neural circuitry for language (whether spoken or signed) operate for linguistic processing independently of language modality, and the ways in which the circuitry is modality bound.

Acknowledgements

This work was supported in part by National Science Foundation grant #BNS-9000407 and National Institutes of Health grant #NS 25149 to Howard Poizner. I thank Lucinda Batch, David Corina, and Edward Klima for helpful discussions of the case of the signer with Parkinson's disease, and Hanna Damasio for interpretation of brain scans and reconstruction of the brain lesions of the signers with unilateral hemispheric damage.

References

Abbs, J.H., Hunker, C.J., & Barlow, S.M. (1983). Differential speech motor subsystem impairments with suprabulbar lesions: neurophysiological framework and supporting data. In W.R. Berry (Ed.), *Clinical dysarthrias* (pp. 21-56). San Diego: College-Hill.

Bellugi, U., Klima, E.S., & Poizner, H. (1988). Sign language and the brain. In F. Plum (Ed.), *Language, communication, and the brain* (pp. 39-56). New York: Raven Press.

Bellugi, U., Poizner, H., & Klima, E.S. (1989). Language, modality and the brain. *Trends in Neurosciences*, **12**, 380-388.

Darley, F.L., Aronson, A.E., & Brown, J.R. (1969). Clusters of deviant speech dimensions in the dysarthrias. *Journal of Speech and Hearing Research*, **12**, 462-496.

Flowers, K.A. (1975). Ballistic and corrective movements on an aiming task: intention tremor and parkinsonian movement disorders compared. *Neurology*, **25**, 413-21.

Flowers, K.A. (1976). Visual 'closed-loop' and 'open-loop' characteristics of voluntary movement in patients with Parkinsonism and intention tremor. *Brain*, **99**, 269-310.

Goodglass, H., & Kaplan, E. (1983). *The assessment of aphasia and related disorders*. (rev. ed.). Philadelphia: Lea and Febiger.

Hallett, M., Khoshbin, S. (1980). A physiological mechanism of bradykinesia. *Brain*, **103**, 301-314.

Jennings, P., & Poizner, H. (1988). Computergraphic modeling and analysis II: three dimensional reconstruction and interactive analysis. *Journal of Neuroscience Methods*, **24**, 45-55.

Johansson, G. (1973). Visual perception of biological motion and a model for its analysis. *Perception and Psychophysics*, **14**, 201-211.

Klima, E.S. & Bellugi, U. (1979). *The signs of language*. Cambridge, MA.: Harvard University Press.

Klima, E.S., Bellugi, U., & Poizner, H. (1988). Grammar and space in sign aphasiology. *Aphasiology*, **2**, 319-328.

Lane, H. & Grosjean, F. (Eds.). (1980). *Recent perspectives on American Sign Language*. Hillsdale, NJ: Lawrence Erlbaum Associates.

Liddell, S.K. (1984). THINK and BELIEVE: sequentiality in ASL. *Language*, **60**, 372-399.

Liddell, S.K. & Johnson, R.E. (1986). American sign language compound formation: process morphology, lexicalization, and phonological remnants. *Natural Language and Linguistic Theory*, **4**, 445-513.

Lillo-Martin, D. (1986). Two kinds of null arguments in American Sign Language. *Natural Language and Linguistic Theory*, **4**, 415-444.

Lillo-Martin, D., & Klima, E.S. (in press). Pointing out differences: American Sign Language pronouns in syntactic theory. In P. Siple (Ed.), *Theoretical issues in sign language research*. New York: Springer-Verlag.

Marsden, C.D. (1982). The mysterious motor function of the basal ganglia. *Neurology*, **32**, 514-539.

Marsden, C.D. (1987). What do the basal ganglia tell premotor cortical areas? In G. Block, M. O'Connor, & J. Marsh (Eds.), *Motor areas of the cerebral cortex* (pp. 282-300). Wiley, Chichester (Ciba Foundation Symposium 132) .

Netsell, R. (1983). Speech motor control: theoretical issues with clinical impact. In W. Berry (Ed.), *Clinical dysarthria* (pp. 1-19). San Diego: College Hill.

Padden, C. (1988). *Interaction of morphology and syntax in American Sign Language*. New York: Garland Press.

Petersen, S.E. & Fox, P.T., Posner, M.I., Mintun, M.A., & Raichle, M.E. (1988). Positron emission tomographic studies of the cortical anatomy of single-word processing. *Nature*, **331**, 585-589.

Poizner, H. (1981). Visual and 'phonetic' coding of movement: evidence from American Sign Language. *Science*, **212**, 691-693.

Poizner, H. (1983). Perception of movement in American Sign Language: effects of linguistic structure and linguistic experience. *Perception and Psychophysics*, **33**, 215-231.

Poizner, H. Bellugi, U., & Lutes-Driscoll, V. (1981). Perception of American Sign Language in dynamic point-light displays. *Journal of Experimental Psychology: Human Perception and Performance*, **7**, 430-440.

Poizner, H., Bellugi, U., & Iragui, V. (1984). Apraxia and aphasia in a visual-gestural language. *American Journal of Physiology*, **246**, R868-R883.

Poizner, H., Bellugi, U., & Klima, E.S. (1990). Biological foundations of language: clues from sign language. *Annual Review of Neuroscience*, **13**, 283-307.

Poizner, H. Kaplan, E, Bellugi, U., & Padden, C. (1984). Visual-spatial processing in deaf brain-damaged signers. *Brain and Cognition*, **3**, 281-306.

Poizner, H., Klima, E.S., & Bellugi, U. (1987). *What the hands reveal about the brain*. Cambridge, MA: MIT Press/Bradford Books.

Poizner, H., Kritchevsky, M., O'Grady, L., & Bellugi, U. (1988, October). *Disturbed prosody in a Parkinsonian signer*. Paper presented at the meeting of the Academy of Aphasia, Montreal, Canada.

Poizner, H., Mack, L., Verfaillie, M., Rothi, L., & Heilman, K. (1990). Three-dimensional computergraphic analysis of apraxia: neural representations of learned movement. *Brain*, **113**, 85-101.

Poizner, H., Wooten, E., & Salot, D. (1986). Computergraphic modeling and analysis: a portable system for tracking arm movements in three-dimensional space. *Behavior Research Methods, Instrumentation, and Computers*, **18**, 427-433.

Posner, M.I., Petersen, S.E., Fox, P.T., & Raichle, M.E. (1988). Localization of cognitive operations in the human brain. *Science*, **240**, 1627-1631.

Stokoe, W., Casterline, D., & Croneberg, C. (1965). *A dictionary of American Sign Language*. Silver Spring, MD: Linstok Press.

Supalla, T. (1985). The classifier system in ASL. In C. Craig (Ed.), *Noun classification and categorization* (pp. 181-214). Philadelphia: Benjamin North America.

Wilbur, R. (1987). *American Sign Language: Linguistic and applied dimensions* (2nd ed.). Boston: Little, Brown.

Cerebral Control of Speech and Limb Movements
G.E. Hammond (editor)

Chapter 11

RELATIONS BETWEEN VERBAL AND GESTURAL EXPLANATIONS

John Annett
University of Warwick

Perceptual-motor and verbal skills (knowing how and knowing that) appear to be supported by distinct neural structures. This paper considers the problem of how the two systems communicate in the process of providing a verbal explanation of a normally non-verbal skill, tying a bow. Observations on the verbal and gestural responses and associated imagery of normal subjects and patients with Parkinson's disease asked to explain how to tie a bow under various experimental conditions are described. A four-stage model of action production provides a source of hypotheses about the interrelationships between verbalisation, image generation and overt gestures. Evidence concerning the nature of the imagery and the relative timing of words and gestures and their form provides some support for a model of action-language interaction which gives the activation of motor schemas a primary role with verbalisation largely dependent on imagery generated as a consequence of motor schema activation. However a firm conclusion may be premature in view of some of the results, notably the failure of some secondary tasks employed in the experiments to suppress imagery.

A distinction is commonly made between skill and knowledge, 'knowing how' and 'knowing that'. It is often difficult to give a verbal description or explanation of skilled actions which can be performed routinely (Annett, 1985, 1986; Berry & Broadbent, 1984). Similar distinctions have been proposed between varieties of memory such as episodic, semantic and procedural (Tulving, 1972) and between verbal and non-verbal coding systems (Paivio, 1969, 1986). Performance on two simultaneous tasks (Allport, Antonis, & Reynolds, 1972; McLeod, 1977) shows less interference between verbal and non-verbal tasks than between pairs of the same type, again suggesting independently functioning motor and verbal subsystems.

Clinical evidence also suggests a substantial degree of independence between the (non-verbal) action system and the language system in the brain. Amnesics have been shown to be able to learn and retain perceptual-motor skills despite gross impairment of memory for episodic and semantic information (Corkin, 1968; Cohen & Squire, 1980). The dissociation between action and language systems is further illustrated in cases of ideomotor apraxia described by Liepmann (1900) and Geschwind and Kaplan (1962). Geschwind and Kaplan's patient could follow verbal instructions such as "show me how you would use a hammer" with the right hand but not with the left, but could produce spontaneous hammering movements or imitate the examiner with either hand. On post mortem examination the anterior four fifths of the corpus callosum was found to be missing, the left hand thus being effectively isolated from the verbal centers of the left hemisphere which could, however, still communicate with the motor centers controlling the right hand.

Despite the extensive evidence for the separation of verbal and non-verbal systems the dissociation is not complete. It is obvious that, to support such everyday activities as following verbal instructions and providing descriptions and explanations of complex actions, the two systems must be linked in some way. Annett (1982) has conceptualized this link as a communication channel, the action-language bridge. Figure 1 represents a crude model of the action-language bridge. Action and language systems are shown as separate parallel channels to the left and right. In the vertical dimension each channel includes mechanisms which are specialized in perceiving and producing these behavior patterns. The human action system is presumed to be specially tuned to recognize the stimulus patterns characteristic of human action and the language system is similarly tuned to recognize linguistic patterns. In both cases the existence of a representational system is implied. Actions are represented as schemata, or generalized motor programs, and the language representational system contains semantic and syntactic elements or 'logogens' employed in language production.

A further assumption is that in both action and language systems there is a high degree of compatibility between the perceptual and the productive mechanisms such that, in general, perceptual analysis complements productive capability. Perceiving a feature of human action (for example a limp) is a prerequisite for being able to produce it and being sensitive to a linguistic feature (for example accent) is a prerequisite for being able to imitate it. Similarly the ability to rearrange and reorganize action schemata mediates the planning of new action patterns just as the manipulation of linguistic representations underlies the production of novel utterances. The model thus reflects in broad terms the 'motor theory of mind' (Weimer, 1977) which asserts an intimate link between perceptual processes and production processes.

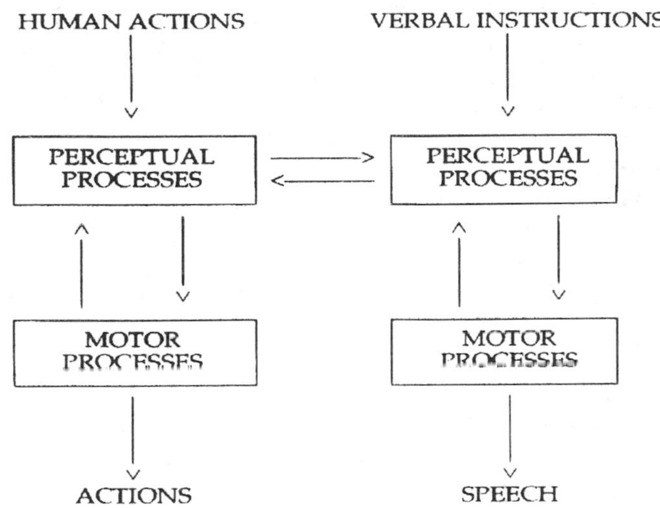

Figure 1. Model of the action-language bridge

Although the perception-action link is seen as particularly close, possibly involving shared cerebral mechanisms, the perceptual/recognition systems can function independently of motor output, as in passively observing the actions of others and in listening or silent reading. They can also act independently of sensory input as a representational, or imagery, system and it is at this level that Annett (1982) suggested the action-language bridge may operate. It is hypothesized that internal representations, or images, of actions are capable of activating their linguistic counterparts and explaining how to perform a task is thus equivalent to giving a running commentary on an internal representation of the task.

The main concern of this chapter is to consider what may be learned about the nature of this action-language bridge by a detailed analysis of the behavior and subjective experience which are observed when subjects attempt a verbal explanation of a familiar but not normally verbalized task. These phenomena include language output, manual and other bodily gestures, and also reports of imagery.

Hypothetical Stages in Action Production

Current theories of action production (e.g. Allen & Tsukahara, 1974; Brooks, 1986) and speech production (e.g. Garrett, 1975, 1984) envisage a series of stages beginning with an *intention* formulated in non-specific terms, through one or more *planning* or *programming* stages in which the behavior (verbal or non-verbal) is organized, sequenced, and co-ordinated with other ongoing activity, through to an *executive* stage which is specific to a particular output system, for example vocal or manual. A possible four stage scheme is as follows.

The Intentional Stage

This may be conceptualized as the interface between the motivational system and the cognitive system. At this stage it is assumed, intentions are formulated in terms of desired goal states. An example would be 'the door (which is currently open) being closed'. Initially intention is represented in terms of desired external states, not yet as specific actions and in this sense the intentional stage may be characterized as abstract or amodal (i.e. neither verbal nor motoric). Activity at the intentional stage requires attention and is typically conscious and unitary.

Planning

To develop a plan the goal states are broken down into a more detailed schedule, e.g. 'get up from chair - walk towards door - push/kick it '. Where simple well learned schemas are available, as in reaching out to grasp a desired object, the necessary programming can be carried out automatically. More complex tasks may require deliberate planning, for example the consideration of alternative methods, or the recall and resequencing of individual actions thus bringing into play the action representation system. Planning may be assisted by the activation of action schemas of the kind described by Schmidt (1975). Action schemas comprise two parts, a 'recall schema' which specifies the initial motor output for an action and a 'recognition schema' which comprises a store of sensory consequences associated with past activations. During planning actions schemas may be available in working memory. A complete plan requires that an output channel be specified (e.g. 'pull bell to summon butler to close door' as an alternative to above) and so the output of the planning stage will activate the appropriate output channel. The issuing of a verbal instruction to someone else is a possible output channel.

Programming

With the output channel specified it is necessary to co-ordinate output with other channels to prevent interference and to co-ordinate detailed sequencing of actions. For the verbal channel, specific words and their order would be specified at this stage. MacKay (1981), for instance, recognizes two substages between a 'propositional' representation and the final motor output in the progressive unfolding of an utterance. These bridge the gap between the initial concept or intention to the choice of a suitable lexical representation, that is, the appropriate noun and verb phrases, and a phonological system which translates these into a sound sequence, or in the case of written language, a sequence of hand/finger movements. For a non-verbal motoric output initial timing/force patterns are specified. Up to this point in the action production system no overt activity has taken place.

Execution

Motor output begins but output mechanisms are partly autonomous. For example, the hand/arm system can vary force output in proportion to felt resistance, can use sensory feedback and can adjust amplitude and timing to synchronize with external events. Execution is progressive; that is, feedback which indicates failure to achieve a specified goal state will result in further output modification. This feedback control may be local and automatic as, for example adjusting force output to take account of resistance, or may involve a longer feedback loop which returns to the planning stage. In this case it may even require a change in the output modality, as in requesting someone else to close the door which (it may have turned out) one cannot physically reach oneself.

Roles of the Action and Language Systems in Generating Explanations

In fulfilling any particular intention one or other channel may be chosen and the output will be either a string of actions or a stream of speech. There are, however, occasions on which both systems may be active and interacting, and providing a verbal explanation of a complex sequence of actions normally carried out without verbalization is one of these. Logical considerations suggest three possibilities. The first is that action and language production are served by entirely separate parallel systems which have their own independent knowledge bases, and planning, programming, and executive functions. The apparent ability to translate between the two is illusory and is no more than could be expected from two systems housed, as it were, in the same organism with a single set of needs and sharing the same environment. The well-known difficulty in providing verbal explanations of even moderately complex skills can be offered as evidence for this option, together with the neuropsychological evidence referred to in the introduction. Gesturing whilst speaking is explained as a rather trivial phenomenon in which the non-verbal motor output system is entrained to speech production in much the same way as any other pair of outputs tend to become temporally synchronized.

A second view, favored by writers such as Butterworth and Hadar (1989) and Feyereisen (1986, 1987) proposes that whilst there are parallel verbal and non-verbal systems they interact, probably in two ways. First, at an early stage there is competition for central processing capacity and the planning of speech production may have the effect of suppressing the non-verbal system, or of allowing it to operate only in an automatic fashion which does not take channel capacity. Interaction can also take place at a later stage where responses are programmed. At this stage different responses (or responses by different body parts) are co-ordinated to prevent conflict. The synchronization of speech and gestures takes place at this stage. Neither of the foregoing accounts offers a functional role for imagery. A coherent explanation must be presumed to be dependent on a separate source of verbal knowledge.

A third possibility is that the planning stage is initially abstract and amodal and common to both verbal and non-verbal systems. At a relatively late stage in its development an amodal action plan can be directed to one or other system which performs relatively low level, modality specific programming and executive functions, and the originally amodal action plan is converted into either a (non-verbal) action sequence or a speech string. This would imply that there exist general action schemas, such as 'door shutting', which share a common representation with their linguistic equivalents, the noun 'door' and the verb 'shut'.

McNeill (1980, 1985) seems to favor a theory of this kind to account for speech-related gestures. He proposes a joint early stage called 'inner speech', from which both speech and gestures arise. This early stage is presumed (despite its name) to be 'amodal' at the level of intention and planning and certainly before programming as defined in the scheme outlined above. For McNeill gestures are essentially linguistic but are somehow linked, perhaps by their common amodal origin, to non-verbal actions. The principal evidence favoring this theory is that speech and gestures are claimed to be affected in the same ways by pathological states, such as aphasia, with no cases of dissociation. This scheme, whilst offering an explanation for the close connection between words and gestures, does not offer any specific role for imagery.

A fourth option is that the non-verbal or action system is primary whilst the verbal system operates only in a secondary role. To provide a verbal explanation (or procedural description) the action system must first actively generate the procedure. This process involves planning and perhaps programming but not execution. The verbal system then translates by acting as an 'observer' of the performance and attaching the appropriate verbal symbols to certain features of the performance. This theory makes two important assumptions, first that actions can be generated in an imaginal form rather than being overtly expressed, and second that this imaginal form of a self-generated action can be 'observed' in much the same way that the actions of another individual can be observed and be described. Describing one's own internally generated actions is taken to be essentially the same as describing actions observed in other individuals and something the verbal system has learned how to do. Logogens in the verbal system are associated with the perceptual features of the motor schemata and these associations are employed in both following instructions and generating explanations.

This theory has some prima facie plausibility in so far as the explanation of actions which are not typically verbalized, for instance explaining how to tie a bow, is commonly mediated by the use of imagery. The concept of a motor schema proposed by Schmidt (1975) includes both motor and sensory components, the latter being the expected sensory consequences of a particular motor output generated under particular initial conditions. According to schema theory, internal or imaginary feedback is available in the absence of external feedback and it is this feedback which could form the imaginal representation of the action. In generating 'inner actions' and images, overt gestures can be constrained with little loss in imagery but the theory suggests that such gestures as are observed ought to be morphologically similar to the real actions to which they refer.

Theories of the relationships between words and gestures (see, for example Nespoulous, Perron, & Lecours, 1986) have been developed on the basis of observations of gestures made during relatively unconstrained communication. Typically the subject is given some general topic to discuss and his behavior is monitored. With the more specific task of explaining how to perform a manual skill the fourth theory outlined above is particularly appropriate, moreover it provides an environment in which it is possible to make direct comparisons between the gestures accompanying speech and actions involved in the actual performance of the task described.

Observational Studies of Explanation

The following observations have been collected over a number of years with different groups of subjects all of whom were required to respond to the instruction "tell me in as much detail as you can how you take two ends of string and tie them together to make a bow". No further instruction is given on the level of detail required nor is any reference made to using or not using gestures or imagery. Verbal responses are recorded on audio tape but in one series video recordings were made of the subject full face and, using a special effects mixer, an oscilloscope trace of the voice channel was superimposed on a corner of the screen and elapsed time in centiseconds on another corner. These recordings, made at 24 frames per second, were then analyzed using a stop frame playback which permitted timing of the onset and duration of speech to the nearest 40 ms.

The basic task was varied in a number of ways in different studies. In some cases subjects were subsequently questioned about their imagery. In some cases subjects were required to carry out a secondary task such as hand tapping, or monitoring a visual or auditory display, whilst others were required to sit on their hands to restrain manual gestures. The bow tying task has the advantage that the gestures spontaneously produced during explanations can be compared with performance on the actual task. Some recordings have been made of subjects tying a bow with two pieces of string attached to a board and some were also instructed to demonstrate bow tying giving a simultaneous commentary. Most of the subjects were normal adults, staff and students and summer visitors to the university but there was also a group of patients suffering from Parkinson's disease and a control group of their (mostly elderly) spouses.

Four fairly distinctive types can be identified in a wide range of response patterns. The most typical (in subjects who had not also been asked to demonstrate) is an initial hesitation, usually accompanied by aversion of the eyes, then a somewhat faltering account taking on average about 35 s and about 50-100 words long, punctuated by some apparently automatized gestures which are typically synchronized with the referent word.

The second type of response is to keep the arms firmly folded or hands tightly clasped and whilst producing a long and detailed account lasting perhaps 2 or three minutes (it normally takes under 10 s to tie a bow). These subjects occasionally lose control either when at a loss for words or towards the end of their ordeal and make small, apparently involuntary, gestures. Some subjects gesture with their head whilst keeping hands firmly clasped.

The third common response pattern, typically by a subject who has just been asked to tie a demonstration bow, is to produce careful and apparently deliberate gestures in synchrony with the verbal explanation. It may not be correct to assume that gestures serve the same function in the latter two cases.

The fourth type of response comes from subjects who apparently find the task difficult and produce a brief and incoherent account. Some can be coaxed into giving a response more like one of the three preceding types but a few (two in over one hundred cases) claim to find it impossible.

Verbal Responses

The majority of explanations describe seven stages in tying a bow. (1) The ends are grasped, (2) they are crossed, (3) twisted together, (4) the ends are pulled to tighten the knot, (5) a loop or loops are formed from the ends, (6) the loops or one loop and a free end are twisted together, (7) the loops are pulled to tighten the knot. A scoring system based on these steps gives up to three points for judged detail and accuracy of each step, a maximum of 21 points. This protocol score, the time taken, and the number of words used are used in various comparisons to be described shortly. A typical protocol is as follows. The slashes represent pauses.

> Er yes I would pick up the string and slide my hands along one to each end/ er bring the ends up to meet one another with my right hand I would put the string over the left hand end/ and then bring it underneath/ and then the piece that I've just brought underneath I would put over the what is now the right hand piece of string/ and fold that over/ and push it through the pull it through the loop/ and pull the whole thing tight.

Although subjects omit to mention some steps, and in this case the description of forming a loop is missing or very obliquely referred to ("and fold that over"), the order is always maintained and subjects usually get to the final step of pulling the knot tight. This feature of the explanations is consistent with the idea that the entire process is being mentally rehearsed but only partly expressed. Since very few subjects fail to reach the end, their failure probably lies in not fully articulating every step. As regards the level of detail, left deliberately vague in the instructions, even those subjects who provide long and elaborate explanations do so more by adding redundant commentary than by providing ever more precise biomechanical detail. For example,

> ... er being right handed I would hold the left hand still/ and take the right hand and pass er/ pass the free end of the string in my right hand over the standing portion of the string in my left hand over and under to produce a a a um/ what would it

be a 360 degree wrap er that would provide the basis for a bow.

If such an explanation is based on the internal rehearsal of a plan, then the plan itself would seem to be more of an outline sketch than a detailed blueprint. For example, protocols rarely refer to body parts other than left or right hands, or to the precise form of the manipulation. In actual bow tying the small finger or side of the hand is often used to keep the string taut whilst another operation is in progress but these secondary actions are rarely mentioned. It is probably uneconomical to store detailed representations of those aspects of actions which are likely to be modified to suit particular circumstances, such as different amounts of tension on the string.

Imagery

In performing this task subjects invariably report the use of imagery (Annett, 1985). Subjects found it relatively easy to describe their imagery with very little probing on the part of the experimenter. In some isolated cases (1-2%) where subjects fail the task completely the principal reason given is the inability to form or retain an appropriate image. Subjects frequently attributed long pauses and restarts to temporary failure of imagery, that is difficulty in attaining or manipulating a clear image.

The imagery reported was predominantly visual rather than tactile, and most subjects could report on the color of the string whilst few reported being able to feel its texture. About half the subjects questioned reported the images as a series of 'stills' and these seemed generally to correspond to discrete stages, such as forming a loop. The remainder reported continuous imagery, like watching a movie. The images are often highly specific, the most common being imagining tying the laces of a specific pair of shoes. In one case the imagery reported was very vivid and comprised not only the shoe, a school gym shoe, but also other visual and olfactory imagery associated with the school gymnasium. In most cases, however, images are restricted to the bare essentials, the string itself and the hands.

Imagery is typically subject-centered, the scene being viewed as if through ones own eyes rather than seeing someone else perform, and is typically accompanied by a feeling of voluntary effort or conviction that one is doing the task, including the voluntary manipulation of the images.

These subjective accounts of imagery are consistent with the view that in producing explanations where there exists no accessible verbal knowledge base, the non-verbal action system plays the primary role by generating internal actions in the form of images which can then be used to support the verbal explanation. These internally generated actions may be envisaged as partially activated motor schemas of the kind described by Schmidt (1975). They have two components, one motor, the recall schema, and one perceptual, the recognition schema in Schmidt's terminology. The recall schemas are generalized motor programs which, when activated, will produce motor activity of a given class, for example grasping movements, whilst recognition schemas are said to contain records of the sensory consequences of past actions. It is tempting to suggest that by partially activating these schemas both images and gestures are generated.

The activation of motor schemas in the absence of external stimuli involves what in another context has been described as working memory (Baddeley, 1986), specifically the visuo-spatial sketchpad (VSSP) or visual working memory (Baddeley & Hitch, 1974; Baddeley & Lieberman, 1980; Logie, 1986; Morris, 1987) and it is from this working memory that the verbal explanation is constructed. A motoric working memory, either separate or working in conjunction with the VSSP, might also be involved and gestures could represent some kind of overflow activity from that part of the motor system involved in motor imagery.

Indirect evidence concerning the nature of these hypothetical processes can be obtained in two ways, first by analyzing the patterns of interference by secondary tasks presumed to involve common mechanisms, and second by analyzing the performance of subjects with well-defined neurological deficits. Results described previously (Annett, 1985, 1986) have failed to show strong interference effects. Using duration of explanation, number of words used, and the content score described above, no interference effects have so far been reliably detected with two visual monitoring tasks and an auditory monitoring task. The visual tasks consisted of (1) watching a slowly moving lissajou figure on a VDU screen - which gives an impression similar to a moving piece of string, (2) watching two lamps flashing on and off alternately in the left and right visual fields. Both these tasks had been shown to produce interference in motor short term memory by Johnson (1982) but neither produced significant decrements in the verbal descriptions or in performance measures such as number of words used and time taken.

There remains a possibility that motor imagery involves the motor output system and so subjects were required to give their explanations whilst carrying out a secondary motor task which consisted simply of tapping alternately between two marks 10 cm. apart on the table top. Surprisingly this task did not significantly affect any of the measures of verbal explanation. In previous studies of VSSP, voluntary movement, including eye movement, has been found to interfere with the encoding of visuo-spatial material in short term memory (Baddeley, Grant, Wight, & Thomson, 1975; Idzikowski, Baddeley, Dimbleby & Park, 1983; Quinn & Ralston, 1986).

Subjects typically report an urge to make hand gestures whilst giving their explanations. This observation also suggests that the motor system is somehow involved in generating explanations either directly or by facilitating the generation of images. A group of 10 subjects was required to sit on their hands whilst giving their explanations. Compared with 10 controls they showed a slight but not significant increase in the number of words used and the time taken, with a slight reduction in the quality of the explanation, but none of these relatively minor effects reached statistical significance. Of course, this involuntary immobilization may not prevent *attempts* to make hand gestures nor does it prevent gestures being made with other body parts, for example the head.

The second approach to the exploration of the mechanisms involved in generating explanations is to compare the performance of subjects with known brain pathology with that of normals. I am indebted to R.J. Smith and R. Phillips of Bradford University for collecting data from nineteen patients suffering from moderately severe idiopathic Parkinson's disease. These patients are of particular interest because the primary neurological deficit is confined to the basal ganglia which are believed to be responsible for various aspects of the programming and execution of motor tasks but presumably not with planning. These subjects were required to explain how to tie a bow and their performance was compared with 9 controls of similar age and socio-economic status, usually a spouse of the patient. Both groups were also required to tie an actual bow. The patients took on average twice as long (20.5 s, SD = 20.3) as the controls (10.0 s, SD = 4.9) to tie a bow but took less time (21.4 s, SD = 11.0) to give their verbal explanations than the controls (29.2 s, SD = 18.8). In fact they were on average (but not significantly) faster in the verbal task without giving significantly less complete or detailed explanations. Unfortunately no record was made of gestures nor were the subjects questioned about their imagery but overall the evidence suggests that the motor schemas necessary to generate a verbal explanation do not involve the basal ganglia but are more probably located in the cortex, possibly in the supplementary motor area (Roland, Larsen, Lassen, & Skinhøj 1980).

Gestures

A series of 54 normal subjects was recorded on video. Subjects were seated, facing a video camera, in a chair without arms so the hands and arms were free to move. Any detectable movement of the hands was recorded as a gesture, but head and body gestures which were sometimes noted are excluded from the current analysis. Four basic performance scores were derived from videotaped records of the subjects. The mean time to complete the explanation (1) was 35.76 s (SD 25.31). The number of words used (2) was on average 85.16 (SD 52.89) and the number of steps in the procedure referred to (3) averaged 5.49 out of 7 (SD 1.36) whilst the mean number of hand gestures (4) was 5.16 (SD 2.19). The number of gestures was found to correlate positively with the number of steps described ($r = 0.31$, $p < .05$).

If gestures were simply an alternative to words as a means of communication one might have expected a negative correlation between gesturing and measures of verbal fluency, but the correlation between gestures and word rate (measure 1 divided by measure 2) was insignificant ($r = -0.01$) and the ratio of measure 2 to measure 3 taken as an index of verbal efficiency did not correlate significantly with the number of gestures ($r = -0.10$). This evidence supports the view that, in general, gestures parallel words; that is to say, we do not find that words and gestures are complementary in the sense of expressing different ideas. Although words referring to actions occur without corresponding gestures and occasionally gestures occur without the corresponding words the general rule is that gestures and words tend to refer to the same actions.

The relative timing of words and gestures could, in principle, provide evidence about the interdependency of the action and language systems. If words were invariably synchronous with gestures this would support the view that they have a common origin, for example McNeill's 'inner speech', whilst if gestures precede words this would suggest that the motor system plays a role in facilitating the retrieval of appropriate words from memory. The video records included an inset oscilloscope trace of the sound channel and so it was possible note the relative timing of the onset of gestures and the words to which they refer. Taking a sample of verbs (grasp, twist, pull etc) with which gestures could be confidently associated, the onset of actions was found to occur on average 89 ms after the onset of the relevant verb. However there was considerable variability, the standard deviation being 0.58 s, so that in many cases actions precede the verbs which denote them. The same subjects were also required to explain how to tie a bow whilst at the same time demonstrating with two pieces of string attached to a board. Under these conditions the onset of action typically precedes the onset of the verb by about 1 s, with the mean difference 1.02 s (SD = 0.32). In the latter case the inference that the words are descriptive of the actions, and dependent on their prior production, is sustainable whilst in the former case the evidence points to a common temporal origin of words and actions.

Whilst McNeill's contention that words and gestures are mostly synchronous (McNeill, 1985) is generally supported there do seem to be occasions when a gesture precedes the relevant word and may have a role in producing it. This appears to be the case when the speaker hesitates and gestures prior to retrieving the appropriate word. A number of instances of this were found in the video records. One subject (S8), who made only two small gestures, both produced at points at which speech was temporarily halted and in both cases the action appeared to help in the production of the sought after word. The phrase "and loop it over so it was divided into ..." was followed after a pause of 0.28 s by a small pointing gesture by the left forefinger and 0.28 s after that by the phrase "... with one third sticking out" which seems to be a modification of the original idea which has been planned during the pause. The same subject hesitated for 0.6 s between "... the hitch and the ..." and "... between the knotted bit ..." making a pointing gesture with the left hand which began 0.3 s after the hesitation began and 0.32 s before the next speech episode.

Subject 4, who gestured much more freely, described taking the two ends of string with both hands raised away from the body, palms upwards and fingers loosely clenched. In a silence of 2.7 s (punctuated by "I") both hands began to move, then 0.6 s later the right hand only rotated, 0.46 s later both hands moved synchronously, 1.1 s later S said "um" and 0.88 s later the left hand began to move again, and finally, a full 6 s after the beginning of the episode, the word "left" began. This seems to be a particularly clear instance of the subject having to produce an action before deciding whether it is correct (i.e., choosing between left and right) before pronouncing the appropriate word. In another case (S13) in a speech hesitation lasting 2.25 s during an attempt to describe how the two pieces of string should be intertwined, first the right and then the left hand began to circle each other. As they finally met the phrase "pass one over the other ..." commenced.

These instances are by no means rare but they account for a relatively small minority of all gestures (McNeill's estimate of 10% is consistent with these data). It is hard to avoid the implication from examples such as these that the gestures have a role in the generation of the explanation rather than representing simply a semi-redundant amplification of verbal expression. Further clues relevant to this question come from an examination of the form of gestures. In the bow-tying data we have additional evidence from recordings of the subjects actually making the movements they are describing and so we can compare the form of real and imaginary bow tying movements.

These gestures can be classified into those which are relatively simple in form and synchronized with an emphasized speech element, and those which are more complex in form and would appear to carry information about the pattern of movement being described. This distinction corresponds to McNeill's 'beat' and 'iconix' gesture types. In an analysis of 27 subjects who made frequent gestures, the latter were nearly 10 times more common, although many of the 'iconix' gestures, being synchronized with speech, may also have served as 'beats'. This is very probably the case in the first and last steps, that is picking up the two ends of string and pulling the knot tight, which are commonly accompanied by morphologically accurate movements of both hands which are also synchronized with speech stresses. The operations of forming loops and twisting strings together are more complex and refer to spatial rather than temporal features of the task and are less likely to be closely synchronized with speech. Gestures occurring during hesitations are characteristically of the iconix type and seem to represent the action for which the appropriate lexical description is currently being sought.

The actual shape of the gestures is of interest. Whilst 'beats' tend to be simple low amplitude oscillations, 'iconix' typically indicate either which hand is to be used, for instance by holding up the appropriate hand, or indicate the direction in which the movement is to be made, often using the index finger to point. Gestures accompanying descriptions of loop formation and twisting together are almost all of this kind and are much more likely to be unimanual.

Gestures which clearly refer to a specific action can be compared with the real actions since subjects were filmed actually tying bows as well as describing the procedure from memory. Whilst some subjects refrained from all gestures, a few deliberately attempted to mime bow tying. Non-gesturing subjects usually clasped their hands or folded their arms as if to deliberately suppress gestures (although they were not asked to do so). This ploy was not always successful and sometimes the clasped hands break free and gesture at a difficult point or towards the end of the explanation. One subject, hands firmly clasped throughout, used head movements to describe the spatial pattern of string manipulation - a nice example of motor constancy !

Gestures, even those made in mime, do not reproduce the actual bow tying movements with any degree of accuracy. In tying a real bow a substantial proportion of hand and finger movements are devoted to holding the string in position in preparation for or during some other activity. These supporting movements are rarely represented in gestures in the absence of real string. The gestural description of forming a loop was analyzed in some detail for 27 subjects. Gestures were classified in terms of their similarity to the actual bow tying movements. Category 1 was very similar to movements made with real string; in category 2 the gesture indicates the shape of the movement of the string (as opposed to the fingers); in category 3 some spatial feature of the string movement is represented but the movement is itself quite different from the actual movement of the fingers; in category 4 the gesture suggests a very abstract concept of loop.

To exemplify the extreme categories, subject 6 made a loop with the right thumb and index finger whilst the left thumb and index finger were used to hold the string in place. With no string present, the right thumb and index finger made a circular movement up and over the left thumb and index finger which were held together as if grasping something. The scale of the movements, a maximum of about three inches, was about the same in both cases. This was classified as category 1. Subject 9, on the other hand, made a real loop with the left thumb and index finger passing the string around the right thumb. The gesture in the absence of string could be described as follows: the left hand, index finger extended, makes an undulating movement about 9 inches to the left of mid line and back again. The right hand was immobile. This was categorized as 4.

Of the 27 subjects in this particular analysis only two produced gestures which could be categorized as very similar to the actual movements. Category 2 had 8 cases, 3 also 8 cases and 9 cases were placed in category 4. We can therefore say with some confidence that the majority of gestures only very loosely resemble the actions they refer to. They normally indicate (a) the hand playing the most significant role and (b) some spatial feature such as the direction of movement and whether it is straight or curved, but detailed finger movement is lost, as is amplitude information, whilst the required movement of the manipulandum (the string) is often represented.

What should we make of these morphological differences between 'real' actions and gestures? If gestures represent the activation of generalized recall schemas then the differences are of no great consequence. The recall schema is not a stored representation of a complete movement pattern but is merely sufficient to initiate an action whose final form will be substantially affected by events in the environment, for example the actual tension on the string in any given instance. Modifications to the general motor program, such as actions required to hold the string in place on a particular occasion, do not form part of the motor schema. The fact that gestures are often recognizable as simpler versions of 'real' actions need not imply that they have become refined into symbols which have a specific semantic function. They probably are quite simply crude and incomplete because they are unconstrained motor schemas.

General Conclusions

The relationship between words and actions is complex and this paper addresses only a limited range of issues, namely how to account for the limited ability to give a verbal account of a well practiced motor skill. Of the four models considered only one gives a reasonably comprehensive account and it allocates a primary role to the motor system. Where there is no readily accessible store of verbal knowledge an explanation can be constructed by partially activating appropriate motor schemas. This process makes images available to the visuo-spatial sketchpad and thus accessible to the verbal system and it is essentially from these images that a verbal explanation is constructed. In terms of the metaphor of a bridge between the action and language systems, the images associated with action schemas constitute a key feature of the bridge by allowing the process of describing actions to occur reflexively as a metacognitive process.

Although this account is plausible there are some problems, the chief of which is the apparent failure of secondary tasks to inhibit explanation. Simple tasks demanding visual attention which, on the basis of recent studies of working memory, would be expected to inhibit imagery and hence explanation, failed to do so. There are several possible reasons for these negative results. First, performance measures such as time, number of words and rating of detail may have been too insensitive. A fine-grain analysis of features such as hesitations and syntactic and prosodic features of the responses might be more revealing of the effects of secondary tasks on the process of constructing an explanation. Furthermore, the secondary tasks themselves may have been too undemanding. For example, in the visual monitoring task eye movements were not recorded so there was no guarantee that the visual system was effectively loaded, and in the tapping task subjects were not given a performance standard to maintain nor was the regularity or spatial accuracy of the tapping responses recorded. The effects of secondary task loading may have been partly concealed by time sharing strategies permitted by the lack of time constraints on the primary task. Further research should be able to deal straightforwardly with these problems.

Another serious difficulty with the proposed model is posed by the data on the relative timing of words and actions. The model predicts that gestures should in general precede the words which refer to them. Whilst this does happen and there are clearly cases in which gestures occur during speech hesitations, apparently as part of the process of searching for the right words, it remains generally true that words and actions are, on average, almost synchronous. The onset of gestures, such as pulling the imaginary string, are preceded by the onset of the word "pull" by just under 0.1 s. This degree of synchrony would suggest that the 'programming' of speech and gestures is governed by a common timing mechanism but the timing is clearly variable as the results of the 'demonstration' condition show. In this condition actions do precede words by 1.0 s on average yet there is no very obvious reason why, if the two sources are independent, that words should not precede actions by a similar amount. It could be argued that this is the natural order of events as predicted by the model but in the situation in which overt actions are not required and speech is the dominant mode, the still partially active motor schema becomes entrained to the programming of speech production.

Gestures, which most people find difficult to suppress, are interpreted in the model as not primarily symbolic or communicative but occurring essentially as a result of the activation of the relevant motor schemas. Gestures, even of the iconix type, are incomplete because motor schemas are not complete actions but simply ways of getting an approximately appropriate action started. Completion depends on response-generated feedback, or in the absence of overt action, a representation of the expected sensory consequences. Motor schemas are associated with the early planning stage of action production, rather than with the detailed programming or execution processes. The finding that patients with Parkinson's disease were able to give as good an explanation of bow tying as normal controls whilst having considerable difficulty with the actual task suggests that motor schemas are represented cortically rather than at any lower level. This would mean that imaginary actions are relatively immune to the effects of concurrent motor activity of a routine kind, but it would not preclude the activation spilling over into a programming stage and thus becoming entrained to speech as suggested above.

Acknowledgements

I should like to thank Jacqui Creasey, Fern Hodges, Chris Neild and Gary Stodel at Warwick University and Rachel Phillips and Bob Smith of Bradford University for their invaluable help in collecting and analyzing the data described in this chapter.

References

Annett, J. (1982). Action, language and imagination. In L. Wankel & R.B. Wilberg (Eds.), *Psychology of sport and motor behavior* (pp. 271-281). Edmonton, Alberta: University of Alberta.

Annett, J. (1985). Motor learning: a review. In H. Heuer, U. Kleinbeck & K-H. Schmidt (Eds.), *Motor behavior: Programming, control and acquisition* (pp. 187-212). Berlin: Springer-Verlag.

Annett, J. (1986). On knowing how to do things. In H. Heuer & C. Fromm (Eds.), *Generation and modulation of action patterns* (pp. 187-200). Berlin: Springer-Verlag.

Allen, G.I., & Tsukahara, N. (1974). Cerebrocerebellar communication systems. *Physiological Reviews*, **54**, 957-1006.

Allport, D.A., Antonis, B., & Reynolds, P. (1972). On the division of attention: a disproof of the single channel hypothesis. *Quarterly Journal of Experimental Psychology* **24**, 225-235.

Baddeley, A.D. (1986). *Working memory*. Oxford: Clarendon Press.

Baddeley, A.D., Grant, W., Wight, E., & Thomson, N. (1975). Imagery and visual working memory. In P.M.A. Rabbitt & S. Dornic (Eds.), *Attention and performance V* (pp. 205-217). London: Academic Press.

Baddeley, A.D., & Hitch, G.J. (1974). Working memory. In G. Bower (Ed.), *Recent advances in learning and motivation, Vol. VIII* (pp. 47-89). New York: Academic Press.

Baddeley, A.D., & Lieberman, K. (1980). Spatial working memory. In R. Nickerson (Ed.), *Attention and performance, VIII* (pp. 521-539). Hillsdale, NJ: Lawrence Erlbaum Associates.

Berry, D.C., & Broadbent, D.E. (1984). On the relationship between task performance and associated verbalisable knowledge. *Quarterly Journal of Experimental Psychology*, **36A**, 209-231.

Brooks, V.B. (1986). *The neural basis of motor control.* Oxford: Oxford University Press.

Butterworth, B., & Hadar, U. (1989). Gesture, speech and computational stages: a reply to McNeill. *Psychological Review*, **96**, 168-174.

Cohen, N.J., & Squire, L.R. (1980). Preserved learning and retention of pattern analyzing skill in amnesia: dissociation of knowing how and knowing that. *Science*, **210**, 207-210.

Corkin, S. (1968). Acquisition of a motor skill after bilateral medial temporal lobe excision. *Neuropsychologia*, **6**, 255-265.

Feyereisen, P. (1986). Lateral differences in gesture production. In J-L. Nespoulous, P. Perron & A.R. Lecours (Eds.), *The biological foundations of gestures: Motor and semiotic aspects* (pp. 77-94). Hillsdale, NJ: Lawrence Erlbaum Associates.

Feyereisen, P. (1987). Gestures and speech, interactions and separations: a reply to McNeill (1985). *Psychological Review*, **94**, 493-498.

Garrett, M.F. (1975). The analysis of sentence production. In G. Bower (Ed). *The psychology of learning and motivation, Vol. 9* (pp. 133-177). London: Academic Press.

Garrett, M.F. (1984). The organization of processing structure for language production: applications to aphasic speech. In D. Caplan, A.R. Lecours & H. Smith (Eds.), *Biological perspectives on language* (pp. 172-193). Cambridge MA: MIT Press.

Geschwind, N., & Kaplan, E. (1962). A human cerebral disconnection syndrome. *Neurology*, **12**, 675-685.

Idzikowski, C., Baddeley, A.D., Dimbleby, R.D., & Park, S. (1983). *Eye movements and imagery*. Paper presented to the Experimental Psychology Society.

Johnson, P. (1982). The functional equivalence of imagery and movement. *Quarterly Journal of Experimental Psychology*, **34A**, 349-365.

Liepmann, H. (1900). Das kranheitsbild der Apraxie (motorischen Asymbolie). *Monatschrift fur Psychiatrie und Neurologie*, **8**, 15-40, 102-32, 182-97.

Logie, R.H. (1986). Visuo-spatial processing in working memory. *Quarterly Journal of Experimental Psychology*, **38A**, 229-247.

McLeod, P. (1977). A dual task response modality effect: support for multiprocess models of attention. *Quarterly Journal of Experimental Psychology*, **29**, 651-667.

McNeill, D. (1985). So you think gestures are nonverbal? *Psychological Review*, **92**, 350-371.

Morris, N. (1987). Exploring the visuo-spatial scratchpad. *Quarterly Journal of Experimental Psychology*, **39A**, 409-429.

Nespoulous, J-L., Perron, P., & Lecours, A.R. (Eds.). (1986). *The biological foundations of gestures: Motor and semiotic aspects*. Hillsdale, NJ: Lawrence Erlbaum Associates.

Paivio, A. (1969). mental imagery in associative learning and memory. *Psychological Review*, **76**, 241-263.

Paivio, A. (1986). *Mental representation: A dual coding approach*. New York: Oxford University Press.

Quinn, J.G., & Ralston, G.E. (1986). Movement and attention in visual working memory. *Quarterly Journal of Experimental Psychology*, **38A**, 689-703.

Roland, P.E., Larsen, B., Lassen, N.A., & Skinhøj, E. (1980). Supplementary motor area and other cortical areas in organization of voluntary movements in man. *Journal of Neurophysiology*, **43**, 118-136.

Schmidt, R.A. (1975). A schema theory of discrete motor skill learning. *Psychological Review*, **82**, 225-260.

Tulving, E. (1972). Episodic and semantic memory. In E. Tulving & W. Donaldson (Eds.), *Organization of memory* (pp. 382-403). New York: Academic Press.

Weimer, W.B. (1977). A conceptual framework for cognitive psychology: motor theories of the mind. In R. Shaw & J. Bransford (Eds.), *Perceiving, acting and knowing: Towards an ecological psychology* (pp. 267-311). Hillsdale, NJ: Lawrence Erlbaum Associates.

PART III

MOTOR PERFORMANCE AND APHASIA

Cerebral Control of Speech and Limb Movements
G.E. Hammond (editor)

Chapter 12

MOTORIC CHARACTERISTICS OF ADULT APHASIC AND APRAXIC SPEAKERS

Malcolm R. McNeil and Raymond D. Kent
University of Wisconsin-Madison

Aphasia, apraxia of speech and dysarthria are the three major impairments of spoken language resulting from damage to the nervous system. Traditional definitions of these disorders imply clear separations in terms of the affected mechanisms or processes. For example, aphasia is assumed to be an impairment of language rather than a disorder of the motor control of speech. However, the contemporary classification of aphasia rests to a large degree on characteristics of speech, perhaps even on characteristics of speech motor control. This chapter examines evidence of motor disturbances in the speech patterns of certain aphasia 'types' and in apraxia of speech. Data from perceptual, acoustic, and physiologic investigations point strongly to the conclusion that movement-level disturbances can be observed in apraxia of speech, Broca aphasia, conduction aphasia and Wernicke aphasia. It is concluded that traditional classifications and descriptions of the aphasia syndromes and of apraxia of speech should be reconsidered in the light of recent perceptually, acoustically and physiologically derived evidence for speech movement-level deficits in speakers with these disorders.

Introduction

Aphasia is, in the simplest sense, an impairment of the cognitive apparatus that performs language. It results from focal brain damage or disease (see Rosenbek, LaPointe, & Wertz, 1989 for a review of the major aphasia definitions and their theoretical infrastructures). Apraxia of speech (AOS) is an impairment in the mechanisms for programming movements for speech production resulting from focal brain damage or disease but without an accompanying impairment of nonspeech functions of the same musculature (see Wertz, LaPointe, & Rosenbek, 1984 and Rosenbek, Kent, & LaPointe, 1984 for detailed discussions of the nature and phenomenology of AOS). Both AOS and aphasia are distinguished from dysarthria, a family of neurogenic speech disorders caused by impairments of neuromuscular systems used for speech (see Darley, Aronson, & Brown, 1975, and Yorkston, Beukelman, & Bell, 1988 for detailed descriptions and mechanisms of the dysarthrias).

Consistent with the definitions of aphasia and AOS, and as a starting premise for this chapter, both aphasia and AOS are viewed as rarely (if ever) involving a total loss of function in any single component of language or speech. Indeed, the general pattern of deficit is a variable or inconsistent performance, frequently, in the case of aphasia, over different modalities and linguistic levels or subcomponents. It has been argued (McNeil, 1984; 1988; McNeil & Kimelman, 1986) that it is misleading to say that speech or language functions are in some sense 'lost'. Dysregulation may be a more suitable term, both for the description of the disorders and for theories of their origin and nature. This chapter will be concerned primarily with two types of aphasia (Broca and Conduction) and with AOS. A primary reason for selection of these two types of aphasia is that they produce a preponderance of speech errors that inform both the understanding of the disorders and their clinical management as well as the development of models of normal speech and language production (cf. Kent, in press).

Most formal definitions of aphasia exclude motor deficits; however, both sensory and motor impairments frequently accompany the language and information processing deficits that define the disorder. Although theoretically inconsistent, the predominant classification schemas for aphasia depend upon these sensory and motor concomitants. Though not desirable or acceptable from either a theoretical or clinical perspective, this union of speech and language is understandable. The differentiation between language and its motoric externalization, *speech*, is not well established in the communication models guiding theoretical developments in both areas, and it would be unlikely that well defined boundaries would have emerged from clinical nosology. This confusion is apparent in the characteristics of spoken language commonly used to distinguish fluent and nonfluent aphasic patients (Benson, 1967; Kerschensteiner, Poeck, & Brunner, 1972). The behaviors used to characterize *nonfluent* aphasia (slow rate, dysarthria, effort, short phrase length and poor melody; Benson, 1967) are most likely deficits at the level of movement control, while those used to characterize *fluent* aphasia (e.g. normal rate, good articulatory agility, long phrases, good melody, verbal and literal paraphasias) rely on the presence of language level (semantic and syntactic) behaviors as well as speech that is perceived as normal. The presence or absence of motoric level deficits also forms an essential portion of the characteristics used to differentiate the aphasic syndromes (Broca, Wernicke, Conduction, Anomic, Transcortical Sensory and Transcortical Motor Aphasia) using the classification methods of Goodglass and Kaplan (1983). Poor melodic line, poor articulatory agility, short phrases, poor repetition and paraphasias in running speech (defined in part, as sound substitutions) are all features of speech that are potential, if not likely, attributes assignable to motoric level impairments of the speech apparatus.

Apraxia of speech (AOS), also referred to as verbal apraxia, speech apraxia, phonetic disintegration and a host of other terms (for a complete list of AOS synonyms see Wertz, LaPointe, & Rosenbek, 1984) is a speech disorder, prescribed by its label to be a disorder of motor programming. Although there is still controversy surrounding the most appropriate term for the disorder (Schiff, Alexander, Naeser, & Galaburda, 1983) and the complete phenomenological description of the disorder, there is emerging agreement as to the existence and isolability of the syndrome and for the phonetic/motoric locus of the speech deficits. Perhaps the point of greatest controversy presently lies in the characterization of the speech deficits that form a necessary part of the syndrome of Broca Aphasia. Whether the speech of the Broca Aphasic is apraxic in origin is the topic of continuing debate and experimentation. What is known, however, is that the majority of literature amassed on the nature, assessment and treatment of AOS has been derived from persons who have been classified as having Broca Aphasia. This fact may not be inharmonious with the notion of aphasia if the speech deficits of the Broca Aphasic are assumed to originate from phonologic mechanisms. The incongruity occurs if the speech errors of the Broca Aphasic are generated from a phonologic code that is representationally intact and properly selected and sequenced for motor programming, but somehow misspecified at the level of the speech motor programmer or at the movement execution level. If in fact the latter interpretation is accurate, as assumed by the use of the term and the emerging AOS literature, it may be more accurate to say that in order to be classified as a Broca Aphasic (at least according to the criteria specified by Goodglass & Kaplan, 1983), one *must* demonstrate a motor speech deficit in addition to some behaviors (e.g. mild auditory comprehension deficit, agrammatic or paragrammatic speech) that might otherwise be considered as aphasic. If the nature of this motor speech deficit is apraxic, as opposed to dysarthric, then it would follow that AOS plus agrammatic aphasia and relatively well preserved auditory comprehension would form the general description of the syndrome of Broca Aphasia. In this sense, one not only *can* have AOS if identified as having Broca Aphasia, but one *has* to have AOS in order to be a Broca Aphasic.

With the high probability of motoric deficits coexisting with, or actually accounting for, many of the deficits labeled as aphasic, it is reasonable that the speech motor control abilities of aphasic populations should have received experimental attention. A number of studies have employed perceptual (e.g. phonetic transcription), acoustic (e.g. spectral and temporal), and physiologic (e.g. aerodynamic, electromyographic, kinematic and force) analyses in order to assign linguistic and/or speech motor control mechanisms to the errors produced by aphasic populations. The following sections review both studies designed to describe the speech motor control abilities of these populations and studies designed specifically to address the linguistic versus motor mechanisms for the speech errors. Apparent in all of these studies is the need for speech to be viewed within the superordinate behavior of language.

In the traditional view of disorders of speech, a two or three (Itoh & Sasanuma, 1984) stage model has been invoked to account for segmental errors. Those segmental speech errors that are produced by aphasic populations are ascribed to the phonologic level because aphasic errors are, by definition, generated at the linguistic level of production. Those segmental and suprasegmental errors produced by apraxic speakers are, by definition, errors generated at the motor programming level. Segmental and suprasegmental errors produced by dysarthric subjects are, by definition, attributed to the level of movement execution after the phonologically intact form has been retrieved and after the muscles have received an otherwise intact set of commands from the motor speech program. With the explication of the mechanisms for these labels, the question becomes not whether aphasia is a disorder of phonologic selection/sequencing or whether AOS is a disorder of motor programming, but rather one of whether the label has been applied correctly to the pathological population or individual (one of diagnostic accuracy). This three stage model, and its associated neurogenic population (broken arrows), is shown in Figure 1. Figure 2 shows the same three stage model with the redirection of arrows (solid lines) based on the evidence derived from the studies reviewed below.

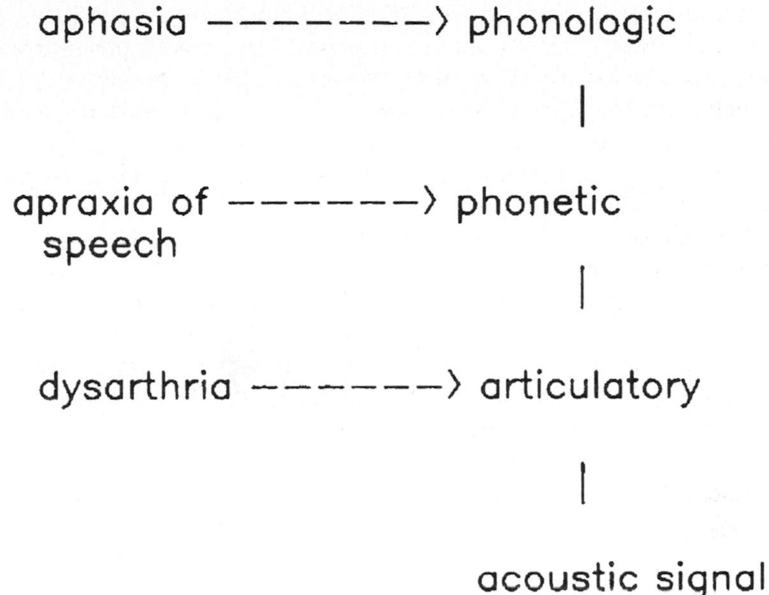

Figure 1. Traditional three-stage model of neurogenic speech production disorders.

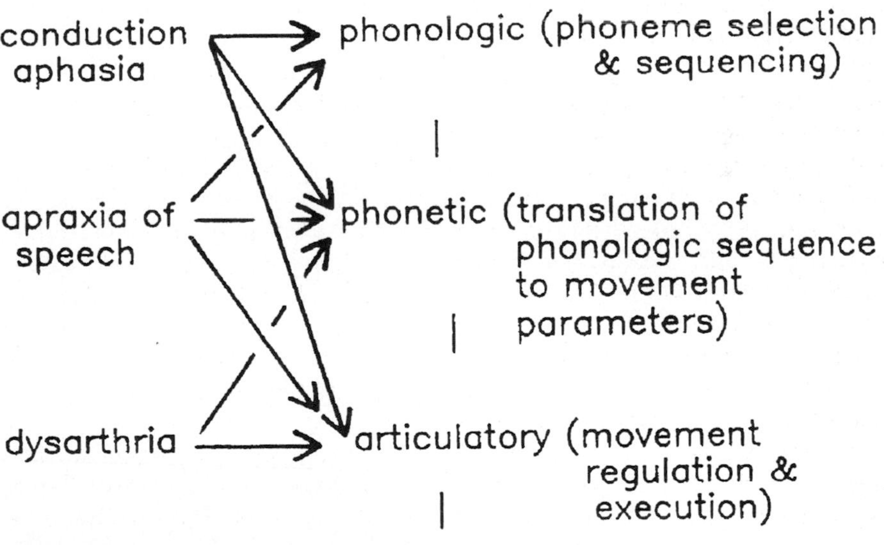

Figure 2. Reformulated three-stage model of neurogenic speech production disorders.

Although the third stage of the model (dysarthric-articulatory) is crucial to the eventual attribution of errors from the aphasic and apraxic populations, a review of the data supporting this level of the model is beyond the scope of this chapter and will, therefore, not be systematically reviewed.

The evidence presented from these three levels of breakdown, derived from these three general pathologic populations may appear to be the eminent example of a tautology (i.e., defining the origins of the errors by the group from whom the errors were generated). While that possibility does exist, care has been exercised by most researchers in the interpretation of their data relative to this potential.

The majority of literature that has investigated speech production in aphasic populations has focused on Broca Aphasic subjects, because this group produces the majority of speech sound errors (both segmental and suprasegmental) that are arguably motoric (programming) in origin. To a lesser extent, and more recently, the speech of the Conduction Aphasic population has received experimental attention from which linguistic versus motoric explanations have been debated. Those studies providing evidence for a motoric level explanation for the speech errors in these populations are reviewed in the following section. For the purposes of this review, the data from the speech of the Broca Aphasic are combined with the data from the subjects labeled as apraxic speakers. The data reviewed for the aphasic groups are derived from subjects other than Broca aphasic subjects.

Perceptual (Analysis) Studies

Many of the errors in aphasic and apraxic speech have been classified as segmental or phonemic errors; that is, errors in which a phoneme is omitted, added, or substituted for another phoneme, or one that is transposed with another phoneme in the same sequence. As will be discussed in the following, the assumption that these errors are phonemic, as opposed to phonetic or motoric, should not be made baldly. However, special attention has been given to these so-called phonemic errors, and their description in aphasic and apraxic speech has strongly affected the understanding of these disorders.

Phonemic errors in neurologically disordered speech have a counterpart in the production errors in normal speech. Corpora of normal speech errors have been collected and/or analyzed by a number of investigators (Boomer & Laver, 1968; Fay & Cutler, 1977; Fromkin, 1971; Garrett, 1975; D.G. MacKay, 1970; Nooteboom, 1969; Shattuck-Hufnagel, 1979; Stemberger, 1982). These production errors in normal speech are lawful, at least statistically so. For example, exchange errors (transpositions, such as 'nake mote' for 'make note') tend to preserve certain features of the target. That is, exchanges occur between elements in each of the following categories: (a) nouns, (b) verbs, (c) stressed syllables, (d) unstressed syllables, (e) consonants, (f) vowels, (g) syllable-initial consonants, and so on. However, exchanges do not usually occur between elements that cross these categories, for example, between consonants and vowels or between elements in stressed and unstressed syllables. A number of different units are involved in slips of the tongue, but these errors are typically described in terms of sounds (phonemes), syllables or parts of syllables, morphemes, words or phrases. Errors also have been categorized as syntagmatic or contextual errors versus paradigmatic or noncontextual errors. In the former type of error, there is evidence of a misordering of elements in a string. Exchanges, anticipations, perseverations, shifts, anticipatory or perseveratory additions and certain deletions all are described as syntagmatic or contextual errors. On the other hand, some errors cannot be readily described as having a source in the utterance in which the error occurs. These paradigmatic or noncontextual errors include noncontextual substitutions, blends, additions and deletions.

The primary interest in normal production errors lies in the belief that they can be used to infer organizational properties of the speech production process. Very little attention has been given to phonetic or motoric errors in normal speech, almost as though it has been implicitly assumed that such errors do not occur. We suspect that phonetic or motoric errors do occur in normal speech but they are difficult to identify because they are infrequent and not as perceptually striking as phonemic errors.

Research on normal speech errors is a foundation for research on errors in aphasic and apraxic speech. It is of interest to know if the speech errors in neurologic populations differ from normal speech errors in kind, number or both. For example, one might ask if the slipping units (the elements involved in speech errors) are the same for normal speakers and for aphasic or apraxic speakers (some similarities have been described by Kent, in press). It is also important to know if the aphasic or apraxic errors include error types that have not been observed in normal speakers. It is clear from the studies of normal speech that errors occur with some frequency. Apparently, speaking is vulnerable to disruption. What we need to learn from analyses of aphasic or apraxic errors is whether the disruption associated with neurologic disorders is basically an exaggeration of the occasional disruptions in normal speech. Perceptual analyses of normal, aphasic, and apraxic speech have taken many forms including broad and narrow phonetic transcription, phonologic process, distinctive feature, coarticulatory and a variety of other analyses. A review of the findings relevant to the understanding of the nature of apraxic and aphasic speech derived from these procedures follows.

Broad Phonetic Transcription

The overwhelming majority of descriptions of both apraxic and aphasic suprasegmental and segmental (phoneme level) speech have been obtained from broad phonetic transcriptions. With this method, apraxic speakers' consonant productions have been found to be more often substituted than added, omitted, repeated or distorted for target sounds (Shankweiler & Harris, 1966; Johns & Darley, 1970; Sasanuma, 1971; Trost & Canter, 1974; LaPointe & Johns, 1975). Aphasic speakers' consonant productions have also been found to be predominated by substitution errors (Blumstein, 1973; Shinn & Blumstein, 1983; Blumstein & Baum 1987; Nespoulous, Joanette, Ska, Caplan, & Lecours, 1987). Though other explanations are possible, the general interpretation of these findings has been that the errors are most consistent with a linguistic-level impairment. The primary problem with this interpretation is in the assignment of substitution errors to *any* level of the model. While substitution errors can be generated by motoric mechanisms (programming and execution) such as uncoordinated synergistic muscle action (Buckingham, 1979; Itoh, Sasanuma, Hirose, Yoshioka, & Ushijima, 1980; Keller, 1987; Rosenbek, Kent, & LaPointe, 1984), gesture reduction (Keller, 1984) or phoneme sequence simplification (Keller, 1984; Shankweiler & Harris, 1966), they can also be generated by linguistic (selection and sequencing) mechanisms and are therefore difficult to interpret unambiguously (see Blumstein & Baum (1987) for a discussion of this issue).

Vowel errors have been investigated and occur less frequently than consonant errors in both apraxic and aphasic populations. However, individuals within groups have been shown to vary greatly from the group means (Darley, 1982; Keller, 1978: LaPointe & Johns, 1975; Lebrun, Buyssens, & Henneaux, 1973; Trost & Canter, 1974). Very little work has been done on the nature of the vowel errors that provides evidence for linguistic, phonetic or motoric mechanisms. Keller (1978) classified the vowel errors of Broca Aphasic patients as either syntagmatic (those resulting from the phonological environment and surrounding sounds) or paradigmatic (those not obviously influenced by environment). Theoretically, syntagmatic errors might be assigned to a phonetic/motoric level impairment while paradigmatic errors would more likely be generated by a segment selection or ordering impairment. Paradigmatic errors predominated (83%). This finding, at first measure, appears to support a linguistic (selection) interpretation. However, as with consonant substitutions, most vowel substitutions cannot be interpreted unambiguously relative to the model. Keller also reported a tendency for low vowels to be substituted for higher vowels, a finding potentially consistent with the explanation of motoric gesture reduction. Béland (1985) observed that the majority of vowel substitutions made by aphasic subjects (various aphasic syndromes) occurred in un-accented positions (72.5%).

Narrow Phonetic Transcription

Using narrow phonetic transcription of mono-, bi- and tri-syllabic word repetitions, Odell, McNeil, Rosenbek, and Hunter (in preparation) reported that their four AOS subjects (without concomitant aphasia or dysarthria) produced more consonant distortions (25%) than substitutions (6%). This finding flies in the face of the great majority of literature supporting the description of AOS as a disorder predominated by consonant substitutions. Furthermore, of all of the consonant substitutions, an equal number (50%) were perceived as distortions as were judged as pure substitutions. Of all of the distorted consonants, 66% were perceived as abnormally prolonged. Eleven percent were judged as devoiced and the following types each accounted for less than 6% of the distortions: juncture, labialized, voiced, backed, aspirated, palatalized, derhotacized, velarized, shortened, dentalized and on/off glide. Errors that can be more confidently attributed to linguistic or articulatory implementation levels (e.g. regressive assimilation errors (Blumstein & Baum, 1987), and anticipatory and perseveratory substitutions (Shattuck-Hufnagel, 1987)) never occurred in this speech sample with these subjects.

Using narrow phonetic transcription of the same mono-, bi-, and tri-syllabic word repetitions by the same AOS subjects used in the Odell et al. (1990) study, McNeil, Hunter, Rosenbek, and Fennell (1987) reported a nearly equal number of total vowel (30%) and consonant errors (33%). Both segmental error classes were further subdivided into substitution, distortion, addition and omission errors. No vowels were omitted, although 8% of the consonants were. It should be remembered, however, that an omitted vowel would be realized as an omitted syllable; a fact that makes direct comparison of vowels and consonants difficult. The percentage of vowel and consonant errors was very similar across all error types, with the exception that slightly more vowels (19%) than consonants (13%) were substitutions. Of all of the vowel errors, 62% were judged as substitutions. Both additions and distortions accounted for 19% of the vowel errors. Of the vowels judged as substitutions, 63% were judged to be distorted. One subject produced distortions that were characterized as 'retracted tongue body' (54% of all distorted vowels). One subject produced distortions reflecting 'raised tongue body' (23%) and two subjects produced distortions that were perceived as 'vowel lengthening' (23%).

The vowel distortion errors can, perhaps, be assigned to a motoric level of the speech production mechanism with relative confidence. However, as with those of the consonants, the other error types (including the substitutions) cannot, with any degree of confidence, be attributed to either a motoric, phonetic or linguistic level deficits.

Phonological Process

Phonologic process analysis is a method of speech analysis that seeks to determine underlying processes or regularities (e.g. metathesis, haplology, epenthesis, elision - I.R.A. MacKay, 1978) involved in speech errors that cross sound classes. The clinical utility of the procedure for managing AOS has been espoused (Crary & Fokes, 1979), and data illustrating (Kearns, 1980) and quantifying (Bowman, Hodson, & Simpson, 1980) disturbed processes have been presented. However, as with many (or perhaps most) of the other analyses, there is no unambiguous way of assigning linguistic versus phonetic/motoric mechanisms to the processes. In fact, the theoretical underpinnings of process analysis are so strongly rooted in linguistic theory (phonologic rule violation) that it may be viewed as untenable to adherents to suggest possible motoric mechanisms for identified processes.

Distinctive Features

Like process analysis, distinctive feature analysis (e.g., place features such as labial, dental, velar; manner features such as stop, affricate, fricative, glide; voiced/unvoiced; nasal/oral) is rooted in linguistic theory. Inter-phoneme speech errors that can be ascribed to a feature or set of features are often interpreted as evidence for a linguistic (sublexical speech planning) locus for the errors. Arguments such as Shattuck-Hufnagel and Klatt's (1979), that errors appearing to involve a change in even a single distinctive feature are actually whole-segment errors rather than feature errors *per se*, have tended to reinforce this linguistic interpretation of featural data. However, distinctive features have been used descriptively, acknowledging potential motoric mechanisms for errors crossing sound classes. From studies using both broad and narrow phonetic transcriptions of the speech of Broca aphasic and AOS subjects, there have emerged a number of consistent findings interpreted to reflect motoric mechanisms for the speech errors. If features are represented in the brain, and if a feature can be found to be in error across sound segments (e.g., the place feature), then it would be argued that there is a representational basis for the errors, rather than a phonetic implementation or execution locus for the error.

Errors of place predominate over errors of the other features in the majority of studies (Trost & Canter, 1974; LaPointe & Johns, 1975; Odell, et al., 1990). The relative order of manner, voicing, oral/nasal and combinations of the feature errors varies across studies and across subjects within studies. Voiceless sounds are more often substituted for voiced sounds than the converse (Trost & Canter, 1974; Odell et al., 1990). It must be remembered that in no studies has a feature been found to be consistently impaired across the phonemes in which it appears (in the strong form of the argument, a requirement for assigning the errors to the abstract level of the feature). We interpret this as an absence of support for a linguistic (representational) mechanism for the speech errors of aphasic and apraxic speakers.

Errors are more likely to differ from the target by one phonetic dimension than by more than one (Trost & Canter, 1974; LaPointe & Johns, 1975; Odell et al., 1990). It is argued that error sounds produced with fewer dimensions from the target more likely show evidence for a better representation, selection and sequencing of the target sound (thus, by default, assigning the error to the phonetic/motoric level) than error sounds that are off the target by a greater number of features. However, without knowledge of whether distinctive features are specified in the planning of speech movements (a notion rejected in the slot fillers model of Shattuck-Hufnagel, 1987), such data can be invoked as evidence for a phonemic level deficit or for a phonetic/motoric one. That is, at least theoretically, a target sound /b/ could be specified with one errant feature [voicing], but programmed and executed appropriately resulting in a [p/b] substitution.

Coarticulation

The influence of upcoming speech segments on preceding segments has been well documented. For example, anticipatory coarticulation for the word 'shoe' involves the rounding of the lips prior to the production of the /u/ sound, whereas such lip rounding is not realized acoustically in the production of the word 'she'. These articulatory allophonic alterations produce robust spectral differences in the consonants that are perceptually present, even in brief portions of these phonemes. Ziegler and von Cramon (1985) proposed that if the apraxic speaker had poorly specified information about the upcoming vowel, then this lack of specification should be reflected in the preceding consonant as a lack of coarticulation with the vowel. In their study, normal listeners judged (predicted) from normal speakers and from a single apraxic speaker the upcoming vowel from stimuli that had progressively less acoustic information (using selectively gated portions of the acoustic signal ranging from the consonant with a portion of the vowel, to only small portions of the word-initial consonant) available from which to make the predictions. While the vowels of the normal speakers were predicted accurately with only small portions of the consonant (and no vowel signal), the apraxic speaker's productions were poorly identified with an equivalently gated acoustic signal. The authors concluded that this subject showed a "delayed onset of anticipatory vowel gestures relative to the labial occlusion." and proposed a mechanism of "aberrant phase relationships in hetero-organic speech gestures", which is clearly a phonetic level interpretation for the findings.

Katz (1987) presented productions from Broca, Wernicke and normal subjects to normal listeners that contained only the consonantal acoustic information for CV and CCV monosyllable words contrasting in the /i/-/u/ vowel [si/su, sti/stu, ski/sku, ti/tu and ki/ku]. The listeners predicted the correct vowel significantly greater than chance for each group (normal = 84%, Broca = 78% and Wernicke = 83%). However, differences between the two vowels were not examined despite the fact that a difference in the lip rounded coarticulatory gesture with the vowel /u/ might be predicted from the results of the Ziegler and von Cramon (1985) study. Although no inferential statistical comparisons were made, Katz concluded that there were no differences between the normal and posterior (Wernicke) subject groups but that the perceptual scores for the anterior (Broca) group were lower than for the normal group. This difference was, however, dependent on the phonetic segment.

In order to evaluate the (reliability) significance of Katz' observation, we computed a two sample *t*-test (Minitab, 5.1.3; B.F. Ryan, Joiner, & T.A. Ryan, 1986), on the data from Figure 11-4 (Katz, 1987; p. 234). The result of this computation revealed that there were significant differences ($p< .025$) between the normal and Broca groups on the overall performance across all phonetic segments as well as for the /sk/, /t/ and /k/ contexts. No significant difference was found on the overall measure for the Broca/Wernicke comparison; however, the /sk/ and /t/ segments were predicted significantly less often for the Broca subjects. No significant differences on any segment or on the overall was observed for the normal/Wernicke comparisons. These findings are interpreted as support for the notion that the posterior aphasic subjects showed no evidence of aberrant anticipatory coarticulation, whereas the anterior aphasic subjects showed some evidence of delayed or deficient anticipatory coarticulation.

Other Articulatory Factors

An argument has been posed that apraxic speakers produce more difficult strings of consonant clusters for easier targets (Johns & Darley, 1970; Shankweiler & Harris, 1966). While this argument has importance for nosology (e.g. whether to call the disorder 'phonetic disintegration' or 'AOS') and perhaps for treatment programming, it is not clear that AOS subjects actually do this (Klich, Ireland, & Weidner, 1979) or if they do, whether it argues for a linguistic or motoric mechanism for the error. One could argue that phonetic/motoric errors could (or might be expected to) result in simplification errors. However, Johns and Darley (1970) have argued that errors of the speech motor programmer might be expected to result in errors of complication. As with number of features from the target, errors of complication cannot be interpreted unambiguously relative to the current models of speech production.

Frequency of sounds in the language (Trost & Canter, 1974; Dunlop & Marquardt, 1977), word length (Johns & Darley, 1970; Odell et al., 1990) and several other 'linguistic' variables have been investigated in apraxic speakers. In general, these data tend to demonstrate influences on error rate and type that are variable across subjects, when they occur, and that parallel those of both normal and aphasic speakers. All other things being equal, speech sounds that are used more frequently, like lexical items that are used more frequently, are more likely to be selected and retrieved efficiently and accurately. Sounds that are implemented and executed at the phonetic/motoric level are more likely to be produced efficiently and accurately. Likewise, utterances that are shorter in number of phonemes (e.g. consonant singletons versus clusters) or syllables require less linguistic specification and phonetic/motoric implementation. It is, therefore, difficult to use these data for the differential assignment of mechanisms for the effects.

Sound error position in words (Johns & Darley, 1970; LaPointe & Johns, 1975; Dunlop & Marquardt, 1977; Odell et al., 1990) is one articulatory feature that could shed light on the error generating mechanism if viewed in the context of the slots and fillers model of speech production planning proposed by Shattuck-Hufnagel (1987). Although there is a common belief that apraxic speakers have a predominance of initial position errors and that aphasic speakers make a predominance of speech errors in medial or final utterance positions, there is little consistency across studies that a positional effect in either AOS (including Broca Aphasia) or Conduction Aphasia exists.

A construct that has held a very important position in the definition and differential assignment of speech errors to levels of the processing system has been the consistency and variability with which errors are made. Errors that are made in the same location of an utterance and are produced in the same deviant manner on repeated trials have been used as evidence for both motoric level deficits (dysarthria) and for linguistic (representational) level deficits. Johns and Darley's (1970) pivotal publication on apraxia of speech provided the initial evidence for what has become dogma (cf. Wertz, LaPointe, & Rosenbek, 1984) that apraxic errors are variable while the errors of the dysarthric population are more consistent. Mlcoch, Darley, & Noll (1982) reported a systematic analysis of six 'pure' apraxic subjects' articulatory consistency and variability. *Consistency* was measured as the speaker's tendency to misarticulate the same words across repeated trials of the same discourse. *Variability* was measured as the speaker's tendency to produce different errors in the same words and word positions across repeated contextual speech trials. Subjects demonstrated that they were both consistent and variable. That is, the apraxic subjects misarticulated the same words across repeated trials, and also tended to produce different errors within the same words and word positions across repeated samples. This finding provided support for the variable nature of apraxic speakers articulatory errors. However, a systematic examination of the consistency and variability of dysarthric errors has not been reported. Given that some types of dysarthria, such as ataxic dysarthria, are in part defined by their variability ("irregular articulatory breakdown"; Darley et al., 1975), this feature and its implied level of breakdown is in need of experimental verification. Further, even if errors were found to be consistent and invariable, the issue of level of phonological representational deficits as the source for this consistency will require additional explanation. That is, articulatory errors that are consistent have also been used as evidence for a deficit at a higher linguistic level. In summary, it appears that apraxic speakers are both consistent and variable in their articulatory errors. This variability argues for a speech mechanism that is representationally and biomechanically sound and thus has been used as evidence for a phonetic level deficit. What is not clear is whether the articulatory errors of any type of dysarthria is either consistent or invariable and if they are, whether it argues unequivocally for a motoric level deficit.

MacNeilage (1982) hypothesized that 'marked' sounds (sounds that are not used in the babbling of children, are produced later in the children's words, and that occur less frequently in the world's languages), reveal a motor constraint on them, while 'unmarked' sounds (sounds that are preferred in children's babbling, are produced early in the words of children, and occur more frequently in the world's languages), have a prearticulatory constraint. He tested the notion that marked sounds (taken from infant babbling data) would correlate more highly with the speech substitution errors of aphasic and apraxic speakers if they were of a motoric origin, whereas the substitution errors from these subjects that are of a prearticulatory origin would correlate more highly with unmarked sounds. Results suggested that the sound substitutions of apraxic (Broca aphasic) subjects correlated more highly with marked sounds, whereas sound substitutions of the Wernicke and conduction aphasic subjects correlated more highly (and in the expected direction) with unmarked sounds. Although these data supported a motoric interpretation for the speech errors of the apraxic speaker and a premotoric level interpretation for the other aphasic subjects, MacNeilage cautioned that there was some evidence for errors at multiple levels in all groups.

Perceptual analyses have shaped much of the understanding of the errors in apraxic and aphasic speech. As the foregoing review indicates, the literature is not wholly consistent on several critical questions. One reason for this inconsistency may be listener criterion, particularly with respect to the identification of distortion versus substitutions. Ideally, fine transcription would detect the two error classes. However, it must be kept in mind that perceptual decisions are not always a direct reflection of the acoustic and physiological events in speech. An example of how perceptual analysis may be misleading was described by Edwards and Miller (1989). Their transcribers heard an apraxic speaker to produce a [k] for [t] substitution. However, data from electropalatography (which records tongue contact with the palate) indicated that the supposed [k] articulations had the kind of central alveolar contact typically associated with [t]. But the central alveolar contact was accompanied by a narrowing in the velar region and by asymmetric lateral contacts. Apparently, the transcribers heard the release of the velar closure through the incomplete lateral constriction and therefore judged that a [k] was produced. Obviously, this kind of perceptual analysis does not accurately depict the articulatory error. Instrumental (acoustic and physiological) analyses have been increasingly applied to the study of apraxic and aphasic speech, and the resulting data are reviewed in the following sections.

Acoustic Studies

Segment Durations

Several investigators have measured the durations of vowel or consonant segments in Broca aphasia or AOS. The durations have been compared to those of normal controls or speakers with other types of aphasia (typically Wernicke). When comparisons have been made for the durations of vowels in monosyllables, the usual result has been little or no difference between groups (Duffy & Gawle, 1984; Gandour & Dardarananda, 1984; Mercaitis, 1983; Ryalls, 1984, 1986). Duffy and Gawle (1984) reported that vowel durations were shorter for apraxic speakers than for normal speakers. Bauman (1978) reached a similar conclusion for speakers with Broca aphasia. She reported that vowel durations were shorter than normal in subjects with Broca aphasia, even though their consonant durations were lengthened. Most of these studies also indicated that vowel durations were highly variable in AOS and Broca aphasia.

However, when comparisons of vowel durations are made for multisyllabic words or nonsense utterances, apraxic speakers have lengthened vowels (Collins, Rosenbek, & Wertz, 1983; Kent & Rosenbek, 1983; Mercaitis, 1983; Ryalls, 1981, 1987; Strand, 1987). It appears, then, that the regulation of vowel duration is most abnormal for multisyllabic speech materials. In fact, the sensitivity of vowel duration to syllabic complexity (or some other aspects of utterance complexity) may be an important clinical feature of AOS. In severe AOS, vowels can be lengthened to a remarkable degree (Kent & Rosenbek, 1983).

Consonant durations have not been studied as frequently as vowel durations but it appears that consonants also tend to be lengthened (Bauman, 1978; Kent & Rosenbek, 1983). Systematic research is needed to determine how consonant durations vary with utterance complexity or length. Voice onset time (VOT) is considered separately in a following section because a fairly large literature has developed on this topic.

Increased segment durations are expected from the typical clinical impression that speech rate is reduced in AOS and Broca aphasia. Normal speakers change speaking rate largely by changing the durations of vowel segments, pauses, and some consonant segments. The slow speaking rate associated with AOS and Broca aphasia is related to increased durations of these segments and, in some speakers, to increased transition durations as well (Kent & Rosenbek, 1983). Particularly for connected speech or multisyllabic utterances, speakers with AOS or Broca aphasia tend to demonstrate increased durations of a variety of segments. As these lengthened segments carry no meaning change, it is difficult to attribute these increases to a linguistic level dysregulation. Indeed, the variability of segment lengths from trial to trial with frequent attempts to self-correct the production has been interpreted as evidence for a phonetic/motoric level deficit.

Syllable Amplitude

The literature on this aspect of speech in AOS and Broca aphasia is small, but at least two reports are consistent in their conclusion that the syllable relief tends toward temporal regularity and amplitude uniformity (Lebrun et al., 1973; Kent & Rosenbek, 1983). These acoustic features should correlate with neutralization of stress pattern and dysrhythmia, that is, with dysprosody.

Fundamental Frequency

The fundamental frequency contour of an utterance is a major component of intonational structure. Proper regulation of fundamental frequency contributes to the naturalness of speech and may influence intelligibility. From the usual clinical description of Broca aphasia as intonationally flat, one would expect that the fundamental frequency contours would have a restricted range. Results in accord with this expectation were reported by Ryalls (1982) and by Cooper, Soares, Nicol, Michelow, and Goloskie (1984). However, Danly and Shapiro (1982) found an apparently opposite effect of exaggerated variation in fundamental frequency in Broca aphasia. As Cooper and Klouda (1987) pointed out, the discrepancy in results may reflect differences in measurement procedure. The Danly and Shapiro results pertain to within-word variation in fundamental frequency whereas Ryalls' results pertain to across-sentence variations. Conceivably, the two patterns of results could co-occur if the fundamental frequency variation in words is exaggerated even as the variation across words in a sentence is restricted.

Additional aspects of intonation were studied in Broca aphasia by Danly, de Villiers and Cooper (1979) and Danly and Shapiro (1982). This research indicated that some features of normal fundamental frequency contours are preserved even in utterances with labored articulation and long interword pauses. But the speakers with Broca aphasia differed from normal speakers in not showing utterance-final lengthening. In addition, the contours in Broca aphasia were interpreted to reflect a prosodic programming that was shorter in span for Broca aphasia than for normal speech. Cooper and Klouda (1987) concluded that the dysprosody in Broca aphasia is influenced more by timing abnormalities than by deviant fundamental frequency variation. Moreover, they pointed to evidence that fundamental frequency sometimes is used in a compensatory fashion, for example, in the form of substantial continuation rises on utterance nonfinal words, as though to signal the intent to continue the utterance.

Vocal Response Times

Delay in vocal or verbal response is a frequently noted characteristic of AOS or Broca aphasia. Mercaitis's (1983) study of apraxic, aphasic, and normal control speakers indicated that the apraxic subjects had longer verbal response times for single syllables, syllable pairs and syllable triads. In addition, the apraxic speakers had lengthened intersyllable intervals. Similarly, Strand (1987) determined that apraxic speakers had abnormally long vocal response times for words, word strings, and sentences. Interestingly, the delay in initiating a vocal response was not influenced by preparation interval in Strand's study. That is, having a longer time for utterance preparation did not affect the subjects' response times.

Summary of Global Speech Features

The foregoing sections apply to relatively global aspects of speech and may be taken to define the long-term, intonational properties of multisyllabic utterances in AOS and Broca aphasia. Briefly, these properties include lengthened vowel and consonant segments, variability in segment duration, prolonged pauses or interword intervals, lack of phrase-final lengthening, reduced fundamental frequency and amplitude variation across words in sentences, and delayed initiation of vocal response. These global features are a backdrop for the following sections that consider abnormalities at the segment or microsegment level.

Vowel Formants

Formant frequency measures for vowels are informative on several grounds, but principally to determine (a) the way in which vowels are represented in the speaker's F1-F2 plane or F1-F2-F3 space, and (b) the reliability of a speaker's vowel productions. Concerning the second of these, apraxic and Broca aphasia speakers are more variable than normal controls in their vowel formant frequencies (Keller, 1975; Ryalls, 1981, 1986; Ziegler, 1987). This greater variability in the acoustics of vowels is taken to mean a greater variability in their phonetic/motoric production of the vowels.

As to whether apraxic speakers and speakers with Broca aphasia have a suitable representation of vowels in the formant plane or formant space, the general conclusion appears to be that they do. Any indications to the contrary are rather subtle. Keller (1975) noted a flattening of the vowel area along the F1 axis, with higher F1 values occurring for aphasic speakers. Generally, higher F1 values reflect a larger mouth opening, which can occur as a consequence of reduced speaking rate. Ziegler (1987) interpreted his vowel formant data to mean that apraxic speakers have a deficit in either the temporal or geometric specifications of vowel articulation.

Voice Onset Time

Probably no single acoustic attribute of aphasic and apraxic speech has been studied as frequently as voice onset time (VOT). VOT is one of the simplest acoustic measures but its interpretation is not altogether straightforward. A potentially powerful interpretation of VOT values was proposed by Blumstein, Cooper, Zurif, and Caramazza (1977) and Blumstein, Cooper, Goodglass, Statlender, and Gottlieb (1980). They defined rules by which VOT data could be related to either phonemic or phonetic errors. The rules were based on the distribution of VOT values for normal speakers' productions of voiced and voiceless stops. The distribution is bimodal and, at least for citation-style speech, the ranges of VOT for voiced and voiceless cognates are nonoverlapping.

Blumstein and associates defined a phonemic error as occurring when a VOT value for a target sound (say, for example, the voiceless [t] fell within the normal VOT range for the alternate example, the voiced [d]). A speaker who commits this kind of error would preserve the nonoverlapping bimodal distribution of VOT values and would be judged to make cognate substitutions, such as [d] for [t]. A phonetic error was judged to occur when a VOT value fell in the interval between the ranges for normal voiced and voiceless cognates. Shewan, Leeper, and Booth (1984) used the term "phonetic gap error" for this outcome. A speaker who produces errors of this type would have overlapping VOT values for voiced and voiceless stops.

Blumstein and her colleagues reported that phonemic VOT errors occurred in Wernicke aphasic, whereas phonetic VOT errors were observed in anterior and Broca's aphasia. It was concluded that speakers with Wernicke's aphasia have a phonological impairment whereas apraxic and Broca aphasic speakers have a phonetic or motor programming disorder.

Other studies confirmed the work of Blumstein and associates in showing overlapping VOT distributions for Broca aphasia (Shewan, Leeper, & Booth, 1984; Tuller, 1984) and apraxia of speech (Hoit-Dalgaard, Murry, & Kopp, 1983; Itoh, Sasanuma, Tatsumi, Murakami, Fukusako, & Suzuki, 1982) but nonoverlapping VOT distributions for Wernicke aphasia (Tuller, 1984). However, the error classification strategy used by Blumstein et al. (1977) and Blumstein et al. (1980) has been criticized for what could be a faulty rigidity (Itoh et al., 1982; Tuller, 1984; Ziegler, 1984, 1987; Hewlett, 1985). Blumstein (1981) recognized the difficulty in noting that some phonological errors could be the result of phonetic distortions so extreme that they are perceived as a change in phonetic category (that is, a substitution).

The objections to the phonemic vs phonetic error classification would appear to leave the matter in quandary. Resolution of the issue could take the form suggested by Ziegler (1987), who used a curve-fitting technique with mixed component functions to model VOT distributions. His results were consistent with earlier conceptualizations of the speech disorder in Wernicke aphasia and AOS. Specifically, he concluded that Wernicke aphasia was associated with a "dysfunction affecting the discrete structure in the inventory of phonetic plans" (p. 177), whereas AOS reflected a difficulty in the realization of properly selected phonological units.

It also is clear from the studies conducted to date that both phonemic and phonetic errors can be observed in Broca aphasia, Wernicke aphasia and conduction aphasia (Tuller & Story, 1987). However, speakers with Broca aphasia or AOS tend to make more phonetic errors than do speakers with Wernicke or conduction aphasia.

Articulatory Timing and Phasing

VOT may be regarded as a measure of inter-articulator coordination because it reflects the relative timing of a supra-laryngeal event (consonant articulation) and a laryngeal event (voicing onset). A variety of other acoustic measures have been used to study other kinds of articulatory timing.

In a study of AOS, Ziegler and von Cramon (1986) examined acoustic data for three speech movement patterns: (a) lingual-laryngeal phasing, measured as VOT for voiced and voiceless stops, (b) lingual-velar phasing, measured by the smoothness of the sound pressure level for utterances containing nasal consonants, and (c) lingual-labial phasing, measured by spectral evidence of anticipatory lip protrusion during prevocalic [t]. The apraxic speakers showed evidence of abnormal sequencing for each of the three movement patterns. Ziegler and von Cramon regarded the abnormalities to be a consequence of disturbed inter-articulator phasing and noted that these errors could conceivably give rise to apparent phonemic errors (substitutions).

Related studies by Tuller and Story (1987) and Katz (1987) were undertaken to investigate anticipatory coarticulation, or the anticipation of an articulatory feature in advance of the production of its parent segment. Tuller and Story used acoustic analysis (linear predictive coding) to examine anticipatory coarticulation for a following vowel in fricative segments. Their results for controls, 'fluent' aphasics and 'nonfluent' aphasics indicated that some of the nonfluent aphasic speakers did not show acoustic evidence of anticipatory coarticulation as early as did the normal controls or fluent aphasic subjects.

In contrast to the results of Tuller and Story, Katz (1987) concluded from acoustic and perceptual studies (see the discussion above for a detailed analysis of the perceptual component of this study) of CV and CCV utterances that both anterior and posterior aphasic speakers demonstrated anticipatory coarticulation. Further, no acoustic evidence was seen for a delay in such coarticulation in anterior aphasic speakers. Katz stated that they appeared to initiate the anticipatory movement at least as early as the normal controls.

Summary of Segmental and Microsegmental Effects

The most consistent characteristic of Broca aphasia and AOS in the studies reviewed here is a large variability in the temporal and spectral properties of segments. The variability is evident for segment durations, VOT, vowel formant frequencies and perhaps for the timing (or phasing) of movements in a phonetic sequence. The variability usually has been interpreted as evidence of a motor dysregulation, and is clearly related to what several authors have described as phonetic errors.

Relative Timing

The relative durations of speech units are of interest for several reasons, but three of these are of primary interest here. First, it has been suggested that manipulation of speaking rate is a means by which a speaker's motoric facility can be evaluated (Kent & McNeil, 1987; McNeil, Liss, Tseng, & Kent, 1990). That is, one aspect of motoric competence is the ability to perform a motor act at different rates. The competent motor system usually handles rate manipulations with ease, whereas the compromised system may be limited in its ability to vary rate of performance. Rate variations are particularly attractive in the study of speech and language disorders because their effects can be studied while linguistic properties of an utterance, such as syntactic, semantic and phonological content, are held constant. By this reasoning, rate manipulations are a way of assessing motoric facility. But because absolute segment durations vary with speaking rate, relative measures of duration often have been taken to show how a speaker adjusts for speaking rate changes. A second reason for the study of relative durations is that many neurologically impaired speakers have reduced speaking rates compared to normal controls. It has been suggested that speaking rate variations affect certain details of the motor control of speech (McNeil et al., 1990; Munhall, 1989). If this is true, then direct comparisons of normal and impaired speech movements hold the risk of a confound between speaking rate and integrity of the speech motor control system. That is, conceivably, a speaker with a neurologic impairment could appear to have abnormal temporal patterns because he or she is using an abnormally slow speaking rate. A third reason for the study of relative durations is that these measures have been used to investigate local and nonlocal changes in the temporal structure of an utterance as a speaker varies speaking rate or stress pattern.

Kent and McNeil (1987) and McNeil et al. (1990) examined the relative durations of various speech units for utterances produced at different rates by normal controls, AOS and conduction aphasic speakers.

Although significant differences among groups for the relative timing measures were not shown, in both studies the apraxic *and* aphasic speakers were less effective than the normal controls in adjusting speaking rate. The apraxic speakers were less proficient than the conduction aphasics in making the rate adjustments. Under the assumption that variation in speaking rate for the same speech sample stresses primarily the phonetic or motoric level of speech production, Kent and NcNeil (1987) and McNeil et al. (1990) interpreted their data to indicate a phonetic-motoric disruption in both AOS and conduction aphasia. This conclusion was supported by observations of other apparent motoric abnormalities in the speech patterns of the apraxic and aphasic speakers (such as abnormal VOT values, variability in formant trajectories, and long pauses).

Studies of apraxic speakers have shown that, despite their typically long absolute segment durations, they make suitable adjustments in relative duration for linguistic properties of the utterance (Collins, Rosenbek, & Wertz, 1983; Strand & McNeil, 1987a,b). These results have been interpreted to mean that AOS affects primarily the motoric aspects of speech production rather than operations at the phonological level. In other words, temporal abnormalities in AOS appear to reflect motoric disturbances rather than deficiencies in the phonological representation of linguistic strings. Furthermore, Weismer and Fennell (1985) reported that neurologically impaired speakers, including two with apraxic characteristics, demonstrated stability in the relative temporal structure of sentences across speaking rates, even in the face of abnormal segment, word, and phrase durations.

Taken together, the studies of relative durations in AOS point to motoric rather than phonological abnormalities. The temporal abnormalities are not easily explained as the consequence of a deviant phonological representation or a disruption at a phonologic planning (selection or sequencing) level. A particularly interesting feature of AOS is the severely limited ability of apraxic speakers to accomplish changes in speaking rate.

Physiologic Studies

Force and Position Control

Clinical examination of persons with impaired speech production resulting from central or peripheral nervous system damage by neurologists and speech-language pathologists typically involves assessing maximum force (strength) for a particular speech structure such as the tongue, lips or jaw. If weakness is detected with these nonspeech tasks, there is a high likelihood that the resultant speech will be attributed to a dysarthria, not to AOS or aphasia. Cases that present with AOS or aphasia but without concomitant dysarthria are, on clinical examination, routinely judged to produce normal maximum forces in the speech structures. However, control of small nonspeech isometric forces by oral structures has been found to be significantly poorer in AOS than in normal subjects (McNeil, Weismer, Adams, & Mulligan, 1990). Isometric force control in conduction aphasic subjects was not significantly different from either normal, AOS or ataxic dysarthric subjects, leaving the possibility that their fundamental motor control may be impaired to a degree that they overlap with dysarthric and AOS subjects.

In the above reported study, McNeil and associates also reported results of fine position control in the same normal, apraxic, ataxic dysarthric and conduction aphasic subjects used in the force control study. In this study, the ability to sustain various displacements of the lips, tongue and jaw was assessed. Results generally paralleled those of the force study, with the dysarthric and AOS subjects performing significantly more poorly than the normal subjects but not differing significantly from one another. Likewise, the conduction aphasic subjects were not different from any of the other groups, leaving the possibility of a fundamental motor control deficit accompanying or perhaps accounting for the perceived speech production deficits of these subjects.

Intra-articulator Kinematics: Movement Duration, Velocity, Displacement, Dysmetria

Although acoustic studies are relatively abundant (as reviewed above), few kinematic studies of apraxic or aphasic speech have been performed, hence, few data have amassed from which to judge the duration of speech movements compared to normal or other pathologic groups. The general conclusion from the perceptual and acoustic evidence is that speech movements from Broca aphasic and AOS individuals are slower than those for normal controls or Wernicke aphasic individuals. However, the explanations for these extended durations and intersegment intervals have ranged from those attributable to (1) a conscious compensatory strategy to (2) a motor programming disorder to (3) a motor execution disorder in which there is a decrease in movement speed (velocity). However, as suggested by McNeil, Caliguiri, and Rosenbek (1989), other kinematic variables could account for the finding of slower speech. A gesture with a greater displacement could take longer to execute, especially if the normal peak velocity and displacement relationship were not achieved. Movements could take longer to execute because of variation in the movement trajectory in the absence of longer peak velocity or greater displacement. Attempts to separate these alternative accounts for the slowness of speech have been investigated by direct measurement of the movement. Using an x-ray microbeam device, Itoh, Sasanuma, Hirose, Yoshioka, and Ushijima (1980) reported lingual peak velocities for one apraxic subject that were approximately one-half of the value of the fast rate of the normal speakers and were similar to the peak velocity values of a patient with amyotrophic lateral sclerosis. Using a light-emitting diode system of measurement, Itoh and Sasanuma (1987) reported peak velocities for the lip and jaw for five young normal, five aged normal, five Broca (apraxic) and three Wernicke aphasic subjects. They found that overall "... patients with Wernicke's aphasia ... showed no sign of deviated articulatory behaviors in terms of peak velocity and displacement ..." (p. 159). On the other hand, the apraxic speakers were characterized by inconsistency in terms of articulatory velocity and/or displacement. The normal reciprocal relationship between peak velocity and displacement was occasionally violated (compared to the ranges for the normal subjects) by the apraxic subjects. Apparently, the apraxic speakers assigned too little velocity to a displacement or too much velocity and displacement simultaneously.

McNeil et al. (1989) compared labiomandibular kinematic durations, displacements, velocities and dysmetrias in four apraxic and four normal controls subjects using strain gauge transducers. Overall duration of the movement for the opening and closing gesture from the /a/ vowel in 'stop' to the /æ/ vowel in 'fast' in the phrase 'stop fast' was significantly longer in the apraxic subjects. The average peak velocity was not significantly different between groups; however, the average displacement of the lower lip + jaw was significantly greater for the apraxic subjects. The velocity/displacement relations was not examined in this study.

While the average peak velocity was not significantly different between groups in the McNeil et al. (1989) study, it was recognized that the peak velocity does not describe, in adequate detail, the many potential differences that could exist in the overall velocity profile. A visual inspection of the velocity traces revealed a great deal of variability in the morphology of the contour for the apraxic subjects. This variability was characterized by multiple peaks, differences in the timing of the peaks and the relative smoothness of the trajectories between peaks. In order to quantify some aspects of this observation, the number of zero acceleration crossings (termed dysmetrias) was counted and compared between groups. There was a significantly larger number of acceleration crossings in the traces of the apraxic subjects. In addition, there was a moderately high correlation coefficient (.70 for the apraxic subjects and .53 for the control subjects) between the number of dysmetrias and the duration of the gesture. Although the McNeil et al. (1989) study has been replicated, this finding calls for further investigation to determine if the number of zero axis crossings was an artifact of the slow rate of the apraxic speakers.

Preliminary analysis of these additional data provide some support for a rate/zero acceleration crossing relationship. Normal subjects' productions of speech at rates that are were not significantly different from the speech rates of the apraxic subjects (measured by total utterance duration) revealed zero axis crossings that were not significantly different in number from those of the apraxic subjects.

McNeil and Adams (in press) compared total duration from both the opening and closing phases of a lower lip + jaw gesture, the peak velocity, maximum displacement, time to peak velocity, total utterance duration, and the velocity/displacement profile across normal, apraxic, conduction aphasic and ataxic dysarthric speakers. There was no significant difference across groups in peak velocity or in maximum displacement. However, intergroup differences were significant for the time of the measured closing phase from the first diphthong plus consonant in 'buy bobby' in the phrase 'Buy Bobby a Poppy', except that the aphasic and dysarthric subject groups were not significantly different from each other. The apraxic subjects produced significantly longer closing segment durations than all other groups, while the conduction aphasic and ataxic dysarthric subjects produced significantly longer durations than the normal subjects. Group comparisons for total utterance duration paralleled those for the segment durations. The only significant intergroup difference for time taken to reach peak velocity occurred for the apraxic subjects compared to the normal subjects, where the AOS subjects took longer. Substantial differences in the velocity/displacement relationships were noted for all of the pathologic subject groups, and especially for the conduction aphasic subjects. Based on these findings, the authors concluded that none of these pathologic groups evidenced movements that were limited in the peak velocity with which the movement was executed, and hence not slow in the fundamental sense that bradykinesic patients are slow, although absolute durations were long in all pathologic groups compared to normal controls. Given that both the apraxic and conduction aphasic speakers' performance on these kinematic measures was significantly different from that of normal subjects, they further concluded that

> ... it is difficult to attribute aberrant control of velocity relative to amplitude to a phonemic selection level of production. At present, the best interpretation for the differences in all three pathological groups is one placed squarely in the motor programming and, perhaps execution domains.

Robin, Bean, and Folkins (1989) replicated the previously summarized findings for AOS and normal speakers on average peak velocity but they failed to find a difference on the peak velocity/displacement relationships. They reported lower-lip velocities and movement onsets for six apraxic speakers that fell within the ranges produced by their single normal speaker. There were no systematic effects of speech rate, correct versus incorrect productions, or whether the jaw was blocked (lower lip only) or unblocked (lower lip + jaw) on the peak velocity/displacement profile.

Inter-articulator Kinematics: Timing and Coordination

Itoh, Sasanuma, and Ushijima (1979) were perhaps the first researchers to use kinematic analyses to investigate the temporal patterning of speech movements in AOS and aphasic speakers. Itoh and Sasanuma (1984) synthesized a number of experiments conducted in their laboratory, including the Itoh et al. (1979), Itoh, Sasanuma, Hirose, Yoshioka and Ushijima (1980), Itoh, Sasanuma, Tatsumi, Murakami, Fukusako, and Suzuki (1982) and Itoh, Sasanuma Hirose, Yoshioka, and Sawashima (1983) studies. In this synthesis, as in the studies they summarized, they reported using fiberscopic analyses of the speech structures of one 'pure' apraxic, two Wernicke aphasics and one normal control subject. Their results revealed a breakdown of the normally tight temporal patterning between velar and tongue tip movements for the apraxic subject. Although the aphasic subjects produced sound substitutions, there was clear evidence from the appropriate anticipatory velar lowering and raising that errors were "... due not to an impairment at the level of articulatory programming but to an error in the selection or retrieval of a target phoneme." The mistimings of the component movements produced by the apraxic subjects marked perceptual changes such that sound substitutions were perceived (e.g. /d/ for /n/ substitution). Marked inter-articulator (velar, labial and lingual) movement timing errors along with marked trial-to-trial variability characterized the speech movements for the same 'pure' apraxic subject using the x-ray microbeam instrumentation originally developed at the Research Institute of Logopedics and Phoniatrics, University of Tokyo (Kiritani, Itoh, & Fujimura, 1975). As discussed above, the voice onset time (VOT) studies also provide information on the inter-articulator timing between the larynx and upper airway articulators. Evidence for such mistiming was also reported by Itoh and colleagues (1982).

Fromm (1981) collected simultaneous acoustic (accelerometer); movement (upper lip, lower lip + jaw, and jaw) and EMG (orbicularis oris superior, orbicularis oris inferior, depressor labi inferior and mentalis) recordings from three apraxic and three normal control subjects. Descriptive analyses across the structures and levels of analysis revealed instances of upper lip and jaw movements for the intended speech gesture without associated voicing, temporal and spatial discoordination among the three articulators, movement additions and apparent groping for correct articulatory productions. Instances were also noted for all three subjects whereby no abnormal movements were observed for individual utterances. As the same systematic descriptive analyses was not undertaken with the control subjects, little can be concluded relative to these finding's representation of 'pathological' behavior or whether they even represent a more frequent occurrence of them. The method of this investigation is a potentially important one, however, and the observations are quite consistent with subsequent findings of inter-articulator discoordination.

Using electropalatography, Hardcastle (1987) reported evidence of a general dyscoordination of the tongue tip, blade and body in one apraxic speaker. This dyscoordination was manifest in problems achieving "... smooth transitions between successive articulatory gestures ..." and frequently involved difficulty achieving normal anticipatory coarticulation among lingual components.

Using strain gauge movement transducers, McNeil, Tseng, Adams and Weismer (in preparation) compared the timing of upper and lower lip onsets, time to peak velocities and offsets among normal, apraxic, conduction aphasic and ataxic dysarthric subjects. Although there were some utterance differences among the groups, the general finding was that the upper lip initiated the movement, reached peak velocity and achieved offset prior to the lower lip significantly more often than the reverse in the normal subjects; a finding consistent with other reports of normal subjects (e.g. Gracco, 1988). As with the normal subjects, the apraxic and conduction aphasic subjects' upper lip led the lower lip in time to peak velocity and time of offset significantly more frequently than the lower lip led the upper. However, upper lip movement onset did not lead the lower lip significantly more frequently than the lower lip led the upper. As with the other three subject groups, the ataxic dysarthric subjects achieved upper lip offset leads significantly more frequently than lower lip leads, however, the time to peak velocity and movement onsets of the upper lip did not lead the lower lip significantly more frequently. These results are consistent with the notion of inter-articulator movement dyscoordination in the ataxic dysarthric and the apraxic subjects (for movement onset), and support the notion that such factors may also be present in the conduction aphasic individual.

Electromyographic

Shankweiler, Harris and Taylor (1968) presented electromyographic data from surface recordings of the tongue (anterior, middle and posterior) and of the upper and lower lips and on what is presumably the digastric muscle (described as the area above the hyoid bone) in two patients described as having 'phonetic disintegration' or AOS. Compared to the EMG activity of a normal control subject, the apraxic subject showed indistinct labial peaks for bilabial stop consonants with peaks across structures occurring at the same point in time. That is, the expected temporal differentiation among articulators was not found. The authors concluded that there was "... a striking reduction of the capacity for independent movement of the articulators." (p. 8). In addition to the kinematic data summarized above, Fromm (1981) described intramuscular EMG signals recorded from the orbicularis oris superior (OOS) and inferior (OOI), the mentalis (MTL) and the depressor labi inferior (DLI). She reported antagonistic muscle co-contraction, continuous undifferentiated activity and EMG shutdown which were interpreted as evidence for a motor control level deficit in her three apraxic patients. Again, it should be remembered that the normal subject's data were not described or quantified and thus did not actually serve as controls. These features could have been present in these subjects as well. Thus, the mere presence of these EMG features may not signal abnormal EMG activity. This limitation of the study motivated a quantitative analysis of antagonistic co-contraction of normal and apraxic, as well as conduction aphasic and ataxic dysarthric subjects by Forrest, Adams, and McNeil (in press). Using a procedure of correlating EMG activity between muscle pairs, it was found that all groups evidenced co-contraction between antagonist muscles (OOI/DLI) as well as reciprocal activity between agonist muscles (e.g. OOS/OOI) and that no between group differences existed on this or the other two EMG features.

More recently, Hough and Klich (1987) investigated the timing relationships of EMG activity underlying the vowel shortening rule researched by Collins et al. (1983) and discussed above. The premise of the study was that the shortened duration of the vowel in the stem syllable that accompanies the increase in syllable number (e.g. suit/suitable/suitability) should be manifest in the timing of lip EMG activity during the lip rounding gesture for the vowel production. Results from two AOS and two normal control subjects indicated that word length affected relative measures of EMG onset in similar ways for both the normal and apraxic subjects. Relative measures of EMG offset were also affected by word length, however, the effect was observed less systematically in the apraxic subjects. The authors concluded that there are detectable linguistic (word length) influences on EMG lip rounding onset activity and that these influences were preserved in the AOS subjects. Further, relative measures of EMG offset were less consistently applied by the AOS compared to the control subjects.

In summary, the EMG studies with aphasic and AOS subjects are meager and in desperate need of replication and careful comparison with equivalent data from normal control subjects and from other pathological subjects who share speech symptomatology and lesion specificity. Until these data are available, the EMG data now available must be interpreted with the greatest of caution.

Summary

Although the data presented in this chapter may be interpreted to provide a rather convincing argument for fundamental movement level deficits in apraxic, conduction aphasic and even Wernicke aphasic speakers, other interpretations of many of the findings are possible. Folkins (1985, 1988), for example, has proposed an interactive model of speech production in which deficits at one level of the linguistic mechanism could conceivably produce speech kinematic deviances. Indeed, Folkins (1988) has argued that

> Finding a difference between apraxic and normal speakers on physiological measure does not indicate necessarily that they have a motor deficit -- physiological differences could result directly from linguistic disabilities, or they could be plastic responses of the motor system to minimize the effects of linguistic limitations (such as reduced speed of linguistic processing).

He goes on to suggest that validation of the physiological measurements can be accomplished by interpreting the physiological measures in relation to perceptually defined differences in the adequacy of speech behavior and by the exploration of forced-variation flexibility (developing tasks that force the motor system to show its limits).

The aspectual theory of linguistics (Trager & Smith, 1961) may be a useful direction for future efforts at linguistic description of these neurological speech and language disorders. The aspectual model is a tripartite hierarchy, with three strata: (1) Phonology, or the sound system of a language; (2) Morphology, or the distribution of sounds into shapes; and (3) Semology, or the sense of the language. Each stratum is in turn composed of three levels, and each level has three aspects. The most relevant stratum for present purposes is Phonology, which includes the three levels of articulation, phonetics and phonemics. Under the level of articulation, three aspects are considered: (1) the prelinguistic, physiological characteristics of the speech apparatus, including pertinent pathology; (2) inventories of features, phones and phonemes; and (3) distributional data pertaining to permissions and prohibitions of syllable sound patterns, from which feature bundlings for segments can be derived. Under the level of phonetics, the aspects are (1) identification of phone types (e.g., stops, spirants, etc.); (2) classification of phones in phonetic tables; and (3) inventory of phones and appropriate use of diacritic symbols to describe deviations of segmental phones from cardinal positions of the tables derived in (2) above. Finally, under phonemics, the aspects determine phonemic classes. Minimal lexical pairs are used to identify segmental phonemes of consonants, vowels and semivowels. Then, intonation patterns combined with segmental minimal pairs are the basis for identifying the suprasegmental phonemes of stress, pitch and juncture. Finally, permissions and prohibitions of distribution for segmental and suprasegmental phonemes are determined.

An advantage of aspectual theory is that it affords a structured descriptive system that carefully identifies the various levels of language. The information derived at each level of analysis can be considered against the information at other levels. Ideally, the sound corpus should contain all structural units of the standard language. Bross (in press) described a concise test procedure, the Quantitative Rating of Performance test, which elicits all structural contrasts for American English. This corpus may be useful as a standard component of speech analysis, not only because it samples all structural units of the standard language but also because it can be analyzed according to the framework of aspectual theory. If the speech sample were used to obtain acoustic and/or physiological data, a highly informative data set would be available for the identification of errors and the assignment of the errors to various levels.

We have reviewed elsewhere (Kent & McNeil, 1987) an information processing model of utterance formulation and production as it might apply to the evaluation of speech in neurologically impaired subjects. The model recognizes the interactions among various aspects of processing (e.g., between syntactic and semantic, and between semantic and phonological). The model also emphasizes the temporal dependencies of utterance formulation and execution, for example, taking into account that speakers begin to produce an utterance before it is completely formulated syntactically and semantically. This model provides a framework for developing and understanding tasks that challenge the systems of utterance formulation and production. In this sense, the model is consistent with Folkins' recommendations noted earlier in this section.

It is a verity that interactive models of speech production should receive the developmental effort that the study of apraxic and aphasic speech has received. Ultimately, and only through the development of such experimental frameworks as that outlined by Folkins and given structure by such theories as the aspectual theory of Trager and Smith, will the appropriate questions be asked and the appropriate experimental tasks be explicated for assigning the speech errors of the apraxic and aphasic speaker to identifiable levels of the speech-language production mechanism.

The literature reviewed provides evidence that the assumptions underlying the speech errors from these pathologic populations (especially from the aphasic populations) are in need of serious reconsideration. The data, although incomplete, are sufficient to force a re-examination of the traditional classifications and descriptions of these disorders. Particular attention should be given to the motoric aspects of speech production, including careful description of speech and the development of consistent frameworks for the interpretation of abnormalities that appear.

Acknowledgements

This work was supported in part by Public Health Service Research grants NS18797 and NS22458. Appreciation is also expressed to Chin-Hsing Tseng for his creative assistance in formulating the visual representations of the models used in this manuscript and to Milly Boyer for clerical assistance.

References

Bauman, J.A. (1978). *Sound duration: a comparison between performances of subjects with central nervous system disorders and normal speakers.* Unpublished Doctoral Dissertation, University of Colorado.

Béland, R. (1985). *Constraintes syllabiques sur les erreurs phonologiques dans l'aphasie.* Unpublished Doctoral Dissertation, Université de Montreal.

Benson, D.F. (1967). Fluency in aphasia: correlation with radioactive scan localization. *Cortex*, **3**, 373-394.

Blumstein, S.E. (1973). *A phonological investigation of aphasic speech.* The Hague: Mouton.

Blumstein, S.E. (1981). Phonological aspects of aphasia. In M.T. Sarno (Ed.), *Acquired aphasia* (pp. 129-155). New York: Academic Press.

Blumstein, S.E., & Baum, S. (1987). Consonant production deficits in aphasia. In J.H. Ryalls (Ed.), *Phonetic approaches to speech production in aphasia and related disorders* (pp. 3-22). Boston: College-Hill.

Blumstein, S.E., Cooper, W.E., Goodglass, H., Statlender, S., & Gottlieb, J. (1980). Production deficits in aphasia: a voice-onset time analysis. *Brain and Language*, **9**, 153-170.

Blumstein, S.E., Cooper, W.E., Zurif, E.B., & Caramazza, A. (1977). The perception and production of voice-onset time in aphasia. *Neuropsychologia*, **155**, 371-383.

Boomer, D.S., & Laver, J.D.M. (1968). Slips of the tongue. *British Journal of Disorders of Communication*, **3**, 1-12.

Bowman, C.A., Hodson, B.W., & Simpson, R.K. (1980). Oral apraxia and aphasic misarticulations. In R.H. Brookshire (Ed.), *Clinical aphasiology* (pp. 89-95). Minneapolis, MI: BRK Publishers.

Buckingham, H.W. Jr. (1979). Explanation in apraxia with consequences for the concept of apraxia of speech. *Brain and Language*, **8**, 202-226.

Bross, R. (in press). An application of structural linguistics to intelligibility measurement of impaired speakers of English. In R.D. Kent (Ed.), *Intelligibility in speech disorders: Theory, measurement and management*. Philadelphia, John Benjamins.

Collins, M., Rosenbek, J.C., & Wertz, R.T. (1983). Spectrographic analysis of vowel and word duration in apraxia of speech. *Journal of Speech and Hearing Research*, **26**, 224-230.

Cooper, W.E., & Klouda, G.V. (1987). Intonation in aphasic and right-hemisphere-damaged patients. In J.H. Ryalls (Ed.), *Phonetic approaches to speech production in aphasia and related disorders* (pp. 59-77). Boston, College-Hill.

Cooper, W.E., Soares, C., Nicol, J., Michelow, D., & Goloskie, S. (1984). Clausal intonation after unilateral brain damage. *Language and Speech*, **27**, 17-24.

Crary, M.A., & Fokes, J. (1979). Phonological processes in apraxia of speech: a systematic simplification of articulatory performance. *Aphasia-Apraxia-Agnosia*, **1**, 1-12.

Danly, M., de Villiers, J.G., & Cooper, W.E. (1979). Control of speech prosody in Broca's aphasia. In J.J. Wolf & D.H. Klatt (Eds.), *Speech communication: Papers presented at the 97th meeting of the Acoustical Society of America* (pp. 259-263). New York: Acoustical Society of America.

Danly, M., & Shapiro, B. (1982). Speech prosody in Broca's aphasia. *Brain and Language*, **16**, 171-190.

Darley, F.L. (1982). *Aphasia*. Philadelphia, W.B. Saunders.

Darley, F.L., Aronson, A.E., & Brown, J.R. (1975). *Motor speech disorders*. Philadelphia: W.B. Saunders.

Duffy, J.R., & Gawle, C.A. (1984). Apraxic speakers' vowel duration in consonant-vowel-consonant syllables. In J.C. Rosenbek, M.R. McNeil & A.E. Aronson (Eds.), *Apraxia of speech: Physiology acoustics, linguistics, management* (pp. 167-196). San Diego, College-Hill.

Dunlop, J., & Marquardt, T. (1977). Linguistic and articulatory aspects of single word production in apraxia of speech. *Cortex*, **13**, 17-29.

Edwards, S., & Miller, N. (1989). Using EPG to investigate speech errors and motor agility in dyspraxic patients. *Clinical Linguistics and Phonetics*, **3**, 111-126.

Fay, D., & Cutler, A. (1977). Malapropisms and the structure of the mental lexicon. *Linguistic Inquiry*, **8**, 505-520.

Folkins, J.W. (1985). Issues in speech motor control and their relation to the speech of individuals with cleft palate. *Cleft Palate Journal*, **22**, 106-122.

Folkins, J.W. (1988, November). *Acquired apraxia of speech in adults: physiological studies.* Paper presented to the Annual Convention of the American Speech-Language-Hearing Association. Boston, MA.

Forrest, K., Adams, S., & McNeil, M.R. (submitted). *Perioral EMG activity in aphasic, apraxic and dysarthric speakers.* Paper submitted for presentation to the 1990 Clinical Dysarthria Conference, San Antonio, TX.

Fromkin, V. A. (1971). The nonanomolous nature of anomolous utterances. *Language*, **47**, 27-52.

Fromm, D. (1981). *Investigation of movement/EMG parameters in apraxia of speech.* Unpublished Masters Thesis, University of Wisconsin-Madison, Madison, WI.

Gandour, J., & Dardarananda, R. (1984). Prosodic disturbance in aphasia, Vowel length in Thai. *Brain and Language*, **23**, 206-224.

Garrett, M.F. (1975). The analysis of sentence production. In G.H. Bower (Ed.), *The psychology of learning and motivation* (pp. 133-177). New York: Academic Press.

Goodglass, H., & Kaplan, E. (1983). *The assessment of aphasia and related disorders.* Philadelphia: Lea and Febiger.

Gracco, V.L. (1988). Timing factors in the coordination of speech movements. *The Journal of Neuroscience*, 8, 4628-4639.

Hardcastle, W.J. (1987). Electropalatographic study of articulation disorders in verbal dyspraxia. In J.H. Ryalls (Ed.), *Phonetic approaches to speech production in aphasia and related disorders* (pp. 113-136). Boston, College-Hill.

Hewlett, N. (1985). Phonological versus phonetic disorders: some suggested modifications to the current use of the distinction. *British Journal of Disorders of Communication*, **20**, 155-164.

Hoit-Dalgaard, J., Murry, T., & Kopp, H.G. (1983). Voice onset time production and perception in apraxic subjects. *Brain and Language*, **20**, 329-339.

Hough, M.S., & Klich, R.J. (1987). Effects of word length on lip EMG activity in apraxia of speech. In R.H. Brookshire (Ed.), *Clinical aphasiology* (pp. 271-276). Minneapolis, MI: BRK Publishers.

Itoh, M., & Sasanuma, S. (1984). Articulatory movements in apraxia of speech. In J.C. Rosenbek, M.R. McNeil, & A.E. Aronson (Eds.), *Apraxia of speech: Physiology, acoustics, linguistics, management* (pp. 135-166). San Diego: College-Hill.

Itoh, M., & Sasanuma, S. (1987). Articulatory velocities of aphasic patients. In J.H. Ryalls (Ed.), *Phonetic approaches to speech production in aphasia and related disorders* (pp. 137-162). Boston: College-Hill.

Itoh, M., Sasanuma, S., Hirose, H., Yoshioka, H., & Sawashima, M. (1983). Velar movements during speech in two Wernicke aphasic patients. *Brain and Language*, **19**, 283-292.

Itoh, M., Sasanuma, S., Hirose, H., Yoshioka, H., & Ushijima, T. (1980). Abnormal articulatory dynamics in a patient with apraxia of speech: X-ray microbeam observation. *Brain and Language*, **11**, 66-75.

Itoh, M., Sasanuma, S., Tatsumi, I., Murakami, S., Fukusako, Y., & Suzuki, T. (1982). Voice onset time characteristics in apraxia of speech. *Brain and Language*, **17**, 193-210.

Itoh, M., Sasanuma, S., & Ushijima, T. (1979). Velar movements during speech in a patient with apraxia of speech. *Brain and Language*, **7**, 227-239.

Johns, D.F., & Darley, F.L. (1970). Phonemic variability in apraxia of speech. *Journal of Speech and Hearing Research*, **13**, 556-583.

Katz, W.F. (1987). Anticipatory labial and lingual coarticulation in aphasia. In J.H. Ryalls (Ed.), *Phonetic approaches to speech production in aphasia and related disorders* (pp. 221-242). Boston: College-Hill.

Kearns, K.P. (1980). The application of phonological process analysis to adult neuropathologies. In R.H. Brookshire (Ed.), *Clinical aphasiology* (pp. 187-195). Minneapolis, MI: BRK Publishers.

Keller, E. (1975). *Vowel errors in aphasia.* Unpublished Doctoral Dissertation, University of Toronto.

Keller, E. (1978). Parameters for vowel substitutions in Broca's aphasia. *Brain and Language*, **5**, 265-285.

Keller, E. (1984). Simplification and gesture reduction in phonological disorders of apraxia and aphasia. In J.C. Rosenbek, M.R. McNeil & A.E. Aronson (Eds.), *Apraxia of speech: Physiology, acoustics, linguistics and management* (pp. 221-256). San Diego: College-Hill.

Keller, E. (1987). Ultrasound measurements of tongue dorsum movements in articulatory speech impairments. In J.H. Ryalls (Ed.), *Phonetic approaches to speech production in aphasia and related disorders* (pp. 93-112). Boston: College-Hill.

Kent, R.D. (in press). The acoustic and physiologic characteristics of neurologically impaired speech movements. In W.J. Hardcastle & A. Marchal (Eds.), *Speech production and speech modelling.* Amsterdam: Kluwer.

Kent, R.D., & McNeil, M.R. (1987). Relative timing of sentence repetition in apraxia of speech and conduction aphasia. In J.H. Ryalls (Ed.), *Phonetic approaches to speech production in aphasia and related disorders* (pp. 181-220). Boston: College-Hill.

Kent, R.D., & Rosenbek, J.C. (1983). Acoustic patterns of apraxia of speech. *Journal of Speech and Hearing Research*, **26**, 231-249.

Kerschensteiner, M., Poeck, K., & Brunner, E. (1972). The fluency-nonfluency dimension in the classification of aphasic speech. *Cortex*, **8**, 233-247.

Kiritani, S., Itoh, K., & Fujimura, O. (1975). Tongue-pellet tracking by a computer-controlled x-ray microbeam system. *Journal of the Acoustical Society of America*, **57**, 1516-1520.

Klich, R.J., Ireland, J.V., & Weidner, W.E. (1979). Articulatory and phonological aspects of consonant substitutions in apraxia of speech. *Cortex*, **15**, 451-470.

LaPointe, L.L., & Johns, D.F. (1975). Some phonemic characteristics in apraxia of speech. *Journal of Communication Disorders*, **8**, 259-269.

Lebrun, Y., Buyssens, E., & Henneaux, J. (1973). Phonetic aspects of anarthria. *Cortex*, **9**, 126-135.

MacKay, D.G. (1970). Spoonerisms: the structure of errors in the serial order of speech. *Neuropsychologia*, **8**, 323-350.

MacKay;, I.R.A. (1978). *Introducing practical phonetics*. Boston: Little, Brown.

MacNeilage, P.F. (1982). Speech production mechanisms in aphasia. In S. Grillner, B. Lindblom, J. Lubker & A. Persson (Eds.), *Speech and motor control* (pp. 43-60). Elmsford, NY: Pergamon Press.

McNeil, M.R. (1984). Current concepts in adult aphasia. *International Rehabilitation Medicine*, **6**, 347-356.

McNeil, M.R. (1988). Aphasia in the adult. In N.J. Lass, L.V. McReynolds, J. Northern & D.E. Yoder (Eds.), *Handbook of speech-language pathology and audiology* (pp. 738-786). Toronto: B.C. Decker.

McNeil, M.R., & Adams, S. (in press). A comparison of speech kinematics among apraxic, conduction aphasic, ataxic dysarthric and normal geriatric speakers. In T.E. Prescott (Ed.), *Clinical aphasiology*. Boston: College-Hill.

McNeil, M.R., Caliguiri, M., & Rosenbek, J.C. (1989). A comparison of labio-mandibular kinematic durations, displacement, velocities and dysmetrias in apraxic and normal adults. In T.E. Prescott (Ed.), *Clinical aphasiology* (pp. 173-193). Boston: College-Hill.

McNeil, M.R., Hunter, L., Rosenbek, J.C., & Fennell, A. (1987). Vowel errors and consonant distortion in apraxia of speech. *American Speech-Language-Hearing Association Abstract*, **29**, 124.

McNeil, M.R., & Kimelman, M.D.Z. (1986). Toward an integrative information-processing structure of auditory comprehension and processing adult aphasia. In L.L. LaPointe (Ed.), *Seminars in speech and language: Aphasia - nature and assessment* (pp. 123-146). New York: Thieme-Stratton.

McNeil, M.R., Liss, J., Tseng, C-H., & Kent, R.D. (1990). Effects of speech rate on the absolute and relative timing of apraxic and conduction aphasics' sentence production. *Brain and Language*.

McNeil, M.R., Tseng, C-H., Adams, S., & Weismer, G. (in preparation). Interlabial speech movement coordination in normal, apraxic, ataxic dysarthric and conduction aphasic speakers.

McNeil, M.R., Weismer, G., Adams, S., & Mulligan, M. (1990). Oral structure nonspeech motor control in normal, dysarthric, aphasic and apraxic speakers: isometric force and static position control. *Journal of Speech and Hearing Research.*

Mercaitis, P.A. (1983). *Some temporal characteristics of imitative speech in non brain-injured, aphasic, and apraxic adults.* Unpublished Doctoral Dissertation, University of Massachusetts, Amherst, MA.

Mlcoch, A.G., Darley, F.L., & Noll, D. (1982). Articulatory consistency and variability in apraxia of speech. In R.H. Brookshire (Ed.), *Clinical aphasiology* (pp. 235-236). Minneapolis, MI: BRK Publishers.

Munhall, K.G. (1989). Articulatory variability. In P. Square-Storer (Ed.), *Acquired apraxia of speech in aphasic adults* (pp. 64-84). London: Taylor and Francis.

Nespoulous, J.L., Joanette, Y., Ska, B., Caplan, D., & Lecours, A.R. (1987). Production deficits in Broca's and conduction aphasia: Repetition versus reading. In E. Keller & M. Gopnik (Eds.), *Motor and sensory processes of language* (pp. 53-81). London: Lawrence Erlbaum Associates.

Nooteboom, S.G. (1969). The tongue slips into patterns. In A.G. Sciarone, A.J. van Essen & A.A. Van Raad (Eds.), *Leyden studies in linguistics and phonetics* (pp. 114-132). The Hague: Mouton.

Odell, K., McNeil, M.R., Hunter, L., & Rosenbek, J.C. (1990). Perceptual characteristics of consonant productions by apraxic speakers. *Journal of Speech and Hearing Disorders,* **55**, 345-359.

Odell, K., McNeil, M.R., Rosenbek, J.C., & Hunter, L. (in press). A perceptual comparison of prosodic features in apraxia of speech and conduction aphasia. In T.E. Prescott (Ed.), *Clinical aphasiology, Vol 19.* Austin, YTX: Pro Ed.

Robin, D.A., Bean, C., & Folkins, J.W. (1989). Lip movement in apraxia of speech. *Journal of Speech and Hearing Research,* **8**, 512-523.

Rosenbek, J.C., Kent, R.D., & LaPointe, L.L. (1984). Apraxia of speech: an overview and some perspectives. In J.C. Rosenbek, M.R. McNeil & A.E. Aronson (Eds.), *Apraxia of speech: Physiology, acoustics, linguistics, management* (pp. 1-72). San Diego: College-Hill.

Rosenbek, J.C. LaPointe, L.L., & Wertz, R.T. (1989). *Aphasia, a clinical approach.* Boston: College-Hill.

Ryalls, J.H. (1981). Motor aphasia, acoustic correlates of phonetic disintegration in vowels. *Neuropsychologia,* **19**, 365-374.

Ryalls, J.H. (1982). Intonation in Broca's aphasia. *Neuropsychologia,* **20**, 355-360.

Ryalls, J.H. (1984). Some acoustic aspects of fundamental frequency of CVC utterances in aphasia. *Phonetica*, **41**, 103-111.

Ryalls, J.H. (1986). An acoustic study of vowel production in aphasia. *Brain and Language*, **29**, 48-67.

Ryalls, J.H. (1987). Vowel production in aphasia: towards an account of the consonant-vowel dissociation. In J.H. Ryalls (Ed.), *Phonetic approaches to speech production in aphasia and related disorders* (pp. 23-44). Boston: College-Hill.

Ryan, B.F., Joiner, B.L., & Ryan, T.A. (1985). *Minitab* (2nd ed). Boston: Duxbury Press.

Sasanuma, S. (1971). Speech characteristics of a patient with apraxia of speech. *Annual Bulletin, Research Institute of Logopedics and Phoniatrics*, **5**, 85-89.

Schiff, H.B., Alexander, M.P., Naeser, M.A., & Galaburda, A.M. (1983). Aphemia, clinical-anatomic correlations. *Archives of Neurology*, **40**, 720-727.

Shankweiler, D., & Harris, K.S. (1966). An experimental approach to the problem of articulation in aphasia. *Cortex*, **2**, 277-292.

Shankweiler, D., Harris, K.S. , & Taylor, M.L. (1968). Electromyographic studies of articulation in aphasia. *Archives of Physical Medicine and Rehabilitation*, **1**, 1-8.

Shattuck-Hufnagel, S. (1979). Speech errors as evidence for a serial-ordering mechanism in sentence production. In W.E. Cooper & E.C.T. Walker (Eds.), *Sentence processing, psycholinguistic studies presented to Merill Garrett* (pp. 295-342). Hillsdale, N.J.: Lawrence Erlbaum Associates.

Shattuck-Hufnagel, S. (1987). The role of word-onset consonants in speech production planning: new evidence from speech error patterns. In E. Keller & M. Gopnik (Eds.), *Motor and sensory processes of language* (pp. 17-51). Hillsdale, N.J.: Lawrence Erlbaum Associates.

Shattuck-Hufnagel, S., & Klatt, D.H. (1979). Minimal use of features and markedness in speech production. *Journal of Verbal Learning and Verbal Behavior*, **18**, 41-55.

Shewan, C.M., Leeper, H.A. Jr., & Booth, J.C. (1984). An analysis of voice onset time (VOT) in aphasic and normal subjects. In J.C. Rosenbek, M.R. McNeil & A.E. Aronson (Eds.), *Apraxia of speech* (pp. 197-220). San Diego: College-Hill.

Shinn, P., & Blumstein, S.E. (1983). Phonetic disintegration in aphasia: acoustic analysis of spectral characteristics for place of articulation. *Brain and Language*, **20**, 90-114.

Stemberger, J.P. (1982). The nature of segments in the lexicon: evidence from speech errors. *Lingua*, **56**, 235-259.

Strand, E.A. (1987). *Acoustic and response time measures in utterance production, A comparison of apraxic and normal speakers.* Unpublished Doctoral Dissertation, University of Wisconsin-Madison, Madison, WI.

Strand, E.A., & McNeil, M.R. (1987a). Evidence for a motor performance deficit versus a misapplied rule system in the temporal organization of utterances in apraxia of speech. In R.H. Brookshire (Ed.), *Clinical aphasiology* (pp. 260-270). Minneapolis, MI: BRK Publishers.

Strand, E.A., & McNeil, M.R. (1987b). Vowel durations in apraxic speech utterances. *American Speech-Language-Hearing Association Abstract*, **29**, 124.

Trager, G.L., & Smith, H.L. Jr. (1961). An outline of English structure (4th printing). *Studies In linguistics: Occasional papers 3.* Washington, D.C: American Council of Learned Societies.

Trost, J.E., & Canter, G.J. (1974). Apraxia of speech in patients with Broca's aphasia. A study of phoneme production accuracy and error patterns. *Brain and Language*, **1**, 65-79.

Tuller, B. (1984). On categorizing aphasic speech errors. *Neuropsychologia*, **22**, 547-557.

Tuller, B., & Story, R.S. (1987). Anticipatory coarticulation in aphasia. In J.H. Ryalls (Ed.), *Phonetic approaches to speech production in aphasia and related disorders* (pp. 243-260). Boston, College-Hill.

Weismer, G., & Fennell, A.M. (1985). Constancy of (acoustic) relative timing measures in phrase-level utterances. *The Journal of Acoustical Society of America*, **78**, 49-57.

Wertz, R.T., LaPointe, L.L., & Rosenbek, J.C. (1984). *Apraxia of speech in adults: The disorders and its management.* Orlando, FL: Grune and Stratton.

Yorkston, K.M., Beukelman, D.R., & Bell, K.R. (1988). *Clinical management of dysarthric speakers.* San Diego: College-Hill.

Ziegler, W. (1984). What can the spectral characteristics of stop consonants tell us about the realization of place of articulation in Broca's aphasia? A reply to Shinn & Blumstein. *Brain and Language*, **23**, 167-170.

Ziegler, W. (1987). Phonetic realization of phonological contrast in aphasic patients. In J.H. Ryalls (Ed.), *Phonetic approaches to speech production in aphasia and related disorders* (pp. 163-180). Boston: College-Hill.

Ziegler, W., & von Cramon, D. (1986). Spastic dysarthria after acquired brain injury: an acoustic study. *British Journal of Disorders of Communication*, **21**, 173-187.

Ziegler, W., & von Cramon, D. (1985). Anticipatory coarticulation in a patient with apraxia of speech. *Brain and Language*, **26**, 117-130.

Cerebral Control of Speech and Limb Movements
G.E. Hammond (editor)

Chapter 13

HEMISPHERIC CONTROL OF ARTICULATORY SPEECH OUTPUT IN APHASIA

Giuseppe Vallar
Università di Milano

The contributions of left and right hemispheric neural mechanisms to residual articulatory speech output in aphasia produced by left-sided lesions and to the recovery process are discussed. The clinical (case reports of left-brain-damaged patients, who suffered a second left- or right-sided lesion; the amobarbital intracarotid technique) and the experimental (lateral asymmetries in mouth opening during spontaneous speech; simple reaction time to lateralized visual stimuli during concurrent verbal activity) evidence is reviewed. The suggestion is made that in right-handed aphasic patients the undamaged regions of the left hemisphere play a main role in the articulatory programming aspects of (recovered and/or residual) speech output, while the contribution of the right hemisphere appears comparatively minor. This pattern may be contrasted with the recovered and residual deficit of speech comprehension of aphasic patients, where the involvement of right hemispheric mechanisms appears to be more substantial.

Since the end of the XIX century, the issue of the hemispheric control of speech output in aphasia has drawn the attention of students of language deficits produced by brain lesions. The theoretical interest of the problem concerns the role of the different cerebral regions spared by the lesion in (a) residual performance -- an issue related to their potential capability of taking over at least in part a function previously performed by the primarily committed regions -- and (b) their role in functional recovery.

In this chapter I shall review the clinical and experimental studies concerning the role of the left hemispheric regions spared by the lesion, and of the right hemisphere, in aphasic speech output. The issue of the neurological mechanisms involved in residual (and recovered) comprehension of aphasic patients will be considered only when relevant to the main aim of the chapter.

1. Clinical Studies

1.1. Double Successive Lesions

As early as in 1895, William Gowers explained recovery from aphasia associated with damage to the left hemisphere in terms of a functional take over by the homologous regions in the right hemisphere (see a related account in Kleist, 1962).[1] Gowers' main empirical argument corroborating the right hemisphere hypothesis was a clinical observation. In a right-handed patient, rendered aphasic by a left hemispheric lesion and in whom some recovery took place, a second lesion located in the right hemisphere produced a worsening of the aphasic deficit.

This hypothesis is based on the following underlying assumption: in the right side of the brain the regions homologous to the left-sided language areas are to some extent involved in language processing, at least in that they have the potential capability of becoming the actual neural correlate of residual and, if amelioration does occur, recovered speech. In the intact brain the linguistic capabilities of the right hemisphere may be inhibited by the dominant left hemisphere (see e.g., Moscovitch, 1976) or a cooperative interaction may occur (Berlucchi, 1982). This issue, very important on its own, is not central to the problem of the role of the right hemisphere in aphasic speech output. The putative right hemispheric contribution may represent the operation of neural networks, inhibited by or cooperating with the left hemisphere in the normal brain, that, in order to take over the defective function, may undergo modifications in their

---

1. Kleist (1962) suggested a left-to-right functional shift in order to explain the preserved comprehension of patient Spratt, who suffered a large left temporal lesion. Repetition was on the contrary disrupted, since the pathway from the right temporal lobe to the left frontal lobe was interrupted by the left temporal lesion. Kleist, however, related the possibility of this takeover by the right hemisphere to atypical patterns of hemispheric lateralization, since Spratt was ambidextrous. This explanation, therefore, may not apply to the generality of right- handed aphasic patients.

patterns of connections and at a more basic molecular level. It should be noted, however, that there seems not to be neurophysiological evidence suggesting that a given cerebral area may inhibit the homologous or other contralateral areas via the commissural projections (Berlucchi, 1982).

Table 1. The effect of a second lesion upon the aphasic output deficit produced by a unilateral lesion.

Case	I Lesion	Recovery	II Lesion
1 (F)	Rh, A	no	Lh, A not
Lesions:	- left I (F2, F3, i atrophic)		worsened (2 yrs)
	- right I (F3 post, T perisylvian, i, lent. n.)		
2 (F)	Rh, A	yes	Lh, A*
Lesions:	- left I (F2, F3)		(11 yrs)
	- right I (F3, P, T3)		
3 (M)	mild Rh, A	yes (paraphasias)	Lh, A (output:
Lesions:	- left (F2, F3)		'Ah')
	- right (F2, F3)		(10 days)
4 (F)	Rh, motor A	yes (complete)	Lh, A
Lesions:	- left (i, put, ic)		(1 yr)
	- right (F3, lent. n., ic, i)		
5	A	yes	A
Lesions:	- left-first (F, Broca's region)		(5 yrs)
	- left-second (F, abscess)		
6 (F)	Rh, motor A	yes (dysarthria)	Lh, motor A
Lesions:	- left H (F subc [Broca's region])		(9 yrs)
	- right I (F subc [Broca's region], lent. n., i)		
7 (F)	Rh, A	yes	Lh, only alexia (5 yrs)
8 (M, left-handed)	Lh, A	yes (complete)	Rh, only right-hand agraphia (7 months)

Table 1 continued overleaf

Table 1 cont. The effect of a second lesion upon the aphasic output deficit produced by a unilateral lesion.

Case	I Lesion	Recovery	II Lesion
9 (M)	Rh, A mute	yes (complete)	mute
Lesions:	- left I (mid. post F [Broca's region])		(1 year)
	- right I (more extensive: inf F, T)		
10 (F)	Rh, mute	yes (incomplete)	mute
Lesions:	- left I (large, FTP perisylvian)		(9 years)
	- right I (less extensive, ant FTP perisylvian)		

* In this case recovery after the second lesion again occurred; a third and a fourth stroke six years after the second produced a complete and permanent aphasia.

Notes: In cases 1-7 and 9-10 the first lesion involved the left hemisphere. The second lesion was in the right hemisphere in cases 1-4, 6-7, 9-10; and in the left hemisphere in case 5. In case 8, a left-handed patient, the first and second lesion involved the right and the left hemisphere, respectively. In cases 7 and 8 no pathological data are available and the side of the cerebral lesions may be inferred from the clinical neurological deficits.
Legend: A: aphasia; R/Lh: right/left hemiplegia; I: infarction; H: hemorrhage; F: frontal; T: temporal; P: parietal; subc: subcortical; lent. n.: lenticular nucleus; i: insula; ic: internal caspule; put: putamen; ant: anterior; post: posterior; mid: middle. The time interval between the first and the second lesions is in brackets.
Sources: [1]: Vulpian & Mongie (1866), cited in Moutier (1908, p. 278); [2]: Charcot & Dutil (1893), cited in Moutier (1908, p. 288); [3]: Barlow, cited in Nielsen (1946, p. 106-107); [4] Kuttner (1930); [5] Morsellis, cited in Kuttner (1930); [6] Nielsen (1946, pp. 146-151); [7] Ibidem, p. 154; [8] Ibidem, p. 155; [9]: D.N. Levine & Mohr (1979), case 1; [10]: Ibidem, case 3.

A perusal of the few published cases of patients with speech output deficits produced by left hemispheric damage, followed by a successive contralateral or, in a few cases, ipsilateral lesion does not allow, however, unequivocal conclusions. As shown in Table 1, in a number of patients rendered aphasic by a left-sided lesion, a second right-sided lesion, occurring after a more-or-less complete recovery of function, indeed brought about an aphasic deficit. This was not systematically the case, however.

1.2. The Amobarbital Intracarotid Injection Technique

The problem has been approached by the Wada technique, where the intracarotid injection of sodium amytal produces the temporary inactivation of one cerebral hemisphere. The interpretation of results obtained by this technique is broadly similar to that of the successive stroke cases, with the main difference that the amobarbital injection affects, albeit temporarily, the whole hemisphere.

In an early study, Mempel, Srebrzynska, Subczynska, and Zarski (1963) examined four left-brain-damaged patients in whom some recovery from aphasia had occurred. In one patient with a traumatic lesion, a right-sided injection produced aphasia; in three patients with left hemispheric tumors, however, this effect was much less pronounced. Kinsbourne (1971) observed a temporary arrest of speech in two left-brain-damaged aphasic patients after right-sided administration of amobarbital; a left-sided injection, that was also given to a third case, did not produce major modifications in the patients' speech output. Czopf (1972) examined a larger series of 25 right-handed aphasics, with non-homogeneous etiologies (cerebrovascular attacks, tumors, traumatic lesions, one case with cerebral atrophy) and duration of illness. In 22 cases specific effects of the injections were observed: (a) in ten patients with a severe deficit and a variable but often long duration of illness (3 weeks - 13 years) speech output was abolished by a right-sided injection; in two such cases a left-sided injection had minor and comparatively shorter effects; (b) in nine patients with a less severe and more recent deficit (the duration of disease ranged from 12 days to two years) a right-sided injection produced a slight worsening of the aphasic deficit; similar effects were observed in four patients of this subgroup after a left-sided injection; (c) finally, in three patients with slight and very recent aphasic deficits (the duration of disease was less than 30 days), the right injection had no effects; in one of these patients a left-sided injection produced a severe aphasia.

1.3. Comment

The observations reviewed above do not provide unambiguous information; they suggest instead that, under specific circumstances, both the undamaged regions of the left hemisphere and/or the right hemisphere may take over language function. There are, in addition, specific problems, that make the interpretation of such studies even more complex. The clinical material summarized in Table 1, with the exception of cases 9 and 10, suffers first of all from an inadequate assessment of language function, that, in a number of cases, is limited to basic information such as the presence or absence of aphasia. The two patients recently studied by Basso,

Gardelli, Grassi, and Mariotti (1989) were however given a complete standard language examination after both the first and the second stroke. These two female cases became global aphasics following a large left hemispheric lesion and showed a remarkable degree of recovery of both speech comprehension and production. After a second stroke in the right hemisphere a definite worsening of both receptive and expressive aspects of language occurred. The amobarbital technique, on the other hand, produces a complete temporary inactivation of the injected hemisphere, and does not allow more detailed specification of the contribution of the two sides of the brain to aphasic speech output.

Let us consider now the issue in the light of current functional models of speech production: they are conceived as multi-component systems, with different levels of representation, such as the message, functional, positional, phonetic and articulatory levels of Garrett (1982), or the semantic, prosodic, lexical, syntactic and phonological assembly systems of Butterworth (1980). These different levels of processing may have discrete neural correlates (see, e.g., Cappa, Cavallotti & Vignolo, 1981; Petersen, Fox, Posner, Mintun, & Raichle, 1989) and brain damage may disrupt speech output by selectively interfering with the operation of one or more such levels. In addition, the role of the undamaged regions of the left hemisphere and of the entirely spared right hemisphere may not be identical for all such levels. For instance, data from split-brain and left hemispherectomy patients suggest that the profile of linguistic competence of the isolated left hemisphere is characterized by good receptive lexical semantics, with limited syntax and phonology (Zaidel, 1985). On the basis of evidence of this sort, one might extrapolate that during the recovery process the takeover by the right hemisphere may be more effective at the semantic or message level than, say, at the more peripheral phonological/articulatory levels.

That the takeover of function by the right hemisphere is not an all-or-none process, but may involve some, but not all components of the language systems, is illustrated by a case reported by Nielsen (1946). The patterns of impairment produced by both the first left and the second left- or right-sided lesions are related to factors such as the site and the extension of the cerebral damage. A woman (case Lulu L., Nielsen, 1946, pp. 152-154) suffered a left hemispheric stroke that left her with an auditory comprehension disorder. After recovery, three months later, she had a second stroke, that produced a total impairment of speech output, but did not affect comprehension of spoken language. A post-mortem examination of the brain revealed old temporal and recent frontal left-sided lesions, involving Wernicke's and Broca's areas, respectively. Nielsen, in line with Gower's original suggestion, argued that the neural mechanism of recovery from the auditory comprehension deficit produced by the first stroke involved functional takeover by the temporal areas in the right hemisphere homologous to Wernicke's region. This mechanism easily explains why the second stroke, which destroyed Broca's area, affected only speech output without disrupting auditory comprehension, which was then supported by the right hemisphere. This position also predicts that in a patient recovered from a Wernicke-type aphasia produced by a left temporo-parietal lesion, a second successive lesion located in the homologous right hemispheric regions should produce a similar aphasic deficit. A few clinical observations, where the lesions were localized by CT Scan, indicate that this may indeed be the case (Lee, Nakada, Deal, Lin, & Kwee, 1984; see also related evidence in Mazzocchi & Vignolo, 1979, pp. 633-634).

When the clinical material summarized in Table 1 is considered in the light of multi-component models of the sort mentioned above, it is clear that the role of the undamaged left and right hemispheric regions in recovery of speech output in aphasia cannot be easily specified. The only conclusion that may be safely drawn is that, in a number of patients, the right hemisphere contributes to aspects of aphasic speech output. A similar line of reasoning may be applied to the amobarbital studies. Since this method produces a global, albeit temporary hemispheric inactivation, the worsening of aphasic speech after a right-sided injection indicates a right hemispheric contribution to speech output. When in a given patient, such as in Kinsbourne's (1971) cases, a left sided injection has little or no disrupting effect, the conclusion may be drawn that aphasic speech production processes are implemented in the right hemisphere.

Finally the temporal dimension should be considered. A given function, such as the component processes of the speech production system, may be taken over after left hemispheric damage due to a cerebrovascular attack by the undamaged right hemisphere in an early post-lesional phase. However, the undamaged regions of the left hemisphere may again become involved in that function in a later stage, after the more-or-less complete regression of the diaschisis phenomena that take place mainly in the hemispheric regions ipsilateral to the focal structural lesion (see, e.g., Vallar, Perani, Cappa, Messa, & Fazio, 1988a).[2] This pattern of recovery may occur when the cerebral region(s) primarily

---

2. The term 'diaschisis' (Monakow, 1914) is at present used to refer to the (typically temporary) more or less complete inactivation, as revealed by reduction of rCBF and metabolism, of a cerebral region. The neural mechanisms of diaschisis involve the structural damage of afferent neural pathways to a given cerebral area, that, although not directly injured, at least at the anatomical level, is functionally deranged (see Feneey & Baron, 1986).

committed to a given function is structurally spared, but temporarily dysfunctional due to the diaschisis produced by the damage of a remote, but connected, region. If this is the case, the evidence for a right or left hemispheric involvement in speech output might be related to the interval between the onset of the disease and the time of assessment by the Wada test, or the natural experiment provided by a second lesion. A different pattern of impairment may take place when the left hemispheric lesion involves a primarily committed region. In this latter case a comparatively minor recovery may occur, and the contribution from the undamaged right hemisphere may be more substantial (see an illustrative example of such patterns in Knopman, Rubens, Selnes, Klassen, & M.W. Meyer, 1984).

In the extreme case of large left hemispheric lesions, involving the whole language area and surrounding regions, any recovery may be attributable to the undamaged right hemisphere (e.g., Cummings, Benson, Walsh, & H.L. Levine, 1979). In such circumstances, however, the possible contribution of spared subcortical structures should not be entirely disregarded (see a related discussion in Vallar et al., 1988a).

2. Experimental Studies of the Hemispheric Contributions to Aphasic Speech Output

In the clinical studies mentioned above the conclusion that aphasic speech output is based on right (or left) hemispheric mechanisms is not based on a direct measure of hemispheric activity, but inferred from the behavioral effects of a brain lesion. Two recent studies have used behavioral techniques that allow assessment of left and right hemispheric contributions to the articulatory processes of speech production. These methods, initially used in normal subjects to explore the normal patterns of performance, have been subsequently employed in aphasic patients.

2.1. Lateral Asymmetries in Mouth Opening During Spontaneous Speech

Graves and coworkers have recently observed that over 80% of normal right-handed individuals show a more frequent right-sided mouth opening during speech; this mouth asymmetry occurs, they argue, as the contralateral left hemisphere controls articulation (see Graves, Goodglass & Landis, 1982; Graves, 1983). If this is the case, the technique may be used to assess the hemispheric control of speech output in aphasia. The persistence of a right-sided mouth asymmetry would indicate left hemispheric control, as in normal subjects; a lack of asymmetry or a reversed (left-sided) asymmetry would suggest, on the contrary, a shift of the speech output control systems to the right hemisphere, even though the potential bias produced by the co-occurrence of a right-sided facial palsy should be considered.

Graves and Landis (1985) examined 20 right-handed aphasics, with an average disease duration of 15 months. Fifteen out of 20 patients had a fluent aphasia. Mouth opening was photographed during a variety of speech production conditions, that included, according to the Jacksonian dichotomy of two levels of language organization (e.g., Jackson, 1915), 'voluntary/propositional' tasks (spontaneous speech, repetition, word list generation) and 'automatic' tasks (counting 1 to 10, reciting the days of the week, singing). Fifteen out of 20 patients showed a right-sided mouth opening in the propositional tasks, in spite of the right-sided facial palsy present in 16 patients. This makes an interpretation in terms of lesion effects highly implausible (see also below).

During the automatic tasks, a left-sided mouth asymmetry was observed in 19 out of 20 patients. Given the co-occurrence of a right-sided facial palsy this finding cannot be safely taken as an indication of a right hemispheric control. Graves and Landis note however that eight patients showed a crossover interaction, with right and left-sided mouth openings in the propositional and automatic tasks, respectively, while a reversed crossover was never observed. Taken together, these data might indicate at least a less complete control by the left hemisphere of these automatic tasks compared with the propositional tasks. It should however be noted that normal control data for the automatic tasks were lacking in Graves and Landis' study, while for the propositional tasks reference was made to previous experiments in normals (e.g., Graves et al., 1982). The lack of a right-sided asymmetry might therefore be interpreted in terms either of a left-to-right functional shift concerning automatic speech or of a hemispheric pattern also present in normal subjects, namely: a more relevant role of the right hemisphere in automatic, as compared to propositional, speech. Consistent with this latter view, in subjects without evidence of focal lesions early studies (Larsen, Skinhøj, & Lassen, 1978; see also Ryding, Bradvik & Ingvar, 1987) of regional cerebral blood flow (rCBF) by Xenon133 have shown bilateral hemispheric activation during automatic tasks (counting repeatedly 1-20, reciting the days of the week). A more recent study (Petersen et al., 1989) performed in normal subjects using Positron Emission Tomography has found that a propositional (see Graves and Landis, 1985) repetition task produces hemispheric activation (assessed by rCBF change compared with a baseline condition) in a number of cerebral areas, including: the rolandic mouth cortex and the supplementary motor area, bilaterally; opercular cortex in the left hemisphere, near Broca's area; and a portion of the lateral sylvian cortex in the right hemisphere. This study, while showing that speech output, as assessed by a repetition task, involves a bi-hemispheric contribution, indicates a specific role of the premotor regions of the left hemisphere, as classically maintained.

As noted above, most patients had fluent aphasia, even though information concerning the time course of the deficit was not provided. It may then prove to be the case that in such patients the more peripheral aspects of speech output processes (such as articulatory programming) were relatively spared. If mouth asymmetry provides an indication of hemispheric control of speech output at the level of articulatory programming, as Graves and Landis seem to argue, their results might refer to the operation of an articulatory component that was spared in their patients from the beginning of their disease, and therefore remained lateralized to the left hemisphere. If this is the case, the observation of the normal right-sided mouth opening in the speech of a group of mainly fluent aphasics would not provide evidence for a left-to-right functional shift, simply because the functional (articulatory) component under investigation was never disrupted by brain damage. Graves and Landis do not mention any mouth asymmetry difference between fluent and nonfluent aphasics, but the nonfluent group might have been too small to allowing the observation of a specific pattern.

2.2. Simple Reaction Time to Lateralized Visual Stimuli During Concurrent Verbal Activity

It has long been known (see e.g., Berlucchi, Heron, Hyman, Rizzolatti, & Umiltà, 1971, and references therein) that simple manual reaction time to lateralized unstructured visual stimuli is shorter when the stimulus is presented in the same half-space as the responding hand (uncrossed conditions: left visual half-field/left hand; right visual half-field/right hand), as compared with the crossed conditions (left visual half- field/right hand; right visual half-field/left hand). This advantage of the ipsilateral responses in simple reaction time has been attributed to the callosal transfer of information that is required in the case of manual responses to contralateral stimuli (Berlucchi et al., 1971). Interpretations in terms of spatial compatibility are unlikely, since the advantage of the anatomically uncrossed conditions, that do not require callosal transfer, is not affected by experimental manipulations whereby the responding hands are crossed, namely: the left hand in the right half-space and the right hand in the left half-space. In such conditions the relative effects of anatomical and spatial compatibility may be contrasted. The crucial experiment has been performed by Anzola, Bertoloni, Buchtel & Rizzolatti and Berlucchi, Crea, Di Stefano, & Tassinari in 1977. Normal subjects show shorter latencies in the anatomically compatible, but spatially incompatible conditions (e.g., left-sided stimulus/left hand in the right half-space), as compared with the anatomically incompatible, but spatially compatible conditions (e.g., left-sided stimulus/right hand in the left half-space).

The anatomical pathways involved in these simple manual reactions to unstructured visual stimuli, such as dots or flashes of light, have been elucidated in some detail. Unstructured stimuli do not require complex visual processing. It is therefore likely to be the case that these simple motor reactions make use of a direct pathway that projects from the peristriate areas to the premotor regions, which, in turn, connect reciprocally with the ipsilateral motor cortex (Pandya & Kuypers, 1969). This route may be used in the case of uncrossed reactions, such as a right-hand response to a stimulus presented in the right half-field. In the case of crossed reactions a callosal transfer is needed. There is no callosal connection between the motor areas corresponding to the hand (Karol & Pandya, 1971; but see Gould, Cusik, Pons, & Kaas, 1986). The premotor region, on the contrary, contains a heavy concentration of callosal terminations (Karol & Pandya, 1971) and may be the locus of the callosal transfer.

The hypothesis of a premotor locus of the transfer is consistent with two sets of empirical data. Berlucchi et al. (1971) argued that, were the callosal connections of the visual cortex involved in the transfer, the difference between crossed and uncrossed reactions should increase when the stimulus is moved out of the region of the visual field connected by the corpus callosum (see a recent review of the organization of callosal connections in Berlucchi, Tassinari & Antonini, 1986). Contrary to this prediction, in humans the difference between crossed and uncrossed responses in simple manual reaction time is constant, independent of the degree of eccentricity of the stimulus (Berlucchi et al., 1971). Secondly, Vallar, Sterzi and Basso (1988b) found that in patients with unilateral left hemispheric lesions, mainly involving the posterior regions (as inferred from CT Scan data and the lack of motor deficits), the difference between crossed and uncrossed reactions (1.87 ms) was broadly comparable to the normal data: 2-3 ms in normal young subjects (Jeeves, 1969; Berlucchi et al., 1971), 8 ms in elderly individuals (Tassinari, 1981). Conversely in left-brain-damaged paretic patients with a major involvement of the frontal regions an abnormally high interhemispheric transmission time (23.33 ms) was found (see related data in Tassinari, 1981). This increase of the difference between crossed and uncrossed reactions in the paretic group cannot be attributed to nonspecific effects of brain damage, as the overall average latencies were comparable in the paretic and nonparetic patients. This lengthening of the interhemispheric transmission time in the group with anterior lesions may be easily explained by assuming that the callosal transfer takes place between the two homologous premotor areas. Were such areas or connections damaged, alternative longer routes, possibly involving subcortical structures (Jeeves, 1969) or back through more posterior regions, would be used. The possibility of ipsilateral corticospinal projections should also be considered (Kinsbourne and Fisher, 1971). To summarize, in normal individuals the anatomical pathways involved in simple reaction time to unstructured stimuli are likely to be the following: (1) striate and peristriate cortex; (2) premotor areas; (3a) ipsilateral motor cortex, for uncrossed (ipsilateral) responses; (3b) callosal transfer to contralateral premotor areas and then to motor cortex for crossed (contralateral) responses.[3]

Rizzolatti and his coworkers have recently investigated the effects of a variety of concurrent tasks on this simple visuo-motor reaction time paradigm. One of their findings has proved to be relevant to the issue of the hemispheric lateralization of speech output in aphasia. Rizzolatti, Bertoloni and Buchtel (1979) reported that in normal right-handed subjects a concomitant verbal task (counting backwards aloud) produces an increase of latencies to unstructured stimuli (circles of light) presented in the right visual half-field, as compared with left-sided stimuli. The effect is independent of the responding hand, occurring with both the left and the right hand. In the anatomical flow-chart of simple visuo-motor reaction time described above, the interference takes place in the left premotor cortex. The motor cortex is unlikely to be the locus of the effect, as there is no difference between the responding hands. The visual regions are also improbable loci of interference. Concurrent verbal memory tasks not only do not negatively affect the performance of the left hemisphere in dot detection, but, if anything, may bring about some improvement (Davidoff, 1977). More specifically, Rizzolatti et al. (1979) mentioned in the discussion of their experiments that the counting backwards task had no differential half-field effects on the detection of near-threshold lateralized spots. The motor programming nature of the interfering effect has been subsequently corroborated by a series of experiments of Rizzolatti, Bertoloni and De Bastiani (1982), who assessed the effects of three concurrent tasks on simple reaction time to lateralized unstructured stimuli: the attentional task required the detection and repetition of a letter among strings of four digits or three digits and one letter; the memory task required the retention of four digit strings; the shadowing task required immediate repetition of single digits. The 'attention' and 'memory' tasks produced an overall lengthening of latencies, without any interference with the performance of

---

3. In Vallar et al. (1988b, p. 518, lines 19-21) we inadvertently wrote that the pathway involved in simple visuo-motor reactions included the 'prefrontal', instead of the 'premotor' frontal regions. We take advantage of this opportunity to amend this error.

the left hemisphere. In fact, the memory task brought about an advantage for right-sided stimuli (see also Davidoff, 1977), that can be explained in terms of facilitatory activation of the left hemisphere by the verbal nature of the stimuli and the task (see Kinsbourne, 1970; Hellige & Cox, 1976). On the contrary, the shadowing task, that required continuous motor programming and speech production, had comparatively minor general effects, but produced a selective lengthening of latencies to stimuli presented in the right visual half-field, an interference with the performance of the left hemisphere in the primary simple reaction time task.

Taken together, these experiments offer a paradigm that may provide information concerning the hemispheric lateralization of the motor programming stage of speech production in both normal subjects and aphasic patients, as Rizzolatti et al. (1979) indeed suggested. The logic of the experiment is similar to that of the mouth-opening study of Graves and Landis (1985). If in aphasic patients, like in normal right-handed individuals, the motor programming stage of speech output is located in the left hemisphere, a verbal concurrent activity should produce a greater lengthening of latencies to stimuli presented in the right visual half-field. On the contrary, had a left-to-right shift of the hemispheric components involved in aphasic speech output taken place, the verbal concurrent task should either produce no hemi-field asymmetries or bring about a right half-field advantage: this would suggest a takeover by the right hemisphere. An obvious limitation to the utilization of this technique in investigating the hemispheric lateralization of speech output in brain-damaged patients is that only individuals without visual field defects are suitable for the investigation, as the visual stimuli should be presented in both half-fields. This limits the generality of the conclusions that can be drawn on the basis of such a paradigm.

This experiment was done by Vallar et al. (1988b), who examined 20 right-handed aphasic nonhemianopic left-brain-damaged patients, in a chronic stable phase. On the basis of a standard language examination (Basso, Capitani & Vignolo, 1979) ten patients were classified as 'nonfluent' (Broca's aphasics) and ten as 'fluent' (Wernicke, amnestic and conduction aphasics) at the time of testing. Approximately two thirds of the patients had shown a clinically relevant improvement of their expressive deficit. Rizzolatti et al.'s (1979) paradigm was adapted to the patients' characteristics. The manual responses were given only by the nonparetic left hand, ipsilateral to the damaged left hemisphere. The interfering concurrent verbal activity was titrated according to the patients' output abilities, ranging from counting one-to-ten in the more severely impaired nonfluent patients to counting backwards by 2's in mild fluent aphasics.

The results are shown in Figures 1-A (control simple reaction time) and 1-B (simple reaction time during the verbal concurrent task).

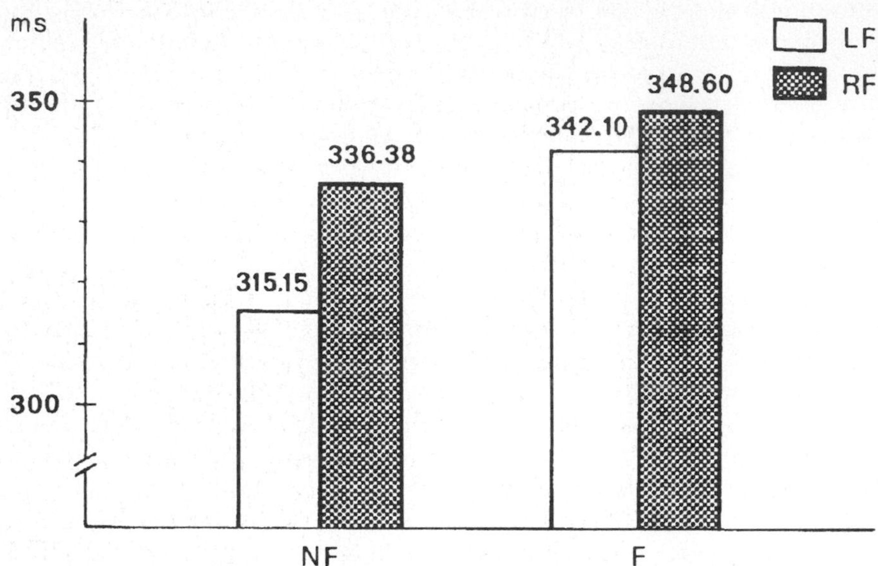

Figure 1-A. Control task. Simple reaction time in ms of nonfluent (NF, N = 10) and fluent (F, N = 10) aphasics, by half-field of presentation of the stimulus (RF = right half-field; LF = left half-field). All patients responded with their unaffected left hand.

As expected, in the control test patients showed reduced latencies in the uncrossed (left-sided visual stimulus/left hand) as compared with the crossed condition (right-sided visual stimulus/left hand). In the concurrent task both fluent and nonfluent patients showed not only the predictable overall increase of latencies, but also slower responses to stimuli presented in the right half-field. The advantage of the left visual half-field increased from 13.8 ms in the control task to 35.64 ms in the concurrent task.

This result was expected in the case of the fluent patients, in whom the articulatory programming components were assumed to be relatively spared, and, therefore, still implemented in the left hemisphere. The observation of a similar pattern in the nonfluent group, in which the articulatory programming components were more likely to have been disrupted by the left-sided brain damage, was less obvious. This latter finding also indicates that in patients with articulatory difficulties, the premotor components of speech output are implemented in the undamaged regions of the left hemisphere.

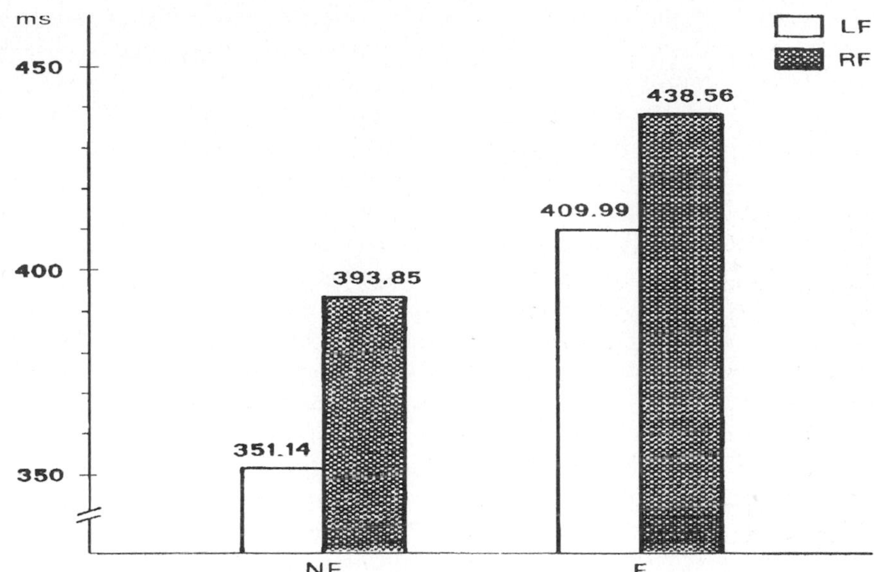

Figure 1-B. Concurrent task. Counting backwards during simple visuo-motor reaction time. Figures reprinted from Vallar et al. (1988b) with permission of Pergamon Press.

The left visual half-field advantage in the concurrent task with respect to the control increased in 19 out of 20 patients, the one exception being a 57 year-old Broca's aphasic who showed a reduction of the left visual half-field advantage from 11.88 ms in the control task to 4.25 ms in the concurrent task, suggesting a minor involvement of the undamaged regions of the left hemisphere in residual speech production. This patient, who had received speech therapy over a six-month period, had a poor oral output. A very similar 55 year-old Broca's aphasic, however, who also had poor speech output, showed a 27.53 ms increase of the left visual half-field advantage from the control to the concurrent task, suggesting in this case a left hemispheric contribution to speech production. Data of this sort raise the possibility that the relative contributions of the right hemisphere and of the undamaged regions of the left hemisphere may not be constant across different patients, but are related to individual variability. This issue clearly needs to be explored.

The interpretation of the Vallar et al.'s (1988b) data should also consider that the clinical distinction between fluent and nonfluent patients does not reflect only the presence or absence of articulatory difficulties, but also parameters such as rate of speech and phrase length that are not necessarily related to the articulatory programming component investigated by the reaction time task. As articulatory difficulties were present in the nonfluent but not in the fluent group, however, the articulatory programming component assessed by the experimental task was likely to be impaired in the former, and not in the latter patients. The localization of the left hemispheric lesions comports with this view. The nonfluent patients had a major involvement of the frontal regions that were comparatively spared in the fluent group (see comparable anatomo-clinical data in Benson, 1967; Mazzocchi & Vignolo, 1979).

The concurrent task methodology used in this experiment is open to the objection that the increase of latencies to dots presented in the right visual half-field (left hemisphere) may represent a nonspecific lesion effect. According to this hypothesis, the verbal task overloads the damaged left hemisphere, producing a larger difference between crossed (stimulus in the right visual half-field) and uncrossed (stimulus in the left visual half-field) responses given by the left hand. Some indication that the results of Vallar et al. (1988b) cannot by attributed to a nonspecific effect of brain damage is provided by the performance of four right-handed right-brain- damaged patients in the simple reaction time tasks given to the 20 aphasic left-brain-damaged patients. The four patients with lesions in the right hemisphere had neither visual field deficits nor left-sided spatial neglect and used their unaffected right hand to respond. In the control simple reaction time task the average latencies to dots ipsilateral (presented in the right visual half-field) and contralateral (presented in the left visual half-field) to the responding hand were 366.9 ms and 394.72 ms, respectively, with an advantage of the uncrossed reactions amounting to 27.82 ms. The advantage of the uncrossed reactions, that do not require callosal transfer, is the expected finding in both normal individuals (see e.g., Bisiach, Mini, Sterzi, & Vallar 1982) and in brain-damaged patients (Vallar et al., 1988b). In this latter group it might be traced back, at least in part, to a nonspecific effect of the lesion, as the uncrossed reactions (right-sided stimuli/right hand) engage only the undamaged left hemisphere, while the crossed reactions (left-sided stimuli/right hand) involve also the injured right hemisphere. An indication that this might indeed be the case is provided by the size of the interhemispheric difference (27.82 ms) found in the four right-brain-damaged patients, higher than the 8 ms value observed by Tassinari (1981) in his elderly control group. When the four right brain-damaged patients were engaged in the verbal articulatory task of counting backwards, their average latencies to dots ipsilateral and contralateral to the responding hand were however 432.57 ms and 412.45 ms, respectively, with a 20.12 ms advantage of the crossed responses. This pattern cannot be explained in terms of a nonspecific lesion effect. This would have produced an increase of the disadvantage of the crossed reactions (left-sided stimuli/right hand), that engage the right hemisphere. The longer latencies to dots presented in the right visual half-field in the concurrent task condition are, on the contrary, entirely compatible with the view that the counting activity has a specific effect, which involves left hemispheric components, and therefore interferes with the processing of stimuli directly delivered to this hemisphere. The data from these four right-brain-damaged patients render improbable the hypothesis that the hemispheric effects of concurrent verbal activity in simple reaction time are attributable to nonspecific lesion effects.

3. A Conclusion

The two experimental studies reviewed above have made use of very different behavioral techniques that allow determination of the hemispheric lateralization of the components involved in the motor programming of aphasic speech output. The results converge in showing that the undamaged regions of the left hemisphere, rather that the contralesional right hemisphere, play a main role in the motor programming aspects of aphasic speech production.

On the other hand, both the clinical data from patients with two successive left and right hemispheric lesions, and the observations in patients who underwent the intracarotid amytal test, suggest that in a not negligible number of cases the right hemisphere may play a relevant role in aphasic speech output.

How can these divergent sets of data be reconciled? One possible interpretation is that the takeover by the right hemisphere does not concern the programming articulatory component assessed by the mouth opening and reaction time studies discussed above, but more central subsystems. Most production systems have a hierarchical organization, whereby the relatively peripheral phonological and articulatory output systems are controlled by and receive input from the more central prosodic, syntactic, lexical and semantic systems, to which they may provide feedbacks (see e.g., Butterworth, 1980; Bock, 1982). Given this hierarchical organization, a dysfunction of the more central components would produce a disturbance, or at least a reduction, of speech output. Consider the hypothetical case of a left-brain-damaged aphasic patient, who in the early post-stroke phase had speech production difficulties, including deficits at the articulatory programming level, and who subsequently showed recovery of speech output. The neural mechanism of such a recovery might comprise a reorganization of the motor programming components in the undamaged left hemispheric regions, while the right hemisphere might take over aspects of the more central semantic and lexical components of the production system. This is not a remote possibility, as the right hemispheric linguistic capabilities seem to be more developed at the lexical-semantic level (see a review by Zaidel, 1985). A second right hemispheric lesion might then affect such more central systems, producing what would clinically manifest as a deficit of speech production. This might clearly be the case when the worsening of aphasic speech output is produced by a global, albeit temporary, inactivation of the right hemisphere, such as in the intracarotid amytal test. This hypothesis clearly applies to patients, such as the two global aphasics of Basso et al. (1989), who recovered from a severe aphasic deficit produced by a left hemispheric lesion, and showed a worsening of both receptive and expressive aspects of speech, after the second right hemispheric stroke.

An alternative possibility is that the second lesion affects speech output because the primary articulatory motor components of the production system are disrupted, even though the articulatory programming system itself is spared. This hypothesis should be taken into consideration, as it is well known that bilateral lesions involving the perirolandic regions (including the motor area) may produce a total deficit of overt articulation that may not be associated with aphasic deficits (see e.g., Villa & Caltagirone, 1984; Vallar & Cappa, 1987; Mao, Coull, Golper, & Rau, 1989). In Vallar & Cappa's (1987) patient, the phonological level was assessed in detail: the processing, short-term storage, and articulatory rehearsal components were spared and the deficit was confined to the grapheme-to-phoneme (phonological recoding) process. These data suggest that the complete absence of speech output in these anarthric non-aphasic patients reflects the impairment of a component concerned with the actual implementation of articulated speech, rather than the deficit of a more central articulatory programming system. In such patients with a selective deficit of overt articulation, not associated with aphasic disorders, speech output may be abolished by bilateral lesions, that have occurred in two successive steps. In a number of patients the first lesion produced a transient dysarthria, that showed a rapid and nearly complete recovery. This, for instance, was the case of the patient of Villa and Caltagirone (1984), in whom a right hemispheric lesion was followed by a left-sided stroke, and of the case studied by Cappa, Guidotti, Papagno, and Vignolo (1987), who vice-versa suffered a left hemispheric stroke followed by a contralateral vascular lesion (see other case reports and reviews of the neurological literature in Mariani, Spinnler, Sterzi & Vallar, 1989; and in Mao et al., 1989). These data indicate that the hemisphere contralateral to the first lesion may successfully take over the articulatory realization of speech, at a stage more peripheral than the motor programming component assessed by the mouth asymmetry and reaction time methods discussed above. The similarity of the effects of left-right compared to right-left successive lesions suggests that the articulatory realization of speech involves bilateral and symmetrical contributions from the two hemispheres. By contrast, the articulatory programming component appears to be strongly lateralized to the left hemisphere. The neural mechanisms of recovery after the first lesion in these purely anarthric patients have not been elucidated in detail, but they are likely to involve the utilization of pathways descending to the ipsilateral motor nuclei in the brainstem (see a review of the anatomical evidence in Brodal, 1981).

In nonfluent aphasic patients, taken as a group, the pattern of deficit is usually not confined to the articulatory components, but may involve at least the syntactic level in the clinical syndrome of Broca's aphasia (see e.g., Berndt Sloan & Caramazza, 1980) and a more widespread disruption of the different levels of language processing in patients clinically classified as global aphasics. In aphasic patients of this sort, who, after some recovery of speech output, suffered a second right hemispheric stroke, the two factors discussed above may co-occur in disrupting recovered speech. In the case of recovered global aphasics, for instance, the disruption of both the more central semantic-lexical components and the more peripheral motor systems might contribute to the worsening of the speech output deficit produced by the second lesion in the right hemisphere. In the individual patient with double successive left- and right-sided lesions, the relative role of these two factors will then be related to the site and size of the two lesions.

The conclusion, suggested by the data of both Graves and Landis (1985) and Vallar et al. (1988b) that the right hemisphere has a comparatively minor role in the motor programming aspects of residual and recovered speech output is also broadly consistent with data from split brain patients, in whom the capabilities of the two hemispheres can be assessed in the absence of their major neural connection, the corpus callosum. The early seminal studies strongly suggested that linguistic expression is organized almost exclusively in the left hemisphere, while language comprehension may be also represented in the right hemisphere (Gazzaniga & Sperry, 1967). This tenet has been subsequently mitigated by the observation that, at least in a few patients, right hemispheric speech production may develop (see Gazzaniga, Volpe, Smylie, Wilson, & LeDoux, 1979; Gazzaniga, Nass, Reeves, & Roberts, 1984; Gazzaniga, Smylie, Baynes, Hirst, & McCleary, 1984), but the conclusion that the disconnected right hemisphere is more proficient in receptive than in expressive linguistic skills can nevertheless be maintained. In a broadly similar fashion, right-handed adult patients who underwent a left hemispherectomy for cerebral malignancy, show a substantial recovery of language comprehension, while the deficit of voluntary propositional speech remains more severe (see Smith, 1966; Gott, 1973; Burklund & Smith, 1977). It is worth noting here that in these left hemispherectomy patients singing recovered better than ordinary propositional speech; this finding is consistent with the Graves & Landis' (1985) observation that 'automatic' tasks, including singing, produce a left mouth opening asymmetry. These findings, while confirming that the contribution of the right hemisphere to aphasic speech output is rather limited, as compared with its role in the language comprehension processes, limit the generality of the conclusion to the 'propositional', 'non-automatic' aspects of speech production. The recent findings of Benke and Kertesz (1989), who examined the abnormalities of a variety of speech output parameters produced by unilateral hemispheric lesions, are also broadly consistent with this distinction. Slurring, phonemic errors and rate reduction were more severe and more frequently associated with left hemispheric damage than with right-sided lesions. By contrast, an opposite pattern was found in the case of dysprosody.

Indirect evidence for a greater role of the right hemisphere in recovery of the receptive aspects of language, as compared to speech production, is also provided by the better recovery of auditory comprehension than verbal expression in left-brain-damaged aphasic patients (see Vignolo, 1964; review and references in Sarno Taylor, 1981). This differential recovery is consistent with the view that a major neural network, including both left and right hemispheric regions may be available for restoration of language comprehension processes, as compared with speech production.

A more complete evaluation of the relative contributions of the right and left hemispheric regions to residual or recovered aphasic language requires the consideration of other sources of evidence, that mainly concern aspects of the neural mechanisms involved in aphasic comprehension of language, but also provide some indirect information as to the hemispheric mechanisms of aphasic speech production.

(1) Divided field (W.H. Moore & Weidner, 1974) and dichotic listening (e.g., W.H. Moore & Weidner, 1975; Pettit & Noll, 1979; Papanicolau, B.D. Moore, Deutsch, Levin, & Eisenberg, 1988; B.D. Moore & Papanicolau, 1988) studies have shown that aphasic patients may show left visual half-field and left ear superiorities in the report of verbal stimuli, while the typical findings in normal subjects are right visual half-field and right ear advantages. In such studies interpretations in terms of nonspecific lesion effects should be seriously taken into consideration as the left half-field or left ear advantages could be explained in terms of a superior efficiency of the undamaged hemisphere. Lesion effect hypotheses have however been rejected, at least in some studies, as a crossover interaction was present: the overall level of performance was comparable in the control and aphasic groups (W.H. Moore & Weidner, 1974, 1975; B.D. Moore & Papanicolau,

1988; Papanicolau et al., 1988), and sensory processing, as assessed by physiological indexes, was preserved (Papanicolau et al., 1988).

Both divided field and dichotic listening tasks do not specifically assess the production systems and have a major input analysis component, while the involvement of the articulatory output system is comparatively minor, or absent, when a pointing-among-alternatives response modality is adopted; therefore, conclusions drawn on the basis of tasks of this sort and concerning ear or visual half-field dominance cannot be confidently extended to the hemispheric lateralization of the normal -- and aphasic -- production systems.

(2) Evidence for a right hemispheric contribution to aphasic language also comes from studies where the evoked potential correlates of verbal tasks such as memorizing words, detecting and repeating words on the basis of phonological and semantic cues, and shadowing (Papanicolau, B.D. Moore, Levin & Eisenberg, 1987; Papanicolau et al., 1988) indicate a right hemispheric involvement in aphasic patients, while control subjects show the expected left hemispheric activation. It is worth noting, however, that all such tasks have a major verbal input analysis component, that, as mentioned above, may be taken over by the right hemisphere. The interpretation of these right hemispheric effects is therefore not straightforward, in that they might reflect a right hemispheric involvement in both analysis and production processes. There might also be a problem concerning the sensitivity of the technique in detecting hemispheric activation. In the shadowing tasks (repetition of sequences of words) that have an important motor programming component with comparatively minor analytic demands, Papanicolau et al. (1988) found no activation of the right hemisphere in aphasics, but also no left hemispheric activation in the normal control group. Conversely, in Rizzolatti et al.'s (1982) experiments the shadowing concurrent activity produced a significant left hemispheric interference.

(3) The divided field, dichotic listening and evoked potential studies provide evidence for a right hemispheric contribution to aphasic language, at least as analysis and comprehension processes are concerned. The evidence from physiological approaches capable of measuring regional cerebral blood flow (rCBF) and metabolism, on the contrary, is less unequivocal. In two left-brain-damaged aphasic patients who had partially recovered from aphasia, Yamaguchi, J.S. Meyer, Sakai, & Yamomoto, (1980) reported, during activation, an increase of rCBF in a right hemispheric region homologous to Broca's area. The recent study by Demeurisse & Capon (1987), in which rCBF was measured in aphasic patients during behavioral activation by an object naming task, argues for a role of both left and right hemispheric regions: recovered patients showed a widespread bi-hemispheric, mainly left-sided, pattern of cortical activation. The

conclusion that a good recovery requires a contribution from the undamaged regions of the left hemisphere is also supported by the results of Knopman et al. (1984). In a study involving activation by a language comprehension task, they found a correlation between good recovery of auditory comprehension and activation of the left posterior-temporal and inferior-parietal areas in patients with infarctions sparing these regions. In the early studies, performed within three months after stroke onset, these patients had a mildly defective comprehension and the activation procedures produced a diffuse increase of rCBF in the right hemisphere. In the later studies, performed about seven months after stroke onset, behavioral activation was associated with an increase of rCBF in the left posterior-temporal inferior-parietal regions. Conversely, in the patients with posterior-temporal inferior-parietal lesions, in whom the auditory comprehension deficit was more severe and recovery was not complete, an increase of rCBF in the right frontal regions was observed only in the later studies. These data, at least as auditory comprehension is concerned, seem to indicate that a good or complete recovery requires the anatomical integrity of the cerebral region primarily committed to a given function, in Knopman et al.'s (1984) study the left inferior-temporal posterior-parietal areas (see clinical - CT Scan correlation data consistent with this view in Selnes, Knopman, Niccum, Rubens, & Larson, 1983).

The view that good recovery requires the integrity of the primarily committed regions is also supported by a recent study of Bosley, Dann, Silver, Alavi, Kushner, Chawluck, Savino, Sergott, Schatz, and Reivich (1987), who found that recovery from hemianopia took place only when the occipital lobe was spared and was related to an improvement of hypometabolism in the striatal cortex. Patients who recovered had hemianopia and occipital hypometabolism in the recent post-stroke phase. Conversely, patients with structural (CT assessed) occipital lesions did not display any recovery from hemianopia. Data of this sort seem to indicate that a good or nearly complete recovery of linguistic functions such as auditory comprehension, or more basic neurological processes such as vision, may require the anatomical integrity of the primarily committed regions. When this is the case, regression of diaschisis (see Feeney and Baron, 1986) is likely to be the main neural correlate of the recovery process.

A comparative evaluation of the Knopman et al.'s (1984) and Bosley et al.'s (1987) data also indicates that in the case of complex cognitive linguistic functions such as auditory comprehension some, albeit far from complete, takeover by areas different from the primarily committed left hemispheric regions, such as the right hemisphere, may occur. In the case of more basic neurological deficits the possible contribution to recovery by non-primarily committed regions, such as the contralateral hemisphere, appears comparatively minor. Consistent with this view, Hier, Mondlock, and Caplan (1983) reported that recovery is more rapid and complete in the case of cognitive deficits (e.g., spatial neglect, denial of illness and prosopagnosia) as compared with more basic and elementary neurological deficits (e.g., hemiplegia and hemianopia). Taken together, these data suggest that in the case of complex cognitive activities a more extensive neural network, involving both hemispheres, may be involved in residual function and in the recovery process, even though some primarily committed regions play a major role (e.g., Wernicke's area in the process of auditory comprehension: Knopman et al., 1984)

Coming back after this digression to the issue of residual and recovered speech output in aphasia, a number of anatomo-clinical observations in aphasic patients with speech output difficulties, including articulatory deficits, are consistent with the views discussed above. On the basis of a literature review and data from four patients with bilateral cerebral infarctions and aphasia, D.N. Levine and Mohr (1979) conclude that bilateral lesions of the third frontal gyrus (Broca's area) are frequently not associated with a permanent lack of speech output and good recovery may occur. This, together with the marked recovery of output deficits in patients with unilateral lesions confined to the third frontal gyrus of the dominant hemisphere (see Mohr, Pessin, Finkelstein, Funkenstein, Duncan, & Davis, 1979; see also a review in Cappa & Vignolo, 1983), is taken as evidence for a role of the adjacent areas of this hemisphere, rather than of the homologous regions of the nondominant hemisphere. On the other hand, a more extensive fronto-parietal damage would be needed to producing a more severe and persistent impairment of speech output, although some recovery may occur. In this case the limited recovery that may take place would be mediated by the nondominant hemisphere, as a second right hemispheric lesions may abolish speech output (see case 3 of D.N. Levine & Mohr, 1979). These cases illustrate the complex pattern of interactions between the undamaged regions of the left hemisphere and the right hemisphere in the recovery process of aphasic speech output. Additional evidence for a role of left hemispheric regions is provided by the longitudinal study of Knopman, Selnes, Niccum, Rubens, Yock, & Larson (1983) who found that persistent nonfluency in left brain-damaged aphasic patients was associated with lesions in the left rolandic region and in the underlying subcortical white matter. Nonfluent patients in whom recovery took place had less extensive lesions, while the crucial rolandic regions were largely spared in fluent patients. Consistent with these data Schiff, Alexander, Naeser, & Galaburda, (1983) found an association of small frontal lesions involving the lower half of the primary motor cortex (precentral gyrus), the posterior portion of the inferior frontal gyrus, and the underlying white matter with persisting dysarthria without aphasia.

The study of Knopman et al. (1983) included patients with vascular lesions, in whom speech fluency was assessed one month post-onset and up to five months after stroke. A main role of the left hemisphere in the recovery process is also suggested by a study of men who had sustained penetrating head injuries resulting in nonfluent aphasia within six months following the trauma. These patients were examined fifteen years after the injury by a comprehensive language examination, and their cerebral lesions were assessed by CT Scan. Nonrecovered patients had larger left hemisphere lesions, while the volumes of the right hemisphere lesions did not differ significantly in the two groups. More specifically, in more than two thirds of both recovered and nonrecovered patients, the anterior cortical regions of the left hemisphere, including Broca's area, were affected. Nonrecovered patients, however, showed a greater involvement of the retrorolandic cortical regions of the left hemisphere, including Wernicke's area, of the underlying white matter, and of the left basal ganglia. These data, while confirming the association between left frontal lesions and nonfluency, indicate that the recovery process relies heavily upon left hemispheric neural systems (Ludlow, Rosenberg, Fair, Buck, Schesselman & Salazar, 1986). More detailed suggestions concerning the role of the damage of specific subcortical white matter regions of the left hemisphere in producing nonfluency in aphasia have been recently made by Naeser, Palumbo, Helm-Estabrooks, Stiassny-Eder and Albert (1989).

The observation that large left hemispheric frontal-anterior parietal lesions prevent good recovery of speech output broadly corroborates the view that the effectiveness of the right hemisphere takeover is far from complete. The interpretation of these clinical correlations should of course consider that the clinical notion of 'fluency' encompasses, in addition to impaired articulation, effortful and amelodic speech and impoverishment of grammatical form (see e.g., Knopman et al., 1983). The implications of these anatomo-clinical studies to the interpretation of the experimental approaches to the issue of the hemispheric mechanisms of aphasic speech output are, therefore, far from direct. Both lines of evidence, however, concur to suggest an important role of the ipsilesional left hemispheric regions to aphasic speech output, without, of course, ruling out some contribution from the undamaged right hemisphere.

The available empirical data concerning the hemispheric mechanisms of residual and recovered speech output in aphasia may be summarized as follows:

(1) Both the undamaged regions of the left hemisphere and the contralateral right hemisphere may participate in the recovery process. Although this bi-hemispheric contribution involves both speech comprehension and production, the overall available evidence appears to indicate that the role of the right hemisphere is comparatively more

relevant in the analysis and comprehension aspects of linguistic processing (see reviews by Searleman, 1977; Zaidel, 1985)

(2) The clinical studies of patients with two successive lesions and the method of temporary inactivation of one hemisphere by the amobarbital intracarotid injection support the view that the right hemisphere may contribute to speech production, but do not allow detailed specification of the precise role of the two hemispheres in the various aspects of this complex multi-component process.

(3) The two available experimental methods that probably assess in a more specific fashion the operation of the articulatory motor programming components of speech output (asymmetry of mouth opening, laterality differences in simple visuo-motor reaction time during concurrent overt articulation) concur to indicate that aphasic speech output is mediated in most patients by the undamaged regions of the left hemisphere. On the other hand, the contribution of the right hemisphere to the more central (lexical-semantic) aspects of speech production may be more substantial, but less direct relevant evidence is available.

Acknowledgements

I am grateful to Dr. Stefano Cappa and Dr. Geoff Hammond for their useful suggestions on an early version of this paper.

References

Anzola, G.P., Bertoloni, G., Buchtel, H.A., & Rizzolatti, G. (1977). Spatial compatibility and anatomical factors in simple and choice reaction time. *Neuropsychologia*, **15**, 295-302.

Basso, A., Capitani, E., & Vignolo, L.A. (1979). Influence of rehabilitation on language skills in aphasic patients: a controlled study. *Archives of Neurology*, **36**, 190-196.

Basso, A., Gardelli, M., Grassi, M.P., & Mariotti, M. (1989). The role of the right hemisphere in recovery from aphasia. Two case studies. *Cortex*, **25**, 555-566.

Benson, D.F. (1967). Fluency in aphasia: correlation with radioactive scan localization. *Cortex*, **3**, 373-394.

Benke, T., & Kertesz, A. (1989). Hemispheric mechanisms of motor speech. *Aphasiology*, **3**, 627-641.

Berlucchi, G. (1982). Una ipotesi neurofisiologica sulle asimmetrie funzionali degli emisferi cerebrali dell'uomo. In C.A. Umiltà (Ed.), *Neuropsicologia sperimentale* (pp. 95-133). Milano: F. Angeli.

Berlucchi, G., Crea, F., Di Stefano, M., & Tassinari, G. (1977). Influence of spatial stimulus-response compatibility on reaction time of ipsilateral and contralateral hand to lateralized visual stimuli. *Journal of Experimental Psychology: Human Perception and Performance*, **3**, 505-517.

Berlucchi, G., Heron, W., Hyman, R., Rizzolatti, G., & Umiltà, C. (1971). Simple reaction time of ipsilateral and contralateral hand to lateralized visual stimuli. *Brain*, **94**, 419-430.

Berlucchi, G., Tassinari, G., & Antonini, A. (1986). The organization of the callosal connections according to Sperry's principle of supplemental complementarity. In F. Lepore, M. Ptito, & H.H. Jasper (Eds.), *Two hemispheres - one brain: Functions of the corpus callosum* (pp. 171-188). New York: A.R. Liss.

Berndt Sloan, R., & Caramazza, A. (1980). A redefinition of the syndrome of Broca's aphasia: implications for a neuropsychological model of language. *Applied Psycholinguistics*, **1**, 225-278.

Bisiach, E., Mini, M., Sterzi, R., & Vallar, G. (1982). Hemispheric lateralization of the decisional stage in choice reaction time to visual unstructured stimuli. *Cortex*, **18**, 191-198.

Bock, J.K. (1982). Toward a cognitive psychology of syntax: information processing contributions to sentence formulation. *Psychological Review*, **89**, 1-47.

Bosley, T.M., Dann, R., Silver, F.L., Alavi, A., Kushner, M., Chawluck, J.B., Savino, P.J., Sergott, R.C., Schatz, N.J., & Reivich, M. (1987). Recovery of vision after ischemic lesions: positron emission tomography. *Annals of Neurology*, **21**, 444-450.

Brodal, A. (1981). *Neurological anatomy*. New York: Oxford University Press.

Burklund, C.W., & Smith, A. (1977). Language and the cerebral hemispheres. *Neurology*, **27**, 627-633.

Butterworth, B. (1980). Some constraints on models of language production. In B. Butterworth (Ed.), *Language production, Vol. 1: Speech and talk* (pp. 423-459). New York: Academic Press.

Cappa, S.F., Cavallotti, G., & Vignolo, L.A. (1981). Phonemic and lexical errors in fluent aphasia: correlation with lesion site. *Neuropsychologia*, **19**, 171-177.

Cappa, S.F., Guidotti, M., Papagno, C., & Vignolo, L.A. (1987). Speechlessness with occasional vocalizations after bilateral opercular lesions: a case study. *Aphasiology*, 1, 35-39.

Cappa, S.F., & Vignolo, L.A. (1983). CT Scan studies of aphasia. *Human Neurobiology*, **2**, 129-134.

Cummings, J.L., Benson, D.F., Walsh, M.J., & Levine, H.L. (1979). Left-to-right transfer of language dominance. A case study. *Neurology*, **29**, 1547-1550.

Czopf, J. (1972). Über die Rolle der nicht dominanten Hemisphäre in der restitution der Sprache der Aphasischen. *Archiv für Psychiatrie und Nervenkrankheiten*, **216**, 162-171.

Davidoff, J.B. (1977). Hemispheric differences in dot detection. *Cortex*, **13**, 434-444.

Demeurisse, G., & Capon, A. (1987). Language recovery in aphasic stroke patients: clinical, CT and CBF studies. *Aphasiology*, **1**, 301-315.

Feeney, D.M., & Baron, J.C. (1986). Diaschisis. *Stroke*, **17**, 817-830.

Garrett, M.F. (1982). Production of speech: observations from normal and pathological language use. In A.W. Ellis (Ed.), *Normality and pathology in cognitive functions* (pp. 19-76). New York: Academic Press.

Gazzaniga, M.S., & Sperry, R.W. (1967). Language after section of the cerebral commissures. *Brain*, **90**, 131-148.

Gazzaniga, M.S., Volpe, B.T., Smylie, C.S., Wilson, D.H., & LeDoux, J.E. (1979). Plasticity in speech organization following commissurotomy. *Brain*, **102**, 805- 815.

Gazzaniga, M.S., Nass, R., Reeves, A., & Roberts, D. (1984). Neurologic perspectives on right hemisphere language following surgical sections of the corpus callosum. *Seminars in Neurology*, **4**, 126- 135.

Gazzaniga, M.S., Smylie, C.S., Baynes, K., Hirst, W., & McCleary, C. (1984). Profiles of right hemisphere language and speech following brain bisection. *Brain and Language*, **22**, 206-220.

Gott, P.S. (1973). Language after dominant hemispherectomy. *Journal of Neurology, Neurosurgery and Psychiatry*, **36**, 1082-1088.

Gould, H.J., Cusik, C.G., Pons, T.P., & Kaas, J.H. (1986). The relationship of corpus callosum connections to electrical stimulation maps of motor, supplementary motor and the frontal eye fields in owl monkeys. *Journal of Comparative Neurology*, **247**, 297-325.

Gowers, W. (1895). *Manuale delle malattie del sistema nervoso*. Milano: Vallardi.

Graves, R. (1983). Mouth asymmetry, dichotic ear advantage and tachistoscopic visual field advantage as measures of language lateralization. *Neuropsychologia*, **21**, 641-649.

Graves, R., Goodglass, H., & Landis, T. (1982). Mouth asymmetry during spontaneous speech. *Neuropsychologia*, **20**, 371-381.

Graves, R., & Landis, T. (1985). Hemispheric control of speech expression in aphasia: a mouth asymmetry study. *Archives of Neurology*, **42**, 249-251.

Hellige, J.B., & Cox, P.J. (1976). Effects of concurrent verbal memory on recognition of stimuli from the left and right visual fields. *Journal of Experimental Psychology: Human Perception and Performance*, **2**, 210-221.

Hier, D.B., Mondlock, J., & Caplan, L.R. (1983). Recovery of behavioral abnormalities after right hemisphere stroke. *Neurology*, **33**, 345-350.

Jackson, J.H. (1915). On the nature of the duality of the brain. *Brain*, **38**, 80-103.

Jeeves, M.A. (1969). A comparison of interhemispheric transmission times in acallosals and normals. *Psychonomic Science*, **16**, 245- 246.

Karol, E.A., & Pandya, D.N. (1971). The distribution of the corpus callosum in the rhesus monkey. *Brain*, **94**, 471-486.

Kinsbourne, M. (1970). The cerebral basis of lateral asymmetries in attention. In A.F. Sanders (Ed.), *Attention and performance III* (pp. 193-201). Amsterdam: North Holland.

Kinsbourne, M. (1971). The minor cerebral hemisphere as a source of aphasic speech. *Archives of Neurology*, **25**, 302-306.

Kinsbourne, M., & Fisher, M. (1971). Latency of uncrossed and of crossed reaction in callosal agenesis. *Neuropsychologia*, **9**, 471-473.

Kleist, K. (1962). *Sensory aphasia and amusia*. Oxford: Pergamon Press.

Knopman, D.S., Rubens, A.B., Selnes, O.A., Klassen, A.C., & Meyer, M.W. (1984). Mechanisms of recovery from aphasia: evidence from serial xenon 133 cerebral blood flow studies. *Annals of Neurology*, **15**, 530-535.

Knopman, D.S., Selnes, O.A., Niccum, N., Rubens, A.B., Yock, D., & Larson, D. (1983). A longitudinal study of speech fluency in aphasia: CT correlates of recovery and persistent nonfluency. *Neurology*, **33**, 1170-1178.

Kuttner, H. (1930). Über die Beteiligung der rechten Hirnhälfte an der Sprachtfunction. *Archiv für Psychiatrie und Nervenkrankheiten*, 91, 691-693.

Larsen, B., Skinhøj, E., & Lassen, N.A. (1978). Variations in regional cortical blood flow in the right and left hemispheres during automatic speech. *Brain*, **101**, 193-209.

Lee, H., Nakada, T., Deal, J.L., Lin, S., & Kwee, I.L. (1984). Transfer of language dominance. *Annals of Neurology*, **15**, 304-307.

Levine, D.N., & Mohr, J.P. (1979). Language after bilateral cerebral infarctions: role of the minor hemisphere in speech. *Neurology*, **29**, 927-938.

Ludlow, C.L., Rosenberg, J., Fair, C., Buck, D., Schesselman, S., & Salazar, A. (1986). Brain lesions associated with nonfluent aphasia fifteen years following penetrating head injury. *Brain*, **109**, 55- 80.

Mao, C-C., Coull, B.M., Golper, L.A.C., & Rau, M.T. (1989). Anterior operculum syndrome. *Neurology*, **39**, 1169-1172.

Mariani, C., Spinnler, H., Sterzi, R., & Vallar, G. (1980). Bilateral perisylvian softenings: bilateral anterior opercular syndrome (Foix-Chavany-Marie syndrome). *Journal of Neurology*, **223**, 269-284.

Mazzocchi, F., & Vignolo, L.A. (1979). Localisation of lesions in aphasia: clinical - CT scan correlations in stroke patients. *Cortex*, **15**, 627-654.

Mempel, E., Srebrzynska, J., Subczynska, J., & Zarski, S. (1963). Compensation of speech disorders by the nondominant cerebral hemisphere in adults. *Journal of Neurology, Neurosurgery and Psychiatry*, **26**, 96.

Mohr, J.P., Pessin, M.S., Finkelstein, S., Funkenstein, H.H., Duncan, G.W., Davis, K.R. (1979). Broca's aphasia. *Neurology*, **28**, 311-324.

Monakow, C. von. (1914). *Die Lokalisation im Grosshirn.* Wiesbaden: Bergmann.

Moore, W.H., & Weidner, W.E. (1974). Bilateral tachistoscopic word perception in aphasic and normal subjects. *Perceptual and Motor Skills*, **39**, 1003-1011.

Moore, W.H., & Weidner, W.E. (1975). Dichotic word-perception of aphasic and normal subjects. *Perceptual and Motor Skills*, **40**, 379-386.

Moore, B.D., & Papanicolau, A.C. (1988). Dichotic-listening evidence of right-hemisphere involvement in recovery from aphasia following stroke. *Journal of Clinical and Experimental Neuropsychology*, **10**, 380-386.

Moscovitch, M. (1976). On the representation of language in the right hemisphere of right-handed people. *Brain and Language*, **3**, 47-71.

Moutier, F. (1908). *L'aphasie de Broca.* Paris: Steinheil.

Naeser, M.A., Palumbo, C.L., Helm-Estabrooks, N., Stiassny-Eder, D., & Albert, M.L. (1989). Severe nonfluency in aphasia. *Brain*, **112**, 1-38.

Nielsen, J.M. (1946). *Agnosia, apraxia and aphasia* (2nd ed.). New York: Hafner.

Pandya, D.N., & Kuypers, H.G.J.M. (1969). Cortico-cortical connections in the rhesus monkey. *Brain Research*, **13**, 13-36.

Papanicolau, A.C., Moore, B.D., Levin, H.S., & Eisenberg, H.M. (1987). Evoked potential correlates of right hemisphere involvement in language recovery following stroke. *Archives of Neurology*, **44**, 521-524.

Papanicolau, A.C., B.D. Moore, B.D., Deutsch, G., Levin, H.S., & Eisenberg, H.M. (1988). Evidence for right-hemisphere involvement in recovery from aphasia. *Archives of Neurology*, **45**, 1025-1029.

Petersen, S.E., Fox, P.T., Posner, M.I., Mintun, M., & Raichle, M. (1989). Positron emission tomographic studies of the processing of single words. *Journal of Cognitive Neuroscience*, **1**, 153-170.

Pettit, J.N., & Noll, J.D. (1979). Cerebral dominance in aphasia recovery. *Brain and Language*, **7**, 191-200.

Rizzolatti, G., Bertoloni, G., & Buchtel, H.A. (1979). Interference of concomitant motor and verbal tasks on simple reaction time: a hemispheric difference. *Neuropsychologia*, **17**, 323-330.

Rizzolatti, G., Bertoloni, G., & De Bastiani, P.L. (1982). Interference of concomitant tasks on simple reaction time: attentional and motor factors. *Neuropsychologia*, **20**, 447-455.

Sarno Taylor, M. (1981). Recovery and rehabilitation in aphasia. In M. Sarno Taylor (Ed.), *Acquired aphasia* (pp. 485-529). New York: Academic Press.

Schiff, H.B., Alexander, M.P., Naeser, M.A., & Galaburda, A.M. (1983). Aphemia: clinical-anatomic correlations. *Archives of Neurology*, **40**, 720-727.

Searleman, A. (1977). A review of right hemisphere linguistic capabilities. *Psychological Bulletin*, **84**, 503-528.

Selnes, O.A., Knopman, D.S., Niccum, N., Rubens, A.B., & Larson, D. (1983). Computed tomographic scan correlates of auditory comprehension deficits in aphasia: a prospective recovery study. *Annals of Neurology*, **13**, 558-566.

Smith A. (1966). Speech and other functions after left (dominant) hemispherectomy. *Journal of Neurology, Neurosurgery and Psychiatry*, **29**, 467-471.

Tassinari, G. (1981). *Misura del tempo di trasferimento interemisferico per mezzo di tempi di reazione visuo-motori semplici: osservazioni in cerebrolesi focali e controlli adulti.* (Tesi di Specializzazione in Neurologia). Pisa: Università di Pisa, Facoltà di Medicina.

Vallar, G., & Cappa, S.F. (1987). Articulation and verbal short-term memory. Evidence from anarthria. *Cognitive Neuropsychology*, **4**, 55-78.

Vallar, G., Perani, D., Cappa, S.F., Messa, C., & Fazio, F. (1988a). Recovery from aphasia and neglect after subcortical stroke: neuropsychological and cerebral perfusion study. *Journal of Neurology, Neurosurgery and Psychiatry*, **51**, 1269-1276.

Vallar, G., Sterzi, R., & Basso, A. (1988b). Left hemisphere contribution to motor programming of aphasic speech: a reaction time experiment in aphasic patients. *Neuropsychologia*, **26**, 511-519.

Villa, G., & Caltagirone, C. (1984). Speech suppression without aphasia after bilateral perisylvian softenings (bilateral rolandic operculum syndrome). *Italian Journal of Neurological Sciences*, **5**, 77-83.

Vignolo, L.A. (1964). Evolution of aphasia and language rehabilitation: a retrospective exploratory study. *Cortex*, **1**, 344-367.

Yamaguchi, F., Meyer, J.S., Sakai, F., & Yamomoto, M. (1980). Case reports of three dysphasic patients to illustrate rCBF responses during behavioral activation. *Brain and Language*, **9**, 145-148.

Zaidel, E. (1985). Language in the right hemisphere. In D.F. Benson & E. Zaidel (Eds.), *The dual brain: Hemispheric specialization in humans* (pp. 205-231). New York: The Guilford Press.

Cerebral Control of Speech and Limb Movements
G.E. Hammond (editor)

Chapter 14

THE RELATIONSHIP BETWEEN PANTOMIME EXPRESSION AND RECOGNITION IN APHASIA: THE SEARCH FOR CAUSES

Robert J. Duffy
University of Connecticut

and

Joseph R. Duffy
Mayo Clinic

Impairments in pantomime expression and pantomime recognition commonly occur as part of the syndrome of aphasia. Deficits in pantomime expression and recognition are highly correlated with each other and with the verbal symptoms of aphasia. To understand the interrelationships among these deficits, it is necessary to focus on the causes of pantomimic deficits. The search for these causes has been the goal of much research for over 25 years. In the first part of the chapter, we review the background and descriptions of current theories of the causes of pantomimic deficits. In the second part, we critically review some of the limitations of the research methods used in testing causal theories. And in the third part, we present a description of causal modeling, a strategy for the testing of causal theories. Seven different causal models hypothesized to explain deficits in both pantomime expression and recognition are presented and tested using path analysis, a type of causal modeling.

Terminology

To avoid any uncertainty of meaning in our presentation, it is important to define the terms used. *Word* refers to any lexical item in a natural language dictionary; words can be in any form -- spoken, written, tactile, etc. Ordinarily, we are referring to natural spoken languages such as English. However, *word* can refer also to the signs that form the lexicon of non-oral languages such as American Sign Language, the natural language of the deaf. *Verbal* refers to any task or behavior in which words, spoken or written, are used in either the presentation of a stimulus or in a response. *Nonverbal* refers to behaviors or tasks in which there is no *overt* use of words either as a stimulus or response; it does not rule out the possibility that words may be used covertly or subvocally. In our discussion, the nonverbal tasks and behaviors that we refer to are, unless otherwise indicated, restricted to those used for communication; other nonverbal tasks, such as problem solving, are not intended. *Pantomime* is a subset of nonverbal behavior and refers to the deliberate use of manual or bodily movement intended to convey a message in the absence of speech. *Gesture* is more generic than pantomime; it refers to any bodily movements, used communicatively or otherwise, in either the presence or absence of speech.

Background and Theories

Structural Theories

Theories of aphasia and brain functioning have always been closely related. In the nineteenth century, neurologic models and 'diagrams' were used frequently in the development of theoretical models intended to explain the processes producing the verbal symptoms of aphasia. Specific aphasic disorders in speaking, auditory comprehension, reading, and writing were accounted for by lesions in specific areas of the brain thought to be the neural substrate for the motor, sensory, and linguistic processes involved in the performance of these behaviors. These cerebral structures are dedicated to and identified with specific verbal behaviors. Extraverbal symptoms were generally considered to be the result of damage to cerebral areas outside of and different from those producing verbal symptoms.

Initially, nonverbal deficits were considered irrelevant to the study of aphasia and generally were ignored in the formulation of theories of aphasia. The co-occurrence of nonverbal neuropathological symptoms with verbal symptoms was usually explained as resulting from a lesion large enough (or several lesions scattered enough) to damage simultaneously the neural substrates of these two distinct behaviors.

Nonverbal impairments generally were viewed as a symptom of general intellectual loss that may accidentally accompany the verbal symptoms of aphasia. Historically, this approach to the explanation of neuropathological symptoms in terms of brain structures has been referred to as 'localizationist' or 'neurological'. Weisenburg and McBride (1935) used the term 'structural' to refer to such theories. And we also will use the term 'structural' to designate the neurological approach to the study of aphasic behaviors. Currently, the structural approach is one of two major theoretical orientations to the explanation of co-occurrence of verbal and pantomimic deficits in the symptom-complex of aphasia.

Central Theories

Early in the history of aphasia, there emerged an alternative to the more popular structural explanations of aphasic symptoms. This second major theoretical orientation has been characterized as 'psychological', 'central', 'preverbal', and 'cognitive'. We shall to use the term 'central' to refer to these theories. Central psychological theories have attempted to explain the coexistence of verbal and pantomimic deficits as the result of a single preverbal dysfunction of some cognitive process that normally underlies propositional communication. The Noetic school of clinician-researchers believed that structural explanations were inadequate to account for the behaviors typically observed in the symptom-complex of aphasia. They emphasized that the symptoms of the aphasic were not restricted to the domain of verbal behaviors and proposed various psychological explanations to account for the simultaneous occurrence of nonverbal communication deficits. Noetic theorists stressed that the concurrent disorders in pantomime typically observed in aphasia were an essential -- and not an incidental or accidental -- component of the aphasic syndrome. Frequently, they cited their clinical observations of aphasics unable to communicate by pantomime or other types of nonverbal modes (e.g., drawing) as evidence of an impairment more extensive than loss of verbal ability. Whereas structuralists view aphasia as a disorder of the perceptual, motor, or linguistic form of words themselves (with intact preverbal cognitive abilities), centralists locate the disorder in the preverbal cognitive processes essential to the *function* of words -- propositional communication. Consistent with the centralist view, therefore, any behavioral forms (verbal or nonverbal) used for the purpose of symbolic representational communication would be compromised as a result of impaired cognitive/symbolic processes. Simultaneous verbal and nonverbal deficits are seen as the homologous effects of a common central disorder. For the structuralists, however, the impairment is in the neural processes involved in the instantiation of the verbal forms themselves.

Various specific central impairments have been proposed: Hughlings Jackson, 1874, (Head, 1915, p. 114) referred to this central problem as 'loss of the power to propositionize'; Finkelnburg, 1870, (R.J. Duffy & Liles, 1975) as 'asymbolia'; Head (1926, p. 210) as a problem in 'symbolic formulation and expression'; Marie, 1906, (Cole & Cole, 1971, p. 54) as 'diminution in intelligence'; Goldstein (1948, p. 56) as 'impairment of abstract attitude;' Critchley (1970, p. 236) as a disorder of the 'preverbitum'; and Bay (1964) as an impairment in the 'differentiation' and 'actualization of concepts'. In a variation of Bay's notion, Gainotti (1988, p. 153) has suggested "... either a disruption of the information stored in the conceptual representation or of an inability to fully access this representation". Centralists typically do not deny that specific perceptual, motor, and linguistic impairments can occur as a confounding condition along with the central problem. Goldstein (1948, pp. 24-25), for example, referred to such specific neural dysfunctions as disturbances in the 'instrumentalities of speech' and warned centralists not to ignore them when describing the clinical syndrome of aphasia.

Searching for Causes

Despite the critical and controversial role that pantomimic deficits has held in the long-standing differences between the structural and central explanations of aphasia, it was not until 1963 that Goodglass and Kaplan published the first empirical investigation of gesture/pantomime in aphasia. Their study, and all subsequent studies (with rare exception), have firmly established that aphasics typically exhibit significant pantomimic and gestural deficits. Goodglass and Kaplan also established the fact of significant covariance between pantomime and verbal deficits; this strong association between verbal and pantomimic deficits has been reported by almost all subsequent investigators. Tables 1 and 2 present measures of association between verbal and nonverbal impairments obtained in previous investigations of pantomime expression and recognition.

The studies presented in Tables 1 and 2 are all *post hoc* observational studies of aphasics performing specific test tasks as a measure of their pantomimic abilities. Typically, pantomime recognition is tested by having the subject select an item from an array of pictures or objects which corresponds to the pantomimed use of that item as demonstrated by the examiner; pantomime expression is tested by having the subject pantomime the use of common objects. Although bearing on the question of the relationship between verbal and nonverbal deficits, other types of studies of nonverbal communicative impairments have been omitted from this review. For example, we have not included studies of spontaneous use of gestural behaviors (see, for example, Glosser, Wiener, & Kaplan, 1986) or experimental studies concerned with training aphasics in the use of nonverbal communicative behaviors (for a review, see Coelho & R.J. Duffy, 1987).

Table 1. Correlation coefficients from studies of the relationship between pantomime recognition and measures of verbal deficits for groups of aphasic subjects. Number of subjects is shown in parentheses.

	VERBAL MEASURES					
PANTOMIME RECOGNITION STUDIES	INPUT		OUTPUT			OVER-ALL
	Aural Compr.	Read	Speech	Naming	Write	
Pickett 1972 (28)	.86[A]	.91[B]		.75[C]		
Pickett 1974 (28)			.83[D]		.69[E]	.89[F]
R.J. Duffy et al. 1975 (44)	.83			.58		.79[F]
Gainotti & Lemmo, 1976 (53)	.54					
Kadish 1978 (6)						.86[G]
Varney 1978 (4)	.61	.87		.60		
Seron, van der Kaa, Remitz, & van der Linden 1979 (27)	.48	.64				
Ferro, Mariano, Castro-Caldas, & Santos, 1980 (111)	.51[H] .68	.49[I] .59[J]				
R.J. Duffy & J.R. Duffy 1981 (47)	.73			.50		.73[F]
Feyereisen, Seron, & De Macar 1981 (20)	.71	.86				
Daniloff, Noll, Fristoe, & Lloyd 1982 (20)	.59 .32*	.32* .16*				
J.R. Duffy & Watkins 1984 (20)	.74[K] .50[L]					
Netsu & Marquardt 1984 (15)	.44[G]					.60[P]

* = not significant (.05 level)

Superscript notations are found at the bottom of Table 2.

Table 2. Correlation coefficients from studies of the relationship between pantomime expression and measures of verbal deficits for groups of aphasic subjects. Number of subjects is shown in parentheses.

PANTOMIME EXPRESSION STUDIES	VERBAL MEASURES					
	INPUT		OUTPUT			OVER-ALL
	Aural Compr.	Read	Speech	Naming	Write	
Goodglass & Kaplan 1963 (20)						.39[M] .66[N]
Pickett 1972 (28)	.72[A]	.77[B]		.79[C]		
Pickett 1974 (28)			.83[D]		.67[E]	.84[F]
Kadish 1978 (6)						.89[G]
R.J. Duffy & J.R. Duffy 1981 (47)	.63			.78		.89[F]
Netsu & Marquardt 1984 (15)			.45			.60[P]

A - Mean r's for PICA VI, X
B - Mean r's for PICA V, VII
C - PICA IV
D - Mean of PICA I-IV
E - Mean of PICA A-F
F - PICA OA Mean
G - Boston Aphasia Test
H - Token Test
I - Word Identification (WI)
J - Word-Object Ident. (WO)
K - Related Foils
L - Unrelated Foils
M - Simple Pantomime
N - Complex Pantomime
P - Combined score for pantomime recognition and expression

In some cases, the correlation coefficients in Tables 1 and 2 have been selected from among several correlations in the same modality. For example, Pickett (1974) presented a table of 62 correlation coefficients among pairs of verbal and pantomimic behaviors, and we have selected only seven of these for our tables. Wherever a coefficient was selected from among several, a subscript is used to identify which of the original coefficients is presented.

Two general impressions may readily be gained from Tables 1 and 2. The first is the consistently high and significant correlations found between the pantomimic and the verbal measures. The second impression is the relative uniform magnitude of the correlations across distinctly different *forms* (i.e., modalities) of behavior, both within and across verbal and nonverbal types. The tables show high correlations between both pantomime expression and recognition and all forms of verbal behaviors -- speech, reading, auditory comprehension, writing. And Table 3 shows the high degree of relationship between pantomime expression and pantomime recognition.

Table 3. Correlation coefficients from studies of the relationship between pantomime recognition and pantomime expression for groups of aphasic subjects. Number of subjects is shown in parentheses.

Studies	correlation coefficient
Pickett 1974 (28)	.70[A]
Kadish 1978 (6)	.85[B]
R.J. Duffy & J.R. Duffy 1981 (47)	.68

A - Pantomime tasks G1 and G4

B - Pantomime tasks G1 and G5

The empirical evidence of pantomimic deficits in association with aphasic verbal symptoms has been demonstrated so consistently that the question is no longer whether nonverbal deficits occur in the symptom-complex of aphasia or whether they are associated with aphasic verbal deficits. The question of interest now is the nature of the association between the verbal and nonverbal behaviors; the answer is being sought in investigations of the causes of the pantomimic deficits.

Analysis by Inspection

Investigations of the causes of pantomimic deficits in aphasia typically have provided descriptive bivariate correlational data. Some studies have used only two or three variables; others have used more. Table 4 is an example of a correlational matrix resulting from an investigation with four causal and two pantomimic (effect) variables. The method of analysis used to uncover evidence of causal relationships has consisted primarily of inspection of the patterns of correlations across pairs of variables. Correlational data have been scrutinized to discern whether there is a pattern of relationships among the variables that supports either the structural or central theory. Investigators have analyzed the correlational data in two ways.

The first way in which correlational data have been inspected and analyzed is *across verbal and pantomimic behaviors*. Conclusions regarding the nature of causal factors are reached on the basis of whether there appears to be a pattern of association or dissociation between these two response classes. Tables 1 to 3 are good examples of the kind of correlational data used to search for patterns of association or dissociation. Centralists would look for a pattern of strong *association* between all verbal and pantomimic responses regardless of specific modality, because they are all effects of the same underlying cognitive dysfunction. In general, centralists would find support from Tables 1 to 3, in the number of uniformly high and significant correlations between both pantomime expression and recognition and the various modalities of verbal behaviors. Structuralists, on the other hand, would predict an opposite pattern, one of *dissociation* between pantomimic and verbal behaviors, because these two response classes are presumed to be the result of distinct neural systems. A qualification of this expectation occurs, however, if the pattern of correlations shows stronger correlations between selected verbal and pantomimic behaviors that may be viewed as structurally related. That is, if a verbal and a pantomimic behavior can be related anatomically, then a high correlation between them may be interpreted as support for a structural interpretation. For example, Varney (1978) noted a significantly stronger correlation of pantomime recognition with reading than with either auditory comprehension or confrontation naming (see Table 1). He interpreted these results as support for the view that these two behaviors, pantomimic and verbal, were affected by the same modality-specific (structural) factor, i.e., visual processing.

The second way in which descriptive correlational data have been inspected and analyzed is in regard to the relative strength of the relationships *between specific causal variables and pantomimic deficits (effects)*. Table 4 is an example of a matrix of correlations showing the strength of relationship between pairs of specific causal and pantomimic deficits.

Centralists predict low or nonsignificant covariance between deficits in specific motor and sensory processes and pantomimic deficits. For example, R.J. Duffy and J.R. Duffy (1981) reported only a small (although significant) correlation of .38 (severity of aphasia partialled out) between limb apraxia and pantomime expression, which they interpreted as evidence against the structural theory. For reasons explained in Addendum A, centralists also expect strong correlations between severity of aphasia and pantomime expression and/or recognition deficits, and interpret such correlations as indications of a symbolic impairment. Structuralists, however, expect strong associations between measures of specific motor dysfunction (e.g., limb apraxia) and pantomime expression and specific sensory dysfunction (e.g., visual agnosia) and pantomime recognition.

Attempts to draw conclusions regarding the cause of pantomimic deficits by inspection of simple correlations is a loose form of inferential inquiry. Such an approach allows for a wide range of alternative interpretations and speculation. Studies with just a few variables create only a narrow window into what is probably a complex structure of relationships; and, they can result in an incomplete, if not distorted, causal interpretation of the data. Studies using an adequate number of variables and more objective and comprehensive methods of statistical analyses are needed to achieve a more rigorous and quantitative inferential interpretation of correlational data.

Cause or Causes

Reviews of causal studies of pantomimic deficits often tend to emphasize their results as supporting either a structural or a central theory. Selective emphasis on certain results may make it appear that the empirical evidence clearly favors one or the other theory. However, the results are more mixed than is often indicated. For example, Goodglass and Kaplan (1963) are frequently cited for their conclusion that limb apraxia accounted for gestural/pantomimic expressive deficits with no mention of their other conclusion that intellectual loss also may be a causal factor. Again, Varney's (1978) conclusion that there is a modality specific factor underlying the relationship between pantomime recognition and reading, is often cited without mention of the other half of his conclusion: that there is a "... supralinguistic impairment (asymbolia?) which also affects nonverbal abilities" (p. 567). And R.J. Duffy and J.R. Duffy's (1981) strong centralist conclusions are based on their findings of very high correlations between aphasia and both pantomime expression and recognition. Their conclusions have been cited without also mentioning their support for a contribution to pantomime expression from limb apraxia. They stated:

> ... limb apraxia may not be the usual or most potent cause of pantomimic impairment in aphasic persons as a group, but it may be a contributing factor in some instances (p. 82).

They also mentioned several other observations supportive of modality specific contributions to pantomimic impairments (p. 77). Care must be taken in reviewing the results and conclusions of causal studies; interpreters of the data may be more partisan than the data themselves.

The Search for Causes

Despite the increasing interest in nonverbal aphasic behaviors and the numerous investigations of the past 25 years, causal explanations of pantomimic deficits remain more theory than fact. Although Goodglass and Kaplan (1963) convincingly demonstrated the existence and prominence of gestural/ pantomimic deficits in aphasia, they were less successful in resolving the question of cause. Subsequent investigators also have experienced difficulty in determining the causes of aphasic pantomimic deficits. The decades since Goodglass and Kaplan have seen an advance in the development of new tests and measures employed in the investigation of pantomimic deficits; the primary causal theories, however, have remained generally the same, and there has been little change in the analytic methods employed to deduce the causes of pantomimic deficits.

We have already discussed the inspection of correlational data as a method for the identification of causes of pantomimic deficits. Related to the question of the adequacy of such an approach to the analysis of causal relations is the question of the adequacy of the statistical methods used to obtain the correlations themselves, and how accurate they are as estimates of covariance. The adequacy and strength of the research procedures employed must be taken into account when evaluating the results of any study. And the conclusions drawn from any study must be judged by the adequacy of the measures and analytic strategies employed in arriving at those conclusions. In the next section, we review the problems of estimating covariance. The purpose of our review is to indicate the need for better analytic strategies to advance the investigation of the causes of pantomimic deficits. The review will serve also as a background to the last section of the chapter that will describe the research strategy of 'causal modeling'. Causal modeling holds promise for resolving a number of problems that have been encountered in investigations of the causes of pantomimic deficits.

Review of Research Methods

As already demonstrated, investigations of the causes of pantomimic deficits have made heavy use of correlational descriptive statistics. This is because correlation meets one of the four conditions requisite for inferring causal relationships in *post hoc* observational investigations. Unlike experimental studies in which the experimenter can control the causes and observe the effects, studies of pathology require the investigator to observe only *post hoc* effects from which he must infer the causes rather than control them.

A relationship is referred to as causal if one variable *explains* or *predicts* another variable. The four conditions necessary to characterize a relationship as causal are: (a) spatial contiguity, (b) temporal priority, (c) covariance, and (d) necessary connection. (See J.R. Duffy, Watt, & R.J. Duffy, 1981, pp. 476-477, for additional discussion of these conditions.) The condition of covariance is demonstrated by obtaining significant correlations between cause and effect variables. Covariance is expected in a cause-effect relationship in that a change in the level of the cause should predict a corresponding change in the effect. Absence of significant covariance between two variables is taken as negative evidence regarding causality. Significant covariance is requisite to the claim of causality.

The typical research strategy in the study of pantomimic deficits has been to obtain correlations between variables hypothesized to be causal (e.g., limb apraxia, visual agnosia, severity of aphasia, intellectual loss) and measures of pantomimic deficits (effects). Ideally, what investigators have looked for is a clear pattern to emerge in which a high correlation is obtained between *one* of the causal factors and the pantomimic deficit and, conversely, nonsignificant correlations for all of the other causal factors. If such results were obtained, it would be easy to infer which variable is the cause of the pantomimic deficit. The history of the search for causal relationships, however, has shown that simple relationships between cause and effect do not obtain. This was demonstrated in the earliest study of pantomimic deficits by Goodglass and Kaplan (1963).

Problems in the Estimation of Covariance

Goodglass and Kaplan (1963) measured the expressive gestural/pantomimic ability of 20 aphasics. They investigated the relationship between gestural/pantomimic performance (effects) and three causal factors: (a) intelligence (WAIS Performance Scale), (b) severity of aphasia, and (c) limb apraxia. (See Addendum A for an explanation of the sense in which aphasia is hypothesized to 'cause' pantomimic deficits.) Using rank order correlations and other nonparametric statistical procedures, they attempted to estimate the covariance between two of the causal variables and the measures of gesture/pantomime. (No attempt was made to estimate the covariance with the third causal variable, limb apraxia.) They discovered that the problem was not one of failure to obtain significant covariance between causes and effects. The problem was the existence of significant correlations among *all* pairs of variables, thereby making the estimate of true covariance difficult. This embarrassment of riches, in which all variables are strongly correlated, requires additional statistical analysis to estimate and distinguish true from spurious covariance. (Spurious covariance is one in which the tendency for two scores to covary arises in part from another factor strongly related to each.)

As an example of the numerous and significant correlations typically found in causal studies, presented in Table 4 are the correlation coefficients between causal variables and pantomimic deficits obtained from our investigation described in Addendum B.

Table 4. Pearson r correlation coefficients among variables in a study of pantomimic deficits in aphasia. See Addendum B for a description of the subjects and the variables.

	Post-erior	Apraxia	Intellect Loss	Pantomime Expression	Pantomime Recognition
Aphasia	.54	.56	.49	.81	.65
Posterior	-	.54	.46	.66	.74
Apraxia	-	-	.47	.73	.42
Intellectual Loss	-	-	-	.47	.44
Pantomime Expression	-	-	-	-	.68

All correlations are significant ($p < .001$)

There are four causal measures (limb apraxia, aphasia, intellectual loss, and posterior lesion) and two nonverbal effects: pantomime expression and recognition. In Table 4, all of the variables are intercorrelated and all correlations are statistically significant ($p < .001$). And, with the exception of intellectual loss, these correlations are high for psychological variables.

The extensive intercorrelations found in studies of brain-damaged behaviors should not be surprising given the interrelatedness and interdependence of the linguistic, cognitive, and neurological processes involved.

When faced with many significant zero-order bivariate correlations as in Table 4, the problem for the investigator seeking to infer causal relationships is to obtain an estimate of true covariance from among the many intercorrelations. Failure to obtain an accurate estimate of the strength of cause-effect relationships can easily lead to erroneous conclusions. Few studies have used statistical analyses appropriate to the control of spurious covariance. Instead of using statistical procedures appropriate to the identification of spurious covariance, most studies have confined their results to simple zero-order correlations, and have attempted to interpret the results without benefit of further statistical inference. To better understand the problems encountered in the determination of covariance, we will review some of the methods used in past studies. Some of the problems are concerned with the adequacy of measurement used in describing the variables; others are concerned with the choice and limitations of the statistical analyses employed in the estimation of covariance.

Levels of Measurement

Difficulty in estimating covariance and inferring causal relations is often related to the level of measurement (nominal, ordinal, interval) employed in describing the original variables. The use of interval level measures allows the widest range of useful statistical analyses. The use of nominal (categorical) or ordinal measures generally requires the use of nonparametric statistical procedures (e.g., phi, Spearman rho), which are less powerful and more difficult to interpret. Obviously, if the original data are nominal or ordinal, then nonparametric analyses must be used. However, it is difficult to defend the practice (which is not uncommon) of reducing original interval level data (e.g., test scores) to rank order or nominal data for description and inferential statistical analyses. For example, a common practice is to take scores obtained on a test of aphasia (interval) and convert them to rank order scores. Or interval test scores may be converted to nominal level by dichotomizing the distribution of scores into groups, such as 'normal' and 'defective', based on an arbitrary cut off score (often the lowest score of normal subjects).

Estimates of covariance derived from such dichotomized or categorical groupings (e.g., 2 X 2 or 2 X 3 contingency tables) can vary greatly depending on the point at which the cutoff between groups is made. Tests with extremely high degrees of reliability in classifying the subjects are required for reliable estimates of covariance derived from nominal data. Tests with small numbers of items and limited range of sensitivity are likely to be very unreliable in their ability to consistently and repeatedly distinguish normal from pathological performance. Ferro, Mariano, Castro-Caldas, and Santos (1980), for example, used only 12 items in their test of gesture recognition ability. This test was so simple that 85% of normal control subjects made a perfect score and 94% made only one or two errors. Based on these results, Ferro et al. chose a score of 10 as the cutoff between normal and 'impaired' performance and concluded that 57% of 111 aphasics 'were free from gestural impairment'. Using such a limited measure, any estimate of the covariance between aphasia and gestural recognition impairment would be heavily dependent on the precision and reliability of their test and their choice of cutoff score. Unfortunately, it is a common practice to omit from reports any data concerning the reliability of the testing and measures used, thereby making it difficult to judge the confidence that one can have in the results and their interpretation.

The conversion of scores from an interval to an ordinal or nominal level is a waste of data and a disregard of valuable and useful information. For example, in discussing 2 X 2 cells of dichotomized data, J. Cohen and P. Cohen (1983, p. 309-310) state:

> It is intuitively obvious that when one reduces a graduated many-valued scale to a two-point scale, one is willfully throwing away information. This has immediate negative consequences to the amount of variance such a crippled variable can account for and concomitantly to the power of the statistical test of its contribution. ... There is no need whatever for the abuse of the data required to cast it into 2 X 2 factorial design form that then results in reduced variance accounting, power, and significance.

Estimates of covariance based on rank order or nominal categories are possible, but can be quite different from the estimate based on interval level measures for the same data. Another problem with the use of nonparametric measures of correlation, such as rank order and contingency, is that they require more difficult statistical analyses and are harder to interpret when used in regression analyses. And regression analyses are essential procedures for estimating true covariance and controlling spurious covariance, and they are best carried out with interval level measures.

Need For Regression Analyses

An early example of the need for the control of spurious covariance is found in Goodglass and Kaplan's (1963) original study of gestural/pantomimic deficits. They encountered the problem of distinguishing spurious from true covariance when attempting to interpret the correlation coefficients obtained between pantomimic deficits and the two causal factors of intelligence and aphasia. They obtained significant Spearman rho rank order correlations among all pairs of variables as shown in Table 5.

Table 5. Correlation coefficients from two studies of expressive pantomime deficits. The coefficients in parentheses are partial correlations as explained in the text.

	Goodglass & Kaplan (1963)		R.J. Duffy & J.R. Duffy (1981)	
	Intelligence	Simple Pantomime	Intelligence	Pantomime
Aphasia	.42	.39	.60	.89 (.85)
Intelligence	-	.48	-	.50 (.07)*

* - nonsignificant. All other correlations are significant. ($p < .05$; one-tailed test)

Their problem was to decide whether aphasia or intellectual level was the cause of the pantomimic deficits. They stated that the data:

> ... indicate that the Gesture and Simple Pantomime scores are related to intellectual efficiency to about the same degree as they are related to severity of aphasia. However, the fact that intellectual efficiency and severity of aphasia are also correlated raises the question as to which variable is carrying the burden of the correlation obtained with gestural proficiency. The strong relationship between Scaled Score (WAIS) and the Gesture-Pantomime scores for the control group (in the absence of aphasia) suggests that intellectual efficiency is the primary determinant and hence one may conclude that increasing *severity* of aphasia has little influence on gestural ability, beyond the effects of the accompanying drop in intellectual efficiency present in this sample (p. 711).

Had their zero-order correlations been subjected to partial regression analysis, it would have been easy to answer the "...question as to which variable is carrying the burden of the correlation obtained with gestural proficiency". This is exactly the question that multiple regression analysis addresses -- what is the true strength of covariance. Without the benefit of statistical analyses to identify spurious covariance, Goodglass and Kaplan (1963) were forced to speculate about the nature of the underlying relationships. They ultimately concluded that intellectual efficiency was 'the prime determinant' and that severity of aphasia had 'little influence on gestural ability'.

The opposite conclusion was reached by R.J. Duffy and J.R. Duffy (1981), who were faced with the same question and the same intercorrelations among the variables of intelligence, aphasia, and pantomimic deficit. Their data are presented in Table 5 for comparison with the Goodglass and Kaplan data. R.J. Duffy and J.R. Duffy used partial regression analysis to arrive at their conclusion that the significant Pearson r of .60 obtained between intellectual loss and pantomimic deficit was spurious; the zero-order correlation of .60 dropped to a nonsignificant .07 when the effect of aphasia was partialled out. And, conversely, the correlation of .89 between aphasia and pantomimic deficit dropped to only .85 when intellectual loss was partialled. Thus, partial regression analysis clearly identified the 'false' covariance between intellectual loss and pantomimic deficit. Additional examples of the effects of partial and multiple regression analyses on the interpretation of zero-order correlations between causal factors and pantomimic deficits may be found in R.J. Duffy and J.R. Duffy (1981).

The only investigation of pantomime to use regression analyses to control for spurious covariance between cause and effect variables has been R.J. Duffy and J.R. Duffy (1981). All others used only zero-order correlations to infer the strength of causal relationships, a practice that can be misleading as indicated from our example above.

Summary of Review of Research Methods

We have reviewed some of the problems encountered in studies attempting to identify causal factors in pantomime recognition and expression. Correlational statistics are essential to the induction of causal relationships in retrospective observational studies. However, the problem for the investigator is the multitude of strong zero-order correlations typically found among the variables of interest, as seen in Table 4. Statistical analyses appropriate to the estimate of true covariance -- a condition necessary to infer causality -- usually have not been employed in causal studies of pantomime. Heavy reliance on speculation and ratiocination has substituted for statistical inference.

Even the best of techniques, partial and multiple regression analyses, are limited in that they can consider only rather simple models of cause and effect in which a single effect (dependent variable) can be explained as a result of several causal (independent) variables, thereby leaving much of the results to the subjective interpretation of the investigator. With complex human behaviors it is to be expected that there may be *several* causal factors and *several* effects occurring simultaneously in a dynamic interactional relationship. And the interpretation of the causes of pantomimic deficits in brain-damaged persons is a complex problem.

What is needed is a research strategy that can handle complex hypotheses, and can process two or more causes and two or more effects in a single interactive analysis, and also can provide strong statistical support for inferences regarding the interpretation of the results. Such procedures do exist and are referred to as 'causal modeling'. According to J. Cohen and P. Cohen (1983, p. 14):

> Causal model analysis provides a formal calculus of inference which promises to be as important to the systematically observing scientist as is the paradigm of the controlled experiment to the systematically experimenting scientist.

Although this procedure has been used extensively in other areas of social science, rarely has it been employed in neuropsychology (Francis, 1989). The remainder of the chapter will be devoted to demonstrating the use of causal modeling in the investigation of pantomimic expression/recognition deficits in aphasia.

Causal Models

The procedure known as causal modeling is directly applicable to the study of pantomimic deficits, because it facilitates the extraction and identification of causal relationships from the complex matrix of correlational data that is typically obtained in such studies. We will demonstrate the application of causal modeling to the investigation of pantomimic deficits in aphasia. No attempt will be made to provide a technical or extensive description of the procedures. Relevant information and references can be found in a recent review by Francis (1989), whose purpose was to stimulate neuropsychologists' interest in the use of causal modeling. Our presentation of causal models is intended as a general illustration of the application of causal modeling to the study of pantomimic deficits, and we have omitted any discussion of the specific calculations used in the procedures.

Causal Models of Deficits in Pantomime Expression and Recognition

Using the data described in Addendum B and in Table 5, we present seven models representing various structural and central hypotheses concerning the causes of deficits in pantomime recognition and expression in aphasia. Three structural, two central, and two combined structural-central models were tested and compared for their adequacy or plausibility in explaining the data obtained in our investigation. Path analysis, a type of causal modeling, was used for these models. J.R. Duffy, Watt, and R.J. Duffy (1981) have provided a detailed description of path analysis with examples of the specific calculations involved.

Basic to any causal analysis is the identification and measurement of the variables that serve as causes and as effects. In our study, impairments of pantomime expression and pantomime recognition were the two effects whose causes we were trying to identify. Specific descriptions of each of the variables used in the models are presented in Addendum B. The causes hypothesized by the central theorists are intellectual loss and central symbolic deficit (asymbolia); therefore, variables representing intellectual loss (INTELL) and aphasia (APHASIA) were obtained. (As mentioned earlier, Addendum A discusses the sense in which aphasia is said to 'cause' pantomimic deficits.) Structural theorists posit that limb apraxia (APRAXIA) is a cause of expressive pantomimic deficits and visual perceptual and/or visuomotor (POSTERIOR) impairment is a cause of recognition deficits.

The first step in path analysis is to draw a (path) diagram that makes explicit the network of relationships (including causal relationships) that are hypothesized to exist among all of the variables. This is a fundamental and important part of causal modeling, because it requires that the theorist make explicit and graphic his explanatory model. The statement of the rationale for the model meets one of the four conditions for a causal relationship -- necessary connection. Necessary connection is a clear statement of why the cause variable(s) should influence the effect variable(s). The model is then tested using the causal and other paths that have been drawn to represent the rationale of the model.

Path models must make explicit which of three types of relationships among the variables is posited: causal, unanalyzed, or null. *Causal* relationships between variables are indicated by a straight line from the cause with an arrow head to the effect. In Model 1, there are two causal relationships indicated by an arrow from APRAXIA to PANTEXP and from POSTERIOR to PANTREC. *Unanalyzed* covariance among other variables is indicated by a curved line with an arrow at both ends indicating ambiguity about the nature of the covariance between the two variables. Unanalyzed covariance is one in which the theorist posits that there is covariance, but is unwilling to assume whether is it is causal or spurious. In Model 1, unanalyzed covariance is indicated by a curved arrow between APHASIA-APRAXIA, APHASIA-POSTERIOR, and APRAXIA-POSTERIOR. A *null* relationship is one in which no covariance is expected, and is indicated by an absence of any lines drawn between variables. The absence of a path between PANTEXP and PANTREC is an example of null covariance.

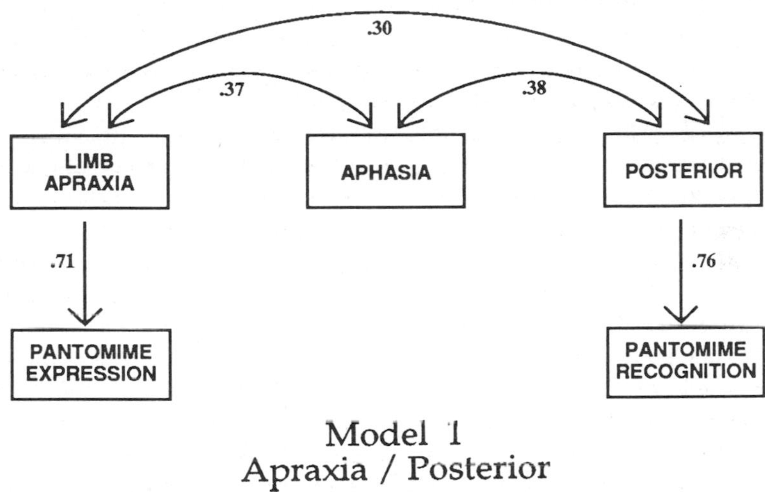

Figure 1. Deficits in Pantomime Recognition and Expression in Aphasia: Model 1

As mentioned earlier, one of the four conditions necessary for inferring a causal relationship is that cause must precede the effect in time ('temporal priority'). In our diagrams, time is represented spatially from top to bottom. Variables at the top are temporally prior to those at the bottom. Thus, in Model 1, the temporally prior causes (APRAXIA and POSTERIOR) are at the top and the effects (PANTEXP and PANTREC) are at the bottom of the diagram.

After the paths have been drawn, the model represents an explicit statement of the causal and other relationships that are hypothesized to exist among all of the variables. The next step is to use the model to estimate the strength of the relationship along the paths between the variables. Partial correlations are used to obtain the coefficients for the unanalyzed paths, and the beta weights from multiple regression analyses are used for the causal paths. In Model 1, for example, the two causal paths are APRAXIA-PANTEXP and POSTERIOR-PANTREC. The obtained coefficients are placed on the path model for inspection and the coefficients are tested for statistical significance.

The first three models presented below represent the three traditionally hypothesized causes of pantomimic deficits in aphasia: apraxia/visuomotor, central symbolic (asymbolia), and intellectual loss. They are presented as single-cause models in which only a single cause is proposed for each effect.

Model 1 - Apraxia/Posterior

In this model (Figure 1), two distinct but coincidental neuropathologic (structural) causes of deficits in pantomime expression and recognition were hypothesized. Limb apraxia was hypothesized as the cause of the pantomime expression deficits and factors represented by a posterior lesion as the cause of the pantomime recognition deficits. The verbal deficits of aphasia were present, but were not causally related to pantomimic deficits.

In the interpretation of the path model, the first thing examined is the significance level of the estimated coefficients. If the correlation coefficient of any path is not statistically significant, then the model is not an accurate one in that the covariance hypothesized by the model is not actually obtained. In Model 1, all coefficients were significant ($p < .05$). Also, strong correlations were obtained between the hypothesized causal paths (APRAXIA-PANTEXP and POSTERIOR-PANTREC).

And it is at this point in the procedure that path analysis demonstrates its advantage as a procedure for determining the adequacy of a model. To accept a model as adequate or plausible, it is not enough that all of the covariances are significant and strong along the hypothesized causal paths. It is also necessary to determine how well the model explains or accounts for the covariances among the *other* variables in the original study. Using path analysis, one can test the degree to which the theory embodied in the model corresponds to *all* of the original facts, that is, all of the original correlations in the study. This is done by identifying all of the paths by which each pair of variables in the model covaries, using regression analyses to compute the covariance contributed by each of these paths, and then summing the results. If the model is to be accepted as plausible, the sum of the covariances derived from the model should approximate the zero-order correlations obtained from the data (as in Table 5). Any significant discrepancy between the estimates derived from the model and the correlations obtained from the original data indicates that the model is inadequate. J.R. Duffy, Watt, and R.J. Duffy (1981) have presented detailed information about the calculations involved in these procedures.

In Model 1, there were four correlation coefficients in the original data that were significantly different ($p < .05$) from the coefficients estimated from the model (APHASIA-PANTEXP, APHASIA-PANTREC, POSTERIOR-PANTEXP, and PANTEXP-PANTREC). They were all hypothesized to be null covariances in the model. Model 1, therefore, was rejected as implausible because it did not generate results that were consistent with the 'facts', that is, with the original data.

Model 2 - Asymbolia

In this model (Figure 2), a causal relationship between aphasia and both pantomime recognition and expression was hypothesized. This was a test of the central symbolic deficit hypothesis (asymbolia) in which both verbal and nonverbal disorders are the result of an inability to engage in representational symbolic functions regardless of the specific behaviors involved.

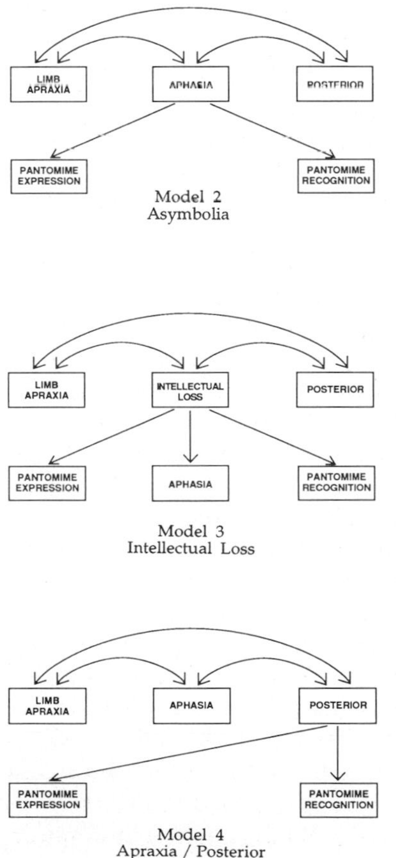

Figure 2. Deficits in Pantomime Recognition and Expression in Aphasia: Models 2, 3, and 4

Model 2 proved to be implausible because it failed to regenerate the original correlations of POSTERIOR-PANTEXP and POSTERIOR-PANTREC, which were hypothesized in the model as null.

Model 3 - Intellectual Loss

In this model (Figure 2), a single cause, intellectual loss, was hypothesized to cause deficits in pantomime expression, pantomime recognition, and aphasia. This theory holds that simultaneous deficits in pantomime expression, pantomime recognition, and aphasia are the result of an absence or distortion of the concepts that are represented by pantomime or by words; if a concept is deficient, both its verbal and nonverbal symbol will be deficient. In this model, aphasia, as well as pantomime expression and recognition, was hypothesized to be impaired by intellectual loss. Model 3 also proved to be implausible because of its failure to regenerate the original significant correlations of APHASIA-PANTEXP, APHASIA-PANTREC, APHASIA-APRAXIA, APRAXIA-PANTEXP, POSTERIOR-PANTEXP, and POSTERIOR-PANTREC.

Thus far, we had tested three single-cause models that attempted to account for pantomimic deficits as the result of either posterior lesion, limb apraxia, symbolic deficit, or intellectual loss. The procedures of causal modeling lead us to reject all three models as implausible, because none could adequately account for the correlations obtained in the original data. The next reasonable step was either to try other versions of structural or central hypotheses or to combine the previous models and determine whether combinations of causes (multimodal models) were plausible explanations of the obtained data. We next examined two other structural models, a single-cause in Model 4 and a dual cause in Model 5. Models 6 and 7 were then tested as combinations of structural and central causal factors.

Model 4 - Apraxia/Posterior

This was a second structural model (Figure 2) that hypothesized that *both* pantomime expression and recognition were the result of a posterior lesion with no effect on pantomime expression from limb apraxia. Rothi and Heilman (1985), among others, have proposed that impairment to a visuokinesthetic system in the parietal lobe may produce deficits in both recognition and motor planning. Model 4 also proved to be implausible because of its failure to regenerate the original correlations of APHASIA-PANTEXP, APHASIA-PANTREC, and APRAXIA-PANTEXP.

Model 5 - Apraxia/Posterior

This model (Figure 3) was a combination of Model 4 and an additional path to PANTEXP obtained by adding the causal path from APRAXIA to PANTEXP. It hypothesized that pantomime expression deficits could result from both anterior (APRAXIA) and posterior (POSTERIOR) cerebral lesions. Model 5 also proved to be implausible because it failed to regenerate the original correlations of APHASIA-PANTEXP and APHASIA-PANTREC, and APRAXIA-PANTEXP. Given the failure of the simpler models to prove plausible, it was reasonable to try multicausal models next by combining the most promising of the single-cause models. The next two models presented are multicausal.

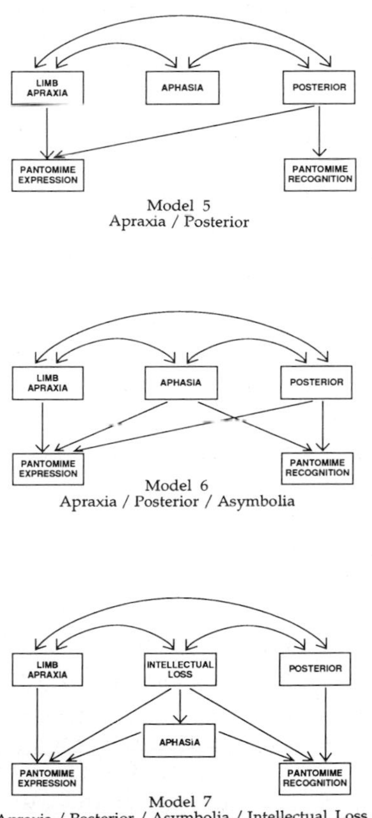

Figure 3. Deficits in Pantomime Recognition and Expression in Aphasia: Models 5, 6, and 7

Model 6 - Apraxia/Posterior/Asymbolia

This model (Figure 3) was a combination of Model 2 (Asymbolia) and Model 5 (Apraxia/Posterior). In this Model 6, there are three causal paths to pantomime expression and two to pantomime recognition. Unlike the previous five models, Model 6 proved to be plausible. All of the path coefficients were significant, and all of the correlations of the original data were regenerated.

At this point in the testing of various models, path analysis has provided objective support for rejecting the first five models and favorably considering Model 6, one that supports the theory that pantomimic deficits in a sample of unselected aphasics are the result of *both* structural and central symbolic disorders. It is important to note that path analysis does not prove that a model is the correct or best one; it simply supports the conclusion that a model, such as Model 6, is not implausible. If more than one model proves to be plausible, then a procedure is needed to choose from among the several plausible models. Path analysis allows a goodness-of-fit procedure that may be used for choosing among plausible models. This goodness-of-fit procedure is described following the presentation of Model 7.

Model 7 - Apraxia/Posterior/Asymbolia/Intellectual Loss.

This model (Figure 3) was a combination of the plausible Model 6 with Model 3, intellectual loss. This is a more complex model and approaches the limits of usefulness of causal modeling when an 'everything causes everything' model can easily be expected to reproduce the original results. Parsimoniously, the best model is the one that accounts for the effects with the least number of causal variables. Not unexpectedly, Model 7 also proved to be plausible and a choice had to be made between it and the other plausible model, Model 6.

Choosing Among Plausible Models

The choice of plausible models is made on the basis of which one most closely regenerates the original correlations. This decision is made using a test of goodness-of-fit of the overall model. An index of the goodness-of-fit is obtained by averaging the differences between the original and the estimated correlation coefficients for each variable. The model with the smaller mean difference between the original and the regenerated coefficients is the better model. The mean difference between original and generated coefficients for Model 6 was 6%, resulting in a goodness of fit of 94%. The overall goodness of fit for Model 7 was 85%. Therefore, on the basis of the quantitative evidence provided by path analysis, we would choose Model 6, the Apraxia/Posterior/Asymbolia model, as the causal model that best explains the data obtained.

Interpretation of Causal Models

In addition to providing a basis for a judgment about the general plausibility of the overall model, path analysis retains information about the relative strength of the contributions of each of the causal factors. The partial and multiple regression coefficients, as shown in Model 1, can be interpreted in terms of the relative strengths of the causal variables. For example, in Model 6, the coefficients for the three causal paths to PANTEXP were APRAXIA, .29; APHASIA, .49; and, POSTERIOR, .28. This means that 8.4% (.29 squared) of the variance in PANTEXP was accounted for by APRAXIA, 24% by APHASIA, and 7.8% by POSTERIOR. Clearly, in this example, APHASIA (24%) is three times more potent in explaining PANTEXP than is either APRAXIA (8.4%) or POSTERIOR (7.8%). Thus, all of the advantages that may be derived from using partial and multiple regression analyses -- discussed in an earlier section -- are retained in the use of path analysis.

Caution is always required in generalizing the results of an investigation to a parent population, and so it is with causal modeling. Causal models are evaluated by how well they can account for the original correlational data obtained from a specific sample of subjects. Of all the models tested, Model 6 best represents the data obtained in our study of a group of *unselected* aphasic subjects. It supports the explanation of pantomimic deficits in aphasics as resulting from *both* a structural and a central origin, but only for unselected aphasics. Obviously, other models that were rejected as implausible for our set of data might be plausible for another set of data obtained from a different and more restricted sample of subjects. For example, if subjects were selected on the basis of type of aphasia, severity of aphasia, site of lesion, or some other clinical characteristics or test performance, it may be that a different model (perhaps one of the single-cause models) would prove to be the best causal model. In the present study, path analysis addressed the question of whether the model fit the data for our group of *unselected aphasics distributed throughout a wide range of severity of aphasia.*

It is also obvious that the validity of the measures chosen to represent the cause and effect factors is an issue that can affect the outcome. For example, in our study the Raven's Progressive Matrices was used as the measure of 'intellectual loss'; it is a commonly used measure because of its nonverbal features. However, the Raven's Progressive Matrices may not measure the kind of cognitive loss associated with pantomime deficits in aphasia. Gainotti (1988), for example, has suggested that variables that represent a disruption at the semantic-lexical level of cognition would be more likely to show stronger degrees of association with pantomimic deficits than would the visual-spatial intelligence assessed by the Raven's.

Causal modeling strategies have much to contribute to neuropsychological research. Whatever modification of subject selection or variable definition is proposed in future studies, casual modeling represents an important advance in the analytic procedures available for the empirical investigation of causal factors responsible for pantomimic deficits in aphasia.

Reprise

Goodglass and Kaplan's 1963 publication of their investigation of gesture/pantomime is recognized as a landmark contribution to neuropsychology and one that stimulated a number of new lines of research. Their opening remarks called attention to an aspect of aphasia that previously had received little serious attention:

> The literature on aphasia from the middle of the 1800's includes references to the ability of aphasic patients to indicate, by means of pantomime, their awareness of certain things which they cannot verbalize, as for example, how to use an object which they cannot name. However, in reality we were impressed with the rarity with which such pantomiming is comprehensible, and the frequency with which it consists of aimless waving which leaves the examiner guessing and the patient frustrated. (p. 703).

Goodglass and Kaplan produced convincing evidence of the reality of gestural/pantomimic problems associated with aphasia -- problems that have been confirmed repeatedly by subsequent studies. Their study also investigated several hypotheses regarding the causes of gesture/pantomime impairments in aphasia. Their conclusion that limb apraxia (and not a central symbolic deficit) was a cause of gestural/pantomimic disorders has been cited frequently in favor of the structuralist theory of pantomimic deficits. So original and persuasive was their study that it was over a decade before other investigations were undertaken.

In the mid 1970s, a number of studies appeared that confirmed Goodglass and Kaplan's observations of aphasic pantomimic deficits, but challenged their generally accepted conclusions, and renewed an interest in the centralist theories of pantomimic disorders. Pickett (1974) reported no support for the conclusion of Goodglass and Kaplan that expressive pantomime deficits were related to limb apraxia. In addition, he reported that pantomime recognition was also impaired and highly correlated with pantomimic expression, and both were highly correlated with severity of aphasia. Consistent with Pickett's results, R.J. Duffy, J.R. Duffy, and Pearson (1975), Gainotti and Lemmo (1976), and Varney (1978) reported significant deficits in pantomime recognition that were highly correlated with severity of aphasic verbal deficits. A renewed interest in pantomimic deficits followed, and a number of studies concerned with identifying the causes of pantomimic deficits were generated with attention focused on central cognitive theories. Investigations of pantomimic deficits have played an important role in the broader area of research concerned with identifying and describing the nature of cognitive deficits in aphasia. Gainotti (1988) recently has provided a review of investigations into the question of cognitive deficits in aphasia that includes the important contributions made by studies of pantomimic deficits.

Despite the last 25 years of research, structuralists and centralists still disagree about the cause of pantomimic deficits. Compelling data have not yet appeared to favor either explanation. The issues are complex and inappropriate psychometric procedures may have contributed to the slow progress. A major limitation of the *post hoc* observational studies of pantomime deficits has been the psychometric level of measurement employed in defining the variables. The frequent use of ordinal and nominal levels of measurement has made the reliable estimation of covariance very difficult. The use of interval level measurements, on the other hand, allows for a relatively easy and straightforward estimate of true covariance by using partial and multiple regression analyses. This is a critical issue because covariance is an essential condition for the deduction of causal relations in retrospective observational studies. The estimation of covariance is a particular problem in studies of pantomimic deficits because of the extensive intercorrelations that are typically obtained among all of the variables studied. To estimate true covariance, the spurious correlations among the variables must be identified and eliminated.

However, even in the best of circumstances when regression analyses can be used to estimate the covariance between cause and effect variables, support for a particular explanation of the data generally reflects a high degree of subjective interpretation. The investigator must interpret the data and reach his conclusions by rationalization without benefit of an objective check on the consistency of his conclusions with the data obtained. Often, there may be several plausible explanations for a given set of results. It would be most important to be able objectively to select the most adequate explanation from among several plausible alternatives. Such an objective procedure, causal modeling, is available, although it has rarely been used in neuropsychology.

We demonstrated the use of path analysis in the testing of seven theoretical models proposed to explain the causes of pantomimic deficits in aphasia. We showed how path analysis objectively assists in the rejection of implausible models and the selection of the best of the plausible models. The model that best explained our data was one that evidenced both a centralist and a structuralist contribution to both pantomimic expression and recognition in our sample of unselected aphasic subjects. Our results emphasize the need for a shift from research paradigms that search for a single cause to ones that allow for the possibility of multiple causal factors. The use of causal modeling strategies in future investigations should greatly advance our understanding of the significance of the various causal factors that may account for the presence of pantomimic deficits in the syndrome of aphasia.

Addendum A: Aphasia as a 'Cause' of Pantomimic Deficits

It was Goodglass and Kaplan (1963) who first proposed that covariance between severity of aphasia and gestural/pantomimic deficits is evidence of a central symbolic cause of these nonverbal deficits. This interpretation has generally been accepted in the psychometric sense that 'cause' means to 'predict' or to 'be associated with'. Strong correlation between aphasia and pantomime indicates covariance between pantomime and aphasia *or something associated with aphasia.* This 'something' is generally interpreted to be a central symbolic or cognitive impairment. Therefore, a correlation with aphasia is interpreted as a correlation with a central deficit. This indirect approach to demonstrating a causal relationship between pantomime and a central deficit would not be necessary if there were available a valid and reliable measure of the 'central deficit'. In summary, it is in the psychometric sense that aphasia 'predicts' or is 'associated with' pantomimic deficits that aphasia is said to 'cause' pantomimic deficits.

Some speculation has been given to the possibility that aphasia may 'cause' pantomimic deficits in an instrumental sense rather than in a psychometric sense. That is, if words are instrumental in and necessary to successful pantomime expression and recognition, then impairment of verbal ability would cause pantomimic deficits. Other examples of instrumental causes are limb apraxia and visual agnosia; it is in the instrumental sense that limb apraxia is hypothesized to cause deficits in pantomimic expression and visual agnosia in pantomimic recognition. This interpretation of verbal causes of pantomimic deficits is referred to as the verbal mediation theory in which words are necessary for the successful production and recognition of pantomime. (See R.J. Duffy & J.R.

Duffy, 1981, p. 82, for further discussion of the verbal mediation theory of pantomimic deficits.) Although investigators have acknowledged the theoretical possibility of the verbal mediation of pantomimic behavior, it has received little support as a plausible explanation. Current practice is to accept the interpretation that covariance between severity of aphasic verbal deficits and pantomimic deficits is supportive of the theory that there exists a central deficit common to both verbal and nonverbal behaviors.

Addendum B: An Investigation of the Causes of Pantomimic Deficits

The subjects and variables described here are from an investigation (R.J. Duffy, Watt, & J.R. Duffy, 1989) of the causes of pantomime expression and recognition deficits in aphasia. These data were originally obtained and reported by R.J. Duffy and J.R. Duffy (1981). We (R.J. Duffy et. al., 1989) have revised and updated the 1981 data in two ways in order to subject them to analysis by causal modeling (path analysis). To avoid confusion with other terms when discussing the variables of our study, we have adopted the convention of placing the names of the variables in capital letters, both in Addendum B and in the text.

In the original 1981 study, APHASIA was operationally defined as the overall mean score of the Porch Index of Communicative Ability (PICA) (Porch, 1981). The overall mean score is the mean of 18 PICA subtests covering speech (I, IV, IX, XII), auditory comprehension (VI, X), reading (V, VII), writing (A, B, C, D), pantomime (II, III), visual matching (VIII, XI), and graphic copying (E, F). This measure of aphasia has been criticized because of the possibility that the inclusion of subtests involving pantomime, visual matching, copying, and even reading and writing, could spuriously inflate the correlations between APHASIA and pantomime recognition or pantomime expression. It has been suggested that the purest measure of verbal impairment in aphasia includes only speech and auditory comprehension. We, therefore, redefined our 1981 measure of APHASIA for the present study and have included only measures of speech and auditory comprehension.

The second change in the data was to add a variable, POSTERIOR, to serve as a hypothesized causal variable for pantomime comprehension deficits.

Subjects

Forty two older left-hemisphere-damaged aphasic subjects (all but three from CVAs) ranging in severity from the 7th to 95th percentile on the PICA, with a median of 52nd percentile, were obtained from six hospitals and treatment centers and were involved in the 1981 study. Additional demographic descriptions of the subjects may be found in R.J. Duffy and J.R. Duffy (1981). Because almost all the subjects were drawn from centers with active treatment programs, our sample may represent a clinical population with few of the very mild forms or infrequently occurring types of aphasia.

Variables

The following two measures of pantomime performance were obtained using the New England Pantomime Tests (R.J. Duffy & J.R. Duffy, 1984). All tests were administered in a standardized manner using nonverbal conditioning procedures to train the subject to perform the task. In addition, the stimulus presentations and subjects' responses required no verbalizations.

PANTREC - the number of items performed correctly on the New England Pantomime Recognition Test (NEPRT). This test consists of 46 items. The examiner pantomimes the use of a common object and the subject points to the object being pantomimed from among a choice of four pictures.

PANTEXP - the overall mean score of the New England Pantomime Expression Test (NEPET). This test consists of 23 items taken from the 46 items of the NEPRT. The subject is nonverbally conditioned to demonstrate the use of an object when shown its picture. A multidimensional scoring system similar to the PICA is used.

Causal Variables

The following four variables served as the independent variables or predictors (i.e, causes) of the dependent or target variables of pantomime expression and pantomime recognition.

APHASIA - the mean of four PICA speech subtests (I, IV, IX, XII) and two auditory comprehension subtest (VI, X).

APRAXIA - the overall mean score of the Limb Apraxia Test (J.R. Duffy, 1974; J.R. Duffy & R.J. Duffy, 1989; also see chapter by J.R. Duffy & R.J. Duffy in this volume). The Limb Apraxia Test is a comprehensive test of unilateral limb praxis. A total of 252 imitative movement components are scored on a 21-point, equal-interval, multidimensional scoring system and an overall mean score obtained. This score reflects impairment of manual motor programming often attributed to lesions of the left frontal lobe motor association areas.

POSTERIOR - the mean of two PICA visual matching subtests (VIII, XI) and two graphic copying subtest (E, copying words, and F, copying geometric forms). This score is a measure of damage to a posterior cerebral area (lower parietal or parietal occipital) hypothesized to interfere with visual recognition and/or motor performance (see Rothi and Heilman, 1985). Although the term POSTERIOR is anatomical (unlike APHASIA, APRAXIA, and INTELL), it represents impairment of processes presumably processed by the posterior cerebral areas. The processes may be visual agnosia, visuokinesthetic motor programming, or a visuomotor disturbance or some combination of these processes. Because we are not attempting to specify which of these processes may be operating, we use the anatomical term to represent them.

INTELL(ectual Loss) - the number of items correct on the Raven's (Standard) Progressive Matrices (Raven, 1960), a visual pattern recognition test used as a measure of general intelligence. This test is frequently used with aphasics because it can be administered and performed nonverbally.

References

Bay, E. (1964). Present concepts of aphasia. *Geriatrics*, **19**, 319-331.

Coelho, C., & Duffy, R.J. (1987). The relationship of the acquisition of manual signs to severity of aphasia: a training study. *Brain and Language*, **31**, 328-345.

Cohen, J., & Cohen, P. (1983). *Applied multiple regression/correlation analysis for the behavioral sciences.* Hillsdale, NJ: Lawrence Erlbaum Associates.

Cole, M., & Cole, M. (1971). *Pierre Marie's papers on speech disorders.* New York: Hafner.

Critchley, M. (1970). *Aphasiology and other aspects of language.* London: E. Arnold Publishers.

Daniloff, J.J., Noll, J.D., Fristoe, M., & Lloyd, L.L. (1982). Gesture recognition in patients with aphasia. *Journal of Speech and Hearing Disorders*, **47**, 43-49.

Duffy, J.R. (1974). Comparison of brain injured and non-brain injured subjects on an objective test of manual apraxia. Ph.D. Dissertation, University of Connecticut.

Duffy, J.R., & Duffy, R.J. (1989). The Limb Apraxia Test: an imitative measure of upper limb apraxia. In T. Prescott (Ed.), *Clinical aphasiology, Vol. 18* (pp. 145-159). Boston: College-Hill.

Duffy, J.R., & Watkins, L.B. (1984). The effect of response choice relatedness on pantomime and verbal recognition ability in aphasic patients. *Brain and Language*, **21**, 291-306.

Duffy, J.R., Watt, J., & Duffy, R.J. (1981). Path analysis: a strategy for investigating multivariate causal relationships in communication disorders. *Journal of Speech and Hearing Research*, **24**, 474-490.

Duffy, R.J., & Duffy, J.R. (1981). Three studies of deficits in pantomimic expression and pantomimic recognition in aphasia. *Journal of Speech and Hearing Research*, **24**, 70-84.

Duffy, R.J., & Duffy, J.R. (1984). *New England pantomime tests*. Austin, Texas: Pro-ed.

Duffy, R.J., Duffy, J.R., & Pearson, K.L. (1975). Impairment of pantomime recognition in aphasics. *Journal of Speech and Hearing Research*, **18**, 115-132.

Duffy, R.J., & Liles, B.Z. (1975). A translation of Finkelnburg's (1870) lecture on aphasia as 'asymboly' with commentary. *Journal of Speech and Hearing Disorders*, **44**, 156-168.

Duffy, R.J., Watt, J., & Duffy, J.R. (1989). Causal models of pantomime expression and recognition deficits in aphasia. Unpublished data.

Ferro, J.M., Mariano, M.G., Castro-Caldas, A., & Santos, M.E. (1980). Gesture recognition in aphasia. *Journal of Clinical Neuropsychology*, **2**, 277-292.

Feyereisen, P., Seron, X., & De Macar, M. (1981). L'interprétation de différentes catégories de gestes chez les patients aphasiques. *Neuropsychologia*, **19**, 515-521.

Francis, D.J. (1989). An introduction to structural equation models. *Journal of Clinical and Experimental Neuropsychology*, **10**, 623-639.

Gainotti, G. (1988). Nonverbal cognitive disturbances in aphasia. In H. Whitaker (Ed.), *Contemporary reviews in neuropsychology* (pp. 129-158). New York: Springer-Verlag.

Gainotti, G., & Lemmo, M. (1976). Comprehension of symbolic gestures in aphasia. *Brain and Language*, **3**, 451-460.

Glosser, G., Wiener, M., & Kaplan, E. (1986). Communicative gestures in aphasia. *Brain and Language*, **27**, 45-359.

Goldstein, K. (1948). *Language and language disturbances*. New York: Grune & Stratton.

Goodglass, H., & Kaplan, E. (1963). Disturbance of gesture and pantomime in aphasia. *Brain*, **86**, 703-720.

Head, H. (1915). Hughlings Jackson on aphasia and kindred affections of speech. *Brain*, **38**, 1-189.

Head, H. (1926). *Aphasia and kindred disorders of speech, Vol. 1*. Cambridge: Cambridge University Press.

Kadish, J. (1978). A neuropsychological approach to the study of gesture and pantomime in aphasia. *South African Journal of Communication Disorders*, **25**, 102-177.

Netsu, R., & Marquardt, T. (1984). Pantomime in aphasia: effects of stimulus characteristics. *Journal of Communication Disorders*, **17**, 37-46.

Pickett, L. (1972). An Assessment of Gestural and Pantomimic Deficit in Aphasic Patients. MA Thesis, University of New Mexico.

Pickett, L. (1974). An assessment of gestural and pantomimic deficit in aphasic patients. *Acta Symbolica*, **3**, 69-86.

Porch, B. (1981). *Porch index of communicative ability.* Palo Alto, CA: Consulting Psychologists Press.

Raven, J.C. (1960). Guide to the standard progressive matrices. London: H.K. Lewis.

Rothi, J.G., & Heilman, K.M. (1985). Ideomotor apraxia: gestural discrimination, comprehesion, and memory. In E.A. Roy (Ed.), *Neuropsychological studies of apraxia and related disorders* (pp. 65-74). Amsterdam: North-Holland.

Seron, X., van der Kaa, M.A., Remitz, A., & van der Linden, M. (1979). Pantomime interpretation and aphasia. *Neuropsychologia*, **17**, 661-668.

Varney, N. (1978). Linguistic correlates of pantomime recognition in aphasic patients. *Journal of Neurology, Neurosurgery, and Psychiatry*, **41**, 564-568.

Weisenburg, T., & McBride, K. (1936). *Aphasia: A clinical and psychological study*. Philadelphia: The Commonwealth Press.

Cerebral Control of Speech and Limb Movements
G.E. Hammond (editor)

Chapter 15

THE DISSOCIATION OF APHASIA FROM APRAXIA OF SPEECH, IDEOMOTOR LIMB, AND BUCCOFACIAL APRAXIA

Paula A. Square-Storer
University of Toronto

Eric A. Roy
Waterloo University

and

Sharon C. Hogg
University of Toronto

The purpose of this chapter is to provide theoretical arguments and empirical evidence which point to the separateness of the disorders aphasia and apraxia. The literature concerning ideomotor limb and oral (buccofacial) apraxia is critically re-evaluated, emphasizing the possible contamination of out interpretation of apraxia by aphasic disturbances. Results of our work are discussed, emphasizing dissociations of the two disorders. Finally, we conclude by providing evidence for the hypothesis that a central praxis mechanism may exist which controls volitional movement in the limb, oral nonspeech, and speech modalities.

This chapter discusses the relationship of aphasia and the apraxias, the latter including apraxia of speech, ideomotor limb, and buccofacial. In this context, *aphasia* is defined as a reduced ability to use linguistic and representational symbols. The ability to apply rule systems governing the arrangement and connection of language symbols - semantic, syntactic, and phonological - is also disordered. Both the encoding and decoding of representational and linguistic symbols and rules are affected, albeit to different relative degrees contingent upon site and extent of damage to the language dominant hemisphere. Like Schuell (Jenkins, Jimenez-Pabon, Shaw, & Sefer, 1975) and Darley (1982), it is our belief that *all* language modalities of expression - including verbal, written, and, where applicable, symbolic and/or linguistically rule-governed manual 'sign language' expression - and *all* modalities of language comprehension - including auditory-verbal, reading, and, where applicable, symbolic and/or linguistically rule-governed manual 'sign language' comprehension - are affected in *each* aphasic patient; most standardized aphasia batteries, however, are insensitive to subtle modality disturbances and, thus, some may appear preserved. We also believe that the relative degree of impairment for each linguistic rule system - syntactic, semantic, and phonological - depends on site and extent of damage to the language-dominant hemisphere. Furthermore, it is our belief that both expression and comprehension of representational gestures is disrupted in aphasia. Hence, we view aphasia as a disruption of the ability to efficiently use representational and linguistic symbols and rules for both expressive and receptive communication; this disruption crosses all modalities of communication.

We view *apraxia* as a disorder which is distinct from aphasia. The apraxias - including ideomotor limb, buccofacial, and apraxia of speech - are disorders of the motor system.

Finally, we believe that there *may* be a central motor programming system which controls all 'modalities of action' - limbs, orofacial nonverbal, and vocal tract-facial speech movements.

In this chapter we will present constructs for our conceptualizations of the disorders of aphasia and apraxia as well as arguments in favor of their separateness. Where appropriate, previous literature will be critically reviewed. Finally, the results from our individual investigations and joint studies undertaken in the Neuropraxis Research Laboratory in Toronto will be presented.

Levels of Motor Control

Similar to the beliefs of Paillard (1983), we feel that there are several levels of control for intentional movement of the limbs and orofacial and vocal tract mechanisms - planning, programming and execution. While some believe that motor control is organized hierarchically (for example, see Marsden, 1982), others believe that motor behavior is controlled coalitionally (for example, see Kelso & Tuller, 1981). These levels of motor control are reviewed in our other chapter in this volume; that review highlights our conceptualization of the disorder, apraxia, as being motoric in nature, and thus distinct from aphasia.

Levels of Control for Communication

For efficient symbolic communication, either by gesture or speech, certain cognitive processes precede the motoric operations requisite for intentional movements of the limbs and/or orofacial structures and vocal tract. The major antecedent process involves the translation of a 'designatum' (idea, feeling, percept, etc.) into a representational communicative 'symbol' or 'sign' (word, phrase, iconic gesture, pantomime etc). Most certainly this stage of *representational translation* precedes the planning/programming and motor execution processes necessary to transmit the message. Nonetheless, these same motor control processes are used to communicate the representation regardless of whether the transmission is by speech, writing, pantomime, or gesture. In the disorder of aphasia, there is ample evidence that the expression and comprehension of gestural symbols is generally *not* preserved (see reviews by Feyereisen & Seron, 1982a, b; Peterson & Kirshner, 1981). In some aphasic individuals, however, gestural expression and/or comprehension may be relatively less impaired than expression and/or comprehension of linguistic symbols (see examples of aphasic cases who learned sign and/or iconic gestural communication systems as reviewed by Peterson & Kirshner, 1981).

But how may the process of representational translation go awry? One of many ways in which representational symbols are stored systematically in memory is with regard to their relatedness of meaning (semanticity). Thus, *inaccessibility of 'semantic memory stores'* or *malselection of a symbol once within a 'semantic memory store'* (substitution) are examples of deficits in representational translation. Motor plans/programs will be generated for the 'representational symbol' selected, whether that symbol is correct or not. The motor plan/program for the malselected symbol may be entirely appropriate. That is, the general plan as well as the specific temporal program of neural impulses necessary to achieve the motor plan may be entirely correct, but the 'wrong' communicative representation may have been selected during the representational translation process.

Thus, if the wrong semantic representation is selected, a wrong movement will be substituted for the target, e.g., 'sawing' motion for 'screwing' motion in the pantomimed use of tools. Or, if access to the memory store is completely blocked, an undifferentiated response such as a gross waving action of the hand and arm may occur or no response at all may be given.

To our way of thinking, 'aphasic' errors of verbal expression, specifically verbal paraphasias, may be explained similarly. In aphasic verbal expression (or manual sign expression), the wrong lexical item may be selected from the lexico-semantic memory file (see Luce & Pisone, 1988, for a review of theories of lexical storage). For example, the wrong word in the 'words for tools' lexico-semantic memory file may be selected, e.g., 'saw' for 'screwdriver', an instance of a semantic paraphasia (substitution).

The issue arises, then, as to whether we should consider production of a 'wrong' representational gesture an 'apractic' error in patients with left-hemisphere (or dominant-hemisphere) damage. We should not be so presumptuous as to assume that errors of this type are apractic (motor) errors since, if produced in their entirety and with motor fluidity, they most probably reflect higher cognitive symbolic selection disorders. As stated above, these higher cognitive selection disorders represent malselections from or inaccessibility to memory files whether semantically organized or organized in other fashions. Likewise, amorphous movements and 'no responses' may reflect 'aphasic' rather than 'apractic' responses.

The manner in which limb and buccofacial apraxia has been traditionally tested also has resulted in contamination of praxis performance with aphasic impairment. Most tests of praxis are heavily laden with items which require performance to auditory-verbal command. Since auditory-verbal comprehension disturbances are a hallmark of aphasia, it is nearly impossible to ferret out the effects of aphasic comprehension disturbances versus motor planning/programming disruptions, i.e., apraxia, when this method of testing is used.

Incorrect, undifferentiated and amorphous limb (and/or orofacial and vocal tract) responses, however, may also result from *motor* planning/programming disturbances. As reviewed by Roy (1982), 'slips of action' occur when there is unintentional activation of similar and/or associated movements for the intended action. Omissions, additions, and misordering of elements as well as the blending together of actions may also occur. Many of these types of errors may be context- or situation-dependent in that the environment, by virtue of the association between stimuli and responses within it, precipitates the intrusion of an error or the omission or misordering of elements necessary to the intended action or action sequence. In these cases, representational processes may be operating efficiently, but motor *planning* appears to go awry. In the verbal output of aphasic individuals, some literal paraphasic errors (phoneme substitution errors) and paragraphic errors (grapheme substitution errors) may represent disruptions to motor planning while others may be reflective of symbolic representational disruptions. Finally, distorted actions, added or omitted features of action or the blending together of features from two subcomponents of an action sequence may arise due to errors in motor programming. That is, the spatial and temporal aspects of a movement may be deviant because of a disruption to the ability to set out the internal program for timing of neural impulses to the muscles.

It is the process of *programming* which has most frequently been implicated as deviant in the disorder of apraxia of speech (Darley, Aronson, & Brown, 1975; Kent & Rosenbek, 1983; Square-Storer, 1989; Square-Storer & Hayden, 1989) and, recently, Square-Storer, Qualizza, and Roy (1989) have implicated *programming* as the level of dysfunction in oral apraxia. However, with regard to motor speech disorders, deviant motor programming may not only characterize apraxia of speech but may also be characteristic of some of the dysarthrias such as ataxic, hyperkinetic, and hypokinetic dysarthria.

From our preceding discussion of levels of control for communication, it becomes evident that, within our construct, 'language/symbolic' processing is independent of 'motor processing'. With this thesis in mind we will reinterpret the literature concerning the relationship of aphasia and apraxia.

The Literature Re-reviewed

Aphasia and Apraxia are Due to 'Asymbolia'

In 1870, Finkelnberg (R.J. Duffy & Liles, 1979) put forth the notion that damage to the dominant hemisphere resulted in a generalized disturbance to express or comprehend 'symbols' in any modality. Broca (1861) expressed a similar view nine years earlier; he described the 'general language faculty' as the mechanism responsible for establishing "... a constant relationship between an idea and a sign, whether or not the sign is a gesture, a figure, or some kind of diagram." Others agreeing with the position that aphasia is a disorder of verbal and extraverbal symbolization have included Critchley (1939), Goldstein (1948), and Bay (1964). As reviewed by R.J. Duffy in a previous chapter, results of his work and that of his colleagues (1975, 1977, and 1981) have lent strong support to the notion that aphasic individuals possess impaired symbolic representational systems in that most demonstrate both pantomimic expression and comprehension deficits and the pantomimic deficits are highly correlated with aphasic 'verbal' impairment (see, for example, R.J. Duffy & J.R. Duffy, 1981). In another large-scale quantitative study, Gainotti and Lemmo (1976) found gesture comprehension to be highly correlated with auditory verbal semantic comprehension among aphasic patients. They concluded that both were due to either a symbolic deficit or a generalized 'semantic' impairment.

It is interesting to note that the majority of investigators reporting that, among aphasic individuals, gesture impairment is highly related to expressive and/or receptive language impairment have utilized self-generated pantomimes or recognition of pantomimed actions correlative to objects as their dependent measures of gestural ability (Pickett, 1974; J.R. Duffy, Watt, & R.J. Duffy, 1975; Kadish et al., 1981). It has been unfortunate that most contemporary investigators of ideomotor and buccofacial apraxia have utilized, to a large extent, pantomimic (e.g., 'Show me how you use a hammer') and/or representational gesture (e.g., salute) when attempting to assess praxis deficits (motor planning/programming deficits). But this means of assessment has been a long-standing historical one (see for example, Liepmann, 1905). In our contemporary literature, much of what we know about limb and orofacial apraxia has been derived from investigations of the abilities of aphasic patients to perform items from 'apraxia' batteries comprised, in large part, of items which require the *self-evocation of symbolic gestures* (Lehmkuhl, Poeck, & Willmes, 1983; Poeck, Lehmkuhl, & Willmes, 1982; Kertesz, Ferro, & Shewan, 1984; Kertesz & Hooper, 1982; Kertesz & Ferro, 1984; De Renzi, Pieczuro, & Vignolo, 1966; Poeck & Kerschensteiner, 1975; Agostini, Coletti, Orlando, & Tredici, 1983; De Renzi, Faglioni, & Sorgato, 1982; De Renzi, Faglioni, Scarpa, & Crisi, 1986; Goodglass & Kaplan, 1963; Haaland & Flaherty, 1984).

Another relevant issue regarding the validity of apraxia testing is the consideration of batteries which require a patient to decipher the meaning of one representational message and then transcode it into another representational message, which is expressed in another modality. For example, in asking a patient to show how he would brush his teeth, we are asking him to decode an auditory-verbal representational message. Not only may auditory-verbal comprehension go awry due to lexical miscomprehension, erroneous syntactic and semantic processing, and/or auditory verbal memory deficits, but the *transcoding* of the command into a pantomimic representation may also be negatively influenced by aphasia. Symbolic transcoding deficits have traditionally been cited as a cornerstone of aphasia (see, for example, Weigl, 1961; Schuell, 1964; Darley, 1982). Fortunately, in the series of studies by Kertesz and colleagues (Kertesz & Hooper, 1982; Kertesz et al., 1984; Kertesz & Ferro, 1984), aphasic patients were not penalized for inability to perform symbolic gestures to verbal command (symbol-to-symbol transcoding) because only imitative responses were used in subsequent analyses; such penalties are given, however, when administering the 'apraxia battery' from the Western Aphasia Battery (Kertesz, 1982).

Others have apparently recognized the inadequacy of testing praxis via methods of symbol-to-symbol transcoding (representational 'word' presented acoustically and transcoded to a representational 'gesture') in that many investigators are now relying strictly on imitation for the testing of praxis among dominant-hemisphere damaged patients (see, for example, De Renzi, Faglioni, Lodesani, & Vecchi, 1983; De Renzi, Motti, & Nichelli, 1980; Basso, Luzzatti, & Spinnler, 1980). Others have included a great number of imitative items for symbolic gesture production on their praxis batteries (see, for example, Goodglass & Kaplan, 1963; Lehmkuhl et al., 1983). This latter method certainly better *approaches* the assessment of praxis per se, but, for aphasic patients, whenever movements are used which evoke recognition of symbols, the risk of contaminating motor performance with verbal mediation deficits exists (R.J. Duffy & J.R. Duffy, 1981, and Luria, as reviewed by Fuson, 1979). That is, mismatching of the demonstrated gesture with its representational lexical symbol, due either to a representational gesture comprehension disruption or to inefficient selection from a lexico-semantic file of the correct lexical label, may lead to erroneous internal verbal mediation of the action.

Finally, some investigators have circumvented the effects of aphasia by using nonrepresentational body movements as stimuli (e.g., 'Bend your head backwards') but have persisted in administering at least a portion of their test via auditory command (see, for example, Poeck et al., 1982). In this latter case, the command section of the praxis test, again, is likely to be influenced by aphasia in that the interpretation of words (representational symbols) and the rule systems governing their arrangements and connections is the essence of aphasia; hence, praxis performance may be contaminated by aphasia.

Apraxia: A Disorder Apart from Aphasia

Although traditionally most investigators have used batteries which have included at least some 'representational symbols' to test for apraxia, there has been a strong contingency which has advocated the hypothesis that apraxia and aphasia are distinct and separate disorders (Wernicke, 1874; Liepmann, 1900; Jackson, 1932; Alajouanine & Lhermitte, 1960; de Ajuriaguerra, Hécaen, & Angelergues, 1960; Geschwind, 1965; Goodglass & Kaplan, 1963; Heilman, Rothi, Campanella, & Wolfson, 1979: De Renzi et al., 1980; Kertesz et al. 1984). The arguments in favor of this position have included the following: (1) severity measures of aphasia as well as severity measures of various aphasic modality disturbances, although highly correlated with apraxia, do not account for praxis deficits, and (2) many cases of dissociations of apraxia and aphasia exist. Each position is discussed further below.

Aphasia does not underlie apraxia

Because traditionally many items on apraxia batteries are elicited by auditory-verbal command, many investigators have been interested in the relationship of aphasic auditory-verbal comprehension deficits and praxis performance. Although auditory-verbal comprehension as well as apraxia have been measured in disparate ways, there has been a strong consensus for Liepmann's (1905) supposition that auditory-verbal comprehension disturbances are not the cause of poor praxis performances among left-hemisphere damaged patients (see, for example, Goodglass & Kaplan, 1963; De Renzi et al., 1982; Kertesz & Hooper, 1982; Lehmkuhl et al., 1983; De Renzi et al., 1986; and Feyereisen & Seron, 1982a and b).

Few researchers have investigated the relationship of aphasia and apraxia beyond the impact of effects of language comprehension on understanding the requirements of the test of apraxia. The notable exceptions have been studies by De Renzi and colleagues in which the effects of 'symbolic disruption' have been minimized by using nonrepresentational (meaningless) as well as representational items. Furthermore, only imitation was evaluated in those studies. Despite an effort to minimize the effects of aphasia, De Renzi et al. (1980, 1983) found a significant relationship between apraxia and aphasia, the latter as measured by a version of the Token Test, an auditory-verbal comprehension test which is extremely sensitive to even subtle aphasic language disturbances. De Renzi and colleagues concluded that praxis and language processes are accommodated by neuroanatomical mechanisms that are in close proximity and thus both processes (language and praxis) are likely to be damaged by a single lesion. Others agreeing with this hypothesis include Lehmkuhl et al. (1983) and Kertesz et al. (1984). More will be said about this hypothesis of neuroanatomical proximity of language and praxis mechanisms below.

Cases in which aphasia and apraxia are dissociated

Reports of cases of dissociation of aphasia and apraxia have had an even greater impact upon the hypothesis that the two disorders are separate and distinct. Most of these case reports have been of patients who were moderately to severely aphasic but who demonstrated no or only mild praxic deficits (see, for example, Heilman et al., 1979; Kertesz et al., 1984). Fewer cases of patients who demonstrate apractic symptomatology but no or mild aphasia have been reported (see, for example, Hécaen, 1978; Selnes, Rubens, Risse, & Levy, 1982; Kertesz et al., 1984; Square, 1981; Square, Darley, & Sommers, 1981, 1982; Square-Storer, Darley, & Sommers, 1988).

The instances of these dissociations have been explained neuroanatomically by several investigators. Kertesz and colleagues (1984) quantitatively investigated the functional-anatomical relationship of aphasia and apraxia. Of their 177 patients, six were found to be severely aphasic with *no* apraxia, the latter being assessed using 15 limb and 5 orofacial items, most highly representational; praxis scores, however, were contingent upon imitation, thereby reducing the confounding effects of auditory-verbal (representational) comprehension disorder. Four of these patients had atypical skull asymmetries indicating that visuokinesthetic patterns may have been represented bilaterally rather than being dominant in the left hemisphere as speculated to be the case for most individuals by Geschwind (1967). The fifth patient had a lesion which spared left premotor, frontoparietal subcortical connections, and callosal connections. The sixth patient had severe Wernicke's aphasia resulting from a small lesion in the superior temporal gyrus sparing occipital, frontal, and parietal lobes and their connections. Thus, each instance of severe aphasia with no or mild apraxia was explained by the intactness of visuokinesthetic processors and their connections; this explanation is appropriate since the test for apraxia was imitative in nature. It would have been of interest, however, to know how these same patients had performed on auditory-verbal command; both methods of assessment were undertaken but performances under the command condition were not reported. We might speculate that each subject with dissociations would have done poorly since auditory-verbal comprehension is impaired in aphasia. Further, in cases of *relatively* preserved auditory-verbal comprehension we might speculate that deviant verbal mediation might have occurred and thus had a deleterious effect on gesture production. That is, internally, a wrong semantic label could have been selected to mediate a gesture, thereby causing the production of a wrong gesture.[1]

A case study by Heilman et al. (1979) might be similarly explained. This was an example of severe global aphasia in which praxis was not disturbed. This patient, however, had (relatively) preserved reading comprehension indicating that representational transcoding was relatively unimpaired for symbolic visual information; that is, visual cortical processors and the pathways utilized for relaying visual information for interpretation by other cortical symbolic areas as well as the symbolic

---

1. The data from the study of De Renzi et al. (1980) in which imitative symbolic and nonsymbolic gestures were performed could potentially answer the question of whether internal verbal mediation deficits underlie apractic deficits when representational gestures are part of the assessment protocol. Paired comparisons for *each* patient's imitative performances on symbolic vs nonsymbolic gestures may provide insights. Unfortunately, De Renzi et al. only report group data.

interpretation centers themselves were unimpaired. In addition, this patient could comprehend and express over 100 Amer-Ind symbols, the latter being a highly iconic gestural communication system. It is interesting to note that other investigators have also noted the relationship of (relatively) preserved reading comprehension (visual symbolic transcoding) and gestural comprehension (Varney, 1978; Seron, van der Kaa, Remitz, & van der Linden, 1979) again implying that for symbolic or representational gesture comprehension neuroanatomical pathways necessary for reading comprehension must remain intact.

Even fewer instances of apraxia *without* aphasia have appeared in the literature. In fact, in the sample of Kertesz et al. (1984), apraxia was never observed in nonaphasic patients. In those studies in which apraxia has appeared as the exclusive disorder (Agostini et al., 1983; Square et al., 1981, 1982; Square-Storer et al., 1988; Square & Mlcoch, 1983), subcortical motor structures have often, but not always, been identified as lesion sites; these sites included basal ganglia and thalamus.[2] Hécaen (1978) felt, as well, that apraxia could occur in the absence of aphasia as the result of a callosal lesion. 'Pure' subcortical apraxias are easily explained from our model of motor programming and the neuroanatomical structures involved described above.

Other pure cases of apraxia without aphasia have been noted as having parietal lobe lesions (Square, 1981; Square et al., 1981, 1982; Square-Storer et al., 1988). Recently, two patients with apraxia of speech, buccofacial apraxia and ideomotor limb apraxia *without* coexisting aphasia have been added to Square's (1981; see also Square et al., 1981, 1982; Square & Mlcoch, 1983; Square-Storer et al., 1988) original series of four 'pure' apractic speakers. These latter two patients as well as two of Square's original patients had lesions of the dominant parietal cortex and, in two cases, lesions extended into the white matter. These 'pure' apractic speakers will be discussed in greater detail in a subsequent section of this chapter.

---

2. Other studies have corroborated the importance of subcortical structures in apraxia but reported also coexisting aphasia (see for example, De Renzi et al. 1986; Cappa & Vignolo, 1979). Metter et al. (1983) suggested, however, that aphasia due to basal ganglia lesions probably results because of the far-reaching metabolic effects of basal ganglia lesions on language cortex.

The common co-occurrence of apraxia and aphasia further explained - neurophysiological correlates

Studies of cortical mapping using electrical stimulation shed further light on the high incidence of co-occurrence yet independence of apraxia and aphasia. Ojemann (1984) provided a succinct review of his numerous cortical mapping studies. His results clearly show that motor and language mechanisms share many common central nervous sites. The two general sites are: (1) ventrolateral nucleus of the thalamus, and (2) the lateral perisylvian cortex of the dominant hemisphere. The latter is further subdivided into two general regions, each subserving *different* language functions: the posterior end of the inferior frontal gyrus, and anterior frontal plus inferior parietal and superior temporal areas. These latter areas are thought to be responsible for sequential motor movements and language decoding. Further, Ojemann (1984) speculated that a 'precise timing mechanism' may underlie certain aspects of language as well as motor control. (Similar views have been put forth by Calvin, 1983; Tallal, 1983; and Tzeng & Wang, 1984.) Finally, Ojemann cautioned that not all perisylvian sites responsible for language are also responsible for motor operations when he stated that "... one should not then expect every lesion that produces a language deficit will also produce a motor apraxia but rather only those that damage the common language-motor system." (p. R902).

Work by Metter, Riege, Hanson, & Phelps (1983) and Metter, Riege, Hanson, Phelps, & Kuhl (1984) corroborates Ojemann's conclusion that motor functions and language processes may share common neuroanatomical sites. Results of their glucose metabolism investigations have indicated that the caudate, a structure traditionally felt to be active in the programming of learned movements, is also active during some language activities, especially some which are traditionally included on aphasia batteries. The important neurophysiological work of investigators such as Ojemann and Metter makes the high co-occurrence yet distinctness of the disorders, apraxia and aphasia, even more understandable.

Apraxia in the Absence of Aphasia

In this section of our chapter we will present detailed descriptions of six patients whom we have studied who were apractic but not aphasic. In the first section, Square's (1981) four patients who evidenced apraxia of speech symptomatology in the absence of aphasia are presented. Unfortunately, limb apraxia was not tested and buccofacial apraxia was assessed only in a cursory way. Thus, little support is provided for our later-developed hypothesis that praxis may be regulated by one central mechanism, damage to which causes disruption in all motor modalities.

In the second section, we will present detailed information on our two most current 'pure' apractic patients. These patients were studied in the Neuropraxis Research Laboratory in Toronto and praxis, as traditionally measured, was assessed for the upper limbs, nonspeech orofacial movements and actions, and speech production. Evidence from our studies of the latter two patients as well as a minimally aphasic patient with apraxia across all three motor modalities provides support for the unitary nature of apraxia.

Finally, results from our recent kinematic studies of limb apraxia, acoustic studies of apraxia of speech, and application of a well-refined error notation system for buccofacial apraxia are presented in order to elucidate our position that apraxia is due to a disturbance in the phasing of spatio-temporal muscle commands.

'Pure' Apraxia of Speech

In an attempt to provide evidence for the hypothesis that apraxia of speech and aphasia are two distinct disorders, Square (1981) studied extensively four patients who demonstrated apraxia of speech symptomatology in the absence of clinical evidence of aphasia, 10 patients with apraxia of speech symptomatology plus aphasia, 10 patients with no apraxia of speech symptomatology but with aphasia, and 11 non-brain-damaged control patients.

Patients were designated as having apraxia of speech if, upon the independent assessments of two highly experienced neurogenic speech/language pathologists, *most* of the symptoms of the disorder as outlined in the literature by Darley et al. (1975) and Wertz (1978) occurred. Those characteristics included: broadly 'perceived' sound substitutions in connected speech; phoneme additions; sound, syllable, and word repetitions; off-target approximations of desired phonemes and syllables; even stressing of syllables; even spacing of syllables; more of the preceding types of errors on phonetically complex stimuli and polysyllabic stimuli; and a slowed speech rate. Of the 12 characteristics, each 'pure' apractic patient and apractic-aphasic patient demonstrated nine or more. In order to ensure clinically that the speech errors were not due to motor execution disturbances (see above), each patient also underwent a complete motor speech examination as prescribed by Darley et al. (1975).

Diagnoses of presence or absence of aphasia was based upon results of administration of the Porch Index of Communicative Abilities (PICA; Porch, 1973), the most psychometrically-sound aphasia test of nine which are frequently used (Skenes & McAuley, 1985); the 62-item Token Test (Boller & Vignolo, 1966), a test sensitive to even mild auditory comprehension disturbances in aphasia; a modified Keenan and Brassell written-sentence-to-dictation test (Keenan & Brassell, 1972); and verbal expression samples as derived from the Cookie Theft Picture (Goodglass & Kaplan, 1972) and the 'J. Smith' picture (Schuell, 1965). Writing samples were carefully analyzed for typical aphasic writing errors such as paragraphias, syntactic and morphosyntactic errors, spelling errors, word substitutions, etc. Similarly, verbal picture descriptions were evaluated for typical aphasic errors including verbal and literal paraphasias, word finding difficulties, syntax and morphosyntactic disturbances, etc. From this thorough pre-protocol inventory, none of the 'pure' apractic speakers demonstrated any clear evidence of aphasia. We thus felt confident that, on typical clinical assessment, none could be considered aphasic. Furthermore, subjects from both aphasic groups were similarly impaired with regard to aphasic severity as measured from PICA overall scores and Token Test scores.

Because both verbal and nonverbal auditory processing disorders have been found to typify aphasia (see Square, 1981 and Riedel, 1981 for reviews), all subjects underwent extensive testing in this area. That is, if our four 'pure' apractic patients were found to be deficient in these areas we might suspect that 'aphasia' was, in fact, responsible for apractic speech symtomatology. Alternatively, we might conclude that a damaged central timing mechanism similar to the one described by Tzeng and Wang (1984) and Tallal (1983) for the decoding of language (with regard to perception of distinctive features of phonemes, particularly) and the production of speech underlies both of aphasia and apraxia. Thus, all subjects were administered 14 tests of speech and nonspeech processing. The processing tests described in detail elsewhere (Square, 1981; Square et al., 1981; Square-Storer et al., 1988) consisted of the following: one of discrimination of temporal ordering of two tones which differed in frequency, fashioned after that of Efron (1963); one task of identification of phoneme-sequencing errors in polysyllabic words; seven tasks of speech recognition / discrimination in which phoneme differences were systematically varied according to speech production dimensions of place or manner of production or voicing or addition or omission of phonemes; two tasks of syllabic recognition and identification of location of occurrence; and three tasks of internal speech discrimination in which patients were required to choose from arrays of five objects the two which began or ended with the same sound or rhymed.

Results of this investigation indicated beyond any doubt that the 'pure' apractic speakers were able to process the speech and nonspeech acoustically-presented tasks as efficiently as non-brain-damaged adult control subjects. Furthermore, for internally-evoked speech as required in the internal speech discrimination tasks devised for this study, analytical phonetic analysis was unimpaired. The two aphasic groups, however, performed *similarly* in most cases as well as inferior to the 'pure' apractic speakers and non-brain-damaged subjects over the 68 variables studied. Square-Storer and colleagues (1988) thus concluded that apraxia of speech is a disorder distinct from aphasia since the 'pure' apractic speakers were free of clinically demonstrable aphasic symptomatology as derived from results on both standardized tests and on the extensive speech and nonspeech processing protocol devised for this study. Furthermore, in most cases aphasic-apractic subjects performed neither worse nor better than subjects with just the disorder of aphasia. Thus, the added disorder of apraxia of speech to the aphasic disorder did not depress performance on the 68 dependent measures. These results call into question the hypothesis of Tallal (1983) and Tzeng and Wang (1984) that a central timing mechanism may underlie both language and motor performance.[3]

Inter-Modality Apraxia in the Absence of Aphasia

As part of a large scale study of sequencing deficits associated with hemispheric damage, Roy and Square assessed 26 left- and 10 right-hemisphere-damaged patients and 15 non-brain-damaged adults (see the chapter by Roy and Square-Storer in this volume for a summary of our sequencing studies). Praxis was assessed in each modality - limb, oral nonverbal, and oral verbal (speech) - using traditional clinical protocols since our concept of 'apraxia' as stated earlier in this chapter and our conception of its valid assessment were in their infant stages. For the assessment of ideomotor apraxia, a 60-item battery was administered which consisted of the following subsets of items: (1) four representational unilateral gestures; (2) four nonrepresentational unilateral gestures; (3) seven axial representational or bilateral pantomimic gestures; (4) four axial nonrepresentational gestures; (5) six transitive items; and (6) two sequenced items each repeated twice. All items on the first four subtests were first administered by verbal command and, when the subset had been completed, were readministered using imitation. The transitive items were administered in subsets first to auditory command, then to imitation, and then to object use. The sequenced items were administered only to imitation.

---

3. Tallal (1983) based her hypothesis upon her studies of language-disordered children with 'phonological' disorders. Also, her tasks of speech perception were psychoacoustic in nature and utilized synthesized speech. The varying methodologies as well as different patient populations may account for the discrepancies between the conclusions of Tallal (1983) and those of Square-Storer et al. (1988).

For the assessment of oral nonverbal (buccofacial) apraxia, a 32-item battery was administered. Sixteen items were representational or pantomimic and 16 were non-representational oral postures or actions. Half of each subset (8 items) was first performed to command and then readministered using imitation.

Finally, for the assessment of apraxia of speech an extended version of the Mayo Screening Battery for Apraxia of Speech (Darley et al., 1975; Wertz, LaPointe, & Rosenbek, 1984) was used. Five types of imitative tasks were included: speech sounds, (phonemes); monosyllabic words; polysyllabic word; words of increasing length; and sentence repetition. Articulatory diadochokinesis for both alternate and sequenced syllables, automatic speech (counting), and discourse comprised the other three subtests. Scoring methods for each battery were devised by Hogg, Square-Storer and Roy (in preparation) and quantitative cut-off criteria for the diagnosis of apraxia were established. For the limb and oral batteries, a three point scoring system was used in which '2' represented an acceptable - unqualified response; '1' represented an acceptable - qualified response; and '0' an unrecognizable or wrong response, refusal or no response. An 'acceptable - unqualified' response was one which was prompt, efficient and complete. The 'acceptable - qualified' response category included recognizable targets which met the pragmatic requirements of the gesture/action requested but were further annotated as delayed, augmented, self-corrected, hesitant or preceded by false-starts, repeated, exaggerated with regard to excursions, and/or non-stereotyped responses which were, nonetheless, considered correct. This 'notation' system was fashioned after the preliminary work of Roy, Square, Adams, and Friesen (1985) and Square-Storer et al., (1989). Inter-judge reliability for the scoring method was established by comparing scores from a judge naive to the purposes of the study and to the disorder of apraxia to those of the investigators. For the limb battery, point-to-point agreement was 90% and for the oral battery, 88%. On these two batteries, a patient was considered 'apractic' if he scored more than two standard deviations (SD) below the mean of the non-brain-damaged group.

Performances on the apraxia of speech battery were scaled independently by two highly experienced neurogenic speech language pathologists. Symptoms of the disorder as derived from the literature (Darley et al., 1975; Wertz, 1978; Wertz et al., 1984; Square, 1987; Square-Storer & Roy, 1989) were listed and reviewed by the two judges. Each subject was observed performing an entire elaborated version of the Mayo Clinic Screening Battery for Apraxia of Speech and performance was rated on a scale of 0 to 5. The score '0' represented occurrence of symptoms no greater than the frequency which would be expected in the normal population. Scores from 1 to 5 represented occurrence of apraxia of speech symptoms greater than expected in the normal population ranging from mild to severe presence with each numeric interval defined. In addition, the speech-language pathologists made another judgement, a yes/no judgement as to whether the apraxia of speech symptoms presented a functional handicap to the patients. Point-to-point agreement for the two judges was 97% over 36 comparisons.

Although it is not within the scope of this chapter to completely review the results of this study, it is of relevance to report that *coexistence of the three apraxias* occurred for 19 of the 23 left-hemisphere damaged subjects who fell within the 'apractic' range established for each battery. Furthermore, severity levels of deficit for the three apraxia modalities were highly correlated. For the four subjects who demonstrated apraxia dissociations, one demonstrated only limb apraxia; however, the patient's score on that battery fell just slightly below 2 SD of the mean of normal and within the range of performance of three normal subjects. Thus, we questioned whether this was a true instance of dissociation. For the three additional subjects, a true dissociation seemed to occur but we query whether these subjects had true 'apraxia', or instead 'disconnection' syndromes; that is, we query whether modality of input lowered overall scores rather than the patients experiencing disruption to a central praxis (motor programming) mechanism.[4] This latter position is elaborated upon by Hogg, Square-Storer, and Roy (in preparation).

Of greater relevance to our current discussion, however, are descriptions of our two 'pure' apractic patients, that is, our patients who demonstrated no indication of clinically discernible aphasia but severe to moderate praxis disruptions across three modalities. Descriptions of both subjects follow.

HM, a 69 year-old white male was studied 19 months post CVA. CT scan indicated that the patient had sustained a large left parietal infarct. Performance on The Western Aphasia Battery (WAB; Kertesz, 1982) was within the normal range in that HM earned an Aphasia Quotient (AQ) of

---

4. Just as we would not consider alexia, in the absence of other language modality impairments, a true aphasia but instead an instance of disconnection between visual receptive and association areas, we hesitate to refer to these three instances of apraxia modality dissociations as true apraxias. While performance patterns and neuroanatomical data are still being examined, we strongly suspect that these three patients with apraxia modality dissociations may have demonstrated dissociated patterns due either to perceptual difficulties and/or contamination of performance by aphasia due to the fact that total test scores were depressed because of performance on command items only.

95.6 on the WAB (normal cutoff = 93.6). On apraxia assessment as described above, the patient scored slightly more than 6 SD below the mean of normals on the limb apraxia test, 7 SD below the mean of normals on the nonverbal oral apraxia test, and was judged to demonstrate a 'functional handicap' with regard to speech praxis in discourse and a 'mild-moderate' severity rating of '2' on performance on the entire apraxia of speech battery. For this patient, there appeared to be clear evidence for the separateness of praxis and language mechanisms. Further scrutiny of this patient's limb and oral praxis performances revealed that on the limb battery, 32 per cent of the items were scored as acceptable - qualified (12%) or unacceptable (20%) responses; on the oral battery 44 per cent of the items were scored as acceptable - qualified (16%) or unacceptable (28%).

Our second patient, MG, a 72 year-old white female, also sustained damage to the left parietal lobe. As verified by CT scan, the cortical area of damage in the antero-inferior quadrant was quite small with the greatest volume of her lesion extending subcortically deep into the white matter in a horseshoe-like pattern. MG's AQ on the WAB was also 95.6, showing her to be nonaphasic on that test. Praxis performance, however, was impaired for all motor modalities tested. Limb praxis was least severely impaired in that MG's score fell just slightly less than 3 SD below the mean of the normal group. Oral nonverbal praxis performance fell between 5 and 6 SD below the mean of the normal group. Finally on speech apraxia testing, MG was considered to be 'functionally handicapped' and moderately impaired with regard to overall severity, attaining a severity score of '3'.

Quality of limb and oral praxis performances indicated that on the limb battery 44 per cent of the items were judged as acceptable-qualified (28%) or unacceptable (16%) while on the oral battery 39 per cent of the items were judged as acceptable-qualified (17%) or unacceptable (22%).

One other patient from the corpus of patients studied in the Neuropraxis Research Laboratory is also of interest. Although he was considered mildly aphasic, praxis impairments in the moderate to mild range were again observed across all three motor modalities. CW, a white male aged 63, was studied 21 months post onset. His large lesion, resulting from tumor resection, was to the left parietal lobe. WAB AQ was 92.6, just 1 point from the normal cutoff. Praxis performances were as follows: limb score was almost 6 SD below the mean of normal; oral was almost 3 SD below the mean of normal; and speech was judged to be 'functionally handicapped' with a severity rating of moderate impairment.

The existence of cases of 'pure' apraxia, few as they may be, indicate to us that the disorders of aphasia and apraxia are independent ones. It would behoove us to study in great depth the motor performances of these individuals, especially across motor systems. We are strongly of the opinion that multimodality kinematic studies and, in the case of speech, acoustic studies from which we can infer spatial and temporal aspects of movement, are areas of study which may greatly enhance our understanding of apraxia. With regard to the kinematics of speech production, Kent and McNeil summarize, in another chapter, the results of their exciting studies which reveal that various sites of lesion believed to contribute to motor programming may result in kinematic disruptions. These disruptions are quite similar across different diagnostic groups including apraxia of speech, ataxic dysarthria (cerebellum) and conduction aphasia, the latter believed to be usually due to parietal lobe lesions. Of course, each of these areas is thought to influence motor programming. In our own lab, we are also embarking on kinematic and acoustic studies to further describe apractic deficits. These are the topics of our next section.

Parameters of Deviant Movement in Apraxia: Kinematic, Acoustic, and Error Notation Studies

In concluding this chapter, we feel compelled to provide evidence which supports our hypothesis that apraxia is a motor disturbance of phasing the spatio-temporal components of movements. Phasing disruptions occur regardless of the nature of the movements - representational or nonrepresentational, operative or symbolic, linguistic or nonlinguistic. We will discuss evidence from each of the three modalities - limb, speech, and oral nonverbal. Although we have not undertaken correlative studies in these three areas, pilot instrumental work for the study of praxis correlatively across motor modalities has been initiated.

Limb apraxia

Recently we completed a pilot study (Charlton, Roy, MacKenzie, Marteniuk, & Square-Storer, 1986) of reaching in an apractic patient with a large left parietal lesion using the WATS-MART sel spot system. The WATS-MART sel spot system allows analyses of velocity and acceleration of limbs by video recording and analyzing on a microcomputer the trajectories of light-emitting diodes attached to the limb. Comparisons of our apractic patient's performance to that of a normal, age-matched control revealed that the shape and velocity profile for the transport or proximal component of reaching were much the same for both subjects, but the apractic patient was much slower. For the apractic patient, the distal or grasp component was different in several respects. The opening of the hand occurred much *earlier*, the maximum aperture was achieved much *earlier*, and the fingers were open more *widely*. Thus, the distal grasp component was poorly coordinated with the proximal transport component and was spatially imprecise.

Apraxia of speech

We have recently completed two acoustic studies of 'pure' apraxia of speech, i.e., apraxia of speech *not* accompanied by aphasia or clinically-discernible dysarthria. The first was a coarticulation study of the speech of MG (Scholten & Square-Storer, in preparation). Similar to the results of a study by Ziegler and von Cramon (1986) of coarticulation in an aphasic-apractic subject, we found our pure apractic speaker to be delayed in the onset of coarticulatory behavior compared to a normal speaker, as measured from vowel formant changes at relative periods of stop-vowel transitions. Furthermore, there was a consistent effect of the identity of the vowel upon coarticulation latency; in contexts in which both mandible and tongue are presumably making a contribution to vowel production rather than the tongue alone, the apractic speaker demonstrated greater motoric variability than the normal speaker. We speculated that this may have been due to greater motoric demands for temporal coordination.

In our second acoustic study of apraxia of speech (Square-Storer & Apeldoorn, in preparation), MG, as well as two apractic speakers from the Square-Storer et al. (1988) study were used. Because most of our findings paralleled those of Kent and Rosenbek (1983) for apractic-aphasic speakers, we concurred with their conclusion that apraxia of speech is a motor programming disorder in which spatio-temporal phasing is disrupted. However, we found that site of lesion appeared to be a significant differentiator with regard to certain behaviors. Our patient with a lesion restricted to parietal cortex demonstrated all acoustic symptoms of apraxia of speech with the exception of *slowness* of movement as evidenced by durations of vocalic segments and continuant consonants which were wholly normal. Our two patients with extensive subcortical involvement demonstrated all symptoms previously cited in the literature and significant slowness. We speculate that one explanation for our results may be that subcortical involvement of the motor programming circuitry may result in programming-execution disturbances, whereas parietal cortex involvement may lead only to programming disruptions.

Oral apraxia

Square-Storer et al. (1989) applied a well-refined system of oral movement notation to oral posture production as isolated tokens and as members of sequences. Eight left-hemisphere damaged patients and four age-matched normal controls were studied. None of the brain-damaged subjects demonstrated significant weakness, slowness, or incoordination of the speech musculature nor tone aberrations as demonstrated from the results of a complete motor speech examination (Darley et al., 1975) That is, no subject was diagnosed clinically as dysarthric. Nonetheless, results from the oral posture production protocol demonstrated that 'additional errors' and 'errors of spatial alignment' prominently characterized the performances of both groups but the *frequency* of these errors among the left-hemisphere damaged subjects was dramatically higher. Furthermore, the quality of the production of these gestures within sequences of increasing length deteriorated significantly among the left-hemisphere damaged subjects but not among the normal subjects. Results clearly demonstrated that the inferior performances of the left hemisphere damaged subjects on both individual tokens and within sequences were due to exaggerated augmentations and spatial targetting deficits; thus, the level of dysfunction implicated was motor programming.

Conclusions

In this chapter we have attempted to present evidence from both the existing body of literature as well as our own investigations which supports the following three positions.

1. Aphasia and apraxia are separate and distinct disorders although they most often coexist. Their coexistence is probably due to the neuroanatomical proximity of the areas of the brain responsible for each.

2. Apraxia represents a disorder of motor system most probably at the level(s) of programming, planning, or both, but the extent to which this disorder is distinct compared to the other movement disorders requires further study.

3. A central mechanism may mediate praxis control over all motor modalities since spatio-temporal disruptions of movement are common to limb, buccofacial, and speech apraxia and the three disorders commonly co-occur.

We look forward to results from future studies which provide evidence for support for or negation of these hypotheses.

References

Agostini, E. Coletti, G., Orlando, G., & Tredici, G. (1983). Apraxia in deep cerebral lesions. *Journal of Neurology, Neurosurgery, and Psychiatry*, **46**, 804-808.

Ajuriaguerra, J. de, Hécaen, H., & Angelergues, R. (1960). Les apraxies, varietes cliniques et lateralisation lesionnelle. *Revue Neurologique*, **102**, 566-594.

Alajouanine, T., & Lhermitte, F. (1960). Les troubles des activities expressives du langage dans l'aphasie, leurs relations avec les apraxies. *Revue Neurologique*, **102**, 604-629.

Basso, A., Luzzatti, C., & Spinnler, H. (1980). Is ideomotor apraxia the outcome of damage to well-defined regions of the left hemisphere? *Journal of Neurology, Neurosurgery and Psychiatry*, **43**, 118-120.

Bay, E. (1964). Principles of classification and their inference on our concepts of aphasia. In A.V.S. De Reuck & M. O'Connor (Eds.), *Disorders of language* (pp. 122-139). London: Churchill.

Boller, F., & Vignolo, L.A. (1966). Latent sensory aphasia in hemisphere damaged patients. An experimental study with the Token Test. *Brain*, **89**, 815-830.

Broca, P. (1861). Remarques sur le siege de la faculte du langage articulé, suivies d'une observation d'aphemie. *Bulletin de la Société Anatomique*, **36**, 330-357.

Calvin, W. (1983). Timing sequences as a foundation for language. *Behavioral and Brain Sciences*, **6**, 210-211.

Charlton, J., Roy, E.A., MacKenzie, C., Marteniuk, R.G., & Square-Storer, P.A. (1986). Impairments to sequencing and motor control in apraxia. *Canadian Psychology*, **27**.

Critchley, M. (1939). *The language of gesture.* London: Edward Arnold.

Darley, F.L. (1982). *Aphasia.* Philadelphia: W.B. Saunders.

Darley, F.L., Aronson, A.E., & Brown, J. (1975). *Motor speech disorders.* Philadelphia: W.B. Saunders.

De Renzi, E. Faglioni, P. Lodesani, M., & Vecchi, A. (1983). Performance of left brain-damaged patients on imitation of single movements and motor sequences. Frontal and parietal-injured patients compared. *Cortex*, **19**, 333-343.

De Renzi, E., Faglioni, P., Scarpa, M., & Crisi, G. (1986). Limb apraxia inpatients with damage confined to the left basal ganglia and thalamus. *Journal of Neurology, Neurosurgery and Psychiatry*, **49**, 1030-1038.

De Renzi, E., Faglioni, P. & Sorgato, P. (1982). Modality specific and supramodal mechanisms of apraxia. *Brain*, **105**, 301-312.

De Renzi, E., Motti, F., & Nichelli, P. (1980). Imitating gestures: a quantitative approach to ideomotor apraxia. *Archives of Neurology*, **37**, 6-10.

De Renzi, E., Pieczuro, A., & Vignolo, L. (1966). Oral apraxia and aphasia. *Cortex*, **2**, 50-73.

Duffy, J.R., Watt, F., & Duffy, R.J. (1981). Path analysis: a strategy for investigating multivariate causal relationships in communication disorders. *Journal of Speech and Hearing Research*, **24**, 474-490.

Duffy, R.J., & Duffy, J.R. (1981) Three studies of deficits in pantomimic expression and pantomimic recognition in aphasia. *Journal of speech and Hearing Research*, **46**, 70-84.

Duffy, R.J., & Liles, B.Z. (1979). A translation of Finkelnberg's (1870). Lecture on aphasia as 'asymboly' with commentary. *Journal of Speech and Hearing Disorders*, **44**, 156-168.

Efron, R. (1963). Temporal perception, aphasia, and déjà vú. *Brain*, **86**, 403-424.

Feyereisen, P., & Seron, X. (1982a). Nonverbal communication and aphasia: a review. Part I. *Brain and Language*, **16**, 191-221.

Feyereisen, P., & Seron, X. (1982b). Nonverbal communication and aphasia: a review. Part II. *Brain and Language*, **16**, 223-226.

Fuson, K.C. (1979). The development of self-regulating aspects of speech: a review. In G. Zivin (Ed.), *The development of self-regulation through private speech* (pp. 135-217). New York: Wiley.

Geschwind, N. (1965). Disconnexion syndromes in animals and man. *Brain*, **88**, 237-294, 585-644.

Geschwind, N. (1967). The apraxias in phenomenology of will and action. In E. Strauss & R. Griffits (Eds.), *The second Lexington conference on pure and applied phenomenology*. Pittsburgh: Duquesne University Press.

Geschwind, N. (1975). The apraxias: neurological mechanisms of disorders of learned movements. *American Scientist*, **63**, 188-195.

Gainotti, G., & Lemmo, M.N. (1976). Comprehension of Symbolic Gestures in aphasia. *Brain and Language*, **3**, 451-460.

Goldstein, K. (1948). *Language and language disturbances*. New York: Grune and Stratton.

Goodglass, H., & Kaplan, E. (1972). *The assessment of aphasia and related disorders*. Philadelphia: Lea and Febiger.

Goodglass, H., & Kaplan, E. (1963). Disturbance of gesture and pantomime in aphasia. *Brain*, **86**, 703-770.

Haaland, K., & Flaherty, D. (1984). The different types of limb apraxia errors made by patients with left vs. right hemisphere damage. *Brain and Cognition*, **3**, 370-384.

Hécaen, H. (1978). Les apraxies ideomotrices. Essai de dissociation. In H. Hécaen & M. Jeannerod (Eds.), *Du contrôle moteur à l'organisation du geste*. (pp. 343-358). Paris: Masson.

Heilman, K., Rothi, L. Campanella, D., & Wolfson, S. (1979). Wernicke's and global aphasia without alexia. *Archives of Neurology*, **36**, 129-133.

Hogg, S.C., Square-Storer, P.A., & Roy, E. (in preparation). Co-occurrence of limb, orofacial and verbal apraxia and their dissociation from aphasia.

Jackson, H. (1932). Affections of speech. In F. Taylor (Ed.), *Selected writings of John Hughlings Jackson, Vol. 2*. London: Hodder and Stroughton.

Jenkins, J., Jimenez-Pabon, E., Shaw, R., & Sefer, J. (1975). *Schuell's Aphasia in Adults: Diagnosis, prognosis and treatment*. Hagerstown, MD: Harper and Row.

Kadish, J. (1978). A neuropsychological approach to the study of gesture and pantomime in aphasia. *South African Journal of Communication Disorders*, **25**, 102-117.

Keenan, J.S., & Brassell, E. (1971). Comparison of minimally dysphasic and minimally educated subjects in a writing task. *Cortex*, **8**, 93-105.

Kelso, J.A.S., & Tuller, B. (1981). Toward a theory of apractic syndromes. *Brain and Language*, **12**, 224-245.

Kent, R., & Rosenbek, J. (1983). Acoustic patterns of apraxia of speech. *Journal of Speech and Hearing Research*, **26**, 231-249.

Kertesz, A. (1982). *The Western Aphasia Battery.* New York: Grune and Stratton.

Kertesz, A., & Ferro, J. (1984). Lesion size and location in ideomotor apraxia. *Brain*, **107**, 921-933.

Kertesz, A., Ferro, J., & Shewan, C. (1984). Apraxia and aphasia: the functional-anatomical basis for their dissociation. *Neurology*, **34**, 40-47.

Kertesz, A., & Hooper, P. (1982). Praxis and language: the extent and variety of apraxia in aphasia. *Neuropsychologia*, **20**, 275-286.

Lehmkuhl, G., Poeck, K., & Willmes, K. (1983). Ideomotor apraxia and aphasia: an examination of types and manifestations of apraxic syndromes. *Neuropsychologia*, **21**, 199-212.

Liepmann, H. (1905). Die linke Hemisphare und das Handeln. *Münchner Medizinische Wochenscrift*, **49**, 2375-2378.

Liepmann, H. (1900). Das krankheitsbild der Apraxie (motorischen Asymbolie). *Monateschrift für Psychiatrie und Neurologie*, **8**, 15-44, 102-132, 182-17.

Luce, P.A., & Pisone, D. (1987). Speech perception: new directions in research, theory and applications. In H. Winitz (Ed.), *Human communication and its disorders: A review - 1987* (pp. 1-87). Norwood, NJ: Ablex.

Marsden, C.D. (1982) The mysterious function of the basal ganglia: The Robert Wartenberg Lecture. *Neurology*, **32**, 514-539.

Metter, E.J., Riege, W.H, Hanson, W.R., & Phelps, M.E. (1983). The use of (F-18) fluorodeoxyglucose positron computed tomography in the study of aphasia. In R. Brookshire (Ed.), *Clinical aphasiology* (pp. 262-275). Minneapolis, MN: BRK Publishers.

Metter, E.J., Riege, W.H., Hanson, W.R., Phelps, M.E., & Kuhl, D.E. (1984) Local cerebral metabolic rates of glucose in movement and language disorders from positron tomography. *American Journal of Physiology*, **246**, R897-R900.

Ojemann, G. (1984). Common cortical and thalamic mechanisms for language and motor functions. *American Journal of Physiology*, **246**, R901-R903.

Paillard, J. (1983). Introductory lecture: The functional labelling of neural codes. In J. Maisson, J. Paillard, W. Schultz, & M. Weisendanger (Eds.), *Neural coding of motor performance* (pp. 1-19). Berlin: Springer-Verlag.

Peterson, L.N., & Kirshner, H.S. (1981). Gestural impairment and gestural ability in aphasia. *Brain and Language*, **14**, 333-348.

Pickett, L. (1974). An assessment of gestural and pantomimic deficit in aphasic patients. *Acta Symbolica*, **5**, 69-86.

Poeck, K., Lehmkuhl, G., & Willmes K. (1982). Axial movements in ideomotor apraxia. *Journal of Neurology, Neurosurgery and Psychiatry*, **45**, 1125-1129.

Poeck, K., & Kerschensteiner M. (1975). Analysis of sequential motor events. In K. Zulch, O. Creutzfeldt, & G.C. Galbraith (Eds.), *Cerebral localization* (pp. 98-111). Heidelberg: Springer Verlag.

Porch, B. (1973). *Porch Index of Communicative Ability.* Palo Alto, CA: Consulting Psychologists Press.

Riedel, K. (1981). Auditory comprehension in aphasia. In M.T. Sarno (Ed.), *Acquired aphasia* (pp. 215-269). New York: Academic Press.

Roy, E. A. (1982) Action and performance. In A. Ellis (Ed.), *Normality and pathology in cognitive function* (pp. 265-297). London: Academic Press.

Roy, E.A., Square-Storer, P.A., Adams, S., & Friesen, H. (1985). Error/movement notation systems in apraxia. *Semiotic Inquiry*, **5**, 402-412.

Scholten, L., & Square-Storer, P.A. (in preparation) Coarticulation within CV syllables in an apractic patients.

Schuell, H. (1965). *The Minnesota Test for the Differential Diagnosis of Aphasia.* Minneapolis, MN: University of Minnesota Press.

Schuell, H., Jenkins, J., & Jimenez-Pabon, E. (1964). *Aphasia in adults.* New York: Harper and Row.

Selnes, O.A., Rubens, A.B., Risse, G.L., Levy, R.S. (1982) Transient aphasia with persistent apraxia: uncommon sequelae of massive left hemisphere stroke. *Archives of Neurology*, **39**, 122-126.

Seron, X., van der Kaa, M., Remitz, A., & van der Linden, M. (1979) Pantomime interpretation and aphasia. *Neuropsychologia*, **17**, 661-668.

Skenes, L., & McAuley, R. (1985). Psychometric review of nine aphasia tasks. *Journal of Communication Disorders*, **18**, 46-474.

Square, P.A. (1981). *Apraxia of speech in adults: speech perception and production.* Unpublished doctoral dissertation, Kent State University.

Square, P.A., Darley, F.L., & Sommers, R.K. (1981). Auditory and speech perception among patients demonstrating apraxia of speech, aphasia, and both disorders. In R. Brookshire (Ed.), *Clinical aphasiology* (pp. 83-88). Minneapolis, MN: BRK Publishers.

Square, P.A., Darley, F.L., & Sommers, R.K. (1982). An analysis of the productive errors made by pure apractic speakers with differing loci of lesions. In R. Brookshire (Ed.), *Clinical aphasiology* (pp. 245-250). Minneapolis, MN: BRK Publishers.

Square, P.A., & Mlcoch, A. (1983). The syndrome of subcortical apraxia of speech: an acoustic analysis. In R. Brookshire (Ed.), *Clinical aphasiology* (pp. 239-243). Minneapolis, MN: BRK Publishers.

Square-Storer, P.A. (Ed.). (1989). *Acquired apraxia of speech in aphasic adults*. London: Taylor and Francis.

Square-Storer, P.A., & Apeldoorn, S. (in preparation). An acoustic study of apraxia of speech in patients with different lesion loci.

Square-Storer, P.A., Darley, F.L., & Sommers, R.K. (1988) Nonspeech and speech processing skills in patients with aphasia and apraxia of speech. *Brain and Language*, **33**, 65-85.

Square-Storer, P.A., & Hayden, D. (1989) The PROMPT system. In P.A. Square-Storer (Ed.), *Acquired apraxia of speech in aphasic adults* (pp. 190-219). London: Taylor and Francis.

Square-Storer, P.A., Qualizza, L., & Roy, E.A. (1989). Isolated and sequenced oral motor posture production under different input modalities by left-hemisphere damaged adults. *Cortex*, **30**, 371-386

Square-Storer, P.A., & Roy, E.A. (1989). The apraxias: commonalities and distinctions. In P.A. Square-Storer (Ed.), *Acquired apraxia of speech in aphasic adults* (pp. 20-63). London: Taylor and Francis.

Tallal, P. (1983). A precise timing mechanism may underlie a common speech perception and production area in the perisylvian cortex of the dominant hemisphere. *Behavioral and Brain Sciences*, **6**, 219-220.

Tzeng, O.J.L., & Wang, S.Y. (1984). Search for a common neuro-cognitive mechanism for language and movements. *American Journal of Physiology*, **246**, R904-R911.

Varney, N. (1978). Linguistic correlates of pantomime recognition in aphasic patients. *Journal of Neurology, Neurosurgery, and Psychiatry*, **41**, 564-568.

Weigl, E. (1961). The phenomenon of temporary deblocking in aphasia. *Zeitschrift für Phonetik, Sprachwissenschaft und Kommunikationforschung*, **14**, 337-364.

Wernicke, K. (1874). *Der aphasische Symptomenkomplex*. Breslau: Cohn and Weigert.

Wertz, R. (1978). Neuropathologies of speech and language: an introduction to patient management. In D. Johns (Ed.), *Clinical management of neurogenic communication disorders* (pp. 1-101). Boston: Little, Brown.

Wertz, R.T., LaPointe, L.L., & Rosenbek, J.C. (1984). *Apraxia of speech in adults: The disorder and its management*. New York: Grune and Stratton.

Ziegler, W., & von Cramon D. (1986). Disturbed coarticulation in apraxia of speech: acoustic evidence. *Brain and Language*, **29**, 34-47.

Cerebral Control of Speech and Limb Movements
G.E. Hammond (editor)
Elsevier Science Publishers B.V. (North-Holland), 1990

Chapter 16

EVIDENCE FOR COMMON EXPRESSIONS OF APRAXIA

Eric A. Roy
University of Waterloo

and

Paula A. Square-Storer
University of Toronto

Apraxia is a disturbance in the performance of movements or gestures which has been identified for the speech, non-verbal oral, and limb movement systems. Although much work has focused on the nature of each of these apraxias, relatively little research has been devoted to their similarities and differences. This chapter examines the degree and nature of the association among these apraxias. The chapter begins by considering evidence which suggests some degree of commonality. The discussion then turns to a consideration of factors which may be important in determining how these commonalities might arise: the presence of aphasia, the location of the lesion, and the nature of the control processes involved. Considering the evidence, the association among the apraxias does not arise from aphasia or comprehension deficits but rather may reflect some common disorder in motor control in that similar types of errors and performance deficits seem to be exhibited in all the apraxias. It is argued that some clue to the common nature of these apraxias may come from carefully examining these disorders as they relate to the location of brain damage and the task demands. The processes involved in the preparation and execution of movement should be the focus of these investigations using measures which will afford a detailed description of the temporal and spatial dimensions of performance.

Apraxia is a disturbance in the performance of movements or gestures which cannot be explained on the basis of motor weakness, ataxia, dementia or poor comprehension in aphasia. This disorder has been identified for the speech, non-verbal oral, and limb motor systems. These three impairments have been referred to as apraxia speech or verbal apraxia, oral, buccofacial, or buccolingual facial apraxia, and limb apraxia, respectively. While considerable research has focused on describing the nature of each of these apraxias (see Haaland & Yeo, 1989; Roy, 1985; and Square-Storer 1987, 1989 for reviews), relatively little research has been directed toward studying the similarities and differences among the apraxias observed in these three movement systems. The purpose of this chapter is to examine the degree and nature of the association among these apraxias. In our discussion the apraxias are defined using the traditional methods of evaluation. Although there are a number of problems related to comprehension and the symbolic nature of many of the gestures (see Square-Storer, Roy, & Hogg, this volume), the majority of work which we will review has used these methods. In the first part of the chapter we present evidence which suggests some degree of commonality in the apraxias. One view of this commonality is that it arises because the brain lesion involves distinct but adjacent brain areas involved in the control of limb, oral, and verbal praxis. Another is afforded through examining similarities in the behavioral expression of apraxia in the three movement systems. This latter perspective is more revealing as to the neurobehavioral bases for the common occurrence of apraxia across the movement systems. Evidence from both of these approaches is reviewed. Some recent work from our laboratory focusing on the relationship among the apraxias and among disorders in the sequencing of limb, oral, and verbal movements is presented. The second part of the chapter turns to a consideration of a number of factors which may be important in determining how these commonalities might arise.

Relationships Among the Apraxias

In considering the relationship among the apraxias it is important to evaluate the relative incidence of the disorders as well as similarities among the apraxias in terms of behavioral characteristics of the disorder. The latter analyses may provide more insight into the commonalities among the apraxias. That is, even though the apraxias may co-occur it is not necessarily the case that the same mechanism may underlie each type.

Coincidence of the Apraxias

Very few investigations have examined the co-occurrence of the apraxias in the same group of patients. One of the first studies to do so (De Renzi, Pieczuro, & Vignolo, 1968) did not specifically identify verbal apraxia but rather looked at aphasic patients with severe phonemic-articulatory disorders finding that almost 70% of the patients with this speech disorder had a severe oral apraxia. Aphasic patients without this phonemic-articulatory disorder, on the other hand, did not exhibit oral apraxia. De Renzi et al. (1968) also reported a high coincidence between limb and oral apraxia although not as clear a relationship as was evident between phonemic-articulatory disorders and oral apraxia.

In a study of Broca's aphasics, Trost (1970) examined the patients' performances on an oral apraxia test. She was also interested in the relationship between the number of speech errors made by the Broca's aphasic patients and performance on the oral apraxia test. She examined performance on the oral praxis test both to verbal command and imitation. On imitation the aphasic patients performed normally. On verbal command, however, they exhibited severe impairments. In addition, as the number of speech errors increased the patients' performance on the oral apraxia test decreased, although this correlation was not statistically significant. Trost interpreted these findings to suggest that the production of speech and non-verbal oral movements may be subserved by different or separate motor areas, although these areas may be in close proximity. The other point of interest in this study was the role played by the modality of performance. Her finding supported the hypothesis proposed by Geschwind (1965) that oral apraxia was most apparent in aphasic patients when they were required to perform to verbal command. This point about the modality of input in performing gestures will be discussed later in the chapter.

The coincidence of articulatory errors and oral apraxia was also examined by Poeck and Kerschensteiner (1975). They suggested that both verbal and non-verbal movements which require precise control may be subserved by similar brain mechanisms since they observed such a strong relationship between the articulatory and oral praxis disorders.

Mateer and Kimura (1977) also found a strong relationship between articulatory speech disorders and oral apraxia. In their study the aphasic patients exhibiting the greatest speech impairments (non-fluent aphasics) were also the most impaired on the production of both isolated oral movements and oral sequences. They suggested that there may be two mechanisms, one concerned with the production of single gestures and phonemes and the other with making the transitions between these gestures or phonemes in a sequence.

Studies by LaPointe and Wertz (1974) and Marquardt and Sussman (1984) have examined the coincidence of verbal, oral and limb apraxia. In their study, LaPointe and Wertz (1974) found that 77% (10/13) of the verbal apractic patients exhibited an impairment in performing isolated oral movements and 85% (11/13) demonstrated a marked impairment in producing sequences of oral gestures.

In their study of 15 Broca's aphasic patients, Marquardt and Sussman (1984) observed that all of the patients demonstrated a marked oral apraxia. Twelve of the patients demonstrated a verbal apraxia but only five exhibited a limb apraxia, suggesting that the co-occurrence of verbal and oral apraxia is higher than that between verbal and limb and oral and limb apraxia. This higher degree of co-occurrence between verbal and oral apraxia may relate to the fact that the same motor system is being used in the production of both verbal and oral gestures.

In our companion chapter we have reviewed a study (Square-Storer, Roy, & Hogg, 1990) we recently completed which focused on the coincidence of limb, oral and verbal apraxia (see Square-Storer, Roy, & Hogg this volume for details). The incidence of apraxia was very low in the right-hemisphere patients, with 10% (1/10) showing limb and verbal apraxia and 30% (3/10) showing oral apraxia. The incidence of apraxia in the left-hemisphere patients was significantly higher. Limb apraxia was observed in 85% (22/26), oral apraxia in 81% (21/26), and verbal apraxia in 77% (20/26) of the cases. Analyses of the coincidence revealed that 73% (19/26) of the cases demonstrated all three types. In 2 of the cases (8%) two types of apraxia were observed, with one showing limb and oral apraxia and the other oral and verbal apraxia. A further two cases showed only one type, limb apraxia. The remaining three cases did not exhibit any of the apraxias.

A number of studies have examined the relationship between impairments in oral and limb gestures outside of the context of verbal apraxia. Kolb and Milner (1981) examined impairments in the performance of meaningless oral and limb gestures in patients who had the frontal, temporal, or parietal areas removed from the left or right hemisphere for the treatment of intractable epilepsy. They compared the performance of single and sequenced limb and oral gestures. They found that single oral gestures were most impaired in the frontal patients, while single limb gestures were most impaired in the parietal patients. Sequencing of oral gestures was impaired in patients with frontal damage regardless of laterality and in patients with left parietal damage. Sequencing of limb gestures was impaired only in patients with left hemispheric damage. Both frontal and parietal damage was associated with an impairment, although parietal damage lead to more severe deficits.

More recent work by Kimura (1982) also examined performance of limb and oral gestures and found that left frontal damage was associated with impairments in the performance of oral gestures both in isolation and in sequence. Left parietal damage was associated with impairments in the performance of single manual gestures and sequences of oral and manual gestures.

Taken together these latter studies suggest that disruptions in oral and limb gestures may occur together. It would appear, however, that this commonality is mediated by factors such as task demands (e.g., single gestures vs sequences) and the location of the brain lesion. These issues will be examined more closely in the last section of the paper.

Similarities in the Behavioral Characteristics of the Apraxias

Square-Storer and Roy (1989) have discussed some common behavioral characteristics observed in the apraxias. Here, then, we will only highlight what they have presented augmenting this with descriptions of some of our recent work.

Movement speed

To some extent all the apraxias involve a reduction in the rate or speed of movement. In apraxia of speech a reduced rate of speaking is a frequently noted characteristic (Kent & Rosenbek, 1982, 1983; Wertz, 1985; Wertz, LaPointe, & Rosenbek, 1984). This slow rate of speaking has been explained, to some extent, in terms of articulatory prolongation of steady states of both consonants and vowels and of the transitions between them. This type of prolongation has been verified both acoustically (e.g. Collins, Rosenbek, & Wertz, 1983) and using electropalatography (Washino, Kasai, Uchida, & Takeda, 1981). Articulatory prolongation has also been related to a reduction in articulatory velocities identified using the microbeam analysis (Itoh, Sasanuma, Hirose, Yosioka, & Ushijima, 1980), velar fiber optics (Itoh, Sasanuma, & Ushijima, 1979) and movement transducers (Fromm, Abbs, McNeil, & Rosenbek, 1982; Barlow, Cole, & Abbs, 1983). Articulatory hiatuses have also been used as an explanation for the slower speaking rate of apraxia of speech. (Kent & Rosenbek, 1982, 1983; Square & Mlcoch, 1983). Syllable segregation involving the temporal isolation of syllables and syllable dissociation have been identified as two types of articulatory breaks which may occur in apraxia of speech.

Slowing in the rate of movement has not been well studied in either oral or limb apraxia. Some reference has been made to a slowing of movement in oral apraxia (De Renzi et al., 1968; LaPointe & Wertz, 1974; Tognolo & Vignolo, 1980). In our work we found that about 2% of all the errors observed in oral praxis in the left-hemisphere damaged patients were characterized as a prolongation of the time to complete a gesture (Square-Storer, Qualizza, & Roy, 1989). Limb apraxia work by Haaland, Porch, and Delaney (1980) suggests that the apractic patients demonstrate decreased rate of movement on complex tasks such as grooved peg board and maze coordination which require the integration of sensory and motor information. Also a study by Charlton, Roy, Marteniuk, MacKenzie, and Square-Storer (1988) which examined reaching and grasping movements in apraxic patients found that the rate of movement was considerably slower for these patients.

The issue of the rate and regularity of movement control was addressed in a recent study examining performance on a finger tapping task in patients with left (N = 28) and right (N = 22) hemispheric damage and in a group of age matched controls (N = 15). In this study (Roy, Clark, Aigbogun, & Square-Storer 1990) the tapping task involved tapping as rapidly as possible for a 10-s period for a series of ten trials. The brain-damaged patients used their ipsilesional hand, while the controls tapped with both hands, half beginning with the right. The dependent measures were the number of taps and the mean and variance of the intertap intervals. The brain-damaged patients were also examined on a limb apraxia battery. The results indicated no differences between the controls and the right-hemisphere patients on any of the tapping measures. The left-hemisphere patients, however, exhibited significantly fewer taps, a significantly larger mean intertap interval and a significantly larger intertap interval variance than either the controls or the right-hemisphere patients. Damage to the left hemisphere, then, disrupted the speed and regularity of tapping. While virtually all of the left-hemisphere patients were impaired on this tapping test, only two exhibited limb apraxia. Further, these two patients were not more impaired on the tapping task than the non-apractics. This disorder in the speed and regularity of fine motor control, then, appears to be independent of apraxia.

Although this impairment in fine motor control appears to be independent of apraxia, disruptions in this type of fine motor reciprocal tapping task may be seen in both the oral and limb motor systems. That is, just as there is evidence that the apraxias may co-occur across the motor systems, so there may be a coincidence in this type of fine motor control deficit, although these deficits may not be related to the apraxias. In order to investigate this question we (Square-Storer & Roy, 1990) examined reciprocal finger and tongue movements in groups of left- and right-hemisphere-damaged patients. Preliminary results suggest that the rate and regularity of finger and tongue tapping is markedly impaired relative to a group of age-matched controls in both brain-damaged groups, but particularly in the left-hemisphere group.

Movement initiation

Another problem which is often seen in all three apraxias is a difficulty in initiating movement. In apraxia of speech this is characterized in a number of ways. One involves the silent delays preceding the initiation of movement (e.g., Square, 1981; Square, Darley, & Sommers, 1982; Trost, 1970). Another involves groping and re-approaches in attempting to make the appropriate sound. A third problem of initiation has been termed 'struggle behavior' which may involve both inaudible and audible components. As operationally defined by Square et al. (1982), the inaudible struggle is characterized by facial grimacing which occurs during a silent period following the presentation of the stimulus for repetition. The audible struggle is characterized by sounds produced during a period after stimulus presentation which are not perceived to be phonemic in nature. Square (1981) and Square et al. (1982), using videotaped analyses, found that these struggle behaviors occurred quite frequently in their verbally apractic patients. Repetition of a phoneme, syllable or word may be a fourth characterization of an initiation disturbance in apraxia of speech. (See Square, 1981; Square et al., 1982; Trost, 1970).

In oral apraxia, disturbances of initiation of movement have often been described. Unlike the work in verbal apraxia, many of the studies of oral apraxia have viewed these disturbances holistically with few attempts to consider subcategories of initiation disorders. De Renzi et al. (1968), Tognolo and Vignolo (1980) and LaPointe and Wertz (1974) characterized initiation errors in oral apraxia as being pauses which preceded correct performance during which unsuccessful attempts at the gesture may have been made. These initiation errors, however, were among the least frequently occurring errors in oral apraxia. In looking more closely at oral apraxia using an error system which provided some insight as to how the oral gesture was performed, Square-Storer et al. (1989) identified seven of nineteen types of behavior which related to initiation. Delays, groping, repetitions and self-corrections were all observed.

Disruptions in the initiation of movement have not been well studied in limb apraxia. In many cases, however, patients with an apraxia do experience difficulty with movement initiation. Delays in the onset of movement which may be filled with a verbal response and groping movements are frequently seen in limb apraxia (Haaland & Flaherty, 1984; Lehmkuhl, Poeck, & Willmes, 1983; Friesen, Roy, Square-Storer, & Adams, 1987).

Sequencing of movement

Disruptions in the sequencing of movement is seen to some extent in all the apraxias. These disorders may be reflected in either misordering the movement elements in the sequence or in perseverations. In apraxia of speech, while errors of sequencing have traditionally been described as part of the disorder (Johns & Darley, 1970; Trost & Canter, 1974), errors characteristic of a sequencing problem (metathetic, perseverative and anticipating errors) have not been consistently found. (e.g., LaPointe & Johns, 1975; Sasanuma, 1971). Furthermore, posterior aphasics who are less frequently verbally apractic have been found to make more phonemic sequencing errors than anterior aphasics (Canter, Trost, & Burns, 1985). These findings seem to suggest that patients with verbal apraxia may have more difficulty with the temporal coordination of the movements involved in the speech rather than with the sequencing of phonemes (see below).

Impairments in the sequencing of oral and limb gestures have been examined by a number of investigations. This work has been concerned more with the association of these deficits with lesion location than with the presence or absence of apraxia. Impairments in the performance of movement sequences have been observed most frequently in patients with left hemispheric damage for both oral (LaPointe & Wertz, 1974; Mateer, 1978; Mateer & Kimura, 1977) and limb (Jason, 1983a, b, 1985, 1986; Kimura, 1977, 1982; Roy, 1981) sequences. One of the characteristic errors observed involves a perseveration in which the patient repeats a movement element in the sequence. Kimura (1977, 1979) argued that the predominance of preservative errors suggested that left hemispheric damage does not lead to a problem in sequencing per se but rather in making transitions between elements in the sequence.

Work by Roy (1981) looked more closely at the nature of the sequencing errors. Sequencing errors were broken down into their order and position components and the relative combination of these components were examined in the left- and right-hemisphere-damaged patients. These sequencing errors were categorized into simple or complex errors. The simple sequencing errors were ones involving two position errors and one order error. The complex sequencing errors involved higher combinations of these components. In examining the performance of the left- and right-hemisphere-damaged patients Roy (1981) found a higher incidence of simple sequencing errors for the right-hemisphere patients but a higher frequency of complex sequencing errors for the left-hemisphere patients. Thus, while there were no differences between the left- and right-hemisphere-damaged patients in the total incidence of sequencing errors, there was a difference when considering the complexity of these errors, with the left-hemisphere patients making complex sequencing errors more frequently.

Several studies have looked at the intrahemispheric location of brain lesions in relation to the impairment to movement sequencing (Kimura, 1982; Kolb & Milner, 1981; Mateer, 1978; Mateer & Kimura, 1977). This work generally suggests that frontal damage is associated with impairments in the performance of sequences of oral and limb movements as well as single oral movements. More posterior (parietal) damage is associated with disruptions to the performance of oral and limb sequences and single limb gestures.

Work by Roy (1981) has suggested that the impairment to movement sequencing may be somewhat task specific. He found that patients with left hemispheric damage were particularly impaired in the performance of movement sequences when these had to be generated from memory. In this study the movement elements in the sequence were presented as a series of pictures. Each trial involved two components, one in which the series of pictures was continually present throughout performance, the other in which the pictures were removed and the patient performed the sequence from memory. When performing with the pictures present the left-hemisphere patients were able to learn the sequence in the same number of trials as the right-hemisphere patients. When performing from memory, however, the left-hemisphere patients took significantly more trials to learn the sequence and they made significantly more errors than the right-hemisphere patients.

More recent work by Jason (1983a, b) provides support for this finding. In these studies Jason compared the performance of left- and right-hemisphere-damaged patients on various gestural sequencing tasks. In one study the tasks involved performing the sequence under two conditions. In the first the sequence of hand postures were demonstrated and the patient performed them from memory. The focus here was on learning the sequence with the criterion being the number of trials to reach a criterion of three consecutive correct trials. On this tasks the left-hemisphere patients took significantly more trials to learn the sequence and made more errors. In the other condition the patients were required to imitate the sequence performed by the examiner by successively copying each hand gesture as it was demonstrated. The time interval between each gesture in the sequence was controlled by a metronome such that these intervals became successively shorter over trials. Performance was reflected as the shortest interresponse time interval before an error was made in the sequence. In this case there were no demands placed on memory; however, the sequencing demands were considerable. In contrast to the first condition there were no differences between the brain-damaged groups on this task. In concert with Roy's (1981) initial findings, these results suggest that the impairment in sequencing with left hemispheric damage arises only when the sequence must be generated from memory.

The role of memory in movement sequencing deficits with left hemispheric damage has been more recently examined in our laboratory (Roy, Square-Storer, Adams, & Friesen, 1989). Several factors were investigated in this study: the length of the sequence (2, 3 or 4 movements), the motor system involved (limb, oral nonverbal or oral verbal) and the modality in which the sequence was performed. This latter dimension involved performing the sequence without any memory demands, in which case pictures depicted the sequence of movements to be performed, or with memory demands, in which the sequence was performed to imitation or to verbal command. In the imitation condition the examiner demonstrated the sequence while in the command condition the sequence of movements was described verbally (e.g., point, slide, turn) to the patient. In both conditions the patient had to generate the sequence from memory. In this study groups of left- (N = 28) and right-hemisphere-damaged (N = 15) patients and normal controls (N = 10) were examined.

Several phases of testing were involved. The movements in the sequence were first demonstrated according to the modality condition involved. In the command condition, for example, the movement associated with each verbal label was demonstrated. Following this demonstration the patient had to perform five consecutive repetitions of each movement element. In the next phase the individual movement elements were presented in a random order and the patient was required to perform each movement. The patient had to achieve a criterion of 80 percent correct in order to move on to the third phase, performing the movement sequence. In this phase seven trials of the sequence were performed and the patient had to achieve a criterion of at least two correct sequences before moving on to the next higher sequence length. If the patient did achieve this criterion, another movement was added and the three phases were repeated for this next sequence length.

Performance was examined in terms of the percent correct single movements, the percent correct sequences and the percentage of distortions of the single movements. Distortions were aberrations in the performance of the individual movements (e.g., mouth opened too wide, wrong hand orientation or posture) which were otherwise correct. Only performance of the limb and oral sequences are reported here since analyses of the verbal sequences are not yet complete. These findings are based on preliminary statistical analyses. Looking first at the single movements, percent correct movements was greater for the normal control group, but there were no differences between the brain-damaged groups. The percentage of distortions of the single gestures when performed in isolation was higher for the brain-damaged groups, but again there were no between-group differences. Turning now to the sequences, an effect of the performance modality was apparent. In the picture modality there were no differences among the groups in terms of the sequence attained, or the percentage of correct sequences. For the two memory modalities, on the other hand, differences between the groups were apparent. The left-hemisphere patients performed more poorly than the other two groups, attaining a lower sequence length and a lower percentage of correct sequences. The right-hemisphere and normal groups were not different. Looking at the distortions of the single gestures in the sequences, again the brain-damaged patients made more distortions than the normals. In contrast to the distortions of the single gestures when performed in isolation, the percentage of distortions was significantly higher for the left-hemisphere patients.

These preliminary findings provide some interesting insights into the nature of the deficits in movement sequencing. First, in accord with previous work (Jason, 1983a; Roy, 1981) impairments in sequencing in patients with left hemispheric damage are most apparent when the task places demands on memory. This is the case for both the oral and limb sequences, suggesting that there is some problem in sequencing which is common to both movement systems.

Comparisons of performance in the second phase of testing in which the patient had to perform the individual movements in a random order to that in the third phase where movement sequences were involved provide some insight into the nature of this sequencing deficit. In the second phase the patient was required to perform a sequence of sorts in that he had to perform each individual movement when prompted. There were demands placed on memory as the patient had to generate each individual movement from memory in the imitation and command modalities. The left hemisphere patients were not impaired on this task, however. In the third phase they were not impaired in performing the sequences in the picture modality condition. Only in the third phase where the sequence involved generating a series of movements in succession from memory did the deficit appear. These patients then seem able to select the appropriate response from memory providing that they do not need to generate a series of movements (phase two performance) and they can perform a sequence of movements providing that they do need to select the movements from memory (picture modality in the third phase). It is only when these two aspects are both required in the task that the impairment appears. As Jason (1986) has suggested, processes involved in response selection in the context of a sequence seem to be important factors in this deficit, although it is not yet clear how these processes are affected.

While these findings suggest that damage to the left hemisphere leads to deficits in sequencing, there also appears to be some impairment to the performance of the individual movements in the sequence as evidenced in the distortions to these movements. This impairment appears not only with left hemispheric damage but the right-hemisphere patients also exhibit distortions. What does seem unique to left hemispheric damage, however, is that the incidence of these distortions increased in the context of the sequence. These findings suggest that damage to either hemisphere may lead to some impairment in the control of the individual movements in the sequence. With damage to the left hemisphere, however, this impairment increases when demands for movement sequencing are added. This increased incidence of distortions in the sequence may reflect a greater effect of movement context on the performance of the individual movements with left hemispheric damage and may provide a key to understanding another basis for the sequencing problem in these patients.

Considerable work in motor control in recent years has focused on the effect of context on the planning and control of movement. In reaching, for example, analyses of the velocity profile of the reaching movement (i.e., trajectory of the wrist movement) have shown that the time after peak velocity increases as target size decreases, suggesting that the time in deceleration increases with the demands for spatial precision (Soechting, 1984). These effects of context have also been observed in a two-element sequence. The time in deceleration in picking up a small disk (the first movement) was greater if the subsequent movement required the subject to place the disk into a small receptacle as opposed to throwing it into a box (Marteniuk, MacKenzie, Jeannerod, Athenes, Dugas, 1987). The precision demands of the second movement, then, affected the planning and control of the first.

Given this work on context, the distortions of any individual movement in the sequences may reflect the influence of the other movements on the planning and control of this movement. The deficits in sequencing observed in this study, then, may arise to some extent from these context effects as defined by the task demands of each movement. In the limb sequence, for example, the hand posture and orientation (grasp vs index finger pointing), the direction of the movement (slide across vs pull down) and the type of action (point vs turn vs slide vs pull) for a particular movement in the sequence may all serve to influence the planning and control of previous and subsequent movements. This effect of context in sequencing might be best reflected in the strong tendency for these left-hemisphere patients to perseverate. In this case some dimension of the previous movement is carried over into the performance of the subsequent movement resulting in a repetition of either the entire response or this dimension of it. In this study a closer examination of the distortions on the limb sequencing task in several of the left-hemisphere patients provided some support for this point. Many of the distortions of the otherwise correct movements involved repeating either the posture or the action from the previous movement. For example, one movement in the sequence involved grasping a knob on the sequencing board and sliding it horizontally across a short groove. The previous movement may have been one where the patient pointed at the top of the previous knob with the extended index finger or grasped and turned the knob. In many of the patients the slide movement was made correctly but it was distorted either in terms of the posture used (an extended index finger instead of a grasp) or the action (a turning movement occurred simultaneously with the slide). These findings indicate the importance of movement context on sequencing performance and suggest that we must look more closely at these effects to understand the nature of the movement sequencing deficit associated with left hemisphere damage. This point will be raised again in the final section of the chapter.

Coordination of movement components

A number of studies using instrumental analyses of the performance of verbal apractic speakers suggest that the impairment may involve disruptions in the temporal coordination of speech movements or speech subsystems (e.g., articulation with resonance). Analyses of the coordination of voice onset times (VOT) with supralaryngeal articulation have suggested that many of the voicing errors perceived in apractic speech may result from disruptions in the temporal coordination of laryngeal movements with articulation (e.g., Freeman, Sands, & Harris, 1978; Fromm et al., 1982; Itoh, Sasanuma, Tatsumi, Murakami, Fukusako, & Suzuki, 1982; Kent & Rosenbek, 1983). Work by Itoh et al. (1980) examining movements of the articulators using x-ray microbeam analyses revealed a dyscoordination among several articulators (lower lip and incisor, tongue dorsum and lower surface of the velum) in their apractic subject. More detailed analyses using electromyography provided support for this finding of poor temporal coordination among the articulators (e.g., Fromm et al., 1982; Keller, 1984; Shankweiler, Harris, & Taylor, 1968). Finally, acoustic analyses have revealed disruptions of anticipatory coarticulation in apractic speech (Scholten & Square-Storer, 1990; Ziegler & von Cramon, 1985, 1986).

Few studies have examined the temporal coordination of movements in oral apraxia in the detail used in the analyses of apraxia of speech. Our recent work (Square-Storer et al., 1989), however, noted two types of errors which may reflect disorders in temporal coordination. One type, inappropriate reciprocity of oral structures, constituted 5% of the errors observed. For the gesture 'tongue out', for example, the mandibular and tongue movements occurred as two separate movements as opposed to a smooth coordination of movements of the two structures. The other type, uncoordinated facial and/or lingual symmetry which was not due to hemiparesis, characterized 1% of the errors.

In limb apraxia disruptions in the coordination of movement components has been suggested by Friesen et al. (1987) and Charlton et al. (1988). In demonstrating a salute gesture the apractic patient made the appropriate axial and proximal postures but assumed an incorrect hand posture, a clenched fist. Charlton et al. (1988) argued that the patient had difficulty coordinating the distal (hand) segment of the gesture with the proximal (arm) and axial (body) components. This proposition was tested more formally by observing the same patient performing a reach and grasp task using a three dimensional movement analysis system. This prehension task involves the coordination of a distal grasp component using the hand with a proximal transport component involving movement of the arm. They found that, although the patient moved more slowly than a normal control, the velocity profile for the transport component was much like that of the normal. However, the coordination between the transport and grasp components and the grasp component itself was considerably different from the normal. Initial opening of the grasp and maximum grasp aperture occurred much earlier in time and the hand was opened more widely. These findings are similar to those using fibreoptic and x-ray microbeam analyses which demonstrated impairments in the spatiotemporal coordination of movement in verbal apraxia (Itoh et al., 1980, 1982).

Spatial disorders

All movements are made within a spatial coordinate system. There is some evidence that disruptions in this spatial coordinate system may be observed in each apraxia. A number of studies of apraxia of speech suggest that substitutions and distortions observed in speech may arise from deficits in placing the articulators in the appropriate spatial locations (e.g., LaPointe & Johns, 1975; Johns & Darley, 1970; Shinn & Blumstein, 1983; Trost & Canter, 1974) and/or achieving the correct lingual postures (Itoh et al., 1979). The groping behavior observed in verbal apraxia may also represent a deficit in spatial targeting (Washino et al., 1981).

Few studies have focused on spatial errors in oral apraxia. Our recent study (Square-Storer et al., 1989), however, identified two types of spatial errors. Overexcursion and insufficient excursion of oral structures constituted respectively 12% and 2% of the errors observed in the left-hemisphere-damaged patients performing meaningless oral gestures.

Spatial errors seem to be important in limb apraxia. Work by Haaland and Flaherty (1984), Rothi, Mack, Verfaillie, Brown, & Heilman (1988), Roy, Square, Adams, & Friesen (1985) and Friesen et al. (1987) identified a number of spatial errors, for example, arm/hand location and hand orientation. Furthermore, patients generally make more errors in performing gestures such as salute and comb which are centered on the body than in gestures such as hammer and saw which are performed in allocentric space away from the body (Cermak, 1985; Roy, 1982). In fact Kimura (1977, 1979) has argued that limb apraxia involves impairments in making transitions between positions and/or postures in body-centered space.

Common Expressions of Apraxia: The Bases of the Relationship

Given the work reviewed above there is considerable evidence that common expressions of apraxia occur across the limb, buccofacial and speech motor systems. In this section we will focus on why and/or how such commonalities might arise. A number of factors are of potential importance here. One relates to the presence of aphasia. As we discussed in our companion chapter apraxia frequently occurs in conjunction with aphasia. It is possible, then, that disruptions to praxis in the three motor systems may occur because all are in some way related to a common aphasic deficit. If this were the case, one might expect that the co-occurrence of the apraxias would be most frequently observed in aphasic patients. While comparisons of aphasics and non-aphasics have been made with regard to the incidence of one type of apraxia (Lehmkuhl et al., 1983), little work has been done on the coincidence of the apraxias in aphasia. Our recent study (Hogg, Square-Storer & Roy, 1990; see Square-Storer et al., this volume, for details), found that the majority of patients who exhibited all three apraxias were aphasic. Nevertheless, two left-hemisphere patients exhibiting all three apraxias were not aphasic. Further, two of the aphasic patients exhibited only limb and oral apraxia and one exhibited only limb apraxia. Finally, one of the right-hemisphere patients exhibited limb and oral apraxia but was not aphasic. These latter findings argue against the notion that aphasia is a necessary condition for the coincidence among the apraxias. The cases showing a relationship between aphasia and the apraxias may reflect, then, the proximity of neuroanatomical regions subserving praxis and language/speech functions such that a single lesion would encroach on both areas (cf. De Renzi, Motti, & Nichelli, 1980; De Renzi, Faglioni, Lodesani, & Vecchi, 1983).

Although the presence of aphasia does not seem to explain the coincidence among the apraxias, some subtle deficit in verbal and/or gestural comprehension may lead to the selection of the wrong response (see Square-Storer et al., this volume), given the symbolic nature of many of the gestures used in the typical apraxia examination and the fact that performance is frequently assessed in response to verbal command. One might, then, expect that patients with more severe verbal and/or gestural comprehension impairments would more frequently demonstrate multiple apraxias. Although no studies have addressed this question with regard to the coincidence of the apraxias, some research has focused on the relationship between limb apraxia and verbal/gestural comprehension.

Work examining verbal comprehension has lead to somewhat inconsistent findings with some research (e.g., Kertesz & Hooper, 1982) finding an association and other work (e.g., Lehmkuhl et al., 1983) finding no relationship between limb apraxia and verbal comprehension.

Work by Heilman, Rothi and Valenstein (1982) examining the recognition of gestures found that ideomotor apractic patients with posterior damage were impaired in recognizing and discriminating among gestures, while those with anterior lesions exhibited no such recognition disorders. These posterior apractic patients were also found to have more difficulty in comprehending the meaning of gestures (Rothi, Heilman, & Watson, 1985). These findings lead to the notion that there may be two types of ideomotor apraxia (Heilman et al., 1982). One involves posterior (parietal-occipital) damage, is associated with impairments in gestural recognition and comprehension, and results from destruction of visuokinesthetic engrams. The other involves anterior damage, is not associated with such recognition/comprehension deficits, and results from a disconnection between the visuokinesthetic engrams in the parietal area and the motor area responsible for the control of movement.

This work suggests an association between gestural comprehension and apraxia. A more recent study (Rothi, Mack, & Heilman, 1986), however, has found patients with impairments in pantomime recognition who were not apraxic. These findings lead this group to suggest (Rothi et al., 1986) that there may be two distinct regions in the visual association cortex in the dominant hemisphere, one (inferior) which is crucial for gesture comprehension and another (superior) which may be critical for imitating a pantomime based on a visual presentation of the gesture. The apractic deficit, then, may not be due to impairments in gestural comprehension. Rather, the association may arise because the brain lesion encroaches on both these areas.

Taken together these studies do not clearly support an association between deficits in gestural/verbal comprehension and limb apraxia. Thus, it is unlikely that a coincidence among the apraxias would be associated with such comprehension deficits. Nevertheless, more work needs to be done to assess the potential association between such gestural/verbal comprehension deficits and impairments in limb, oral, and verbal praxis.

Another more indirect approach to studying the effects of verbal comprehension on praxis is to compare performance between verbal command and imitation, the logic being that poorer performance to verbal command may arise from comprehension deficits. While comparisons between performance to command and imitation may reveal something of the role of comprehension, these conditions differ in ways other than the need to understand the verbal command. Performance to verbal command requires that the patient generate the movement from memory, while imitation requires the patient to copy the gesture presented by the examiner. The command condition, then, places more demands on the processes of response selection and response organization (De Renzi, 1985; Roy & Square, 1985). If verbal comprehension deficits or problems in response selection/organization processes underlie the co-occurrence of the apraxias, it might be argued that the common expression of apraxia across the motor systems would arise primarily when performing to verbal command. A number of studies have examined this question as it relates to single apraxias. Work on limb (e.g., De Renzi et al. , 1968) and oral (e.g., Trost, 1970) apraxia has demonstrated that the most errors are made when performing to verbal command. The only study to date which has addressed these issues with reference to the coincidence of the apraxias (Hogg et al., 1990) has found little support for this hypothesis. While significantly fewer oral and limb gestures were performed correctly to verbal command, performance to verbal command did not give rise to all three apraxias in all the aphasic patients.

A second factor which may throw light on the association among the apraxias is lesion localization. The co-occurrence of the apraxias may arise because the lesion encroaches simultaneously on a brain region (or regions) involved in the control of limb, oral, and verbal praxis. Just as disruptions to neostriatal function in Parkinson's disease lead to a common expression of impairments in limb, body, and speech movements, damage to particular brain areas may give rise to a common expression of apraxia. Studies which have focused on commonalities among the apraxias measured in the traditional way suggest that a coincidence between articulatory speech disorders and oral apraxia frequently arise with lesions to the frontal lobe (Poeck & Kerschensteiner, 1975), while apractic impairments in all three movement systems frequently involve parietal damage (see Square-Storer et al., this volume).

Studies examining the performance of nonrepresentative oral and limb gestures provide further insight on the importance of these brain areas. Although there are clear differences among these studies in the nature of brain damage and the types of tasks used, this work has revealed several inter- and intra-hemispheric effects (e.g., Jason, 1983a, b; 1985, 1986; Kimura, 1982; Kolb & Milner, 1981). Damage to the left hemisphere most frequently gives rise to impairments in the performance of single and multiple oral and limb movements. Within the left hemisphere the effects of the location of brain damage is somewhat dependent on the movement task. Performance of a sequence of oral or limb movements is impaired with either frontal or parietal damage. Single oral movements, however, are more impaired with frontal lesions, while single limb gestures are more affected by parietal lesions. Both frontal and parietal areas would then seem to be important in the control of limb and oral gestures, with task demands (single versus sequenced gestures) being an important factor.

Given these findings, the coincidence among the apraxias might depend on the location and size of the brain lesion as well as the nature of the task. With circumscribed lesions affecting either the frontal or parietal areas the coincidence between impairments to limb and oral praxis as measured by single oral or limb gestures might be small. As measured by sequences of limb and oral gestures, however, the coincidence might be high, since both of these areas appear critical for such sequential tasks. With large lesions, on the other hand, one might expect a substantial coincidence regardless of the nature of the task since the larger the lesion the greater the likelihood it would involve both frontal and parietal regions.

A third factor addressed somewhat indirectly above which may be important in determining the degree of association among the apraxias concerns the nature of the task. Both the characteristics of the control system and the demands of the task are important. Looking first at the motor control systems limb gestures require the control of multi-joint movements against gravitational, inertial and reactive forces arising from movement itself in concert with the control of postural movements to maintain stability. While oral and verbal gestures require the control of multiple movement components, these movements do not need to be coordinated with postural movements and the effects of gravity and other forces are much less important. Given the differences in what must be controlled it seems surprising that common expressions of apraxia occur.

Although the biomechanical properties of limb movements differ from verbal and oral movements, there are a number of similarities in the control processes involved which might explain the potential for a common occurrence of apraxia. Work on movement programming indicates that for both limb and verbal tasks, as the number of movement elements increase the time to prepare the sequence increases (e.g., Sternberg, Monsell, Knoll, & Wright, 1978). Sequences composed of similar elements are prepared more quickly than those with dissimilar elements (e.g., Klapp & Wyatt, 1975; Sternberg et al., 1978).

Both speech and limb movements also exhibit what has been termed motor equivalence. For both repetitive finger-thumb apposition movements and bilabial speech movements a perturbation to one of the effectors caused considerable variability in the movements, but the goal of the movement was always successfully achieved (Abbs, Gracco, & Cole, 1984; Cole & Abbs, 1986).

Finally, both speech and limb movements seem to involve a type of context-dependent control. Inter- and intra-articular coarticulation in speech demonstrates the influence of context reflected in the vowel-to-consonant and consonant-to-vowel transitions. Intra-articular context effects indicate that the observed movement of an articulator is affected by the extent and direction of the preceding (carry-over effects) and subsequent (anticipatory effects) movements of that articulator. These effects are expressed both in spatial and temporal measures. Several studies of the spatial effects have revealed, for example, that tongue movements in the horizontal plane during an intervocalic stop consonant closure tend to be in the direction of the tongue position for the subsequent vowel (Gay, 1977; Perkell, 1969). Work focusing on the temporal effects has shown, for example, that during the contact period for a velar stop the tongue dorsum will begin to move sooner if the following vowel is open than if it is closed (e.g., Parush, Ostry, & Munhall, 1983).

Context-dependent control of limb movements has been revealed in work on reaching movements. The goal of the movement (e.g., speed vs. accuracy, Fisk & Goodale, 1989; pointing vs grasping, Marteniuk et al., 1987;) and the constraints in the environment (e.g., target size, Soechting, 1984) have been shown to affect the control of movement as expressed in the velocity profile of the trajectory of the reach movement. An effect comparable to the VCV transition effect in speech has been observed in work by Marteniuk et al. (1987) involving a sequence of two reaching movements.

This notion of context-dependent control suggests that movement control arises out of constraints (e.g., Arbib, 1985). These constraints serve to define the task demands. The degree to which these constraints or task demands are shared across the praxis tasks may determine the degree of coincidence among the apraxias. Ostensibly, this proposition suggests that the greater the similarity in constraints the more likelihood one might observe a common expression of apraxia. However, it may be very difficult to define these constraints a priori across the movement systems in order to examine this hypothesis. For example, if we use the dichotomy employed in the study of non-representational gestures alluded to in the work above (e.g., Kimura, 1982; Kolb & Milner, 1981), that is, single versus sequenced or multiple gestures, one might argue that the potential for coincidence among apractic impairments across the movement systems would be greater for gestures within a type (i.e., single or sequenced) than for gestures which are of different types. The problem here is that there are many constraints which may serve to further differentiate among gestures within each of these rather global types. These constraints may be equally important in determining the potential for coincidence among the apraxias. Considering oral gestures, while 'smile' and 'blow out a candle' are both single gestures, the latter is somewhat more complex in that the facial movement (lip rounding) must be coordinated with an expiration of airflow. In a similar vein while the limb gestures 'salute' and 'comb your hair' are both single gestures, the latter is again more complex in that the movement of the hand toward the head must be followed by a reciprocal movement of the hand about the head in the saggital plane. Given these examples might one expect more of a coincidence in apraxias for single gestures which exhibit equivalent complexity? Clearly, much more work needs to be done on identifying the important constraints within each of these movement systems before we can begin to understand the commonalities and dissociations among limb, oral, and verbal apraxia.

Taken together the evidence suggests that the association among the apraxias does not arise from aphasia or comprehension deficits. Rather, this co-occurrence may reflect some common disorder in motor control in that similar types of errors and performance deficits seem to be exhibited in all the apraxias. The characteristics of this common disorder are by no means clear, however. Some clue to the nature of this disorder may come from carefully studying disruptions to praxis as they relate to the location of brain damage and the task demands. The analyses here should focus on the processes involved in the preparation and execution of movement using measures which will afford a detailed description of the temporal and spatial dimensions of performance. Such studies may provide a clearer view of commonalities in the control of gestural movements across the three systems. For example, kinematic and acoustic analyses of speech in verbal apraxia suggests that the disorder may be characterized to some extent as a dyscoordination of multiple movement subcomponents (e.g., Itoh et al., 1979, 1980). Work by Charlton et al. (1988) using a comparable level of analysis suggests that a similar disorder may characterize limb apraxia.

While these studies may provide more insight into the commonalities among the apraxias, one must keep in mind, as Saltzman and Kelso (1987) point out, that the kinematic measures used may not reflect what is being controlled by the nervous system. The patterns of performance observed through these kinematic measures may emerge from control principles that are only indirectly related to these measures. These patterns, then, may indicate something about the underlying motor control processes without necessarily revealing the specific parameters of movement programmed by the nervous system. Recognizing this caveat, it is nevertheless important to do these types of correlative kinematic studies as a first step in more clearly delineating the common expressions of apraxia.

Acknowledgement

Preparation of this manuscript was partially funded through a grant from the Natural Sciences and Engineering Research Council of Canada to Dr. Roy.

References

Abbs, J.H., Gracco, V.L., & Cole, K.J. (1984). Control of multimovement coordination: sensorimotor mechanisms in speech motor programming. *Journal of Motor Behavior*, **16**, 195-231.

Arbib, M.A. (1985). Schemas for the temporal organization of behavior. *Human Neurobiology*, **4**, 63-72.

Barlow, S., Cole, K.J., & Abbs, J. (1983). A new head-mounted lip-jaw movement transduction system for the study of motor speech disorders. *Journal of Speech and Hearing Research*, **26**, 283-288.

Canter, G.J., Trost, J.E., & Burns, M.S. (1985). Contrasting speech patterns in apraxia of speech and phonemic paraphasia. *Brain and Language*, **24**, 204-222.

Cermak, S. (1985). Developmental dyspraxia. In E.A. Roy (Ed.), *Neuropsychological studies of apraxia and related disorders* (pp. 225-250). Amsterdam: North Holland.

Charlton, J., Roy, E.A., Marteniuk, R.G., MacKenzie, C.L., & Square-Storer, P.A. (1988). Disruptions to reaching in apraxia. *Society for Neuroscience Abstracts*, **14**, 1234.

Cole, K.J., & Abbs, J.H. (1986). Coordination of three-joint digit movements for rapid finger-thumb grasp. *Journal of Neurophysiology*, **55**, 2318-2330.

Collins, M., Rosenbek, J.C., & Wertz, R. (1983). Spectrographic analysis of vowel and word duration in apraxia of speech. *Journal of Speech and Hearing Research*, **26**, 224-230.

De Renzi, E. (1985). Methods of limb apraxia examination and their bearing on the interpretation of the disorder. In E.A. Roy (Ed.), *Neuropsychological studies of apraxia and related disorders* (pp. 45-64). Amsterdam: North Holland.

De Renzi, E., Motti, F., & Nichelli, P. (1980). Imitating gestures: a quantitative approach to ideomotor apraxia. *Archives of Neurology*, **37**, 6-10.

De Renzi, E., Pieczuro, A., & Vignolo, L.A. (1968). Oral apraxia and aphasia. *Cortex*, **2**, 50-73.

De Renzi, E., Faglioni, P., Lodesani, M., & Vecchi, A. (1983). Performance of left brain-damaged patients on imitation of single movements and motor sequences: frontal and parietal-injured patients compared. *Cortex*, **19**, 333-343.

Fisk, J.D., & Goodale, M.A. (1989). The effects of instructions to subjects on the programming of visually directed reaching movements. *Journal of Motor Behavior*, **21**, 5-19.

Freeman, F., Sands, E., & Harris, K. (1978). Temporal coordination of phonation and articulation in a case of verbal apraxia. *Brain and Language*, **6**, 106-111.

Friesen, H., Roy, E.A., Square-Storer, P.A., & Adams, S. (1987) *Apraxia: interrater reliability of a new error notation system for limb apraxia*. Poster presentation at the annual meeting of the North American Society for the Psychology of Sport and Physical Activity, Vancouver, B.C.

Fromm, D., Abbs, J.H., McNeil, M.R., & Rosenbek, J.C. (1982). Simultaneous perceptual-physiological method for studying apraxia of speech. In R. Brookshire (Ed.), *Clinical aphasiology* (pp. 251-262). Minneapolis, MN: BRK Publishers.

Geschwind, N. (1965). Disconnexion syndromes in animals and man. *Brain*, **88**, 237-294, 585-644.

Gay, T. (1977). Articulatory movements in VCV sequences. *Journal of the Acoustical Society of America*, **62**, 183-193.

Haaland, K.Y., & Flaherty, D. (1984). The different types of limb apraxia errors made by patients with left or right hemisphere damage. *Brain and Cognition*, **3**, 370-384.

Haaland, K., & Yeo, R. (1989). Neuropsychological and neuroanatomic aspects of complex motor control. In E.D. Bigler, R.A. Yeo & E. Turkheimer (Eds.), *Neuropsychological function and brain imaging* (pp. 219-244). New York: Plenum.

Haaland, K., Porch, B.E., & Delaney, H.D. (1980). Limb apraxia and motor performance. *Brain and Language*, **9**, 315-323.

Heilman, K.M., Rothi, L.J., & Valenstein, E. (1982). Two forms of ideomotor apraxia. *Neurology*, **32**, 342-346

Hogg, S., Square-Storer, P.A., & Roy, E.A. (1990). *Co-occurrence of limb, orofacial and verbal apraxia and their dissociation from aphasia*. Manuscript submitted for publication.

Itoh, M., Sasanuma, E., & Ushijima, T. (1979). Velar movements during speech in a patient with apraxia of speech. *Brain and Language*, **7**, 227-239.

Itoh, M., Sasanuma, S., Hirose, H., Yosioka, H., & Ushijima, T. (1980). Abnormal articulatory dynamics in a patient with apraxia of speech. *Brain and Language*, **11**, 66-75.

Itoh, M., Sasanuma, S., Tatsumi, I., Murakami, S., Fukusako, Y., & Suzuki, T. (1982). Voice onset time characteristics in apraxia of speech. *Brain and Language*, **17**, 193-210.

Jason, G. (1983a). Hemispheric asymmetries in motor function: I. Left hemisphere specialization for memory but not performance. *Neuropsychologia*, **21**, 35-46.

Jason, G. (1983b). Hemispheric asymmetries in motor function. II. Ordering does not contribute to left hemisphere specialization. *Neuropsychologia*, **21**, 47-58.

Jason, G. (1985). Manual sequence learning after focal cortical lesions. *Neuropsychologia*, **23**, 35-46.

Jason, G. (1986). Performance of manual copying tasks after focal cortical lesions. *Neuropsychologia*, **23**, 41-78.

Johns, D.F., & Darley, F.L. (1970). Phonemic variability in apraxia of speech. *Journal of Speech and Hearing Research*, **13**, 556-583.

Keller, E. (1984). Simplification and gesture reduction in apraxia and aphasia. In J.C. Rosenbek, M. McNeil & A. Aronson (Eds.), *Apraxia of speech: Physiology, acoustics, linguistics and management* (pp. 221-256). San Diego, CA: College Hill.

Kent, R., & Rosenbek, J.C. (1982). Prosodic disturbance and neurologic lesion. *Brain and Language*, **15**, 259-291.

Kent, R.D., & Rosenbek, J.C. (1983). Acoustic patterns of apraxia of speech. *Journal of Speech and Hearing Research*, **26**, 231-249.

Kertesz, A., & Hooper, P. (1982). Praxis and language. The extent and variety of apraxia in aphasia. *Neuropsychologia*, **20**, 275-286.

Kimura, D. (1977). Acquisition of a motor skill after left hemisphere damage. *Brain*, **100**, 527-542.

Kimura, D. (1979). Neuromotor mechanisms in the evolution of human communication. In H.D. Steklis & M.J. Raleigh (Eds.), *Neurobiology of social communication in primates* (pp. 197-219). New York: Academic Press.

Kimura, D. (1982). Left-hemisphere control of oral and brachial movements and their relationship to communication. *Philosophical Transactions of the Royal Society of London*, **B298**, 135-149.

Klapp, S.T., & Wyatt, E.P. (1976). Motor programming within a sequence of responses. *Journal of Motor Behavior*, **8**, 19-26.

Kolb, B., & Milner, B. (1981). Performance of complex arm and facial movements after focal brain lesions. *Neuropsychologia*, **14**, 491-503.

LaPointe, L.L., & Johns, D.F. (1975). Some phonemic characteristics in apraxia of speech. *Journal of Communication Disorders*, **8**, 259-269.

LaPointe, L.L., & Wertz, R.T. (1974). Oral movement abilities and articulatory characteristics of brain-injured adults. *Perceptual and Motor Skills*, **39**, 39-46.

Lehmkuhl, G., Poeck, K., & Willmes, K. (1983). Ideomotor apraxia and aphasia. An examination of types and manifestations of apraxic syndromes. *Neuropsychologia*, **21**, 199-212.

Marquardt, T.P., & Sussman, H. (1984). The elusive lesion-apraxia of speech link in Broca's aphasia. In J.C. Rosenbek, M. McNeil & A. Aronson (Eds.), *Apraxia of speech: Physiology, acoustics, linguistics and management* (pp. 91-112). San Diego, CA: College Hill Press.

Marteniuk, R.G., MacKenzie, C.L., Jeannerod, M., Athenes, S., & Dugas, C. (1987). Constraints on human arm movement trajectories. *Canadian Journal of Psychology*, **41**, 365-378.

Mateer, C. (1978). Impairments of nonverbal oral movements after left hemisphere damage: a follow-up analysis of errors. *Brain and Language*, **6**, 334-341.

Mateer, C., & Kimura, D. (1977). Impairments of nonverbal movements in aphasia. *Brain and Language*, **4**, 262-276.

Parush, A., Ostry, D.J., & Munhall, K.G. (1983). A kinematic study of lingual coarticulation in VCV sequences. *Journal of the Acoustical Society of America*, **74**, 1115-1125.

Perkell, J.S. (1969). Physiology of speech production: results and implications of a quantitative cineradiographic study. In *Research Monograph No. 53*, Cambridge, MA: MIT Press.

Poeck, K., & Kerschensteiner, M. (1975). Analysis of sequential motor events in oral apraxia. In K.J. Zulch, O. Creutzfeldt, & G.C Galbraith (Eds.), *Cerebral localization* (pp. 98-111). Berlin: Springer-Verlag.

Rothi, L.J.G., Heilman, K.M., Watson, R.T. (1985). Pantomime comprehension and ideomotor apraxia. *Journal of Neurology, Neurosurgery and Psychiatry*, **48**, 207-210.

Rothi, L.J.G., Mack, L., & Heilman, K.M. (1986). Pantomime agnosia. *Journal of Neurology, Neurosurgery and Psychiatry*, **49**, 451-454.

Rothi, L.J.G., Mack, L., Verfaillie, M., Brown, P., & Heilman, K.M. (1988). Ideomotor apraxia: error pattern analysis. *Aphasiology*, **2**, 381-387.

Roy, E.A. (1978). Apraxia: a new look at an old syndrome. *Journal of Human Movement Studies*, **4**, 191-210.

Roy, E.A. (1981). Action sequencing and lateralized cerebral damage: evidence for asymmetries in control. In J. Long & A.D. Baddeley (Eds.), *Attention and performance IX* (pp. 487-498). Hillsdale, NJ: Lawrence Erlbaum Associates.

Roy, E.A. (1982). Action and performance. In A. Ellis (Ed.), *Normality and pathology in cognitive function* (pp. 265-298). New York: Academic Press.

Roy, E.A. (Ed.). (1985). *Neuropsychological studies of apraxia and related disorders*. Amsterdam: North Holland.

Roy, E.A., & Square, P.A. (1985). Common considerations in the study of limb, verbal and oral apraxia. In E.A. Roy (Ed.), *Neuropsychological studies of apraxia and related disorders* (pp. 111-159). Amsterdam: North Holland.

Roy, E.A., Square, P.A., Adams, S., & Friesen, H. (1985). Error/movement notation systems in apraxia. *Recherches Semiotiques/Semiotics Inquiry*, **5**, 402-412.

Roy, E.A., Square-Storer, P.A., Adams, S., & Friesen, H. (1989). Disruptions to central programming of sequences. *Canadian Psychology*, **30**, 423.

Roy, E.A., Clark, P., Aigbogun, S., & Square-Storer, P.A. (1990). *Disruptions to fine motor control associated with lateralized brain damage.* Manuscript submitted for publication.

Saltzman, C., & Kelso, J.A.S. (1987). Skilled actions: a task-dynamic approach. *Psychological Review,* **94**, 83-106.

Sasanuma, S. (1971). Speech characteristics of a patient with apraxia of speech. *Annual Bulletin, Research Institute of Logopedics and Phoniatrics.* Tokyo: University of Tokyo, 5, 85-89.

Scholten, L. & Square-Storer, P.A. (1990). *Coarticulation within CV syllables in apractic patients.* Manuscript in preparation.

Shankweiler, D., Harris, K., & Taylor, M.S. (1968). Electromyographic studies of articulation in aphasia. *Archives of Physical Medicine and Rehabilitation,* **49**, 1-8.

Shinn, P., & Blumstein, S.E. (1983). Phonetic disintegration in aphasia: acoustic analysis of spectral characteristics for place of articulation. *Brain and Language,* **20**, 90-114.

Soechting, J.F. (1984). Effect of target size on spatial and temporal characteristics of a pointing movement in man. *Experimental Brain Research,* **54**, 121-132.

Square, P.A. (1981) *Apraxia of speech in adults: speech perception and production, Unpublished doctoral dissertation.* Kent State University.

Square, P.A., & Mlcoch, A.G. (1983), The syndrome of subcortical apraxia of speech: an acoustic analysis. In R. Brookshire (Ed.), *Clinical aphasiology* (pp. 239-243). Minneapolis, MN: BRK Publishers.

Square, P.A., Darley, F.L., & Sommers, R.K. (1982). An analysis of the productive errors made by pure apractic speakers with differing loci of lesions. In R. Brookshire (Ed.), *Clinical aphasiology* (pp. 245-250). Minneapolis, MN: BRK Publishers.

Square-Storer, P.A. (1987). Acquired apraxia of speech. In G. Winitz (Ed.), *Human communication and its disorders* (pp. 88-159). Norwood, NJ: Ablex.

Square-Storer, P.A. (Ed.). (1989). *Acquired apraxia of speech in aphasic adults.* London: Taylor and Francis.

Square-Storer, P.A., & Roy, E.A. (1989). The apraxias: commonalities and distinctions. In P.A. Square-Storer (Ed.), *Acquired apraxia of speech in aphasic adults* (pp. 20-63). London: Taylor and Francis.

Square-Storer, P.A., & Roy, E.A. (1990) [Disruptions to reciprocal tapping performance: manual, oral-nonverbal and oral-verbal movements compared]. Work in progress, Neuropraxis Research Program, Universities of Toronto and Waterloo.

Square-Storer, P.A., Darley, F.L., & Sommers, R.K. (1988). Speech processing abilities in patients with aphasia and apraxia of speech. *Brain and Language,* **33**, 65-85.

Square-Storer, P.A., Qualizza, L., & Roy, E.A. (1989). Isolated and sequenced oral motor posture production. *Cortex*, **30**, 371-386.

Sternberg, S., Monsell, S., Knoll, R., & Wright, C. (1978). The timing of rapid movement sequences. In G.E. Stelmach (Ed.), *Information processing in motor control and learning* (pp. 117-152). New York: Academic Press.

Tognolo, G., & Vignolo, L.A. (1980). Brain lesions associated with oral apraxia in stroke patients: a clinico-neuroradiological investigation with the CT scan. *Neuropsychologia*, **18**, 257-272.

Trost, J.E. (1970) *Patterns of articulatory deficits in patients with Broca's aphasia.* Unpublished doctoral dissertation, Northwestern University.

Trost, J.E., & Canter, G.J. (1974). Apraxia of speech in patients with Broca's aphasia. *Brain and Language*, **1**, 63-79.

Washino, K., Kasai, Y., Uchida, Y & Takeda, K. (1981). Tongue movements during speech in a patient with apraxia of speech. *Current Issues in Neurolinguistics: A Japanese Contribution* (Supplement to *Language Sciences*). Tokyo: International Christian University.

Wertz, R.T. (1985). Neuropathologies of speech and language: an introduction to patient management. In D.F. Johns (Ed.), *Clinical management of neurogenic communicative disorders* (pp. 1-96). Boston: Little, Brown.

Wertz, R.T., LaPointe, L.L., & Rosenbek, J.C. (1984). *Apraxia of speech in adults: The disorder and its management*. New York: Grune and Stratton.

Ziegler, W., & Von Cramon, D. (1985). Anticipatory coarticulation in a patient with apraxia of speech. *Brain and Language*, **26**, 117-130.

Ziegler, W., & Von Cramon, D. (1986). Disturbed coarticulation in apraxia of speech: acoustic evidence. *Brain and Language*, **29**, 34-47.

Cerebral Control of Speech and Limb Movements
G.E. Hammond (editor)

Chapter 17

THE ASSESSMENT OF LIMB APRAXIA: THE LIMB APRAXIA TEST

Joseph R. Duffy
Mayo Clinic

and

Robert J. Duffy
University of Connecticut

Limb apraxia has long been recognized as an impairment of purposive limb movements associated primarily with left hemispheric pathology. Its clinical assessment, however, typically has been highly subjective and variable. In this paper we discuss factors that are important to the assessment of limb apraxia, including the basic nature and categorization of movements to be assessed, methods for eliciting responses, the potential influence of aphasia on representational limb movements, salient response characteristics, and scoring of performance. We then describe the item, subtest structure, and scoring of the Limb Apraxia Test (LAT), an 80-item test of imitative unilateral upper limb movement, which was designed to meet the need for a valid and reliable quantitative measure of limb apraxia. Finally, we summarize the LAT performance of normal, right-hemisphere-damaged and left-hemisphere-damaged-aphasic groups, emphasizing data which demonstrate the reliability, validity, and usefulness of the test.

Apraxia, a deficit in the performance of purposive movements without impairment of strength, mobility, sensation, or coordination, has been recognized as a sign of brain injury since the 1800s. The first clinical description of the disorder by Jackson in 1866 (Brain, 1961; Weisenberg & McBride, 1964; Wilson, 1908-09) focused on the disorder's nonverbal oral manifestations. Most subsequent attention in the neurological literature, however, has been devoted to its effect on limb movements. This focus is reflected in Liepmann's (1900) historically dominant and widely accepted conceptualization of apraxia and, contrary to ongoing debate about whether apraxia can affect speech production, there has been almost no dispute about whether apraxia can exist in the upper limbs.

The acceptance of limb apraxia as a distinct clinical entity, the relative historic stability of concepts about its types, and the ongoing focus of investigations of its psychologic, physiologic, and anatomic bases stand in contrast to Poeck's (1986) observation that: "no standardized battery of tasks is available for the clinical examination of motor apraxia. The diagnosis is made mainly on the basis of personal experience and intuition." (p. 130).

The state of assessment is not quite this anarchistic because tasks and scoring criteria have been described (e.g., Agostini, Coletti, Orlando, & Tredici, 1983; Borod, Fitzpatrick, Helm-Estabrooks, & Goodglass, 1989; De Renzi, Faglioni, Lodesani, & Vecchi, 1983; De Renzi, Pieczuro & Vignolo, 1968; J.R. Duffy, 1974; R.J. Duffy & J.R. Duffy, 1981; Gonzalez-Rothi & Heilman, 1984; Haaland, Porch, & Delaney, 1980; Kertesz & Hooper, 1982; Lehmkuhl, Poeck, & Willmes, 1983; Poeck, 1986; Rapcsak, Croswell, & Rubens, 1989). However, the validity and reliability of many of these measures are questionable or untested, and it is defensible to conclude that assessment generally is highly variable and subjective. Finally, the fact that limb apraxia is a 'silent' neurobehavioral sign, one detected only during performance of tasks specifically designed to elicit it (Brain, 1961; Critchley, 1971; De Renzi, 1985; Heilman, 1979; Liepmann, in Brown, 1988), compounds the problems created by the absence of a well-developed assessment tool.

In this chapter we will discuss several issues which are important to the assessment of limb apraxia and will describe those characteristics of a valid and reliable test that could assess the disorder in clinically and theoretically meaningful ways. We will also describe such a test, and will summarize data which help to document its clinical and research usefulness.

Assessing Limb Apraxia - Fundamental Issues

Motor and Sensory Prerequisites and Basic Nature of Movements

Underlying any assessment of limb apraxia is the assumption (requirement) that elementary motor and sensory functions necessary for performance are accounted for or intact. This is typically addressed prior to actual assessment and will not be discussed further here.

By definition, detection of limb apraxia requires the assessment of purposeful movement. Although the meaning of 'purposeful' (versus 'automatic') is difficult to specify in absolute terms, it presumably includes: awareness of the limb to be used; an image of the spatial relationship between limb and objects (if objects are involved); awareness of temporal order and sequence; knowledge of the purpose of the activity; and a feeling of effort (Mayer-Gross, 1936). These characteristics influence the selection of assessment tasks and lead logically to the traditional use of imitation or command/request (verbal or nonverbal) as modes for eliciting movement.

Types of Apraxia

It has been traditional to test for 'types' of apraxia, most often using Liepmann's categories of ideational, ideomotor, and limb kinetic apraxia. It may be helpful at this point to define these types briefly. Ideational apraxia is the

> defective performance of a complex sequence of gestures, due to incorrect programming of the entire sequence: while the single partial acts, taken one by one, may be correctly performed, their logical sequence is severely disturbed. (De Renzi et al., 1968, p. 41).

Thus, in ideational apraxia the 'ideational outline' of the act is inadequate. Ideomotor apraxia involves impairment of even simple gestures because of faulty transmission of commands to motor centers, as if the ideational plan and motor elements are separated. In limb kinetic apraxia (which some argue should not be considered apraxia), simple and practiced movements may be clumsy or awkward because of a failure to distinguish or remember constituent elements of a movement, as if limb-kinetic 'engrams' or 'kinesthetic images' are lost (De Renzi et al., 1968; Liepmann, in Brown, 1988).

Although the above definitions provide a general sense for Liepmann's types of apraxia, it is important to recognize that these types have had a variety of definitions, with considerable overlap or inconsistency across tasks and the behavioral characteristics associated with each type.

Liepmann himself (1913) felt that separation of apraxia into three types was 'diagrammatic', and he admitted that he schematized more than was justified.

Although the underlying processes implied in the various categories of apraxia may be useful in parsing the psychological 'stages' involved in movement programming and control, it seems more productive - at least for assessment - to focus on the characteristics of the movements being assessed and the description and categorization of the abnormal movements which may occur. At the least, it is important to operationalize the definition of tasks and behaviors which constitute various types. An operational definition of types of apraxia was perhaps first pursued by De Renzi et al., (1968), and their work has influenced the subsequent development of 'tests'.

Categorization of movements

Traditional descriptions of apraxia are based as much on the tasks used to elicit the behavior as they are on apraxic behavior itself. De Renzi (1985) has cogently discussed the broad categories into which meaningful movements can be grouped. We will rely heavily on his ideas in this section.

Transitive and intransitive movements

Movements may be *transitive* (involve object manipulation) or *intransitive* (which De Renzi describes as involving the expression of ideas and feelings). Operationally, it is probably more appropriate simply to distinguish these categories as involving or not involving object use, because ideas and feelings can be expressed both with and without objects.

De Renzi points out that transitive movements are usually used to assess ideational apraxia, and that demonstration of object use (e.g., show how to use a toothbrush) can be of value because it taps the lower limits of performance. However, these tasks are often replaced in apraxia batteries by the more difficult task of pantomiming object use in the actual object's absence, a requirement "which calls for an effort of imagination" (p. 47). (Note, however, that pretending to use the actual object also requires 'imagination', although to a lesser degree.) Such tasks are difficult to place in the object - no object dichotomy; they involve objects conceptually, but do not employ them behaviorally.

Intransitive movements traditionally have been used to assess ideomotor apraxia. They usually can be labelled and are overlearned or conventional (e.g., salute; signify a bad smell). De Renzi rightly points out that such movements are 'symbolic' when produced out of context, and he questions whether the requirement to conjure up their movement patterns is significantly different than the requirement to pretend to use objects with or without their actual presence. Thus, while the transitive - intransitive distinction is defensible as an operational one, it is not clear how meaningful (representational) movements with- versus without-objects represent the different levels of conceptual breakdown presumed to underlie ideational and ideomotor apraxia.

Meaningfulness

Assessment is often confined to meaningful (i.e. symbolic, representational) transitive or intransitive movements. However, De Renzi argues that meaningless movements - because they are not overlearned - may be more easily disrupted by brain damage because they probably require greater volitional motor control than conventional, overlearned movements. In support of this, he refers to the finding of Pieczuro and Vignolo (1967) that left-brain-damaged patients had more difficulty with meaningless than meaningful movements on imitation tasks. In addition, De Renzi, Motti, and Nicheli (1980) found that meaningless and meaningful movements were equally sensitive to the presence of limb apraxia in left-brain-damaged patients. Thus, it appears that meaningless movements are valid and potentially sensitive tasks even though, as De Renzi notes, they do not lend themselves to elicitation by command or request; they can, however, easily be used in imitation tasks and may be a 'purer' measure of motor control than meaningful movements. This latter assertion will be discussed in the section on the influence of aphasia on limb movements.

Sequencing demands

Voluntary movements can also be categorized according to their sequencing demands. It has been argued that only sequential movements are affected by apraxia (Kimura & Archibald, 1974), or that lesion site influences the effects of apraxia on single versus sequential movements (Kimura, 1982). There are also data that suggest that single movements can be impaired (Pieczuro & Vignolo, 1967) and that single versus sequential movements are not differentially influenced by lesion site (De Renzi et al., 1983). These issues, and the face validity of the concept that sequencing requirements influence motor control, justify the inclusion in limb apraxia tests of items with variable demands on sequencing ability.

Methods for Eliciting Responses

The assessment of limb apraxia typically relies on commands/requests for movements or the imitation of movements performed by an examiner. Although it has been recommended that both methods be used (Poeck, 1986), it is atypical that the same items are used for both elicitation modes (i.e. pantomimes may be requested, but meaningless movements are imitated); if they are, scores are often based on the best response elicited in either mode (e.g., Kertesz & Hooper, 1982).

The choice of imitation versus request for eliciting responses has an important bearing on the validity of assessment, given our current level of understanding of limb apraxia. Although it has been suggested that there may be no substantial difference in performance to verbal command or imitation (Poeck, 1986), studies have found performance differences, usually in favor of imitation tasks (e.g., De Renzi, Faglioni, & Sorgato, 1982; Graff-Radford, Welsh, & Godersky, 1987; Lehmkuhl, Poeck, & Willmes, 1983), or different degrees of correlation between imitation scores and command scores with other deficits, such as language or visuospatial skills (e.g., Foster, Chase, Patronis, Gillespie, & Fedio, 1986). In addition, some connectionist models of the disorder predict differences between responses to imitation and command for some patients (e.g., Watson & Heilman, 1983).

It may be useful to use both imitation and command stimuli when the same items are used for both elicitation modes and when aphasia is not present or is minimal. When aphasia is present, however, we believe that imitation tasks must be relied on for assessment. The reasons for this are rooted in some important theoretical issues, as well as some data that suggest that aphasia may have a significant impact on (i.e., be a cause of) pretended actions in response to verbal or nonverbal command.

The Potential Influence of Aphasia on Voluntary Limb Movements

The most obvious influence of aphasia on limb apraxia assessment is that it may impair the ability to comprehend a verbal request for movement. This reason alone has been used frequently to support the use of imitation in apraxia assessment (e.g., De Renzi, 1985; Head, 1926), especially for the assessment of aphasic patients with more than mild verbal comprehension impairment .

A more difficult issue is related to the role of aphasia in the actual faulty 'expression' of limb movement, even when comprehension of the task is intact. De Renzi (1985) suggests that classification of movements in assessment is based on whether the motor act is: "... meant to manipulate objects, *to communicate ideas, to express feelings, or is devoid of any pragmatic or symbolic value*". (p. 46, italics ours.) This reference to communicative intent and pragmatic and symbolic value, as well as the 'effort of imagination' required to pretend to use objects, suggests that aphasia - if one accepts the notion that aphasia may affect symbolic communication in any output modality - may have an impact on performance on measures of limb apraxia. Head (1926), for example, referred to the 'profound difficulty' that must often arise in distinguishing between the effects of limb apraxia and aphasia on symbolic limb gestures. He also noted that difficulty in executing complex actions might be due to an inability to formulate the intention or goal of the task, and that this might be labelled ideational apraxia. He argued, however, that such a disturbance could also be interpreted as a defective use of symbols, rather than to a loss of the concept of the movements comprising the symbols: "A high-grade disturbance of function of this order obviously belongs to defects of symbolic formulation and is not due to lack of ideas of movement, however general." (p. 101). Luria (1966) suggested that the capacity to select movements consistent with an overall goal is dependent on the regulating influence of verbal associations, and Ettlinger (1969) considered apraxia a 'language-dependent disorder' because voluntary motor acts rely on events which take place in neural systems concerned with language. De Renzi et al., (1968) concluded that ideational apraxia could be thought of as: "... one of the manifold manifestations of the impairment of 'concept formation' which is typically found in aphasia ..." (p. 51). Finally, evidence derived from recent studies of pantomime recognition and expression in aphasia demonstrates a strong relationship between pantomime expression deficits (primarily deficits in the ability to demonstrate the use of objects in non-imitative tasks) and severity of aphasia, even when the effects of limb apraxia are controlled (R.J. Duffy & J.R. Duffy, 1981). These data and arguments, along with estimates that ideomotor and ideational apraxia are associated with aphasia about 90% of the time (Hécaen & de Ajuriaguerra, 1964), indicate that the influence of aphasia must be considered in the development of apraxia tests and in their interpretation.

The simplest way to deal with these issues is to use imitation tasks, especially if the test is to be used primarily with aphasic patients. To summarize the reasons for this, there are several disadvantages to using commands: (1) they require verbal comprehension, a problem of consequence for most aphasic patients; (2) poor performance is ambiguous about whether it is due to defective recall of movement patterns or to inadequate execution (De Renzi, 1985); (3) poor performance might also be due to inadequate recall or formulation of the concept or 'meaning' underlying the movements, a problem more closely related to aphasia than apraxia. Use of imitation avoids the first problem, and helps to disambiguate the second and third. And, it does not compromise what De Renzi states is the most crucial factor in assessment, the artificial conditions under which movements are elicited.

We are not suggesting that tasks which request production of meaningful and communicative limb movements should be abandoned. On the contrary, they are extremely important to the examination and understanding of nonverbal communication in those with aphasia as well as limb motor control disturbances. However, they potentially measure both limb apraxia and the effects of aphasia or related cognitive deficits. Such tasks should be used with some prior measure of a 'purer' index of limb praxis, one not so influenced by factors that may not be confined to motor programming, if they are to be interpreted properly.

Response Characteristics and Scoring

Remarkably little attention has been paid to the qualitative characteristics of responses which reflect apraxic behavior. That is, numeric indices of impairment are typically based on the sum of plus-minus scores on a test. This is surprising, because many early reports contain exquisite descriptions of inadequate movements, and several investigators have noted the potential discriminative value of qualitative analysis (e.g., De Renzi, 1985; Lehmkuhl, Poeck, & Willmes, 1983; Poeck, 1986).

Many terms and phrases have been used to describe the flawed character of apraxic limb movements (e.g., uncertainty, fumbling, delays, awareness of errors, incomplete, mirror image reversals, spatial disorientation, jerky, rough, garbled, formless, amorphous, exchanged motions, perseveration, omission of movements, use of one object as if it were another, parts of actions left out or done ahead of time, incorrect position of the gesture leading it to a final incorrect attitude, use of a body part as an object). These descriptors indicate that a host of deficient behaviors are encompassed by the disorder.

Attempts to capture qualitative information in numeric indices of performance have been limited and often either identify only a limited number of response dimensions or include more than one dimension in a particular score. For example, several studies have used measures in which from 0 to 5 points are awarded depending on the number of stimulus repetitions that are necessary for a correct response to be achieved (De Renzi et al., 1982; De Renzi et al., 1980; De Renzi et al, 1983). This approach identifies the need for extra stimulation or practice but loses information about other response characteristics. Others have attempted to capture the degree or type of response inadequacy by awarding different values to responses which are, for example: "impaired but recognizable", "poor but approximate", (Kertesz & Hooper, 1982; Kertesz, Ferro, & Shewan, 1984); characterized by hesitation or delay in which wrong responses occur, conceptually correct but somewhat inaccurate or awkward (Basso, Luzzatti, & Spinnler, 1980); or adequate or partially adequate (Borod, Fitzpatrick, Helm-Estabrooks, & Goodglass, 1989; Foster, Chase, Patronas, Gillespie, & Fedio (1986). These behaviors usually are vaguely defined, particularly with respect to crucial descriptors like 'impaired', 'approximate', 'somewhat', 'partially', etc. This vagueness tends to generate unreliability in scoring, with further potential compromise of reliability because many measures employ only a small number of items. It is unfortunate, therefore, that only rarely have inter-judge and test-retest reliability been reported for measures of limb apraxia (cf. Haaland, Porch, & Delaney, 1980).

It is possible that a scoring system designed to capture information about several dimensions of performance would increase a test's sensitivity to the presence of the disorder, assist in distinguishing among apraxia types, and contribute to our understanding of the underlying nature of the disorder. For such a measure to be of value, however, its parameters must have face validity and be operationally defined and reliably identified. We have developed a test that uses such a scoring system and is a reliable and valid measure of imitative movements of the upper limbs. This test will be described in the next section.

A Measure of Limb Apraxia

The Limb Apraxia Test (LAT; J.R. Duffy, 1974) is an objective, quantifiable, reliable and valid measure of the ability to imitate unilateral upper limb movements. It is an outgrowth of our interest in nonverbal communication in aphasia and a recognition that limb apraxia has been one of the major explanations for impairments in symbolic upper limb movements (pantomime, signing, etc.) in those with dominant hemisphere lesions and aphasia. Although the LAT was designed with aphasic individuals in mind, it can and has been used with other pathologies.

A general guiding principle in the design of the LAT was that it should assess unilateral upper limb movements (to bypass the effects of hemiparesis) and avoid apparent heavy demands on intelligence, education, and physical prowess. In addition, item selection was based on correspondence or similarity to tasks frequently described in the literature as essential to the diagnosis of apraxia.

Imitation as the Mode for Eliciting Responses

Like many measures of limb apraxia, the LAT is imitative. There are three reasons for this:

(1) Imitation avoids verbal stimuli and eliminates the effects of verbal comprehension deficits on performance. The test also employs nonverbal training and practice items to ensure that the nature of the task is understood (we have not yet encountered an alert aphasic patient with a unilateral left hemisphere lesion who could not be conditioned to the nature of the LAT tasks).

(2) Imitation allows response requirements to be precisely defined, so responses can be scored on movement characteristics rather than meaningfulness or communicative effectiveness, response parameters that may be influenced by deficits other than limb apraxia (e.g., aphasia).

(3) Imitation eliminates or reduces the symbolic or representational 'intent' of meaningful limb movements, even though some LAT subtests include 'pantomimes' with and without objects. This helps to isolate the 'motor programming' aspects of performance from the conceptual, symbolic, or long term recall demands of tasks which request that acts be performed out of context. We believe that deficiencies on such 'higher-level' tasks probably should not be encompassed under the heading of limb apraxia. To assess performance on such tasks is important, but it may be best to do so without a claim that they assess only limb apraxia.

Task Characteristics

Scrutiny of items often used to assess limb apraxia suggest that at least three binary contrasts can be examined. The LAT is organized on this basis. These contrasts are described below:

Object - no object

Tasks in which objects (comb, pencil, blocks, etc.) are handled, as opposed to those in which objects are not used.

Simple - complex

Tasks in which one or only a small number of movements are required, as opposed to those in which a larger number are required. Simple items are operationally defined as having three or fewer movement components. Complex items have four to six components. A component is defined as a movement of the arm, hand, wrist, or fingers to a new position in space. The transition from one component to another (in any item with more than one component) is signalled by a change in the direction of movement. For example, extending the arm parallel to a table, and then lowering it until it touches the table, is a two component item. Using this system of classification, the components comprising each item can be predefined and scored individually.

Segmented - sequenced

The third feature is related to memory, retention, attention, and sequencing ability, factors often noted to play a role in apraxic behavior (e.g., De Renzi et al., 1968; Wilson, 1908-09). These are tasks in which demands on memory or sequencing capacity are minimal (Segmented), as opposed to those in which they are maximized (Sequenced). Segmented was operationally defined as simultaneous imitation (one component at a time) of the examiner. In Sequenced tasks, the subject responds only after the examiner completes all components of an item.

Subtest Structure

The LAT contains eight 10-item subtests with each subtest characterized by the binary features described above. The subtest characteristics are summarized in Table 1 and are briefly described below:

Table 1. Summary of LAT subtest structure (10 items per subtest)

			Features		
Subtest	Components		Components	Sequenced(+)	Complex(
+)	Object(+)				
	Per Item	Per Subtest	Segmented(-)	Simple(-)	NoObject(-)
I	1-3	17	+	-	-
II	1-3	17	+	-	+
III	4-6	46	+	+	-
IV	4-6	46	+	+	+
V	1-3	17	-	-	-
VI	1-3	17	-	-	+
VII	4-6	46	-	+	-
VIII	4-6	46	-	+	+

Total test components = 252

Subtest I

Items are Sequenced, Simple, and require No Object. They require movements ranging from one (e.g., touch thumb and index finger) to three components (e.g., extend hand in fist; bend fist up; bend fist down). Imitation follows completion of the entire item by the examiner.

Subtest II

Items are Sequenced, Simple, and use Objects. They require the manipulation of a block(s) and/or cup, or the positioning of the limb in relation to a block(s) or cup. The number of components per item ranges from one (e.g., place one block on top of another) to three (e.g., turn cup over to cover a block; put another block on cup; lift cup). Imitation follows completion of the entire item by the examiner.

Subtest III

Items are Sequenced, Complex, and require No Object. They are interpretable as pantomimic acts demonstrating the use of common objects (e.g., key, scissors, screwdriver). The number of components per item ranges from four (extend hand as if to grasp salt shaker; lift and rotate imaginary shaker so it faces down; shake in up and down motion several times; place imaginary shaker back on table) to six (e.g., grasp imaginary screw driver so thumb and index finger are facing downward; rotate hand clockwise; rotate hand counterclockwise to original position; rotate hand clockwise; rotate hand clockwise to original position; rotate hand clockwise). Imitation follows completion of the entire item by the examiner.

Subtest IV

Items are identical to those in Subtest III, but actual objects are used.

Subtest V

Items are identical to those in Subtest I, but administration and imitation are Segmented.

Subtest VI

Items are identical to those in Subtest II, but administration and imitation are Segmented.

Subtest VII

Items are identical to those in Subtest III, but administration and imitation are Segmented.

Subtest VIII

Items are identical to those in Subtest IV, but administration and imitation are Segmented.

The binary contrast features and subtest structure of the LAT avoid *a priori* assumptions about different types of apraxia while providing a framework for examining variables which influence performance. For example, the Simple - Complex contrast permits comparisons between

Simple and Complex subtests and, therefore, examination of the effect that complexity (as defined by the contrast) has on performance.

To the extent that classifications of types of apraxia are based on the types of tasks used for assessment, some LAT subtests may be sensitive to specific apraxia types. For example, ideational apraxia, often associated with complex actions demonstrating object use, can be contrasted with ideomotor apraxia, often associated with more basic movements not necessarily associated with pretended use of objects. From this standpoint, the Complex subtests (III, IV, VII, and VIII) may be more sensitive to ideational apraxia, while the Simple subtests (I, II, V, and VI) may be more sensitive to ideomotor apraxia. Similarly, the Object subtests (II, IV, VI, and VIII) may be more sensitive to ideational apraxia, while the No Object subtests (I, III, V, and VII) may be more sensitive to ideomotor apraxia. Or, if as some definitions suggest, ideational apraxia is consequence of memory, attention, or sequencing ability, Sequenced subtests (I, II, III, and IV) may be more sensitive to ideational apraxia than Segmented subtests (V, VI, VII, and VIII). Finally, limb kinetic apraxia, if considered a true apraxia, would likely be manifest in all subtests, although perhaps more prominently on Complex (III, IV, VII, and VIII) than Simple (I, II, V, and VI) subtests. The reader is cautioned, however, that the LAT was not designed for the purpose of detecting apraxia types. The incorporation of features associated with apraxia types was a consequence of our intention to ensure coverage of the broad range of tasks which have been used to measure limb apraxia, regardless of type.

Scoring

A 21-point scoring scale (see Table 2) was developed to capture as many salient response characteristics as possible. The scale was derived from the multidimensional scoring system used in the *Porch Index of Communicative Ability* (PICA; Porch, 1967), a test with established sensitivity to pathological behavior.

Dimensions of response

The PICA scoring scale evaluates five dimensions of performance: accuracy, responsiveness, completeness, responsiveness, and efficiency. These dimensions appeared suitable for evaluating responses to the LAT.

Following are basic explanations of the five dimensions of response which combine to form the 21-point LAT scoring scale.

Table 2. Category names, characteristics, and point value for the 21 categories of the LAT scoring scale

CATEGORY NAME	DIMENSIONAL CHARACTERISTICS	POINT VALUE
Complete	Accurate, Responsive, Complete, Prompt, Efficient	21
Distorted	Accurate, Responsive, Complete, Prompt, Distorted	20
Delay	Accurate, Responsive, Complete, Delayed, Efficient	19
Incomplete	Accurate, Responsive, Incomplete, Prompt, Efficient	18
Del-Dis	Accurate, Responsive, Complete, Delayed, Distorted	17
Inc-Dis	Accurate, Responsive, Incomplete, Prompt, Efficient	16
Corrected	Accurate, Corrected, Complete, Prompt, Efficient	15
Inc-Del	Accurate, Responsive, Incomplete, Delayed, Efficient	14
Repeated	Accurate, Repeated, Complete, Efficient	13
Corr-Dist	Accurate, Corrected, Complete, Distorted	12
Inc-Del-Dist	Accurate, Responsive, Incomplete, Delayed, Distorted	11
Rep-Dis	Accurate, Repeated, Complete, Distorted	10
Corr-Inc	Accurate, Corrected, Incomplete, Efficient	9
Rep-Inc	Accurate, Repeated, Incomplete, Efficient	8
Corr-Inc-Dis	Accurate, Corrected, Incomplete, Distorted	7
Rep-Inc-Dis	Accurate, Repeated, Incomplete, Distorted	6
Related	Inaccurate, Almost Accurate	5
Error	Inaccurate	4
Perseveration	Inaccurate, Repetition of previous items or component	3
Unintelligible	Inaccurate, Does not resemble stimulus in any way	2
No Response	Inaccurate, Item is rejected or not responded to	1

Accuracy. Judgments of accuracy are generally based on the angle of a movement or target posture. Movements or postures more than 90° different from the stimulus target are scored as Inaccurate. Movements which are less than 90° off target, but inadequate in other dimensions, are still scored as Accurate, with other deficiencies captured in scores reflecting inadequacies in other dimensions. Accurate responses receive higher scores than Inaccurate ones. Several categories of inaccuracy are also included in the scale, to reflect degrees or types of inaccuracy (see Table 2).

Completeness. This dimension also focuses on angles of movement or postures. Accurate responses that are less than 90° but 45° or more off target are scored as Incomplete. Responses that are less than 45° off target are neither inaccurate nor Incomplete, and are essentially 'lost' to quantification. Complete responses are scored higher than Incomplete ones.

Promptness. This dimension refers to the immediacy of completion of a movement. Responses that are not Prompt are considered Delayed. Prompt responses receive higher scores than Delayed ones.

Responsiveness. This dimension refers to the amount of information required to elicit a response. If a stimulus repetition is requested or required to elicit a response, it is considered inadequate in the responsiveness dimension. Responses not requiring stimulus repetition are Responsive and receive higher scores than those preceded by a Repeated stimulus.

Efficiency. This refers to the 'smoothness' or awkwardness of responses. Awkward or clumsy responses, even if Accurate and Complete, are called Distorted. Efficiently (smoothly) executed responses receive higher scores than Distorted ones.

Validation of the scale's ordering and interval characteristics

The ordering of the scoring categories and interval level score values for them were established through a paired comparison experiment by J.R. Duffy (1974). In the same investigation, J.R. Duffy also found high correlations (0.99) between LAT scores derived from the interval values and scores based on easier-to-use ordinal values (given in Table 2). Therefore, the ordinal scale has been adopted for all subsequent scoring and analyses, including parametric statistics.

Computation of scores

Each of the 252 movement components of the LAT (i.e. all of the individual components of each item in the test) is scored. An item score is the average of its component scores. A subtest score is the average of its item scores. The total LAT score is the average of the subtest scores. These scores permit comparisons among components within items, comparisons among items, and comparisons across subtests for individuals, subjects within groups, and across-groups. The multidimensional scoring system permits analysis of those dimensions of response which are most salient in characterizing and distinguishing defective performance among items and subtests within subjects, among subjects within groups, and across groups.

Administration

Standard, nonverbal conditioning procedures (with minimal verbal direction) are used prior to each subtest to ensure the understanding of the nature of the subtest. Scoring is time consuming because reliable scoring currently requires videotaping of responses and scoring at a later time. Scoring of each movement component in a response frequently requires viewing a response more than once. (Time demands may be reduced in the future by the development of a short form of the test (J.R. Duffy, R.J. Duffy, & Uryase, 1989).

The Limb Apraxia Test (LAT) - Reliability, Validity, and Application

This section summarizes some of the data which bear on the LAT's validity and reliability, and reviews the results of some of the uses to which the test has been put.

Subjects

The LAT has been administered to three groups of subjects, and the data to be summarized are derived from the performance of these groups or portions of these groups. A more complete description of subject characteristics can be found in J.R. Duffy (1974), R.J. Duffy and J.R. Duffy (1981), and J.R. Duffy et al. (1989).

Normals (N = 30)

Hospitalized adults without neurological deficits or significant visual impairment. The group's mean age was 62.4 years (SD = 12.1). Mean educational level was 9.3 years (SD = 2.4).

Right-hemisphere-damaged (RHD; N = 44)

Hospitalized adults with single, unilateral right-hemisphere lesions without significant visual acuity deficits who were willing and able to cooperate with testing. Their mean age was 63.4 years (SD = 9.6). Mean educational level was 10.8 years (SD = 3.0).

Left-hemisphere-damaged aphasic (LHDA; N = 77)

This group is made up of three smaller subgroups of adults (tested at different points in time) with single unilateral left- hemisphere lesions and aphasia, without significant visual acuity deficits. The total group's mean age was 61.5 years (SD = 12.5). Mean educational level was 11.1 years (SD = 3.2).

a. The first subgroup (LHDA1) contained 20 adults on whom the test was initially developed (J.R. Duffy, 1974).

b. The second subgroup (LHDA2) contained 36 adults who were tested as part of a larger investigation of pantomime abilities in aphasia (R.J. Duffy & J.R. Duffy, 1981).

c. The third subgroup (LHDA3) contained 21 adults who were tested as part of an investigation to establish a short form of the LAT (J.R. Duffy et al., 1989).

There were no significant differences among the control, RHD, and LHDA groups in age or educational level. There were no significant differences between the RHD and LHDA groups in time post-onset, which ranged from 2 weeks to 26 years.

Reliability

Test-retest and intra-judge reliability

Test-retest comparisons yielded high test-retest correlations and only small differences between test and retest scores. Similarly, Intra-judge comparisons for tests scored at different points in time yielded high correlations and only small differences between test scores. These acceptably high indices of test-retest and Intra-judge reliability were established by J.R. Duffy (1974), and the reader is referred to his study for details of the reliability procedures and results.

Internal consistency (relationships among subtests and overall LAT scores)

Table 3 summarizes the correlations between each LAT subtest and the overall LAT score. The correlations are corrected for spurious overlap and, therefore, reflect the relationship between each subtest and a composite score for the remainder of the test.

All correlations are significant and high, with the highest correlations generally obtained for the LHDA group and the lowest for Normals. These high correlations attest to the LAT's internal consistency, as do intersubtest correlations, which were also quite high. The relatively lower correlations in the RHD and Normal groups very possibly reflect attenuation due to reduced range of scores in those groups.

The LAT's reliability was also assessed by J.R. Duffy (1974) through an analysis of variance technique (Winer (1971). The reliability of the test, considered as a measure comprised of eight subtests, was high for Normals (N = 20), RHD (N = 20), and LHDA1 groups, respectively. These indices indicate that the mean error of measurement across LAT subtests is small, resulting in scores which are a reliable estimate of the magnitude of the trait measured by the test.

Table 3. Correlations* between LAT subtests and overall LAT scores for each group

Group	Subtest							
	I	II	III	IV	V	VI	VII	VIII
LHD	.85	.84	.92	.91	.89	.80	.92	.86
RHD	.64	.82	.84	.71	.67	.84	.83	.80
Normal	.67	.71	.74	.74	.56	.32	.59	.62

* corrected for spurious overlap; all r's reliable ($p < .001$)

Right versus Left Limb Performance

To establish if the use of the right versus left limb has an appreciable effect on LAT performance, J.R. Duffy (1974) compared the performance of 10 normal subjects who used their left hand on the test with that of 10 who used their right. There were no significant differences between hand performance on any subtest. This suggests that comparisons among Normal, RHD, and LHDA groups are not likely to be influenced by the exclusive use of the dominant or non-dominant hand in brain-damaged groups.

J.R. Duffy (1974) also administered the Purdue Pegboard (1961) to his Normal (half using the right hand, half using the left), RHD (using their right hand), and LHDA (using their left hand) subjects. The Purdue Pegboard is a timed measure of manual speed and dexterity which requires the rapid, repetitive placement of pegs into a board. Comparison among the groups failed to reveal significant differences in performance. Assuming that the speed and dexterity demands of the LAT are no greater than those required for the Purdue Pegboard (the LAT is not intended to measure speed of movement or simple dexterity), the equivalence of the RHD and LHDA groups on the Purdue Pegboard suggests that differences between the two groups on the LAT are likely due to factors other than speed of movement and simple dexterity. That is, differences between the groups on the LAT would more likely be explainable by differences in ability to sequence non-repetitive movements, difficulty positioning the limb in a correct spatial configuration, difference in moving the limb in an appropriate direction, etc. In addition, if speed and dexterity are thought of as a function of strength, basic coordination, and the absence of increased tone or adventitious movements, then the similarity between the groups on the Purdue Pegboard helps to rule out these basic movement parameters as a primary source of group differences on the LAT.

Relationship of Age and Education to LAT Scores

J.R. Duffy (1974) examined correlational data between the LAT and age and education for his Normal, RHD, and LHDA1 groups. Age did contribute to variance of scores in the Normal group but not in the brain-injured groups. Education was not importantly related to LAT performance in any of the groups. These findings are desirable for a test designed to be sensitive primarily to factors associated with brain injury.

Comparisons Among Three LHDA Groups

The replicability of a test is important to its reliability and usefulness. Therefore, before comparing the entire LHDA group to the Normal and RHD groups, it is appropriate to ask if similar results are likely to be obtained across similarly chosen groups of LHDA patients.

Analysis of variance of the overall LAT scores of the three LHDA subgroups was not statistically significant (J.R. Duffy & R.J. Duffy, 1989). This indicates that group performance is replicable across independent samples of LHDA patients. Because of this, the performance of the three LHDA subgroups was combined for subsequent comparisons with Normal and RHD groups.

Performance of Normal, RHD, and LHDA Groups

Table 4 summarizes the performance of the Normal, RHD, and LHDA groups on the overall LAT, and Table 5 summarizes their performance across the eight LAT subtests.

The performance of Normal subjects was uniformly high, although never perfect (i.e., no Normal subject received a maximum score of 21). The distribution of scores (albeit narrow) among normal subjects is desirable because it reflects a degree of challenge in the test, reduces ceiling effects, and makes detection of mildly abnormal performance more likely.

The distribution of scores in the RHD group was similar to that of the Normals, although 27% of the RHD patients performed more than 2.58 standard deviations below the Normal's mean (i.e. encompassing more than 99% of the normal distribution); all Normals fell above this cutoff level. This finding of 'deficient' performance in some of the RHD patients is unexpected on the basis of the predicted dominance of the left hemisphere for motor control, but it may reflect the general effects of brain injury, and perhaps oversensitivity of the LAT to such effects. However, De Renzi et al., (1980) classified 20% of their RHD patients as apraxic on an imitative measure of ideomotor apraxia. Most of their apraxic RHD patients were only mildly impaired, but a few were "remarkably poor" and indistinguishable from LHDA patients with comparable impairment.

Table 4. Distribution and summary of overall LAT scores for normal, RHD, and LHD groups (% of subjects within each group given in parentheses)

Scores	Control	RHD	LHD
20.0 - 21.00	21 (70)	15 (34)	7 (9)
19.0 - 19.99	9 (30)	17 (39)	18 (23)
18.0 - 18.99		3 (7)	13 (17)
17.0 - 17.99		8 (18)	11 (14)
16.0 - 16.99		1 (2)	11 (14)
•			
•			
11.0 - 15.99			15 (19)
•			
•			
1.0 - 10.99			2 (3)
n	30	44	77
M	20.17	19.40	17.36
S.D.	0.45	1.10	2.63
Range	19.32 - 20.85	16.60 - 20.83	7.73 - 20.89

None of our RHD patients was markedly deficient but we also are unable to distinguish their performance characteristics from those of LHDA patients with similar degrees of impairment. The similarity of our findings to those of De Renzi et al. help establish the concurrent validity of the LAT and suggest that further assessment of RHD patients on measures of limb apraxia is warranted.

Table 5. Performance of the Normal, RHD, and LHDA groups across the eight LAT subtests (# of subjects in parentheses)

		GROUP		
Subtest		Normal (30)	RHD (44)	LHDA (77)
I	M	19.4	18.8	16.5
	SD	1.1	1.4	3.3
	Range	16.7-20.9	14.9-20.8	7.3-21.0
II	M	20.1	18.9	17.3
	SD	0.8	1.9	3.0
	Range	18.3-21.0	11.9-21.0	6.4-21.0
III	M	19.8	19.1	15.5
	SD	1.0	1.5	4.0
	Range	16.8-21.0	15.3-20.9	4.7-20.9
IV	M	20.5	19.6	17.2
	SD	0.5	1.7	3.5
	Range	19.2-21.0	14.6-21.0	5.7-21.0
V	M	20.3	19.8	18.3
	SD	0.7	1.2	2.5
	Range	18.7-21.0	16.6-21.0	9.5-21.0
VI	M	20.3	19.4	18.3
	SD	0.6	1.5	2.4
	Range	18.8-21.0	16.2-20.9	9.0-21.0
VII	M	20.5	19.9	17.7
	SD	0.7	1.2	2.7
	Range	18.2-21.0	16.6-21.0	8.3-21.0
VIII	M	20.5	19.8	18.1
	SD	0.3	1.2	2.7
	Range	19.7-21.0	16.4-21.0	9.2-21.0

In contrast to the Normal and RHD groups, LHDA scores were much more variable, with 68% of the LHDA group scoring below the cutoff of

2.58 standard deviations below the Normal's mean, and a substantial number of subjects performing very poorly. This incidence figure is higher than that reported by Hécaen and de Ajuriaguerra (1963) and De Renzi et al. 1968. This suggests that difficulties with imitation of limb movements occurs more frequently than is often reported and that the LAT is sensitive to such deficits.

Comparisons among the Normal, RHD, and LHDA groups (ANOVA and appropriate *post hoc* comparisons) indicated that the LHDA group was inferior to both the Normal and RHD groups, but that the Normal and RHD groups did not differ from one another (this does not reduce the value of examining the performance of RHD patients who perform more poorly than Normal subjects, as discussed above). Thus, these results are in agreement with the consistent report of limb apraxia as primarily a sign of left hemisphere damage, and further establish the concurrent validity of the LAT (although true concurrent validity can only be established by direct comparison with other measures of the disorder).

The pattern of group differences across the eight LAT subtests is similar to those for the overall LAT. Multivariate ANOVA and appropriate *post hoc* tests indicated that the Normal and RHD groups did not differ on any of the subtests and that the LHDA group was inferior to both Normal and RHD groups on all subtests.

Influence of Subtest Characteristics on LAT Performance

We have examined some of the influences of the binary contrast features on LAT performance in 64 subjects in the LHDA group. To do this, we averaged the scores on subtests characterized by each feature as an index of performance for that feature. That is, the mean of subtests I - IV was compared to the mean of subtests V - VIII to compare the Sequenced and Segmented features, the mean of subtests I, II, V, and VI was compared to the mean of subtests III, IV, VII, and VIII to compare the Simple and Complex features, and the mean of subtests I, III, V, and VII was compared to the mean of subtests II, IV, VI, and VIII to compare the No Object with the Object features.

Comparisons with *t*-tests indicate that Sequenced tasks are more difficult than Segmented tasks and that No Object tasks are more difficult than Object tasks. In addition, the difference between Sequenced and Segmented tasks was significantly greater than the difference between Object and No Object tasks, suggesting that Sequenced tasks have a greater influence on reducing performance adequacy than movements without Objects. There were no differences between Simple and Complex tasks. These results indicate that some of the features characterizing LAT subtests do influence task difficulty and that some features may be more influential than others. These findings validate the inclusion of the features in the test's design.

Analysis of Qualitative Performance

Table 6. Percentage of responses in each scoring category across the 252 LAT movement components for the normal, RHD, and LHDA groups

Scoring Category	Control (N=30)	RHD (N=44)	LHD (N=77)
21. Complete	86	75	55
20. Distorted	4	6	7
19. Delay	3	5	6
18. Incomplete	3	5	7
17. Del-Dist	<1	1	3
16. Inc-Dist	<1	<1	1
15. Corrected	1	1	1
14. Inc-Del	<1	<1	<1
13. Repeated	<1	1	<1
12. Corr-Dist	<1	<1	<1
11. Inc-Del-Dist	0	0	<1
10. Rep-Dist	<1	<1	<1
9. Corr-Inc	<1	<1	<1
8. Rep-Inc	<1	<1	<1
7. Corr-Inc-Dist	<1	<1	<1
6. Rep-Inc-Dist	0	0	<1
5. Related Error	2	4	11
4. Error	1	2	6
3. Perseveration	0	0	1
2. Unintelligible	0	0	<1
1. No Response	0	0	<1

Table 6 summarizes the percentage of responses in each of the scoring categories across the 252 LAT movement components for the Normal, RHD, and LHDA groups. Analysis of this distribution sheds some light on the kind of information retained by the LAT multidimensional scoring system.

For the Normal group, 86% of their responses were Complete (i.e. completely adequate). Only about 2.5% of their responses were Inaccurate, and most were Related to the target. Deficient responses in the dimensions of Responsiveness, Completeness, Promptness, and Efficiency occurred infrequently, and rarely in combination with one another.

RHD patients performed similarly to Normals, although a smaller percentage of the responses were Complete (75%). About 7% of their responses were Inaccurate, although most of those were Related. Deficient responses in other dimensions occurred a bit more frequently than in Normals, but rarely in combination with one another.

The basic profile of response across scoring categories for the LHDA group is also (surprisingly) similar to Normals, although with some notable increases and decreases in some categories. Only 55% of the LHDA group's responses were Complete and, because of this, they had a larger percentage of inadequate responses in all other response categories, although usually not in combination with one another. Most notably, about 18% of their responses were Inaccurate. Like the other groups, most errors were Related, but a relatively higher proportion were not; that is, although the proportions are very small, they are the only group to show Perseveration and errors so far off target to be called Unintelligible.

These data indicate that the multidimensional scoring system retains descriptive information about responses which, by themselves, differentiate groups from one another. Scoring the LAT on the basis of Accuracy alone would have differentiated the groups, but would not have retained the observations that both brain-injured groups, especially the LHDA group, gave less efficient responses, needed more time to respond accurately, and failed more often to meet the full requirements of the task. That some LHDA subjects were deficient in ways not observed in the other groups (Perseveration and Unintelligible responses) would also have been lost. Finally, the occurrence of few responses in a number of categories (particularly in the dimension of responsiveness) suggests that the scoring scale could be modified to reflect the relative insignificance (i.e., lack of salience) of some response categories (see J.R. Duffy et al., 1989 for a description of some short form versions of the LAT). This would also make the scoring of the test more efficient, and probably more reliable.

Relationship of LAT Performance to Aphasia

We have discussed the notion that disturbances in representational movements can be difficult to interpret relative to the 'causal' influence of limb apraxia compared to aphasia. In fact, this was one of the primary reasons for establishing imitation as the mode for eliciting responses for the LAT; that is, imitation reduces the influence of symbolic processes on performance and permits a 'purer' examination of motor programming influences on movement. Ideally, one would hope to generate no relationship between measures of aphasia and limb apraxia with a measure of limb apraxia that is relatively free of the influence of verbal language or general symbolic deficits.

Unfortunately, this is not the case for the LAT. Using the subjects in the LHDA2 group, R.J. Duffy and J.R. Duffy (1981) found a significant correlation of 0.63 between performance on the LAT and the PICA (a measure of overall aphasia severity). Furthermore, they found a significant correlation of 0.70 between the LAT and a measure of pantomime expression ability (essentially a test of ability to demonstrate object use in response to pictures). These correlations establish that the relationships among limb apraxia, aphasia, and pantomime ability are complex and not easily explained descriptively or by simple correlational analyses. It is not our purpose here to discuss the results of efforts to clarify the nature of these relationships (see R.J. Duffy & J.R. Duffy, 1981 for such discussion). We do wish, however, to point out that the success of any retrospective effort to understand hypothesized causal relationships among neurobehavioral deficits is partially dependent upon reliable, valid measures of the deficits in question. Such measures should be as free as possible from the influence of other deficits, particularly those that are part of the relationships under study. The measurement of limb apraxia is as important to this enterprise as the measurement of aphasia and other deficits.

Summary

We have discussed several issues that are relevant to the assessment of limb apraxia. Assessment historically has been highly subjective and variable and only recently have investigators attempted to operationalize task characteristics that appear important to the identification of the disorder. Even with some agreement about the types of tasks which should be used, most measures use scoring methods that evaluate only accuracy - which is variably defined - without attention to other response characteristics that may represent salient features of apraxia. The use of a small number of test items and failure to establish scoring reliability further compound problems of assessment.

Commands to elicit the pretended use of objects or other nonverbal 'ideas' require the retrieval and formulation of symbols which are then expressed through limb movements. Performance on such tasks can be influenced by aphasia, if aphasia is viewed as a disorder which can affect the use of symbols in any modality, including limb movement. Because the effects of limb apraxia and aphasia may be very difficult to distinguish in a given patient, it seems prudent to use imitation as the elicitation mode for assessing limb apraxia, at least in patients with aphasia, and at least until the specific influence and behavioral manifestations of each disorder is better understood.

We have described the Limb Apraxia Test (LAT), a measure which requires imitation of simple and complex movements, movements requiring and not requiring the use of objects, and movements which are sequenced in their entirety or one component at a time. The test also employs a multidimensional scoring scale which retains information about response characteristics that seem relevant *a priori* to salient features of the disorder.

Use of the LAT with Normal, right-hemisphere-damaged (RHD) and left-hemisphere-damaged aphasic (LHDA) groups has established that the measure identifies the LHDA group as inferior, consistent with the accepted dominance of the left hemisphere for praxis. The ability of the test to separate LHDA from Normal and RHD patients is consistent and replicable, insofar as similar deficient performance has been obtained in three separate samples of LHDA patients. In addition, the test yields incidence rates for limb apraxia in LHDA patients that are higher than several reported in the literature; this attests to its sensitivity, something which may reflect a combination of its comprehensive sampling of behavior, its multidimensional scoring system, and its test-retest reliability and internal consistency.

The LAT's multidimensional scoring system preserves information about response characteristics that occur with varying frequency across Normal, RHD, and LHDA groups. Analysis of the effect on performance of the features characterizing subtests indicates that Sequenced tasks are more difficult than Segmented tasks, that No Object tasks are more difficult than Object tasks, and that Simple and Complex tasks do not differ in difficulty. These findings suggest that the test can be used to examine the influence of these factors on performance across groups and suggest that such comparisons may be useful in the analysis of individual performance.

The LAT is not importantly related to age, education, manual dexterity, or use of the nonpreferred limb. It is, however, correlated with aphasia severity. This correlation underscores the complex relationships that exist among deficits in nonverbal (limb) symbolic communication, limb apraxia, and aphasic verbal impairment, and it reinforces the need to isolate the influence of aphasia from limb apraxia in attempts to understand the nature of each disorder's potential influence on nonverbal deficits in those with aphasia. The LAT's structure, scoring system, and reliability make it a useful measure for identifying the presence and degree of difficulty in imitating limb movements, for analyzing the factors which influence performance, and for describing the behaviors characterizing performance. To that extent, it can contribute to the understanding of limb apraxia, as well as to understanding the nature of other neurobehavioral deficits, particularly those related to communication ability manifested through limb movements.

Finally, it should be recognized that any test of limb apraxia may not be adequate for answering all questions about the disorder or about its relationship to other variables. Nor should any test substitute for a comprehensive definition and theory of the disorder. The assessment of limb apraxia, however, should provide information that is reliable and sensitive to those behaviors - and only those behaviors - which are consistent with one's definition and understanding of the disorder.

References

Agostini, E., Coletti, A., Orlando, G., & Tredici, G.(1983). Apraxia in deep cerebral lesions. *Journal of Neurology, Neurosurgery, and Psychiatry*, **46**, 804-808.

Basso, A., Luzzatti, C., & Spinnler, H. (1980). Is ideomotor apraxia the outcome of damage to well-defined regions of the left hemisphere? *Journal of Neurology, Neurosurgery, and Psychiatry*, **43**, 118-126.

Borod, J.C., Fitzpatrick, P.M., Helm-Estabrooks, N., & Goodglass, H. (1989). The relationship between limb apraxia and the spontaneous use of communicative gesture in aphasia. *Brain and Cognition*, **10**, 121-131.

Brain, R. (1961). *Speech disorders*. Washington, DC: Butterworth.

Brown, J.W. (Ed.), (1988). *Agnosia and apraxia: Selected papers of Liepmann, Lunge, and Potzl*. Hillsdale, NJ: Lawrence Erlbaum Associates.

De Renzi, E. (1985). Methods of limb apraxia examination and their bearing on the interpretation of the disorder. In E.A. Roy (Ed.), *Neuropsychological studies of apraxia and related disorders* (pp. 45-64). Amsterdam: North-Holland.

De Renzi, E., Faglioni, P., Lodesani, M., & Vecchi, A. (1983). Performance of left brain-damaged patients on imitation of single movements and motor sequences: frontal and parietal-injured patients compared. *Cortex*, **19**, 333-343.

De Renzi, E., Faglioni, P., & Sorgato, P. (1982). Modality-specific and supramodal mechanisms of apraxia. *Brain*, **105**, 301-312.

De Renzi, E., Motti, F., & Nichelli, P. (1980). Imitating gestures: a quantitative approach to ideomotor apraxia. *Archives of Neurology*, **37**, 6-10.

De Renzi, E., Pieczuro, A., & Vignolo, L.A. (1968). Ideational apraxia: a quantitative study. *Neuropsychologia*, **6**, 41-52.

Duffy, J.R., Duffy, R.J., & Uryase, D. (1989). The limb apraxia test: development of a short form. In T.E. Prescott (Ed.), *Clinical aphasiology, Vol. 18* (pp. 161-171). Boston: College-Hill.

Duffy, J.R. (1974). *Comparison of brain-injured and non-brain-injured subjects on an objective test of manual apraxia.* Unpublished doctoral dissertation, University of Connecticut.

Duffy, J.R. & Duffy, R.J. (1989). The limb apraxia test: an imitative measure of upper limb apraxia. In T.E. Prescott (Ed.), *Clinical aphasiology, Vol. 18* (pp. 145-159). Boston: College-Hill.

Duffy, R.J., & Duffy, J.R. (1981). Three studies of deficits in pantomime expression and pantomime recognition in aphasia. *Journal of Speech and Hearing Research*, **46**, 70-84.

Ettlinger, G. (1969). Apraxia considered as a disorder of movements that are language-dependent: evidence from cases of brain bisection. *Cortex*, **5**, 285-289.

Foster, N.L., Chase, T.N., Patronas, N.J., Gillespie, M.M., & Fedio, P. (1986). Cerebral mapping of apraxia in Alzheimer's disease by positron emission tomography. *Annals of Neurology*, **19**, 139-143.

Gonzalez-Rothi, J.L. & Heilman, K.M. (1984). Acquisition and retention of gestures by apraxic patients. *Brain and Cognition*, **3**, 426-437.

Graff-Radford, N.R., Welsh, K., & Godersky, J. (1987). Callosal apraxia. *Neurology*, **37**, 100-105.

Haaland, K.Y., Porch, B.E., & Delaney, H.D. (1980). Limb apraxia and motor performance. *Brain and Language*, **9**, 315-323.

Head, H. (1926). *Aphasia and kindred disorders of speech, Vol. I.* New York: MacMillan.

Hécaen, H., & de Ajuriaguerra, J. (1964). *Left handedness.* New York: Grune and Stratton.

Heilman, K.M. (1979). Apraxia. In K.M. Heilman & E. Valenstein (Eds.), *Clinical neuropsychology.* London: Oxford University Press.

Kertesz, A., Ferro, J.M., & Shewan, C.M. (1984). Apraxia and aphasia: the functional-anatomical basis for their dissociation. *Neurology*, **34**, 40-47.

Kertesz, A., & Hooper, P. (1982). Praxis and language: the extent and variety of apraxia in aphasia. *Neuropsychologia*, **20**, 275-286.

Kimura, D. (1982). Left hemisphere control of oral and brachial movements and their relation to communication. *Philosophical Transactions of the Royal Society*, **B298**, 135-149.

Kimura, D., & Archibald, Y. (1974). Motor functions of the left hemisphere. *Brain*, **97**, 337-350.

Lehmkuhl, G., Poeck, K., & Willmes, K. (1983). Ideomotor apraxia and aphasia: an examination of types and manifestations of apraxic symptoms. *Neuropsychologia*, **3**, 199-212.

Liepmann, H.K. (1900). Das Krankheitsbild der Apraxie (motorischen Asymbolie). *Monatsschrift für Psychiatrie und Neurologie*, **8**, 15-44, 102-132, 182-197.

Liepmann, H.K. (1913). Motor aphasia, anarthria, and apraxia. *Transactions of the 17th International Congress of Medicine, Section XI, Part II*, 97-106.

Luria, A.R. (1966). *Higher cortical functions in man*. New York: Basic Books.

Mayer-Gross, W. (1936). Further observations on apraxia. *Journal of Mental Science*, **82**, 744-762.

Poeck, K. (1986). The clinical examination for motor apraxia. *Neuropsychologia*, **24**, 129-134.

Porch, B. (1967). *Porch Index of Communicative Ability*. Palo Alto, CA: Consulting Psychologists Press.

Purdue Research Foundation. (1961). *The Purdue Pegboard*. Chicago, IL: Science Research Association, Inc.

Rapcsak, S.J., Croswell, S.C., & Rubens, A.B. (1989). Apraxia in Alzheimer's disease. *Neurology*, **39**, 664-668.

Pieczuro, A., & Vignolo, L.A. (1967). Studio sperimentale sull ápraxssia ideomotor. *Sistema Nervoso*, **19**, 131-143.

Watson, R.T., & Heilman, K.M. (1983). Callosal apraxia. *Brain*, **106**, 391-403.

Weisenberg, T.J., & McBride, K.E. (1935). *Aphasia: A clinical and psychological study. Vol. 1.* New York: The Commonwealth Fund.

Wilson, S.A.K. (1908-09). A contribution to the study of apraxia with a review of the literature. *Brain*, **31**, 164-216.

Winer, B.J. (1971). *Statistical principles in experimental design* (2nd ed.) New York: McGraw-Hill.

PART IV

INTERACTIONS OF SPEECH AND MANUAL PERFORMANCE

Cerebral Control of Speech and Limb Movements
G.E. Hammond (editor)

Chapter 18

INTERACTION OF VOCAL AND MANUAL MOVEMENTS

Michael Peters
University of Guelph

The relation between the control of the vocal apparatus and the hands is tracked across different levels of structure and function. While differences in structure and function at the level of the final motor outflow are considered, the principal focus is on the commonalities between the systems at a level where volitional intent is transformed into action. Particular attention is paid to dual task paradigms that pit the demands for attention of the two control systems (for voice and hand movements) against each other. It is concluded that at the higher levels of praxis control a unitary mechanism channels action commands into the two different outflow paths. Relative independence between vocal and manual control is observed at lower levels.

The juxtaposition of motor control for speech and limb movements presupposes that something useful can be said about the topic. It is clear from the outset that the most interesting link between speech and manual control will be found at a level several steps removed from the execution of movement. In Lakoff's (1978, p. 277) terms, we consider movement as the source domain of purpose and it is primarily through speech and movements of the hands that conscious volition makes itself known. One of the most intriguing approaches to the question of how volition selects its channel of expression is through interference paradigms that pit the speech apparatus and the limb musculature against each other. The consideration of such interference paradigms, then, is at the center of this discussion.

However, in order to provide a somewhat broader background for the evaluation of interference paradigms, it is useful to first consider a number of neuropsychological aspects of the organization of motor control for the speech and limb effectors.

The most natural point of departure for our exploration is the observation that in most humans the side of the brain that appears to be involved in the management of speech is also the side that is involved in the control of the preferred hand. However, whatever joy early neurologists may have derived from this relationship dissipated as soon as it was realized that there are exceptions to this rule. Indeed, the departures from the rule were discovered just about at the same time as the rule itself (Harris, in press). Because of these exceptions, the relation between speech and hand motor control is not a simple one and this is why the present chapter will have to look at the issue from various perspectives.

First, if only for reasons of completeness, some basic background information will be provided for the two systems. It is clear, a priori, that the mode of operation of the two systems at the level of execution is quite different. However, to the extent that certain aspects of function and structure of the two systems have some bearing on their interrelation as agents of volition, this basic background information is of importance in understanding higher order interactions. Second, some general similarities and differences between the two systems will be pointed out. Third, the degree of association in terms of common lateral localization will be examined and, finally, in an attempt to integrate the various aspects of interaction between speech and hand control, higher-level commonalities will be discussed in the context of interference paradigms.

Motor Control of Speech: Brief Background

From modest beginnings, where the larynx functioned as little more than a valve to ensure that air goes hither and food thither, the speech apparatus in man has reached an impressive complexity. Indeed, such are the specialized needs for speech production that sacrifices had to be made in the design of the human larynx both in terms of reduced efficiency of respiration and danger of food lodging in the larynx (Lieberman, 1972, p. 34). No fewer than six of the cranial nerves are needed in order to ensure proper phonation and articulation (trigeminal, facial, auditory, glossopharyngeal, vagus and hypoglossal). The interplay of the laryngeal muscles underlying abduction (posterior cricoarytenoid), adduction (interarythenoid, lateral cricoarytenoid and thyroarytenoid) and control of stiffness of the vocal folds is a study in motor complexity all by itself. In order to achieve adequate integration of speech with respiration, an exception to the rule that direct corticospinal tract endings on spinal motor neurons are mostly found on neurons that supply the distal musculature of the limbs had to be made: direct synaptic contacts of the corticospinal tract are also found on the neurons that supply the thoracic musculature used to power inhalation and exhalation. Sears (1977) states that

> ... we can see that by analogy with the small muscles of the hand, the muscle spindles of the rib-cage are admirably suited to the task of regulating sub-glottal pressure during speech and song. (p. 92).

The delicacy required for faultless operation of the speech machinery is such that even minor problems in the central nervous system lead to disruption. For instance, in persons with severe or profound mental retardation, clearly articulated speech is extremely rare.

In controlling the speech production machinery, the cortical areas responsible likely do not 'compose' individual speech sounds but address the lower motor neurons by means of a short hand code that results in the production of laryngeal 'gestures'. Such gestures constitute the basic units of speech production. Whether or not phonemes as commonly defined constitute such basic units is unclear, but it is obvious from the study of people who have a facility in speaking backwards that they do use the phoneme as basic unit in accomplishing their feat (Cowan, Leavitt, Massaro, & Kent 1982). Kelso, Tuller, and Harris (1983) have argued that the speech machinery, in producing utterances, is constrained by coordinate linkages between participating muscle groups. Direct and compelling evidence for this has been provided by Gracco and Abbs (1986), who made kinematic recordings of the movements of the jaw and upper and lower lips during speech. They suggested that the consistency of the timing relations between these elements during speech was indicative of the operation of pattern generators such as have been found to be active in the control of locomotion. What is the case for the easily observed movements of the lips and jaw very likely also applies to the activation of tongue, pharynx and larynx because it is inconceivable that invariance in the timing relationships should only be observed between the outer elements of the speech apparatus. To the extent that the movements of the tongue, pharynx and laryngeal components are less directly experienced than movements of lips and jaws, it would be even more important for the former to be operated in the form of coordinated linkages than the latter.

The very nature of coordinated linkages suggests that the motor cortex does not control speech gestures via the individualized control of particular muscle movements, but rather through the activation of constellations of such movements, or even only indirectly through the activation of subcortical structures. This appears to contradict known principles in the organization of columns in the primary motor cortex (Asanuma, 1973) whereby single cortical motor neurons project predominantly only to one muscle. Asanuma's findings have generally been supported, although it is now also quite clear that single cortical motor neurons do provide collateral branches to spinal motor neurons subserving different muscles (Phillips, 1986, p. 118-124). Particularly in speech, where the production of speech sound is realized through the assumption of laryngeal postures that are based on the concurrent activation of a complex array of muscles (Sawashima & Hirose, 1983) the principle of coordinated linkages of different muscle groups must hold.

Motor Control of the Hands: Brief Background

In an evolutionary sense, the speech apparatus of humans is highly specialized in terms of structural and functional differentiation that allows coactivation of oral region, tongue, pharynx, larynx and innervation of the thoracic musculature. In case of the hands, the structural differentiation, apart from the opposable thumb, is less impressive. At least at a very superficial glance, the human hand seems to represent the basic ground plan of the vertebrate five-digited forepaw, resembling the hand of a salamander more than that of more specialized higher mammals. The functional specialization, however, is profound. As is the case for the speech machinery, much of the specialization lies in the cortex. A comparatively enormous amount of cortical surface is devoted to the motor and sensory mapping of the hand. In the somatosensory cortex, the amount of cortex devoted to mapping the thumb is roughly comparable to the area devoted to mapping of the entire torso! Partly because of the initial segmental layout of the basic animal, the cortical areas responsible for movement of the hand and the mouth region are in close proximity. Compared to the mapping of sensory areas, a full understanding of how the cortical columns in the motor cortex relate to each other, and how they are organized themselves, lags far behind. It is clear that pyramidal tract fibers that innervate the hand of higher primates differ from other such fibers in that they make direct contact with motor neurons that control finger movements. This arrangement is particularly conducive to managing what has been called 'fractionated' movements of the fingers.

By fractionated one means that individual fingers are freed from the constraints of whole hand movements, such as seen in grasping, and can in that way be selectively addressed. This creates the sort of flexibility that is the foundation of all skilled manual movement. Having said this, it should be recognized that even within the hand there are limitations as to the degree of voluntary control that can be exercised by the individual fingers; they are not all equally accessible and responsive to voluntary control. The ring finger and the small finger are less capable of rapid independent movement than the other fingers, partly because of the nature of tendon articulation and partly because of muscular factors. From a neurophysiological point of view, the role of the motor cortex in activating the movements of individual fingers is not well understood. The functional demands of rapid integrated finger movements would suggest that cortical motor neurons are active in organizing particular constellations of finger movements, and the branching of corticospinal axons and their termination on different motor neurons in the spinal cord would be conducive to such a mode of operation. Nevertheless, Muir and Lemon's (1983) work suggests that the degree of divergence is quite restricted in functional terms. Although direct corticospinal connections play a very important role in movements of the distal musculature, it is clear that fractionated movements do not take place in a vacuum. Arbib, Iberall, and Lyons (1985) make it clear that in the case of precision movements of the hand there is involvement of supportive extrapyramidal action. Muir (1985), after studying individual hand muscles after cortical ablation, came to the conclusion that even after destruction of the primary motor cortex, descending input to spinal motor neurons was capable of providing individual hand muscles or combinations of these with activating input.

Differences Between Speech and Hand Control Systems

One of the most striking differences between the two control systems is the fact that the entire innervation of the larynx, both motor and sensory, is accomplished through the inferior and superior laryngeal branches of the vagus nerve which, after all, is part of the autonomic nervous system. The autonomic nervous system is not normally thought of as the carrier of voluntary action. The autonomic influence has a deep phylogenetic root. Lieberman (1972) has emphasized that in those primates for which a detailed study has been carried out, the inability to modulate the cross-sectional area of the larynx restricts the ability of these animals to produce the entire range of human speech sounds. But what is more striking than the structural restrictions is the fact that subhuman primates have difficulties in bringing their vocalizations under voluntary control. Although they vocalize readily and with a great variety of sound patterns (Peters & Ploog, 1973), the vocalizations tend to be associated with given emotional states that underlie, e.g., alarm calls, food calls and contact calls. Monkeys have difficulties in producing any of these calls outside their proper 'limbic state' context, even if rewarded for doing so. The observation that removal of the cortical larynx area in monkeys does not produce noticeable problems in vocalization (Jürgens, 1984) supports this view. In man, infringement on this area produces dysarthria. Humans have excellent voluntary control over speech mechanisms, but the autonomic influence manifests itself in a variety of ways. Those who have difficulties with speech fluency, such as stutterers, are clearly responsive to social context in their speech behavior (Carlisle, 1985). Nonstutterers, under extreme emotional stress will also have difficulties in speaking without basic pitch being affected and in some cases they may be rendered speechless temporarily.

This aspect of disruption of vocal control should not be overstated and does not allow a categorical distinction because emotional states also affect movements of the limbs. Analogies to 'be rendered mute' can be found in persons who are rendered 'frozen with fear', or going 'weak kneed'. Whether or not the mechanisms for loss of control in the vocal system are similar to those affecting the limbs (where large amounts of peripherally circulating adrenaline play a role) is unclear.

The other major difference, beside the difference in neurological access to the target musculature, lies in the symmetry of the executive structures. The vocal apparatus is meant to be activated synchronously and while the tongue in particular is capable of asymmetric movement along the midline axis during eating and chewing, during speech it is meant to move symmetrically along the midline axis. We do not normally, as it were, speak with a forked tongue and some portions of the machinery underlying speech, such as the thoracic musculature when engaged in breathing, are altogether incapable of nonsymmetric movement. The hands, in contrast, are meant to move asymmetrically. There is no speech equivalent of handedness as far as the final motoric outflow is concerned.

Similarities Between Speech and Hand Control Systems

Whether or not there are similarities between the two systems, and how much one is to make of such similarities, depends on the level at which a comparison is drawn.

Lateral Congruence of Speech and Preferred Hand Control: What is it that is Lateralized?

It is quite impossible to discuss speech and hand movement control without reference to hand preference, because the lateral specialization is common to both. Unfortunately, this section has to begin with a caution regarding handedness classification. Handedness is classified by preference choices or performance or both, and it is not possible at this point to relate handedness phenotype to handedness genotype for either of the currently popular genetic models of handedness (Annett, 1985; McManus, 1984). For instance, McManus quite frankly admits that his model does not permit on a priori grounds a description of the heterozygote phenotype and a similar problem is also seen in Annett's model. Worse, in both models a significant proportion of individuals have a genotype that does not specify hand preference and the hand preference that eventually emerges in these individuals may be suggestive of either a right-hander or a left-hander. Again, it is not possible at this point to distinguish clearly between a person who is right-handed because he or she has the genotype that specifies a dextral bias from a person who is lacking such a specification. This debate is not idle contemplation because whatever statements one finds in the literature regarding, e.g., the prevalence of aphasia among right- and left-handers depends ultimately on a reasonable classification scheme for handedness. The only saving grace is that there is a fair amount of agreement with regard to some quite important associations between handedness and language lateralization. Various critical reviews of the issue have come to the conclusion that aphasia in right-handers after right hemisphere lesions is very rare (Segalowitz & Bryden, 1983; McManus, 1984). In view of the lack of an absolute correspondence between genotype and phenotype for handedness, it is not even certain that these few cases are, in fact, genotypic right-handers. The recent report by Henderson (1983) of three completely right-handed right-handers (as determined by scores of 100 on the Oldfield questionnaire) with fluent aphasia after right hemisphere lesions suggests that such cases exist. However, handwriting and drawing samples, done with the preferred right hand by all three patients show extremely poor motor control both for the writing and the drawing samples. It is possible that (see discussion on apraxia below) the patients had their praxis specialization on the right side and this might be an explanation of the poor performance. One patient had a tremor in the right hand and this would account for at least one aspect of the poor performance, but of the three, one had no indication of limb apraxia and the other two, including the one with the tremor, did not have severe cases of apraxia. The lateral neglect seen in the patients would not as such account for the poor motor execution. The fact that these patients had the traditional spatial neglect problems after the right hemisphere lesion (which indicates that both speech and language function and the sort of spatial functions normally attributed to the right hemisphere were on the right) and the poor motor performance of the right hand makes one wonder what the status of the left hemisphere in these patients was. Could these persons really be considered typical right-handers ?

Segalowitz and Bryden (1983) also point out that patients in whom bilateral language representation is found are practically never right handed. This leads to the conclusion that departures from a lateral congruence between language and speech lateralization and hand preference are to be found in left-handers. In left-handers, the largest single block of individuals has a left-sided speech lateralization, with a smaller proportion reportedly having bilateral or right-sided specialization (Segalowitz & Bryden, 1983). What is one to make of this ? Some (Bryden, 1982, p. 171) have concluded that there is only a weak relation between handedness and speech lateralization while the models of others (e.g. McManus, 1984) even postulate independence between these two specializations. However, the fact that in some individuals there is a lack of lateral congruence must not necessarily mean that there is a weak relation between handedness and speech lateralization. Indeed, the uncertainty as to the interrelation between the two reveals a fundamental weakness in theories of handedness which normally can be glossed over but which in applications like this becomes a nuisance. The weakness is found in the lack of a real understanding of why it is that people prefer one hand over the other for certain activities. In terms of formal requirements of theories in the scientific domain, theories of handedness are extremely weak in the sense that they do not lend themselves to powerful predictions about 'hand behavior' and because they are difficult to falsify.

Let us assume, for instance, that there are several levels of lateral specialization, across different anatomical substrates, that underlie handedness (Peters, 1983). To the extent that skilled movements of the digits are operated by the contralateral hemisphere, it is reasonable to assume that in right-handers the left hemisphere manages the final motor outflow to the right hand. It appears that in most discussions of the relation between speech/language and handedness the lateralization argument for handedness is based simply on the basic fact that the activities of the preferred hand have their executive motor machinery in the hemisphere contralateral to the hand. The question is: does the lateral specialization reside only in the system that manages final execution or does it reside also in a higher order system that feeds into the executing level of the hand control system? There is reason to believe that lateral specialization in the executing systems will eventually be found for both speech and manual control. Once the cruder methods of counting descending fibers or looking at which side crosses above the other in the crossing of the pyramidal tracts at the brainstem level have given way to more sophisticated methods, lateralized specialization of the final motor outflow path will likely be documented. The work of Scheibel (1984) on patterns of dendritic branching in the opercular region of right-handers and non-right-handers points the way for this new generation of investigations. Scheibel has demonstrated subtle lateral specializations for the region involved with speech and there is no reason why such specializations should not be found in the hand motor region of the preferred hand. In a nice complementary study that is entirely behavioral,

Wolf and Goodale (1987) have shown that oral asymmetries during speech in right-handers are clearly indicative of a left hemisphere predominance, and these asymmetries increase in clarity with increasing complexity of the movements.

If there is a lateral specialization for both lower and higher order motor control systems it is quite possible to have a lateral specialization for speech and language and higher order manual movement programming on the left side, while the final common path that is used to guide the preferred left hand is in the right hemisphere. In other words, in the case described one would have a phenotypic left-hander who prefers the left hand but the higher order planning of movements for the left hand is guided by the left hemisphere. In such a hypothetical case there would or there would not be a discrepancy between speech and handedness lateralization, depending on which level of hand motor control one wishes to look at. The first question to be considered in relating speech/language to handedness, then, is whether or not the different levels of the control systems are necessarily lateralized on the same side of the brain and under what circumstances they are not. It should be noted that this question is of some additional interest in those cases where there is some suspicion that brain pathology has led to a switch in hemispheres responsible for speech and hand control (Simon & Sussman, 1987). There is some reason to believe that when there is a switch, *both* hand preference and speech lateralization switch together (Rasmussen & Milner, 1977) but it is not clear at all whether such a switch implies a switch of all levels of control, i.e., final outflow and praxis.

In order to address this question, a closer look has to be taken at the theoretical underpinnings of the speech/handedness connection. Some investigators have toyed with the idea of independence between the two (McManus, 1984), some have suggested the relation to be weak (Bryden, 1982) and some (Annett, 1985) have felt that the two have co-evolved and efforts to separate them out in terms of which caused which are not likely to be fruitful. Nevertheless, numerous writers have attempted to draw causal links. For instance, Hewes (1973) believed that speech evolved secondarily from an already lateralized system of communication with manual gestures that, in turn, was secondary to a lateral manual specialization for manual precision movements in the manufacture and use of tools. The argument about the specialization underlying precision movements can be turned around. Peters (1988) has suggested that the primate mouth shows motor specializations during oral exploration and manipulation of objects that are analogous to the skilled use of the hands. There can be little question that in an evolutionary context the role of the mouth in exploration and the precise control of force that is characteristic in feeding and chewing must precede lateral hand specialization. An argument was made that consistent manual lateralization is the byproduct of the advantages of combining specialized control systems for oral manipulation and vocalization with attentional mechanisms that serve to focus attention on a single volitional goal.

Kimura's work (Kimura, 1979, 1982) on the close relation between gestures of the preferred hand and the hemisphere thought to be specialized for speech/language might be seen to be in direct support of Hewes' ideas. However, Kimura also focuses on the common motoric requirements of the speech machinery and the hands; she has attempted to isolate underlying motor specializations in terms of the requirement for fast and precise timing of postural transitions. Kimura makes the case for a commonality between the two motor systems in an explicit form:

> One can reasonably conclude that there is some system common to the control of both free movements and speaking and that this system, for most people, is based primarily on the left hemisphere. (Kimura, 1973a, p. 49).

The 'free movements' refer to hand movements that accompany speech and that do not involve touching the body. These movements clearly favor the right hand in right-handers. In left-handers the situation is more complex; left-handers with language functions that are inferred to be localized on the left (by dichotic listening test) do not show any clear bias towards free movements in either the left or right hand while left-handers shown to have a right hemisphere language specialization tend to favor the left hand when carrying out free movements during speaking. As an aside, it can be noted that hand movements are not, of course, the only gestural concomitant of speech as head movements have been shown to have a very close relationship to various speech features (Hadar, Steiner, & Rose, 1984). Because the motor control system for the head is quite apart from that of the hands, it is suggested that the integration of hand and head movement in support of speech is due to a superordinate level of motor control that is common to both - and which does not reside within the specific executing mechanism for hand or head. Such a model of a superordinate system is also inherent in the account by Steklis and Raleigh (1979) who suggest that gestural language need not have preceded vocal language and who feel that it is more reasonable to assume that early hominids would have employed both vocal and manual means in cooperation, using one channel in order to avoid difficulties in another.

Indirect experimental support for the contention of a higher level interaction comes from the dual task study by Rey, Dellatolas, Baucaud, and Talairach (1988) who examined the interference effects of speech on concurrent speaking in a large sample of right- and left-handers. Left-handers show stronger interference effects in the left hand than in the right hand. It is not possible to explain this with reference to the expected interference of right hemisphere speech with right hemisphere control of the left hand because the majority of left-handers have left hemisphere specialization for speech. Rey et al. (1988) suggest that the data may be explained on the basis of ipsilateral control of the left hand. However, in the absence of any convincing evidence of ipsilateral motor control for rapid fine movements of the distal musculature, the more appropriate interpretation is that interference occurs between a left-sided praxis center for the left hand (in the sense of Liepmann's model) and the speech control machinery, and *not* between the speech machinery and the final executive path for the control of the left hand which can be assumed to originate from the right hemisphere.

In this brief examination of lateralization of speech and hand motor control, I have so far neglected any mention of singing. Singing adds another level of complexity because lateralization for singing and speech need not necessarily be congruent. Bogen and Gordon (1971) studied singing performance in patients who were given injections of sodium amytal into either the left or right carotid artery. Of the eight patients, seven showed a significant loss of singing performance after right carotid injections even though in all but one speech was relatively unaffected. Smith and Burkland (1966) reported a converse situation. After left hemispherectomy, their patient showed severe losses in speech but was able to sing quite adequately. At a more peripheral level, anesthesia of the vocal folds will allow the affected person to speak intelligibly, but singing will be very severely affected (Harvey, 1985, p. 309). These selected references show that the situation with regard to singing and speech is complex. Whether or not singing is more complex than speaking depends on a number of factors. If singing rests on an overlearned vocal pattern it might well be that singing can be viewed as primarily tonal/musical rather than verbal, and it might be that a person can, as Smith and Burkland (1966) show, sing but not speak. If the singing involves the generation of new (produced 'on-line') verbal patterns, as in Guiard's (1989) study, singing may be viewed as speaking with an additional level of complexity added. Whatever the complexities, from the point of view of motor production, the occasional dissociation of speaking and singing shows that the speech musculature can be accessed by control systems from either the left or right hemisphere. Both hemispheres can presumably access the final motor path to the vocal box but the specific ability to address it from the left or the right side depends on other specializations that are prerequisite to vocal control in the case of voluntary speech (i.e., on-line transition of thought into speech action vs. superimposing musical parameters on an already known verbal base) and singing. It should be noted that the situation as it emerges from clinical investigations of speaking and singing after brain damage or brain manipulations needs to be reconciled with demonstrations of lateralized specialization at the level of the final common motor path to the speech machinery (Scheibel, 1984).

If gestural support is notable during speech it is, of course, practically inseparable from singing where there are far more clearly defined pauses and stresses that can be complemented by gestural elaboration. The general assumption that the relation between speech, singing, and gestural support, be it through hand or head, is at a level above the executing level moves the entire argument towards the notion of a common underlying machinery for praxis.

Praxis of Hands and Speech Machinery

Ever since Liepmann (1908), there has been an acceptance of the idea that there is a superordinate level of control that does not reside in the final cortical outflow to the spinal motor neurons for the hands, and that it is from this level that the organized and integrated sequences of instructions necessary for skilled hand movement are issued. This, of course, relates back to our discussion of what it is that is lateralized in hand preference. To the extent that Liepmann believed that the machinery for praxis is concentrated in the left hemisphere, it is only reasonable to ask whether there is some connection between praxis of speech movements and praxis of hand movements. Kimura (1982) summarizes data that suggests a close link between the two. Patients with left anterior hemisphere lesions showed a marked impairment in tasks that required oral and manual praxis. They performed much worse on these tasks than patients with right hemisphere lesions. Significantly, patients with left hemisphere lesions showed their greatest deficit when required to perform series of movements and in this case both multiple oral and multiple manual movement sequences were equally badly affected.

A more detailed look at the data revealed that the left anterior region of the brain appears crucial for oral praxis, be it in the context of speech or non-speech movements. Kimura concluded that the left frontal and the left parietal areas are very important both in oral and manual praxis, with some dissociation between the two localizations, depending on whether single or multiple movement sequences are required. In the case of the parietal lobe, the correlation between difficulties in multiple oral and manual gestures is impressively high. As might be expected because of the specialized region for oral praxis in the anterior brain half, there is a high correlation between impairment for single and multiple oral gestures; the primarily executive role of the oral praxis region makes it likely that the problems in multiple oral gestures are caused by problems in oral praxis in general. The patterns of intercorrelations suggest that the overlap between oral and manual control is more clearly expressed in the parietal lobe than in the anterior lobe. In the anterior lobe there is presumably a clearer separation between the two. Whether or not this differentiation is due to a genuine difference in organization or due to the nature of insult to the frontal and parietal regions is unclear.

Kimura's findings parallel an earlier study by Poeck and Kerschensteiner (1975). These researchers again emphasized the important role of the motor requirements of the movements involved; the association between verbal and non-verbal problems was particularly close when the movements demanded precision in execution. More broadly conceived surveys (Kertesz, 1984) conclude that particularly in cases with severe aphasia, apractic problems were almost invariably found whereas the association was not as striking in patients with less severe aphasia. Kertesz is conservative in terms of attributing the linkage to a common underlying neural structure and points out that the areas sensitive to apractic and aphasic disturbances lie largely in the irrigation area of the middle cerebral artery. In other words, a stroke that affects language might very well also affect the areas underlying praxis - and thus give rise to the illusion that a common mechanism is at work. Kimura (1982), however, has argued that the finer dissociations between region and specific task tested do not support a single 'size of lesion' type of explanation for the complex association between apraxia and aphasia.

At present, there seems to be some support for Kimura's contention that the parietal lobe of the left hemisphere has some general programming function that covers both oral and manual movement. As Faglioni and Basso (1984) point out, this is precisely the conclusion Kleist (1934) came to in his modification of Liepmann's scheme.

To summarize a somewhat complex and contradictory literature, there is some evidence that there is a superordinate mechanism - Faglioni and Basso (1984) and De Renzi (1984) feel that it is a circumscribed region - that lies outside classical sensory-motor cortex and which is active in praxis of both oral and manual movements. An additional anterior region that is more specific to oral praxis, be it in the context of verbal or non-verbal movements, is less clearly associated with praxis in general. The literature is agreed that there is some degree of lateralization in these regions. The indirect evidence from surveys of apraxia shows that the left hemisphere is predominantly involved. The question arises: what is one to think of those cases where aphasia is observed without apraxia and, conversely, where apraxia is seen without aphasia - regardless of any aspects of lateralization? Does this mean there is in fact independence between speech and manual machinery, and that the observed associations are merely epiphenomena due to the anatomy of the systems involved in brain damage? Unfortunately, no clear answer can be given to such a question, if levels proximal to the final motor outflow are considered. Aphasic disturbances, as De Renzi (1984) points out, are much more salient in a patient's behavior and have received much more detailed attention in clinical research. The level of sophistication of work dealing with apraxia has, until recently, lagged behind work on aphasia. For this reason, the understanding of apraxia and its subclassifications compares poorly with the current understanding of aphasia. Adding to this the problems in anatomical documentation of clinical cases, it is perhaps premature to conclude that cases with aphasia with no apraxia exist. Only if limb apraxia is tested exhaustively, perhaps by means of a list of error categories for limb apraxia such as described in the thoughtful analysis of Roy and Square (1985, p. 148) can conclusive statements be made.

In examining the relation of praxis in the hands relative to speech and language mechanisms, an interesting confound of manual praxis in writing can be demonstrated. A lateral asymmetry of negative slow potentials favoring the left side in right-handers was found during writing, regardless of whether the writing was done with the left or the right hand (Jung, 1984). Jung was also able to show that in 10 out of 12 left-handed writers there still was also a lateral asymmetry favoring the left hemisphere. It seems that this particular measure is more sensitive to the lateralized language aspects of writing than to the final motoric outflow involving the motor cortex that directs the contralateral hand.

An additional line of evidence concerning the relation of praxis of speech and hand motor control comes from work with stutterers. Stutterers have speech production problems that cannot be related to aphasic disturbances and it may be assumed that their problems are caused by difficulties at levels very near the final motor execution of speech. The question is: Does the problem experienced by stutterers manifest itself in speech only or is there a more pervasive difficulty in motor control that can be attributed to a higher-order motor mechanism, common to speech and manual control? Because stutterers perform single handed tasks that occur normally in everyday life quite well, the issue has not received much attention.

However, problems in the performance of single handed tapping sequences have been identified (Webster, 1989). Even more striking is the performance deficit of stutterers on a bimanual writing task (Webster, 1988), although there is some disagreement on the exact performance patterns observed for various samples of stutterers (Greiner, Fitzgerald, & Cooke, 1986). On a task where subjects were required to perform two concurrent motor tasks (turning a knob at a rate determined by an auditory signal with the left hand while at the same time producing a tapping sequence with the right hand) stutterers did again more poorly than nonstutterers on a number of different performance measures. In a recent study, Vaughn and Webster (1989) were able to show that when stutterers had to perform bimanual activities that involved consecutive actions of the two hands, their performance was as good as that of nonstutterers. Only when the bimanual activities required bimanual and basically incompatible actions did the stutterers show marked deficits. Webster (1989) attributes the difficulties experienced by stutterers to problems involving the supplemental motor area and its interhemispheric connections. The emphasis on bilateral interactions between the supplemental motor (SMA) areas of both sides reflects Goldberg's belief (1985) that the interhemispheric connections between the SMA are of importance to both speech and manual activities. It is at this level where bilateral influences come to bear on the final lateralized motor outflow.

Bilateral vs. Unilateral Control of Hand and Speech Movement

In various approaches to the lateralization of motor function, notably electrical brain stimulation (e.g., Ojemann, 1983) and the sodium amytal injection technique, a unilateral disturbance can be documented in the final motor path. Similarly, in the discussion of apraxias it was shown that praxis specialization appears quite clearly lateralized. An extensive body of work on cerebral blood flow during various activities also gives evidence of lateralization. Roland (1985) summarizes a wide array of evidence that shows lateralized increase in metabolic rate in certain brain areas, but not others, during specific activities. For instance, in fluent descriptive speech, Broca's area on the left side shows a much greater increase than the corresponding area in the right hemisphere. Although others (e.g., Gur & Reivich, 1980; Larsen, Skinhøj, & Lassen, 1978) also report such an asymmetry, dissenting studies exist. A careful recent study by Formby, Thomas, and Halsey (1989) fails to show cerebral asymmetries in blood flow during singing, humming and speaking.

The complexity of this particular question is brought out even better by the observations made with the Bereitschaftspotential (readiness potential). Deecke, Engel, W. Lang, and Kornhuber (1986) observed a bilateral readiness potential (RP) but just in the final 100 ms before onset of speech they noted a lateral asymmetry favoring the left hemisphere. Localization of bilateral activation patterns has by and large been focused on the supplementary motor area (SMA), also called the 'supramotor area' by Orgonozo and Larsen (1979). Beginning with Eccles (1982), a number of researchers (Kornhuber, 1984; Goldberg, 1985; Grözinger, Kornhuber, & Kriebel, 1979; Kornhuber & Deecke, 1985; Deecke et al., 1986; Deecke, Kornhuber, W. Lang, M. Lang, & Schreiber, 1985) have emphasized the role of the SMA as an area that is related to the control of movement, regardless of whether it is movement of the oral region or the limbs. Kornhuber and

Deecke (1985) summarize much of the work on the RP by stating that it precedes voluntary movement maximally in the SMA for movements of the fingers, hand, toes, mouth, tongue, speech in general and eye movement. This appears to support the contention by Orgonozo and Larson (1979) that the SMA is a superordinate motor area. In attempting to specify further the role of the SMA in movement, Kornhuber and Deecke (1985) and Deecke et al. (1985) speculate that the SMA is particularly concerned with *when* a particular movement is to take place in accord with a variety of internal and external conditions. For instance, when two fingers are to tap synchronously, their mutual coordination is very important and according to Kornhuber and Deecke this is the sort of task for which the SMA is specialized.[1]

Goldberg (1985) suggests that even in the case of unimanual activities, there is an information exchange between the SMAs of the two brain halves. Presumably there is a tendency for bilateral symmetry in actions (Cernacek, 1961; Schott, 1980) that, under normal conditions, is successfully suppressed. Evidence that Goldberg's suggestion is correct derives from studies in which an artificial disturbance reveals the bilateral symmetry. Brinkman (1984), in a much-cited study, showed that monkeys with lesions of the premotor cortex had a tendency to mirror purposive movements made in one hand with the other hand, but that this mirror movement ceased after anterior callosal lesions.

This, incidentally, points out another basic difference between manual and speech motor control because in the normal skilled use of the hands, the movement trajectories of the hands differ and mirror imaging in movement is bound to interfere. Thus, at least at the level of execution, there is a considerable advantage in keeping specific information from one hand from interfering with movement control of the other. To the extent that peripheral feedback is important in hand control, it is understandable why there is very little direct transcallosal connection between the primary sensory and motor areas serving the hands. In the case of speech there is no particular reason why mirror imaging should have a deleterious effect at least at a level one step removed from execution. Certainly, the sodium

---

1. It is important to note that the sort of timing discussed by Kornhuber and his colleagues is quite different from what one might call 'process timing', that is, timing that is inherent in the running of the actual motor machinery. This is a topic that is neglected here but brief reference can be made to the cerebellum as principal actor in this domain (Ivry & Keele, 1989) and it would be interesting to see if the lateralizations observed for hand and speech control might in the end also find reflection in cerebellar function. This is a promising area of future research.

amytal studies show that an intact bilateral machinery, even though it might normally be operative, is *not needed* for successful activation of speech machinery.

In summarizing the previous sections, we can state that speech and hand motor control interact at various levels, and that a common control mechanism that doles out movement initiations to lower order mechanisms seems to exist. Perhaps, if further work is supportive of this, there may even be agreement on an anatomical focus (SMA).[2] Having established that there is a common mechanism, the psychologically interesting question of how such a common mechanism deals with the demands of focusing attention on hands and mouth when competition arises. This will be dealt with in the following section.

Competition for Attention Between Speech and Manual Movement

This section is concerned most directly with competition for attention in the volitional control of speech and manual movement. The unsuspecting reader will likely be taken aback when faced with an extensive discussion of attention and how attention is focused on action before competition paradigms are introduced, and I feel the need to justify this approach. At the very outset, it was stated that the most interesting aspects of the interrelation between speech and manual movement lie at levels that are superordinate to actual control mechanisms for the two. The issue is how movement intent expresses itself in action. For methodological reasons, this can be approached best in paradigms where there is competition for 'resources' (of whatever kind) because it is under these conditions where choices and strategies of the systems that direct attention and initiate action become visible. In a way, this is a uniquely psychological concern, known as the 'how is it possible for a unitary acting self to do two things at the same time?' question. While it is true that neurophysiologists and neuroanatomists can define likely structures that might underlay the realization of a movement intent, they cannot with their methods address the question of how attention selects its object and how priorities are chosen. Kornhuber (1984) is not shy in talking about free will and the supplementary motor area in the same breath, and how it might be

2. Lest the impression is given that there is universal consensus concerning the role of the SMA, it should be noted that this area has been implicated in the support functions of adjusting body posture in correspondence with the voluntary activity as well as with initiation of movement (M. Wiesendanger, & R. Wiesendanger, 1984).

involved in the choice of what movement is initiated. But the dynamics of how this is done can be explored only through behavioral techniques. Because such techniques involve, implicitly or explicitly, the concept of attention, the consideration of how attention relates to concurrent activities is central to the entire discussion of 'doing two things at the same time'.

The Essential Elements of Doing Two Things at the Same Time

First, one needs to consider what one means by 'the things' that are done at the same time. Nobody is surprised that a person can walk and talk at the same time, or walk while looking about. Similarly, the pianist who accompanies him or herself on the piano while singing a song fails to astound the onlooker because of this feat. When asked why this is so, the observant layman (who is as trustworthy as any academic on these matters) may observe that in the first instances a person performs activities that do not need much attention and that in the last example the two concurrent activities complement each other. Our hypothetical layman has isolated two important factors in concurrent motor behavior: (a) the degree to which component activities are automatic, and (b) the degree to which concurrent behaviors are in mutual support rather than competition. These factors will be considered below. So much for the 'things' that can be done at the same time. What about the innocent, but on closer observation rather tricky, statement of two things being done 'at the same time'?

Dividing attention

An example that seems to hold some powerful attraction because both Hebb (1966) and Ryle (1949) use it in this context is talking and driving a car at the same time. Presumably these two activities are unrelated and both authors make the assumption that one can simultaneously attend to driving and talking. In order to account for the ability to do so, psychologists have invoked the idea of dividing attention, divisibility being considered a property of attention (Kahneman, 1973; Posner, 1973). I must confess that I have great difficulty with the idea of dividing attention, because of the connotations of 'divided'. If a stream is divided, the resulting branches carry the same stuff that is present in the main body, but less of it. The underlying assumption for 'divided' is that the stuff that is in the parts is qualitatively the same stuff that constitutes the undivided whole. Once attention is divided, how are changes in attention managed? Is there still an undivided attention that presides over divided parts (much like a thing splitting itself, but only so far)? Can attention be directed at something and at the same time initiate a switch to another location? Ryle raises the question in the context of introspection: can we attend, at the same time, to the act and the content of introspection (Ryle, 1951, p. 165)? Polanyi (1962) was concerned with the same point: "The conception in question is the focus of attention, in terms of which we attend subsidiarily both to the text and the objects indicated by the text." (p. 92). These questions show that in considering concurrent speaking and skilled manual movement, the concept of divided attention is not likely to be of great use and, in particular, it can give us no help in trying to understand how people can talk and steer the car at the same time.

Switching attention / time sharing

Others (Broadbent & Gregory, 1963; Duncan, 1979) have similar problems with divided attention, for different reasons. There are attractive alternatives to the idea of managing two different streams of movement through division of attention. One of these is simple alternation, expressed quite clearly by Ryle (1951): "... though some people would describe the division of attention as a rapid to-and-fro switch of attention, rather than a synchronous distribution of it." (p. 164). Alternating attention to its varying objects may be a useful strategy in some contexts, but there must be limitations when there is time pressure, because, as Titchener had already described it in 1908, attention needs time to grasp its object and it also needs time to switch its object - in Titchener's (p. 242) terms, 'accommodation' and 'inertia' of attention. The more current term for alternation is 'time-sharing' and there is a conception of time-sharing ability as a particular skill. Ackerman, Schneider, and Wickens (1984), for instance, suggest that time-sharing is a skill that is different from the skills required to perform the component tasks in isolation. Part of this assumption rests on the conviction (Duncan, 1979) that dual tasks involve emergent qualities that are not predictable on the basis of what is known about the demands of the component tasks. Time-sharing is by no means a unitary concept. Damos and Wickens (1980) allow for parallel processing, serial processing and attention switching - all under the general rubric of time-sharing - and Navon and Gopher (1979) amplify this point by stating that it is not possible to identify a particular mode of operation of time-sharing at a given time.

In spite of these difficulties, time-sharing, or switching attention to different objects is of some use in looking at the feat of talking and doing something with the hands at the same time, provided that the two activities do not overlap in time. If they do, this does not exclude time-sharing, but an additional concept needs to be introduced: automaticity.

Automaticity

An implicit idea underlying time-sharing as an explanation of how two things may be done at the same time is that they are not, in fact, done at the same time but in such rapid alternating succession that from a behavioral perspective they appear to be done at the same time. Some behaviors do, however, involve true concurrence of movement, as in the concurrent singing while playing the piano, and any sort of alternation of attention strategy is likely insufficient. How are these behaviors maintained?

The concept of 'automaticity', introduced with the example of concurrent walking and eating, offers one possibility. The idea here is that motor activities range from those that are under constant 'on-line' volitional control to those that take place in a somewhat self-sufficient way. Presumably, it is possible to combine one activity that requires constant volitional monitoring and guidance with an activity that does not have such requirements. As in the case of 'dividing attention' and 'time-sharing' it becomes immediately obvious, that the concept of automaticity is fraught with difficulties as well. There is perhaps no better way of illustrating these difficulties than with reference to a paper that claims to have excluded automaticity as explanation for the rapid and complex concurrent performance of reading a text and writing a different text to dictation at the same time. Hirst, Spelke, Reaves, Caharak, and Neisser (1980) report on the ability of subjects to do this quite well and conclude that their performance excludes automaticity as meaningful explanation of what they do. Somewhat extravagantly, the authors also conclude that subjects are potentially able to devote attention to an unlimited number of different tasks at the same time. The problem is this: in both the case of reading and writing, not all activities are under constant attentional control. For instance, the experienced reader does not have to attend to each and every word and letter while scanning for meaning. Similarly, the experienced writer does not have to attend to each and every letter of each word. In both cases part of the activity is 'on-line' and under attentional control while part of the activity is automatic. For instance, in writing the word 'and' the placing of the first letter relative to the previous word likely involves focused attention while the shaping of the subsequent letters involves various degrees of preprogrammed trajectories.

For this reason, it is impossible for Hirst et al. (1980) to exclude automaticity as a factor in the concurrent performance of reading and writing by their subjects; unless one could catch at a glimpse as to what happens during reading at the very same time as the first letter of a new word is place on the line, one cannot possibly exclude automaticity or, for that matter, rapid time-sharing, as means of maintaining performance.

Kahneman and Treisman (1983) formally acknowledge the problems with the unitary term 'automaticity' by introducing the subcategories of strong, partial and occasional automaticity. The searching questions that Kahneman and Treisman have raised with regard to strong automaticity on the basis of their own work and that of others invite the further question of when strong automaticity can be demonstrated. Because support of the claim for strong automaticity rests on proven insensitivity of performance to attentional processes, generally valid claims will be hard to make. After all, such independence of performance can only be shown with a particular selection of performance criteria and manipulations of attentional processes. Thus, performance may be automatic with reference to a particular measure (e.g. errors) but not to another (e.g., evidence of mutual interaction in time).

What about partial automaticity? Kahneman and Treisman apply the term in cases where performance can be carried out without attention but where allocation of attention can have a beneficial effect on the task. The question of how attention comes to bear on automated performance is controversial. Automatization of actions avoids attentional demands and imparts speed and precision to those processes that have been automated. It is difficult to imagine a situation where the performance of a truly automated response or process is aided by attention. Quite the contrary view has been articulated by Kimble and Perlmuter (1970):

> Assuming that one of the consequences of the process of automatization is the elimination of the attention previously paid to the response, will calling attention to such a bit of behavior interfere with it? (p. 377)

In the minds of researchers in the area, automaticity is by and large always defined with reference to attentional processes, regardless of the fact that their precise relation to each other has not been specified. The matter is complicated by the observation (Shiffrin, Dumais, & Schneider, 1981) that: "All tasks normally encountered are accomplished with a mixture of controlled and automatic processes." (p. 229). In other words, even if one conceives of automatic and controlled processes as categorically distinct, in their normal mode of appearance they are inextricably interwoven.

Combining time-sharing and automaticity as factors in the maintenance of concurrent speaking and manual activity seems a fairly satisfactory solution for the problem of overlapping activities. For instance, in the Hirst et al. (1980) study, it is quite conceivable that in writing to dictation, the subject initiates the first letter of a word and completes the rest in an automatic mode. While producing the first letter, the subject may not, in fact, actively read for meaning, while during the production of the latter part of the word, resources for active reading are freed. In such a manner the subject may skip back and forth between reading and writing, using controlled and automatic modes of action during the process. But there remains a problem, and this is probably the most interesting one raised so far. When the hands and the mouth are concurrently active in an interference paradigm, there is an asymmetry in the magnitude of the interference effect, depending on which hand does what. None of the concepts previously discussed are of any help in accounting for this observation.

The Interference Paradigm

In their discussion of experimental designs that ask subjects to speak and perform manual activities at the same time, Kelso et al. (1983) dispute the usefulness of terms like competition and interference between two systems that in their view must be viewed as a coordinated system. They continue to say that: "... we do want to illustrate that apparent competition and interference between the subsystems for speaking and manual performance may be more correctly viewed as an effect of their mutual collaboration." (p. 149). It is quite true that in most naturally occurring vocal and manual activities, the two systems are either not in conflict (as in walking and talking), or are manifestly integrated. There is a great human tradition of songs that complement a variety of work activities and in these cases the musical rhythm is entirely supportive of the work rhythm. Indeed, some of the anthropological literature goes so far as to suggest that body work rhythms play a significant role in the evolution of musical structure (Bücher, 1902). In this case it is entirely legitimate to emphasize coordination, and the work of Kelso et al. underlines the predisposition of mutual entrainment between the vocal and manual systems. However, it is equally true that under some conditions, one or the other system makes such extreme demands that no resources for the independent operation of the other remain. In this case it is justified to speak of interference or competition. To give a common and accessible example, modern opera singers are expected to accompany their singing with as much supporting gestural and general movement support as possible. They do so successfully, and to great effect. Nevertheless, when particularly difficult passages are to be sung, or in the case of single demanding notes such as the high 'C', practically all body movement ceases. There can be no talk of 'doing two things at the same time' on these occasions and it is of little usefulness to talk of coordination between the vocal and manual or body gestural system if the latter systems are entirely shut down. In intermediate cases, and these are studied extensively in the experimental psychology literature, there are varying degree of controlled interference between vocal and manual activities and their interpretation and significance will be discussed here.

By no means the first interference study, but one that serves as the point of departure for most current investigations, was carried out by Kinsbourne and Cook (1971). They had subjects balance a dowel rod with one hand while speaking at the same time. They found that balancing performance of the right hand significantly declined during speaking but that no such interference effect was seen for the left hand. Not everybody found such an asymmetry (Majeres, 1975), but after a number of years of research with this and similar paradigms, the basic effect can be considered established, both in adults and in children (Kinsbourne & Hiscock, 1983; Kinsbourne & McMurray, 1975; Hiscock, Antoniuk, Prisciak, & von Hessert, 1985; Hiscock, Kinsbourne, Samuels, & Krause, 1985; Thornton & Peters, 1982). Various similar paradigms have been used and Kreuter, Kinsbourne, and Trevarthen (1972) even tested the interference paradigm with a person whose callosum had been split. In this case, too, there was interference between right hand tapping and speaking while the tapping performance of the left hand was unaffected.

Kinsbourne and Hicks (1978) interpreted these effects within the framework of competition in 'cerebral space'. Their influential account was based on the assumption that because both speaking and the control of movements of the right hand were guided by the left hemisphere, the demands for concurrent attention by the two processes in the same hemisphere lead to interference. A corollary of this model is that if two control processes are managed by different hemispheres, less interference would take place. The model is reminiscent of Pavlov's idea of 'irradiation', i.e., that if different stimuli were close to each other in terms of cortical mapping, the conditioned effects of one would more likely be seen in the other than in the case of wide cortical separation.

Kinsbourne and Hicks do not specify at what level competition in cerebral space takes place. If interference between speech and hand movement takes place between the executing levels, one would expect that left-handers, as a group, to show interference effects between speaking and movements of *the right hand*. This is so because left-handers as a group have left hemisphere specialization for speech and it is presumably the left motor cortex that constitutes the final motor outflow for the movements of the right hand. Earlier work failed to show convincing interference effects for left-handers (Hicks, 1975) and thus at least did not contradict the functional cerebral space model (everybody appears satisfied with the explanation that things are odd with left-handers). However, an extensive and careful study of interference effects with a large sample of left-handers by Rey et al. (1988) showed that left-handers experienced an interference effect in the *left* rather than the right hand. If the competition in functional cerebral space is to be salvaged in the face of these data, one has to assume that competition between concurrent speech and finger tapping does not take place at the level where the final motor commands to the spinal motor neurons to the right hand are issued.

Once the idea of competition in functional cerebral space is accepted, it seems only natural to invoke the concept of divided attention in accounting for concurrent performance, with the additional assumption that such a division is harder to maintain when the controlling cortical areas are in close proximity. However, it is not necessary to invoke the idea of divided attention in the context of these interference paradigms. This is so both because of the basic reservations that were previously expressed with regard to the concept, and because alternate explanations are possible. This can be illustrated with reference to a simple set of studies. Peters (1977) examined the interference paradigm with three basic variations. In the first, subjects performed the concurrent speaking and tapping task that is quite common in the literature. In the second, they tapped a rhythm with one hand while tapping as quickly as possible with the other and in the third they were asked to recite a nursery rhyme while at the same time tapping out a simple rhythm with the hand.

The last task demanded of subjects that they did not change the normal pace and rhythm of the nursery rhyme while tapping, and that the tapping rhythm should not be affected by the concurrent speaking performance. Unlike the other interference tasks, where subjects showed a relative loss in performance in one or the other task (acknowledging that assessing the loss of speaking performance is usually more difficult), in the present task, subjects were not able to perform the task as demanded. That is, if the rhyme was recited adequately, the finger tapping rhythm was totally disrupted and vice versa. Importantly, it did not matter which hand did the tapping; performance in the left was just as badly off as performance in the right. This results showed that humans, who can perform the most intricate feats of concurrent performance (as in playing a fugue) fail at such a relatively simple task. In this, and subsequent experiments, timing constraints were held to be absolutely limiting.[3]

Hiscock and Chipuer (1986) used a paradigm in which they manipulated the rhythmic content of the speech that accompanied tapping. In one condition, the sentence spoken had the simple pattern of a iambic pentameter while in the other the rhythm was irregular. Subjects were asked to tap in a simple iambic pattern while reciting either the rhythmic or irregular sentence. When tapping rate was used as performance index, the left hand was quite unaffected by the concurrent speaking tasks, regardless of whether the sentence had a regular rhythm or not, relative to the control single hand performance. In contrast, the right hand showed a severe performance drop in the two speaking conditions relative to the single hand control condition. When the variability of performance was used as

---

3. In 1985, I wrote to Roger Sperry, asking him to try the task with a split-callosum patient. In his reply, he stated that he had tried the task on a casual basis with a patient who was unable to perform the task.

the performance index, both the right and the left hand tapped as regularly while reciting the sentence with the regular rhythm as they did in the single hand control condition, but both showed a clear increase in variability of tapping when asked to tap rhythmically while reciting the sentence that had a rhythm incompatible with the tapping task.

Hiscock and Chipuer felt that they had isolated two different aspects of manual/speaking interference. The first was due to a capacity limitation in the sense of the functional space model proposed by Kinsbourne and Hicks while the second - timing constraints - was of a more general nature that would apply to any concurrent activities. Depending on the nature of the interference task, one could expect at least some interference effect to manifest itself in the performance of either hand if this second factor has general validity. Indeed, Todor and Smiley (1985) point out that this is the case.

The observed asymmetry under certain conditions allows us to return to the question of divided attention. If Hiscock and Chipuer had only measured tapping rate one could have easily concluded that left hand performance was unaffected - leading to the conclusion of quite independent left hand performance and invoking with some justification the concept of divided attention. As it turned out, the variability of performance measure did not discriminate between the two hands. Why was the left hand capable of maintaining a reasonable rate in spite of the increase in variability of tapping? Does this not argue in favor of some division of attention at least in case of speaking and left hand performance?

How the Interference Paradigm for Speaking and Manual Activities Relates to Levels or Varieties of Attention

In order to address this question, it is necessary to examine the mode of manual interactions during concurrent bimanual activities, because when this is done, a new concept has to be introduced in the discussion of how attention comes to bear on action. As Kinsbourne and Hicks (1978) have noted, Welch (1898) had already described that when the two hands are performing concurrently, on a task that promotes independence of hand actions, the interference effects depend on which hand does what. In Welch's task, subjects had to exert a steady tracking force with one hand while exerting pressure rhythmically with the other hand. When the left hand had to change its pressure rhythmically, it interfered more with the ability of the right hand to exert a steady pressure than was the case for the converse arrangement. As Kinsbourne and Hicks note themselves:

> This leads to the paradoxical proposition that the functional distance from the control center of the right hand to the control center of the left hand is greater than that from the

control center of the left hand to the control center of the right hand. (p. 57).

This is clearly an unsatisfactory explanation of the effect. In a subsequent series of experiments, Ibbotson and Morton (1981) and Peters (1981; 1984; 1985a; 1985b; 1987) showed that it does indeed matter what hand does what in bimanual interference tasks and that the interference effects are not equal in each direction. In studies of this kind it is, of course, always possible that the task demands interact with the competences of the right and the left hand to perform a certain task. As an example, if one hand had to write and the other had to track a specific force target, one could a priori predict an asymmetrical interference effect because the left hand of the right-handers is totally ill-adept at writing. To counter this possibility, Peters (1984; 1985; 1987) designed experiments that eliminated task characteristics as possibly confounding variables and manipulated only the direction of attention, i.e., which hand would receive focused attention. These experiments showed that in the right-hander, there is a clear tendency to focus attention to the preferred right hand.

What happens to the left hand under these conditions? A number of researchers and theorists have commented that the hands, in collaboration towards a common goal, show a role differentiation (Bruner, 1968; Guiard 1987; Peters, 1981). The specific assignment of hand roles in such collaborative efforts is as sure an indicator of hand preference as are preferences for unimanual tasks (Peters, 1981). However, the most interesting aspect is the attentional disposition. While it is true that the preferred hand receives focused attention, it cannot be said that the nonpreferred hand does not receive any attention.

And this is where the new (of course, not really new, cf. James, 1893) concept comes in: levels, or varieties of attention. One of the reasons why the concept 'automaticity' was not used by earlier psychologists was their ready acceptance of the notion of different levels of attention. Thus, what puzzled Hebb about the apparent automaticity in changing gears while talking would be dealt with rather simply by Titchener (1908) by means of allocating 'subconscious' attention to the process of changing gears.

When the term 'levels' is used as a metaphor, a number of loosely defined meanings can be attached to that metaphor. Usually, the meanings are implicit but it is of interest to spell out some possible meanings. 'Levels' implies that the constituent parts are part of an interconnected whole. There is also an allusion to hierarchy in the sense that operations at level X may have more importance for operations at level Y than vice versa, and an allusion to interdependence in the sense that operations at one level may not be independent of operations at other levels. In addition, different levels may differ qualitatively; they are similar in the sense that they serve the same common goal but different in the sense that their structural substrate in the brain may differ and that their relation to conscious intent may differ.

Unfortunately, the above account of meanings of 'level' is by no means exhaustive. In Treisman's (1979) critical examination of the implications of the term level in the context of processing, it becomes quite clear that there is an embarrassment of riches of meanings that can be attached to 'levels'. Moreover, it is very hard to decide what is a legitimate meaning and what transcends the normal understanding of the term. For instance, is it reasonable to equate levels with stages and is the concept of nesting a legitimate part of the concept of levels ? In order to avoid the problem of carrying an unwanted burden of meanings that is part of the term 'levels', it may be desirable to look for more appropriate terms.

William James talked about varieties of attention in his *Principles of Psychology* (James, 1893, p. 416) and although his examples overlap and there may be category mistakes in his listing of six varieties of attention, the term has an appealing neutrality. 'Varieties', or 'kinds' will be used here to denote differences in the quality of attention that are defined in terms of differences of function and differences in the degree to which awareness of the content of attention is implicated. The terms do not preclude interdependence, hierarchical structure or even continuity rather than polarity.

In establishing the varieties of attention, James used representation in consciousness as one of the differentiating criteria. Earlier writers were not entirely clear on how the things attended to were experienced. Some saw conscious experience represented in terms of discrete and different levels while others allowed for a gradient that went from clear and focused to diffuse and peripheral (Titchener, 1908, pp. 220-241). James addresses the subject of different levels of attention indirectly in his chapter on the 'Stream of Thought' where he refers to the awareness of elements that receive only marginal attention: "Of most of its relations we are only aware in the penumbral nascent way of a 'fringe' of unarticulated affinities about it." (James, 1893, p. 259).

Wundt (1907) expresses this in a rather similar way: "Dabei sind aber in der Regel die indirekt gesehenen Teile des Objektes die dunkler bewussten." (p. 261). Freely translated, this reads "as a rule, the indirectly perceived aspects of the object come less clearly to the fore of awareness".[4] Wundt uses the term 'dunkler' (darker) with the connotation of less clearly defined, less visible, in the background. The visual metaphor is more clearly expressed in Jung's (1978) searchlight model of selective attention,

---

4. Wundt's language is a wonderful illustration with regard to some of Lakoff's (1978) ideas about the use of metaphor.

where the focus of the beam determines the content of conscious experience. In Jung's model, as in the earlier expositions, there is a fringe of awareness that is outside the focus. Attention and awareness are considered to have a different relationship in this fringe than they do in the focus.

However cumbersome this interpretation, it gives a better and intuitively more appealing account of how the nonpreferred hand stands in relation to the focus of attention than any other current description. The left hand does receive attention but this attention is of a different kind than the attention received by the preferred hand. Thus, during bimanual skilled activities, and particularly those in the very complex actions performed in music (Peters, 1986), the left hand most commonly operates in a quasi-independent mode. The term 'quasi-independent' can be justified by the behavior of the subjects. For instance, in a task where the left hand had to tap slowly and regularly while the right hand tapped out a rhythm (Ibbotson & Morton, 1981), that included two quick 1/8 note taps, the left hand would lengthen the duration of a slow tap just so that the two 1/8 note taps could fit within the boundaries marked by the onset and offset of the slow tap (Peters, 1985a, p. 186). Thus, while in general the slow tapping pace of the left hand was done quite independently, on those occasions where the right hand tapped more quickly, the actions of the left hand where affected in a subtle way.

Interference effects of this kind need not be precise in time in the sense that one discrete event in one hand always has a discrete local effect on the actions of the other. Peters (1985b) asked subjects to smoothly accelerate the tapping pace of one hand while tapping slowly and regularly with the other hand. Subjects did this task better when accelerating with the right hand. As they accelerated, the pace of the left hand slowed down - with no point to point correspondence of the actions of the two hands. Thus, interference effects in this case took place at a level one step removed from the final motor outflow.

Performance in various dual tapping tasks was better when attention was focused on the preferred right hand and under these conditions the performance advantage applied to both hands. For instance, in a task where subjects had to tap twice in one hand against every one tap in the other (where the hand doing double time inevitably receives attention), performance of both the right (2 taps) and left hand (1 tap) was better than the performance of the left (2) and the right (1) tap. Significantly, the right hand (1 tap) performance was worse than the left (1 tap) performance under these conditions (1987).

A manual/speech interaction under these conditions was shown by Peters and Schwartz (1989), who asked subjects to perform a 3:2 polyrhythm, with one hand producing three taps against every two in the other. In accordance with previous work it was found that subjects spontaneously chose the preferred hand for the faster 'three tap' chain. Subjects were then asked to count along with either the faster or the slower chain, while trying to maintain regular tapping performance. Performance was very much worse in terms of regularity of inter-tap intervals when attention (through counting) was directed at the slower chain - a distribution of attention that went against the natural preference of the subjects. In this case, as in the 2:1 task (Peters, 1987), subjects did better in both hands when attention was directed in accordance with the natural preferences.

Kinsbourne and Hicks (1978, p. 353) cite an unpublished study in which the interaction between hand and voice was even more directly addressed. In their study, trained musicians had to play two orthogonal tunes with each hand. When able to do so, they were asked to hum along with either the tune played by the left or that played by the right hand. Accuracy of playing as well as quality of humming were best when the pianists hummed the tune played by the right hand. Most of the errors consisted of an entrainment of the hand that played the tune unaccompanied by humming by the hand that was accompanied. Again, Kinsbourne and Hicks interpreted this along the lines of functional cerebral space; presumably the humming was managed by the same hemisphere which guided the playing by the right hand.

This particular effect can be more thoroughly examined in a beautiful study by Guiard (1989), who used a related paradigm. Guiard used trained pianists as subjects. They had to play the first four bars of the Second Prelude of J. S. Bach's *Well-tempered Klavier*. These bars are characterized by the fact that the notes played by the two hands show complete synchronicity in rhythm; each hand plays a note exactly when the other plays it - but the notes are different. The pianists were asked to sing the names of the notes (in the appropriate pitch) along with the notes as they are played. They were asked to either sing along with the notes played by the left hand or with the notes played by the right hand. Guiard found a clear-cut asymmetry in that the pianists were quite good at singing the notes played by the right hand, but they had a very hard time singing the notes played by the left hand. Thus, Guiard, with a somewhat different arrangement, showed the same basic asymmetry cited in the Kinsbourne and Hicks review. Moreover, Guiard found that long-term practice did not markedly improve the situation, suggesting a deeper source for these asymmetries.

Errors were mostly found to be in the vocal rather than the manual response. Guiard interprets this as indicating that priority was assigned to the manual response. Alternatively, it could be suggested that the pianists found the manual part of the tasks relatively easier and were able to maintain it while struggling with the vocal demands. The nature of the errors was very interesting, in that the *name* of the note was usually given correctly but the pitch was incorrect - most often the pitch corresponded not to the note played by the left hand, but to the note played by the right hand. Another form of error consisted in the appropriate name being given to the note, but by speaking it rather than, as required singing it. It appears that the demand of singing introduced one more level of complexity to the process, and that subjects were able to maintain performance by reducing complexity. It is not clear how the Kinsbourne and Hicks model of functional cerebral space could account for this finding, particularly in view of the fact that there is at least some suggestion of singing and humming involving right hemisphere function as well.

In attentional terms, the experiment by Guiard makes it quite clear that the concepts of divided attention and time sharing do not suffice to explain what happens here. The additional factor of how the various effector channels are related to each other, and which uses which as reference (Guiard, 1987) need to be brought into any explanatory attempt. Guiard (1988) uses the metaphor of a serial assembly of two motors, where the second uses the first as reference, in order to explain the relationship of interdependence between the hands or between hands and the vocal apparatus. Guiard (1989) observes:

> Whereas it is quite easy to improvise rhythms vocally (using constant utterance and a constant pitch) while tapping the beat with the hand (either the left hand or the right hand, or both), it is virtually impossible, without some practice, to improvise rhythms with the hand (either the left hand or the right hand, or both) while marking the beat vocally, a phenomenon displayed both by nonmusicians and musicians. (p. 307).

The system of precedence is such that when the left hand and the right hand are active together in this context, the right hand will be the improvising hand. This is something that is quite well known particularly to Jazz musicians (Sudnow, 1981), and emerges clearly in the bare bones paradigms of Peters (1985a). In a pairing between voice and the right hand the right hand marks the beat while the voice improvises. Guiard interprets this in terms of a fairly stable linkage with specified directions of priority between hands and between hands and vocal organ. However, the fact that practice does have an impact suggests that one deals with attentional biases rather than firmly entrenched structural relations. Whichever way one looks at this problem, one does not really get around the concept of a central unitary scheduler, the unitary acting self, that assigns priorities and determines which of two concurrent activities is in the foreground of attention. What language one uses in describing this is relatively unimportant, the fact is that somehow priorities are assigned that may be described either in terms of focal and subsidiary (for lack of a better term) attention or the serial ordering of motors in a kinematic chain. The nature of the tasks determines the assignment of priorities and because there is a natural distribution of attention to the two hands in normally occurring bimanual activities (Peters, 1981), some inherent biases make some priority assignments more likely than others. To the extent that such a unitary scheduler must also give movement initiation to the effectors, the timing and assignment of such initiations if virtually synonymous with the assignment of priorities. It will be recalled that at the level of the initiation of timing of two concurrent activities, the unitary scheduler reveals itself to be just that - when the timing demands of two separate activities cannot be brought into a harmonic structure, they cannot be satisfied at the same time (Peters, 1977, Experiment 3).

Kornhuber's (1984) description of the supplementary motor area as the region that determines the right moment for starting movement with respect to internal and external cues, and Kornhuber and Deecke's (1985) emphasis on the fact that the readiness potential in the supplementary motor cortex precedes activity in the primary motor cortex especially when the coordination of the two hands is essential, sound suspiciously like the identification of just such a central scheduler. As in all of these cases, it is not likely that in the end one single circumscribed anatomic locus turns out to be the home of a psychological construct, and it is more reasonable to assume that the functions attributed to the supplementary motor cortex are distributed in nature. Nevertheless, there is no reason to doubt that the SMA does represent a focal point for the initiation and coordination of volitional activities in the hands and the voice, and it is through this area that the will to act seeks its channels of expressions.

Finally, a higher order feature that is common to hand movement and speech control has to be pointed out. In the collaboration of the two hands in skilled activities, such as using a tool, the component activities of the two hands complement each other and have full meaning only with reference to each other. To the extent that the different hands may use different aspects of the physical environment into account in order to compute their individual movement trajectories, there is some reason to believe that the two hemispheres each provide different sorts of information to the two hands (cf., Carson, 1989). Although it is conceivable that each hand control system has its own complete representation of the goal of the collaborative movement it is more reasonable to assume that the full representation of the goal that is used to coordinate the activities of the two hands does not reside in the control systems of the hands but is most likely a unitary process, that is not bilaterally localized.

A similar situation holds with regard to language as expressed through speech. Here, too, there is a collaborative effort which relies on information from both hemispheres in order to generate the final outflow. For instance, there is reason to believe that some aspects of linguistic processing (broader context, metaphorical expression) are contributed from the right hemisphere (Gardner, Ling, Flamm, & Silverman, 1976). Just as it is possible to do things with the preferred right hand alone, it is possible to do linguistic things with the left hemisphere alone, but in each case there is a loss in quality of outcome and, if one looks hard enough, one will find things that cannot be done at all. The delicate business of feeding complementary information into a dominant process in order to make it complete is common to both speech and skilled hand movement. Little information is available about how this is accomplished and through what avenues. However, it is clear that at least for the hands the interhemispheric exchange will not likely take place between the primary sensory-motor that maps the hand because of the paucity of transcallosal connections between these areas, indicating that higher order motor control regions must be involved.

Summary

In humans, thoughts are so far emancipated from the specific motor pathways through which we make thought known that there is no fixed linkage between higher cognitive processes and particular effectors. Thus, in a paraplegic person the full complexity of thought may be coded through changes in respiration that trigger a computer input element, or even only through opening and closing ('on', 'off' code) of the eyelids. That having been said, the evolution of complex communication systems and the ways in which we can impose our will on the external world rest heavily on the motor effectors of the vocal apparatus and the hands. Similarities and differences in the way in which voice and hands are controlled were pointed out. To the extent that the realization of our will involves the composition of entirely new combinations of pre- existing basic motor commands, both systems are suited to (a) show maximal flexibility in the acquisition of new combinations and to (b) learn these new combinations in such a way that new combinations themselves can eventually be automated. Such automatization implies that entire chains of responses can be run off without 'on-line' volitional control, making life miserable for those who are looking for point-to-point mutual interference in competition paradigms.

Simple experimental competition paradigms show that when 'on-line' control is required, as in the case when independent timing chains are to be issued for both mouth and hands at the same time, clear evidence for a unitary scheduler emerges: in the motor system, under these circumstances, two things *cannot* be done at the same time, and this limitation is absolute. Recent work shows that when there are partially conflicting demands, asymmetries can be observed in the way in which voice and hands collaborate. Such asymmetries are a function of handedness and relate to the way in which the preferred and nonpreferred hands are able to operate with or without the benefit of focussed attention.

Acknowledgement

The author gratefully acknowledges support by the National Sciences and Engineering Research Council of Canada (Grant No. A 7054).

References

Ackerman, P., Schneider, W., & Wickens, C.D. (1984). Deciding the existence of a time-sharing ability: a combined methodological and theoretical approach. *Human Factors,* **26**, 71-82.

Annett. M. (1985). *Left, right, hand and brain: The right shift theory.* London: Lawrence Erlbaum Associates.

Arbib, M.A., Iberall, T., & Lyons, D. (1985). Coordinated control programs for movements of the hand. In A.W. Goodwin & I. Darian-Smith (Eds.), *Hand function and the neocortex* (pp. 110-129). Berlin: Springer-Verlag.

Asanuma, H. (1973). Cerebral cortical control of movement. *Physiologist,* **16**, 143-166.

Bogen, J.E., & Gordon, H.W. (1971). Musical tests for functional lateralization with intracarotid sodium amytal. *Nature,* **230**, 524-525.

Brinkmann, C. (1984). Supplementary motor area of the monkey's cerebral cortex: short- and long-term deficits after unilateral ablation and the effects of subsequent callosal section. *Journal of Neuroscience,* **4**, 918-929.

Broadbent, D.E., & Gregory, M. (1963). Division of attention and the decision theory of signal detection. *Proceedings of the Royal Society London,* **B158**, 222-231.

Bruner, J.S. (1968). Processes of cognitive growth: infancy. Worcester, MA: Clark University Press.

Bryden, M.P. (1982). *Laterality.* New York: Academic Press.

Bücher, K. (1902). *Arbeit und Rhythmus.* Leipzig: B. G. Teubner.

Carlisle, J.A. (1985). *Tangled tongue.* Toronto: University of Toronto Press.

Carson, R.G. (1989). Manual asymmetries: feedback processing, output variability and spatial complexity - resolving some inconsistencies. *Journal of Motor Behavior,* **21**, 38-47.

Cernacek, J. (1961). Contralateral motor irradiation-cerebral dominance: its changes in hemiparesis. *Archives of Neurology*, **4**, 165-172.

Cowan, N., Leavitt, L.A., Massaro, D.W., & Kent, R.D. (1982). A fluent backward talker. *Journal of Speech and Hearing Research*, **25**, 48-53.

Damos, D.L., & Wickens, C. (1980). The identification and transfer of time sharing skills. *Acta Psychologica*, **46**, 15-39.

Deecke, L., Engel, M., Lang, W., & Kornhuber, H.H. (1986). Bereitschaftspotential preceding speech after holding breath. *Experimental Brain Research*, **65**, 219-223.

Deecke, L., Kornhuber, H.H., Lang, W., Lang, M., & Schreiber H. (1985). Timing function of the frontal cortex in sequential motor and learning tasks. *Human Biology*, **4**, 143-154.

De Renzi, E. (1984). Methods of limb apraxia examination and their bearing on the interpretation of the disorder. In E.A. Roy (Ed.), *Neuropsychological studies of apraxia and related disorders* (pp. 45-64). Amsterdam: North-Holland.

Duncan, J. (1979). Divided attention: the whole is more than the sum of its parts. *Journal of Experimental Psychology: Human Perception and Performance*, **5**, 216-228.

Eccles, J.C. (1982). The initiation of voluntary movements by the supplementary motor area. *Archiv für Psychiatrie und Nervenkrankheiten*, **231**, 423-441.

Faglioni, P., & Basso, A. (1984). Historical perspectives on neuroanatomical correlates. In E.A. Roy (Ed.), *Neuropsychological studies of apraxia and related disorders* (pp. 3-44). Amsterdam: North-Holland.

Formby, C., Thomas, R.G., & Halsey, J.H. (1989). Regional cerebral blood flow for singers and nonsingers while speaking, singing and humming a rote passage. *Brain and Language*, **36**, 690-698.

Gardner, H., Ling, P.K., Flamm, L., & Silverman, J. (1976). Comprehension and appreciation of humorous material following brain damage. *Brain*, **98**, 399-412.

Goldberg, G. (1985). Supplementary motor area structure and function: review and hypotheses. *Behavioral and Brain Sciences*, **8**, 567-616.

Gracco, V.L., & Abbs, J.H. (1986). Variant and invariant characteristics of speech movement. *Experimental Brain Research*, **65**, 156-166.

Greiner, J.R., Fitzgerald, H.E., & Cooke, P.A. (1986). Bimanual writing in right-handed and left-handed stutterers. *Neuropsychologia*, **24**, 441-447.

Grözinger, B., Kornhuber, H.H., & Kriebel, J. (1979). Participation of mesial cortex in speech: evidence from cerebral potential preceding speech production in man. In O. Creutzfeldt, H. Schleich, & C. Schreiner (Eds.), *Hearing mechanisms and speech* (pp. 189-192). Berlin: Springer-Verlag.

Guiard, Y. (1989). Failure to sing the left-hand part of the score during piano performance: loss of the pitch and stroop vocalizations. *Music Perception*, **6**, 299-314.

Guiard, Y. (1988). The kinematic chain as a model for human asymmetrical bimanual cooperation. In A. Colley & J. Beech (Eds.), *Cognition and action in skilled behavior* (pp. 205-228). Amsterdam: North-Holland.

Guiard, Y. (1987). Asymmetric division of labor in human skilled bimanual action: the kinematic chain as a model. *Journal of Motor Behavior*, **19**, 486-517.

Gur, R.C., & Reivich, M. (1980). Cognitive task effects on hemispheric blood flow in humans: evidence for individual differences in hemispheric activation. *Brain and Language*, **9**, 78-92.

Hadar, U., Steiner, T.J., & Rose, F.C. (1984). Involvement of head movement in speech production and its implications for language pathology. In F.C. Rose (Ed.), *Advances in Neurology, Vol. 42, Progress in aphasiology* (pp. 247-261). New York: Raven Press.

Harris, L.J. (in press). Cerebral control for speech in right-handers and left-handers: an analysis of the views of Paul Broca, his contemporaries, and his successors. *Brain and Language*.

Harvey, N. (1985). Vocal control and singing: a cognitive approach. In P. Howell, I. Cross, & R. West (Eds.), *Musical Structure and Cognition* (pp. 287-332). Orlando, FL: Academic Press.

Hebb, D.O. (1966). *The organization of behavior*. New York: Wiley.

Henderson, V.W. (1983). Speech fluency in crossed aphasia. *Brain*, **106**, 837-858.

Hewes, G.W. (1973). Primate communication and the gestural origin of language. *Current Anthropology*, **14**, 5-24.

Hirst, W. Spelke, E.S., Reaves, C.C., Caharak, G., & Neisser, U. (1980). Dividing attention without alternation or automaticity. *Journal of Experimental Psychology: General*, **109**, 98-117.

Hiscock, M., & Chipuer, H. (1986). Concurrent performance of rhythmically compatible or incompatible vocal and manual tasks: evidence for two sources of interference in verbal-manual timesharing. *Neuropsychologia*, **24**, 691-698.

Hiscock, M., Antoniuk, D., Prisciak, K., & von Hessert, D. (1985). Generalized and lateralized interference between concurrent tasks performed by children: effects of age, sex and skill. *Developmental Neuropsychology*, **1**, 29-48.

Hiscock, M., Kinsbourne, M., Samuels, M., & Krause, A.E. (1985). Effects of speaking upon the rate and variability of concurrent finger tapping in children. *Journal of Experimental Child Psychology*, **40**, 486-500.

Ibbotson, N.R., & Morton, J. (1981). Rhythm and dominance. *Cognition*, **9**, 125-138.

Ivry, R.B., & Keele, S.W. (1989). Timing functions of the cerebellum. *Journal of Cognitive Neuroscience*, **1**, 136-152.

James, W. (1893). *The principles of psychology, Vol 1.* New York: Henry Holt.

Jung, R. (1984). Electrophysiological clues of the language-dominant hemisphere in man: slow brain potentials during language processing and writing. In O. Creutzfeldt, R.F. Schmidt, & W.D. Willis (Eds.), *Sensory-motor integration in the nervous system* (pp. 430-450). Berlin: Springer-Verlag.

Jung, R. (1978). Perception, consciousness and attention. In P.A. Buser & A. Rogeul-Buser (Eds.), *Cerebral correlates of conscious experience* (pp. 15-36). Amsterdam: North-Holland.

Jürgens, U. (1979). Neural control of vocalization in nonhuman primates. In H.D. Steklis & M.J. Raleigh (Eds.), *Neurobiology of social communication in primates* (pp. 11-44). New York: Academic Press.

Kahneman, D. (1973). *Attention and effort.* Englewood Cliffs, N.J.: Prentice-Hall.

Kahneman, D., & Treisman, A. (1983). Changing views of attention and automaticity. In R. Parasurman, R. Davies, & J. Beatty (Eds.), *Varieties of attention* (pp. 29-61). New York: Academic Press.

Kelso, J.A.S., Tuller, B., & Harris, K.S. (1983). A 'dynamic pattern' perspective on the control and coordination of movement. In P.F. MacNeilage (Ed.), *The production of speech* (pp. 137-173). New York: Springer-Verlag.

Kertesz, A. (1984). Apraxia and aphasia. Anatomical and clinical relationship. In E.A. Roy (Ed.), *Neuropsychological studies of apraxia and related disorders* (pp. 163-178). Amsterdam: North-Holland.

Kimble, G.A., & Perlmuter, L.C. (1970). The problem of volition. *Psychological Review*, **77**, 361-405.

Kimura, D. (1982). Left hemisphere control of oral and brachial movements and their relation to communication. *Philosophical Transactions of the Royal Society of London*, **B298**, 135-149.

Kimura, D. (1979) Neuromotor mechanisms in the evolution of human communication. In H.D. Steklis & M.J. Raleigh (Eds.), *Neurobiology of social communication in primates* (pp. 197-219). New York: Academic Press.

Kimura, D. (1973a). Manual activity during speaking - right-handers. *Neuropsychologia*, **11**, 45-50.

Kinsbourne, M., & Cook, J. (1971). Generalized and lateralized effects of concurrent verbalization on a unimanual skill. *Quarterly Journal of Experimental Psychology*, **23**, 341-345.

Kinsbourne, M., & Hicks, R.E. (1978). Functional cerebral space: a model for overflow, transfer and interference effects in human performance. In J. Requin (Ed.), *Attention and performance VII* (pp. 345-362). Hillsdale, NJ: Lawrence Erlbaum Associates.

Kinsbourne, M., & Hiscock, M. (1983). Asymmetries of dual-task performance. In J. B. Hellige (Ed.), *Cerebral hemisphere asymmetry* (pp. 255-334). New York: Praeger.

Kinsbourne, M., & McMurray, J. (1975). The effect of cerebral dominance on time sharing between speaking and tapping by preschool children. *Child Development*, **46**, 240-242.

Kleist, K. (1934). *Gehirnpathologie vornehmlich auf Grund der Kriegserfahrungen*. Leipzig: Barth.

Kornhuber, H.H. (1984). Attention, readiness for action and the stages of voluntary decision - some electrophysiological correlates in man. In O. Creutzfeldt, R.F. Schmidt, & W.D. Willis (Eds.), *Sensory-motor integration in the nervous system* (pp. 420-429). Berlin: Springer-Verlag.

Kornhuber, H.H., & Deecke, L. (1985). The starting function of the SMA. *Behavioral and Brain Sciences*, **8**, 591-592.

Kreuter, C., Kinsbourne, M., & Trevarthen, C. (1972). Are deconnected hemispheres disconnected channels? A preliminary study of the effect of unilateral loading on bilateral finger tapping. *Neuropsychologia*, **10**, 453- 461.

Lakoff, G. (1978). *Women, fire and dangerous things*. Chicago: The University of Chicago Press.

Larsen, B., Skinhøj, E., Lassen, N.A. (1978). Cortical activity of left and right hemispheres during automatic speech. *Brain*, **101**, 193-209.

Lieberman, P. (1972). *The speech of primates*. The Hague: Mouton.

Liepmann, H. (1908). *Drei Aufsätze aus dem Apraxiegebiet*. Berlin: Karger.

Majeres, R.L. (1975). The effect of unimanual performance on speed of verbalization. *Journal of Motor Behavior*, **7**, 57-58.

McManus, I.C. (1984). Genetic of handedness in relation to language disorder. In F.C. Rose (Ed.), *Advances in neurology, Vol. 42: Progress in aphasiology* (pp. 125- 138). New York: Raven Press.

Muir, R.B. (1985). Small hand muscles in precision grip: a corticospinal prerogative? In A.W. Goodwin & I. Darian-Smith (Eds.), *Hand function and the neocortex* (pp. 155-174). Berlin: Springer-Verlag.

Muir, R.B., & Lemon, R.N. (1983). Corticospinal neurons with a special role in precision grip. *Brain Research*, **261**, 312-316.

Navon, D., & Gopher, D. (1979). The economy of the human-processing system. *Psychological Review*, **86**, 214-255.

Ojemann, G. A. (1983). The intrahemispheric organization of human language, derived with electrical stimulation technique. *Trends in Neurosciences*, **6**, 184-189.

Orgonozo, J.M., & Larson, B. (1979). Activation of the supplementary motor area during voluntary movement suggests it works as a supramotor area. *Science*, **206**, 847-850.

Peters, M. (in preparation). Two subgroups of nonpathological left-handers pose problems for theories of handedness.

Peters, M. (1988). The primate mouth as agent of manipulation and its relation to human handedness. *Behavioral and Brain Sciences*, **11**, 729.

Peters, M. (1987). A nontrivial motor performance difference between right-handers and left-handers: attention as intervening variable in the expression of handedness. *Canadian Journal of Psychology*, **41**, 91-99.

Peters, M. (1986). Hand roles and handedness in music: comments on Sidnell. *Psychomusicology*, **6**, 29-33.

Peters, M. (1985a). Constraints in the coordination of bimanual movements and their expression in skilled and unskilled subjects. *Quarterly Journal of Experimental Psychology*, **37A**, 171-196.

Peters, M. (1985b). Performance of a rubato-like task - when two things cannot be done at the same time. *Music Perception*, **2**, 471-482.

Peters, M. (1984). Initiation and termination of movement in dual tasks. *Annals of the New York Academy of Sciences*, **423**, 628-629.

Peters, M. (1983). Differentiation and lateral specialization in motor development. In G. Young, C. Corter, S.J. Segalowitz, & S. Trehub (Eds.), *Manual specialization and the developing brain: Longitudinal studies* (pp. 141-159). New York: Academic Press.

Peters, M. (1981). Attentional asymmetries during concurrent bimanual performance. *Quarterly Journal of Experimental Psychology*, **33**, 95-103.

Peters, M. (1977). Simultaneous performance of two motor activities: the factor of timing. *Neuropsychologia*, **15**, 461-465.

Peters, M., & Ploog, D. (1973). Primate communication. *Annual Review of Physiology*, **35**, 221-242.

Peters, M., & Schwartz, S. (1989). Coordination of the two hands and effects of attentional manipulation in the production of a bimanual 2:3 polyrhythm. *Australian Journal of Psychology*, **41**, 215-224.

Phillips, C.G. (1986). *Movements of the hand.* Liverpool: Liverpool University Press.

Poeck, K., & Kerschensteiner, M. (1975). Analysis of sequential motor events in oral apraxia. In K.J. Zulch, O. Creutzfeldt, & B.C. Galbraith (Eds.) *Cerebral localization* (pp. 98-111). Berlin: Springer-Verlag.

Polanyi, M. (1962). *Personal knowledge.* London: Routledge & Kegan Paul.

Posner, M.I. (1973). *Introduction to cognition.* Glenview, IL: Scott, Foresman.

Rasmussen, T., & Milner, B. (1977). The role of left-brain injury in determining lateralization of cerebral speech function. *Annals of the New York Academy of Sciences*, **299**, 355-369.

Rey, M., Dellatolas, G., Baucaud, J., & Talairach, J. (1988). Hemispheric lateralization of motor and speech functions after early brain lesion: a study of 73 epileptic patients with intracarotid amytal test. *Neuropsychologia*, **26**, 167-172.

Roland, P.E. (1985). Cortical organization of voluntary behavior in man. *Human Neurobiology*, **4**, 155-167.

Roy, E.A., & Square, P.A. (1985). Common considerations in the study of limb, verbal and oral apraxia. In E.A. Roy (Ed.), *Neuropsychological studies of apraxia and related disorders* (pp. 111-162). Amsterdam: North-Holland.

Ryle, G. (1949). *The concept of mind*. London: Hutchinson.

Sawashima, M., & Hirose, H. (1983). Laryngeal gestures in speech production. In P.F. MacNeilage (Ed.), *The production of speech* (pp. 11-36). New York: Springer-Verlag.

Scheibel, A.B. (1984). A dendritic correlate of human speech. In N. Geschwind & A.M. Galaburda (1984). *Cerebral dominance* (pp. 43-52). Cambridge, MA.: Harvard University Press.

Schott, G.D. (1980). Mirror movements of the left arm following peripheral damage to the preferred right arm. *Journal of Neurology, Neurosurgery, and Psychiatry*, **43**, 768-773.

Sears, T.S. (1977). Some neural and mechanical aspects of singing. In M. Chritchley & R.A. Henson (Eds.), *Music and the brain* (pp. 78-94). London: William Heinneman.

Segalowitz, S.J., & Bryden, M.P. (1983). Individual differences in hemispheric representation of language. In S.J. Segalowitz (Ed.), *Language functions and brain organization* (pp. 341-372). New York: Academic Press.

Shiffrin, R.M., Dumais, S.T., & Schneider, W. (1981). Characteristics of automatism. In J. Long & A. Baddeley (Eds.), *Attention and performance IX* (pp. 223-238). Hillsdale, NJ: Lawrence Erlbaum Associates.

Simon, T.J., & Sussman, H.M. (1987). The dual task paradigm: speech dominance or manual dominance? *Neurospychologia*, **25**, 559-569.

Smith, A., & Burkland, C.W.B. (1966). Dominant hemispherectomy. *Science*, **153**, 1280-1282.

Steklis, H.D., & Raleigh, M.J. (1979). Requisites for language: interspecific and evolutionary aspects. In H.D. Steklis & M.J. Raleigh (Eds.), *Neurobiology of social communication in primates* (pp. 283-314). New York: Academic Press.

Sudnow, D. (1981). *Ways of the hand*. New York: Harper.

Titchener, E. B. (1908). *Lectures on the elementary psychology of feeling and attention*. New York: MacMillan Co.

Thornton, C., & Peters, M. (1982). Interference between concurrent speaking and sequential finger tapping: both hands show a performance decrement under both visual and non-visual guidance. *Neuropsychologia*, **20**, 163-169.

Todor, J.I., & Smiley, A.L. (1985). Performance differences between the hands: implications for studying disruption to limb praxis. In E.A. Roy (Ed.), *Neuropsychological studies of apraxia and related disorders* (pp. 309-344). Amsterdam: North-Holland.

Treisman, A. (1979). The psychological reality of levels of processing. In L.S. Cermak & F.I.M. Craik (Eds.), *Levels of processing and human memory* (pp. 301-330). Hillsdale, NJ: Lawrence Erlbaum Associates.

Vaughn, C.L.D., & Webster, W.G. (1989). Bimanual handedness in adults who stutter. *Perceptual and Motor Skills*, **68**, 378-382.

Webster, W.G. (1989). Sequence initiation performance by stutterers under conditions of response competition. *Brain and Language*, **36**, 286-300.

Webster, W.G. (1988). Neural mechanisms underlying stuttering: evidence from bimanual handwriting. *Brain and Language*, **33**, 226-244.

Welch, J.C. (1898). On the measurement of mental activity through muscular activity and the determination of a constant of attention. *American Journal of Physiology*, **1**, 283-306.

Wiesendanger, M., & Wiesendanger, R. (1984). The supplementary motor area in the light of recent investigations. In O. Creutzfeldt, R.F. Schmidt, & W.D. Willis (Eds.), *Sensory-motor integration in the nervous system* (pp. 382-392). Berlin: Springer-Verlag.

Wolf, M.E., & Goodale, M.A. (1987). Oral asymmetry during verbal and non-verbal movements of the mouth. *Neuropsychologia*, **25**, 375-396.

Wundt, W. (1907). *Grundriss der Psychologie*. Leipzig: Verlag von Wilhelm Engelmann.

Cerebral Control of Speech and Limb Movements
G.E. Hammond (editor)

Chapter 19

COMPARATIVE INVESTIGATIONS OF SPEECH AND OTHER NEUROMOTOR SYSTEMS

Anne Smith and Howard Zelaznik
Purdue University

Investigators searching for principles underlying the control and coordination of complex movement sequences recently have explored a variety of experimental paradigms in which measures from performance of different effector systems are compared. These comparative methodologies have yielded data relevant to a number of significant theoretical issues in motor control, for example, the question of shared features of temporal and spatial organization in speech and limb movements. In this chapter, we review studies that have implemented analyses of a broad range of motor behaviors: finger tapping, speech, bimanual coordination in the production of American Sign Language, repetitive 'voluntarily-controlled' movements of finger, forearm, and jaw, and finally, relatively 'automatic' repetitive behaviors, respiration and mastication. Evidence from these studies converges to suggest that the central nervous system employs common strategies to generate the movement sequences that give rise to speech sounds and those that accomplish a variety of other goals.

Results of investigations in which characteristics of the coordination of two or more effectors are compared have significant implications for a number of different theoretical perspectives. From a general motor control perspective, identifying features of motor performance that are shared across different output systems provides clues concerning general principles that underlie the control and coordination of movement. In addition, such investigations may reveal classes of movements that share features not found in other types of movements.

From another perspective, that of the scientist particularly interested in the production of speech, results of comparative investigations of speech and other motor output systems bring important insights on this question: Is the production of speech special? The idea that speech production, because of its linguistic component, is a special behavior employing neural mechanisms that are distinct from those underlying the performance of other motor tasks has been articulated and debated repeatedly (e.g., Liberman, Cooper, Shankweiler, & Studdert-Kennedy, 1967; Abbs, 1986). The 'speech is special' argument has had a strong impact on investigations of speech motor organization. Until the 1970s, electromyographic and kinematic studies of speech production took place largely in isolation from the general motor control literature, and the explicit goals of many studies were to identify the invariant physiological correlates of linguistic units, such as phonemes (individual speech sounds) and syllables. MacNeilage (1970) reviewed this work, which, rather than revealing invariant physiological correlates of speech sounds, indicated that variability in motor output was ubiquitous. This conclusion led MacNeilage to propose a target-based model of speech production that was developed within the context of general motor control models of the time. The trend for investigators of speech motor organization to build working hypotheses within the general motor control framework has continued, and a number of investigators have embraced the point of view that speech production shares principles of organization with other motor behaviors (e.g., Abbs, 1986; Moll, Zimmermann, & Smith, 1977). Within this theoretical framework, a major challenge is to determine what features of motor organization speech shares with other motor behaviors.

These theoretical underpinnings have motivated a number of experiments undertaken in the motor control and speech laboratories at Purdue. In this chapter, we will describe some of our investigations comparing motor control characteristics of different effector systems. These investigations are related to a number of general issues, including temporal and spatial constraints on movements occurring in dual-task paradigms, the question of whether different motor tasks share common timing mechanisms, and the question of whether common neural sources drive muscles in speech and in 'automatic' behaviors such as metabolic breathing and mastication.

Simultaneous Performance of Speech and Finger Movements

In Smith, McFarland, and Weber (1986), we explored interactions in the frequency and amplitude domain of simultaneously performed tasks, speaking and finger tapping. The direct motivation for this experiment came from work by Kelso, Tuller, and Harris (1981). They challenged traditional motor control theories, which are based on computer and control system metaphors, and argued that traditional theories should be replaced by a 'dynamic pattern' perspective. Under this view, ;muscles are organized into functional synergies called coordinative ;structures that are constrained to act as a unit. Coordinative structures are proposed to behave as limit-cycle oscillators, that is, they have a preferred frequency and amplitude of oscillation. Coordinated motor behaviors arise from the coupling or cooperation of limit-cycle oscillators, and evidence of cooperation can be obtained by examining the frequency and amplitude of oscillations. Kelso et al. cited results of studies of locomotion and two-handed movements in human subjects as evidence for their point of view.

An additional claim made by Kelso et al. was that even apparently independent motor-control processes, such as speaking and moving a finger, will be produced by coupling the underlying oscillatory processes for each behavior. They provided examples in which changes in the rate and amplitude of finger movements were coupled with changes in simultaneously produced speech. Likewise, changes in speech produced predictable changes in finger movements. Indeed, the two behaviors were found always to be entrained, so that they occurred at the same frequency, or at two frequencies that were harmonically related. This was evidence, in Von Holst's (1973) terminology, of *absolute* coordination of the speech and finger movement systems. Kelso et al. did not report any quantitative analysis of these data and implied that absolute coordination was obvious and always present.

The major thrust of our investigation (Smith et al., 1986) was to attempt to quantify the degree of coupling between speech and finger movements. Therefore we used the same tasks as Kelso et al., vertical finger tapping and repeating the word 'stock', and recorded finger displacement and the amplitude envelope of the speech acoustic signal. The degree of coupling between the two behaviors was assessed in the frequency domain by computing the spectrum to obtain the ;repetition rate of each behavior. An index of the relative phase of the two behaviors was computed after a method described by Von Holst (1973). For analysis of the covariance of the amplitude of the behaviors, correlations were used.

In the frequency domain, the results revealed strong evidence of absolute coordination (1/1 rate ratios and strong phase locking) when the two tasks were performed together without any perturbation away from the preferred rate. However, instructions to change the rate of one of the behaviors produced frequency ratios that were not obviously harmonically related (e.g., 3.8/1.0, 4.5/1.2) and consistently reduced the phase locking between the two behaviors. Correlations computed between the amplitude of temporally adjacent cycles indicated that varying the amplitude of finger movement did not have predictable effects on speech amplitude. In contrast, varying the speech amplitude produced consistent modulation of the amplitude of finger movements. Results for one subject are illustrated in Figure 1.

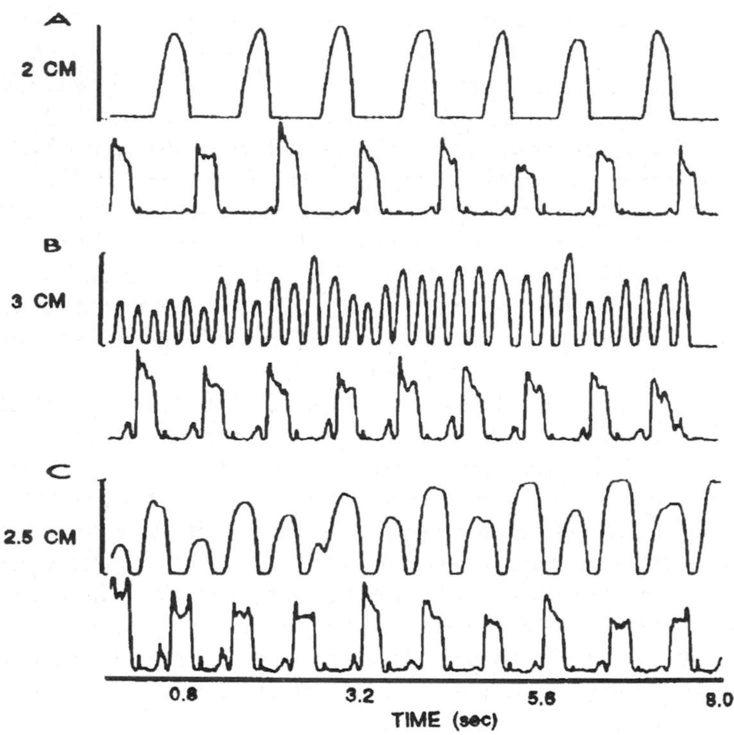

Figure 1. Data from one subject performing three experimental conditions. In all panels the upper trace is the vertical displacement of the finger, and the lower trace is the rectified and smoothed speech acoustic waveform. Panel A shows performance of the control condition (behaviors performed together at subject's preferred rate); B, the condition in which the instruction was to change the rate of finger tapping from its preferred rate; C, the condition in which the instruction was to produce alternating large and small finger movements.

The data in panel A are from the condition in which the two behaviors were performed together at the subject's preferred rate. The tasks are performed at the same frequency (finger, 1.0 Hz and speech, 1.0 Hz), and the index of phase coupling is very high (100%). Instructions to vary the rate of the finger movement away from the preferred rate produced the records in panel B. In this case, the ratio of the repetition rates of the two tasks was 3.75 (4.5 Hz for the finger, 1.2 Hz for speech), and the index of phase coupling dropped to 60%. Panel C shows the effect of instructions to produce alternating large and small finger movements. The subject does produce the required amplitude pattern in the finger displacement, but there is no clear effect on the speech amplitude. The correlation between amplitudes of temporally adjacent speech and finger cycles was -.39.

The results of Smith et al. (1986) were, in a general sense, compatible with the dynamic pattern hypothesis, that when an organism performs two tasks at once, they are not organized independently. However, the claims of Kelso et al. for pervasive, *absolute* coordination in the face of rate and amplitude modulation were not supported. When one behavior was shifted away from the preferred frequency or amplitude, the shift had *quantitative* effects on the other behavior and indicated what Von Holst called *relative* coordination. On the basis of Von Holst's experiments and writings, this result was not unexpected. Absolute coordination is rare, and Von Holst developed a number of creative methods for assessing the quantitative influences of one rhythm on another.

The results of our investigation and those of a study by Chang and Hammond (1987) of the same two tasks provide evidence in support of the central claim of the dynamic pattern perspective, that co-produced behaviors are scaled or organized as a single unit. This offers an important challenge to traditional motor control theories. If speech and finger movements are the products of separate motor programs, it seems possible that they could be performed without quantifiable influences on each other. The results imply that, although it may be theoretically possible to program any act, the motor system appears to control and coordinate events, even those involving parts of the body that are not constrained biomechanically to cooperate, so that their control is interactive.

Spatial Constraints in Bimanual Coordination

The previously discussed work examined temporal and amplitude coupling between effectors. Coordinated activity involves not only the blending of temporal aspects of movement but spatial topological aspects as well. In a dual-hand Fitts' law task in which subjects must move each hand to a target possessing a different index of difficulty (ratio of movement distance to target width), the movement time for the 'easy' hand increased to accommodate the increased movement time for the hand performing the difficult Fitts' law task (Kelso, Southard, & Goodman, 1979). Kelso, Putnam and Goodman (1983) argued that the hands are governed by the same processes that scale the movement in space and in time, while preserving the relative spatial-temporal form of the movement.

Previous investigations of bimanual tasks by Kelso and his colleagues assessed coupling by examining the structure of the temporal organization of bimanual performance. In the work to be described, the spatial coupling between the two hands will be examined. Because movements are produced in space and time, and many theorists have attributed spatial form as an *essential* aspect of motor control (Turvey, 1977), the analysis of the spatial-topological rules of coordinated activity was undertaken.

As a first test of the notion that coordination is influenced by the spatial form of the two tasks, we (Franz, 1988; Franz & Zelaznik, 1990) asked subjects to either draw circles with both hands, draw lines with both hands, or draw a line with one hand and a circle with the other hand. The choice of these two tasks was based upon consideration of movement topology and joint dynamics. A priori, circles and lines possess different spatial topologies. To make a line from a circle involves 'breaking' a circle. A circle is a closed form, while the line is an open form. Furthermore, there is considerable controversy (see Hollerbach & Atkeson, 1986) whether straight-line or curved trajectories are a basic element of control. Straight-line trajectories support the idea that movements are planned in external spatial coordinates, while curved-line trajectories support the idea that movements are planned in joint coordinates. Thus, it should be difficult to produce a circular and a linear movement simultaneously.

Kinematic information about the pen's trajectory was collected via a WATSMART infrared recording technique. The subject initiated a dual-hand trial by performing one of two tasks with only one hand. Five seconds later, the other hand initiated its task, and then, for the remainder of the 20-s trial, both hands performed their respective tasks. All single-hand control conditions were employed; in addition, all dual-task conditions were counterbalanced for hand (left/right), direction, and which hand began the dual-hand trial.

Figure 2 displays a typical dual-hand trial when both hands were drawing circles, and when both hands were drawing lines.

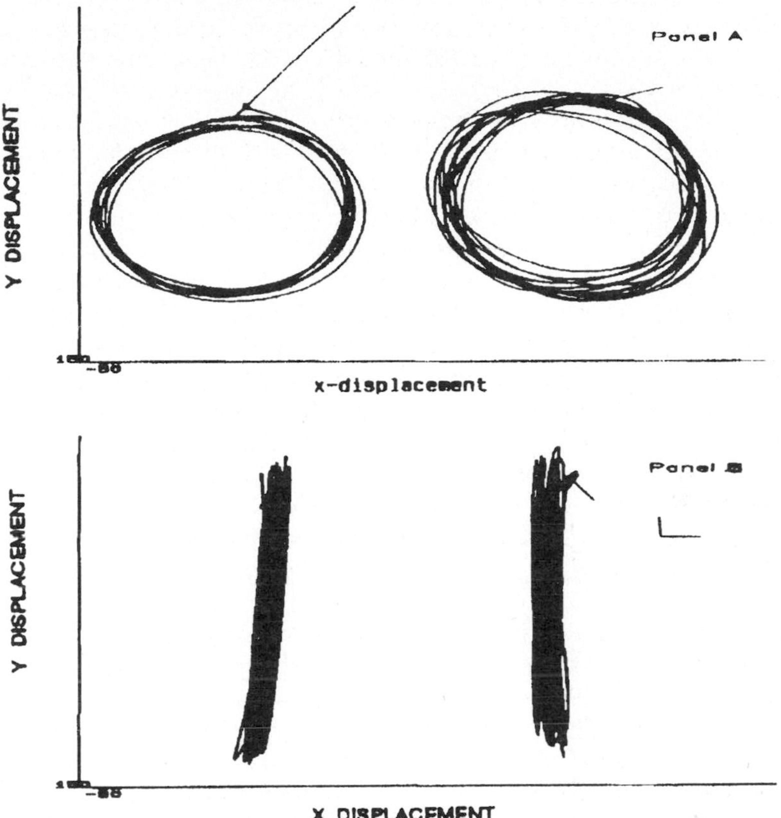

Figure 2. Description of dual-task performance when both hands are performing circles (Panel A) and when both hands are performing lines (Panel B). Each set of trajectories represents 15 seconds of continuous performance. The axes represent the X and Y dimensions. The calibration corner represents 2 cm in the X and Y dimensions.

Figure 3 displays a typical trial of circle-task performance when the circle was performed for the first five seconds (Panel B), and a line task was added for the last 15 s of the trial; and a line task when it was being performed for the first five seconds alone, followed by addition of a circle task (Panel A). In both cases the movement of the single hand being depicted was performed alone for the first five seconds (number 1 in each panel), and then performed in dual-task conditions for the latter two five-second intervals (numbers 2 and 3). In the latter two five-second intervals, the shape of either the circle (Panel B) or line (Panel A) appears to change to accommodate the different shape of its partner hand.

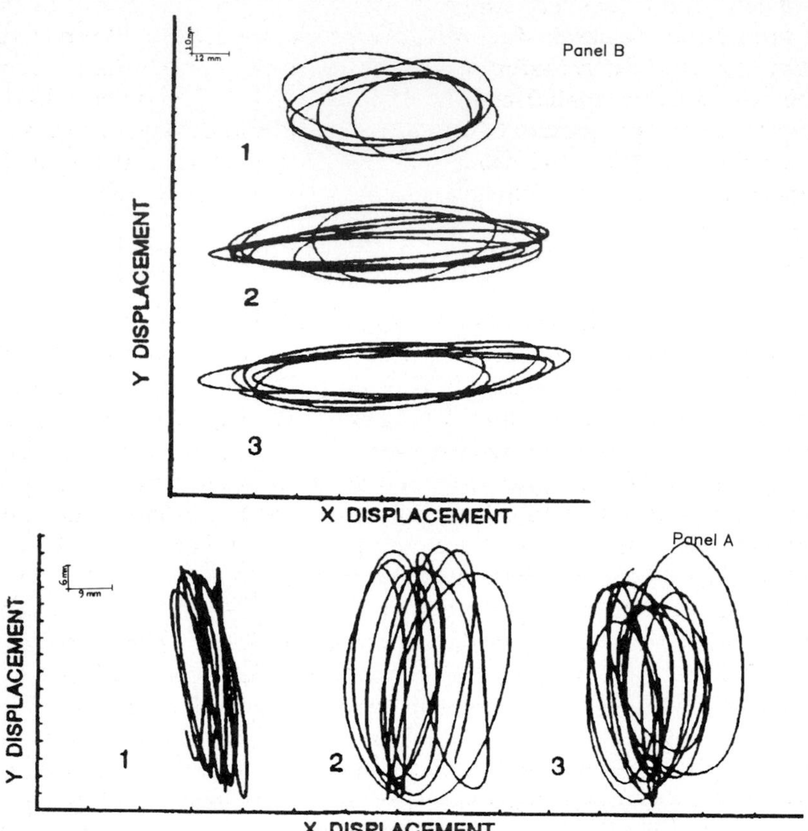

Figure 3. Description of a line task (Panel A) and a circle task (Panel B) when each was performed in conjunction with a task with the other spatial form. The plot in each panel (labeled 1) represents the first five seconds of the task, when only one hand was producing a movement. The second two sets of records in each panel (labeled 2 and 3) represent the next ten seconds, when the other hand (not shown) had begun simultaneous performance of the second task. The axes represent the X and Y dimensions.

To analyze these observations numerically, a quantitative measure of circularity and linearity was employed. For a perfect circle, the ratio of any two diameters always is 1.00. A perfect line will have no radius in its minor axis of motion and thus will produce a ratio of 0.00 (assuming the minor-axis radius is the numerator). Compared to single-hand conditions the ratio of lines increased when paired with a circle, and the ratio of the circle diameters decreased when paired with lines (Franz & Zelaznik, 1990).

These results are very similar to those of Smith et al. (1986) in that in the Franz and Zelaznik dual-task conditions involving different spatial forms, one hand *did not* adopt the spatial form of the other hand. Instead, there was relative spatial coordination of the two limbs, but the linear movement still appeared to be linear, and the circular movement appeared to be circular. Thus, the same principles apply to both the spatial and temporal domain for coordinated activity of two effector systems.

Coordination in American Sign Language

Virtually all of the above cited work involved the performance of two tasks that are well-learned and easy. However, we know very little about the *development* of coordination and coupling for unpracticed and difficult activities. In a different line of research, Lupton and Zelaznik (1990) examined the learning of American Sign Language (ASL). ASL is a distinct language with its own grammar, syntax, and morphology. For present purposes ASL is interesting because it involves the learning, not only of language, but of new motor behaviors that must be coordinated in space and time to produce informative movements.

Kinematic data were gathered with a WATSMART system from two ASL students during a 15-week first course in ASL. Prior to the course, neither subject had any experience in ASL. Subjects produced signed utterances that were either one-hand signs or two-hand signs. Subjects were tested during Week 2, Week 9, and Week 15 of the course. These students reduced sign duration and increased sign consistency during the course of the semester. However, of particular interest to the present chapter, is the qualitative analysis of the development of coordination in these one-handed and two-handed signs.

The phase portrait of a one-handed sign YOU-ALL exhibits essentially the same qualitative limit-cycle behavior for all three testing sessions (i.e., over the 15-week course). However, as seen in Figure 4, for the two-handed sign, SIGN-LANGUAGE, the phase portrait undergoes a marked qualitative change across the three testing sessions. Furthermore, during the first session, the two-handed sign phase portrait does not appear to be derived from a common oscillatory process that is emergent during testing-session one. By the third session, the phase portraits for the index finger of each hand appear to be coupled, derived from a common oscillatory mechanism, because the phase-portrait of each hand appears to be of a similar shape. In other words, coupling might be one of the consequences of learning and skill development.

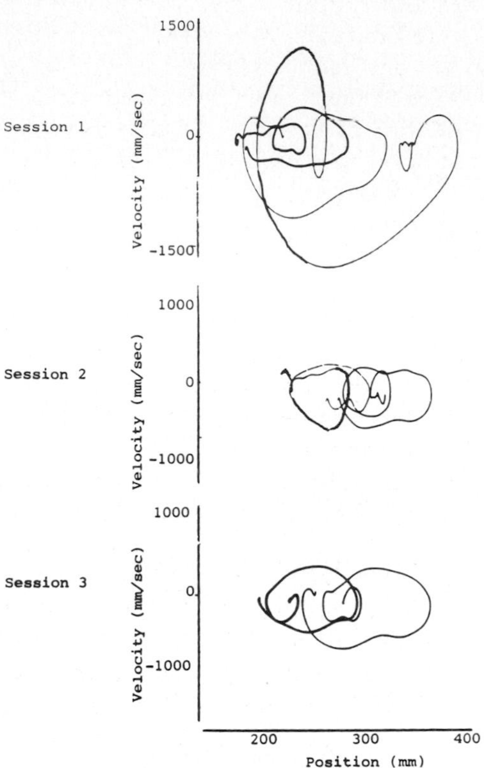

Figure 4. A plot of displacement (x) versus velocity (y) [phase portrait] of the index finger of each hand for the ASL sign, SIGN-LANGUAGE, across three testing sessions. The bold line is a record of one index finger, and the lighter line represents the index finger of the other hand.

Most studies of coordination, whether between speech and limb movements, or within limbs or speech, examine well learned or practiced behaviors. The inference is that these constraints provide a window to some *fundamental aspect* of motor behavior. Although this might be the case, the Lupton and Zelaznik work on the learning of ASL suggests that constraints develop into one of the fundamental properties of movement after extensive practice and experience. We might even argue that coordination involves the learning or development of these constraints.

Comparisons of Non-simultaneous Tasks

In the search for shared principles of speech and limb motor control, dual-task paradigms, such as simultaneous finger tapping and speaking, have provided and will continue to yield important experimental results. Such experiments are limited in one sense, however, due to the somewhat artificial demand for one central nervous system to perform two tasks at once. It could be argued that, if performed separately, the two tasks might not show any evidence of common organization. In other words, the experimental paradigm may artificially introduce the constraints on production that we interpret as evidence of common organizational principles. In recent years, we have begun to explore features of repetitive motor behaviors of different effector systems without coupling them by concurrent performance.

Our approach is derived directly from the work of Keele and his colleagues (Keele, Pokorny, Corcos, & Ivry, 1985; Keele, Ivry, & Pokorny, 1987). In a series of experiments, they have explored the question of whether different effectors share common timing mechanisms by determining if timing variance was correlated across different effectors, finger, forearm, and foot. They found correlations of approximately .45 for finger and foot tapping (Keele et al., 1985) and .90 for finger and forearm tapping (Keele et al., 1987). Subjects who were consistent at tapping with the finger were also more consistent at tapping with the foot and forearm. Keele et al. (1985) have suggested that these results are consistent with a 'modular' systems view of motor control. A module (Fodor, 1983) is defined as a self-contained set of processors that accomplish a specific operation. Keele and colleagues infer that the significant correlations were the result of a common timing module that controls the timing of the onset of successive actions, and the same module is used for different effector systems.

Using analyses of movement, we have examined cycle durations of repeated utterances, nonspeech jaw movements, finger tapping, and forearm 'tapping' (Franz, Zelaznik, & Smith, in preparation). This investigation focused on timing variability assessed in different effectors and different tasks, and employed the same experimental paradigm as Keele and co-workers (Keele et al., 1985; Keele et al., 1987) to determine if hypothesized timing processes are also shared by the speech production system. The question addressed was whether timing variability would be correlated across four repetitive tasks: finger tapping (FINGER), forearm tapping (ARM), non-vocalized opening and closing movements of the jaw (JAW), and repeating the syllable 'pa' (SPEECH). Subjects were required to synchronize their tapping, speech, or jaw movement to a click that occurred every 400 ms. After 20 clicks, the pacing beat was turned off, and subjects continued to do the task until they had produced 30 non-paced cycles of the behavior. They then stopped, and after a brief pause, the pacing beat was turned on again, and new trial began. For each of the four tasks, 39 subjects completed 24 trials. The last 20 trials for each task were analyzed.

Cycle durations were measured, and the within-subject standard deviation of the cycle duration of each task was computed. Correlations between standard deviations on all possible task pairs were computed across subjects. These correlations are presented in Table 1.

As Table 1 indicates, all correlations were positive and significant (p .05). The highest correlations were found for FINGER and ARM (.48) and ARM and JAW (.48); the lowest correlation was observed for SPEECH and JAW (.36). The significant positive correlations for standard deviations between speech and the other three tasks were surprising, because the speech task, unlike the others, required management of the breathstream. Put simply, subjects had to pause to take breaths in order to produce the syllable 'pa' repetitively. This requirement presumably introduced a source of variance in cycle duration not present in the other tasks. Despite this additional source of cycle variation in speech, subjects who are 'good timers' with the arm or finger tend also to be 'good timers' in speech.

Table 1. Correlations of standard deviations for all possible task pairs

	FINGER	ARM	JAW
ARM	.48	-	-
JAW	.38	.48	-
SPEECH	.38	.41	.36

(All correlations are significant, $p < .05$)

These results indicate that some common processes underlie timing variability in speech, nonspeech oro-facial movements, and limb movements. What might these shared processes of timing control be? It is tempting to speculate that these results have implications for recent debates concerning extrinsic and intrinsic theories of timing control in speech and other motor behaviors (e.g., Fowler, 1980). The finding that variability in speech timing is correlated with variability in timing of other motor tasks might be interpreted to support extrinsic timing theories of speech production.

Under extrinsic theories, the stored representations of utterances do not include time. Only in translation from stored 'canonical forms' (such as bundles of phonetic features) does the linguistic unit acquire the durational parameters necessary to actualize the unit in production. Perhaps the shared feature of timing control is a 'translator', a process that translates the abstract representation of a motor act into an executable motor plan that includes the detailed timing information necessary for implementation. Many different motor behaviors share this 'translator module', which, within a subject, contributes a consistent amount of timing variability regardless of the effector system employed. In essence, we are proposing an alternative process that may be contained in a timing module and that may account for the common cycle-to-cycle variability observed in different tasks.

Fowler (1980) argued strongly against the viability of extrinsic timing theories and suggested that stored 'canonical forms' are four-dimensional. These stored representations of motor acts include time ('intrinsic timing') and therefore do not need a translation step. While the present results do seem to suggest that there is some process external to the specific plan for a motor behavior that contributes to timing control of different classes of motor acts, including speech, the idea of a shared translator is only one of many possible speculations concerning the nature of the shared timing process. To perform these tasks, subjects were required to initiate new cycles of behavior at appropriate intervals of time. The timing measure we used, cycle duration, is a global one that does not necessarily reflect variability in the relative timing of the numerous neuromuscular events required to perform each cycle of behavior. Thus, it may be inappropriate to speculate on the basis of such global measures about the specific mechanisms involved in generating the detailed motor plan for each behavior. As Keele et al. (1985) have suggested, it may be that the initiation of each new cycle of a behavior depends on a process that is extrinsic to the specific plan for the motor act, and that the module contains a mechanism for cycle initiation. Of course, another possibility is that the common cycle-to-cycle variability arises both from shared processes for cycle initiation and from shared processes that produce the relative timing of events within a cycle. These questions could be addressed to some extent by determining if correlations across subjects are observed in the relative timing of events within cycles of behavior, as well as on the more global measure of cycle duration.

Common Drive to Motoneuron Pools

This volume, and indeed this chapter, are devoted primarily to the comparative study of classes of speech and limb movements usually thought to be executed under 'voluntary' control. It is worthwhile to note, however, that useful insights on speech and limb motor control may also be derived from the study of relatively automatic behaviors such as mastication and respiration. We know very little about the neural mechanisms that produce coordinated muscle output for speech and 'voluntarily-controlled' limb movements. In contrast, behaviors such as locomotion, mastication, and respiration are thought to arise from the activation of neuronal networks in the brain stem or spinal cord. Such networks, usually referred to as central pattern generators (CPGs), interact with sensory information to produce behavior that is centrally patterned, but adaptive in the face of alterations in the environment (Rossignol, Lund, & Drew, 1988).

In the case of speech, which involves activity in muscles that are driven by CPGs for some behaviors, two speculations have been offered to account for the relationship between speech production and the CPG-driven behaviors. One suggestion is that brainstem CPGs are by-passed, and the neural control of speech arises in special circuitry in the cortex. This argument has been made for the neural control of metabolic and speech breathing by Euler (1981). Another suggestion is that the neural processes controlling speech actually take advantage of pattern generation circuitry; it has been proposed, for example, that the control of jaw movements in speech involves the masticatory CPG (Grillner, 1981; Gracco & Abbs, 1988).

In a recent investigation (Smith & Denny, 1990), we attempted to determine if there were common sources of synaptic drive to motoneuron pools during the execution of different motor tasks. We exploited a method developed by investigators studying respiratory pattern generation circuitry in experimental animals (e.g., Bruce, 1988; Cohen, 1973; Richardson & Mitchell, 1982). In a number of studies, activity of pairs of i respiratory nerves and muscles has been found to contain correlated oscillations in two frequency ranges, approximately 20-60 Hz and 60-110 Hz. On the basis of recordings of activity of brainstem respiratory neurons, in addition to a variety of other kinds of experimental evidence, it has been hypothesized that the wide-spread, correlated oscillations in the 60-110 Hz band arise from operation of the respiratory CPG (Bruce, 1988; Cohen, 1979, Euler, 1986).

Bruce and Ackerson (1986) explored the possible presence of correlated high frequency oscillations (HFOs) in human subjects. They recorded activity of the diaphragm from the right and left lower ventrolateral surface of the rib cage during the rising phase of inspiration. Coherence functions were computed between right and left EMG pairs. Coherence, computed for each frequency, ranges between 0 and 1, and represents the squared cross correlation between the two signals at each individual frequency (Jenkins & Watts, 1968). Bruce and Ackerson (1986) found significant bilaterally-correlated HFOs in the 60-110 Hz range during voluntarily controlled deep breathing. Further, they found that significant coherence was not present in coactivation of bilateral muscle pairs not normally driven by a CPG, for example, in sternomastoids or biceps, and when respiratory muscles were activated in postural maneuvers.

Smith and Denny (1990) computed coherence functions between bilateral pairs of EMGs of respiratory and jaw muscles to address these questions: (1) Would correlated HFOs present for deep metabolic breathing also be observed during activation of the diaphragm during speech breathing and during a task in which speech breathing was simulated by breathing in phase with a tracking wave? (2) If correlated oscillations are present in the human respiratory system, are they also a feature of another behavior thought to be CPG-driven, i.e. mastication? (3) Are correlated oscillations present in a bilateral pair of mandibular muscles (masseters) during their activation for speech and clenching? Coherence functions computed from bilateral EMG recordings of the diaphragm during deep metabolic breathing replicated Bruce and Ackerson's (1986) earlier observations of significant, correlated oscillations in the 60-110 Hz frequency range. In speech and speech-like breathing, a within-subjects statistical analysis revealed that correlated oscillations in the 60-110 Hz band were significantly reduced. This result supports the hypothesis that the neural circuitry characterized by high frequency oscillations in the 60-110 Hz range, possibly a respiratory CPG, is not the primary source of drive to respiratory motoneuron pools in speech.

The analysis of the coherence of EMGs of bilateral masseter activity revealed highly correlated oscillations during chewing.

Significant coherence values occurred in the range of 20-140 Hz, with consistent, very large peaks in the 20-60 Hz band (illustrated for one subject in the panel labeled CH in Figure 5). In contrast to the respiratory system, there had not been previous studies in experimental animals that linked HFOs in the masticatory system with the operation of a CPG. By analogy with the respiratory data and in light of studies of rhythmic jaw movements elicited by cortical stimulation in experimental animals, it could be proposed that the highly correlated oscillations consistently present in human subjects in the 20-60 Hz band arise from a central command system, such as a masticatory pattern generator.

Coherence functions computed from the other tasks with the mandibular system, speech and clenching, did not reveal any consistent pattern across subjects. Figure 5 shows the coherence functions calculated from the bilateral recordings of masseter for chewing (CH), clenching (CL), and speech (SP) for one subject, and the average coherence function computed across all subjects for the mandibular tasks (AVG). In speech and clenching, coherence functions were highly variable with significant values of coherence scattered throughout the frequency range analyzed (20-230 Hz). As the coherence functions averaged across subjects indicate, coherence values for speech were generally higher than those observed for clenching. A majority of the subjects showed significant (nonzero) coherence in the 20-60 Hz band in the speech and clenching conditions, but a within-subjects statistical analysis revealed that coherence in this band was significantly reduced in speech and clenching compared to chewing.

In general, such results are compatible with the hypothesis that a stereotypic, stable source characterized by consistent, widely distributed oscillations contributes to the high levels of coherence observed in chewing, and that, if this source contributed correlated inputs for speech and clenching, it is a less dominant source of input for these tasks.

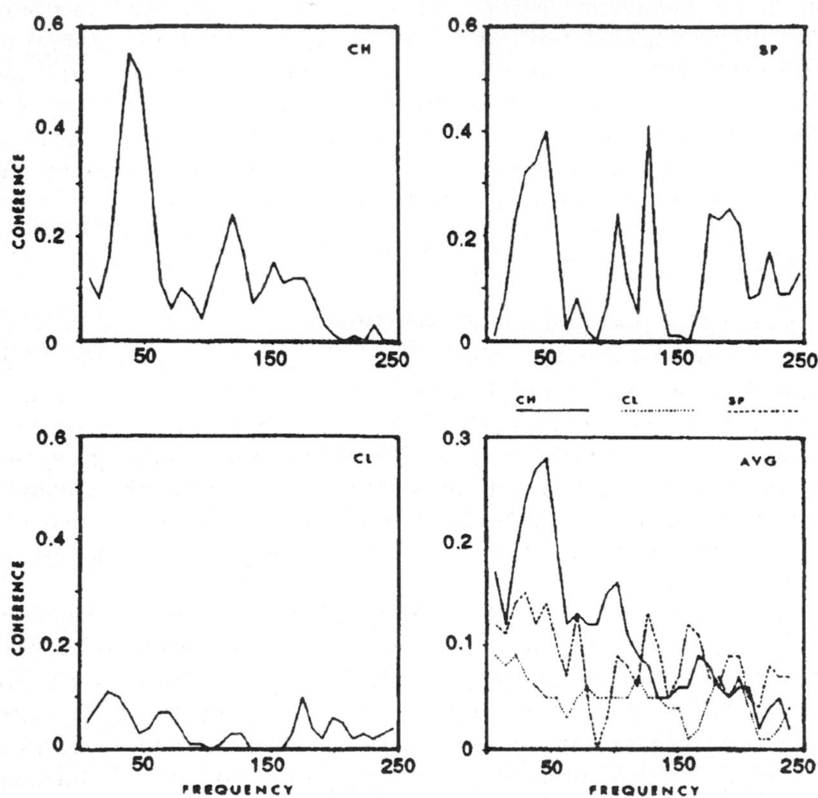

Figure 5. Coherence between EMG recordings of right and left masseter muscles for one subject in the chewing (CH), clenching (CL), and speech (SP) conditions. The lower right panel, labeled AVG, shows the coherence functions averaged across all subjects for the three conditions.

The level of analysis employed in this experiment focuses on the details of the synaptic drive to motoneuron pools during motor behavior, and as such, is quite different from the level of analysis in the experiments discussed above. Despite the difference in methodological approach, it would seem that the method employed in this experiment is particularly promising for the search for common processes in control in different effector systems. This method essentially produces an index of the degree of common drive to different motoneuron pools. Further, if a particular neural source is characterized by a tendency to oscillate in a specific frequency range, evidence of correlated drive in this range is in some sense a 'signature' of that source. Our preliminary findings and those of Bruce and Ackerson (1986), indicate that these coherent HFOs are characteristic of human motor behaviors that are likely to involve pattern generation circuitry, respiration and mastication. They also provide some support for the proposal that neural control of speech production is not accomplished by taking advantage of this pre-existing circuitry. It seems likely that requirements for speech production are so different from those of metabolic breathing or mastication, that the patterns generated by this circuitry would not be appropriate for the generation of speech.

Conclusion

The results of the work reviewed in this chapter lead to the general conclusion that the central nervous system employs some common mechanisms to generate the movement sequences that give rise to speech sounds and those that accomplish a variety of other goals, for example, leading an orchestra or lifting a glass. It also seems that, although speech production employs the same effector systems used in metabolic breathing and mastication, there are substantial differences in the nature of the neural inputs that drive the muscle systems for speech compared to chewing and nonspeech breathing.

Using traditional tools of analysis of human motor behavior, electromyographic and kinematic analysis, considerable progress has been made in identifying the control characteristics that speech production shares and does not share with other motor behaviors. These investigations have proceeded without the assumption that progress in understanding speech production depends on making a connection between linguistic units and the control of movement. Ultimately, of course, we would like to understand the nature of the relationship between linguistic structure and organization of the motor processes that underlie speech production. Similarly, in the case of moving a glass, we would like to understand the connections between the performer's intent and the motor system's implementation of the act. At present, these questions are in the province of cognitive science and philosophy.

For the scientist with a focus on the control of muscles and movement, there are a number of new directions of research opened by advances in recent years. Our increased understanding of shared principles of motor control, coupled with improved technology for kinematic analysis, has led to the recognition of potentially rich new sources of data. For example, in recent years, we (Lupton & Zelaznik, 1990) and other investigators (Bellugi, Poizner, & Klima, 1989) have begun to study the kinematic properties of manual sign language, a motor behavior in which linguistic goals are implemented via different effector systems than those usually employed. Previous research has compared the same effector systems engaged in motor tasks with different goals (e.g., speech and chewing). Investigations of manual sign language production now provide the opportunity to examine the relationship between different effector systems that are organized to accomplish a common goal, linguistic communication.

Comparative work on different effector systems also has led to important new insights concerning disorders of movement. Over the past two years, we have initiated a research program on stuttering, which is often characterized as a disorder of timing (Kent, 1984; Van Riper, 1982). The demonstration that timing characteristics are shared across motor systems has implications for a question that has been posed by researchers for many years: Is stuttering a movement disorder that is specific to the speech motor system, or is it associated with a generalized timing disorder? We believe that progress on these and many other questions will arise from continuing study of a variety of effector systems engaged in a broad range of behaviors.

Acknowledgements

We would like to thank Margaret Denny and Elizabeth Franz for their help in preparation of this manuscript. This work was supported by grants NS 19173 and DC 00559 from the National Institutes of Health.

References

Abbs, J.H. (1986). Invariance and variability in speech production: a distinction between linguistic intent and its neuromotor implementation. In J.S. Perkell & D.H. Klatt (Eds.), *Invariance and variability in speech processes* (pp. 202-223). Hillsdale, NJ: Lawrence Erlbaum Associates.

Ackerson, L.M., & Bruce, E.N. (1983). Bilaterally synchronized oscillations in human diaphragm and intercostal EMGs during spontaneous breathing. *Brain Research*, **271**, 346-348.

Bellugi, U., Poizner, H., & Klima, E.S. (1989). Language, modality and the brain. *Trends in Neurosciences*, **12**, 380-388.

Bruce, E.N. (1988). Correlated and uncorrelated high-frequency oscillations in phrenic and recurrent laryngeal neurograms. *Journal of Neurophysiology*, **59**, 1188-1203.

Bruce, E.N., & Ackerson, L.M. (1986). High-frequency oscillations in human electromyograms during voluntary contractions. *Journal of Neurophysiology*, **56**, 542-553.

Chang, P., & Hammond, G.R. (1987). Mutual interactions between speech and finger movements. *Journal of Motor Behavior*, **19**, 265-274.

Cohen, M.I. (1973). Synchronization of discharge, spontaneous and evoked, between inspiratory neurons. *Acta Neurobiology*, **33**, 189-218.

Cohen, M.I. (1979). Neurogenesis of respiratory rhythm in the mammal. *Physiological Reviews*, **59**, 1105-1173.

Euler, C. von. (1981). The contribution of sensory inputs to the pattern generation of breathing. *Canadian Journal of Physiology and Pharmacology*, **59**, 700-706.

Euler, C. von. (1986). Brain stem mechanisms for generation and control of breathing pattern. In A.P. Fishman (Ed.), *Handbook of physiology: Sec. 3. The respiratory system: Vol. II. Control of breathing, Pt.* 2 (pp. 1-68). Bethesda, MD: American Physiological Society.

Fodor, J. (1983). *The modularity of mind.* Cambridge, MA: The MIT Press.

Franz, E.A. (1988). *Spatial and temporal constraints in bimanual coordination tasks.* Unpublished Masters Thesis, Purdue University.

Franz, E.A., & Zelaznik, H.N. (1990). *Spatial topological constraints in bimanual coordination.* Manuscript submitted for publication.

Franz, E.A., Zelaznik, H.N., & Smith, A. (in preparation). Evidence for a timing module for different effector systems.

Gracco, V.L. & Abbs, J.H. (1988). Central patterning of speech movements. *Experimental Brain Research*, **71**, 515-526.

Grillner, S. (1981). Possible analogies in the control of innate motor acts and the production of sound in speech. In S. Grillner, P. Lindblom, J. Lubker, & A. Persson (Eds.), *Speech motor control* (pp. 217-230). New York: Pergamon Press.

Hollerbach, J.M., & Atkeson, C.G. (1986). Characterization of joint-interpolated arm movements. In H. Heuer & C. Fromm (Eds.), *Generation and modulation of action patterns* (pp. 41-54). Berlin: Springer-Verlag.

Keele, S.W., Ivry, R., & Pokorny, R.A. (1987). Force control and its relation to timing. *Journal of Motor Behavior*, **19**, 96-114.

Keele, S.W., Pokorny, R.A., Corcos, D.M., & Ivry, R. (1985). Do perception and motor production share common timing mechanisms: a correlational analysis. *Acta Psychologica*, **60**, 173-191.

Kelso, J.A.S., Southard, D.L., & Goodman, D. (1979). On programming and coordinating two-handed movements. *Journal of Experimental Psychology: Human Perception and Performance*, **5**, 229-238.

Kelso, J.A.S., Putnam, C.A., & Goodman, D. (1983). On the space-time structure of human interlimb coordination. *Quarterly Journal of Experimental Psychology*, **35A**, 83-92.

Kelso, J.A.S., Tuller, B., & Harris, K.S. (1981). A 'Dynamic Pattern' perspective on the control and coordination of movement. In P.F. MacNeilage (Ed.), *The production of speech* (pp. 137-173). New York: Springer-Verlag.

Kent, R.D. (1984). Stuttering as a temporal programming disorder. In R.F. Curlee & W.H. Perkins (Eds.), *The nature and treatment of stuttering: New directions* (pp. 283-302). Boston MA: College Hill Press.

Liberman, A.M., Cooper, F.S., Shankweiler, D.P., & Studdert-Kennedy, M. (1967). Perception of the speech code. *Psychological Review*, **74**, 431-461.

Lupton, L.K., & Zelaznik, H.N. (1990). Motor learning in sign language students. *Sign Language Studies*.

MacNeilage, P.F. (1970). The motor control of serial ordering in speech. *Psychological Review*, **77**, 182-196.

Moll, K.L., Zimmermann, G.N., & Smith, A. (1977). The study of speech production as a human neuromotor system. In M. Sawashima & F.S. Cooper (Eds.), *Dynamic aspects of speech production* (pp. 107-127). Tokyo: University of Tokyo Press.

Richardson, C.A., & Mitchell, R.A. (1982). Power spectral analysis of inspiratory nerve activity in the decerebrate cat. *Brain Research*, **233**, 317-336.

Rossignol, S., Lund, J.P., & Drew, T. (1988). The role of sensory inputs in regulating patterns of rhythmical movements in higher vertebrates: a comparison between locomotion, respiration, and mastication. In A. Cohen, S. Rossignol, & S. Grillner (Eds.), *Neural control of rhythmic movements in vertebrates* (pp. 201-283). Washington, DC: Wiley.

Smith, A., & Denny, M. (1990). High frequency oscillations as indicators of neural control mechanisms in human respiration, mastication, and speech. *Journal of Neurophysiology*.

Smith, A., McFarland, D.H., & Weber, C.M. (1986). Interactions between speech and finger movements: an exploration of the dynamic pattern perspective. *Journal of Speech and Hearing Research*, **29**, 471-480.

Turvey, M.T. (1977). Preliminaries to a theory of action with reference to vision. In R. Shaw & J. Bransford (Eds.), *Perceiving acting and knowing: Toward an ecological psychology* (pp. 211-265). Hillsdale, NJ: Lawrence Erlbaum Associates.

Van Riper, C. (1982). *The nature of stuttering*. Englewood Cliffs, NJ: Prentice-Hall.

von Holst, E. (1973). *The behavioral physiology of animal and man: The collected papers of Erich von Holst, Vol. 1*. (R. Martin, Trans.). London: Methuen. (Original work published 1937, 1939).

Cerebral Control of Speech and Limb Movements
G.E. Hammond (editor)

Chapter 20

DEVELOPMENT OF SENSORIMOTOR CAPACITIES RELEVANT TO SPEECH AND CONCURRENT TASK PERFORMANCE

Gerald Turkewitz
Hunter College and Albert Einstein College of Medicine

Lisa Ecklund-Flores
City University of New York

and

Darlynne A. Devenny
New York State Institute for Basic Research in Developmental Disabilities

Development in general, and speech development in particular, are viewed as the result of sensorimotor limitations and coordinations interacting with a dynamically changing environment. A framework for describing early speech development in relation to more general aspects of sensorimotor development is presented. Within this framework, concurrence of functioning is considered in two ways. First, concurrence in developmental time is illustrated with examples from early speech development as it occurs in the context of changing sensorimotor and affective development. Second, concurrence of functioning in real time is illustrated by methods entailing the simultaneous elicitation of different behaviors to examine the underlying structure of behavioral and neural organization.

It is our belief that the concurrent development of the multiple sensorimotor functions in the young infant has a profound influence on the development of speech. This belief is guided by the view that development and evolution can both be productively approached within Francois Jacob's formulation of evolution as a tinkerer rather than as an engineer (Jacob, 1977). In this metaphor evolutionary outcomes are the products of the modification and recombination of existing elements rather than the result of a plan to produce a predetermined end product with parts designed and fabricated specifically for an ultimate purpose. Although we believe this to be a useful metaphor it can be misleading if it is not combined with Oppenheim's recognition of the requirement that at all stages of development (we would add `and at all stages of evolution') the organism be adapted to its circumstances (Oppenheim, 1984). This stricture places constraints on both evolution and development which are not characteristic of those placed on tinkerers, namely that evolutionary and developmental processes are not free to disassemble the organism. Instead, the processes involved must always maintain the integrity of the organism while producing change through the modification and reorganization of existing parts. According to this view the characteristics of the butterfly can only be understood with reference to the characteristics of the caterpillar while the caterpillar cannot be understood as a defective or incomplete butterfly. It should be noted, however, that the evolutionary requirement for successful reproduction gives the butterfly a role in shaping the caterpillar and this aspect of the process of change introduces a teleology which adds complexity to the study of both evolution and development.

The analogy of evolution with ontogenetic development is relevant to the issues which we will consider, as functions such as speech can arise from organizations and components which are largely independent of speech during early stages of their development. Speech is a function which is late in evolving and, therefore, utilizes structures which evolved for other, primarily vegetative, functions. That is, the primary functions of the structures utilized in articulation are feeding and mastication; the function of the glottis is as a valve to facilitate lifting and evacuation by allowing the accumulation of intrathoracic pressure; the function of the respiratory system is first for the exchange of gases before it is used as a source of energy for voice. Ontogenetically, the vegetative functions develop prior to utilization of these same structures for speech (DeVito, Giattino, & Schon, 1975). As in the metaphor of the tinkerer, evolution has utilized structures already present and adapted them for more elaborate functions (Lieberman, 1975).

Development has at least two components, one which is linear or quantitative and one which is non-linear, involving reorganization. It is the utilization of available part processes to create organized and adapted integrations and reintegrations as conditions change which gives development its discontinuous or stage-like appearance. Continuity within this discontinuous framework is provided by linear processes yielding incremental improvements in structure or function during either evolution or development. The development of speech undoubtedly involves a complex interplay between organizational and quantitative processes with both constrained by the dictates of current function within a structured and integrated organism. Although structures subserving speech can be modified through development and evolution, the modification is constrained by the requirement for the structure to maintain the earlier function.

Thelen (1990) offers a view of speech development which exemplifies these non-linear/reorganizational and linear/quantitative processes. Speech development is linear in that behavior changes over real time and is therefore necessarily progressive. However, underlying parallel and interacting processes reorganize elements according to task demands, ultimately transforming pre-speech sounds into intelligible speech. Particular stages of anatomical and functional maturation constrain and direct the natural sounds which emerge from the oral, facial, respiratory, and ingestive apparatus. At the same time, the level of functioning achieved in the perceptual systems increases the sensitivity of the infant to the linguistic environment, as well as to self-produced sounds. Neither of these processes occur independently, however, in that the developing infant is continually matching the task demands of the perception-action environment with the self-organizing capabilities of its own perception-action system. In depicting speech development in this way, the constant reorganization of related elements according to the demands of the task and the constraints of the system provide a progressive sequence of behavior leading to the acquisition of intelligible speech. For example, changes in the size of the oral cavity, mobility of the tongue and lips, and development of the jaw muscles are seen as functionally driven by such non-speech behaviors as sucking, swallowing and crying (Fletcher, 1973). Such anatomical changes make possible the production of a variety of sounds and afford new multidimensional matching capabilities in response to input from the linguistic environment. The result is a reorganization of structure-function relationships to accommodate these elemental changes, and the emergence of a new pre-speech 'stage'.

Speech-motor functioning can be understood as a component of a larger organization of the motor system. Studies of the relationship between speech-motor processes and other complex motor processes provide a mounting body of evidence of similarities across motor systems. Similarities in speech and limb systems have been found to exist in relative timing patterns with changes in rate (Tuller, Kelso, & Harris, 1982), characteristics of kinematic patterns (Ostry & Cooke, 1987; Ostry, Keller, & Parush, 1983), and responses to unexpected perturbations (Kelso, Tuller, Vatikiotis-Bateson, & Fowler, 1984). Such similarities in multimovement coordination across motor systems have led to the classification of certain speech and non-speech motor processes as coordinative, synergistic structures, possessing comparable underlying sensorimotor mechanisms. Abbs, Gracco, and Cole (1984), have proposed that the motor production system is composed of coordinative motor processes which are task-dependent and operate flexibly and dynamically in response to the peculiarities of the situation. Intermovement coordinative actions rely on a predictive feedforward process, compensating for perturbations in an ongoing manner. Sensorimotor-based intermovement adjustment determines the final contribution of an individual movement to the multimovement goal. Applied specifically to speech-motor processes, afferent information of predictive value in this feedforward process may be available prior to movement onset, maybe even prior to muscle contraction, from mechanoreceptors of the facial skin and lingual-oral mucosa. Representation of the relationship between these afferent signals and synergistic motor output is experience-based, implicating the importance of the variety of pre-verbal vocal experimentation by infants in the emergence of articulation of intelligible speech. In other words, the role of experience is in the 'calibration' of the relationship between afferent and efferent signals. Recalibration must occur continuously throughout development in accord with developmental change in the size and relationship of the oral cavity structures.

In this chapter we hope to provide a framework for describing early speech and language development in relation to more general aspects of sensorimotor development. We will examine concurrence of function in developmental time as well as concurrence in real time in which competing demands of a situation determine functional relationships. Within this framework we will consider some sensorimotor characteristics of infants and the way in which these may shape the foundations of cognition. In that we are trying to propose a method of viewing and studying aspects of development we are highly selective in the literature reported and have made no attempt to be comprehensive. We will not attempt to parcel development into separate influences of genetics and environment as we believe that it is counterproductive to conceive of development in dichotomous terms. In that all organisms are constructed from interactions between phenotype and environment and not, as is frequently stated, between genotype and environment, any attempt to assign differential weight to one or the other interactants must result in oversimplification (see Johnston, 1987, and Oyama, 1985, for recent treatments of some of the problems involved in utilizing dichotomies).

Sensorimotor Development Concurrent with Speech

We will first examine the development of capacities which are concurrent in developmental time and relate them to functions which come into play in some close, regular temporal relationship to each other. Concurrent development is differentiated from other types of development in that it is not conceptualized as being part of a causal sequence with temporal regularity stemming from the dependent relationships between the functions. Rather, the temporal association is thought to stem primarily from the development of a substrate which is common to simultaneously emerging functions. Such concurrence of different functions can be related to the emergence of structures (neural, muscular, or cognitive) which are fundamental to the appearance of emerging functions. Good examples of the latter are provided by Piaget whose stage theory involves the appearance of a variety of functions following the development of particular psychological structures (Piaget, 1954).

Developmental milestones which emerge concurrently may be useful indices of developing brain organization. This is especially the case with speech development and the development of other sequential processing abilities (e.g., motoric) which are felt to come under the control of the dominant hemisphere. Ramsay offers extensive research in this area, concentrating on the developmental co-occurrence of milestones in hand preference and pre-linguistic milestones for speech acquisition. When tested for unimanual hand preference after the advent of stable duplicative syllable babbling, clear right hand preferences were found to follow the onset of duplicative syllable babbling in the majority of infants studied (Ramsay, 1980a). Additionally, Ramsay found that 7-month-old infants who demonstrated duplicated syllable babbling (e.g., 'baba') also showed clear hand preference while 5-month-old infants had not achieved either milestone (Ramsay, 1980b). When a different group of infants, all of whom were 6 months old, were tested he found that those who had duplicative babbling showed preferential handedness while those who were not babbling in this manner showed no clear hand preference (Ramsay, 1983). While earlier results showed the babbling-hand preference relationship to be equivocal for girls, subsequent research found the predicted trends in unimanual had preference in both sexes. For both girls and boys Ramsay suggests that the right hand preference loses robustness as the left hand becomes increasingly used in bimanual manipulation of objects. This is followed by a return of handedness in tasks of bimanual manipulation concurrently with the advent of dissimilar syllable use (Ramsay, 1984). Ramsay has speculated that the curvilinear pattern of hand preference moving from unimanual to bimanual hand use, concurrent with developmental achievements in duplicative and dissimilar syllable use in speech acquisition, may reflect progressive levels of expression of asymmetric brain organization and control at the sub-cortical and cortical levels.

More recently, Bloom has presented data concerning the relationship between speech and emotional behavior. In a series of studies Bloom and her associates (Bloom, 1990; Bloom, Beckwith, & Capatides, 1988) have found changing patterns of association between speech and affect. Towards the end of the first and beginning of the second year of life there is a negative association between the expression of affect and speech such that those infants who spend more of their time in neutral affect say their first words at an earlier age, show an earlier verbal spurt, and use multiword utterances earlier than do those who spend more of their time exhibiting positive or negative affect. Furthermore, they found that at younger ages speech is more likely to occur in the absence of affect whereas later (and particularly with respect to more familiar words), mild affect is more likely to accompany speaking. Bloom attributes these relationships and developmental changes to the effortful nature of expressing both speech and affect and their competing demands for attention which are reduced when speaking is no longer so effortful.

Elicitation of Function Through Concurrent Activity

The second sense in which concurrent tasks will be used concerns not the emergence of functions in developmental time but rather the influence of one type of function on another in real time. Concurrent elicitation of multiple functions can result from developmental changes in the nervous system. For example, the spread of excitation is, in part, a function of degree of myelination of the neural tissue. Since unmyelinated fibers have a greater potential for spread of firing via non-synaptic conduction (i.e., ephaptic transmission), maturational changes in myelin deposition can affect concurrent activation of adjacent neural areas (Arvanitaki, 1942; Katz & Schmitt, 1940; Purpura, 1969; Rasminsky, 1981). In that cerebral areas have different rates of myelination, effects of concurrent elicitation can show different developmental trajectories in accordance with the particular functions involved. These differences can be rather marked as myelination of some regions is completed before birth whereas the corpus callosum is not fully myelinated until about 11 years of age (Yakovlev & Lecours, 1967).

To provide a background against which to consider the use of concurrent tasks for understanding the role of sensorimotor capacities in the development of speech we will present a brief description of the major relevant theoretical position with respect to this issue. In a model developed by Kinsbourne, performing a task activates not only the region specific for that task but, due to the spread of neural activation from that site, activates adjacent cerebral areas as well (Kinsbourne & Hiscock, 1983; Lassen & Roland, 1983). Spreading activation is presumed to be graded in accord with proximity to the site activated. Thus, in the mature brain, sites within a hemisphere have a closer functional relationship to one another than to corresponding sites in the opposite hemisphere.

According to this model, either facilitation of or interference with function can occur as a consequence of the spatial proximity of areas of concurrent cortical activation. Facilitation occurs when an area of the brain is activated by the spread of neural activity from an adjacent region of the brain. The facilitatory effect is a function of the nature of the tasks involved and their degree of difficulty. If simultaneous tasks are easy and not incompatible their simultaneous execution is facilitatory. If, however, the tasks are difficult, execution of the task results in interference and, consequently, impaired performance. According to this model, impairment in functioning occurs for complex tasks or incompatible tasks because overflow activity interferes with areas of specific cortical control. The prototypical example of such effects are provided by Kinsbourne and Cook (1971) and Hicks (1975) who found that speaking (a left hemispheric function) interfered with simultaneously balancing a rod on the right but not left index finger. Presumably, movements of the right index finger are controlled in the left hemisphere and it is the use of the same hemisphere for speaking and balancing on the right index finger which led to a decrement in performance.

The facilitatory effects of temporal priming have been viewed as stemming from the activation of a hemisphere by the immediately preceding utilization of that hemisphere for another function. Such facilitation of activity is a consequence of a state of depolarization with enhanced readiness for firing amplifying sensory input (Lassen & Roland, 1983). Such enhancement effects have been reported for motor activity. For example, Kimura (1973) reported greater spontaneous right hand movements during speaking than during silence.

It should be noted that an extension of the Kinsbourne model would suggest different consequences for the concurrent elicitation of the same behaviors at different stages of development. Thus one might anticipate shifts from interference to facilitation as tasks shifted from difficult and effortful to easy and skillful during the course of development. So, for example, the previously mentioned facilitation of right arm movement seen during speaking (Kimura, 1973) might characterize stages during which speech is well developed, but right arm movement during early stages in speech development may produce an interference with speaking, or vice versa. Bloom's finding that the relationships between speech and affect shifted from a stage in which speech was less likely to occur to one in which familiar words were more likely to occur in conjunction with mild affect suggests a developmental shift from interference to facilitation with changes in the effortfulness of speech.

Concurrent task performance has been utilized experimentally to reveal underlying relationships. Measurement of facilitatory or inhibitory influences of concurrent tasks provide some measure of the componential structure of the various facets of behavior. In one of the few studies of infants which explicitly utilized the presentation of concurrent tasks to examine the influence of processing sensory input on the execution of a sensorimotor task, Lewkowicz and Turkewitz (1982) examined the effect in infants of presenting speech or music to either the left or the right ear on reaching. In this study six- and eight-month-old infants were presented with speech or music through earphones to either their right or left ear and immediately subsequent to the onset of the sound were presented with an attractive object. It was anticipated that the two types of auditory input would engage mechanisms having different cortical loci, and they would have different effects when presented at the different ears. That is, if speech activated left-hemisphere and music activated right-hemisphere mechanisms of attention or processing it was anticipated that presenting speech to the right ear or music to the left ear would have more marked effects on reaching than would presenting speech to the left ear or music to the right ear. Although it was initially expected that differential activation of the two hemispheres might influence the hand used in reaching for the object, there was no effect of type of auditory input or of ear of presentation on the hand used for contacting the object. There was, however, an effect of both of these factors as well as of gender and age on the latency to contact the object. These effects included a longer latency for six-month-old boys to contact the objects when speech was presented to the left ear than was the case when music was presented to that ear or when speech was presented to the right ear. Although no such effects were found for six-month-old girls, eight-month-old girls tended to show the anticipated pattern of longer latencies to contact when speech was presented to the right ear or music to the left ear than was the case when those directions of presentation were reversed. At this age the boys no longer exhibited differential responses to speech but did to music with the presentation of music to the right ear resulting in a longer latency to contact than did its presentation to the left ear.

These data are so complex that they do not lend themselves to any very clear or compelling interpretation with regard to the nature of the relationships between processing speech and the infants' sensorimotor capacities. They do, however, indicate that the characteristics of the input affects a sensorimotor behavior, such as reaching, and does so in relation to the hemisphere to which it is more strongly presented. At a somewhat less general level the data also suggest a non-linear path of development for hemispheric specialization. That is, the data for the boys suggests an early-appearing left ear (right hemisphere) effect of the speech stimulus used and a somewhat later-appearing right ear (left hemisphere) effect of music together with the disappearance at that age of the differential ear effect for speech. In that older boys and adults typically show the reverse pattern, i.e., a right ear speech and left ear music advantage, the data suggest a shifting pattern of hemispheric specialization during development. It is still unclear whether the pattern observed in the girls represents a simpler developmental pattern with the typical pattern of hemispheric specialization for speech and music beginning to emerge at around 8 months. Data from other studies, however, which indicate lateralized differences in response to speech and music in much younger female infants suggests that the pattern of relationships between processing requirements and sensorimotor functions in females is not likely to be any simpler than that seen in males (Turkewitz, 1988). These and similar findings led Molfese and Betz (1987) to conclude that 'specific behaviors that are part of the same structure may show parallels in development but not all parallel behaviors are structurally related and not all behaviors that become structurally related develop at the same point in time.' (p.265)

The use of the concurrent tasks of sensory processing and manual production to examine early hemispheric specialization has revealed a complex profile of development. To understand such complexity it is necessary to analyze newly emerging behaviors in terms of the previously existing part processes of which they are constituted and to view the new behavior as a reorganization of these parts to meet the demands placed upon the infant while functional integrity is maintained. The questions to be answered are not when does the adult behavior appear, but rather, what functional demands does the emergent behavior fulfil at a given point in developmental time, and what lower level processes are integral to its emergence. To do this for sensory processing and manual production requires understanding the developmental history of both types of tasks and relating them, theoretically, at different times in development.

Implications of Early Sensory Limitation

Turkewitz has recently proposed a model for the development of perceptual and cognitive processes in relation to hemispheric specialization. This model attempts to unify a number of factors in development including the consequences of limited sensory capacities of the fetus and infant, the requirements of concurrent information processing, and the circumstances in which the development is occurring

(Turkewitz, 1990). During very early development the fetal acoustic environment changes as the transmission characteristics of the expanding uterus change (Fifer & Moon, 1988). That is, the fetal acoustic environment shifts from one characterized by a preponderance of internally-generated noises (gastrointestinal, cardiovascular, etc.) to one with considerably more externally-generated sounds, including speech. Maternal speech is particularly salient during the latter part of gestation as it is propagated to the uterus via bone conduction as well as air conduction and is accompanied by concomitant tactile stimulation resulting from diaphragmatic movements of the speaking mother. Changes in acoustic characteristics of the intrauterine environment are associated with maturational changes in the development of the cerebral hemispheres of the fetus. The two hemispheres develop at different rates with the right hemisphere beginning development somewhat earlier (see Galaburda, 1984, and Turkewitz, 1990, for reviews of evidence supporting this progression). Best (1988) has suggested a somewhat more complicated developmental scheme with the right-left gradient of development being only one of several axial gradients. The interaction of these gradients results in a changing set of relationships between and within the hemispheres. Although it seems likely that this scheme is a more accurate reflection of developmental changes in the hemispheres than any based on a relatively simple right-left gradient of development, for purposes of the present exposition it is sufficient to note that there is evidence for differential rates of development of the two hemispheres. In the absence of any clear timetable with regard to the age at which shifts in the relative development of relevant areas of the two hemispheres occur and an equal uncertainty concerning the timing of transitions in the acoustic characteristics of the intrauterine environment, it is sufficient to note that any difference in the timing of maturation of the two hemispheres, even a very slight one, has potential consequences for the development of hemispheric specialization. Although, as previously indicated, even small temporal differences can have marked consequences, in their study of postnatal development Thatcher, Walker, and Giudice (1987) provide electrophysiological evidence of substantial differences in rates of development of the hemispheres which were not functionally equivalent from the earliest age measured (2 months).

The proposed developmental model is based on two assumptions for determining hemispheric specialization. First, depending on the relative degree of development, new functions are assumed by the relatively more advanced or more rapidly developing hemisphere. Second, concurrent processing demands set conditions between hemispheres such that the simultaneous processing of different types of input within the same hemisphere is unlikely because of interference effects from competition for the same neural space. It is proposed, therefore, that because the right hemisphere is leading in development during the period of gestation when the predominant sound in the uterus is internally-generated noise, the right hemisphere becomes specialized for processing such sounds. In early gestation the fetal acoustic environment is characterized by maternal heartbeat and the pulsing of the fetal artery, both of which are rhythmical and organized but without profound dynamic change. During the latter part of gestation when maternal speech is more likely to be transmitted and salient, the left hemisphere of the fetus is undergoing a period of rapid and extended neuronal development. This, together with the involvement of the right hemisphere in the processing of fetal environmental sounds (which are still present as a component of the intrauterine acoustic environment) results in the left hemisphere becoming specialized for processing speech. In that females appear to develop earlier than males this model may account for some of the gender differences with regard to specialization which have been reported.

The processing requirements of early concurrent sensorimotor functioning have consequences not only for the development of specialization for speech but also for other functioning. We propose that the infant's left hemispheric specialization for speech, which is present at birth, together with limitations of the infant's visual system, have consequences for the development of a hemispheric specialization for processing faces and possibly for ultimately determining characteristic modes of cognitive functioning. Because the limited depth of field of the infant constrains visual functioning (Aslin, 1987), it is likely that if an adult signals his or her approach by speaking to the infant, there will be effective auditory stimulation prior to the face becoming an effective stimulus. Given the infant's left hemispheric specialization for processing speech in this situation the left hemisphere is relatively unavailable for the processing of the facial information when it does become available. Furthermore, although limited myelination tends to increase the spread of neural excitation within a hemisphere, this same paucity of myelination of callosal nerve fibers is likely to depress interhemispheric communication. The activation of the left hemisphere, then, is not likely to interfere with the function of the right hemisphere and leaves it available for the processing of the facial information.

The proposed model also predicts the type of processing which will develop in the cerebral hemispheres. As the infant's visual system shows poor contrast sensitivity to high and even middle frequency spatial information, the available information for the infant consists, primarily, of low spatial frequency information. While such information is adequate for the identification of individual faces (Sergent, 1986) the identification would be based on configuration (the location of features and the external contour of the face) rather than the characteristics of specific facial features for which high frequency spatial information would be required. This would then result in the infant developing a right hemispheric specialization for recognizing faces based upon their configuration. As the infant visual system develops there is an increase in the depth of field and an increase in the availability of middle and high frequency spatial information (Aslin, 1977). When the face of the parent is clearly visible to the infant from a distance, the temporal priority of voice in face-voice presentation changes with the face having increased salience. At this stage of development, the featural information contained in faces would be newly available, at the same time that configurational information would be concurrently available. In the proposed model, the right hemisphere would be engaged with the configurational information it had become specialized for processing, leaving the relatively unengaged left hemisphere available for processing the featural information. This could give rise to an analytic approach which is said to characterize the functioning of the left hemisphere. Ross-Kossak and Turkewitz (1986) have suggested a similar progression in the adults' familiarization with initially unfamiliar faces. That is, initially there is right-hemisphere advantage for processing faces in which the face is identified on the basis of its crude configurational characteristics. With increased familiarity with the face and subsequent processing, there is a left-hemisphere advantage and an analytic mode of processing followed by the integration of the two modes in the right hemisphere.

We believe that the proffered model of the development of hemispheric specialization is a useful framework for understanding development in general. It is likely that the emergence and modification of developmental functions are driven by continually changing requirements for dealing with increasingly complex concurrent tasks associated with changing sensorimotor capacities. These changes are based upon both linear and organizational ontogenetic influences. That is, quantitative changes in the development of the hemispheres in association with quantitative shifts in the developing organism's stimulus ecology may give rise to major organizational differences in the characteristics of the functioning of the two hemispheres. As noted at the outset, our position is that any explanation of development must not violate the requirement that the organism be at least adequately functioning at all stages of development and furthermore that structures and functions constructed in the service of one stage of development are available for utilization in new organizations and are capable of producing new functions when reorganized. In that speech motor production is primarily a left hemispheric function it is relevant to examine factors in development which contribute to the specialization of the left hemisphere. The exploration of such developmental factors will be facilitated by careful examination of changes in the ecology of the fetus, infant, and child, together with consideration of the sensory limitations in early development.

We have addressed two related themes; the consequences for development of the concurrent demands of changing circumstances and the use of methods entailing the concurrent elicitation of different behaviors to examine the underlying structure of behavioral and neural organization. Both of these themes require a consideration of the changing sensorimotor characteristics of the developing infant. By providing a framework and using examples from infancy we have tried to indicate ways in which sensorimotor limitations interact with a dynamically changing environment to promote new, emergent structures.

Acknowledgements

This work was supported in part by funds from the New York State Office of Mental Retardation and Developmental Disabilities. The authors would like to thank Judith M. Gardner and David Lewkowicz for their helpful comments on the chapter.

References

Abbs, J.H., Gracco, V.L., & Cole, K.J. (1984). Control of multimovement coordination: sensorimotor mechanisms in speech motor programming. *Journal of Motor Behavior*, **16**, 195-231.

Arvanitaki, A. (1942). Effects in an axon by the activity of a contiguous one. *Journal of Neurophysiology*, **5**, 89-108.

Aslin, R.N. (1987). Visual and auditory development in infancy. In J.D. Osofsky (Ed.), *Handbook of infant development* (pp. 5-98). New York: Wiley.

Best, C.T. (1988). The emergence of cerebral asymmetries in early human development: a literature review and a neuroembryological model. In D.L. Molfese & S.J. Segalowitz (Eds.), *Brain lateralization in children* (pp. 5-34). New York: The Guildford Press.

Bloom, L. (1990). Developments in expression: affect and speech. In N. Stein, B. Leventhal, & T. Trabasso (Eds.), *Psychological and biological approaches to emotion*. Hillsdale, NJ: Lawrence Erlbaum Associates.

Bloom, L., Beckwith, R., & Capatides, J. (1988). Developments in the expression of affect. *Infant Behavior and Development*, **11**, 169-186.

DeVito, J.A., Giattino, J., & Schon, T.D. (1975). *Articulation and voice: Effective communication*. Indianapolis, IN: Bobbs-Merrill.

Fifer, W.P., & Moon, C. (1988). Auditory experience in the fetus. In W.P. Smotherman & S.R. Robinson (Eds.), *Behavior of the fetus* (pp. 175-190). Telford, NJ: Caldwell.

Fletcher, S.G. (1973). Maturation of the speech mechanism. *Folia Phoniatrica*, **25**, 161-172.

Galaburda, A.M. (1984). Anatomical asymmetries. In N. Geschwind & A.M. Galaburda (Eds.), *Cerebral dominance: The biological foundations* (pp. 11-25). Cambridge, MA: Harvard University Press.

Hicks, R.E. (1975). Intrahemispheric response competition between vocal and unimanual performance in normal adult human males. *Journal of Comparative and Physiological Psychology*, **89**, 50-60.

Jacob, F. (1977). Evolution and tinkering. *Science*, **196**, 1161-1166.

Johnston, T. (1987). The persistence of dichotomies in the study of behavioral development. *Developmental Review*, **7**, 149-182.

Katz, B. & Schmitt, O.H. (1940). Electrical interaction between two adjacent nerve fibers. *Journal of Physiology*, **97**, 471-488.

Kelso, J.A.S., Tuller, B., Vatikiotis-Bateson, E., & Fowler, C.A. (1984). Functionally specific articulatory cooperation following jaw perturbations during speech: evidence for coordinative structures. *Journal of Experimental Psychology: Human Perception and Performance*, **10**, 812-832.

Kimura, D. (1973). Manual activity during speaking: I. Right handers. *Neuropsychologia*, 11, 45-50.

Kinsbourne, M., & Cook, J. (1971). General and lateralized effects of concurrent verbalization on a unimanual skill. *Quarterly Journal of Experimental Psychology*, **23**, 341-345.

Kinsbourne, M., & Hiscock, M. (1983). The normal and deviant development of function lateralization of the brain. In P. Mussen, M. Haith, & J. Campos (Eds.), *Handbook of child psychology* (pp. 157-280). New York: Wiley.

Lassen, N.A., & Roland, P.E. (1983). Localization of cognitive function with cerebral blood flow. In A. Kertesz (Ed.), *Localization in neuropsychology* (pp. 141-152). New York: Academic Press.

Lewkowicz, D.J., & Turkewitz, G. (1982). The influence of hemispheric specialization in sensory processing on reaching in infants: age and gender related effects. *Developmental Psychology*, **18**, 301-308.

Lieberman, P. (1975). The evolution of speech and language. In J.F. Kavanagh & J.E. Cutting (Eds.), *The role of speech in language* (pp. 83-106). Cambridge, MA: MIT Press.

Molfese, V.J. & Betz, J.C. (1987). Language and motor development in infancy: three views with neuropsychological implications. *Developmental Neuropsychology*, **3**, 255-275.

Oppenheim, R.W. (1984). Ontogenetic adaptations in neural development: toward a more 'ecological' developmental psychobiology. In H.F.R. Prechtl (Ed.), *Continuity of neural function from prenatal to postnatal life* (pp. 16-30). Philadelphia: Lippincott.

Ostry, D.J. & Cooke, J.D. (1987). Kinematic patterns in speech and limb movements. In E. Keller & M. Gopnik (Eds.), *Motor and sensory processes of language* (pp. 223-235). Hillsdale, NJ: Lawrence Erlbaum Associates.

Ostry, D.J., Keller, E. & Parush, A. (1983). Similarities in the control of the speech articulators and the limbs: kinematics of tongue dorsum movement in speech. *Journal of Experimental Psychology: Human Perception and Performance*, **9**, 622-636.

Oyama, S. (1985). *The ontogeny of information: Developmental systems and evolution*. Cambridge, England: Cambridge University Press.

Piaget, J. (1954). *The construction of reality in the child.* New York: Basic Books.

Purpura, D. (1969). Mechanisms of propagation: intracellular studies. In H.H. Jasper, A.A. Ward, & A. Pope (Eds.), *Basic mechanisms of the epilepsies* (pp. 441-451). London: Little Brown.

Ramsay, D.S. (1980a). Onset of unimanual handedness in infants. *Infant Behavior and Development*, **3**, 377-385.

Ramsay, D.S. (1980b). Beginnings of bimanual handedness and speech in infants. *Infant Behavior and Development*, **3**, 67-77.

Ramsay, D.S. (1983). Unimanual hand preference and duplicative syllable babbling in infants. In G. Young, C. Corter, S.J. Segalowitz, & S. Trehub (Eds.), *Manual specialization and the developing brain* (pp. 161-176). New York: Academic Press.

Ramsay, D.S. (1984). Onset of duplicative syllable babbling and unimanual handedness in infancy: evidence for developmental change in hemispheric specialization? *Developmental Psychology*, **20**, 64-71.

Rasminsky, M. (1981). Hyperexcitability of pathologically myelinated axons and positive symptoms in multiple sclerosis. In S.G. Waxman & J.M. Richie (Eds.), *Advances in neurology, Vol. 31: Demyelinating disease: basic and clinical electrophysiology* (pp. 289-297). New York: Raven Press.

Ross-Kossak, P. & Turkewitz, G. (1986). A micro and macro developmental view of the nature of changes in complex information processing: a consideration of the changes in hemispheric advantage during familiarization. In R. Bruyer (Ed.), *The neuropsychology of face perception and facial expression* (pp. 125-145). Hillsdale, NJ: Lawrence Erlbaum Associates.

Sergent, J. (1986). Structural processing of faces. In A.W. Young & H.D. Ellis (Eds.), *Handbook of research on face processing* (pp. 57-91). Amsterdam: Elsevier Science Publishing.

Thatcher, R.W., Walker, R.A. & Giudice, S. (1987). Human cerebral hemispheres develop at different rates and ages. *Science*, **236**, 1110-1113.

Thelen, E. (1990). Motor aspects of emergent speech. In N. Krasnegor (Ed.), *Biobehavioral foundations of language.* Hillsdale, NJ: Lawrence Erlbaum Associates.

Tuller, B., Kelso, J.A.S. & Harris, K.S. (1982). Interarticulator phasing as an index of temporal regularity in speech. *Journal of Experimental Psychology: Human Perception and Performance*, **8**, 460-472.

Turkewitz, G. (1988). A prenatal source for the development of hemispheric specialization. In D.L. Molfese & S.J. Segalowitz (Eds.), *Brain lateralization in children* (pp. 73-81). New York: The Guilford Press.

Turkewitz, G. (1990). Perinatal influences on the development of the hemispheric specialization and complex information processing. In M.J. Weiss & P.R. Zelazo (Eds.), *Newborn attention: Biological constraints and the influence of experience.* Norwood, NJ: Ablex.

Yakovlev, P.I. & Lecours, A.R. (1967). The myelogenetic cycles of regional maturation of the brain. In A. Minkowski (Ed.), *Regional development of the brain in early life* (pp. 3-70). Oxford, England: Blackwell Scientific Publications.

Cerebral Control of Speech and Limb Movements
G.E. Hammond (editor)

Chapter 21

IS TIME SHARING ASYMMETRY A VALID INDICATOR OF SPEECH LATERALIZATION? EVIDENCE FOR LEFT HANDERS

Merrill Hiscock
University of Houston

Marcel Kinsbourne
Shriver Center and Harvard Medical School

and

Adele Green
Youngstown State University

Numerous studies have shown that speaking disrupts concurrent right-hand more than left-hand performance in right-handers. This asymmetry of interference is commonly accepted as evidence of left lateralized speech control. Two early and three recent studies of left-handers have yielded the opposite asymmetry of interference. The earlier studies drew no sweeping theoretical conclusions. On the assumption that left-handers are rarely right lateralized for speech, the recent investigators concluded either that many left-handers have ipsilateral cortical control of hand movement or else that time-sharing asymmetries reflect manual preference rather than speech dominance. We review these recent studies of left-handers in detail and find that they do not convincingly support either manual preference or ipsilateral motor control, as against central interference. The nature and variability of their brain organization disqualify left-handers from serving as a reference group to validate any laterality paradigms, the dual-task paradigm included.

The Problem

Relatively little attention has been given to concurrent-task interference in left-handers, who are thought to have a less uniform pattern of left-hemisphere speech representation than right-handers (Rasmussen & Milner, 1975; Satz, 1980). Hicks (1975) reported more left than right interference (that is, a reversed pattern) for left-handers with familial sinistrality, and so did Parlow and Kinsbourne (1981) for left-handers whose handwriting posture was noninverted. In both studies the alternate subgroup of left-handers exhibited no significant asymmetry of interference. Recently, three studies have yielded an apparently more general reversed (left-greater-than-right) asymmetry of verbal-manual interference in left-handers (Orsini, Satz, Soper, & Light, 1985; Simon & Sussman, 1987; van Strien & Bouma, 1988). The authors have suggested that interference asymmetries reflect manual dominance rather than speech dominance (Orsini et al., 1985; van Strien & Bouma, 1988) or, alternatively, that movement of the left hand in left-handers is controlled by the ipsilateral (left) hemisphere (Simon & Sussman, 1987).

We shall examine the studies of left-handers to determine whether the evidence demands either of these conclusions. We shall even question whether the brain organization(s) of left-handers is well enough understood to justify using them for a validity check on any laterality paradigm, be it dual-task or any other. We shall briefly summarize the arguments for the interpretation of asymmetric verbal-manual interference, based on lateralized speech representation, to determine whether this concept is still viable.

Background

Since the early 1960s asymmetric performance on tests of dichotic listening (Kimura, 1961) and visual half-field perception (Bryden, 1964) has been used to infer the language lateralization of various normal and clinical populations. Subsequently, unimanual and bimanual (dichhaptic) methods have yielded converging evidence (Rudel, Denckla, & Spalten, 1974; Witelson, 1974).

Although these input laterality paradigms have yielded an immense amount of data, some conceptual and methodological problems have tempered their contributions to our understanding of hemispheric specialization. For example, asymmetry scores of individuals tend to be unstable over time (Blumstein, Goodglass, & Tartter, 1975; Teng, 1981) and laterality scores from different tests tend not to be highly correlated (Eling, 1983). Moreover, the proportion of normal, right-handed subjects who show the expected right-sided advantage for identification of linguistic stimuli is typically much lower than the proportion known from clinical studies to have left hemispheric language representation (Satz, 1975). But some investigators have successfully modified the standard paradigms so as to eliminate artifacts and to increase reliability and validity and more closely approximate the known distribution of lateralization *in right-handers* (Bryden, Munhall, & Allard, 1983; Geffen & Caudrey, 1981; Oscar-Berman, Rehbein, Porfert, & Goodglass, 1978; Schmuller & Goodman, 1979; Wexler & Halwes, 1983). Another paradigm now receiving critical attention is the concurrent-task (time-sharing) method of Kinsbourne and Cook (1971).

Concurrent-task Performance as a Laterality Measure

The multitask paradigm is an important research method in the study of attention (Posner, 1982), and in human factors research (Alluisi, 1967). Kinsbourne and Cook's (1971) original contribution was their finding (in right-handers) that the interaction between two concurrent tasks -- one manual, the other vocal -- differed according to the hand performing the manual task. Specifically, speaking disrupted right-hand but not left-hand performance. Kinsbourne and Cook had predicted this asymmetric effect, based on the differential specialization of the cerebral hemispheres. They proposed that, in the case of concurrent speaking and right-hand performance, "mutual interference between main and secondary task in the left cerebral hemisphere ... sets up an overall decrement in performance on [the right] side" (Kinsbourne & Cook, 1971, p. 345). Numerous subsequent studies have confirmed that speech disrupts concurrent right-hand activity more than left-hand activity (see Kinsbourne & Hiscock, 1983, for a review) and have supported the suggested mechanism, based on Kinsbourne and Hicks' (1978) functional cerebral distance model (Urbanczyk, Angel, & Kennelly, 1988).

Although the details of the link between asymmetric interference and left-hemispheric speech representation remains to be established, there is considerable indirect evidence that such a link exists. Right-greater-than-left asymmetry of interference is found only when verbal tasks are used. Nonverbal tasks concurrent with finger tapping either disrupt left-hand performance more than right (Dalby, 1980; Hatta & Minagawa, 1982; Hellige & Longstreth, 1981; Kee, Bathurst, & Hellige, 1984; McFarland & Ashton, 1975, 1978b, 1978c; Piazza, 1977) or else disrupt the left and right hands about equally (Bowers, Heilman, Satz, & Altman, 1978; Hiscock, Antoniuk, Prisciak, & von Hessert, 1985; McFarland & Ashton, 1978a; White & Kinsbourne, 1980). There is also evidence that asymmetries are related to dichotic listening asymmetries (McFarland & Geffen, 1982; Hellige, Bloch, & Taylor, 1988). Further evidence that asymmetrical interference in manual performance reflects central rather than peripheral (e.g. handedness) factors derives from a verbal-manual interference study by Kee, Bathurst, & Hellige (1983). Among strongly right-handed subjects they found a greater asymmetry of interference in those who did not have sinistral relatives. Corresponding findings have been reported for dichotic and hemifield asymmetry (e.g., Hannay & Malone, 1976; McKeever & VanDeventer, 1977).

Concurrent-task Interference in Left-handers

Insofar as left-handers are heterogeneous with respect to cerebral speech representation (Rasmussen & Milner, 1975; Satz, 1980), one would expect on the average to find little lateralization of interference between speaking and manual performance in a sample of left-handers. The evidence available prior to 1985 did, in fact, suggest comparable left- and right-hand interference among left-handers (Hicks, 1975; Lomas & Kimura, 1976; Sussman, 1982; Parlow & Kinsbourne, 1981). No studies have reported greater right than left interference in left-handers (except for a questionable subgroup that, though preferring the left hand, was more dextrous with the right -- unpublished studies from their laboratory cited by Hellige & Kee, 1990). But some differences among subgroups have been reported. Hicks (1975) found differential effects for left-handed males depending on whether they had a first-degree relative who was left-handed. For the nine left-handed subjects with familial sinistrality (FS+), speaking disrupted the performance of the left hand more than that of the right hand. The 13 left-handers without familial sinistrality (FS-) showed slightly more right-hand interference. Using a larger sample, Parlow and Kinsbourne (1981) found no asymmetry for 34 left-handers who used inverted hand posture for writing, but reverse asymmetry (greater left than right interference) for 39 left-handed noninverters. Left-handed sample sizes were small in the two other studies. Lomas & Kimura (1976) tested 12 males and 12 females and Sussman (1982) three males and seven females. Neither study yielded asymmetric interference.

The absence of lateralized interference in these small samples of left-handers can be reconciled quite readily with clinically-based estimates of the incidence of left- and right-sided speech representation in left-handed adults. Even if the true incidence of left-sided speech in left-handers is as high as 70% (Rasmussen & Milner, 1975), one should not expect statistically significant interference *asymmetry* in a random sample of 10 or 20 left-handers. But one would expect significant right-greater-than-left asymmetry in larger samples of left-handers, which afford greater statistical power. The magnitude of the asymmetry should be reduced, relative to right-handers, but there should be asymmetric interference nonetheless. Instead, the opposite asymmetry, such that speaking disrupts left-hand performance significantly more than right-hand performance, was obtained in three larger-scale studies of left-handers (Orsini et al., 1985; Simon & Sussman, 1987; van Strien & Bouma, 1988). If the findings are accepted at face value, then either the concurrent-task paradigm is not a valid indicator of cerebral speech dominance, or else the neural organization of left-handers in the general population deviates markedly from that posited by Rasmussen and Milner (1975) on the basis of their brain-damaged population.

The Orsini, Satz, Soper, and Light (1985) Study

Orsini et al. (1985) used two dual tasks as well as dichotic listening in their investigation of familial sinistrality effects on the laterality of 215 right-handed and 257 left-handed adults. Subjects performed a word fluency test while finger tapping with either the left or right hand, and they read silently while tapping. Even though (contrary to Hicks, 1975) familial sinistrality failed to influence the asymmetry from either the dichotic listening or the dual task procedures, there was a significant difference on each test between right- and left-handers. On dichotic listening, there was, as expected, a stronger right-ear advantage (REA) for right-handers than for left-handers. Nearly 89% of the right-handers and about 75% of the left-handers showed a REA. But on the dual tasks, right-handers showed a significant right-greater-than-left asymmetry of interference and left-handers showed a significant left-greater-than-right asymmetry. One way of characterizing these data is that preferred hand performance was disrupted more than nonpreferred hand performance. Right-greater-than-left interference was observed in 62.8% of right-handers and 43.6% of left-handers on the tapping-and-speaking test and in 57.2% of right-handers and 42.8% of left-handers on the tapping-and-reading test.

According to data tabulated by Orsini et al., speaking slowed concurrent finger tapping much more than silent reading did (approximately 11% versus 2%). Also, there was a significant sex difference for speaking-and-tapping that was absent for reading-and-tapping. Although speaking tended to interfere with the preferred hand more than the nonpreferred hand irrespective of the subject's handedness, this effect was seen more often in male right-handers than in male left-handers or females.

The Simon and Sussman (1987) Study

In the Simon and Sussman study, left- and right-hand finger tapping was conjoined with each of three speech tasks -- describing a picture, reading aloud, speaking extemporaneously -- and the data were averaged across tasks. Of the 260 normal subjects, 140 were right-handed and 120 were left-handed. Each handedness group comprised equal numbers of males and females and equal numbers of subjects with and without familial sinistrality. The finding of primary interest was a significant handedness by hand interaction, which reflected greater slowing of the preferred hand than the nonpreferred hand during the concurrent-task conditions. As in the Orsini et al. study, this asymmetry of interference did not vary with familial sinistrality. Although females showed significantly greater interference than males in the concurrent-task conditions, this sex difference was additive across the left and right hands. The overall magnitude of interference was 5.4%, which falls between the 2% interference for silent reading and the 11% interference for speaking in the Orsini et al. (1985) study. The proportion of right- and left-handers showing different interference patterns was not reported by Simon and Sussman, but the dissertation from which their data were obtained (Simon, 1984) indicates that 66.4% of right-handers and 37.5% of left-handers showed right-greater-than-left interference. This difference is somewhat more marked than the comparable differences reported by Orsini et al.

Though they closely resemble those of Orsini et al., the Simon and Sussman findings are qualified by three ancillary results. First, among left-handers, only males showed the left-greater-than-right pattern of interference. Interference was approximately symmetric in left-handed females. The second qualification pertains to speed of finger tapping in the control (single-task) conditions. Simon and Sussman identified the subjects whose single-task tapping speed placed them in the top or bottom quartile of their respective sex x handedness cell. The 66 fast tappers (irrespective of handedness) showed significantly greater right-hand interference than left-hand interference, whereas the 66 slow tappers tended to show the opposite asymmetry. Finally, interference asymmetries in both right and left-handers depended on the degree to which tapping was asymmetric in the control (single-task) conditions. Subjects with relatively symmetric single-task tapping failed to show significant asymmetry of interference in the concurrent-task conditions. Right-handers with the most asymmetric single-task tapping showed significant right-greater-than-left interference in concurrent-task tapping, and left-handers with the most asymmetric single-task tapping showed significant left-greater-than-right interference in concurrent-task tapping.

The van Strien and Bouma (1988) Study

In the first of two experiments, van Strien and Bouma examined the effects of three vocal tasks -- repetition, word fluency, and reading aloud -- on repetitive and sequential finger tapping in right-handed adults. The mean percentage of disruption in tapping appears to be under 6.5% for each combination of vocal and manual task. Irrespective of the vocal task being performed, repetitive tapping with the right hand was slowed more than repetitive tapping with the left hand. In contrast, sequential finger tapping revealed no lateralized effects.

The second experiment was identical to the first except that subjects were left-handed and the vocal repetition task was omitted. The 60 left-handers in this experiment were grouped according to sex, familial handedness and writing posture (inverted versus noninverted). Analysis of variance for repetitive finger tapping showed that the vocal tasks slowed the left hand significantly more than the right. This left-greater-than-right asymmetry characterized three of the four sex by hand posture cells, with only the male inverters failing to show a significant degree of asymmetry (in partial confirmation of Parlow & Kinsbourne, 1981). As in Experiment 1, sequential finger tapping failed to show any asymmetry of interference.

FS+ left-handed males tapped faster than FS+ left-handed females in both control and concurrent-task conditions. Thus, although van Strien and Bouma found sex differences among their left-handed subjects, these sex differences diverge from those reported by Orsini et al. (1985) as well as from those reported by Simon and Sussman (1987).

Averaged across vocal tasks, the overall reduction in left-handers' rate of repetitive tapping in the concurrent-task conditions was 5.6%, a figure very similar to that reported by Simon and Sussman (1987). The van Strien and Bouma report does not indicate the proportion of left-handed subjects who showed left-greater-than-right interference. The laterality effect is greater in magnitude (r^2=.23) than the comparable effect reported by Simon and Sussman (r^2=.15) and appreciably greater than the effects reported by Orsini et al. (r^2=.03), but the difference might be attributable to van Strien and Bouma's use of raw scores rather than proportional change scores. Without an adjustment for differences between the hands in single-task tapping rate, the interference asymmetry in van Strien and Bouma's study may be augmented by a range restriction, i.e., the relatively poor performance of the right hand in the single-task condition may leave little room for further deterioration (see Hiscock, 1982).

When van Strien and Bouma examined intertask interference in the 'opposite direction', i.e., the effect of finger tapping on verbal fluency, they found no lateralized effect. The number of words produced during episodes of right-hand tapping did not differ significantly from the number during left-hand tapping. For both right- and left-handers, however, sequential tapping disrupted verbal fluency more than did repetitive tapping.

In addition to the dual tasks, the 60 left-handers in Experiment 2 were administered a dichotic listening test consisting of 80 pairs of digit names presented in sets of four pairs each. It yielded a significant right-ear advantage (REA) that was comparable to the REA obtained in right-handers on the same test. However, the outcome for left-handers was qualified by the absence of a significant ear asymmetry in FS+ inverted writers.

Interpreting the Evidence from Left-handers

The results from these three recent studies of left-handers were construed in two fundamentally different ways. One interpretation is Orsini et al.'s suggestion that "some factor or factors more closely related to manual dominance than language may be involved in the observed dual task result" (p. 230). A similar explanation is offered by van Strien and Bouma (1988), with the additional speculation that "the motor areas for the dominant hand may occupy more space than those for the nondominant hand and hence have a greater chance to interfere with the motor areas for speech" (p. 153). But according to Simon and Sussman (1985), "the greater left-than-right hand concurrent task interference in sinistrals might possibly be due to left hemisphere ipsilateral involvement in control of the left hand tapping" (p. 566). It is important to distinguish between these alternative explanations as they have dissimilar implications for the validity of the concurrent-task paradigm as a measure of speech lateralization. The Orsini et al. and van Strien and Bouma explanations imply that the concurrent-task paradigm may not indicate speech lateralization in either right-or left-handers, whereas the Simon and Sussman explanation implies that the paradigm does indicate speech lateralization in right-handers and left-handers also, but by a different mechanism in the latter. This mechanism is implausible. If hemispheric control of manual activity were ipsilateral in left-handers, this would be apparent in the relationship between side of brain injury and side of paralysis in such diseases as stroke. Such an observation has never been reported, and the proposed relationship can be rejected out of hand on neurological grounds.

Left-handers and Other Laterality Paradigms

Suppose we apply the test of validity by sinistral outcome to that most time-honored laterality paradigm, dichotic listening. What do we conclude from the following? *Left-handers overall* show a right-ear advantage (Fennell, Bowers, & Satz, 1977; Satz, Achenbach, & Fennell, 1967; Satz, Achenbach, Pattishall, & Fennell, 1965) or a left-ear advantage (Conrad, J.E. Obrzut, & Boliek, 1990; Hugdahl & Andersson, 1984; J.E. Obrzut, Boliek, & A. Obrzut, 1986). *Subgrouping by strength of handedness* yields a left advantage for weak and right advantage for strong left-handedness (Dee, 1971), or the exact opposite (Knox & Boone, 1970). *Subgrouping by familial sinistrality* yields a variety of outcomes. For FS-, there is either a right-ear advantage (Lake & Bryden, 1976; Lishman & McMeekan, 1977; Zurif & Bryden, 1969) or no asymmetry (J. Demarest & L. Demarest, 1980; L. Demarest & J. Demarest, 1981; Higgenbottam, 1973; McKeever & VanDeventer, 1977); for FS+, there may be a right-ear advantage (Lake & Bryden, 1976), reduced right-ear advantage (Lishman & McMeekan, 1977), no asymmetry (Higgenbottam, 1973; Zurif & Bryden, 1969), or left-ear advantage (L. Demarest & J. Demarest, 1981). Based on this confusion, we would have to dismiss the dichotic listening paradigm in short order. Yet no one has made this preposterous suggestion for dichotic listening. The situation is just as chaotic for visual-half field viewing (J.L. Bradshaw, 1980) and dichhaptic identification (Nilsson, Glencross, & Geffen, 1980) in left-handers.

Whereas the standard laterality paradigms have successfully distinguished between task (right versus left hemispheric) and subject (personal and familial handedness) variables, they have in general not been successful in reflecting the proportionate incidence of the several existing patterns of brain lateralization (Satz, 1975). To expect dual-task outcomes to map *quantitatively* on to the relative prevalence of left, right and bilateral speech representation in left-handers is unreasonable, given that other laterality tasks generally do not do so. Much remains to be learned about the relationship between interference patterns and sinistral brain organization.

We now revert to the three studies under review. Are they representative of concurrent-task laterality studies? Can their results be generalized to other concurrent-task procedures? Or might idiosyncratic aspects of these studies have led to spurious outcomes?

Methodological Issues

Measurement of Manual-to-Nonmanual Interference

Additional information might have been helpful in interpreting the recent findings. Neither Orsini et al. (1985) nor Simon and Sussman (1987) ascertained whether interference occurred in the reverse direction, i.e., the manual-to-nonmanual direction. Did finger tapping interfere with speaking or reading and, if so, was tapping by one hand more disruptive than tapping with the other hand? Did interference asymmetries in the manual-to-nonmanual direction differ between right-and left-handers? Without this information, it is difficult to interpret interference asymmetries in the nonmanual-to-manual directions. Although van Strien and Bouma (1988) measured word production in the concurrent-task conditions involving finger tapping and verbal fluency, the lack of a single-task verbal fluency condition limits the usefulness of this information.

In the absence of information about manual-to-nonmanual interference, it is impossible to rule out a differential trade-off such that the greater reduction in dominant hand tapping speed is matched by greater disruption of verbal performance when tapping is being performed by the nondominant hand. Such a trade-off appears in the data of Crossley and Hiscock (1989) who required right-handed adults of different age levels to perform maze tasks while tapping with either the left or right hand. Contrary to expectations, performing the maze tasks slowed right-hand tapping more than left-hand tapping. However, performance on the maze tasks was more severely disrupted by left-hand tapping. An outcome such as this undermines conclusions about the laterality of interference based on finger tapping data alone. The Orsini et al., Simon and Sussman, and van Strien and Bouma studies could, to an unknown extent, be misrepresenting the relative severity of right- versus left-hemisphere interference in their subjects.

Task Emphasis

All three studies of left-handers lack a task emphasis manipulation, such that finger tapping is emphasized on some trials and vocal performance on others. Without this manipulation, the subject is given complete latitude to 'protect' one task or the other and to change at any time the priority given to each task. When performance on only the tapping task is measured, there is no way of knowing whether decreased tapping speed represents increased interference or merely a shift of attention toward the nonmanual task (Navon & Gopher, 1979). Greater interference in the dominant hand than the nondominant hand could represent a tendency to allocate more attention in the dual-task situation to the nondominant hand. Available evidence from right-handers suggests that interference asymmetries, as reflected in tapping speed, are relatively constant irrespective of which task is emphasized (e.g., Hiscock, 1982; Hiscock, Cheesman, Inch, Chipuer, & Graff, 1989), but the effect of task emphasis manipulations on interference asymmetries in left-handers is unknown.

Magnitude of Interference

Manipulating task emphasis usually changes the amount of intertask interference by only a few percentage points (e.g., Hiscock et al., 1989). Consequently, a task emphasis manipulation is unlikely to compensate entirely for choosing tasks that yield too little interference. If rate of tapping is used to infer lateralized effects, it is possible that a reliable right-greater-than-left effect for verbal tasks in left-handers can be observed only with an effortful task that substantially disrupts concurrent manual activity. Theoretically, the imbalance in hemispheric activation varies with the difficulty of the verbal task. Thus, if a left-handed person (left lateralized for language) performs a verbal task while tapping with the right hand, there should be some threshold level of verbal task difficulty, beyond which left hemispheric capacity is exceeded and the performance of the right hand should begin to deteriorate more rapidly than the performance of the left hand. As we have pointed out, the overall magnitude of interference (i.e., slowing of tapping) in the three studies of left-handers ranged from approximately 2% to 11%. Although this range is typical of the interference obtained in studies of right-handed adults (e.g., Hellige & Longstreth, 1981; Hiscock et al., 1989), it nonetheless may be suboptimal for the purpose of demonstrating interference asymmetries. Verbal tasks that produce high levels of interference (15% or more) may provide more reliable and valid measures of speech lateralization in right-handers (Green, Schweda-Nicholson, Vaid, & White, 1989a).

At low levels of interference, asymmetries may depend on a differential reduction of less than a single tap. For instance, Lomas and Kimura (1976), studying right-handed adults, reported that speaking reduced the number of right-hand taps by 2.61 and the number of left-hand taps by 2.25 over an interval of 10 sec. Thus, the rate-reduction scores for the two hands differed by a statistically nonsignificant 0.36 taps. Especially when the tapping apparatus or scoring procedure is imprecise, a small difference between hands may not be detected reliably (Green & Weller, 1989). Low interference levels would be expected to diminish the reliability of measurement and thus decrease the likelihood of finding significant asymmetry. Green et al. (1989b) found a shadowing task to produce significantly less overall disruption of finger tapping than did a paraphrasing task. Accordingly, only the paraphrasing task yielded lateralized interference scores with satisfactory retest reliability.

Poor reliability cannot account for the reported differences in asymmetry between left-and right-handers, but it could account for the relatively small proportion of right-handers who show the expected asymmetry. As we previously noted, the silent reading task of Orsini et al. (1985) yielded right-greater-than-left asymmetry in only 57.2% of right-handers. The overall level of interference, irrespective of hand, was 2%. In contrast, Hiscock (1982), who achieved an overall interference level of 28.8% by requiring right-handed children to recite a tongue-twister while engaging in finger tapping, reported that 85.5% of subjects showed right-greater-than-left interference. Similarly Green (1986) obtained an overall interference level of 21.5% in adult males by conjoining finger tapping with object naming and picture description tasks. Of 24 right-handed monolingual English speakers in this study, 87.5% showed a right-greater-than-left asymmetry of interference. Green et al. (1989b), using verbal tasks that yielded interference levels of 11.4 and 17.4%, obtained right-greater-than-left interference in 79% of their monolingual subjects.

Although the dramatic difference between Orsini et al. (1985) and other studies with respect to the incidence of right-greater-than-left asymmetry might be attributed to the greater reliability of measurement at higher interference levels, it is also possible that different mechanisms operate at different levels of interference. For instance, range effects -- consequences of a difference between hands in single-task tapping rate -- may be less prominent at higher levels of interference. Hiscock (1982), using regression analyses to relate left-and right-hand interference to baseline tapping rate with the respective hand, found that less than 0.2% of the variance associated with either left- or right-hand interference was attributable to single-task tapping rate. In contrast, Simon and Sussman (1987) reported that hand differences in single-task tapping rate exerted a significant influence on the asymmetry of interference. The overall level of interference in the Simon and Sussman study was 5.4%, as compared with 28.8% in the Hiscock study.

Choice of Manual Task and Dependent Variable

In each of the three recent studies of left-handers, interference was manifested as a change in the rate of finger tapping. Although reasonable, this manual task and dependent variable were not the only possible choices. In the words of Hiscock et al. (1989):

> Subjects have been told to tap as fast as possible, as regularly as possible, or as fast and regularly as possible. They have tapped a single key repetitively, two keys in alternation, or three or more keys in sequence. Both the rate and variability of tapping have been used as dependent variables. This lack of standardization has been identified as a problem (Green & Vaid, 1986; Hiscock, 1986), but there is almost no empirical basis for choosing one procedure over another (p. 2).

One can only speculate as to whether other choices of task and dependent variable might have yielded different results for left-handers.

We do know that, in some instances, concurrent-task asymmetries for right-handers have been influenced markedly by varying the tapping task (Hicks, G.J. Bradshaw, Kinsbourne, & Feigin, 1978; Lomas & Kimura, 1976), the dependent variable (Hiscock & Chipuer, 1986; Kee, Morris, Bathurst, & Hellige, 1986), or both the task and the dependent variable (McFarland & Ashton, 1978c). Hiscock and Chipuer (1986) argued that rate reduction and variability increments reflect independent mechanisms of concurrent-task interference.

The most direct evidence regarding the importance of the dependent variable in studies of left-handers comes from a recent experiment by Hiscock and Inch (1990) in which 48 left-handed adults engaged in speeded or regularly paced finger tapping while reading aloud from a textbook. Both the speed and variability of finger tapping were measured. As expected, concurrent reading decreased the rate of speeded tapping and increased the variability of paced tapping. However, the two dependent variables yielded *opposite* asymmetries. Consistent with other findings for left-handers (Orsini et al., 1985; Simon & Sussman, 1987; van Strien & Bouma, 1988), reading reduced tapping speed in the left hand more than in the right hand. Reading also increased the variability of tapping, but in the right hand more than the left. This striking dissociation between asymmetry of rate change and asymmetry of variability change implies that, at least in left-handers, it is inadvisable to rely on either dependent variable as the sole indicator of asymmetric interference.

Order Effects

Some investigators have noted that the magnitude of interference asymmetries is significantly smaller for right-handed subjects tested initially with the left hand than for subjects tested initially with the right hand (Hicks, Provenzano, & Rybstein, 1975; Hiscock & Kinsbourne, 1978, 1980). Presumably this finding reflects transfer of training such that the second hand to be tested in the concurrent-task situation benefits from the practice gained by the first hand. The importance of testing order is illustrated by data from Green's (1986) 24 right-handed monolingual anglophones, 16 of whom had right-hand interference scores that exceeded left-hand scores by more than 3 percentage points when finger tapping was conjoined with object naming and picture description tasks. Of the eight subjects whose left-and right-hand scores differed by less than three percentage points, seven had performed left-hand tapping first.

Clearly, an order effect such as that found in Green's (1986) data is capable not only of reducing but also of amplifying or reversing asymmetries of interference. Since the order of left- and right-hand testing was counterbalanced across subjects in each of the recent studies of left-handers, one can appeal to order effects as an explanation for the left-greater-than-right asymmetry of interference only if transfer of training is itself asymmetric. This appears to be so. Parlow and Kinsbourne (1989) found asymmetry in intermanual transfer during acquisition of a motor skill (inverted and reversed writing). This asymmetry interacted with hand preference.

Conclusions

In spite of methodological shortcomings in the three recent studies of left-handers, their basic finding is unlikely to be attributable to methodological artifact. The primary issue is not one of reproducibility but of generality. Across studies, greater left interference is frequent but far from invariable. Until left-handers are studied with other combinations of tasks and other dependent variables, and until the role of subject factors such as sex and familial handedness is clarified, left-greater-than-right interference in left-handers should not be over-interpreted. To attribute the interference pattern to as simple and static a subject variable as hand preference is certainly inadequate and probably misconceived.

Additional concurrent-task studies of left-handers are needed to determine the generality of left-greater-than-right interference across tasks and dependent variables, and to isolate the mechanism(s) of lateralized interference in left-handers. Does asymmetric interference depend on asymmetric manual skill in the single-task situation, as suggested by the data of Simon and Sussman (1987)? Is its extent predictable from the baseline initial value? (Apparently not, according to Harrison, 1990.) Are males more likely than females to show asymmetric interference, as found by Orsini et al. (1985) and Simon and Sussman (1987)? Is the effect of nonverbal tasks on concurrent-task interference patterns in left-handers also mirror image to their effect in right-handers, i.e., more interference with nonpreferred hand performance? Do left-handers show a right-greater-than-left pattern of interference if interference is defined in terms of increased variability rather than decreased speed (Hiscock & Inch, 1990)?

In the cognitive psychological literature, interference between concurrently performed tasks is often ascribed to competition for a finite supply of some hypothetical nonspecific capacity or resource (Holtzman & Gazzaniga, 1982; Norman & Bobrow, 1985), a concept that has been described as vacuous (Navon, 1984). Be that as it may, verbal-manual interference seems to result not from a shortage of general capacity but from response competition or cross-talk between two unrelated responses (Kinsbourne & Hicks, 1978; Urbanczyk, Angel, & Kennelly, 1988). It is very difficult to perform two simultaneous tasks that require responses conforming to different rhythms (Hiscock & Chipuer, 1986; Klapp, 1979;

Peters, 1977; Thornton & Peters, 1982). Subjects attempt to reconcile temporally disparate activities by performing both at the same pace or with the same rhythm (e.g., Hiscock, 1982; Hiscock & Chipuer, 1986; Hughes & Sussman, 1983). Hiscock et al. (1989), for instance, found that speaking (reading aloud) increased the rate of simultaneous slow tapping and decreased the rate of simultaneous fast tapping. In a sample of right-handed adults, both the acceleration of slow tapping and the deceleration of fast tapping were significantly more pronounced in the right hand. These finding, along with similar findings for left-handers (Hiscock & Inch, 1990), suggest that the temporal linkage between speaking and hand movement is stronger in the dominant hand than in the nondominant hand. Thus, interference between speaking and finger tapping may be viewed as a consequence of attempting to synchronize the two activities. If so, interference asymmetries may be attributable to a learned association between speaking and hand movement (i.e., writing). These 'synchronization' asymmetries may mask interference based on intrahemispheric cross-talk, which might be revealed more clearly using tasks that do not require speaking.

Whatever mechanisms underlie asymmetric time sharing, there is an empirical approach that may be informative. We noted that the distribution of interference asymmetries, as reported by Orsini et al. (1985) and by Simon (1984), deviated substantially from the expected distributions. In particular, far too few right-handers showed the expected right-greater-than-left pattern, and this discrepancy made the data for left-handers especially difficult to interpret. As Green (1986) and Green et al. (1989b) showed, it is possible to create a concurrent-task situation in which a high percentage of right-handers show the expected asymmetry of interference. If this combination of tasks were used with left-handers, the resultant distribution of asymmetry scores might be less ambiguous. One could go one step further and rank verbal tasks according to proportion of right-handers who show a right-greater-than-left asymmetry pattern. If the tasks that yield the highest incidence of right-greater-than-left asymmetry in right-handers also yield the highest incidence of the reverse asymmetry in left-handers, then an explanation in terms of manual dominance would be supported. Alternatively, if such tasks yield little asymmetry in left-handers, one could argue that speech lateralization at least contributes to the outcome.

The recent attention to left-handers should not detract from findings that support the validity of concurrent-task interference as an index of speech lateralization in right-handers. As we noted previously, nonverbal activities disrupt the left hand more than the right (Dalby, 1980; Hatta & Minagawa, 1982; Hellige & Longstreth, 1981; Hillis & Hiscock, 1989; Kee et al., 1984; McFarland & Ashton, 1975, 1978b, 1978c; Piazza, 1977) or disrupt the left and right hands equally (Bowers et al., 1978; Hiscock et al., 1985; McFarland & Ashton, 1978a; White & Kinsbourne, 1980). These findings provide strong support for the conclusion that the right-greater-than-left asymmetries obtained with verbal tasks derive from left hemispheric representation of language.

Interpretation of verbal-manual interference asymmetries in terms of speech lateralization is supported by recent findings of Hellige et al. (1988), who tested 120 right-handed adults on five laterality tasks, two of which were dual tasks entailing the conjunction of finger tapping with syllable repetition and anagram solving, respectively. Of the intercorrelations among laterality indices for the different tasks (with data from the dual tasks pooled), the only significant correlation was .27 between dichotic listening asymmetry and concurrent-task asymmetry. Stronger REAs were associated with larger right-greater-than-left interference asymmetries. There was a more dramatic relationship between auditory and concurrent-task laterality at the extreme ends of the dichotic listening distribution. The ten subjects with the largest REAs in dichotic listening showed a right-greater-than-left difference in concurrent-task interference of six percentage points, whereas the subjects with the largest left-ear advantages (LEA) showed a left-greater-than-right difference in interference of nearly five percentage points. The difference between groups in laterality of interference was statistically significant. The 98 subjects with ear difference scores that fell between those extremes showed a right-greater-than-left difference in concurrent-task interference of approximately two percentage points. Insofar as all 120 subjects were right-handed, these findings cannot be attributed to manual dominance effects.

The question posed in the title of this paper, i.e., whether concurrent-task asymmetry is a valid index of speech lateralization, must be addressed separately for right- and left-handers. For the former, its validity is as solidly based as that of the earlier input laterality paradigms, dichotic listening and hemifield viewing. For left-handers, the findings of Orsini et al. (1985), Simon and Sussman (1987), and van Strien and Bouma (1988) argue that concurrent-task asymmetry is not always a valid index of speech lateralization. But this is not new. McFarland and Geffen (1982) tested interference in seven subjects known to be right-hemisphere lateralized for language based on their dichotic monitoring test, which had previously been validated against speech lateralization determined directly by intracarotid amytal injection (Geffen & Caudrey, 1981). They found bilaterally symmetrical, not greater left-sided, interference. Left-handers may be unstable with respect to which hemisphere they use for verbal tasks, or alternatively, their choice of hemisphere may not be domain specific (verbal versus nonverbal), but task-specific within a domain. The dual-task interference paradigm is one of several methodologies that hold promise for clarifying hemisphere utilization in left-handers.

The issue is further complicated by highly contradictory models of language representation in the brains of left-handers (cf. Carter, Hohenegger, & Satz, 1980; Rasmussen & Milner, 1975). With clinically-based estimates of exclusive left-hemispheric language representation in left-handers ranging from 24% to 70%, it is difficult to specify the distribution of dual-task interference asymmetries that one would expect to observe in a sample of left-handers. More serious still, if the meta-analysis of Carter et al. (1980) is correct in its conclusion that in excess of two-thirds of left-handers have bilateral speech representation, then no viable prediction as to side of interference between verbal and manual behavior can be made. This is because in many bilateralized sinistrals, the two hemispheres subserve different verbal behaviors varying between individuals (Rasmussen & Milner, 1975), and the side of maximum interference might depend on the specific verbal task that is being performed.

In summary, the findings of Orsini et al., van Strien and Bouma, and Simon and Sussman can be considered to be steps toward the elucidation of brain organization in sinistrals. But they fail to contribute to an appraisal of the validity of the dual-task paradigm in lateralizing cognitive processes in the right-handed majority.

References

Alluisi, E.A. (1967). Methodology in the use of synthetic tasks to assess complex performance. *Human Factors*, **9**, 375-384.

Blumstein, S., Goodglass, H., & Tartter, V. (1975). The reliability of ear advantage in dichotic listening. *Brain and Language*, **2**, 226-236.

Bowers, D., Heilman, K.M., Satz, P., & Altman, A. 1978). Simultaneous performance on verbal, nonverbal and motor tasks by right-handed adults. *Cortex*, **14**, 540-556.

Bradshaw, J.L. (1980). Right-hemisphere language: familial and nonfamilial sinistrals, cognitive deficits and writing hand position in sinistrals, and concrete-abstract, imageable-nonimageable dimensions in word recognition. A review of interrelated issues. *Brain and Language*, **10**, 172-188.

Bryden, M.P. (1964). Tachistoscopic recognition and cerebral dominance. *Perceptual and Motor Skills*, **19**, 686.

Bryden, M.P., Munhall, K., & Allard, F. (1983). Attentional biases and the right-ear effect in dichotic listening. *Brain and Language*, **18**, 236-248.

Carter, R.L., Hohenegger, M., & Satz, P. (1980). Handedness and aphasia: an inferential method for determining the mode of cerebral speech specialization. *Neuropsychologia*, **18**, 569-574.

Conrad, P.F., Obrzut, J.E., & Boliek, C.A. (1990). Verbal and nonverbal auditory processing among left- and right-handed good readers and reading disabled children. *Neuropsychologia*.

Crossley, M., & Hiscock, M. (1989). Age-related changes in the concurrent-task performance of normal adults [Abstract]. *Journal of Clinical and Experimental Neuropsychology*, **11**, 71.

Dalby, J.T. (1980). Hemispheric timesharing: verbal and spatial loading with concurrent unimanual activity. *Cortex*, **16**, 567-573.

Dee, H.L. (1971). Auditory asymmetry and strength of manual preference. *Cortex*, **7**, 236-245.

Demarest, J., & Demarest, L. (1980). Auditory asymmetry and strength of manual preference reexamined. *International Journal of Neuroscience*, **9**, 111-124.

Demarest, L., & Demarest, J. (1981). The interaction of handedness, familial sinistrality and sex on the performance of a dichotic listening task. *International Journal of Neuroscience*, **14**, 7-13.

Eling, P. (1983). Comparing different measures of laterality: do they relate to a single mechanism? *Journal of Clinical Neuropsychology*, **5**, 135-147.

Fennell, E.B., Bowers, D., & Satz, P. (1977). Within-modal and cross-modal reliabilities of two laterality tests among left handers. *Perceptual and Motor Skills*, **45**, 451-456.

Geffen, G., & Caudrey, D. (1981). Reliability and validity of the dichotic monitoring test for language laterality. *Neuropsychologia*, **19**, 413-423.

Green, A. (1986). A time sharing cross-sectional study of monolinguals and bilinguals at different levels of second language acquisition. *Brain and Cognition*, **5**, 477-497.

Green, A., Schweda-Nicholson, N. Vaid, J., & White, N. (1989a). Hemispheric involvement in shadowing vs. interpreting: a time-sharing study of simultaneous interpreters and bilingual/monolingual controls [Abstract]. *Journal of Clinical and Experimental Neuropsychology*, **11**, 37.

Green, A., Schweda-Nicholson, N, Vaid, J., & White, N. (1989b, March). *Why task analysis is important in dual task research*. Paper presented at the Neuropsychology: Experimental and Theoretical (NET) meeting, Niagara Falls, NY.

Green, A., & Vaid, J. (1986). Methodological issues in the use of the concurrent activities paradigm. *Brain and Cognition*, **5**, 465-476.

Green, A., & Weller, L. (1989). Do different tapping devices and methods of evaluating output produce different outcomes in dual-task research? [Abstract]. *Journal of Clinical and Experimental Neuropsychology*, **11**, 71.

Hannay, H.J., & Malone, P.R. (1976). Visual-field recognition memory for right handed females as a function of familial handedness. *Cortex*, **12**, 41-48.

Harrison, D.W. (1990). *Concurrent verbal interference of right and left proximal and distal upper extremity tapping.* Manuscript submitted for publication.

Hatta, T., & Minagawa, N. (1982). Sex differences in hemispheric function: Implications from a hemispheric time sharing task. *International Journal of Neuroscience*, **16**, 227-230.

Hellige, J.B., Bloch, M.I., & Taylor, A.K. (1988). Multitask investigation of individual differences in hemispheric asymmetry. *Journal of Experimental Psychology: Human Perception and Performance*, **14**, 176-187.

Hellige, J.B., & Kee, D.W. (1990). Asymmetric manual interference as an indicator of lateralized brain function. In G.R. Hammond (Ed.), *Cerebral control of speech and limb movements* (pp. 635-660). Amsterdam: North Holland.

Hellige, J.B., & Longstreth, L.E. (1981). Effects of concurrent hemisphere-specific activity on unimanual tapping rate. *Neuropsychologia*, **19**, 1-10.

Hicks, R.E. (1975). Intrahemispheric response competition between vocal and unimanual performance in normal adult human males. *Journal of Comparative and Physiological Psychology*, **89**, 50-60.

Hicks, R.E., Bradshaw, G.J., Kinsbourne, M., & Feigin, D.S. (1978). Vocal-manual trade-offs in hemispheric sharing of human performance control. *Journal of Motor Behavior*, **10**, 1-6.

Hicks, R.E., Provenzano, F.J., Rybstein, E.D. (1975). Generalized and lateralized effects of concurrent verbal rehearsal upon performance of sequential movements of the fingers by the left and right hands. *Acta Psychologica*, **39**, 119-130.

Higgenbottam, J.A. (1973). Relationships between sets of lateral and perceptual preference measures. *Cortex*, **9**, 402-409.

Hillis, S.K., & Hiscock, M. (1989). Asymmetric processing of whole and partial faces: a dual-task study [Abstract]. *Canadian Psychology*, **30**, 457.

Hiscock, M. (1982). Verbal-manual time sharing in children as a function of task priority. *Brain and Cognition*, **1**, 119-131.

Hiscock, M. (1986). Lateral eye movements and dual-task performance. In H.J. Hannay (Ed.), *Experimental techniques in human neuropsychology* (pp. 264-308). New York: Oxford University Press.

Hiscock, M., Antoniuk, D., Prisciak, K., & von Hessert, D. (1985). Generalized and lateralized interference between concurrent tasks performed by children: effects of age, sex and skill. *Developmental Neuropsychology*, **1**, 29-48.

Hiscock, M., Cheesman, J., Inch, R., Chipuer, H.M., & Graff, L.A. (1989). Rate and variability of finger tapping as measures of lateralized concurrent task effects. *Brain and Cognition*, **10**, 87-104.

Hiscock, M., & Chipuer, H. (1986). Concurrent performance of rhythmically compatible or incompatible vocal and manual tasks: evidence for two sources of interference in verbal-manual timesharing. *Neuropsychologia*, **24**, 691-698.

Hiscock, M., & Inch, R. (1990). *Asymmetry of verbal-manual interference in left-handers: a dissociation between rate and variability.* Unpublished manuscript.

Hiscock, M., & Kinsbourne, M. (1978). Ontogeny of cerebral dominance: evidence from time-sharing asymmetry in children. *Developmental Psychology*, **14**, 321-329.

Hiscock, M., & Kinsbourne, M. (1980). Asymmetry of verbal-manual time sharing in children: a follow-up study. *Neuropsychologia*, **18**, 151-162.

Holtzman, J.D., & Gazzaniga, M.S. (1982). Dual task interactions due exclusively to limits in processing resources. *Science*, **218**, 1325-1327.

Hugdahl, K., & Andersson, L. (1984). A dichotic listening study of differences in cerebral organization in dextral and sinistral subjects. *Cortex*, **20**, 135-141.

Hughes, M., & Sussman, H.M. (1983). An assessment of cerebral dominance in language-disordered children via a time-sharing paradigm. *Brain and Language*, **19**, 48-64.

Kee, D.W., Bathurst, K., and Hellige, J.B. (1983). Lateralized interference of repetitive finger tapping: influence of familial handedness, cognitive load and verbal production. *Neuropsychologia*, **21**, 617-624.

Kee, D.W., Bathurst, K., & Hellige, J.B. (1984). Lateralized interference in finger tapping: assessment of block design activities. *Neuropsychologia*, **22**, 197-203.

Kee, D.W., Morris, K., Bathurst, K., & Hellige, J.B. (1986). Lateralized interference in finger tapping: comparisons of rate and variability measures under speed and consistency tapping instructions. *Brain and Cognition*, **5**, 268-279.

Kimura, D. (1961). Cerebral dominance and the perception of verbal stimuli. *Canadian Journal of Psychology*, **15**, 166-171.

Kinsbourne, M., & Cook, J. (1971). Generalized and lateralized effects of concurrent verbalization on a unimanual skill. *Quarterly Journal of Experimental Psychology*, **23**, 341-345.

Kinsbourne, M., & Hicks, R.E. (1978). Functional cerebral space: a model for overflow, transfer and interference effects in human performance. In J. Requin (Ed.), *Attention and performance VII* (pp. 345-362). Hillsdale, NJ: Lawrence Erlbaum Associates.

Kinsbourne, M., & Hiscock, M. (1983). Asymmetries of dual-task performance. In J.B. Hellige (Ed.), *Cerebral hemisphere asymmetry: Method, theory and application* (pp. 255-334). New York: Praeger.

Knox, A.W., & Boone, D.R. (1970). Auditory laterality and tested handedness. *Cortex*, **6**, 164-173.

Klapp, S.T. (1979). Doing two things at once: the role of temporal compatibility. *Memory and Cognition*, **7**, 375-381.

Lake, D.A., & Bryden, M.P. (1976). Handedness and sex differences in hemispheric asymmetry. *Brain and Language*, **3**, 266-282.

Lishman, W.A., & McMeekan, E.R.L. (1977). Handedness in relation to direction and degree of cerebral dominance for language. *Cortex*, **13**, 30-43.

Lomas, J., & Kimura, D. (1976). Intrahemispheric interaction between speaking and sequential manual activity. *Neuropsychologia*, **14**, 23-33.

McFarland, K., & Ashton, R. (1975). The lateralized effects of concurrent cognitive activity on a unimanual skill. *Cortex*, **11**, 283-290.

McFarland, K., & Ashton, R. (1978a). The influence of brain lateralization of function on a manual skill. *Cortex*, **14**, 102-111.

McFarland, K., & Ashton, R. (1978b). The influence of concurrent task difficulty on manual performance. *Neuropsychologia*, **16**, 735-741.

McFarland, K., & Ashton, R. (1978c). The lateralized effects of concurrent cognitive and motor performance. *Perception and Psychophysics*, **23**, 344-349.

McFarland, K., & Geffen, G. (1982). Speech lateralization assessed by concurrent task performance. *Neuropsychologia*, **20**, 383-390.

McKeever, W.F. & VanDeventer, A.D. (1977). Visual and auditory language processing asymmetries: influence of handedness, familial sinistrality, and sex. *Cortex*, **13**, 225-241.

Navon, D. (1984). Resources -- A theoretical soup stone? *Psychological Review*, **91**, 216-234.

Navon, D., & Gopher, D. (1979). On the economy of the human information processing system: a model of multiple capacity. *Psychological Review*, **86**, 214-255.

Nilsson, J. Glencross, D., & Geffen, G., (1980). The effects of familial sinistrality and preferred hand on dichhaptic and dichotic tasks. *Brain and Language*, **10**, 390-404.

Norman, D.A., & Bobrow, D.G. (1985). On data-limited and resource-limited processes. *Cognitive Psychology*, **7**, 44-64.

Obrzut, J.E., Boliek, C.A., & Obrzut, A. (1986). The effect of stimulus type and directed attention on dichotic listening with children. *Journal of Experimental Child Psychology*, **41**, 198-209.

Orsini, D.L., Satz, P., Soper, H.V., & Light, R.K. (1985). The role of familial sinistrality in cerebral organization. *Neuropsychologia*, **23** 223-232.

Oscar-Berman, M., Rehbein, L., Porfert, A., & Goodglass, H. (1978). Dichhaptic hand-order effects with verbal and nonverbal tactile stimulation. *Brain and Language*, **6**, 323-333.

Parlow, S.E., & Kinsbourne, M. (1981). Handwriting posture and manual motor asymmetry in sinistrals. *Neuropsychologia*, **19**, 687-696.

Parlow, S.E., & Kinsbourne, M. (1989). Asymmetrical transfer of training between hands: implications for interhemispheric communication in normal brain. *Brain and Cognition*, **11**, 98-113.

Peters, M. (1977). Simultaneous performance of two motor activities: the factor of timing. *Neuropsychologia*, **15**, 461-465.

Piazza, D.M. (1977). Cerebral lateralization in young children as measured by dichotic listening and finger tapping tasks. *Neuropsychologia*, **15**, 417-425.

Posner, M.I. (1982). Cumulative development of attentional theory. *American Psychologist*, **37**, 168-179.

Rasmussen, T., & Milner, B. (1975). Clinical and surgical studies of the cerebral speech areas in man. In K.J. Zulch, O. Creutzfeldt, & G.C. Galbraith (Eds.), *Cerebral localization* (pp. 238-257). Berlin: Springer-Verlag.

Rudel, R.G., Denckla, M.B., & Spalten, E. (1974). The functional asymmetry of Braille letter learning in normal, sighted children. *Neurology*, **24**, 733-738.

Satz, P. (1977). Laterality tests: an inferential problem. *Cortex*, **13**, 208-212.

Satz, P. (1980). Incidence of aphasia in left-handers: a test of some hypothetical models of cerebral speech organization. In J. Herron (Ed.), *Neuropsychology of left-handedness* (pp. 189-198). New York: Academic Press.

Satz, P., Achenbach, K., & Fennell, E. (1967). Correlations between assessed manual laterality and predicted speech laterality in a normal population. *Neuropsychologia*, **5**, 295-310.

Satz, P., Achenbach, K., Pattishall, E., & Fennell, E. (1965). Order of report, ear asymmetry, and handedness in dichotic listening. *Cortex*, **1**, 377-396.

Schmuller, J., & Goodman, R. (1979). Bilateral tachistoscopic perception, handedness, and laterality. *Brain and Language*, **11**, 12-18.

Simon, T.J. (1984). On sex, hands, handedness, handwriting position, familial handedness, and the cerebral lateralization of language in monolinguals and bilinguals. *Dissertation Abstracts International*, **46**, 968A.

Simon, T.J., & Sussman, H.M. (1987). The dual task paradigm: speech dominance or manual dominance? *Neuropsychologia*, **25**, 559-569.

Sussman, H.M. (1982). Contrastive patterns of intrahemispheric interference to verbal and spatial concurrent tasks in right-handed, left-handed and stuttering populations. *Neuropsychologia*, **20**, 675-684.

Teng. E.L. (1981). Dichotic ear difference is a poor index for the functional asymmetry between the cerebral hemispheres. *Neuropsychologia*, **19**, 235-240.

Thornton, C.D., & Peters, M. (1982). Interference between concurrent speaking and sequential finger tapping: both hands show a performance decrement under both visual and non-visual guidance. *Neuropsychologia*, **20**, 163-169.

Urbanczyk, S.A., Angel, C., & Kennelly, K.J. (1988). Hemispheric activation increases positive manifold for lateralized cognitive tasks: an extension of Stankov's hypothesis. *Brain and Cognition*, **8**, 206-226.

van Strien, J.W., & Bouma, A. (1988). Cerebral organization of verbal and motor functions in left-handed and right-handed adults: effects of concurrent verbal tasks on unimanual tapping performance. *Journal of Clinical and Experimental Neuropsychology*, **10**, 139-156.

Wexler, B.E., & Halwes, T. (1983). Increasing the power of dichotic methods: the fused rhymed words test. *Neuropsychologia*, **21**, 59-66.

White, N., & Kinsbourne, M. (1980). Does speech output control lateralize over time? Evidence from verbal-manual time-sharing tasks. *Brain and Language*, **10**, 215-223.

Witelson, S.F. (1974). Hemispheric specialization for linguistic and nonlinguistic tactual perception using a dichotomous stimulation technique. *Cortex*, **10**, 3-17.

Zurif, E.B., & Bryden, M.P. (1969). Familial handedness and left-right differences in auditory and visual perception. *Neuropsychologia*, **7**, 179-187.

Cerebral Control of Speech and Limb Movements
G.E. Hammond (editor)

Chapter 22

ASYMMETRIC MANUAL INTERFERENCE AS AN INDICATOR OF LATERALIZED BRAIN FUNCTION

Joseph B. Hellige
University of Southern California

and

Daniel W. Kee
California State University, Fullerton

Many concurrent tasks interfere more with the activity of one hand than with the activity of the other hand. The existence of this asymmetric manual interference can provide important insights into attention-related processes. Data from right-handed and left-handed subjects indicate that two factors contribute to the direction and magnitude of asymmetric manual interference: hemisphere-specific competition for attentional resources and hand dominance. Accordingly, when the goal is to use asymmetric manual interference to study one of these factors, it is necessary to control for the other. Procedures are outlined that can accomplish this. When these procedures are employed, it is possible to use asymmetric manual interference to study lateralized brain function and to investigate hypotheses about hemisphere-specific processing capacity.

Concurrent tasks often interfere with ongoing manual activity. Furthermore, some tasks interfere more with the manual activity of one hand than with the manual activity of the other hand. In recent years, explanations of this lateralized manual interference have been formulated in terms of hemisphere-specific competition for information processing resources (e.g. Friedman, Polson & Dafoe, 1988) or for functional cerebral space (e.g. Kinsbourne & Hiscock, 1983). Consequently, the investigation of lateralized manual interference is regarded as a useful tool for the investigation of information processing differences between the left and right cerebral hemispheres (Hellige, 1990). The purpose of the present chapter is to reconsider this point of view in light of recent findings that raise questions about the extent to which asymmetric manual interference is caused by hemispheric asymmetries for cognitive processing.

In order to illustrate the nature of important challenges to the hemisphere-specific competition point of view, it is instructive to consider a typical paradigm for demonstrating asymmetric manual interference. On each trial the subject performs some manual activity with one hand or the other. Manual activities have included such things as single-finger tapping of one key, alternate tapping of two keys and the sequential tapping of four or more keys. The goal is to choose a manual activity such that the movements of each hand are controlled by the contralateral cerebral hemisphere. On some trials (baseline trials) the subject performs only the manual activity. On other trials (dual-task trials) the subject performs some concurrent task at the same time as the manual activity. Of particular importance is a comparison of the manual performance of each hand with and without the concurrent task. In this way, we can determine whether the concurrent task produces asymmetric manual interference; i.e., different amounts of interference for the two hands.

For right-handed subjects, performing a variety of verbal tasks concurrently with a manual activity (e.g., tapping rapidly with a single finger) interferes more with performance by the right hand than with performance by the left hand (for a partial review see Kinsbourne & Hiscock, 1983). Concurrent verbal activities have included such things as reciting nursery rhymes from memory (e.g., Kinsbourne & Cook, 1971), reading aloud and silently (e.g., Hellige & Longstreth, 1981), solving anagram problems (e.g., Kee, Bathurst & Hellige, 1983) and holding words in short-term memory (e.g., Friedman et al., 1988). For right-handed subjects, there is a great deal of evidence that verbal processing involves more left- than right-hemisphere resources. Consequently, the pattern of asymmetrical manual interference is consistent with the position that there is greater interference with the hand controlled by whichever hemisphere is more involved in the concurrent task.

This hemisphere-specific interference interpretation has received support from two other sets of experimental findings. One is that the pattern of asymmetric motor interference for right-handed subjects changes with the specific information processing demands of the concurrent task.

Specifically, a number of investigators have reported greater right- than left-hand interference for a variety of concurrent verbal activities but either equal interference for the two hands or greater left- than right-hand interference for a variety of concurrent nonverbal activities that should, if anything, require greater resources from the right hemisphere than from the left hemisphere (e.g., Dalby, 1980; Hellige & Longstreth, 1981; McFarland & Ashton, 1975, 1978). The other set of experimental findings demonstrates hemisphere-specific interference in dual-task paradigms that do not involve manual activity. For example, concurrent verbal tasks are shown to interfere more with recognition of words and nonsense syllables from the right visual field (left hemisphere) than from the left visual field (right hemisphere) (e.g., Friedman, Polson, Dafoe & Gaskill, 1982; Hellige & Cox, 1976; Hellige, Cox & Litvac, 1979) and more with the recognition of auditory stimuli presented to the right ear (left hemisphere) than to the left ear (right hemisphere) (e.g., Hellige & Wong, 1983; Herdman & Friedman, 1985). The fact that hemisphere-specific competition occurs with these nonmanual dual-task paradigms makes it likely that such competition also contributes to asymmetric manual interference.

Challenges to the Hemispheric Interpretation

The explanation of asymmetric manual interference in terms of hemisphere-specific competition has recently been challenged in two ways. One alternative explanation is that the amount of manual interference shown for each hand is a function of that hand's baseline level of performance on the manual task (e.g., Willis & Goodwin, 1987). For example, on baseline trials, the index finger of the right hand taps at a faster rate than the index finger of the left hand for most right-handed subjects. Willis and Goodwin argue that asymmetric manual interference may be an artifact of these initial hand differences in tapping rate rather than caused by hemispheric lateralization effects. In a subsequent section of this chapter, we discuss the plausibility of this position and consider whether initial hand differences are either necessary or sufficient for the production of asymmetric interference effects.

A second type of alternative explanation suggests that factors related to manual dominance in general are involved in asymmetric interference effects, but not necessarily as an artifact of initial hand differences. This type of explanation has arisen as a result of several recent investigations of the effects of concurrent verbal activity on the manual performance of left-handed subjects. Recent studies have shown opposite interference asymmetries in right- and left-handed groups, with each group showing greater interference for their dominant hand. For reasons considered in detail later in this chapter, this pattern of results is inconsistent with an explanation solely in terms of hemisphere-specific competition. In a subsequent section of this chapter, we review the findings for left-handed subjects and present new data to suggest that more than one factor contributes to the observed pattern of asymmetric manual interference.

The next two sections of the chapter deal with the two complicating factors that have been outlined. Following this, we will consider how these factors have important implications for the design and interpretation of studies of asymmetric manual interference.

Baseline Hand Differences and Statistical Artifact

Kinsbourne and Hiscock (1983) cautioned early that it is crucial to show that at least one category of task does not produce a right-greater-than-left pattern of interference. Only then can one be confident that the consistent asymmetry of interference achieved with verbal tasks is not an invariant property of dual-task performance in humans, for example, an artifact of the disparity between the hands in single-task performance. Thus, the maintenance of an hemispheric specialization interpretation of lateralized finger-tapping interference requires the observation of greater right-hand than left-hand interference produced by verbal concurrent tasks in conjunction with the demonstration of greater left-hand than right-hand interference with nonverbal concurrent tasks--a double dissociation.

An early study by McFarland and Ashton (1975) provides an illustration of this double dissociation. Twenty-one right-handed adult subjects were told to alternately tap two buttons as quickly as possible with the index finger of their left versus right hand. Finger-tapping was recorded during the 10- to 20-s completion intervals required by the different concurrent tasks. Concurrent verbal tasks required sentence construction, word scanning, alphabetic rehearsal, anagram solution, reading a concrete paragraph, and reading an abstract paragraph. The nonverbal tasks included embedded figures, matching line drawings, scanning random shapes, scanning geometric figures, and picture identification. Results showed that verbal concurrent tasks slowed right-hand finger-tapping more than left-hand finger-tapping. In contrast, more slowing of left-hand relative to right-hand finger tapping was associated with the nonverbal concurrent tasks (see also McFarland & Ashton, 1978).

Dalby (1980) has also reported a similar dissociation for verbal and nonverbal concurrent tasks within a single sample of right-handed subjects. Thirty right-handed subjects tapped four typewriter keys in sequence (ring finger, index finger, little finger, and middle finger) with their left versus right hands on 15 s trials. Verbal concurrent tasks included vocal repetition and reading words. Nonverbal concurrent tasks consisted of solving Raven Progressive Matrices problems and Space Relations items from the

Differential Aptitude Test. Results showed that more right-hand than left-hand finger tapping interference was associated with the verbal concurrent tasks, while the opposite pattern--more left-hand than right-hand finger-tapping interference--was found for the nonverbal concurrent tasks.

The foregoing studies by McFarland and Ashton and by Dalby required alternate and sequential tapping of multiple keys, respectively. Hellige and Longstreth (1981) show that when repetitive tapping of a single key is measured, a similar dissociation of the direction of lateralized finger-tapping is also produced by verbal versus nonverbal concurrent tasks. In their experiments right-handed university students were required to tap a single telegraph key as quickly as possible with their left versus right hands on 15-s tapping trials. The verbal concurrent task used in Experiment 1 required paragraph reading and more right-hand than left-hand finger tapping interference was observed. In Experiment 2 the concurrent task required the manual solution of WISC-R block designs with the nontapping hand. In this latter experiment more left-hand than right-hand finger tapping interference was observed.

The preceding studies show that the direction of lateralized finger-tapping performance produced by verbal versus nonverbal concurrent tasks is different. Thus, the greater right-hand than left-hand pattern of lateralized finger-tapping interference usually associated with verbal tasks cannot be attributed solely to an invariant property of dual-task performance in humans. Despite this, Willis and Goodwin (1987) maintain that this pattern of lateralized finger-tapping interference implicating left-hemisphere verbal processing may still be influenced by a statistical artifact:

> This is because research participants are usually right-handed and interhand comparisons of initial (i.e., baseline) tapping rates typically favor the right. Given this initial discrepancy between the hands, differential interference effects associated with the concurrent performance of an unrelated task may be due to initial differences in tapping speed rather than lateralization effects. In this respect, interference might be greater for right- than left-handed tapping because, due to the higher range of initial values for the right hand, there is a higher possible range for reduction. (p. 719)

They argue that this problem is not solved by measuring interference for each hand as a percentage change from the baseline rate for that hand.

A recent study by Kee and Cherry (1989) bears on this issue. They reasoned that if lateralized finger-tapping interference is due to differences in initial values, this asymmetry effect should emerge only when the right-hand advantage -- faster right-hand than left-hand finger tapping -- is present on baseline-tapping trials. In contrast, the hemispheric present on baseline-tapping trials. In contrast, the hemispheric specialization interpretation would be bolstered if the same pattern of lateralized finger-tapping interference was observed regardless of whether the hands differed on baseline tapping trials. Thus, they experimentally manipulated finger-tapping conditions so that a comparison of lateralized interference was provided under two conditions: right-hand advantage present on baseline trials (standard tapping condition) versus right-hand advantage absent on baseline trials (adjusted tapping condition). This comparison was achieved by manipulating both the down-force for a tapping-switch closure and the travel release distance required after a switch closure.

Sixteen right-handed university subjects participated in their study. Subjects were instructed to tap as quickly as possible on a microswitch with the index finger of their left versus right hand. The verbal concurrent task required solution of four single-solution anagrams. Subjects participated in both a standard tapping key condition in which baseline differences were allowed to emerge (faster right- than left-hand finger tapping) and in an adjusted key condition where the baseline differences were removed by the adjustment of down-force and travel release distance. Order of these two conditions was counter-balanced across subjects.

The results of the Kee and Cherry study are displayed in Figure 1. The upper panel of the figure presents the baseline tapping rates as a function of tapping arrangement (standard vs adjusted) and tapping hand. As can be seen, the right-hand advantage in finger tapping associated with right-handed subjects was observed under the standard tapping condition, but this advantage was removed by the adjusted tapping condition. This impression was confirmed by an analysis of variance that indicated a significant Hand by Tapping Condition interaction and by subsequent tests of simple effects that indicated a reliable hand difference in the standard condition, but not in the adjusted condition (alpha = .05).

The lower panel of Figure 1 displays the dual task results expressed as a percentage of baseline change. Notice that the typical pattern of lateralized finger-tapping interference produced by a verbal task--greater right-hand than left-hand disruption--is shown for both the standard and adjusted tapping conditions. Analysis of variance indicated a significant hand main effect and this effect was not qualified by tapping condition. This outcome clearly demonstrates that exactly the same lateralized finger-tapping interference can be observed regardless of whether baseline tapping differences are present.

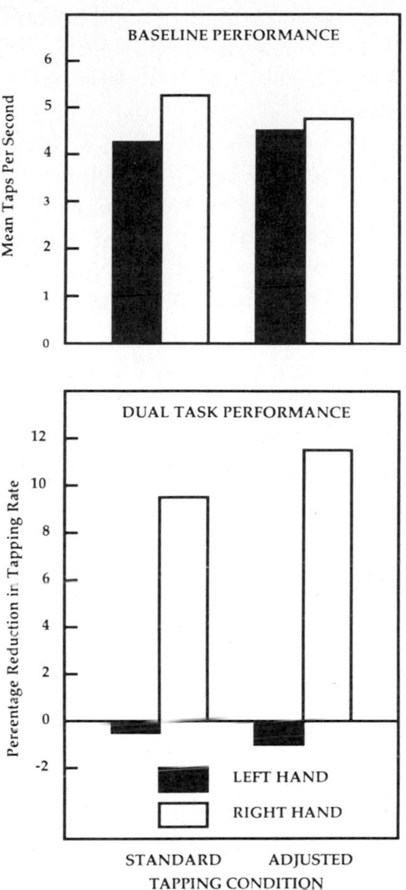

Figure 1. The upper panel shows the mean number of taps per second for each hand during the baseline condition. The results are shown for the standard versus adjusted tapping conditions. The lower panel shows the percentage reduction in tapping rate for each hand during dual-task trials. (From Kee & Cherry, 1989)

The study by Kee and Cherry experimentally manipulated the presence or absence of hand differences on baseline tapping performance. While the dual-task literature indicates that right-handed subjects are usually associated with a right-hand advantage in baseline tapping performance, exceptions occur (e.g., Hiscock & Chipuer, 1986; Hiscock, Cheesman, Inch, Chipuer, & Graff, 1989). For example, a study by Hiscock and Chipuer (1986) tested 42 right-handed adults with dual-task procedures. The finger tapping task consisted of rhythmic tapping with the index finger of the left or right hand. The concurrent task consisted of sentence recitation. No hand differences in baseline tapping rate were observed. Nevertheless, reliable lateralized interference was detected such that sentence recitation interfered more with right-hand finger tapping than left-hand finger tapping rate.

The preceding studies show that the presence of a right-hand advantage in baseline finger-tapping performance is neither a necessary nor a sufficient condition for the observation of more right-hand than left-hand finger tapping interference in right-handed subjects. Such evidence diminishes the validity of the statistical artifact interpretation of asymmetric manual interference. However, this does not necessarily mean that there is no relationship whatsoever between hand dominance and asymmetric manual interference. To the contrary, recent investigations of left-handed subjects indicate that hand dominance is a very important factor.

Studies of Left-Handed Individuals

As noted earlier, questions about the mechanisms responsible for asymmetric manual interference are raised by recent studies of left-handed subjects. If we assume that the motor activity of each hand is controlled by the contralateral cerebral hemisphere, then the hemisphere-specific competition explanation that has been applied to right-handed subjects makes the following predictions. A concurrent task should interfere more with the motor activity of the hand contralateral to the cerebral hemisphere whose resources are taxed most heavily by the concurrent task. For a variety of verbal tasks such as the identification of dichotically presented words, average laterality results for left-handed subjects are frequently in the same direction as for right-handed subjects--although the average left/right asymmetries are typically smaller for left- than for right-handed subjects and frequently fail to be statistically significant. Consequently, the straightforward prediction for left-handed subjects is that concurrent verbal activity should interfere equally with the motor activity of both hands or should interfere more with the activity of the right hand (just as in right-handed subjects).

In fact, some studies that have compared asymmetric manual interference in right- and left-handed subjects reported greater right- than left-hand interference in right-handed subjects and equal interference with both hands in left-handed subjects (e.g., Lomas & Kimura, 1976; Sussman, 1982). However, more recent studies have reported opposite interference effects in right- and left-handed subjects. Such results are difficult to reconcile with a straightforward account in terms of hemisphere-specific competition.

For example, Orsini, Satz, Soper and Light (1985) had right- and left-handed subjects tap with the index finger of the left or right hand as quickly as possible and examined the interfering effects produced by concurrent verbal activities. One activity was a verbal fluency task that required subjects to generate words beginning with a specific letter. The other activity required subjects to read silently. In addition to the manual interference tasks, subjects identified dichotically presented words. The results for right-handed subjects were as expected from previous literature: the concurrent verbal tasks interfered more with right- than with left-hand tapping and there was a significant right-ear advantage for dichotic listening. For left-handed subjects there was again a right-ear advantage, but it was smaller than that shown by the right-handed subjects. In marked contrast to the results for right-handed subjects, for left-handed subjects the concurrent verbal tasks interfered more with left- than with right-hand tapping. The opposite patterns of interference shown by the two handedness groups are not explained by assuming opposite patterns of hemispheric superiority for verbal processing -- at least as measured by ear differences in dichotic listening. Because of this, Orsini et al. suggest that factors related to manual dominance are involved in asymmetric manual interference.

Simon and Sussman (1987) examined the effects of three concurrent verbal activities (describing a picture, reading aloud and speaking extemporaneously) on the rate of single finger tapping in both right- and left-handed subjects. Consistent with the results of Orsini et al. (1985), interference was greater for the right hand in the right-handed group and greater for the left hand in the left-handed group. Simon and Sussman also reported that left/right asymmetries in both handedness groups were present only for those subjects whose hands tapped at different rates during baseline tapping trials (i.e., trials with no concurrent activity) and not for those subjects whose baseline tapping rates were approximately equal for the two hands. This relationship of asymmetry on baseline trials to asymmetric interference merits additional investigation, especially because it is unlikely to be a statistical artifact (e.g., the preceding section of this chapter and Kee & Cherry, 1989).

van Strien and Bouma (1988) examined the effects of three concurrent verbal tasks (vocal repetition of a proverb, verbal fluency and reading aloud) on both single finger tapping and on a sequential tapping task. Their right-handed subjects showed greater interference with right- than with left-hand tapping using the single-finger procedure. Their left-handed subjects showed exactly the opposite pattern of interference. This is not easily attributed to right-hemisphere dominance for verbal processing in the left-handed subjects because, on the average, these subjects showed a right-ear advantage for recognizing dichotically presented digits. Neither group showed asymmetric interference for the sequential tapping task.

Wong, O'Boyle, and Tepin (1989) examined the effects of two concurrent tasks (reading a paragraph aloud; encoding and remembering a nonverbal shape) on single-finger tapping in a group of left-handed subjects who were selected for tapping faster with their left- than with their right-hand on baseline trials. Both tasks produced greater interference with left- than with right-hand tapping. This is in contrast to a previous experiment of theirs that showed the opposite interference effects for right-handed subjects.

These recent investigations of manual interference in left-handed subjects raise several important issues that must be considered in an evaluation of the manual interference paradigm. For example, it is important to consider more completely the relationship between baseline motor asymmetry and asymmetric interference in left-handed subjects. It is also important to examine further the relationships among baseline asymmetry, asymmetric interference and other measures of cognitive lateralization such as ear differences in dichotic listening.

With these issues in mind, we had left-handed university students (15 men, 12 women) perform a set of tasks employed by Hellige, Bloch and Taylor (1988) in an investigation of right-handed university students. A complete description of the tasks can be found in Hellige et al. so that only a brief description is given here.

Of particular importance for present purposes were two dual-task finger-tapping activities. On each of several 15-s trials, subjects tapped a key as quickly as possible with the index finger of one hand. On baseline trials subjects performed only this tapping task. On dual-task trials subjects performed another activity concurrently with finger tapping. One concurrent task (Syllable Repetition) required subjects to say aloud the syllables /ba/, /da/, /ga/, /pa/, /ta/ and /ka/ over and over. The other concurrent task required subjects to solve anagram problems silently while also finger tapping. Subjects performed each concurrent activity twice while the right hand was tapping and twice while the left hand was tapping. For right-handed subjects, both of these concurrent verbal activities interfere more with right- than with left-hand tapping (e.g., Hellige et al., 1988).

Three other tasks were also employed. A dichotic listening task required subjects to identify acoustically presented syllables from the set listed above. Subjects received a total of 120 dichotic pairs, with each pair consisting of two different stimuli from the set of six. For right-handed subjects, a right-ear advantage is found for this task (e.g., Hellige et al., 1988). A tachistoscopic identification task required subjects to identify visually presented versions of these same consonant-vowel syllables.

Hellige et al. found no visual field difference for right-handed subjects on this task. The final task was a free-vision face task developed by Levy, Heller, Banich and Burton (1983a,b). Subjects on each trial indicated which of two chimeric faces looked happier. The two faces on each trial were photographic mirror images of each other. Each face consisted of two half-faces from the same poser -- one with a neutral expression and the other with a happy expression. Thus, the two faces on a single trial differed only with respect to which side of the chimeric face contained the happy expression. For right-handed subjects there is a bias toward choosing the face with the "happy" side toward the viewer's left as looking happier than its mirror image (e.g., Hellige et al., 1988; Levy et al., 1983a,b). Left-handed subjects have been found to show a similar, but reduced bias (Levy et al., 1983a). Preliminary analyses indicated no significant effects of subjects' gender. Thus, the results presented here collapse across gender.

Interference in the dual-task paradigm was computed as a percentage change from the baseline rate for each hand. Specifically, percentage reduction scores were calculated as [(B - D)/B] * 100, where B is the tapping rate in the baseline condition and D is the tapping rate for dual-task trials. Percentage reduction scores were computed for each hand during each of the concurrent activities. The results have been averaged across the two trials with each concurrent activity. In the present experiment with left-handed subjects, there were no significant differences between left-hand and right-hand interference for either concurrent task. During concurrent syllable repetition, the percentage reduction scores were 4.16 and 5.35 for the left and right hands, respectively. During concurrent anagram solution, the percentage reduction scores were 3.55 and 2.77 for the left and right hands, respectively. This is in marked contrast to the results for right-handed subjects reported by Hellige et al. (1988), for which there was significantly greater interference with right-hand tapping for both tasks.

The absence of hand differences in finger-tapping interference for the present group of left-handed subjects is consistent with the absence of a significant ear difference on the dichotic listening task (Right Ear Mean = 67.4%; Left Ear Mean = 63.3%, with 16 of 27 subjects showing better right-ear performance and 11 showing better left-ear performance). By way of comparison, the right-handed subjects studied by Hellige et al. (1988) showed a highly significant right-ear advantage (Right Ear Mean = 70.6%; Left Ear Mean = 58.8%, with 108 of 120 subjects showing better right-ear performance). If the dichotic listening results are taken as an indication of the average language lateralization for the present group of left-handed subjects, then the absence of a significant ear advantage might explain the absence of significant asymmetries in finger-tapping interference. It should also be noted that when the present results for left-handed subjects (i.e., no lateralized interference and no ear advantage) are compared with the

Hellige et al. results for right-handed subjects (i.e., greater right-hand interference and a right-ear advantage) we have converging evidence for an association between lateralized manual interference and ear advantage during dichotic listening--a relationship shown by Hellige et al. to exist within the right-handed population.

As in the Hellige et al. (1988) experiments with right-handed subjects, there were no visual field differences for the tachistoscopic task and it will not be considered further. For the free-vision face task, a bias score was computed as (R - L) / 36, where R is the number of trials on which the face with the happy expression on the viewer's right looked happier, L is the number of trials on which the face with the happy expression on the viewer's left looked happier and 36 is the total number of trials. The mean bias score was -.26. That is, there was a significant bias to choose the face with the happy expression on the viewer's left as looking happier than its mirror image.

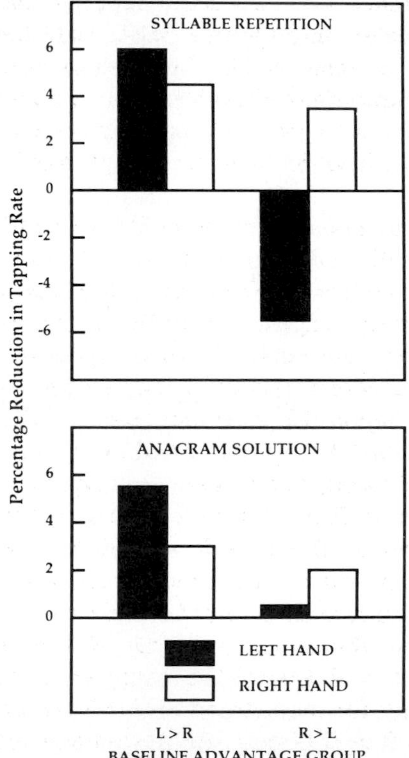

Figure 2. Percentage reduction in tapping rate for each hand during dual-task trials. The results are shown separately for each baseline advantage group and for two different concurrent activities: syllable repetition (upper panel) and anagram solution (lower panel).

All of the subjects in the present experiment wrote with their left hand and were clearly left-handed as indicated by a 10-item handedness questionnaire. Furthermore, the tapping rate during baseline trials averaged faster for the left hand (M = 5.12 taps/s) than for the right hand (M = 4.92 taps/s). However, there was considerable variation in the hand difference on baseline trials. In view of the observation that asymmetric interference may be related to asymmetries of baseline tapping rate (e.g., Kee & Cherry, 1989; Simon & Sussman, 1987; Willis & Goodwin, 1987), we divided the subjects into two groups defined by which hand tapped more quickly on the baseline trials and compared the interference patterns for the two groups. The left hand was faster on baseline trials for 21 subjects (L > R Group) whereas the right hand was faster on baseline trials for 6 subjects (R > L Group). The percentage reduction scores for these two groups are shown in Figure 2. As the figure suggests, there was a statistically significant Group by Hand interaction such that the L > R group tended to show greater interference with left-hand tapping and the R > L Group tended to show greater interference with right-hand tapping. This interaction confirms a relationship between asymmetries of baseline performance and asymmetries of interference (cf., Simon & Sussman, 1987). At least for left-handed subjects, the concurrent verbal activities employed here interfere more with whichever hand taps more quickly on baseline trials.

A similar Group by Hand interaction for left-handed subjects is found in unpublished data collected by Bathurst (1989). She examined the effects of two concurrent verbal tasks (solving anagrams silently, as in the present experiment, and solving anagrams aloud) on single-finger tapping in a group of 64 left-handed subjects. As in the present experiment, for the group as a whole the percentage reduction scores were not significantly different for the two hands (Right Hand Mean = 2.52; Left Hand Mean = 2.62). On baseline trials, 50 subjects tapped faster with their left than with their right hand (L > R Group) and 14 subjects tapped faster with their right than with their left hand (R > L Group). The first thing to note is that the proportion of subjects in the L > R and R > L groups (.78 and .22, respectively) were identical to the proportions found in our study. In addition, when the interference effects in Bathurst's study were examined for these two groups, there was a highly significant Group by Hand interaction. For the L > R Group the percentage reduction scores were nonsignificantly greater for the left hand (M = 3.37) than for the right hand (M = 1.79). For the R > L Group the percentage reduction scores were significantly greater for the right hand (M = 5.11) than for the left hand (M = -.08).

Recent studies of dual-task interference in left-handed subjects have not typically reported how many subjects showed faster left-hand tapping during baseline trials. The present results and those from Bathurst's study suggest that such information should be reported because different interference asymmetries may be found for a group of left-handed subjects depending on the proportion of subjects showing various baseline asymmetries. That is, discrepancies among studies may be caused by different proportions of subjects showing L > R versus R > L baseline asymmetries.

One interpretation of the relationship between baseline asymmetry and asymmetric interference is that asymmetric interference is in some way a statistical artifact of asymmetries in baseline performance (e.g., Willis & Goodwin, 1987; Wong et al., 1989). In an earlier section of this chapter we reviewed data showing that the presence of baseline asymmetries is neither necessary nor sufficient for obtaining asymmetric interference. Therefore, it is important to consider an alternative possibility: that hand asymmetries in the baseline condition may themselves be related to such things as cerebral dominance for making precise rapid movements, for verbal processing or for a predisposition to rely on the resources of one hemisphere more than the other. If this is the case, the existence of a relationship between baseline and interference asymmetries is not merely a statistical artifact. The following aspects of the present study of left-handed subjects illustrate the plausibility of these points.

The ear differences in dichotic listening were different for the L > R and R > L subgroups, with the Group by Ear interaction approaching statistical significance ($p < .09$). In the R > L Group, more syllables were recognized from the right ear (M = 75.6%) than from the left ear (M = 60.6%), with 5 of the 6 subjects showing better right-ear than left-ear performance. In the R > L Group, approximately equal numbers of syllables were recognized from the right ear (M = 63.8%) and from the left ear (M = 63.4%), with only 11 of 21 subjects showing better right-ear than left-ear performance. In fact, the magnitude of the right-ear advantage for the R > L Group is similar to that reported by Hellige et al. (1988) for right-handed subjects. This pattern of results is consistent with the possibility that individual differences in baseline asymmetry are related to individual differences in hemispheric superiority for aspects of verbal processing. If this were the case, then the relationship between baseline asymmetry and interference asymmetry would not necessarily contradict an explanation in terms of hemisphere-specific competition.

Although not significantly different from each other, the bias scores for the free-vision face task also tended to be different for the two groups. Specifically, the leftward bias was larger for the L > R Group (M = -.30) than for the R > L Group (M = -.11). Levy and her colleagues (Levy et al., 1983a,b) have argued that individual differences in the free-vision face task reflect individual differences in arousal asymmetry between the two cerebral hemispheres. That is, the greater the leftward bias, the greater the arousal asymmetry in favor of the right hemisphere. Thus, it is possible that differences in baseline tapping asymmetry also reflect different arousal asymmetries or differences in the tendency to rely on the processes of one hemisphere more than the other. If so, this could contribute to the relationship between baseline and interference asymmetries.

Despite these possibilities, the pattern of results for left-handed subjects is still not explained completely by the hemisphere-specific competition logic that has been applied to the results of right-handed subjects. According to this logic, the pattern of manual interference for left-handed subjects (i.e., for the majority of subjects a variety of concurrent verbal activities interfere more with left- than with right-hand tapping) would indicate that the concurrent verbal activities involve more right- than left-hemisphere resources for the majority of left-handed subjects. This possibility seems unreasonable in view of the fact that the majority of left-handed subjects show a right-ear (left-hemisphere) advantage for the recognition of verbal material (e.g., the present study; Orsini et al., 1985; van Strien & Bouma, 1988) and left-hemisphere superiority for speech production (e.g., Rasmussen & Milner, 1977; Segalowitz & Bryden, 1983). Consequently, these results suggest that factors in addition to or instead of hemispheric superiority for verbal processing determine asymmetric motor interference.

An interesting possibility has been considered by Simon and Sussman (1987). They speculate that the single-finger tapping of both hands is controlled primarily by the left hemisphere in both right- and left-handed subjects. Furthermore, they suggest that ipsilateral control of the left hand by the left hemisphere is sufficiently prevalent in left-handed subjects to account for greater interference with left- than with right-hand tapping. Although Simon and Sussman do not specifically discuss this, in order to account for the reversed pattern of interference in right-handed subjects we would have to assume a lower incidence of ipsilateral control in the right-handed than in the left-handed population. While this possibility preserves the hemisphere-specific competition account of manual interference effects and cannot be ruled out, it cannot be tested adequately without converging evidence about ipsilateral versus contralateral hand control in individual subjects.

Another possible explanation has been suggested by van Strien and Bouma (1988). They question whether lateralized motor interference is determined by hemisphere-specific competition at all. Instead, they argue that the motor control areas for the dominant hand occupy more cerebral space than do the motor control areas for the nondominant hand. As we understand it, they assume that larger control areas are more susceptible to interference. Consequently, concurrent activities are more likely to interfere with the performance of the dominant hand (the right hand for right-handed subjects and the left hand for left-handed subjects). The best measure of hand dominance would seem to be which hand actually performs the experimental task better on baseline trials (rather than the hand used for writing or other activities). Consequently, it is interesting that in the present experiment the pattern of asymmetric interference was related to hand asymmetry in the baseline rate of tapping.

It should be noted that van Strien and Bouma (1988) formulated their arguments in terms of interference between the motor programming required for overt speech and the motor programming required for finger tapping. Given that similar effects of handedness are found when the concurrent task does not require overt speaking (e.g., the silent reading condition used by Orsini et al., 1985 and the silent anagram task used in the present study and by Bathurst) it is clear that their arguments must be broadened in order to account for the accumulated data.

Although the "hand dominance" explanation suggested by van Strien and Bouma (1988) could account for the relationship between baseline tapping asymmetries and asymmetric interference, it cannot account for the fact that different concurrent activities produce different (sometimes opposite) patterns of asymmetric interference in different samples from the same right-handed population (e.g., Hellige & Longstreth, 1981) or within a single sample (e.g., Friedman, Polson & Dafoe, 1988; McFarland & Ashton, 1975,1978). Nor can it account for the relationship between asymmetric manual interference and the ear advantage found in dichotic listening (e.g., Hellige et al., 1988). Thus, the most likely possibility is that asymmetric motor interference is determined by more than one factor, with the observed asymmetry depending on the combined influence of the various factors.

One prediction that comes from this multi-factor point of view is that a specific pattern of asymmetric interference is more likely when both hand dominance and hemispheric dominance lead to the same expected outcome than when they do not. In order to test this prediction in the present experiment, we used ear advantage during the dichotic listening task as an index of hemispheric dominance for verbal processing and hand superiority during baseline trials as an indication of hand dominance for tapping. For 15 subjects (the Consistent Group) hand dominance and ear dominance were either both right-sided (5 subjects) or both left-sided (10 subjects). For the Consistent Group the predictions based on hemisphere-specific competition are identical to the predictions based on hand dominance: the dominant tapping hand should show more interference as measured by percentage reduction scores. In fact, this pattern of results was found in 13 of the 15 subjects ($p < .01$). Averaged across both syllable repetition and anagram tasks the percentage reduction scores were larger for the dominant hand (M = 4.72) than for the nondominant hand (M = 0.77). For the remaining 12 subjects (the Inconsistent Group) hand dominance and ear dominance were for opposite sides of the body (right-hand dominant, left-ear advantage -- 1 subject; left-hand dominant, right-ear advantage -- 11 subjects). For subjects in the Inconsistent Group the prediction based on hemisphere-specific competition (i.e., greater interference with the nondominant hand) is opposite the prediction based on hand dominance (i.e., greater interference with the dominant hand). In fact, for the Inconsistent Group the percentage reduction scores for the dominant hand (M = 5.45) were not significantly different from the percentage reduction scores for the nondominant hand (M = 4.19), $F < 1.0$, with 7 subjects showing larger percentage reduction scores for the dominant hand and 5 subjects showing larger percentage reduction scores for the nondominant hand.

Until the differences between Consistent and Inconsistent subjects are replicated, the results can only be suggestive. What the results suggest, however, is quite consistent with the body of research that has accumulated during the last several years and important for considering the use of asymmetric manual interference for the study of hemispheric asymmetry. It now appears that such asymmetry is determined by at least two factors: hemispheric asymmetry and hand dominance. Consequently, when the paradigm is used to make inferences about hemispheric asymmetry, special care must be taken to rule out interpretations in terms of hand dominance.

Controlling for Hand Dominance Effects

In order to consider how we might control for the effects of hand dominance, it is useful to think about the ambiguity involved in the interpretation of the following finding. The example comes from part of a study reported by Lempert (1989). In one of her conditions (Imagery condition), right-handed subjects (all of whom tapped faster with the right than with the left index finger during baseline trials) either tapped alone (baseline trials) or tapped while visualizing the situation described by a concurrently presented sentence. Using percentage change from baseline as a measure of interference, Lempert found greater interference with right-hand tapping than with left-hand tapping. To what extent can we conclude (based only on the results from this group) that the asymmetric manual interference reflects hemispheric asymmetry rather than manual dominance?

From what we have seen in this chapter, it should be clear that interpretation of these results would be ambiguous. Because all of the subjects showed a right-hand advantage in the baseline condition, a hand dominance explanation (e.g., such as that proposed by van Strien and

Bouma, 1988) could account completely for the pattern of effects. In order to eliminate this sort of explanation, it is necessary to have more information.

A similar problem arises in other paradigms that are used to make inferences about hemispheric asymmetry from behavioral measures of laterality. For example, in tachistoscopic studies, visual half-field asymmetries can be influenced by many things in addition to hemispheric asymmetry (e.g., Hellige & Sergent, 1986). Therefore, it is important to design experiments as much as possible to control for the effects of other variables. Beyond that, it is important to appreciate the value of focusing more attention on Hemisphere-of-Presentation by Task interactions than on the simple effects of hemisphere-of-presentation for any single task. As discussed in detail by Hellige (1983), such interaction patterns can be extremely informative in separating the effects of hemispheric asymmetry from behavioral asymmetries that are produced by other factors. This is true whenever the unwanted factors can be assumed to have the same effect across all tasks and cannot, therefore, produce an interaction between task and hemisphere.

Consider how the same logic applies to separating manual dominance effects from hemispheric effects in the study of asymmetric manual interference. For a single group of adult subjects or for two samples chosen from the same hand-dominance population it is the case that hand dominance is a stable characteristic. That is, hand dominance for writing or for a specific baseline task does not change with the nature of the concurrent task that is imposed on dual-task trials. Therefore, any explanation of interference asymmetries that relies on hand dominance of the subjects must predict that all concurrent tasks will produce the same pattern of asymmetry. Of course, this interpretation is clearest when the overall amount of interference (i.e., averaged across the two hands) is the same for the tasks that are used. (See Hellige, 1983, for discussion of problems that can arise in interpreting interaction patterns.) As a result of this, it is extremely useful to contrast the pattern of manual interference obtained with one concurrent task with the pattern obtained with a different concurrent task. When the patterns are not the same, the resulting Task by Hand interaction cannot be attributed to any effects of the subjects' manual dominance (artifactual or otherwise).

In the example given at the beginning of this section, it would be useful to show that another concurrent task produces a different pattern of asymmetric interference--either equal interference with both hands or greater interference for the left than for the right hand--for these same subjects or for a sample that shows exactly the same pattern of hand dominance on baseline trials. In fact, Lempert (1989) has shown exactly this. In a second condition (Silent Rehearsal condition) a second group of subjects from the same hand-dominance population as the first received exactly the same sentences but were instructed to imagine hearing them over and over while tapping. For both groups of subjects, there were right-hand advantages of equal magnitudes on baseline trials. That is, the two groups showed exactly the same hand dominance. Despite this, they showed different patterns of manual interference; i.e., there was a Task by Hand interaction. As noted earlier, subjects in the Imagery group showed greater right- than left-hand interference. In contrast, subjects in the Silent Rehearsal group showed equal interference with both hands. At least for male subjects, the overall amount of interference was equal for both groups. Thus, the Task by Hand interaction cannot be attributed to hand dominance. Lempert suggests that imagining a visual representation of the situation described by a sentence involved the left hemisphere beyond its role in reading the sentences. Whether this is the correct interpretation or not, the pattern of results is at least consistent with the hypothesis that the Imagery task was more left-hemisphere dominant or less right-hemisphere dominant than the Silent Rehearsal task (for similar results see Lempert, 1987).

The study by Lempert (1989) provides an example of the importance of a Task by Hand interaction in an experiment that used different groups of subjects for each concurrent task. An experiment by Friedman et al. (1988) illustrates such an interaction within a single group of subjects. Friedman et al. examined the effects of reading and remembering nonsense words on single-finger tapping. Each of their 17-s trials was divided into three segments. During the first segment (7 s) subjects tapped while looking at a fixation point. Tapping rate during the last 5 s of this segment was used as the baseline measure for that trial. During the second segment (5 s) subjects read aloud three nonsense words. During the third segment (5 s) the words were replaced by the fixation point and subjects were to hold the words in memory with no overt verbalization. After the end of the 17-s trial subjects reported as many of the nonsense words as they could remember. Subjects were chosen to show a right-hand advantage on baseline tapping trials and a right visual field (left hemisphere) advantage for recognizing nonsense words.

For present purposes, an important result is that reading the nonsense words aloud produced equal interference with both hands whereas holding the words in memory without overt verbalization interfered more with right-hand tapping than with left-hand tapping; i.e., there was a Task by Hand interaction. Furthermore, during the reading aloud task subjects' finger-tapping rate for both hands was sensitive to instructions about whether to emphasize the tapping task or the reading/memory task. There was no such effect of task emphasis for either hand when the concurrent activity was holding the words in memory without overt verbalization.

Friedman et al. (1988) also found that the decrement in recall of their nonsense words was greater after trials involving right-hand finger tapping than after trials involving left-hand finger tapping. There are two things about this result that are relevant to the present discussion. One is that it is not often reported that performance on the nonmanual concurrent task depends on which hand is engaged in the manual activity. Although a variety of explanations have been offered to account for this (e.g, Friedman et al., 1988; Hiscock, 1982), we believe that the most likely explanation is that most investigators have not used measures of nonmanual concurrent task performance that are sensitive enough to reveal the relatively small laterality effects involved. The other point to note is that, when interference with the concurrent task depends on which hand performs the manual task, it is still possible that the laterality effect is caused by hand dominance rather than hemisphere-specific competition. That is, demonstrating this reverse type of interference does not by itself rule out interpretations based on hand dominance. However, in view of the Task by Hand interaction described earlier, it does not seem likely that hand dominance was the critical factor in this case.

Based on this specific pattern of interactions, Friedman et al. (1988) suggest that left-hemisphere resources are required to coordinate movements associated with overt speech and movements associated with finger tapping, regardless of which hand is tapping. Consequently, reading aloud interferes equally with both hands and task emphasis instructions have an effect. During the silent retention interval, no overt speech was required and the fact that there was greater interference with the right-hand than with the left-hand suggests more left-hemisphere involvement in the retention processes, at least relative to the processes involved during the reading aloud interval. Additional discussion of the theoretical points raised by Friedman et al. is beyond the scope of this chapter. However, note that were it not for the presence of the Task by Hand interaction it would be impossible to rule out the possibility that the asymmetric manual interference produced during the retention interval was a product of the subjects' hand dominance rather than related to hemispheric factors.

An important point about interpreting Task by Hand interactions is that the best we can do is to reach conclusions about the hemispheric dominance of one task relative to the hemispheric dominance of another task. Now that we know hand dominance is a factor in producing asymmetric manual interference, we must be much more cautious in reaching conclusions about the absolute hemispheric dominance for any single task. In the same way, we are limited in what we can conclude about differences in the pattern of hemispheric dominance for two individuals or groups of individuals using a single concurrent task. In the first place, if the individuals show different baseline asymmetries then it will be difficult to rule out explanations in terms of hand dominance. Even when the individuals or groups show exactly the same baseline asymmetries we may be limited to reaching conclusions about hemispheric dominance in one individual relative to the other rather than about absolute hemispheric dominance for either individual. As an example, consider a comparison of right-handed males and females contained in Kee, Matteson and Hellige (1990),

Kee et al. (1990) examined lateralized finger tapping interference produced by concurrent block design activity. More specifically, the block design task required subjects to imagine solving block design problems from the WAIS. For males, this concurrent activity interfered more with right-hand than with left-hand finger tapping, whereas for females there was equal interference with both hands. This result could not be accounted for by any difference in hand dominance for males versus females. Therefore, it is reasonable to suggest that during the block design task there was relatively more left-hemisphere involvement for males than for females. However, the absolute direction and magnitude of hemispheric involvement cannot be determined for either group without additional research.

What we have seen in this section is that the existence of hand-dominance effects complicates the interpretation of asymmetric manual interference in terms of hemisphere-specific competition. However, by focusing on Task by Hand interactions and realizing the limitations on the conclusions that can be drawn, it is still possible to use asymmetrical manual interference to test hypotheses about hemispheric asymmetry and hemisphere-specific competition.

The Balance of Hemispheric and Hand Dominance Effects

Previous sections of this chapter have shown that asymmetric manual interference is determined by both hemispheric and hand dominance factors. Furthermore, we have considered how effects of hand dominance might be separated from effects of hemispheric asymmetry via the examination of Task by Hand interactions. In this section we acknowledge the possibility that several aspects of procedure might determine whether the asymmetric manual interference found in a particular experiment is determined more by hand dominance or more by hemispheric asymmetry. We believe that it would be worthwhile in future experiments to determine whether these procedural details are, in fact, important. To do so, it is necessary to compare groups who vary systematically on hand dominance but not on hemispheric asymmetry and vice versa. Among other things, such studies would produce guidelines for the design of studies that minimize the contribution of hand dominance.

The experiments reviewed earlier in this chapter indicate that hand dominance, measured in terms of base-line performance, is a factor that affects the direction of asymmetric manual interference produced under dual-task conditions. This relationship was suggested by dual-task studies that used a repetitive finger-tapping task in which subjects were instructed to tap as quickly as possible on a single key and tapping rate was measured. Other kinds of finger-tapping tasks have also been used to measure manual performance and it remains to be determined whether the relative contribution of hand dominance and hemispheric factors changes with the type of manual task and type of performance measure.

For example, instead of using a single key, some studies have used the alternate tapping of two keys (e.g., McFarland & Ashton, 1975, 1978). With this procedure subjects have sometimes been told to tap as quickly as possible and have sometimes been told to tap as consistently as possible (i.e., at a constant rate). In addition, different performance measures have been used (e.g., tapping rate measures versus measures of the moment-to-moment variability in tapping rate). At the present time, there is little agreement about which combination of tapping instructions and performance measures produce the most reliable interference asymmetries with the two-key procedure (see Kee, Morris, Bathurst & Hellige, 1986; Hiscock et al., 1989). Of particular importance for present purposes is the fact that the effects of hand dominance on baseline trials have not been examined using any of the two-key procedures or other more elaborate sequential tapping procedures (e.g., Lomas & Kimura, 1976). Until this is done, it is difficult to attribute the different patterns of effects that might be obtained using those different manual tasks and performance measures to hemispheric factors. Instead, it might be the case that some tasks/measures are relatively uninfluenced by hand dominance so that the effects of hemisphere-specific competition can be seen more clearly with those tasks/measures.

Just as some manual tasks may be less influenced by hand dominance than others, some concurrent tasks may be less influenced by hand dominance than others. We have seen that a variety of concurrent verbal tasks produce asymmetric manual interference. Furthermore, we have seen that for many (perhaps all) of those tasks, the pattern of asymmetric interference is related to hand dominance on baseline trials. However, there is insufficient data at the present time to determine whether certain characteristics of the concurrent task determine the balance of hemispheric versus hand-dominance contributions to asymmetric manual interference. Future studies that provide such data may help us to determine exactly how it is that hand dominance exerts such a powerful effect.

An additional aspect of procedure that may be important is task emphasis. Some recent investigations of asymmetric manual interference have varied instructions about which of the two tasks to emphasize on dual-task trials (e.g., Hiscock, 1982; Friedman et al., 1988). This has been done for a variety of theoretical reasons that are beyond the scope of the present chapter. To the extent that asymmetric manual interference is determined by both hand-dominance and hemispheric factors, it is important in future studies to determine whether the effects of task emphasis are restricted to one factor or the other and whether the answer to this question depends on other considerations such as the nature of the manual task and concurrent task. Put another way, it is important to know whether the contribution of hand dominance to asymmetric manual interference is reduced with some task-emphasis instructions relative to others. Until we know more about this, it is prudent to be cautious about formulating explanations of task emphasis effects exclusively in terms of hemispheric factors.

Much of the new research recommended here involves further study of the relationship between hand dominance and asymmetric manual interference. When this relationship is examined, it is important to assure that the asymmetric interference estimates are not contaminated by trial-order effects. For example, many dual-task studies counterbalance the order of baseline and dual-task tapping trials across subjects. That is, different subjects receive different orders. If hand dominance is based on these same baseline trials, the order effects removed by the counterbalancing across subjects may be reinstated when the sample is divided into hand-dominance groups (i.e., the proportion of subjects receiving a specific ordering of conditions may not be the same for both groups). At the least, this possibility should be checked. Alternatively, other procedures can be used. For example, the identification of hand dominance can be based on an independent assessment given before the experiment proper. In this way, the ordering of baseline and dual-task trials can be counterbalanced within each of the hand-dominance groups. If the focus is on individual differences, then it would be prudent to use a fixed (i.e., the same) order of trials for all subjects. This fixed order would include the requisite counterbalancing of baseline and dual-task trials.

Concluding Comments

This chapter began with the observation that many concurrent tasks interfere more with the manual activity of one hand than with the manual activity of the other hand. Understanding the mechanisms responsible for this asymmetric manual interference will provide important insights into attention-related processes in neurologically normal humans. The data reviewed in this chapter indicate that two contributing factors are hemisphere-specific competition and hand dominance. Accordingly, when the goal is to use asymmetric manual interference to study one of those factors, it is necessary to control for the other. We have outlined some ways in which this might be accomplished. We believe that, with appropriate care, it remains possible to use asymmetric manual interference as an indicator of lateralized brain function.

Acknowledgements

The preparation of this chapter was supported in part by a grant to the first author from the National Science Foundation (BNS-8908305) and a Faculty Research Grant to the second author from the California State University at Fullerton.

References

Bathurst, K. (1989). *Finger tapping interference produced by concurrent verbal and nonverbal tasks: analysis of individual differences in left-handers.* Unpublished manuscript.

Dalby, J.T. (1980). Hemispheric timesharing: verbal and spatial loading with concurrent unimanual activity. *Cortex*, **16**, 567-574.

Friedman, A., Polson, M.C., & Dafoe, C.G. (1988). Dividing attention between the hand and the head: performance trade-offs between rapid finger tapping and verbal memory. *Journal of Experimental Psychology: Human Perception and Performance*, **14**, 60-68.

Friedman A., Polson, M.C., Dafoe, C.G., & Gaskill, S. (1982). Dividing attention within and between hemispheres: testing a multiple resources approach to limited-capacity information processing. *Journal of Experimental Psychology: Human Perception and Performance*, **8**, 625-650.

Hellige, J.B. (1983). Hemisphere X task interaction and the study of laterality. In J.B. Hellige (Ed.), *Cerebral hemisphere asymmetry: Method, theory and application.* New York: Praeger, 411-443.

Hellige, J.B. (1990). Hemispheric specialization. *Annual Review of Psychology*, **41**, 55-80.

Hellige, J.B., Bloch, M.I., & Taylor, A.K. (1988). Multi-task investigation of individual differences in hemispheric asymmetry. *Journal of Experimental Psychology: Human Perception and Performance*, **14**, 176-187.

Hellige, J.B., & Cox, P.J. (1976). Effects of concurrent verbal memory on recognition of stimuli from the left and right visual fields. *Journal of Experimental Psychology: Human Perception and Performance*, **2**, 210-221.

Hellige, J.B., Cox, P.J., & Litvac, L. (1979). Information processing in the cerebral hemispheres: selective hemispheric activation and capacity limitations. *Journal of Experimental Psychology: General*, **108**, 251-279.

Hellige, J.B., & Longstreth, L.E. (1981). Effects of concurrent hemisphere-specific activity on unimanual tapping rate. *Neuropsychologia*, **19**, 395-405.

Hellige, J.B., & Sergent, J. (1986). Role of task factors in visual field asymmetries. *Brain and Cognition*, **5**, 200-222.

Hellige, J.B., & Wong, T.M. (1983). Hemisphere-specific interference in dichotic listening: task variables and individual differences. *Journal of Experimental Psychology: General*, **112**, 218-239.

Herdman, C.M., & Friedman, A. (1985). Multiple resources in divided attention: a cross-modal test of the independence of hemispheric resources. *Journal of Experimental Psychology: Human Perception and Performance*, **11**, 40-49.

Hiscock, M., Cheesman, J., Inch, R., Chipuer, H.M., & Graff, L.A. (1989). Rate and variability of finger tapping as measures of lateralized concurrent task effects. *Brain and Cognition*, **10**, 87-104.

Hiscock, M., & Chipuer, H.M. (1986). Concurrent performance of rhythmically compatible or incompatible vocal and manual tasks: evidence for two sources of interference in verbal-manual timesharing. *Neuropsychologia*, **24**, 691-698.

Kee, D.W., & Cherry, B. (1989). *Lateralized interference in finger tapping: initial value differences do not affect the outcome.* Manuscript submitted for publication.

Kee, D.W., Hellige, J.B., & Bathurst, K. (1983). Lateralized interference of repetitive finger tapping: influence of family handedness, cognitive load, and verbal production. *Neuropsychologia*, **21**, 617-625.

Kee, D.W., Matteson, R., & Hellige, J.B. (1990). Lateralized finger tapping interference produced by block design activities. *Brain and Cognition*.

Kee, D.W., Morris, K., Bathurst, K., & Hellige, J.B. (1986). Lateralized interference in finger tapping: comparisons of rate and variability measures under speed and consistency tapping instructions. *Brain and Cognition*, **5**, 268-279.

Kinsbourne, M., & Cook, J. (1971). Generalized and lateralized effects of concurrent verbalization on a unimanual skill. *Quarterly Journal of Experimental Psychology*, **23**, 341-345.

Kinsbourne, M., & Hiscock, M. (1983). Asymmetries of dual task performance. In J.B. Hellige (Ed.), *Cerebral hemisphere asymmetry: Method, theory and application* (pp. 255-334). New York: Praeger.

Lempert, H. (1987). Effect of imaging sentence on concurrent unimanual performance. *Neuropsychologia*, **25**, 835-839.

Lempert, H. (1989). Effect of imaging vs. silently rehearsing sentences on concurrent unimanual tapping: a follow-up. *Neuropsychologia*, **27**, 575-580.

Levy, J., Heller, W., Banich, M.T., & Burton, L. (1983a). Asymmetry of perception in free viewing of chimeric faces. *Brain and Cognition*, **2**, 404-419.

Levy, J., Heller, W., Banich, MT., & Burton, L. (1983b). Are variations among right-handed individuals in perceptual asymmetries caused by characteristic arousal differences between hemispheres? *Journal of Experimental Psychology: Human Perception and Performance*, **9**, 329-359.

Lomas, J., & Kimura, D. (1976). Intrahemispheric interaction between speaking and sequential manual activity. *Neuropsychologia*, **14**, 23-33.

McFarland, K., & Ashton, R. (1975). The lateralized effects of concurrent cognitive activity on a unimanual skill. *Cortex*, **11**, 283-290.

McFarland, K., & Ashton, R. (1978). The lateralized effects of concurrent cognitive and motor performance. *Perception and Psychophysics*, **23**, 344-349.

Orsini, D.L., Satz, P., Soper, H.V., & Light, R.K. (1985). The role of familial sinistrality in cerebral organization. *Neuropsychologia*, **23**, 223-232.

Rasmussen, T., & Milner, B. (1977). The role of early left-brain injury in determining lateralization of cerebral speech functions. *Annals of the New York Academy of Sciences*, **299**, 355-369.

Segalowitz, S.J., & Bryden, M.P. (1983). Individual differences in hemispheric representation. In S.J. Segalowitz (Ed.), *Language functions and brain organization* (pp. 341-372). New York: Academic Press.

Simon, T.J., & Sussman, H.M. (1987). The dual task paradigm: speech dominance or manual dominance? *Neuropsychologia*, **25**, 559-570.

Sussman, H.M. (1982). Contrastive patterns of interhemispheric interference to verbal and spatial concurrent tasks in right-handed, left-handed and stuttering populations. *Neuropsychologia*, **20**, 675-684.

van Strien, J.W., & Bouma, A. (1988). Cerebral organization of verbal and motor functions in left-handed and right-handed adults: Effects of concurrent verbal tasks on unimanual tapping performance. *Journal of Clinical and Experimental Neuropsychology*, **10**, 139-156.

Willis, W.G., & Goodwin, L.D. (1987). An alternative to interference indexes in neuropsychological time-sharing research. *Neuropsychologia*, **25**, 719-724.

Wong, T.M., O'Boyle, M.W., & Tepin, M. (1989, November). *Dual-task interference in left-handers.* Paper presented at the Annual Convention of the American Psychological Association, New Orleans, LA.

Cerebral Control of Speech and Limb Movements
G.E. Hammond (editor)

Chapter 23

TEMPORAL CONSTRAINTS ON CONCURRENT TASK PERFORMANCE

Jeffery J. Summers
University of Melbourne

There is considerable evidence to suggest that temporal factors play a critical role in our ability to perform two different motor activities concurrently. Although a number of different mechanisms have been proposed to account for the temporal constraints on concurrent task performance, two theoretical perspectives have dominated. One approach has emphasized limitations in some central timing and/or attentional system. The other has placed the constraints within the motor system, in terms of entrainment between coupled neural oscillators. The results from a series of studies involving bimanual tapping are presented. It is argued that the data are consistent with the view that cognitive processes can influence lower-level oscillatory mechanisms.

When we are required to perform two different motor activities at the same time, interference between the activities is frequently observed. The form and locus of these interference effects have been of long-standing interest to researchers in motor control and coordination.

Two lines of research can be identified as addressing the general question of how concurrent motor activities are integrated. One approach has used the dual task paradigm to investigate the cerebral specialization of cognitive and motor functions. Much of this work has examined the effects of concurrent speech on the performance of various unimanual motor tasks. The other approach has more directly addressed the issue by examining the constraints in coordinating the limbs. Studies involving, for example, bimanual tapping tasks have been used to discover the principles underlying inter-limb coordination. In this chapter I will briefly review the research findings from each paradigm and then discuss some models of concurrent task performance. Finally, the results from a series of experiments examining bimanual coordination will be presented.

Concurrent Speech-Manual Activity

Much of the research using speech-motor activities to examine cerebral specialization of function has been based on the following assumptions: (a) two concurrently performed (orthogonal) activities will interfere with each other to the extent that their cerebral programs compete for resources within the hemisphere (Kinsbourne & Cook, 1971); (b) manual activities for each hand are programmed by the contralateral cerebral hemisphere; and (c) in right-handed persons, speech is primarily a left hemisphere function (Todor & Smiley, 1985).

Support for these hypotheses has been obtained in a number of studies showing that concurrent speech interferes more with right- than left-hand motor tasks, such as dowel balancing and single-finger tapping (e.g., Bowers, Heilman, Satz & Altman, 1978; Hellige & Longstreth, 1981; Kinsbourne & Cook, 1971; Van Strien & Bouma, 1988; Summers & Sharp, 1979).

In contrast some studies has shown bilateral and equal decrement when concurrent verbal tasks are combined with sequential tapping (e.g., Van Strien & Bouma, 1988; Summers & Sharp, 1979). This finding has been interpreted as supporting the suggestion that the left hemisphere controls the sequencing of movements for both hands (Kimura, 1977; Kimura & Archibald, 1974). However, distinguishing between single finger and sequential finger tapping in terms of the demand for rapidly executed postural transitions is questionable (Thornton & Peters, 1982; Todor & Smiley, 1985).

A common problem with studies showing interference effects between speech and motor activity is that the exact nature of the interference is not readily apparent. That is, it is not clear the extent to which the dual task decrements observed reflect cognitive-motor interference as well as motor-motor interference arising from competition between two motor processes (Kinsbourne & Hiscock, 1983). Some support for the existence of cognitive-motor interference has come from studies in which lateralized decrements were obtained with verbal tasks not requiring overt speech, such as silent reading or verbal rehearsal, (e.g., Hellige & Longstreth 1981; Hicks, Provenzano & Rybstein, 1975; Summers & Sharp, 1979). However, when tasks involving covert and overt speech have been compared within the same experimental design, performance decrements are greater under overt speech conditions (e.g., Hellige & Longstreth, 1981). Furthermore, the extent to which tasks such as covert rehearsal are qualitatively different to speaking is debatable (e.g., Elliott & Strawhorn, 1976; Estes, 1973).

Recently, Friedman, Polson and Dafoe (1988) have addressed this issue more directly by employing a verbal memory task consisting of three discrete phases: (a) a 5-s fixation period; (b) a 5-s period in which subjects read aloud a nonsense word; and (c) a 5-s delay interval before recall of the word. It was hypothesized that each phase would involve different processing requirements. Subjects performed the memory task in combination with a single-finger tapping task and were paid to emphasize one task or the other. Relative to single task performance, there was no decrement in tapping performance during the fixation interval. A large bilateral decrement in finger tapping was observed, however, during the reading aloud phase, and a greater slowing of right hand than left hand tapping during the retention interval. Furthermore, when the effects of the task emphasis were examined, a reliable and equal bilateral trade-off in tapping performance was evident in the reading aloud phase only. It was hypothesized that competition between the motor components of speaking and tapping would be primary the source of interference during this phase. The authors interpret the trade-offs observed during the reading aloud phase as indicating that resources from both hemispheres were required during left-handed tapping. Specifically, it was suggested that when tapping is combined with another motor task (e.g., speaking) left hemispheric resources may be needed to coordinate the timing of motor outputs between the two tasks and to resolve scheduling conflicts. Other researchers have also suggested that the interference effects observed between speaking and manual activity should be more properly thought of as reflecting the need to coordinate the timing of the two activities (Kelso, Tuller & Harris, 1983; Thornton & Peters, 1982).

Strong support for the interaction between the motor systems controlling speech and finger movements has been obtained by Chang and Hammond (1987). Interactions between concurrent verbalization (syllable repetition) and cyclic finger movements were examined under three conditions. Subjects were required to maintain either a constant amplitude in both response systems or alternate the amplitude in one response system while attempting to maintain a constant amplitude in the other. The results showed that modulation in either system constrained the output of the other concurrently active system. Furthermore interactions between speech and finger movements were obtained for both right hand and left hand movements.

In sum, recent research suggests that the frequently observed interference between speaking and manual activity may be due to incompatibility of the timing characteristics of the two motor tasks. Further support for the importance of temporal factors in dual task performance has come from studies examining the constraints in coordinating limb movements.

Constraints on Inter-limb Coordination

A common feature of many motor skills is that they require the coordination of different limbs. There appear, however, to be strong constraints on inter-limb coordination. In particular, the ease with which two different motor activities can be performed concurrently depends, to a large extent, on the temporal compatibility between the actions. For example, studies of bimanual tapping have consistently shown that subjects can accurately produce two isochronous sequences simultaneously, one with each hand, as long as they have identical or harmonically related time intervals (e.g., 1 vs 1, 2 vs 1, 3 vs 1). However, when sequences involving non-harmonically related time intervals have to be produced, such as polyrhythms (e.g., 3 vs 2, 4 vs 3, 5 vs 4), interference between the two hands is commonly observed (Deutsch, 1983; Klapp, 1979). In such sequences, one response rhythm often tends to dominate the organization and performance of the other or both hands exhibit mutual interference. Similar response tendencies are evident in the simultaneous coordination of repetitive hand and vocal movements (Chang & Hammond, 1987; Klapp, 1981).

A similar disposition toward simple timing relations in the coordination of the two hands has been observed in tasks where the maintenance of precise timing between movements is not an explicit requirement of the task. For example, Kelso, Southard and Goodman (1979) examined bimanual coordination in a task which placed external spatial constraints on the two limbs. Subjects were required to make two-handed movements to separate targets that differed in size and distance from the resting position. Even though the spatial demands for the two limbs were quite different, subjects appeared to move the limbs in synchrony, so that they arrived at their respective targets at the same time.

In sum, evidence from a variety of tasks and contexts suggest that coordinating the timing of movements of each task is the primary source of limitation on the performance of simultaneous motor actions. The mechanisms underlying the temporal constraints, however, have been a central issue in the continuing debate between the information processing and ecological approaches to motor behavior (see Meijer & Roth, 1988).

The Information Processing Perspective

In general, information processing theorists have appealed to limitations in some central attentional and/or timing system to account for the constraints on dual actions. One prominent line of theorizing considers the joint-performance problem in terms of the deployment of limited attentional resources. In this view there are different types of resources which can be allocated to any task that demands them (Navon & Gopher, 1979). For example, it has been suggested that there is a specific resource for motor control (Gopher & Sanders, 1984). Two tasks that compete for the same type of resource can be performed concurrently without decrement, relative to when they are performed alone, providing that their combined demands do not exceed the available supply. When dual-task demands exceed resources supply, performance decrements on one or both tasks will be observed. Recent work within the multiple resources framework has been concerned with identifying particular resources (e.g., Wickens, 1984), or linking resources to particular brain structures, such as the cerebral hemispheres (e.g., Friedman & Polson, 1981).

Although multiple resource models have been able to account for a wide range of dual-task findings, the specific patterns of interference between concurrent motor actions present problems for resource theory (see Neumann, 1987 for further discussion). For example, proposing a specific resource for coordinating motor outputs between tasks (see previous section) does not provide a satisfactory account of the bias of motor systems toward harmonic timing.

A model that has more explicitly addressed the temporal constraints on dual-task performance is the functional cerebral space model (Kinsbourne & Hicks, 1978). According to this model interference between temporally incompatible motor patterns is the result of spread of activity between the cerebral foci controlling the two activities. Because the brain is a highly linked system, no part of the system can be considered insulated from any other. The degree of interference between activities is an inverse function of the functional distance (i.e., the degree of interconnectedness) between their cerebral control centers. When two functionally close control centers (e.g., the two hands) are required to produce unrelated action patterns (e.g., non-harmonically related time intervals) interference occurs, and one rhythm will tend to dominate the other or both activities will mutually affect each other (Kinsbourne & Hicks, 1978).

Another popular model, with a number of variants, interprets the temporal constraints on concurrent motor performance as indicating the existence of a superordinate timing or controlling mechanism responsible for initiating and coordinating the activities of the motor subsystems (e.g., Keele & Ivry, 1987; Peters, 1985). A common assumption of this view is that the superordinate mechanism is limited in the extent to which it can maintain two differently timed actions at the same time. Peters (1981, 1985) has argued that the central controller copes with this situation by assigning priorities, through the allocation of attention, so that one rhythm dominates the other. He further suggests that in the guidance of bimanual activities, there is a preferential allocation of attention to the preferred hand. Support for this hypothesis has come from a number of studies showing strong performance asymmetries in bimanual tasks (e.g., Ibbotson & Morton, 1981; Peters, 1977, 1981, 1985).

In summary, information processing theorists have tended to place the limitations on concurrent motor performance within a high-level control or timing mechanism. Some have argued that the system or module that controls time is general, being involved in both perceptual and motor functions (Keele & Ivry, 1987).

The Ecological Perspective

The ecological or action system approach offers a radically different account of motor - motor interference. This approach rejects the view that such interference arises from limitations in some central timing system or attentional mechanism, and argues that motor interactions are a consequence of the dynamic behavior of the neuromotor system itself. Action system theorists suggest that the periodicities apparent in cyclic repetitive movements are indicative of oscillatory processes underlying movement. A key concept in this approach is the coordinative structure; a group of muscles often spanning several joints that is constrained to act as a single functional unit (Turvey, 1977). Coordinative structures function as nonlinear, limit-cycle oscillators, each with an intrinsic periodicity and controlling some component of an action (see Kelso, Holt, Rubin, & Kugler, 1981). It is assumed that the motor system constrains hierarchies of coordinative structures which become coupled to produce an overall rhythm in the action.

According to this view the timing constraints on the current performance of motor actions are a consequence of interactions between coupled coordinative structures. Two forms of interaction are seen as important organizational principles in human movement. One form is mutual entrainment that occurs when coupled oscillations with slightly different frequencies become synchronized at an intermediate frequency. The other is subharmonic entrainment that occurs when one oscillator adopts a frequency that is an integer multiple of another to which is coupled (as when two limbs are moved at different rates).

Evidence for mutual and subharmonic entrainment in human motor behavior has come from studies of the coordination of cyclic finger, hand or arm movements (e.g., Baldissera, Cavallari, & Civaschi, 1983; Cohen, 1970; Kelso et al., 1981; Yamanishi, Kawato, & Suzuki, 1980), and in the coordination of speech and finger movements (Chang & Hammond, 1987; Kelso et al., 1983). For example, Yamanishi et al. (1980) required subjects to tap the index finger of each hand at a constant 1000-ms period. The time difference between left and right hand responses was varied systematically from 0 (synchronous tapping) to 900 ms, in 100-ms intervals. Accurate and stable performance was obtained when the two hands were required to tap in synchrony or in an alternating fashion (180 degrees out of phase). Furthermore, intermediate phases produced unstable performance and a tendency to entrain to the nearest stable phase (i.e., synchrony or alternation). These results suggest that only two stable phase-lockings between the hands exist, either in-phase or anti-phase (Kelso & Schöner, 1988). However, other studies have shown that when subjects performing alternating movements of the two hands gradually increase cycling frequency, an abrupt shift to an in-phase mode occurs at a critical frequency (Kelso, 1981, 1984). In-phase movements, therefore, appear to be the more preferred mode of coupling the hands.

The action system approach, therefore, argues that the bias of harmonic timing in inter-limb coordination reflects the entrainment properties of coupled nonlinear oscillators operating at a functionally low-level in the motor system. One advantage of the oscillator model is that it minimizes the need for computational processes in the control of movement. The temporal constraints on concurrent motor performance are a consequence of an organizational style of biological systems, and not the result of interference produced by limitations in some high level control process.

The extent to which the oscillator model can provide a complete account of movement timing and coordination, without recourse to central processes, however, is unclear. For example, repetitive single-finger tapping tasks have frequently be used to investigate the processes underlying the perception and production of rhythm (e.g., Essens & Povel, 1985; Povel, 1981; Summers, Hawkins & Mayers, 1986). A common finding that has emerged from this work is that accurate reproduction of temporal patterns depends upon the temporal structure (i.e., the time relations between intervals) of the presented sequence. Povel (1981), for example, has argued that in such patterns subjects attempt to detect underlying "beats" that occur at equal time intervals throughout a sequence. The beat interval is then used to organize other shorter intervals in the patterns. Although oscillator concepts have been applied to individual rhythmic hand movements (Kelso & Schöner, 1988) extension to temporal patterns with unequal intervals has yet to be attempted.

Another important issue which needs to be addressed by models of inter-limb coordination is skill acquisition. It is clear that the human is able to perform many activities that do not involve either synchronous or alternating movements of the limbs (see Guiard, 1987). This suggests that an important aspect of skill learning is overcoming the temporal constraints in coordinating limb movements. From an information processing perspective this process may involve integrating initially separate activities into a higher-order skill, so that it is no longer a dual task situation (Neumann, 1987). Alternatively, with practice, there may be a reduction in the influence of a higher-level control process that is constrained to handle single inputs from independent timing mechanisms, and the two limbs may achieve some independence (Keele & Ivry, 1987). Shaffer (1982), for example, has argued that the rhythmic interplay between the hands evident in the performance of highly skilled musicians depends on being able to independently time the finger movements of the two hands.

Another possibility is that skill learning involves the development of some form of insulation against mutual interference between temporally incompatible actions. For example, within the framework of the functional cerebral space model, Kinsbourne and Hicks (1978) have proposed two ways in which this may be achieved. One is by delaying the initiation of one activity relative to the other, a process called staggered processing. The other way is to reduce the spread of activity between interconnected control centers by setting up some form of inhibitory barrier. Support for a staggered processing strategy has come from a study in which subjects made simultaneous upper limb movements that differed in their spatiotemporal requirements (Swinnen, Walter, & Shapiro, 1988). High intra- and inter-individual differences were observed in the degree of inter-limb dependence. Some subjects achieved almost complete independence of the two limbs by the end of a long practice session, while for others the limbs appeared to become more coupled. The authors observed that the degree of independence between the limbs appeared to be related to the absolute time differences between initiation of the two limb movements. That is, the larger the initiation difference the greater the decoupling of the limbs achieved. It was hypothesized that the activation of an inhibiting mechanism may underlie the initiation delay, its purpose being to minimize interference between concurrent activities.

Action system theorists have only recently begun to address the question of how temporally incompatible actions, with practice, can be performed successfully. There some evidence that there may be a weakening of the interaction between coupled oscillators with learning. Yamanishi et al. (1980) noted that the entrainment between the hands was much stronger for unskilled than skilled (musically trained) subjects. Motor constraints also appear to have a decreasing influence on bimanual coordination as a function of age (Fagard, 1987). The weakening of entrainment may reflect the increasing influence of higher-control centers. B. Craske and J.D. Craske (1986), for example, have argued that goal-directed action is achieved through a high-level motor controller, capable of translating intention into action "by starting and stopping, and modifying parameters of oscillator mechanisms to which it has access" (p. 122). Kelso and de Guzman (in press) also suggest that patterns of temporal coordination reflect the interplay between environmental forces and intrinsic patterns (in-phase and anti-phase) arising from the organization of subcortical neural networks. When the required relative phase does not correspond to one of the intrinsic patterns, competition between the two forces produces distortions from the required relative phase. With learning, the influence of the intrinsic dynamics disappears as the required new relative phase emerges. Relative phases which are not compatible (e.g., 5 vs 2, 4 vs 3) with the intrinsic patterns, however, are less accurate and more variable than relative phases that do correspond to the intrinsic dynamics.

Studies of Bimanual Coordination

In this section I will briefly describe some experiments we have conducted in an attempt to address the issues discussed above. In this work we examined the basic assumption that both high level cognitive processes and coupled oscillatory mechanisms are involved in bimanual performance. Entrainment between coupled oscillators is responsible for the preferred relationships (i.e., synchrony and alternation) observed between the hands in voluntary activity. Higher-order processes that can influence the oscillator systems, however, produce the adaptability and flexibility of skilled motor performance (Summers, in press; Summers & Burns, in press).

Three of the studies examined the production of polyrhythms. Polyrhythms require the simultaneous production of two conflicting but isochronous movement sequences, one with each hand. They possess a number of features that make them ideally suited to examination of the interaction between cognitive processes and low-level motor constraints. First, they require that the two hands move at different frequencies - a situation that has been shown to produce strong entrainment effects. Second, to successfully perform a polyrhythm necessitates the precise phasing of the two hands: that is, they involve complex, coherent rhythmic structures. Deutsch (1983) has argued that accurate polyrhythm performance requires the development of an internal representation of the patterns as an integrated whole. Last, polyrhythms are extremely difficult to perform, especially for the musically unskilled. However, with extensive practice, people such as highly skilled musicians can perform complex polyrhythms suggesting that central control can be exerted over low-level motor constraints.

Experiment 1

In the first study (Summers, Burns, Gazis & Young, in preparation) we compared the ability of six skilled (i.e., musically trained) and six unskilled subjects to produce simple rhythms (e.g., one vs one, two vs one, three vs one) and more complex polyrhythms. The five polyrhythms studied were: three *vs* two, five vs two, four vs three, five vs three and, five vs four. All subjects were right-handed.

Of particular interest was the degree to which the entrainment effects observed in studies using simple movements of the two hands (e.g., Kelso et al., 1981) would be evident in the performance of complex polyrhythms. To this end, a detailed examination of the phasing relationships between the hands during polyrhythmic performance was undertaken. Previous studies of polyrhythms have not examined systematically the kinematics of the movements of the two hands (e.g., Deutsch, 1983; Jagacinski, Marshburn, Klapp & Jones, 1988; Klapp, Hill, Tyler, Martin, Jagacinski, & Jones, 1985).

The rhythms were presented to subjects as two parallel tone sequences through headphones, one to each ear. Subjects were required to tap out the rhythms on two keys with the index finger of each hand. Each subject was tested over five sessions, with the first session being devoted to the performance of simple rhythms. For each rhythm subjects were first given a series of trials in which they attempted to tap the right hand in synchrony with the tones presented to the right ear and the left hand in synchrony with the tones delivered to the left ear. These synchrony trials were immediately followed by a series of test trials in which subjects were required to tap out the rhythm from memory without the aid of the pacing tones.

Two other factors were manipulated in the experiment: hand arrangement and speed of performance. Subjects performed each rhythm with the right hand taking the faster beat and the left hand the slower beat, and vice versa. Previous research (e.g., Peters, 1977, 1981, 1985) would suggest that performance should be better when the preferred hand (i.e., right hand) takes the faster beat. Subjects also performed each polyrhythm at a slow rate (total period 2250 ms) and a fast rate (total period 1500 ms).

It was predicted that if in the early stages of learning polyrhythms the phasing of the hands is determined primarily by endogenous oscillatory mechanisms, then unskilled subjects should exhibit stronger entrainment effects than skilled subjects.

The main findings of the study were as follows: First, no performance asymmetries with respect to hand arrangement were observed in the reproduction of either the simple rhythms or polyrhythms. Second, in terms of overall performance, musically trained subjects were better at reproducing all the rhythms tested. Third, and of particular importance, was the finding that the response profiles of unskilled subjects during the performance of polyrhythms did not appear to be consistent with an oscillatory-type process operating in the phasing of the two hands. Rather, both skilled and unskilled subjects reproduced the intervals for the fast hand with a high degree of accuracy across all the polyrhythms tested. The main difference between the two groups was in the accuracy of the intervals produced by the slower hand. These results suggest that subjects adopted the strategy of allocating attention to the fast hand and then tried to interlace the movements of the slow hand into movements of the fast hand. Jagacinski et al (1988) have reported a somewhat similar strategy in the performance of a three vs two polyrhythm. By examining the covariances among intertap intervals, integrated (i.e., interleaving the timing of the two hands) versus parallel (i.e., decoupling of the two hands) motor organizations were tested. Support was found for a particular form of integrated motor organization (multiplicative hierarchical model) involving the use of a higher-order (i.e. non-successive) time intervals. It should be noted that subjects in the Jagacinski et al. study received extensive practice at performing the three vs two polyrhythm, whereas subjects in our study received little training on each rhythm. It is possible, therefore, that the strategy observed in our study was a precursor to the development of the integrated task organization observed by Jagacinski et al. (1988). Furthermore, requiring each subject to perform five different polyrhythms may have encouraged the adoption of a similar general strategy for each polyrhythm.

There are, however, several reasons to suggest that in the performance of polyrhythms more complex that three vs two (e.g., five vs three, five vs four) a parallel motor organization would be more efficient (Jagacinski et al., 1988). In such patterns, treating the right hand and left hand sequences as separate may be easier than trying to combine them into a complex integrated structure. Such a strategy should also allow for the generalization to other complex polyrhythms. Furthermore, in learning polyrhythms it has been recommended that each hand first be learned separately before being combined (e.g., Cooke, 1941).

In two experiments we examined the question of whether a parallel motor organization is adopted in the performance of a complex polyrhythm.

Experiment 2

In this study (Summers & Hinton, in preparation) four skilled musicians received extensive training at performing a five vs three polyrhythm, with the right hand taking the faster beat. Following training, subjects performed a series of trials in which a predetermined tap in either the right hand or left hand sequence had to be tapped with more force (i.e., accented) than the other taps. In a previous study using this manipulation (Semjen & Garcia-Colera, 1986), accenting a nominated tap in a single-hand rhythm significantly affected the timing of the sequence. Specifically, it was found that the disruption of timing was localized to the intervals immediately preceding and following the accented tap.

Over the series of test trials, each response in the fast hand and in the slow hand sequence was accented. Of particular interest was the effect of accenting a tap on one hand which immediately preceded or followed a tap with the other hand. It was hypothesized that if a parallel motor organization has been achieved, then the effects of accenting a response on one hand should be localized to the immediately adjacent intervals on that hand, leaving the intervals produced by the other hand unaffected. In contrast, if an integrated motor organization had be adopted, then the effects of stressing an element on one hand should disrupt timing on the other.

The results were consistent with an integrated motor organization. That is, stressing a polyrhythm element was associated with a significant lengthening of the interval prior to the next tap regardless of which hand performed the next tap. This result suggests that, at least for the subjects in this study, the two hands were not functioning independently. It is possible, of course, that a parallel motor organization may only be found among the most highly skilled professional musicians (Jagacinski et al., 1988).

Experiment 3

In the third experiment (Summers & Kennedy, in preparation) we were interested in the effects of two different types of training on the performance of a five vs three polyrhythm. Six skilled (musically trained) and six unskilled subjects were randomly assigned to each training condition. In one training condition (separate) subjects received extensive practice at producing the rhythm for the right hand (one tap every 300 ms) and the left hand (one tap every 500 ms) in isolation. Subjects in the other condition (integrated) also practiced the same single hand patterns but each cycle of a rhythm was initiated by a simultaneous right and left response. Thus, the sequences for the integrated group became 5 vs 1 and 3 vs 1. By the end of training both groups were able to produce their respective sequences accurately, without the aid of pacing tones. Prior to the testing phase subjects in the separate condition were given a short practice session with the 5 vs 1 and 3 vs 1 patterns.

In the test phase subjects in both groups were asked to produce (without pacing tones) a 5 vs 3 polyrhythm with each cycle of the rhythm beginning with a simultaneous tap by the two hands. Subjects of both groups were shown a diagram of the polyrhythm to be produced. Instructions to the integrated group emphasized the production of the rhythm as an integrated whole. In contrast, subjects in the separate condition were instructed to produce the polyrhythm as separate sequences of taps for the left and right hands, synchronizing the hands only at the beginning of each cycle.

The main finding of the study was that none of the unskilled subjects in the separate condition were able to perform the two rhythms concurrently. Instead they either tapped the two hands in synchrony, alternated the hands, or produced five taps with the right hand followed by three taps with the left hand. Two of the skilled subjects in the separate conditions also showed large distortions from the required pattern. One subject accurately reproduced the slow hand intervals but consistently made six taps with the fast hand, so that every third response was a simultaneous tap with both hands. The other subject produced the correct number of taps with each hand, but showed a strong tendency to synchronize the movements of the slow hand with movements of the fast hand.

A comparison of performance in the integrated condition revealed large differences between skilled and unskilled subjects. Unskilled subjects made more sequencing errors and produced the polyrhythms at a much slower rate (2449-ms cycle period) than skilled subjects (1538-ms cycle period). Furthermore, analysis of skilled subjects' response profiles showed similar tendencies to that observed in Experiment 1. That is, accurate reproduction of the fast hand intervals and some distortion of the intervals produced by the slow hand. In contrast, unskilled subjects showed distortion of the intervals produced by both hands. Finally, a comparison of skilled subjects' performance in the integrated and separate (4 subjects) condition, in terms of overall accuracy (average deviation), revealed superior performance in the integrated condition. Subjects in both groups, however, showed similar response profiles (see above).

Experiments 2 and 3, therefore, strongly suggest that in the performance of a complex 5 vs 3 polyrhythm an integrated form of motor organization is adopted. Furthermore, all three studies of polyrhythmic performance suggest that when faced with the task of concurrently performing two differently timed motor sequences, subjects adopt the strategy of allocating attention to the fast hand. By focussing attention on the fast hand, the slower hand beats can then be branched off the faster beat, while the converse is not true (Peters, 1985). The finding that skilled subjects in both training conditions adopted a similar strategy suggests that one effect of musical training is the acquisition of strategies for integrating temporally compatible motor sequences. In contrast, when unskilled subjects in the separate condition attempted to keep the two hands separate, strong entrainment between the hands was observed. These results are consistent with the view that overcoming the temporal constraints on concurrent task performance depends upon the integration of the two activities into a higher-order skill (Neumann, 1987).

Experiment 4

Further support for the notion that high level cognitive processes can override constraints within the motor system has come from another experiment we have recently completed (Summers, Bell & Burns, 1989). The basic task was similar to that used by Yamanishi et al. (1980). Subjects were required to tap each hand at a constant 1200-ms interval, but the phase of one hand lagged the other by a constant amount. The delay between left hand and right hand responses was varied in 100-ms steps. Thus six two-interval sequences were created containing intervals of 100-1,100, 200-1,000, 300-900, 400-800, 500-700, and 600-600 ms. In one condition (between-hand) subjects tapped out the sequences using the right- and left-hand index fingers. For example, when the first response was made with the right hand, the order of taps was: right index - left index - right index. Subjects also produced the sequences with the left hand leading. This response condition was identical to that used by Yamanishi et al., (1980). In another condition (single-hand), subjects tapped out the sequences using one hand only. For each sequence subjects first synchronized their responses with auditory pacing tones before reproducing the sequence without the aid of the pacing signals.

It was predicted that if two-handed tapping is determined by the entrainment properties of coupled neural oscillators, then different response tendencies would be evident in the between-hand condition than in the single-hand condition, where motor interactions are not involved.

The results, however, showed almost identical response profiles for the two response conditions. In particular, the tendencies toward either synchronization or alternation of the hands, reported for similar sequences by Yamanishi et al. (1980), were not evident in the between-hand condition of the present study. Although the pattern with intervals relating as 1:1 (600-600 ms) was reproduced accurately, a general tendency toward an interval relation of 1:2 was evident in the imitation of the other patterns.

These results suggest that the sequences were coded in terms of two perceptual categories of duration, a 'short' and a 'long' duration that relate roughly as 1:2 (Fraisse, 1946, 1956; Essens & Povel, 1985; Povel, 1981). In this experiment perceptual factors, rather than motor factors, appeared to be the main determinant of performance.

Although there were a number of methodological differences between our study and that of Yamanishi et al. (1980) which may account for the different findings obtained (see Summers et al., 1989, for details), our results clearly show that motor interactions are not a necessary consequence of bimanual performance.

Conclusion

In this paper I have reviewed the literature concerning the constraints on the concurrent performance of two motor activities. The general finding that has emerged from this work is that the temporal relationship between the two motor actions is the critical factor in concurrent performance.

Two radically different explanations of the temporal constraints observed in the dual-task situation were outlined. One view argues that these constraints arise from limitations in some central timing mechanism or higher-level control system. Attentional factors are also seen to play an important role in dual-task performance. The other view places the constraints within the motor system. The limitations are assumed to reflect entrainment between coupled neural oscillator systems.

A number of experiments were then presented that appear to suggest that some reconciliation between the two viewpoints is warranted. Specifically, it is proposed that timing in dual-task movements may be a secondary consequence of the entrainment between coupled neural oscillators or it may reflect some higher-level control process. The particular level at which timing is determined will depend upon such factors as the task demands and stage of learning (Summers & Burns, in press). For example, in dual-tasks where the maintenance of precise timing relations between movements is an explicit part of the activity (e.g., playing music), central control may be exerted over low-level oscillatory mechanisms. Motor factors, however, may play a more dominant role in bimanual tasks involving very simple movements, such as cyclical flexion-extension movements performed without externally imposed temporal constraints (e.g., Kelso et al., 1981). Gentner (1987) has similarly concluded that the control of timing can be determined at several levels in the perceptual-cognitive-motor system. An important issue for future research on the simultaneous performance of motor actions is elucidating the processes by which central control can be exerted over lower-level neurological mechanisms.

Acknowledgment

This chapter was written during my stay at the Netherlands Institute for Advanced Study, Wassenaar. I am very appreciative of the opportunities provided by the Institute. The studies of bimanual coordination from my laboratory that are reported in this paper were supported by the Australian Research Grants Scheme, Project No. A 28115899.

References

Baldissera, F., Cavallari, P., & Civaschi, P. (1982). Preferential coupling between voluntary movements of ipsilateral limbs. *Neuroscience Letters*, **34**, 95-100.

Bowers, D., Heilman, K.M., Satz, P., & Altman, A. (1978). Simultaneous performance on verbal, nonverbal and motor tasks by right-handed adults. *Cortex*, **14**, 540-566.

Chang, P., & Hammond, G.R. (1987). Mutual interactions between speech and finger movements. *Journal of Motor Behavior*, **19**, 265-274.

Cohen, L. (1970). Interaction between limbs during bimanual voluntary activity. *Brain*, **93**, 259-272.

Craske, B., & Craske, J.D. (1986). Oscillator mechanisms in the human motor system: investigating their properties using the aftercontraction effect. *Journal of Motor Behavior*, **18**, 117-145.

Deutsch, D. (1983). The generation of two isochronous sequences in parallel. *Perception and Psychophysics*, **34**, 331-337.

Elliott, L.A., & Strawhorn, R.J. (1976). Interference in short-term memory from vocalization: aural versus visual modality differences. *Journal of Experimental Psychology: Human Learning and Memory*, **2**, 705-711.

Essens, P.J., & Povel, D.-J. (1985). Metrical and nonmetrical representations of temporal patterns. *Perception and Psychophysics*, **37**, 1-7.

Estes, W.K. (1973). Phonemic coding and rehearsal in short-term memory for letter-strings. *Journal of Verbal Learning and Verbal Behavior*, **12**, 360-372.

Fagard, J. (1987). Bimanual stereotypes: bimanual coordination in children as a function of movements and relative velocity. *Journal of Motor Behavior*, **19**, 355-366.

Fraisse, P. (1946). Contribution à l'étude du rhythme en tant que forme temporelle. *Journal de Psychologie Normale et Pathologique*, **39**, 283-304.

Fraisse, P. (1956). *Les structures rhythmiques.* Louvain: Universitaires de Louvain.

Friedman, A., & Polson, M.C. (1981). The hemispheres as independent resource systems: limited capacity processing and cerebral specialization. *Journal of Experimental Psychology: Human Perception and Performance*, **7**, 1031-1058.

Friedman, A., Polson, M.C., & Dafoe, C.G. (1988). Dividing attention between the hands and the head: performance trade-offs between rapid finger tapping and verbal memory. *Journal of Experimental Psychology: Human Perception and Performance*, **14**, 60-68.

Gentner, D.R. (1987). Timing of skilled motor performance: tests of the proportional duration model. *Psychological Review*, **94**, 255-276.

Gopher, D., & Sanders, A.F. (1984). S-Oh-R? Oh stages! Oh resources! In W. Prinz & A.F. Sanders (Eds.), *Cognition and motor processes* (pp. 231-253). Heidelberg: Springer.

Guiard, Y. (1987). Asymmetric division of labour in human skilled bimanual action: the kinematic chain as a model. *Journal of Motor Behavior*, **19**, 486-517.

Hellige, J.B., & Longstreth, L.E. (1981). Effects of concurrent hemisphere-specific activity on unimanual tapping rate. *Neuropsychologia*, **19**, 395-405.

Hicks, R.E., Provenzano, F.J., & Rybstein, E.D. (1975). Generalized and lateralized effects of concurrent verbal rehearsal upon performance of sequential movements of the fingers by the left and right hands. *Acta Psychologica*, **39**, 119-130.

Ibbotson, N.R., & Morton, J. (1981). Rhythm and dominance. *Cognition*, **9**, 125-138.

Jagacinski, R.J., Marshburn, E., Klapp, S.T., & Jones, M.R. (1988). Tests of parallel versus integrated structure in polyrhythmic tapping. *Journal of Motor Behavior*, **20**, 416-442.

Keele, S.W., & Ivry, R.I. (1987). Modular analysis of timing in motor skill. In G. Bower (Ed.), *The psychology of learning and motivation* (pp. 183-228). New York: Academic Press.

Kelso, J.A.S. (1981). On the oscillatory basis of movement. *Bulletin of the Psychonomic Society*, **18**, 63.

Kelso, J.A.S. (1984). Phase transitions and critical behavior in human bimanual coordination. *American Journal of Physiology*, **240**, R1000-1004.

Kelso, J.A.S., & de Guzman, G.C. (in press). Order in time: how the cooperation between the hands informs the design of the brain. In H. Haken (Ed.), *Neural and synergic computers*. Berlin: Springer-Verlag.

Kelso, J.A.S., Holt, K.G., Rubin, P., & Kugler, P.N. (1981). Patterns of human inter-limb coordination emerge from the properties of non-linear, limit-cycle oscillatory processes: theory and data. *Journal of Motor Behavior*, **13**, 226-261.

Kelso, J.A.S., & Schöner, G. (1988). Self-organization of coordinative movement patterns. *Human Movement Science*, **7**, 27-46.

Kelso, J.A.S., Southard, D.L., & Goodman, D. (1979). On the coordination of two-handed movements. *Journal of Experimental Psychology: Human Perception and Performance*, **5**, 229-238.

Kelso, J.A.S., Tuller, B., & Harris, K.S. (1983). A 'dynamic pattern' perspective on the control and coordination of movement. In P.F. MacNeilage (Ed.), *The production of speech* (pp. 137-173). New York: Springer-Verlag.

Kimura, D. (1977). Acquisition of a motor skill after left hemisphere damage. *Brain*, **100**, 527-542.

Kimura, D., & Archibald, Y. (1974). Motor functions of the left hemisphere. *Brain*, **97**, 337-350.

Kinsbourne, M., & Cook, J. (1971). Generalized and lateralized effects of concurrent verbalization on a unimanual skill. *Quarterly Journal of Experimental Psychology*, **23**, 341-345.

Kinsbourne, M., & Hicks, R.E. (1978). Functional cerebral space: a model for overflow, transfer and interference effects in human performance. In J. Requin (Ed.), *Attention and performance VII* (pp. 345-362). Hillsdale, NJ: Lawrence Erlbaum Associates.

Kinsbourne, M., & Hiscock, M. (1983). Asymmetrics in dual task performance. In J. Hellige (Ed.), *Cerebral hemisphere asymmetry: Method, theory, and application* (pp. 255-344). New York: Praeger.

Klapp, S.T. (1979). Doing two things at once: the role of temporal compatibility. *Memory and Cognition*, **7**, 375-381.

Klapp, S.T. (1981). Temporal compatibility in dual motor tasks: II. Simultaneous articulation and hand movement. *Memory and Cognition*, **9**, 398-401.

Klapp, S.T., Hill, M.D., Tyler, J.G., Martin, Z.E., Jagacinski, R.J., & Jones, M.R. (1985). On marching to two different drummers: perceptual aspects of the difficulties. *Journal of Experimental Psychology: Human Perception and Performance*, **11**, 814-827.

Meijer, O.G., & Roth, K. (Eds.). (1988). *Complex movement behavior: 'The' motor-action controversy*. Amsterdam: North-Holland.

Navon, D. & Gopher, D. (1979). On the economy of the human processing system. *Psychological Review*, **86**, 214-225.

Neumann, O. (1987). Beyond capacity: a functional view of attention. In H. Heuer & A.F. Sanders (Eds.), *Perspectives on perception and action* (pp. 361-394). Hillsdale, NJ: Lawrence Erlbaum Associates.

Peters, M. (1977). Simultaneous performance of two motor activities: the factor of timing. *Neuropsychologia*, **15**, 461-464.

Peters, M. (1981). Attentional asymmetries during concurrent bimanual performance. *Quarterly Journal of Experimental Psychology*, **33A**, 95-103.

Peters, M. (1985). Constraints in the performance of bimanual tasks and their expression in unskilled and skilled subjects. *Quarterly Journal of Experimental Psychology*, **37A**, 171-196.

Povel, D.-J. (1981). Internal representation of simple temporal patterns. *Journal of Experimental Psychology: Human Perception and Performance*, **7**, 3-18.

Semjen, A., & Garcia-Colera, A. (1986). Planning and timing of finger tapping sequences with a stressed element. *Journal of Motor Behavior*, **18**, 287-322.

Shaffer, L.H. (1982). Rhythm and timing in skill. *Psychological Review*, **89**, 109-122.

Summers, J.J. (in press). Temporal constraints in the performance of bimanual tasks. In D. Vickers & P.L. Smith (Eds.), *Human information processing: Measures, mechanisms and models*. Amsterdam: Elsevier.

Summers, J.J. Bell, R., & Burns, B.D. (1989). Perceptual and motor factors in the imitation of simple temporal patterns. *Psychological Research*, **51**, 23-27.

Summers, J.J., & Burns, B.D. (in press). Timing in human movement sequences. In R.A. Block (Ed.), *Cognitive models of psychological time*. Hillsdale, N.J.: Lawrence Erlbaum Associates.

Summers, J.J., Burns, B.D., Gazis, J., & Young, K.H. (in preparation). The production of polyrhythms.

Summers, J.J., & Hawkins, S.R., & Mayers, H. (1986). Imitation and production of interval ratios. *Perception and Psychophysics*, **39**, 437-444.

Summers, J.J., & Hinton, E. (in preparation). The effects of dynamic stress on the timing of bimanual rhythms.

Summers, J.J. & Kennedy, T. (in preparation). A comparison of two training schemes on the acquisition of a bimanual skill.

Summers, J.J., & Sharp, C.A. (1979). Bilateral effects of concurrent verbal and spatial rehearsal on complex motor sequencing. *Neuropsychologia*, **17**, 331-343.

Swinnen, S.P., & Walter, C.B. (1988). Constraints in coordinating limb movements. In A.M. Colley & J.R. Beech (Eds.), *Cognition and action in skilled behavior* (pp. 127-143). Amsterdam: North-Holland.

Swinnen, S., & Walter, C.B., & Shapiro, D.C. (1988). The coordination of limb movements with different kinematic patterns. *Brain and Cognition*, **8**, 326-347.

Thornton, C.D., & Peters, M. (1982). Interference between concurrent speaking and sequential finger tapping: both hands show a performance decrement under both visual and non-visual guidance. *Neuropsychologia*, **20**, 163-169.

Todor, J.L., & Smiley, A.L. (1985). Performance differences between the hands: implications for studying disruption to limb praxis. In E.A. Roy (Ed.), *Neuropsychological studies of apraxia and related disorders* (pp. 309-344). Amsterdam: North-Holland.

Turvey, M.T. (1977). Preliminaries to a theory of action with reference to vision. In R. Shaw & J. Bransford (Eds.), *Perceiving, acting, and knowing: Toward an ecological psychology* (pp. 211-265). Hillsdale, NJ: Lawrence Erlbaum Associates.

Van Strien, J.W., & Bouma, A.(1988). Cerebral organization of verbal and motor functions in left-handed and right-handed adults: effects of concurrent verbal tasks on unimanual tapping performance. *Journal of Clinical and Experimental Neuropsychology*, **10**, 139-156.

Wickens, C.D. (1984). Processing resources in attention. In R. Parasuraman & R. Davies (Eds.), *Varieties of attention* (pp. 63-101). New York: Academic Press.

Yamanishi, J., Kawato, M., & Suzuki, R. (1980). Two coupled oscillators as a model for the coordinated finger tapping by both hands. *Biological Cybernetics*, **37**, 219-225.

INDEXES

Subject Index

Author Index